International Economics

The Irwin Series in Economics
Consulting Editor
Lloyd G. Reynolds   Yale University

INTERNATIONAL ECONOMICS

Herbert G. Grubel, Ph.D.
Simon Fraser University
Vancouver, B.C.

 1977

RICHARD D. IRWIN, INC.   Homewood, Illinois   60430
Irwin-Dorsey Limited   Georgetown, Ontario   L7G 4B3

First Printing, January 1977

ISBN 0-256-01793-X
Library of Congress Catalog Card No. 76–22260
Printed in the United States of America

To Eric and Heidi

Preface

TEXTBOOK WRITING is an exercise in product-differentiation. In this book I have attempted to be different by degree from competing texts in three important ways.

First, I have stressed the development of the standard analytical tools required for an understanding of the real world and treated relatively lightly topics that are primarily of theoretical interest, such as stability conditions in the pure and monetary models, the foreign repercussions of income and trade multipliers, and the assignment problem.

Second, I present data on world trade, exchange rates, the balance of payments of major countries, the history of tariff negotiations, and international monetary institutions to provide students with an appreciation of the changing environment to which international trade theory has to be applied. At the same time, attention is given to the manner in which abstract ideas of economists influence the real world, as for example, they have in the development of post-war international organizations, tariff policies, the Phillips curve and inflation trade-off, and the monetary-fiscal policy-mix models.

Third, I have tried to incorporate into the standard material recently developed theoretical and empirical knowledge, which increases the usefulness and explanatory power of the more standard models of international economics. Thus, I discuss models of international trade in differentiated products, the concepts of optimum currency areas and exchange rate stability, the determinants of price elasticities, the concepts of risk diversification and knowledge capital as determinants of foreign investment, and the monetarist approach to the balance of payments.

The book has been structured for a two-semester course in which the sequence of real and monetary aspects is not important. For a one-semester course in the pure theory of international trade I would recommend the use of Chapters 1–9 and 25–27. Chapters 10–24 are most suitable for a one-semester course in international monetary economics.

At the end of each chapter are found suggestions for further readings, concepts for review, and questions for further discussion and research. A selected alphabetically arranged bibliography is at the end of the book.

Students interested in a particular topic can find the relevant references by consulting the bibliographic notes appended to the chapter in which the topic is discussed.

The level of difficulty of the text material is one which should be manageable by students majoring in economics at all universities of the world. Almost all theories are developed verbally and with the help of simple geometry. Somewhat more complicated subjects are presented in appendixes, which can be skipped without loss of continuity. The principle of exposition followed involves development of the simplest model to demonstrate some central propositions such as the gains from trade, the neutrality of exchange rates, and the tendency for automatic adjustment to disturbances. These simple models are then modified and extended to make them progressively more useful for understanding real-world phenomenon and policies.

The writing of the sections dealing with the international adjustment mechanism and monetary system presented me with a real dilemma. On the one hand I believe that the recent criticisms of the Keynesian system of analysis, especially its emphasis on nominal rates of interest and the Phillips-curve trade-off, has cast very serious doubt on the usefulness of a number of popular models of international adjustment, such as the monetary-fiscal policy-mix models. Furthermore, I am convinced that much of the controversy over fixed versus freely floating rates is very misleading, as is exemplified by the fruitless attempts to define operationally "fundamental disequilibrium." Therefore, I was tempted to omit such topics from the text. On the other hand, these models and topics are part of the traditional body of knowledge that every student should be familiar with, even if they are misleading. Therefore, I have presented these topics in the traditional way. However, in Chapters 19–20, 22, and 24 I criticize these models and present alternatives to replace them. Chapter 19 draws heavily on my publication "Domestic Origins of the Monetary Approach to the Balance of Payments," *Essays in International Finance,* No. 117, Princeton, N.J.: Princeton University Press, June 1976. Most of Part V of this book contains the same material as my *The International Monetary System,* Harmondsworth, England: Penguin, third edition, 1976. I thank both Princeton University Press and Penguin Books Ltd., for permission to use these materials in this book.

In writing a textbook one draws on a stock of intellectual capital both in the literature and in one's own mind. The bibliography at the end of the book acknowledges my debt to the producers of this capital in the literature. Here I would like to acknowledge my debt to Harry Johnson, Max Corden, Robert Triffin, Milton Friedman, Robert Mundell, and Henry Wallich, who have done much in the past to shape my private stock of knowledge capital.

My students in past courses at the University of Chicago, University of

Pennsylvania, and Simon Fraser University, who have helped me focus and present more clearly the material in this book, deserve my thanks. My thanks also go to the following persons who have read and commented on parts of the manuscript: S. Arndt, R. Baldwin, R. Bharath, P. Callier, J. Cuddington, S. Easton, H. G. Johnson, P. J. Lloyd, J. Martin, J. Newman, L. Reynolds, R. Schwindt, Z. Spindler, and E. Tower. B. Coysh, L. Halstrum, and N. Petersen have efficiently typed different parts of the manuscript. My wife and children have sustained me with their love and understanding during the trials and tribulations encountered in writing this book.

Vancouver, B.C.
December 1976

HERBERT G. GRUBEL

Contents

Products. Differentiated Products: Scale Economies. Differentiated Products: Product Cycles. Labor Value-Added Processes. Summary and Conclusions.

part two
COMMERCIAL POLICIES

POLICIES: The Cost of Protection. Why Not Unilateral Free Trade Policies?
Summary and Conclusions.

part three
FOREIGN EXCHANGE MARKETS AND
BALANCE-OF-PAYMENTS STATISTICS

part four
THE INTERNATIONAL ADJUSTMENT
MECHANISM

Fiscal Policy and Temporary Payments Imbalances. Monetary Policy and Permanent Payments Imbalances. Reserve Currency Country under Managed Exchange Rates. Some Casual Empirical Support of the Monetarist Views. III. OTHER MONETARIST ANALYTICAL APPROACHES: Perfect Competition in Goods Markets. Perfect International Short-Term Capital Markets. Stock-Flow Relationships. IV. SUMMARY AND CONCLUSIONS.

part five
THE INTERNATIONAL MONETARY SYSTEM

Free Market Method. Transactions Demand Method. IV. THE OPTI-
MUM QUANTITY AND COST OF INTERNATIONAL RESERVES. V. MIS-
CELLANEOUS PROBLEMS OF INTERNATIONAL MONETARY ORGANIZATION:
The Role of Monetary Gold. Control over the Adjustment Mechanism. The
Problem of an Intervention Currency and the Future Role of the Dollar.

part six
INTERNATIONAL FACTOR MOVEMENTS AND THE ECONOMICS OF INTEGRATION

1 Introduction

THE LEARNING of any task or body of knowledge is greatly facilitated if the student is properly motivated and knows the ultimate rewards of his labor, if he has a clear notion of the requirements he must meet to attain these rewards, and if he knows the road that will take him to his goal. In this introductory chapter we will lay the groundwork for the study of this book by analyzing the usefulness of international economics for students with many different life careers ahead of them. We will also describe the broad intellectual content of the subject of international economics and explain the strategy of exposition and general philosophy to be followed in this book.

Why Study International Economics?

Students take courses and acquire skills and knowledge for many different reasons, most of which are applicable to the study of international economics. First (and somewhat cynically), they take many courses simply because they need to fulfill certain requirements for graduation, which itself is only a means to high starting salaries and lifetime earnings. International economics, of course, does help to fulfill course requirements, but students who take it for this reason alone have been ill advised, for there are many much less rigorous and less substantial subjects with which these formal obligations can be met.

A second purpose for taking courses is the acquisition of skills and knowledge that will be directly useful in earning a living later on in life. International economics teaches very few skills or knowledge which can be used directly in this manner, except to the relatively small proportion of students who will become professional economists and who will work in the capacity of teachers, researchers, or advisers to government, industry, and international agencies. While the skills and knowledge acquired in international economics are of greatest use in the analysis of problems in international trade and finance, they also benefit general economists because international economics constitutes the field in which general tools of micro- and macroeconomics are applied to specific problems with great rigor and intensity.

Very rarely can students apply the skills and knowledge acquired in a course in international economics directly to the process of becoming successful entrepreneurs and getting rich quickly by operating in international markets for commodities, capital, or currencies. As we will demonstrate, knowledge generally available and therefore written up in this textbook typically has been acted upon by entrepreneurs in the past. Thus existing conditions leave no room for the present generation of students to make extraordinary profits. For this purpose it is necessary for them to create new knowledge by the expenditure of much research effort, guided by a generous dash of luck, some genius, and a thorough understanding of the existing knowledge. The average returns to the study of international economics applied in this direct manner are not high.

Most college courses are taken for a third distinct reason—students expect the skills or knowledge acquired will enrich their lives, make them wiser consumers and more responsible citizens, and in general will improve the quality of the decisions they make in all fields of endeavor. International economics provides its share of benefits in this manner. Newspapers are full of stories about such world crises as starvation, overpopulation, environmental pollution, poverty, inflation, recession, revolution, unemployment, and foreign exchange controls, all of which most students wish to understand because they are concerned about their fellow men and the world in which they live. Most of these enduring problems of mankind are affected by or influence international economic relations in some way, as we will demonstrate in detail in this book.

The study of international economics thus heightens students' understanding and appreciation of the world surrounding them. As tourists, buyers of goods and services, and managers of their own portfolios of assets, liabilities, and human capital, students can use knowledge acquired in this course to maximize benefits and minimize costs and risks. They will know what is likely to happen to the prices of goods, services, and assets located or originating in a country whose currency has just been revalued. They will have good ideas on where to exchange their tourist money to greatest advantage and how to minimize risks of revaluations. As responsible citizens, they will use their understanding of international economics to evaluate political arguments, identify narrow self-interests, and hold up the public interest in casting their votes or taking sides in other ways.

As future businessmen and managers of their own private affairs, students of international economics will also benefit through their familiarity with such concepts as comparative advantage and the gains from specialization and trade. They will profit from their understanding of economic interdependencies and the role of government policies in the determination of exchange rates, interest rates, prices of products and inputs, the balance of payments, competitive conditions, and many other factors affecting the profitability of business and private wealth and income in a world composed of independent nations. International economics, much like economics in general, provides students with a particular way of approaching and solving a wide range of problems. Armed with this knowledge and way of thinking, they will be able to improve the quality of their decisions above what would have otherwise been the case, increase their usefulness to employers, raise their incomes, and maximize the returns to their private wealth holdings and the enjoyment of their consumption expenditures.

The fourth motive underlying the choice of courses by college students often is aesthetics. Literature, the fine arts, and languages are often studied for the sole purpose of increasing awareness and appreciation of the beauty of man's environment, of the power of emotions and feelings, of the symmetry and order in the universe. With the proper attitude, one can find similar sources of aesthetic satisfaction in the study of international economics. There are logical constructs, such as the demonstration of the welfare gains from international trade, which have a beauty and aesthetic quality that is appealing to many persons. Like outstanding games of chess, mathematical proofs, certain laws in physics and chemistry, and proofs of the existence of God by deductive logic, some subjects in international economics would be worth studying even if they had no other more mundane utility.

In this text we will frequently present ideas and concepts of deceptive clarity and simplicity which in fact have been developed during the past 100 years only after the expenditure of large quantities of intellectual resources. Students who are attracted to the aesthetic qualities of international economics can increase their enjoyment by reading historic pieces which show the evolution of ideas, through many detours and blind alleys. Suggested readings are included in the bibliographical notes at the close of each chapter.

In sum, international economics is a field which is likely to provide satisfaction to students who come to it with many different motives. Readers of this text may find greater rewards for their efforts if they try occasionally to think about their own motives, which may differ according to the subject of individual chapters. The process of learning is much more efficient and firm if students have a good idea of the future use of the knowledge and are not just concerned with passing examinations.

Objectives of Study of the Text

There are several broad, important ideas in international economics which this text will present, the understanding of which is the ultimate, direct objective of its study. These ideas can be developed fully only after students have become familiar with certain skills, concepts, and analytical tools, which we list for review and summary at the end of each chapter. Their mastery will enable the student to understand the broad, important ideas. Also at the end of each chapter will be given points for thought and discussion. In answering these questions students will learn to apply the new analytical tools and deepen their understanding of the broader issues of international economics.

We will sketch the basic ideas to be developed fully in this text, in order to provide the student with a clear notion of where his labors are taking him and what he will be expected to know at the end of the course. The first and in some sense fundamental idea of international economics is to show why countries trade, or, put differently, what the gains are from trade and what determines their magnitude. Somewhat subsidiary, but still important, is the question of how these gains are distributed among nations and among the owners of productive factors within each country. Answers to these questions will be provided in Part One of this book at different levels of abstraction, moving from the simplest to progressively more complicated models of the world. We will show that international trade, free from restrictions, tends to maximize the value of income in a world in which factors of production cannot move across the international borders of independent nation-states. We will discuss conditions under which this world income maximization will not be achieved fully and show how trade affects the welfare of individual countries and of groups within countries. The effects of the growth of productive factor supplies on these conclusions is analyzed in the final chapters of Part One.

The findings of Part One will be used to explain that most countries do not permit complete freedom of international trade. They use tariffs, quotas, and other instruments of control to correct alleged or real failures of the market or to acquire benefits at the expense of the rest of the world. We will show how relatively easy it is to make persuasive cases for interference with free trade in particular instances, and how difficult it is to demonstrate the general, worldwide welfare losses accompanying these trade restrictions. In the views of many economists, the case for free trade and the cost of protection represent the socially most valuable insights to be derived from a study of international economics. In this text, they will provide the focus for the first two parts of the book.

A third fundamental idea of international economics is that the theory of comparative statics and growth which is presented in Parts One and

Two is not affected by the existence of money and national currencies, except to the extent that they increase the efficiency of production and trade. In Part Three we will develop a model of the foreign exchange markets capable of proving this point. Much practically useful information about the exchange markets and balance of payments will be presented at the same time.

One of the weakest aspects of the field of international economics concerns the operation of the international economy in a world of uncertainty, random disturbances, and changing expectations about prices. In Part Four we will develop the existing theory in this crucial area, showing how under these circumstances money often becomes a powerful force influencing real variables. We will also show how nations try to deal with disturbances through monetary and fiscal policies and attempt to achieve simultaneously full employment, price stability, and balance in international payments. The tools of analysis and policy recommendations derived in this part of the text underlie most contemporary government actions, and they have to be fully understood by anyone who wishes to influence these policies or to protect his interests against their consequences.

The main idea to be presented in Part Five is that the world of uncertainty in which each nation-state tries to maximize its national income and minimize its fluctuations must be served by an efficient international monetary system. We will develop the characteristics of such a system, contrast it with the ideal blueprints of international monetary organization designed by men, and discuss the real-world shortcomings of each. In this discussion we will provide students with the knowledge needed to understand, interpret, and act upon proposals for the reform of the international monetary system. According to our analysis, these proposals will continue as long as the world is subject to economic disturbances, and economic, political, and military power relations among nations continue to change.

We conclude the book by discussing, in Part Six, the idea that international factor movements in the form of migrating labor, both unskilled and trained, and of capital through the multinational corporations represent forces that are capable of breaking down the nation-states' sovereignty and of equalizing incomes in all parts of the world. As such forces, migration and the multinational corporations are in conflict with existing nation-states and their supporters, but they also have the potential to improve welfare in the world as a whole by equalizing incomes and creating interdependencies among nations which make armed conflict even costlier than it has been in the past. We will discuss in some detail the motives and welfare effects of the international flows of labor, capital, and human capital in order to clarify issues which are likely to attract increasing public concern in the future.

Some Notes on Methodology

The preceding sketch of the main issues and ideas of international economics in the 1970s reveals that we will be approaching the subject in the traditional paradigm of capitalist economics. At the same time, however, the analysis will deal with all of the social issues which are of such great concern to economists and students of the New Left, even if the final policy conclusions may be different. Our analysis will be logically rigorous and therefore refutable with logical or empirical evidence to the contrary. Students who believe that the orthodox international economics does not come up with the right answers to certain problems should welcome the opportunity to learn thoroughly the orthodox body of knowledge, discover its flaws, and correct them, perhaps by the substitution of a new paradigm. They might motivate themselves by remembering the old slogan: Know your enemy before you fight him.

Our analysis will be grounded firmly in the paradigm of traditional economics with which students using this text should be familiar through exposure to at least a one-semester introductory course. In essence, international economics is nothing more than the application of conventional tools to a set of particular problems.

However, these tools have been forged into powerful instruments to be used in the analysis of the special kinds of problems we have sketched. Except for the discussion of capital flows and migration, there are two assumptions most characteristic of international economics: First, the factors of production—land, labor, and real, human, and knowledge capital—are given within each country, and the only exchange possible with the rest of the world is through the trade of goods and services. Second, every nation must make monetary and fiscal policy in a world of interdependent states where foreign policies impinge on domestic conditions, and national policies have repercussions for the rest of the world.

Summary and Conclusions

As a field of study, international economics has much to offer students who wish to use it in later life, both directly to earn a living and indirectly to improve their intellectual capacity and the quality of their decisions in a wide range of endeavors. International economics, however, also may appeal to students interested in the aesthetic qualities of logical thought structures and arguments and who wish to gain a better understanding of the perennial great problems of mankind.

The fundamental problems students must be able to understand after their study of this text in international economics are (1) why nations trade, (2) the cost of protection and the case for free trade, (3) the neutral effects of international currencies on the basic propositions derived in the real sector, (4) the role of money and exchange rates in a world of uncertainty, (5) the need for an international monetary system, and (6) the probable future of nation-states in the presence of human migration and capital flows. The analysis will be presented within the framework of orthodox economics, though most of the problems of concern to the New Left will be considered.

BIBLIOGRAPHICAL NOTES

Textbooks

Some books written specifically for courses in international economics at the advanced undergraduate level and covering roughly the same material as the present one are, in alphabetical order: Caves and Jones (1973) Heller (1973, 1974), Kindleberger (1973), Kreinin (1974), Scammel (1974), Soedersten (1970), Walter (1975). Penguin Books has published a series of inexpensive edition texts covering somewhat more narrowly defined fields: Findlay (1971), on the pure theory of trade; Cohen (1970), on the monetary aspects; Helleiner (1972), on trade and development; Swann (1975), on the Common Market, and Grubel (1975), on the international monetary system. (See the Bibliography at the end of the text for the list of references.)

Treatises

Books reviewing and extending the field of international economics, normally at a higher level of abstraction and assuming more basic knowledge than texts, are, dominantly in the theory of trade, the classics Ohlin (1933), Haberler (1950), Meade (1951, 1952, 1955); and the extensions Caves (1960), Johnson (1961), Mundell (1968), Grubel and Lloyd (1975). In the monetary aspects of trade they are Stern (1973a), Yeager (1966), Johnson (1962), Mundell (1971), Sohmen (1969), Clement et al. (1967). Leamer and Stern (1970) provide a useful survey of the application of quantitative methods in international economics. Cooper (1968) discusses the effects of foreign trade on economic and political interdependence, providing a useful perspective on the pure-theory arguments about the gains from trade.

Mathematical Approach

There is a genre of textbook treating international economics as an integrated field at a high level of abstraction and using mathematics: Kemp (1969), Pearce (1970), Takayama (1972).

Books of Readings

Classics from professional journals have been reprinted in Allen (1965), Ellis and Metzler (1949), and Caves and Johnson (1968). Especially inexpensive and useful collections of basic articles from professional journals are published by Penguin Books in paperback: Bhagwati (1969), on pure theory; Cooper (1969), on monetary aspects; Robson (1971), on the Common Market; and Dunning (1972), on international investment. Somewhat more expensive but also in paperback form are books of readings edited by Meier (1970) on economic development, and Officer and Willett (1969) on the international monetary system.

A book of readings put together especially for undergraduate students is Baldwin and Richardson (1973). A useful mixture of text and original source material is presented by Meier (1973, 1974).

part one

THE PURE THEORY OF
INTERNATIONAL TRADE

2 Gains from Trade in a Classical World

SCIENTIFIC PROGRESS in economics is achieved through the use of simplified models of the world, which are continuously refined and made more realistic by the adoption of more complicated sets of assumptions. This process of refinement is stimulated by findings of inconsistency between the real world and either the assumptions of or the conclusions reached by the model.

In this book we will attempt to replicate this process of scientific advance by starting out with a drastically simplified model of the world, considering its implications, and discovering where it leads to false, incomplete, or misleading conclusions about real-world phenomena. We then make the necessary modification of the assumptions to correct these deficiencies, ending up with complicated logical structures representing the most recent state of knowledge.

In pursuing this process of exposition we follow closely the actual historic evolution of knowledge in the field of international economics. In this chapter we begin with the simple and easy-to-understand models of the classical economists, most notably Adam Smith and David Ricardo, who wrote their main works in the last part of the 18th and first part of the 19th centuries. The work of these economists had been stimulated by the development of industry in England, which drew an increasingly larger proportion of the population out of rural occupations into cities and factory work. This shift of the population from a relatively simple rural life, where purpose and operation could be understood easily, into the complicated social and economic structure of city life based on industry was accompanied by many social hardships and the loss of identity and purpose by individuals. Artisans and peasants who for generations had been supplying their communities with goods found themselves unable to compete with factory output or imported goods. Where previously the welfare of the community as a whole to a large extent guided the actions of individual peasants, artisans, and landlords, the new market-oriented activities were almost exclusively dominated by self-interest.

The natural reaction to these developments was the growth of demand by the public that the government bring order to the apparent chaos by regulating and controlling industry, commerce, and international trade. It is useful to recall these circumstances to appreciate the important insights the classical economists provided to the world by explaining how the apparently selfish pursuit of profits by entrepreneurs raises the welfare of the entire community through the operation of the "invisible hand" of competition in the marketplace. It is a most fundamental insight—which even today many persons have not gained—that the baker who tries to earn a profit for himself will produce the quality product the public wants at the cheapest price possible, in competition with other bakers. The public gains by being able to purchase this competitively priced good of their choice of a quality which the bakers produced for purely selfish reasons.

In this chapter we analyze in the same classical tradition how the selfish pursuit of the profit motive by international traders buying at low and selling at high prices increases world welfare. This insight is as fundamentally valid and important in the 20th century as it was in the 18th century, though in the intervening years many qualifications and exceptions to the rule have been found, as we will show.

Absolute and Comparative Advantage

In our development of the arguments of the classical economists, we assume that the world consists of only two countries, "America" and "Europe," each producing only two goods, wheat and cloth. We also assume initially that no goods, capital, or labor flow between the two countries. Population, tastes, and technology are constant during the period under consideration.

According to classical economists before Ricardo, the existence of beneficial trade opportunities between the two countries depended on labor productivity conditions providing countries with what became known as an "absolute advantage." This can be illustrated by a table comparing output per man per year.

Output of One Man per Year

Product	America	Europe
Wheat	12 bushels	10 bushels
Cloth	4 yards	5 yards

In the context of this example, America is depicted as having an absolute advantage in the production of wheat and an absolute disadvantage in the production of cloth. Europe's absolute advantage and disadvantage are in cloth and wheat, respectively.

In order to understand the development of the terms "absolute advantage" and "disadvantage," we must remember that classical economists believed that the only determinant of the value of a commodity was the labor required in its production. As a result of this theory, labor was the standard of value within countries and in the world as a whole. By this standard Europe could produce a yard of cloth at the price of one fifth of a labor year, and in America one fourth of a labor year would be necessary to do this, giving Europe an absolute advantage in price of 0.05 labor years per yard of cloth. The classical economists argued that these prices provided the incentive for profit-seeking entrepreneurs to buy cloth in Europe and sell it in America, always under the assumption that there are no transportation costs. For analogous reasons it was considered profitable to buy wheat in America and sell it in Europe.

The public gains from this private profit-seeking activity arise from the shift of labor into wheat and out of cloth production in America, and vice versa in Europe. Each unit of labor shifted in this manner produces a net gain in world output of 2 bushels of wheat, because American production rises by 12 and European production falls by only 10 bushels. By the same process, the world production of cloth rises by one yard, as a European's labor increases output by five yards and the American worker's shift lowers it by only four.

This simple argument succeeds in making the main point that trade increases world output through specialization, but it is deficient in many respects. For example, it does not state by what mechanism the world gains in output are distributed among the residents in each country and between the two countries. Furthermore, the model does not explain what happens if one country has shifted all of its labor from one industry into the one in which it enjoys an absolute advantage, while the other country still produces both products. A third problem not dealt with in this model is the determination of the differences in labor productivity. The classical economists hinted at the quantity and fertility of the land, climate, capital, and level of human skills as sources of these differences. In the next chapter we will answer all of these questions by proper modifications of the classical model.

There is one glaring deficiency of the preceding model, which Ricardo remedied by the substitution of the concept of "comparative advantage" for the concept "absolute advantage". The deficiency of the model to which Ricardo's analysis addressed itself can best be seen by consideration of the example of productivity conditions shown in the accompanying table.

Output of One Man per Year

Product	America	Europe
Wheat	12 bushels	6 bushels
Cloth	4 yards	3 yards

In this example America has an absolute advantage in the production of both commodities, and use of the arguments about the incentives for trade and the process of increasing world output leads to the conclusion that trade is not profitable and that gains are ambiguous. In terms of labor years both wheat and cloth are cheapest in America, and according to the preceding argumentation, entrepreneurial incentives to trade are absent. As labor shifts, in America from cloth into wheat production and vice versa in Europe, there is a gain of six bushels of wheat but a loss of one yard of cloth output. What in the previous example yielded unambiguous gains in output under the present circumstances does not yield a clear-cut gain. Like the labor theory of value, the concept of absolute advantage is deficient because it comes up with correct and consistent explanations of the real world only under a limited range of circumstances. As we shall presently note, even under the example of absolute advantage or disadvantage in the production of both goods, there are private incentives for trade and unambiguous increases in world output.

Before we can move to this analysis, it is necessary to understand that the relative productivity of labor in the two industries determines the price at which the two commodities exchange within each country before trade. Thus, in America a yard of cloth must bring three bushels of wheat. If there were a different price, such as one yard of cloth for 4 bushels of wheat, entrepreneurs would profit by shifting labor from the production of wheat, at the sacrifice of 12 bushels, into the production of four yards of cloth. The entrepreneurs could then exchange the four yards of the cloth into 16 bushels of wheat at the hypothesized price of 1 to 4, pay labor its previous income of 12 bushels, and make a net gain of 4 bushels of wheat. Moreover, such entrepreneurial activities would have the effect of increasing the supply of wheat, lowering its price, and decreasing the supply of cloth, thus increasing its price. These price changes would continue until entrepreneurial activity ceases to be profitable, when the market rate of exchange is equal to the ratio of labor productivities (students may wish to verify this for themselves). We now assume that before trade the relative prices in America and Europe are in domestic equilibrium, at the rate of one yard of cloth for three and two bushels of wheat, respectively, in the two countries.

Under these conditions international trade is privately profitable, as can readily be seen by considering the following transactions. Take two bushels of wheat from America to Europe, and exchange them there for one yard of cloth. Return the cloth to America, and obtain three bushels of wheat, and earn a profit of one bushel. Moreover, as a little arithmetic will verify, no such profit could be earned, indeed a loss would be sustained, by the export of cloth from America and of wheat from Europe.

The profitability of trade even in the case where absolute advantage lies with America in both commodities is due to the existence of comparative advantage, which describes the fact that America is *relatively* more efficient in the production of wheat rather than cloth, and vice versa for Europe.

The principle of comparative advantage pervades many motives in everyday life. A business executive may be a better typist than anyone he can hire, but he will not type his own correspondence and instead spends his time in managerial activities in which he has a comparative advantage. Sometimes we observe persons who behave as if they had not grasped the principle of comparative advantage and note that they lose opportunities by engaging in activities in which they are good, but which are not the ones in which they have their comparative advantage. As a result their incomes are lower than they could be, or they have to work harder to attain a given level of income.

Both in international trade and in personal affairs it is important to realize that every country and every person must have a comparative advantage in the production of one good or pursuit of one activity, as long as there are at least one partner and two different goods or activities. No one had to teach Robinson Crusoe the concept of comparative advantage for him to realize the benefits he could derive from sharing chores with Friday, with each doing what he could do relatively best. Yet, often, international trade is opposed by persons who believe that their countries cannot compete with the rest of the world in the production of *any* goods. As we shall see later, such situations may arise when there are money and exchange rates to disguise the real goods exchange and when governments interfere with the market determination of the exchange rate. But the principle remains valid that there always must be some activity in which a country has a comparative advantage. Even if the world consisted only of North America, where wages are high, and Asia, where wages are very low, trade between the two continents would be profitable.

The exploitation of private profit opportunities by traders increases world output. This can be seen by working through our preceding numerical example. The entrepreneurs export wheat from America and induce a shift of labor from cloth into wheat production. One unit of labor shift raises wheat output by 12 and lowers cloth output by 4 units. Analogous adjustments in Europe lower wheat output by six and raise cloth by three units, for a net world gain of six bushels of wheat, but a reduction of one yard in cloth output. Whether or not this combination of gains and losses of the two commodities represents a net gain has to be determined by the relative value of the two commodities. Remember that in the classical model this relative value is determined by the labor input requirements. Using American productivity figures, the net gain in world output is worth one quarter of a man year per unit of labor shifted, because to make up the loss of one yard of cloth requires three bushels of wheat, leaving a net gain of three, which in turn can be produced by the expenditure of one quarter of a man-year. In terms of European labor the net gain of world output is worth two thirds of a man-year per unit of labor shifted. Using these labor gain figures, it is possible also to express the increase in world output in terms of wheat or cloth in America and Europe, simply by calculating how much of each good the net world labor gain could produce.

For many students, and for purposes of analysis, it is sufficient to prove the existence of entrepreneurial incentives and gains from international trade using numerical examples. However, using numerical examples as a tool of analysis is dangerous, since we may be dealing with special cases that have only very limited general validity. The derivation of the concept of absolute advantage as a basis for trade undertaken above illustrates the dangers inherent in the use of numerical examples.

Economists have developed two tools of analysis which avoid the pitfalls of specific cases. Mathematical formulations of functional relationships are the most general. Unfortunately, they also tend to produce normally useless results, because anything is possible in the most general cases. Therefore, the mathematical functions must be restricted in their form by a priori assumptions chosen on the basis of economic theory or empirical facts. Conclusions become more definite and limited in number the more restrictive the assumptions made. In a sense, specific examples are equivalent to mathematical formulations with a maximum amount of restrictive assumptions. The power of mathematical analysis is based on the fact that it can establish the influence on the conclusions stemming from each assumption specified precisely. Only an infinite number of numerical examples and their careful analysis could come to the same insights mathematical analysis obtains directly.

The second form of analysis used by economists to overcome the pitfalls of specific numerical examples involves the use of geometry. The geometric representation of functional forms is equivalent to using a priori restrictions on general mathematical functions, with the convenience that the restrictions do not have to be listed tediously, and the geometric representation yields visual images which can be appreciated with less training than is required for the understanding of mathematical proofs.

In turning to a geometric representation of the classical analysis of the gains from trade, we will be able to arrive at some interesting and important conclusions which could have been derived from numerical examples only with involved and lengthy calculations. In other chapters we will often skip the numerical examples and move directly to geometrical representations. For this reason we will take special care in demonstrating how it is possible to move from numerical examples to graphs. In principle, therefore, students can always construct their own numerical examples from geometric analysis, if they find this useful.

The Gains from Trade: Geometric Analysis

Using the second table of labor productivity set out above, and assuming that Europe and America have a total supply of five and four units of labor, respectively, we can show the maximum combination of wheat and cloth each country can produce during a year. This is done in Table 2–1.

TABLE 2–1
Maximum Combination of Outputs of Wheat
and Cloth

Europe		America	
Wheat	Cloth	Wheat	Cloth
30	0	48	0
24	3	36	4
18	6	24	8
12	9	12	12
6	12	0	16
0	15		

It is easy to understand how these numbers are derived. In Europe, when all labor is devoted to wheat production ($L_w = 5$), output is 30 bushels of wheat, leaving zero labor for cloth production ($L_c = 0$). Shifting one unit of labor away from wheat into cloth production results in outputs of 24 bushels of wheat and three yards of cloth. Using the equations $W = L_w \cdot 6$; $C = L_c \cdot 3$; and $L_c = S - L_w$, where W and C denote quantities of wheat and cloth output, respectively, and S indicates the total supply of labor, other combinations of maximum output can be derived by varying L_w from 5 to 0, inserting the values in the first and third equations, and using the calculated L_c in the second equation. The output combinations available to America can be calculated in the same manner.

We used the numbers in Table 2–1 to draw the graphs in Figure 2–1. Along the horizontal and vertical axis, we measure physical units of wheat and cloth, respectively, showing the production possibilities of Europe in the top panel and of America in the bottom one. As can be seen, the production possibility lines P_eP_e' and P_aP_a' are straight lines. This linear tradeoff between the output of wheat and cloth is due to the assumption that labor productivity is the same at all output levels for each commodity. This constant cost of production is the second outstanding feature of the

FIGURE 2–1
Production Possibility Frontiers

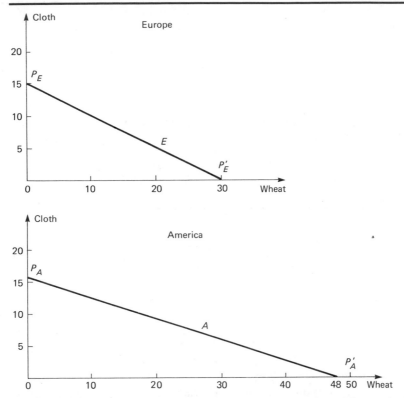

In the top panel of Figure 2–1, the production possibility frontier of Europe is shown as the line $P_E P_E'$. This indicates that Europe can produce a maximum of 30 units of wheat and 0 units of cloth, a maximum of 15 units cloth and 0 units of wheat, or a combination of cloth and wheat, along the line $P_E P_E'$. The combination of 20 units of wheat and 5 units of cloth is the point E, at which, before trade, Europe produced and consumed.

In the bottom panel, the production possibility frontier of America is shown as the line $P_A P_A'$. This indicates that America can produce a maximum of 48 units of wheat and 0 units of cloth, a maximum of 16 units of cloth and 0 units of wheat, or a combination of cloth and wheat along $P_A P_A'$. The combination of 25 units of wheat and 7.5 units of cloth shown as point A indicates America's pretrade point of production and consumption.

classical trade model, and it is a corollary of the assumption of only one input requirement, labor, as discussed above.

For the demonstration of gains from trade we have to make an assumption about the combinations of cloth and wheat the two countries produce and, in the absence of trade, also consume. We have arbitrarily selected the quantities indicated by points E (cloth = 5, wheat = 20) for Europe and A (cloth = 7.5, wheat = 25) for America in Figure 2–1.

Now let us consider Figure 2–2, which was derived from the two parts

FIGURE 2–2
Gains from Trade

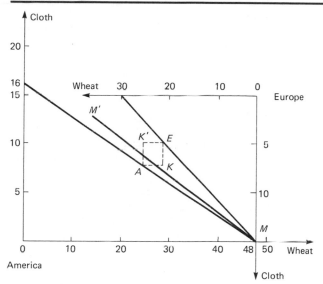

With Europe specializing in the production of cloth and America specializing in the production of wheat, world aggregate output of the two products is at point 0–Europe, equal to 15 units of cloth and 48 units of wheat. With Europe and America continuing at their pretrade levels of consumption at E and A, respectively, there is a net gain in world output available of AK of wheat and KE of cloth. Distribution of the increased world production between America and Europe is indeterminate in the model, but at any point in the area AKEK', both countries can consume at least as much of each good as they did before trade.

of Figure 2–1. The. zero origin of Europe's production possibilities block has been moved to the upper right corner of the panel showing America's production possibilities, so that the two countries' axes measuring the output of wheat and cloth are parallel, and the tips of the two production blocks touch at point M. Considering point M from the point of view of American production possibilities, we can see that it represents America's maximum output of 48 bushels of wheat, achieved at a zero production of cloth. Analogously, point M in Europe's block represents its maximum output of 15 yards of cloth and zero bushels of wheat. Recalling our preceding analysis based on the numerical example, it is clear that under the conditions shown graphically each country specializes fully in the production of the good in which it has a comparative advantage.

With Figure 2–2 we can demonstrate easily and dramatically the world gains from trade and specialization. Under autarchy America produced and consumed, at point A, 25 bushels of wheat; Europe, at point E, consumed 20 bushels of wheat. World output now is at 48 bushels for a gain of 3 bushels, which is represented in Figure 2–2 by the distance AK. By the same method of reasoning, the world gain in the output of cloth can be seen to be equal to two and one half yards—the distance KE in Figure 2–2. In other words, as a result of specialization in production, both countries of the world can continue to consume the same quantities of both goods as under autarchy, at points A and E, and have left over AK wheat and KE cloth.

How are these gains from trade and specialization distributed between America and Europe? This depends on the price ratio at which wheat and cloth are exchanged in international trade. We will defer to the next chapter the analysis of how this world price ratio is determined. However, we can indicate here how it influences the distribution of the gains from trade. For this purpose, consider that the world price stays at the ratio prevailing in Europe before trade. Since nothing in our model implies that Europe's tastes have changed, it is reasonable to conclude that the old consumption pattern is maintained at these prices, and Europe as well as America consumes at point E. Under these conditions all gains accrue to America, which produces only wheat but can exchange 20 bushels of it for 10 yards of cloth at the European price of 2 for 1.

The preceding kind of reasoning can be repeated for any price ratio lying in the wedge between the American and European pretrade conditions. One such price is shown in Figure 2–2 as the line MM'. Exchange can take place anywhere along this line, but only in the area $AKEK'$ do the resultant combinations of goods imply at least pretrade quantities of each commodity for both countries. At point K, for example, America obtains all of the increased output of wheat and Europe all of the increased output of cloth.

Generally, a country's gains from trade and specialization are larger the more the world trade price ratio differs from that prevailing under autarchy. Maximum gains are obtained when the world trade price ratio is exactly equal to the pretrade ratio of the other country. At prices higher than this, the trading partner can attain only a consumption point inside the production frontier, involving lower than pretrade levels of consumption. While this price ratio would be desirable for one of the countries, the other one would not be interested in trading at all. We therefore conclude that the world trade price ratio must lie between the extremes of the two countries' pretrade price ratio.

Two interesting conclusions follow easily from the preceding model and analysis. First, there can be no gains from trade and specialization if the two countries' pretrade price ratios are identical. It can readily be seen from Figure 2–2 that under these conditions the two production possibility frontiers must coincide, and there is no such triangle as AKE. Second, the wedge representing the gains will be larger the more different the pretrade price ratios are. In the real world this difference is determined by all of the production conditions which underly comparative advantage. We will discuss these in the next chapter.

Finally, note that the geometric analysis reveals readily that the gains from trade and specialization are due only to relative labor productivity in the two industries, which we have seen to be the determinant of pretrade prices and of comparative advantage. Absolute labor productivity and absolute advantage do not enter the analysis of the gains. They merely determine the size of the production possibility block, given a country's stock of labor. The greater the absolute labor productivity, the larger the block.

The Small-Country Case

Understanding of the preceding analysis of the gains from trade can be deepened and some additional insights gained by considering the case in which the world is assumed to consist of only two countries, America, which is large, and Luxembourg, which is assumed to be relatively small. In Figure 2–3 we show the initial pretrade equilibrium condition, derived in a manner analogous to that used in connection with Figure 2–2. The origin of America's production block is in the bottom left corner and that

FIGURE 2–3
Trade of a Small Country

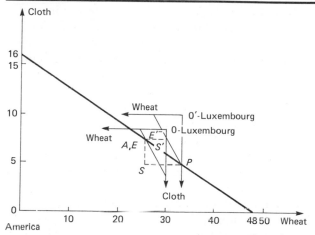

Pretrade world output is at point 0–Luxembourg. After Luxembourg specialized completely in the production of cloth and America moved from point A to point P on its frontier, total output increased to 0'–Luxembourg. With the world price remaining at that prevailing in America before trade, all gains from increased output accrue to Luxembourg, which consumes at point E, trading SE of its cloth output for SP of America's wheat. Through this trade America remains at point A and Luxembourg's gains are equal to ES' of wheat and E'S' of cloth consumption.

of Luxembourg is shown initially as 0–Luxembourg in the upper right corner. In the graph the two production blocks under autarchy have been placed in such a way that the points of domestic production and consumption, A for America and E for Luxembourg, coincide at the point A,E in Figure 2–3. It can readily be seen from the graph that as a result of this construction, total world output and consumption are given by the point 0–Luxembourg.

Now let us consider the effects of opening up trade between these two countries of very unequal size. In the new equilibrium, production is at point P and world output at $0'$–Luxembourg, the latter indicating that in comparison with the original output at 0–Luxembourg, there have been gains from international specialization in production of the sort analyzed above. However, in contrast with the preceding case of trade among roughly equal-sized countries, we can note that while Luxembourg in equilibrium is specialized completely in the production of cloth, America continues to produce both goods. This result is due to the fact that the change in the relative quantities of the two goods offered in America after the opening of trade is so small that it leads to only a marginal change in the relative price, sufficient to bring about the shift along the production locus from point A to point P. Since the domestic relative prices of wheat and cloth in America are the same before and after trade, consumption also remains unchanged at the preferred point A.

As a result of these conditions in America, the small country, Luxembourg, reaps all of the benefits from increased specialization in production and trade. It produces at P but consumes at E, which, if viewed from the proper Luxembourg origin of the trade block, implies a greater consumption of both wheat and cloth than was possible before trade at the point labeled E'. In this trade equilibrium Luxembourg produces $O'P$ of cloth, of which it trades SE for SP of wheat at America's price ratio, permitting the consumption of $O'P$–ES of cloth and SP of wheat in Luxembourg. The analysis shows clearly that a small country unable to affect world prices through its production and consumption decisions can benefit from international specialization, while it affects welfare in the rest of the world only marginally. In anticipation of arguments to be presented below we should note, however, that these potentially large benefits to the small country do not come entirely without cost. The small country is dependent through trade on the willingness of the rest of the world to continue trading. In our simplified example, Luxembourg imports all the wheat it consumes. At the same time, the rest of the world has diversified production and is much less dependent on trade than any small country. The dilemma of choice between gains from trade and specialization in return for greater dependence on the rest of the world haunts the public and politicians in many small countries.

BIBLIOGRAPHICAL NOTES

The reading of important ideas in their original source can provide interesting insights into their background and give a perspective on how difficult it has been to reach the level of sophistication characterizing modern international trade theories. The classic statements of pure trade theory using the labor theory of value are Ricardo (1817), chap. 7; Mill (1848); and Marshall (1879).

CONCEPTS FOR REVIEW

Absolute advantage
Comparative advantage
Gains from trade
Labor theory of value

POINTS FOR FURTHER STUDY AND DISCUSSION

1. What pattern of trade emerges in a Ricardian model of the world in which two countries have identical production functions?
2. Would the concept of absolute and comparative advantage have any meaning for Robinson Crusoe when he was alone? After Friday joined him?
3. Describe the labor theory of value, and explain what is appealing about it and in what applications it could lead to misleading conclusions.
4. Describe and evaluate the advantages and disadvantages associated with being a small country and trading with all the rest of the world or one other large country.

3 The Modern Theory of International Trade

IN THIS CHAPTER we present the complete model of the determinants of and gains from international trade as it has developed in the 20th century, in a tradition started by the Swedish economist Eli Heckscher and his student Bertil Ohlin. In honor of these economists the modern theory of international trade is known as the Heckscher-Ohlin model.

The expositional strategy we have adopted here is to base the model on just one set of assumptions about production functions, tastes, income distribution, and resource endowments, in order to make the general case of the gains from trade and analyze some fundamental implications for factor prices and economic interdependencies. In the following chapter we present modifications and extensions of the model which have been inspired by empirical findings that are inconsistent with the assumptions or conclusions of the simple model.

This chapter is divided into five sections. In the first two sections we derive models of production and consumer behavior within a given country. For most students these sections contain only little more than a review of price theory, though they do lay a very important foundation for the analysis that follows. Section III shows the gains from trade in a single country which faces an exogeneously given world price ratio for the two goods it produces. In Section IV we derive this world price, assuming that there are only two countries. The chapter concludes with a discussion of the factor price equalization theorem. The main objective of the chapter's analysis is to demonstrate the three most fundamental and important implications of the Heckscher-Ohlin model: (1) the efficiency of the free market in the maximization of world welfare; (2) the equilization of factor prices, and (3) the interdependence of the prices of goods, factor supplies, incomes, technology, and price levels.

24

I. PRODUCTION

The classical economists had assumed that only labor needs to be considered in the analysis of production conditions giving rise to international trade, implying that differences in production functions explain differences in labor productivity among countries. In the following analysis we become somewhat more realistic by assuming that production requires two inputs, labor and capital. Of course, in the real world land, human and knowledge capital, and natural resources also enter into production, and climate and cultural and social conditions influence the productivity of these factor inputs. We do not disregard these other influences on production altogether, but we remove them from the analysis by assuming that they are the same in all parts of the world and that they determine the overall productivity of the two primary factors. As a result, differences in fundamental conditions determining productivity in the two countries, A and B that are assumed to make up the world are due only to the relative amounts of capital and labor they possess. In more formal language, the preceding assumption states that production functions are identical in both countries, but that relative factor supplies differ. Later in this book we will analyze the implications this assumption has for the main conclusions to be reached in this chapter.

Production functions indicate precisely what minimum quantities of the inputs, labor and capital, are required to produce different amounts of a given product. This relationship between inputs and output is purely technological and in principle is supplied by engineers. We assume that the production functions for goods X and Y possess certain characteristics, which can easily be specified with the help of Figure 3–1.

The curve labeled XX' shows the combinations of labor and capital required to produce one unit of good X. The curve, known as an isoquant, is convex if viewed from below. This convexity signifies that the removal from the production process of successive one-unit measures of one of the factors can be compensated for only by the addition to the process of increasingly larger amounts of the second factor. This phenomenon is known as involving diminishing marginal rates of substitution and is assumed to be continuous and without limit. Consequently, the curvature of the isoquants in our assumed production function is without kinks, and it becomes asymptotic to the labor and capital axes.

The least cost combination of capital and labor used by producers of the good X is determined by the relative price of the factors and the budget constraint. In Figure 3–1 we show the price of three units of labor for two units of capital by the two straight parallel lines known as budget or iso-outlay lines. The lower of the budget lines, $CL,$ indicates that a given amount of money can purchase either seven and one half units of labor or five units of capital, or any combination of the two found along the line.

FIGURE 3–1
Production Functions

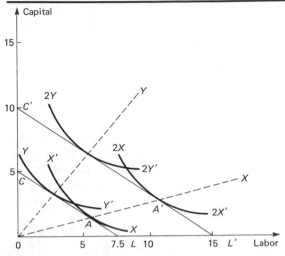

The isoquants XX′ and YY′ show the combinations of capital and labor required to produce one arbitrarily defined unit of goods X and Y, respectively. The iso-outlay line C′ shows that at the assumed relative factor prices it is possible to purchase three units of labor for every two units of capital. Least cost combinations of capital and labor are given by the rays OY and OX for the industries producing goods Y and X, respectively. X is the labor- and Y the capital-intensive industry. The facts that the two budget lines are parallel, the distances OA and AA′ are equal, and the isoquant 2X2X′ represents twice the output of XX′ indicate that the production function is subject to constant returns to scale.

Point A in Figure 3–1 is at the tangency between the isoquant and the budget line and represents the least cost combination of labor and capital to produce one unit of X. Only at that point does the rate at which capital has to be substituted for labor in the production process (known as the marginal rate of substitution) equal the rate at which capital can be exchanged for labor in the market. The incentives on producers to move to this efficient input combination can readily be seen by considering production at a point where the marginal rate of substitution is one unit of capital for three units of labor, while the market exchange takes place at two for three. Taking away three units of labor from the production process and substituting one unit of capital to maintain output at the initial level is profitable because the three labor units bring two capital units, for a net gain of one. The hypothesized substitution of capital for labor changes the marginal rate of substitution in production and comes to an end when all profitable exchange opportunities have ceased to exist and the marginal rate of substitution and relative factor prices are equal.

A further characteristic of our production function is that it exhibits constant returns to scale, which means that the doubling of both inputs at the same relative price leads to a doubling of the output and the use of capital and labor in unchanged proportions. In Figure 3–1, the new budget line is drawn parallel to the initial one, indicating unchanged relative prices; and the new budget line is twice the distance from the origin as the old one, indicating a doubling of outlays. The budget line is tangent to the isoquant 2X2X', which represents twice the level of output as isoquant XX'. The points of tangency between budget lines and isoquants A and A' lie along the ray OX from the origin, indicating unchanged relative physical capital labor requirements at the same relative factor prices.

Production functions of this sort are used frequently in all branches of economics. They have many convenient mathematical characteristics and have been found to exist in many industries. Later in this book we will consider our model using some different forms of the production function.

In Figure 3–1 we also show the production function for good Y. It differs from that for good X in only one important respect: It requires a higher proportion of capital to labor inputs at all relative factor prices. This is shown by the facts that the ray OY is steeper than the ray OX, and the isoquants for the two products each intersect only once. The importance of this assumption will become apparent in the next chapter. In other respects the production functions for X and Y are the same, exhibiting constant returns to scale and diminishing returns to the variable factor. It may be worth noting that doubling of inputs and outputs of the two goods can be represented in Figure 3–1 as taking place on the same budget lines by defining conveniently (but otherwise arbitrarily) the units of output of both goods to be one at the first budget line.

In the following discussion we will occasionally have to refer to the capital/labor intensity of production of a given good. It is clear that this intensity is not absolute and must therefore always involve the comparison of at least two goods. In our example and the illustration in Figure 3–1, good Y is the capital- and X is the labor-intensive product.

The Edgeworth Box Diagram

We will now turn to the derivation of a country's production possibilities frontier, using the production functions specified above and employing the Edgeworth Box diagram. This tool of geometric analysis was named after its inventor, F. Y. Edgeworth, who produced his most important writings in economics in the last decades of the 19th century. The analysis based on the Edgeworth Box diagram is rather involved, but the insights derived from it are very valuable and therefore worth studying carefully.

In the top panel of Figure 3–2 we show a rectangular box which is assumed to indicate the stocks of labor and capital available during a given

FIGURE 3–2

Edgeworth Box Diagram (top) and Production Frontier (bottom)

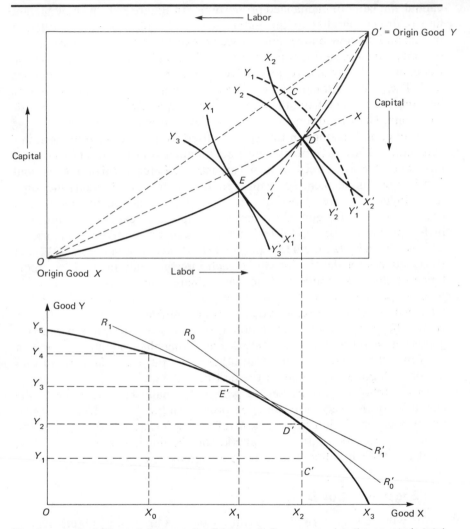

The top panel of Figure 3–2 shows the Edgeworth Box, measuring the country's total stocks of labor and capital along the horizontal and vertical axes, respectively. The output origins of industries X and Y are in the bottom left and top right corners, respectively. Two sets of X and Y isoquants are tangent at points E and D is known as the contract curve and connects all possible points of tangency, such as E and D between X and Y isoquants. If production takes place on the contract curve, then output of one good can be increased only by decreasing output of the other. If output is at any other point such as C, labor and capital are fully used, but a different combination of the inputs allows output of one good to be increased without requiring a decrease in the other good. The slopes of the rays OX and OY indicate the relative factor combinations used in the two industries when output is at point D on the contract curve.

In the bottom panel the quantities of goods X and Y are measured on the horizontal time period in a representative country, A. The horizontal length of the box measures the physical units of labor, and the vertical length represents the units of capital. The bottom left-hand corner of the box is considered to be the zero origin for the production function of good X, as shown in Figure 3–1. In the box the isoquants X_1X_1' and X_2X_2' are representative of the entire production function for X. The further from the origin the isoquants are, the higher the level of output of good X they represent. The subscripts to the X isoquants indicate ranking of output levels but not exact proportionality.

The upper right-hand corner of the box is treated as the origin of the production function map for good Y, and within the box some representative isoquants with the familiar characteristics are shown.

Let us now consider a random point in the box, such as C. It must be on an isoquant for both X and Y, as is shown in Figure 3–2. By producing at this point country A will employ all of its resources, as can readily be discovered by relating input requirements of labor and capital in the production of X_2X_2' and Y_1Y_1' at point C to the total stock of these factors. However, output at point C is not efficient, since it is possible to increase the output of one good without decreasing the output of the other. That this is so can be seen by analyzing the consequences of production at points alternative to C but lying on the isoquant X_2X_2'. At any point between C and D in Figure 3–2 the output of X remains unchanged, while the output of Y is above the initial Y_1. The maximum output of Y, given X_2, is attained at point D.

At point D two isoquants of X and Y are tangent, showing that at this point the marginal rates of substitution of capital for labor in the two industries are the same. Both industries will choose the capital/labor input proportions shown by the lines OX and $O'Y$ and end up at point D if the relative price of capital and labor in the market is equal to this marginal rate of substitution in production. Geometrically we would show this capital/labor price ratio by a budget line going through D and tangent to both isoquants, though we have not done so in Figure 3–2 to keep the drawing as simple as possible.

Point D is just one of a locus of points where the maps of isoquants of the X and Y production functions are tangent. This locus is shown as the curved line running between the two production function origins (O_xEDO_y) and is known as the contract curve. Any point of production on

and vertical axes, respectively. The curve Y_5X_3 represents the maximum combination of the two goods producible with the stock of resources and production functions shown in the top panel. The point D' in the lower panel corresponds to point D in the upper panel, both showing output of X_2 and Y_2. Analogously, there is a correspondence between points E' and E and outputs of X_1 and Y_3.

The two graphs show that relative factor prices and goods prices are jointly and uniquely determined by output. At points D and D' the factor and goods price ratios are given, and they are different from those found at points E and E'.

this contract curve has the characteristic that it involves efficient production in the sense that the output of one product can be raised only by reduction in the output of the other. For later analysis it is important to note that the choice of different combinations of outputs of X and Y, as for example X_1 and Y_3 at point E in contrast with X_2 and Y_2 at D, involves different capital/labor ratios in both industries and therefore also different relative prices of capital and labor. If capital/labor ratio lines analogous to OX and $O'Y$ were drawn through point E, it would be evident that both production processes are more labor intensive than they are at point D. The explanation of this phenomenon is as follows. As we move from point D to E along the contract curve, the output of Y is increased and output of X, is decreased. Every reduction of X output releases a bundle of capital and labor that contains relatively more labor than is required at the initial technique of producing good Y, since we had assumed that X is the labor-intensive product. In order to employ all available labor, the technique of producing both products therefore must become relatively more labor intensive as we move towards increased output of the capital-intensive product.

Why does the contract curve bulge towards the lower right corner? We can answer this question by analyzing why it is not a straight line and why it does not bulge in the opposite direction. First, the contract curve cannot be a straight line running diagonally across the box from one production function origin to the other, because this would imply that the two products require inputs of capital and labor in identical ratios, which violates our assumption that they are different. Second, remember the assumption that X is the labor- and Y is the capital-intensive industry. As we consider the diagonal line across the box, going from one origin to the other, we can see that it provides a convenient common reference slope by which the slopes of the OX and $O'Y$ rays can be judged. Looking from the respective origins, OX is flatter and $O'Y$ is steeper than the diagonal, indicating that the former is relatively labor intensive and the latter relatively capital intensive, consistent with our assumption. Now consider what slopes the OX and $O'Y$ lines would have if the contract line bulge were to the left of the diagonal. We would find OX capital intensive and $O'Y$ labor intensive, which is inconsistent with our assumption. Therefore, the contract curve must bulge below the diagonal.

The Production Frontier

After this analysis of the most important features of the Edgeworth Box, we now move to the bottom panel of Figure 3–2 to explain how the production possibilities frontier is derived from the box diagram. Starting at the origin of good X, we know that output of X is at zero and of Y is at its maximum. This condition is reflected in the fact that the production frontier commences at the vertical Y axis and shows a maximum production of Y_5 with X output at zero. By similar reasoning we find the maximum output of X_3 and zero Y. The production frontier connecting the points X_3Y_5 shows the combination of maximum quantities of X and Y attainable by producing efficiently on the contract curve. Point D on the contract curve is associated with outputs X_2 and Y_2, which are reflected in point D' on the production frontier, and so on for points E and E' and other unlabeled points on the two curves. The inefficient production at C discussed earlier causes the corresponding point C' to lie inside the production frontier, with the distance $D'C'$ representing the gain in output of Y attained by moving to the efficient technologies.

At every point such as D' on the production frontier there exists one unique and efficient relative price for products X and Y. In Figure 3–2 we have shown this price as R_0R_0'. Now consider the adjustment process taking place when the original equilibrium goods price R_0R_0' is changed exogenously to R_1R_1', shown to be tangent to the production frontier at E'. At the new price, X is relatively more expensive than it was before, and producers are induced to increase the output of X. In so doing they require factors of production which are bid away from the Y industry. These adjustments appear in the Edgeworth Box as a movement along the contract curve from point D to point E. As we mentioned above, the shift into the production of the more capital-intensive product requires increased labor intensity of the production processes in both industries. Consequently, there is also an increase in the marginal productivity of capital and a decrease in the marginal productivity of labor, implying a different wage/capital ratio than existed at point D. The important conclusion of this analysis is that the relative price of goods X and Y is interdependent with and determined uniquely and simultaneously by the relative quantity of the two goods produced, the technology used in both industries, and the relative price between capital and labor.

The exact curvature of the production frontier is not important for our purposes of analysis, as long as two characteristics are present. First, the frontier must be downward sloping, thus satisfying the condition established in our discussion of the contract curve that increased output of one good can be attained only at the expense of reduced output of the other. Second, the frontier must be concave from the origin. This condition implies that there are diminishing marginal rates of transformation of one product into the other. Geometrically this condition is revealed by the fact that as output of one product is increased by successive units, reductions in the output of the other become increasingly larger. In Figure 3–2 we show rather crudely that two equal-sized unit increases in the output OX_0 and X_0X_1 lead to successively larger reductions in the output Y_5Y_4 and Y_4Y_3, where $Y_5Y_4 < Y_4Y_3$.

In the Appendix to this chapter we prove geometrically that the assumptions made above about the nature of the production functions, especially the condition of constant returns to scale, must lead to a production frontier having diminishing marginal rates of transformation. That proof follows that presented in an article by K. M. Savosnick (1958) and may be skipped by readers in a hurry. The proof is interesting and important, because it is not immediately obvious why, under conditions of constant returns to scale in production, a country should not be able to trade off one product for the other at a constant rate and thus have a straight-line production frontier. At an intuitive level, the explanation for the phenomenon lies in the diminishing returns to the variable factor. These diminishing returns become operative as capital/labor ratios in both industries change at different output mixes to keep all resources employed, as we analyzed above.

Summary and Conclusions

In this section of Chapter 3 we have derived the production possibilities frontier of a country, starting from a set of assumptions about production functions and specifying a given stock of capital and labor. We have shown that the assumed production functions imply concavity from the origin of the production frontier and that any point on the frontier has a counterpart on the contract curve in the Edgeworth Box diagram. At all points along the contract curve capital/labor ratios in both industries and the equilibrium relative prices of capital and labor are different. This strict interdependence between the mix of output and the relative prices of X and Y and the factor prices and technologies will be seen to be important in our analysis of the effects from the opening of international trade to be discussed below. However, before we can turn to this topic, we need to introduce consumer tastes into the analysis, to explain the choice of output and consumption patterns in the country under consideration.

II. THE COMMUNITY INDIFFERENCE CURVE

An essential element of the proof of the gains from trade in the Heckscher-Ohlin model is the community indifference curve. We will show how it is derived from the individual indifference curve and discuss one of its short-comings, which represents the Achilles heel of this otherwise objective and value-free demonstration of the gains from trade.

The individual indifference curve map is an unambiguous and useful concept. In Figure 3–3, the curve I_0I_0' shows the combination of the goods X and Y whose consumption leaves a given individual at the same level of satisfaction. It can be derived in principle by asking a person to reveal his preferences after introspection. Its shape is determined by the operation of the ubiquitous law of diminishing returns, which in turn is responsible for

FIGURE 3–3
Individual Indifference Curve

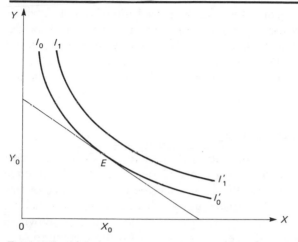

The indifference curve I_0I_0' shows the combination of goods X and Y whose consumption leaves the individual at the same level of welfare. The budget line is tangent to the indifference curve at point E, indicating that at the given relative price of the two goods, and the budget, the highest level of welfare is reached by the consumption of goods X_0 and Y_0. When the budget allows attainment of indifference curve I_1I_1', a higher level of welfare has been reached.

the existence of diminishing marginal rates of substitution of one good into the other. This characteristic is reflected in the convexity from the origin of the indifference curve. In common-sense terms it implies that, typically, the successive removal of equal-sized units of one good will induce a person to ask for increasingly more units of the second good, in order to stay at the same level of welfare.

Every person can be considered as having a complete map of indifference curves such as I_0I_0', each representing a different level of welfare. We have drawn into Figure 3–3 a second indifference curve, I_1I_1', to make two points. First, since I_1I_1' is above and to the right of I_0I_0', it represents a greater combination of goods over the entire range, and therefore it is considered to imply a higher level of welfare for the individual than does the curve I_0I_0'. By the same reasoning, indifference curves below and to the left of I_0I_0' represent lower levels of welfare. Second, indifference curves must not intersect. If they did we would have the nonsensical situation that the point of intersection represents simultaneously two different levels of welfare, since it is common to two indifference curves.

In Figure 3–3 we also show a budget or iso-outlay line, which should be familiar from our discussion of production functions. At point E the individual with given tastes consumes the bundle OY_0 of Y and OX_0 of X and attains the highest level of welfare from his given income, represented by the budget line. At E the marginal rate of substitution in the welfare function of the person is equal to the relative price ratio of X and Y, which is also the rate at which the two goods can be transformed into, or exchanged for, each other in the market. Only when these individual and market rates are equal is it impossible to increase welfare through arbitrage operations of the kind discussed above in connection with production functions.

A Community Indifference Curve

We will now consider a community assumed to consist of only two individuals, whose preferences are given and described by indifference maps of the kind just discussed. We derive the indifference curve of this community by assuming a given distribution of the community's income and a given relative price for the two goods. Individual 1 is shown to consume OX_1 and OY_1 quantities, reaching a level of welfare equal to I_1I_1', as shown in Figure 3–4. The second individual consumes X_1X_2 and Y_1Y_2 quantities to reach his indifference curve, I_2I_2'. In Figure 3–4 the second person's indifference map is drawn with the origin in the upper right-hand corner and the two axes parallel to those of the first individual. Point C, the origin of the second indifference map, reflects the total consumption of OX_2 and OY_2 of the community in the initial situation. The community indifference curve, $I_{1+2}I_{1+2}'$, goes through point C and has a slope equal to the relative goods price line, RR', at point D, where the two individual indifference curves are tangent.

The community indifference curve $I_{1+2}I_{1+2}'$ is derived by considering alternative relative prices of the two goods, finding equilibrium points for each individual on the initial indifference curve, and adding up the combination of X and Y consumed by each, just as was done to find point C. Graphically, this procedure is equivalent to sliding the two individual indifference curves along each other, keeping parallel the two axes in the graph. The origin of the second individual's map then traces out the community indifference curve, $I_{1+2}I_{1+2}'$, as shown in Figure 3–4.

The meaning of this community indifference curve is quite analogous to that of the individual's curve. It shows the combination of goods X and Y which leave the community equally well off. The slope of the curve represents a relative goods price at which both individuals separately are induced to consume quantities of the two goods equal to those available to the community, keeping each at the hypothesized initial level of welfare.

The key problem in the use of community indifference curves arises when for some exogenous reason the community's income is raised and a point such as C' on $I_{1+2}'I_{1+2}''$ becomes attainable. While for the individual such a move to a higher indifference curve always represents an unam-

FIGURE 3–4

Community Indifference Curve

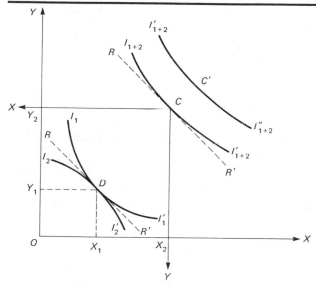

In Figure 3–4 the community indifference curve, $I_{1+2}I_{1+2}'$, is found by placing the origins of two individual indifference maps on the bottom left corner O and upper right corner C of the box and sliding the specific individual indifference curves, I_1I_1' and I_2I_2', along each other, while keeping the axes parallel. The origin, C, traces out the community indifference curve. At any price ratio, such as RR' tangent to $I_{1+2}I_{1+2}'$, the community demands quantities of goods X and Y which can be distributed among the two individuals such that each of them remains at the same level of welfare as at any other relative price and corresponding consumption pattern.

biguous gain, we cannot be certain that it does so in the case of the community. This is so because we do not know from the information given whether or not the increased income was accompanied by any redistribution of income among consumers.

Logically, it is possible in such a case that one consumer's income will remain unchanged and all of the increased income will accrue to the second. The community enjoys an unambiguous gain only if the welfare functions of the two consumers are independent, so that the higher income of the second does not affect adversely the welfare of the first. Such a relationship is normally assumed to exist in economics, though its realism is open to some question. A second possibility is that both consumers will enjoy an increase in income. Here we have an unambiguous gain, except under conditions of interdependent welfare functions and unequal gains.

A third possibility is that the gains in community income may lead to a redistribution such that one person's income decreases absolutely and all of the community's net gains, plus some more, accrue to the second person. This creates the greatest analytical difficulties; it frequently takes place in connection with the opening up of international trade. Modern welfare economics has established that in this situation objective analysis cannot prove that the gains of one person, however great they may be in terms of physical quantities of goods, are sufficient to offset the losses of the second person, even if they involve small numbers of goods. Any estimates of community welfare changes in this sort of instance involve interpersonal comparisons of welfare, which cannot be undertaken legitimately because economists have no objective measuring tool for this task. Thus, even if welfare functions are independent, community welfare is not necessarily increased as long as the gains in output are accompanied by the decrease in income of only one person.

Modern welfare economics has concluded that the only objective way it can be shown that a policy increases overall welfare is if gainers from the policy actually bribe losers into accepting the policy change. A blending of political science and economics in the writings of Anthony Downs (1957) and J. Buchanan (1968) in recent years has suggested that political bargaining processes in legislatures and democratic election processes can be considered as being equivalent to processes whereby losers are bribed into accepting policies which would reduce their welfare but otherwise are in the interest of the community as a whole. In this book we will assume that this political bargaining process works with sufficient efficiency in the countries under examination, so that we can interpret any move to a higher community indifference curve as an unambiguous gain in welfare.

This procedure for overcoming the fundamental difficulty arising from the noncomparability of individuals' personal welfare is not entirely satisfactory. It has to be brought into an analysis in which otherwise there is no government and the assumption about the operation of political processes is itself known to be valid only in a most general way. However, the alternatives to the use of this procedure are even worse.

First, we could reject the proof of gains from trade as being invalid and refuse to base any policy recommendations on it. Governments would not like this solution because if they wish to improve welfare they must act, especially since they are pressed constantly by interest groups to make certain policies, and these interest groups are not reluctant to make interpersonal comparisons of welfare in stating their case. For this reason governments need the advice of economists about the general welfare implications of these policies.

Second, we could assume that all consumers in the community are so similar in their cultural and psychological makeup that they function much like identical "pleasure machines," and they enjoy equal standard units of welfare from the consumption of the same bundles of goods. Moreover, we must assume that consumers do not experience decreasing marginal utility of income. In technical terms, all of these characteristics are embodied in the assumption that the welfare functions of all consumers are identical and linearly homogeneous, where the latter expression describes the constancy of the marginal utility of income in analogy with linearly homogeneous production functions which exhibit constant returns to scale. Under this set of assumptions the transfer of one bundle of goods from one person to the other does not change aggregate welfare, since the gainer and the loser experience equal-sized standard changes in welfare. Net increases in output then raise overall welfare unambiguously.

While this last set of assumptions is technically neat and succeeds in overcoming the problems raised by our inability to make interpersonal comparisons of utility, it does not seem to be very realistic. Especially, the assumption of constant marginal utility of income appears to be unjustified. If it were correct, many important policy conclusions derived from modern economic analysis would be invalid.

Summary and Conclusions

This section of Chapter 3 can be summed up as follows. The concept of the individual indifference curve is unambiguous, allowing us to judge the direction of personal welfare changes resulting from changes in income and prices confronting an individual. The community indifference curve map derived from the indifference curves of two individuals gives rise to some ambiguities in the interpretation of welfare gains, based on the fact that economists have no tool for the interpersonal comparison of welfare. We adopted the assumption that political bargaining processes work sufficiently well to assure that the interests of losers are protected and policies are undertaken only if gainers are made better off after they have compensated the losers. We therefore interpret movements to higher community indifference curves as unambiguous gains in welfare.

III. THE GAINS FROM TRADE

The payoff from an investment in understanding of production functions, the production possibilities frontier, and the community indifference curve now comes easily as we combine these concepts in drawing Figure 3–5. We show our representative country, A, in equilibrium before it engages in any foreign trade. The economy produces and consumes at point C,P on its production frontier. The community reaches a level of welfare indicated by the indifference curve I_0I_0', which is tangent to the production frontier at C,P. The domestic relative price for X and Y is shown by the line RR' going through C,P and tangent to both the indifference curve and the production frontier. From our preceding analysis it is known that under the conditions represented by Figure 3–5, the economy is producing at maximum efficiency and will reach the highest level of

FIGURE 3–5
Gains from Trade

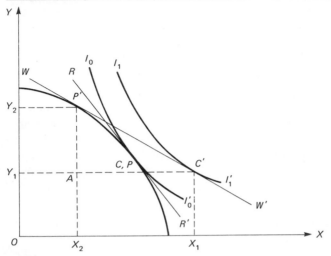

Under autarchy country A produces and consumes at point C,P, reaching level I_0I_0' of welfare at the domestic price ratio RR'. Opening of trade leads to the establishment of the world price, WW'; production at P'; consumption at C', and the higher level of welfare, I_1I_1'. In trade equilibrium country A imports AC' of good X and exports AP' of good Y.

community welfare attainable with the given income distribution. No reallocation of resources within the economy can increase the welfare of one person without decreasing that of another person. This point of maximum efficiency and welfare is attained by the decentralized decisions of individual producers and consumers pursuing their self-interests in a setting constrained by competition and market-determined prices for goods and by the labor and capital they own.

Now consider that this closed economy is opened up to international trade through some exogenous event such as the removal of government obstacles to trade or the drastic lowering of transportation costs. We assume that as a result of this opening of trade the relative price of goods X and Y in country A becomes equal to WW', as shown in Figure 3–5. In the next section of this chapter we discuss the determinants of this world price, but for the moment we assume that it is given exogenously and that it remains unchanged, whatever quantities of the two goods country A exchanges. These characteristics of the world price would be encountered typically by a small country, whose demand and supply are unimportant relative to the quantities produced and consumed in the rest of the world.

According to our analysis in Section I above, the establishment of the world price WW' induces producers in country A to increase output of the good Y, which has become relatively more expensive than good X. In doing so, they decrease output of X and reach the equilibrium mix of output shown as point P' on the production frontier in Figure 3–5.

Consumers facing the new relative world price ratio similarly are induced to change their expenditure patterns. In the new equilibrium they consume at point C' on the world price ratio WW', reaching the higher level of welfare represented by the isoquant I_1I_1'.

As can be seen from Figure 3–5, the new point of consumption lies outside of the production frontier. This is possible because of international trade, which involves the export of the excess of production over consumption of the Y good (i.e., $Y_2Y_1 = OY_2 - OY_1$), for the import of the excess of consumption over production of the X good (i.e., $X_2X_1 = OX_1 - OX_2$). The slope of the budget line WW' forming the hypotenuse of the rectangular triangle $AP'C'$ in Figure 3–5 indicates that the world is willing to exchange exactly $AP' = Y_2Y_1$ of country A's export good Y for $AC' = X_2X_1$ of that country's import good X.

The gains from trade enjoyed by country A are equivalent to the increase in the community's welfare gained by consuming a bundle of goods on the indifference curve I_1I_1', which is above and to the right of the maximum indifference curve II' attainable in the absence of trade. Such gains from trade must take place, given our assumptions about the nature of the production and community welfare functions in country A whenever both products are consumed and produced under autarchy and the world price ratio is different from that under autarchy. For example, if in Figure 3–5 the new world price WW' had been steeper than RR', the new production point would have been closer to the X axis on the production frontier. However, the new world price line then must lie to the right of point C,P and give rise to a new point of tangency with an indifference curve above the original II'. Only when the world and domestic prices under autarchy are identical (i.e., $WW' = RR'$) will there be no increase in welfare from the opening of international trade.

In Figure 3–6 we have reproduced in all essential aspects Figure 3–5, but we have added a world price line W_1W_1', which is parallel to WW' but goes through point C,P. To this new world price line the indifference curve I_1I_1' is tangent at point C_2. It lies between the pretrade curve I_0I_0' and the free trade curve I_2I_2'.

Figure 3–6 allows us to demonstrate that the gains from trade analytically have two components. The first arises from the opportunity to trade at world prices alone. Country A remains at the production point under autarchy, C, P, but trades its output at the world price to reach consumption point C_2 for a gain in welfare from I_0I_0' to I_1I_1'. The triangle C, P, A', C_2 shows the quantities traded at the world price. In this situation the relative prices of the commodities in the markets for consumers and producers are different, because producers stay at point C,P only if the

FIGURE 3-6
Gains from Specialization and Trade

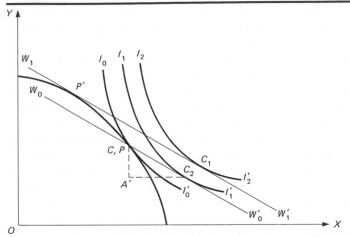

The welfare gains from trade consist of those due to trade at the initial point of production and from specialization in production. Trade gains are from I_0I_1' to I_1I_1' with consumption at C_2, and production gains are from I_1I_1' to I_2I_2' with consumption at C_1.

price ratio is at its pretrade level RR' and consumers are in equilibrium at C_2 only at the world price W_0W_0'. In a later chapter we will discuss techniques, such as tariffs, by which governments can drive such a wedge between domestic and world price ratios.

In Figure 3-6 we also show the equilibrium position of the economy after production has adjusted to the world price W_1W_1' and consumption takes place at C_1. The welfare gain from I_1I_1' to I_2I_2' is due to specialization in production. We conclude, therefore, that what in the preceding analysis we called "gains from trade" can conveniently be considered to consist of the two components of gains from trade and gains from specialization in production.

The Case for Free Trade

Up to this point in this chapter we have made the very fundamental and important case that free trade tends to result in maximum welfare for the population of a country. The proof represents the justification for the recommendations by economists that governments should not interfere with the free international flow of goods and services. As we have seen, the proof is based on a number of clearly specified assumptions about the nature of production functions and consumer tastes, the stocks of capital and labor, forces guiding the maximizing behavior of producers, and consumers and prices in the rest of the world. We have defended the realism of these assumptions, and in later chapters we will discuss what implications result from changes in these assumptions. Except for the problem with interpersonal comparisons of welfare, which imply acceptance of the posttrade income distribution, the tools of analysis we have used involved value-free concepts and reasonably realistic descriptions of the real world.

It is difficult to underestimate the influence this academic exercise and proof of the gains from trade and specialization have had on the world economy and the welfare of nations. Governments in the real world are constantly besieged by labor or the owners of capital to protect them from the adverse effects of foreign trade. Though it is dangerous to use our simple Heckscher-Ohlin model to illustrate real-world phenomena, the analysis of the two-goods case is sufficiently realistic to make the point of how trade and specialization lead to changes in production techniques and the relative returns to labor and capital. Industries and factors of production losing in this process of adjustment tend to be well organized and to be capable of presenting their cases to the government effectively.

The beneficiaries of free trade—consumers and some factors of production—tend on the other hand to be poorly organized and ineffective in their representations to government. This is so because the benefits from free trade often are less obvious than the losses, and it seems to be human nature that actual decreases in welfare call forth more vigorous actions than do the threats of reduced or zero increases. In this world, the unequal pressures on governments to interfere with free trade are equalized by economists who make the case for free trade through direct representations with governments and through public education. In so doing they rely heavily on the insights derived from the kind of rigorous analysis we have presented in this chapter.

In this book we will present many extensions, refinements, and modifications of the basic Heckscher-Ohlin model which underlies our demonstration of the gains from trade and specialization. As a result of this work students should increase their understanding of the real world and discover many special circumstances under which free trade will not maximize welfare. However, most economists believe that all of these special circumstances have failed to destroy the general case for free trade we have just made.

IV. GENERAL EQUILIBRIUM: OFFER CURVES

We now turn to the determination of the equilibrium world trade price, which in Section III we assumed to be given exogenously. To do so we use a geometric technique perfected by James Meade, a British economist who published the first rigorous and complete exposition of the Heckscher-Ohlin model in 1952. In the derivation of the equilibrium world price we develop as intermediate steps of analysis the concepts of the trade indifference curve and the offer curve. The latter concept is used extensively in the analysis of the effects of tariffs to be presented in Part Two.

We assume that the world consists of two approximately equal-sized countries, A and B, endowed with given stocks of capital and labor which are combined to produce production frontiers of the kind discussed in Section III of this chapter. Welfare levels are represented by the familiar community indifference curves. The analysis proceeds by developing first trade indifference and offer curves for country B and then generalizes from them to justify the offer curve for country A. The combination of the two offer curves yields the equilibrium world price ratio and some other valuable insights into adjustments accompanying the exploitation of gains from trade.

The Trade Indifference Curve and Map

In Figure 3–7 the axes measure physical quantities of goods X and Y produced, consumed, and traded by country B. The production frontier of country B is shown to extend into the northwest (upper left) quadrant of the commodity axis instead of the northeast (upper right) quadrant it

FIGURE   3–7
The Trade Indifference Curve

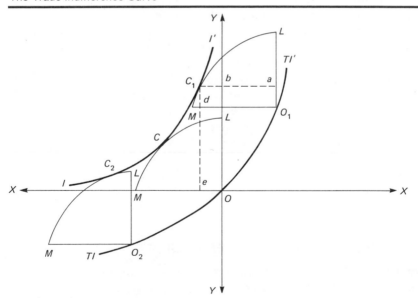

The trade indifference curve $TITI'$ is derived by sliding the production block MOL along the community indifference curve II', holding the axes parallel and having the origin O of the production block trace out the trade indifference curve. In equilibrium at a point such as C_1, country B is producing $O_1 d$ and consuming eO of good X, while it consumes eC_1 and produces dC_1 of good Y. It therefore exports ba of X for the import of ed of Y.

occupied in other diagrams presented above. The reason for this switch will become obvious below. Point C represents pretrade equilibrium and marks the tangency between the indifference curve II' and the production frontier LM.

Let us now slide the production block OML along the indifference curve II' keeping the commodity axes parallel at all times. As we do so, the origin of the production block traces out the line $TITI'$, which is known as the trade indifference curve because it traces out a locus of points along which country B is at the same level of welfare with trade as it is in the initial situation without trade. In order to see this, consider that both points C and C_1 are on the same community indifference curve. While C is attainable without trade, C_1 is reached when the origin of the production block touches the trade indifference curve at O_1, as is shown in Figure 3–7. In this situation country B produces C_1a of good X but consumes only C_1b, thus leaving ba for export. Imports of ed of good Y are required to supplement production of C_1d and permit consumption of C_1e. We can therefore conclude that if country B could exchange ba units of X for de units of Y, it could produce at point C_1 of its production frontier and enjoy the same welfare as without trade. Similar statements about production, trade, and welfare can be made about all points along the $TITI'$ curve. We should note, though we cannot prove it here, that the slope of the trade indifference curve at O_1 is equal to that of the community indifference curve at C_1, and so on for all corresponding points O and C.

Before we can use this trade indifference curve in our further analysis, we need to make the point that $TITI'$ is only one of an entire map of such trade indifference curves. In Figure 3–8 we show three different community indifference curves, the subscripts corresponding to higher levels of welfare. By sliding the production block along each of these community indifference curves in the manner described above, we can trace out a corresponding family of trade indifference curves. These are shown as the broken lines in Figure 3–7, and they represent higher levels of welfare the higher and further to the left they are.

The Offer Curve

In Figure 3–9 this same family of trade indifference curves for country B is replicated, but to keep the drawing simple, other features of Figures 3–7 and 3–8 have been omitted. The straight lines labeled OW_1, OW_2, and so on in Figure 3–9 represent different relative prices for the two goods X and Y, which are also known as the terms of trade. The steeper the line is, the more expensive is X in terms of Y. The price ratio lines are tangent to the trade indifference curves at points O, D, E and F. For the complete map of indifference curves and price ratios, we would find the line OB as the locus of tangency points. This line, OB, is known as country B's offer

FIGURE 3–8
The Trade Indifference Map

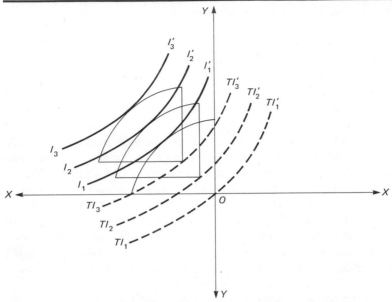

The trade indifference map is derived by repeating the process described in Figure 3–7 at different community indifference curves. Since community indifference curves with higher numbered subscripts represent higher levels of welfare, trade indifference curves with higher numbered subscripts also represent higher levels of welfare.

curve. It indicates what quantities of goods X and Y country B is willing to exchange at different relative prices. For example, at the price implied by the ray OW_4, country B is willing to import OY_4 of Y and export OX_4 of X.

The welfare of country B increases the further away from the origin O on the offer curve it is. This follows directly from our derivation of the trade indifference curves, which imply higher levels of community welfare the higher and further to the left they are. The common-sense explanation of the phenomenon is that at low prices for its export good X, country B obtains few units of Y, keeps trade at a low level, and enjoys only small gains from trade and specialization. In fact, at a whole range of unfavorable terms of trade represented by lines flatter than OW_1, country B could realize no gains from trade at all. This is, of course, why the offer curve does not exist at terms-of-trade lines below OW_1.

Why does the offer curve bend backward, indicating that after some critical terms of trade, further increases in the price of the export good X will induce country B to offer absolutely fewer units of X for more of Y? The answer to this question is implicit in the building blocks of our analysis. Recall from our discussions above that movements along the

FIGURE 3–9
The Offer Curve

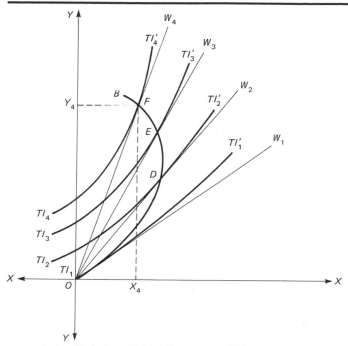

The offer curve, *OB*, is the locus of points at which different world price ratios for goods *X* and *Y* represented by the lines OW_1, OW_2, etc., are tangent to the trade indifference curves TI_1TI_1', TI_2TI_2', and so on. At the world price ratio OW_4, country B reaches its highest trade indifference curve TI_4TI_4', since at this world price it can obtain more of its import good *Y* for a given amount of its export good *X* than at the other world price ratios shown.

production frontier lead to diminishing marginal rates of transformation so that the closer country B gets to complete specialization in the production of *X*, the fewer units of *X* can be obtained for the resources set free by the reduction of a unit output of *Y*. For strictly analogous reasons, as consumers in country B are induced to purchase more and more of good *Y* at the decreasing price, they experience strongly diminishing marginal rates of substitution in their consumption. The combination of these two effects results in the backward bending of the offer curve. In more common-sense terms, but also somewhat inaccurately, we can say that the phenomenon is due to the fact that after a certain amount of export of good *X* it becomes so scarce at home, and the imported good *Y* becomes so abundant, even redundant, that further imports of *Y* will be accepted only in return for an absolute decrease in the export of *X*.

The offer curve is like an ordinary demand curve in that it shows what quantities of goods will be exchanged at what prices if an appropriate seller or trading partner can be found. In the case of the demand curve, equilibrium exchange is determined by the intersection of the demand with the supply curve. In the case of the offer curve the analytical equivalent of the supply curve is the second country's offer curve. In order to derive this offer curve for country A in the X–Y commodity diagram so that it is located in the proper relation to country B's, we initially place country A's production block into the south east (lower right) quadrant, opposite of B's block in Figure 3–7. We will not repeat the steps of analysis which are required to derive country A's offer curve, since they are identical in

FIGURE 3–10
General Equilibrium

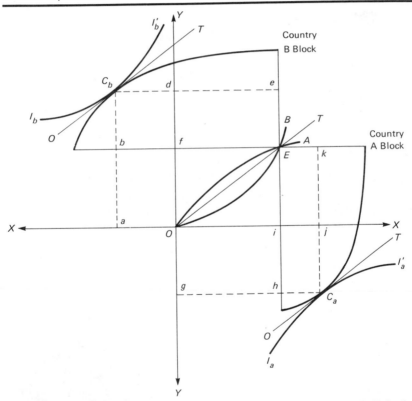

In free trade equilibrium, the world price OT is established and prevails in both countries A and B. The equilibrium is at point E, the intersection of the two countries' offer curves OA and OB. No change of the world price, OT, can increase the welfare of one country without decreasing the welfare of the other.

Country A consumes $C_a j$ and produces $C_a k$ of good Y, leaving jk for export, while it produces $C_a h$ and imports gh of good X, for a consumption of $C_a g$. Analogous reasoning shows that country B reaches C_b by exporting de of X and importing ab of Y. Since $jk = ab$ and $gh = de$, trade is balanced.

every respect to those already carried out for country B. Instead, we turn to Figure 3–10, where the offer curves of the two countries are shown as the lines OA and OB.

Equilibrium Conditions

In Figure 3–10 we bring together in one diagram information about the world terms of trade and equilibrium levels of consumption, production, and trade in both countries. Thus, at the intersection of the two offer curves, point E, the origins of the two countries' production blocks are joined. As we explained above, country B in equilibrium produces $C_b e$ of X and consumes $C_b d$, thus leaving de for export. It imports ab of Y because its consumption is $C_b a$ and its production only $C_b b$. By strictly analogous reasoning we find that country A in equilibrium exports jk of product Y and imports gh of X. As can readily be seen from Figure 3–10, A's exports (jk) equal B's imports (ab) of Y and A's imports (gh) equal B's exports (de) of X. The equilibrium terms of trade shown by the line OT going through E imply that in fact $gh = Oi$ of X can be exchanged for $ab = Of$ of Y. The domestic prices shown as the lines OT in both countries are equal to the world price ratio. Therefore, traders, consumers, and producers all adjust to the same equilibrium price.

It may be useful to summarize these relationships in the following table:

TABLE 3–1

Equilibrium	Country A		Country B
Foreign price ratio	OT		OT
Domestic price ratio	OT		OT
Production of X	hC_a		$C_b e$
Consumption of X	gC_a		$C_b d$
Production − Consumption	$-gh$	$=$	de
Production of Y	$C_a k$		$C_b b$
Consumption of Y	$C_a j$		$C_b a$
Production − Consumption	jk	$=$	$-ab$
Trade good X	Import $gh = Oi$	Export $de = Oi$
Trade good Y	Export $jk = Ei$	Import $ab = Ei$
Ratio of X/Y	$Oi/Ei = OT = Oi/Ei$	

The general equilibrium analysis presented above embodies the very essence of the understanding of the determinants and effects of international trade which the Heckscher-Ohlin model can provide. Even though the analysis may seem excessively complex to many readers, experience has shown that careful study will reveal simple, logical relationships which are easy to follow and remember. Many points in the rest of this book will be based on this model, and it can be expected to deepen students' understanding and appreciation of its structure, implications, and subtleties.

One important aspect of the Heckscher-Ohlin model which Meade's general equilibrium analysis does not cover concerns the effects of international trade on factor prices and incomes. This is the subject of the following section.

V. FACTOR PRICE EQUALIZATION

In our derivation of the production frontier from the Edgeworth Box diagram in Section I of this chapter, we saw that changes in a country's production mix are necessarily accompanied by movements along the contract curve, changes in capital/labor ratios used in both industries, and changes in the marginal productivities and earnings of capital and labor. It therefore follows that a country taking advantage of the gains from trade and specialization is faced with changes in the relative earnings of its factors of production. One of the most startling (and famous) consequences of this process is that in the two-country general equilibrium conditions just discussed, the relative and absolute returns to factors of production in the two countries are fully equalized.

In the following we develop the arguments leading to the conclusion of relative factor price equalization, using a relatively simple geometric technique. In the Appendix to this chapter we present a second technique which is somewhat more difficult than the one used in this text but which also yields some interesting additional results. In the Appendix is also the difficult proof of absolute factor price equalization. In the final part of the text we examine the probability that factor price equalization takes place in the real world, and in the process, we review the main assumptions underlying the basic Heckscher-Ohlin model developed in this chapter.

Relative Factor Prices

In Figure 3–11 the Edgeworth Box diagram (familiar from Section I) is used to represent production conditions in a world consisting of two countries. The Edgeworth Boxes of the two countries are superimposed on each other such that the X origins for both coincide in the bottom left corner. The dimensions of the boxes differ, with country A having a relatively higher capital/labor ratio than country B, so that the Y origins are separate (OY and OY'). The contract curves in both boxes bulge toward the right below the diagonal, consistent with our assumptions made earlier that X is the labor-intensive product and that production functions are the same throughout the world. The pretrade production

FIGURE 3–11
Factor Price Equalization

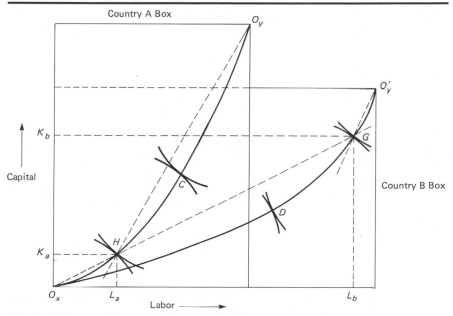

The two Edgeworth Boxes of countries A and B have the common origin O_x for good X but the different origins O_y and O_y' for good Y. At the pretrade equilibrium at points D and C, relative factor prices and factor intensities in production are different. In equilibrium under free trade, country A is at point H with higher output of Y and lower output of X than under autarchy. For country B the trade equilibrium is at point G, with lower output of Y and greater output of X. In both countries the factor intensity of production in industry X is the same, as is shown by the fact that the ray O_xG goes through both equilibrium points H and G. The factor intensity in industry Y is also the same, since the rays O_yH and $O_y'G$ are parallel. With identical, linear homogeneous production functions in both countries, relative factor prices must also be the same.

points on the contract curves are shown as C and D for countries A and B, respectively.

Now consider that international trade is opened up and specialization in production takes place. Consistent with our earlier examples, we assume that country A specializes in the production of Y, and in Figure 3–11 thus moves along its contract curve toward the X origin. We assume that point H corresponds to the equilibrium output position under free trade. The corresponding point for country B is point G.

In this equilibrium at points G and H the capital/labor ratio employed in the production of X is the same in both countries, as can readily be seen by the fact that the two points are on the straight line O_xHG from the origin. The capital/labor ratio in the production of Y is also equal in the two countries, which follows from the fact that the two expansion rays O_yH and $O_y'G$ are parallel. Since, in the case of linear homogeneous production functions, relative factor prices are the same along any expansion ray, and since production functions are identical in the two countries, it therefore follows that relative and absolute factor prices must be the same in both countries. Students interested in a rigorous proof of absolute factor price equalization should turn to the Appendix of this chapter.

A crucial step in the preceding analysis was the assumption that points G and H, with the characteristics described, correspond to output combinations in equilibrium. To prove the validity of this assumption is difficult, but it is possible to do so at an intuitive level of reasoning by considering that if production in the world were at points different from G and H, capital/labor ratios would be different, and opportunities for profitable arbitrage would exist. For example, assume that the production of good X requires three units of capital and one unit of labor in country A, and two units of capital and one unit of labor in country B. Under these conditions a profit of one unit of capital can be earned by shifting a unit of X from country B to country A. Of course, when the capital/labor ratios are different for X they are also different for Y, and arbitrage in the reverse direction is profitable in much the same way indicated in our analysis of the classical model in Chapter 2. Only when the factor input ratios are the same in both countries for each industry are there no more opportunities for profitable arbitrage, and the equilibrium points G and H are arrived at.

Real-World Factor Price Equalization

The factor price equalization theorem discussed above was first presented rigorously by Paul Samuelson in publications in the last half of the 1940s. It shocked many economists, and its real-world implications continue to be far-reaching. Given the large population in the world outside of the industrially developed countries of Europe, North America, and Japan, factor price equalization through trade would mean a drastic fall in wage rates and a sharp rise in the returns to capital in the developed countries and only a relatively small rise in wage rates and sharp rise in the returns to capital in the rest of the world. Many people are quite appalled by this prospect of income distribution towards the owners of capital, even if the total national income of all countries in the world is raised. Because of this fact it is important to consider the problem of how realistic is the prospect that international trade will in fact lead to absolute price equalization.

Of course, the question of realism should be applied not only to the factor price equalization theorem but to all of the other important implications of the Heckscher-Ohlin model. How realistic is it to count on gains from trade and on the interdependence of commodity and factor prices, tastes, and technologies?

It is tempting to argue that the validity of theories should be judged on the basis of the verifiability of their assumptions. Consider, in this light, the assumptions we have made explicitly, or on occasion only implicitly, in our derivation of the Heckscher-Ohlin model in this chapter:

1. There are only two countries, two commodities, two factors of production.
2. The production functions are linearly homogeneous.
3. Production functions are identical in all countries.
4. There are no factor intensity reversals.
5. Both countries are incompletely specialized and continue to produce both products in international equilibrium.
6. Factor supplies are given and do not grow internally or through international migration, either exogenously or in response to trade.
7. Perfect competition prevails in all product and factor markets.
8. There are no costs of transportation or information in carrying on trade.
9. Governments do not interfere with free trade through tariffs, quotas, taxes, or other regulations.

None of these assumptions is entirely realistic, though evidence in their support can be found and has been mentioned in many places in this chapter. However, it is important to realize the methodological point made by Milton Friedman about the usefulness of economic theorizing. All economic analysis must of necessity be based on assumptions which simplify the real world, with all of its known interdependencies and complicated functional relationships among consumers, producers, and nature. Such simplifying assumptions must be unrealistic to some degree. Friedman therefore suggests that the validity of a theory not be judged on the realism or verifiability of its assumptions, but by its ability to produce empirically verifiable theorems.

While this view of the nature of economic analysis is not fully accepted, it has considerable appeal. We might consider briefly whether or not the main theorems of gains from trade and factor price equalization are in obvious conflict with reality. Gains from trade seem to be arising from the importation of goods at prices below those at which domestic substitutes are available. The lowering of the prices of imported goods accompanying international trade raises real incomes of the public not employed in the import-competing industries. We can also observe quite readily that workers displaced by imports tend to find jobs in export industries and therefore they are not unemployed, nor do they necessarily face a drastic fall in income. Broadly based gains from trade therefore seem to be predicted correctly by the theory of international trade.

Similarly, we can observe that relative factor prices are subjected to market pressures which make them move in the theoretically predicted direction. The displacement of labor-intensive textile output in North America by imports tends to release relatively more labor than capital, and the high-technology exports of this region require relatively less labor and more capital, especially human and knowledge capital, as we will discuss in the next chapter. It is more difficult to find casual evidence on the operation of the process of absolute factor price equalization. If it was going on in recent decades, its effect has been swamped by rapid increases in labor productivity in the developed countries, as a result of capital formation and technical progress.

The preceding observations about the correspondence between some theorems of the Heckscher-Ohlin model and the real world are very imprecise; they are intended merely to indicate that the two are not obviously inconsistent. At the same time, we hardly need mention the fact that absolute factor price equalization has not taken place. Why not? The body of knowledge in economics which constitutes an answer to this question is not sufficiently developed and settled that it can be presented simply in a textbook in international economics. No one knows which of the nine simplifying assumptions spelled out above are unrealistic and have prevented factor price equalization. Perhaps government restrictions have been designed explicitly to avoid trade-induced reductions in earnings; they alone could explain the inconsistencies between theory and facts, though this proposition is only speculation.

In the next chapter we will discuss the results of some more precise tests of empirical hypothesis derived from the simple Heckscher-Ohlin model. Some of these tests have revealed the need to modify and extend the model, and we will analyze some suggested modifications and extensions. As a result, the theory of international trade will be more realistic and useful for the analysis of the effects of particular economic policies, but it will also have lost much of the simplicity, rigor, and aesthetic appeal which characterize the basic Heckscher-Ohlin model presented in this chapter.

APPENDIX

Proof of Production Frontier Curvature

In Figure 3A–1 we show an enlarged part of the Edgeworth Box around point D in Figure 3–2 through which run the capital/labor rays OX and OY, as well as the contract curve CC'. The line FF' is the relative price ratio

FIGURE 3A–1
Proof of Curvature of Production Frontier

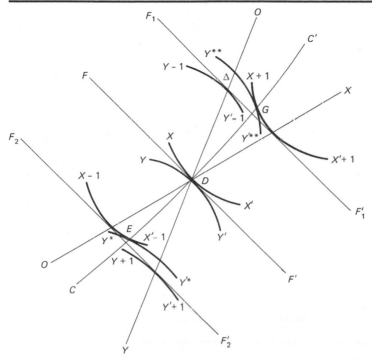

Moving along the ray OY in Figure 3A–1, the distances between isoquants $Y - 1$, Y, and $Y + 1$ are the same. Also, along the ray OX the distances between the isoquants $X - 1$, X, and $X + 1$ are the same. Therefore along each ray output changes between isoquants are identical, and they can be arbitrarily considered to represent one unit of output.

Movement along the contract curve CC' from point E to point D shows that increasing output of X by one unit leads to the reduction of Y output smaller than one unit, since the isoquant $Y^*Y^{*'}$ is closer to the Y origin than the isoquant $Y + 1$. Increasing output of X by another unit by moving to point G on the contract curve leads to a reduction in output of Y greater than one, since the isoquant Y^{**} is closer to the origin than $Y - 1$. Therefore it follows that successive, equal-sized increases of the output of good X lead to consecutively larger reductions in the output of good X, which is exactly what is implied by a production frontier that is concave from below.

prevailing at equilibrium output D. The lines $F_1 F_1'$ and $F_2 F_2'$ are parallel to and equal distances from FF'. The assumption of constant returns to scale implies that with unchanged relative factor prices, such as is indicated by the parallel FF' lines, and two equal-sized reduction in inputs, as· is indicated by the equal distances of $F_1 F_1'$ and $F_2 F_2'$ from FF', factor input proportions remain the same, and output falls by two equal-sized units. For these reasons, the X isoquants tangent to the three FF' lines along the OX ray (as shown in Figure 3A–1) must represent output levels of $X - 1$, X, and $X + 1$ units, respectively, moving from left to right on the diagram.

For analogous reasons we show the three isoquants representing output $Y + 1$, Y, and $Y - 1$ along the OY ray.

Now consider what happens to efficient levels of output of Y as output of X is increased first from $X - 1$ to X and then from X to $X + 1$. The $X - 1$ isoquant involves efficient production at point E on the contract curve, where the isoquant $Y^*Y^{*\prime}$ is tangent to the $X - 1$ isoquant. We notice that this $Y^*Y^{*\prime}$ isoquant intersects the OY ray Δ units of output below the $Y + 1$ isoquant, implying that the first unit increase in the production of X required a reduction of $1 - \Delta$ units of Y output. As we repeat this procedure for point G we find that the second unit increase in the output of X leads to the reduction of $1 + \Delta$ units of Y output. In other words, the first unit increase in the output of X requires the reduction of a smaller quantity of output of Y than does the second unit increase in the output of X.

The characteristic of the tradeoff between X and Y has been described above as diminishing marginal rates of transformation and has been shown to be implicit in the concavity of the production frontier. We have thus established that production functions with constant returns to scale yield production frontiers concave from the origin in models of two goods and two factors.

Alternative Method for Proving Factor Price Equalization Theorem and the Stolper-Samuelson Theorem

A demonstration of relative factor price equalization different from that used in the main body of the text involves a diagram first developed by Abba Lerner (1952). This analysis is presented here because it reveals some aspects of the problem more readily than the box diagram modifications of the Heckscher-Ohlin model used in the main body of the text.

In Figure 3A–2, the vertical axis above the zero origin measures the physical capital/labor ratio (K/L) and the horizontal axis measures the relative price of labor and capital $(P_l/P_k = R)$. Remember from our discussion of production functions surrounding Figure 3–1 that the higher the relative price of labor, the greater will be the ratio of capital to labor used in production, as a measure for economizing on the use of the expensive factor. This simple and intuitively appealing relationship between capital/labor ratios and the labor-capital factor price ratio is represented by the lines XX' and YY' in Figure 3A–2. Consistent with our other assumptions about the production functions of X and Y, the latter industry is more capital intensive than the former, at all relative factor prices.

The horizontal lines AA' and BB' show that country A has a higher overall capital labor ratio than country B. Finally, the line PP' shows an increasing functional relationship between the relative prices of X and Y, measured along the vertical axis below zero, and the labor-capital price

FIGURE 3A–2
Factor Price Equalization, Alternative Method

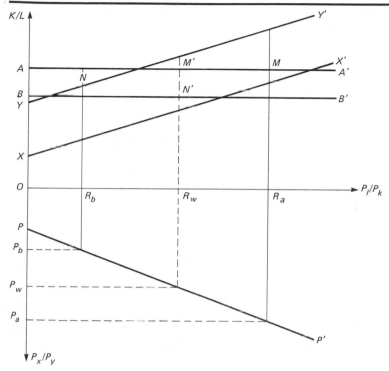

The lines XX' and YY' in Figure 3A–2 show that the K/L (capital/labor) ratio in each industry is an increasing fraction of the ratio of the price of labor and capital. At all factor prices the production of Y is more capital intensive than the production of X. The line PP' shows that the higher the ratio of goods prices, P_x/P_y, the higher is the factor price ratio P_l/P_k. The lines AA' and BB' indicate the overall factor endowment ratios of countries A and B, respectively.

In pretrade equilibrium country B's goods' price and factor price ratios are at P_b and R_b, respectively, while those for country A are at P_a and R_a. Free trade equalizes the goods price ratio in both countries at P_w, which also leads to factor price equalization at R_w.

ratio measured on the horizontal axis. The increasing functional relationship arises from the fact that at the higher prices for X, more of X is produced. Since X is the relatively labor-intensive product, labor is demanded proportionately more than capital, and the returns to labor relative to capital are raised. In a famous article published in 1941, Wolfgang Stolper and Paul Samuelson first proved this functional relationship formally, and it has since been known as the Stolper-Samuelson theorem.

Given these functional relationships in Figure 3A–2, we find that the before-trade position of country A is determined by national tastes and all the other production conditions discussed above. This position is described by the vertical line intersecting the horizontal axis at R_a. The distance OR_a indicates the equilibrium factor price ratio, which, as previous discussion has indicated, is associated uniquely with a commodity price ratio, here shown as P_a. The intersection of the vertical line R_a with country A's endowment ratio, AA', must lie between the two commodity lines XX' and YY'. The point, M, is closer to the X line the larger is the proportion of good X in the output mix of country A. In the extreme, if only X is produced, point M is at the intersection between the lines AA' and XX', signifying that the industry's capital labor ratio is equal to that for the country as a whole. By analogy, country B's pretrade position can be explained. It is shown as the vertical line at R_b.

As international trade is opened up, commodity price ratios in the two countries are equalized, and the world price, P_w, somewhere between P_a and P_b is established. At this common equilibrium price ratio for goods, P_w, we can see that country A is producing at point M', which is relatively closer to the YY' line than point M under autarchy. This signifies that under trade, country A is specialized more in the production of Y. Country B, under trade, is at point N' and is specialized relatively more in the production of X. All of these findings are consistent with the relationships among variables we have found in other graphic models based on the same assumptions. The outstanding feature of the Lerner diagram for present purposes of analysis is that movement of the different pretrade commodity price ratios P_a and P_b toward the common world price P_w implies clearly the equalization of relative factor prices in both countries at R_w.

Proof of Absolute Factor Price Equalization

It is easy to see that it is much stronger analytically and more disturbing for real-world policy makers to show that trade equalizes absolute rather than just relative prices. It is one thing to predict that as a result of trade with China and India, North American income to labor must fall drastically relative to that of capital, but it is quite another thing to predict also that North American labor income must fall toward a common level with the labor income of China and India. Yet this is exactly what the basic Heckscher-Ohlin model implies.

To see this, consider the fact that according to a fundamental proposition in price theory known as Euler's theorem, under the assumption of constant returns to scale the value of total factor payments must equal the value of an industry's output. Thus, in industry X for country A:

$$(O_xL_a)MP_{la} + (O_xK_a)MP_{ka} = (X \cdot P_{xa}), \qquad (3A-1)$$

where O_xL_a is the physical quantity of labor used in producing at point H in Figure 3–11; O_xK_a is the corresponding physical quantity of capital; and

MP_{la} and MP_{ka} are the marginal products of labor and capital, respectively. X is the physical quantity and P_{xa} the price of good X. Equation (3A–1) therefore states that the value of the payments to labor plus those to capital equals the value of the output.

Equation (3A–1) can be divided by the physical quantity of labor to obtain the expression for the average product of labor:

$$\frac{(XP_{xa})}{(O_xL_a)} = MP_{la} + \frac{(O_xK_a)}{(O_xL_a)}MP_{ka} \tag{3A–2}$$

$$= MP_{la}\left(1 + \frac{(O_xK_a)}{(O_xL_a)} \cdot \frac{MP_{ka}}{MP_{lu}}\right) \tag{3A–3}$$

By strictly analogous reasoning, we can find for country B

$$\frac{(XP_{xb})}{(O_xL_b)} = MP_{lb}\left(1 + \frac{(O_xK_b)}{(O_xL_b)}\frac{MP_{kb}}{MP_{lb}}\right) \tag{3A–4}$$

Now, if we can prove that the three ratios in equation (3A–3) have identical counterparts in Equation (3A–4), it must follow that the absolute values of the marginal productivities of labor in countries A and B are identical, since they do not occur in ratio form in the two equations.

From the preceding relative factor price equalization proof we know that $MP_{kb}/MP_{lb} = MP_{ka}/MP_{la}$. By virtue of the fact that in Figure 3–11, in equilibrium the two points H and G lie on a straight line from the origin, it follows that the capital/labor ratios are equal and $O_xK_b/O_xL_b = O_xK_a/O_xL_a$. This leaves the expressions for the average products of labor in the two countries. They are equal because in linearly homogeneous production functions they are the same for constant capital/labor ratios. Thus consider the linearly homogeneous production function known as the Cobb-Douglas:

$$Q = AK^{\alpha}L^{1-\alpha} \tag{3A–5}$$

which after rearrangement says that the average product of labor Q/L is equal

$$Q/L = AK^{\alpha}L^{-\alpha} = A(K/L)^{\alpha} \tag{3A–6}$$

to the capital/labor ratio common to both countries (K/L) times a constant which is also identical in both countries.

Therefore, all three ratios in Equations (3A–3) and (3A–4) are identical and $MP_{la} = MP_{lb}$. Under the normal assumption that factors are paid their marginal product it follows, therefore, that wages are absolutely equal in countries A and B. By analogous reasoning it can readily be shown that returns to capital must also be absolutely equal in the two countries in international equilibrium.

BIBLIOGRAPHICAL NOTES

The Heckscher-Ohlin theory derives its name from the seminal contributions by Heckscher (1919) and Ohlin (1933). Lancaster (1957) uses the Edgeworth Box diagram. Of the many original articles on the use of indifference curves in international trade theory, two are Leontief (1933) and Samuelson (1956). The derivation of the offer curves presented in this book originates with Meade (1952), ch. 2 and 3. Implications of the Heckscher-Ohlin model are discussed by Jones (1956–57), Samuelson (1939) and Johnson (1962), ch. 2. The factor price equalization theorem was derived by Samuelson (1948, 1949). The reference to Lerner is 1952. A good synthesis of the subject is Johnson (1957); more at the level of textbooks is Clement, Pfister, and Rothwell (1967). The curvature of the offer curve has been proved by Savosnick (1958).

Students interested in the history of the development of ideas presented in this and the next chapter should read the survey articles by Bhagwati (1964), Corden (1965), and Haberler (1961).

The theories about economics and political bargaining important for a modern interpretation of community indifference curves are found in Downs (1957) and Buchanan (1968).

CONCEPTS FOR REVIEW

Production function
Isoquant
Efficient production
Contract curve
Capital (or labor) intensity of production
Rate of transformation of good X into Y
Indifference curve for the individual and for the community
Interpersonal comparison of utility
Gains from trade

Budget line
Gains from specialization in production
Trade indifference curve
Small-country assumption
Offer curve
Marginal rates of substitution in consumption
Factor price equalization: Relative and absolute
Stolper-Samuelson theorem
Terms of trade

POINTS FOR FURTHER STUDY AND DISCUSSION

1. The traditional Heckscher-Ohlin model of this chapter exhibits diminishing rates of transformation. What is the rate of transformation of good X into Y in the Ricardian trade model?
2. What conditions are necessary to obtain increasing rates of transformation?
3. What assumption in the text produces the result that the production frontier is smooth and has no bulges, indentations, or inflection points?
4. Use the Savosnick technique to argue that increasing returns to scale in production cause the frontier to be convex from the origin.
5. Derive a community indifference curve for three persons.

6. Since interpersonal comparisons of utility cannot be undertaken scientifically, and since all government policies involve changes in factor incomes, explain whether and why it is ever possible to be certain that any policy increases community welfare.

7. Show the existence of gains from trade when country A's export good is X.

8. Explain why a country's offer curve may turn backward.

9. Interpret the meaning of a straight-line offer curve.

10. Derive an offer curve using the normal trade indifference curves but a Ricardian production frontier.

11. Can there be trade between two countries having identical relative capital/labor endowments and identical production functions for goods X and Y?

12. What do you find to be the most convincing argument why, in the real world, neither relative nor absolute factor price equalization has taken place?

13. Explain the essential difference between the Ricardian and Heckscher-Ohlin trade models.

4 Empirical Tests and Extensions of the Heckscher-Ohlin Model

IN THE FIRST of the three main sections of this chapter we review briefly the most important empirical tests of international trade theory produced since the end of World War II. Extensions and modifications of the simple Heckscher-Ohlin model developed in Chapter 3 which were primarily stimulated by the empirical finding that the United States exports labor-intensive and imports capital-intensive products, the so-called Leontief paradox, are presented in Section II. The chapter concludes with a discussion of contributions to international trade theory which are based on the explicit introduction into the analysis of product differentiation and imperfect competition. The focal point for this discussion is the empirical finding that a very large proportion of international trade is made up of the exchange of goods produced by the same industry and with very similar input requirements.

I. EMPIRICAL TESTS OF INTERNATIONAL TRADE THEORY

All of the empirical tests of international trade theory to be reviewed here involve implications of the models, not of their assumptions. One of the most important implications of both the Ricardian and the Heckscher-Ohlin model is that we can predict what goods individual countries will export and import simply by knowing something about the factors of production available within each country and the input requirements of the goods. If we can predict successfully the commodity composition of trade we will have established that the analytical simplifications of our models are sufficiently general to capture the essence of the determinants of international trade. Consequently, we can have greater confidence in the realism of other implications of the models, which is especially important in the case of implications serving as a basis for policy recommendations to governments. Furthermore, if comparative advantage could be predicted from given resource endowments, we would be able to recommend to governments precisely which industries to support in a program of economic development.

Disregarding many complications and qualifications, we can summarize the empirical hypothesis about the nature of traded products and resource endowments in the Ricardian and Heckscher-Ohlin models as follows. According to the Ricardian model we can explain the commodity composition of exports and imports of two countries simply on the basis of the relative labor productivity each country enjoys in the manufacture of these goods. Each country exports goods in which its labor productivity is the highest and imports those in which it is the lowest. The Heckscher-Ohlin model, on the other hand, implies that the composition of trade is determined by relative labor-capital endowments of countries and the relative factor input requirements of the products. Countries with a relative abundance of capital should export goods produced capital intensively and import goods produced labor intensively, and vice versa for countries with relatively abundant labor supplies. We will review the studies which have attempted to verify these simple empirical hypotheses.

Studies of the Ricardian Model

The pioneering and best known study of the Ricardian trade theory is by G. D. A. MacDougall of Oxford University in England, published in 1951 and 1952. At the time of the study the best data available were those for 1937, concerning production conditions in, and trade of, the United States and the United Kingdom.

MacDougall collected statistics on the output per worker in individual industries in both countries and formed the following ratio: Output per U.S. worker over Output per U.K. worker. As can be seen from Figure 4–1, these ratios, measured along the vertical axis, range from slightly above 1 to about 6. MacDougall also collected information on the exports in these industries of each country to third countries. This trade represented about 95 percent of each country's exports and reflected the competitiveness of the industries in countries in which they faced equal tariffs. (Tariffs between Britain and the United States were very high during this period, so they greatly distorted the trade patterns between these two countries.) MacDougall therefore formed the ratio of U.S. over U.K. exports to third countries for each industry. This ratio, which is measured along the horizontal axis in Figure 4–1, can be seen to range from near 0 to about 8 for the industries under study.

The empirical hypothesis suggested by the Ricardo model is that the

FIGURE 4–1

Labor Productivity and Comparative Advantage

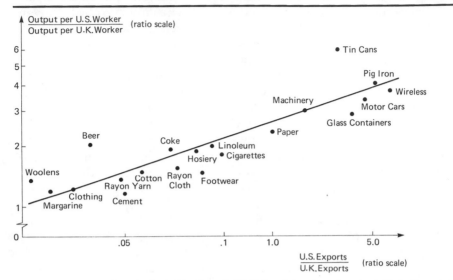

Source: Adapted from G. D. A. Mac Dougall, "British and American Exports: A Study Suggested by the Theory of Comparative Costs," *Economic Journal,* December 1951, p. 703.

relative export success of U.S. over U.K. industries, as measured by the ratio of U.S. over U.K. exports, should be an increasing function of U.S. over U.K. labor productivity, measured as a ratio of the two countries' productivity in each industry. It is obvious that the observations recorded in Figure 4–1 confirm this hypothesis. There is clearly an increasing functional relationship between the two ratios of productivity and exports. Therefore we can conclude that the Ricardian theory of comparative advantages is supported by the evidence.

Following up on Mac Dougall's study, Robert Stern (1962) and Bela Balassa (1963) tested the theory again, using data for different time periods and countries. Generally, they also found strong support for the Ricardian theory of comparative advantage.

Studies of the Heckscher-Ohlin Model

The empirical studies of the Heckscher-Ohlin models can conveniently be separated into two groups. The first consists of studies by Mac Dougall, Irving Kravis, and Lorie Tarshis, while the second comprises those by Wassily Leontief and a number of others who replicated Leontief's approach for other time periods and countries.

MacDougall's (1951, 1952) test of the Heckscher-Ohlin model was based on the statistics of labor input requirements of a number of the industries in the United States and United Kingdom that he had used in his test of the Ricardian model. In order to calculate relevant ratios of capital and labor use by industries, he needed a data series on the capital stocks in each industry. Unfortunately, these data were not available. However, by assuming that there was a high degree of correlation between an industry's capital stock and the amount of horsepower used, he was able to employ the available data on power requirements of each industry as a proxy for the capital stock series. The results of his empirical analysis did not support the Heckscher-Ohlin model of trade. There was no systematic relationship between the ratios of horsepower to labor and U.S. over U.K. exports. In some industries with high horsepower requirements per unit of labor, Britain outsold the United States, and in other industries with low horsepower requirements per unit of labor, the United States outsold Britain.

Kravis (1956) found that wages were higher in U.S. export-competing than in import-competing industries. This finding would be consistent with the Heckscher-Ohlin model if industries with high wages also were characterized by high capital requirements. However, Kravis could not find a systematic relationship between U.S. exports and capital requirements per unit of output. We will show below, in our discussion of explanations of the Leontief paradox, that Kravis's findings are nevertheless consistent with the Heckscher-Ohlin model if we assume that high wages are due to human capital which workers have acquired through schooling, on-the-job training, physical health, or work discipline. According to this view and Kravis's findings, U.S. export performance is explained by U.S. comparative advantage in total including human rather than physical capital alone.

The study by Tarshis (1954) did not concern itself with different input requirements of industries in various countries, as did all of the other studies discussed thus far. Instead, Tarshis focused on the implication of the Heckscher-Ohlin model that the relative prices of final goods in every country should favor the goods using relatively more intensively the factor that is available in relative abundance. Accordingly, Tarshis found that goods produced with capital-intensive methods were relatively cheaper than goods produced with labor-intensive methods in the United States, and the opposite held for some countries with capital endowments per unit of labor presumably lower than those in the United States. These findings are in agreement with the predictions of the Heckscher-Ohlin model if we assume that transportation costs and other impediments to trade prevent perfect relative price equalization of final goods and that tastes are similar in all countries. The justification for the latter assumption will be provided below.

In general, we can conclude that the Heckscher-Ohlin model was supported by the investigations of Tarshis and, with the help of some insights about the nature of human capital developed only in recent years, by that of Kravis. Only MacDougall's study failed to support the Heckscher-Ohlin model.

One of the most influential empirical studies in international economics ever undertaken was that by Leontief, published in 1953 and 1956. Using the then fairly new, mathematically elegant, and theoretically well-developed analytical tool of input-output analysis, Leontief found that in 1947 the United States exported goods that contained relatively more labor than capital, as compared with goods it imported. Leaving out nontraded services and goods that are not produced in the United States, such as tea, coffee, and jute, and taking account of all the input requirements of intermediate products entering into the traded goods, Leontief found that on average a million dollars of U.S. exports required 182 man-years and the services of $2.6 million of capital, or $14.3 thousand of capital per man-year. On the other hand, on average a million dollars of U.S. imports could have been produced domestically employing 170 man-years and the services of $3.1 million capital, or $18.2 thousand of capital per man-year.

The surprising result that the U.S. exported labor-intensive and imported capital-intensive products stimulated much theoretical work, the results of which we will discuss in the next section of this chapter. It also stimulated Leontief-type empirical studies for other time periods in the United States and for other countries. Leontief himself redid his calculations with data on trade from 1951, presumably a year less subject to distortions caused by war than 1947 was. Robert Baldwin (1971) used U.S. input-output coefficients from 1958 and trade data from 1962. Both studies reconfirmed the earlier Leontief results.

R. Bharadwaj (1962) found that India's trade with the rest of the world involved labor-intensive exports and capital-intensive imports, as the Heckscher-Ohlin model predicts in the case of a labor-abundant and capital-scarce country such as India. However, Bharadwaj found that the bilateral trade of India with the United States consisted of labor-intensive imports and capital-intensive exports.

In a study of Japan's trade, M. Tatemoto and S. Ichimura, (1959) found that country importing labor-intensive and exporting capital-intensive goods, which is inconsistent with the Heckscher-Ohlin model if we consider that Japan in the 1950s was a country with high population density and a relatively small capital stock. However, when the authors broke down Japan's trade by regions they discovered that bilateral trade with the United States had characteristics consistent with the Heckscher-Ohlin model.

Wolfgang Stolper and K. Roskamp (1961) found East Germany's trade with its relatively capital-poor partners in the eastern European bloc involved the export of capital-intensive and import of labor-intensive products, consistent with the Heckscher-Ohlin theory. D. F. Wahl's (1961) study of Canada's international trade, which is mostly with the United States, revealed a pattern of capital-intensive exports and labor-intensive imports. In an imaginative study of trade between the Southeast section of the United States and the rest of the country, John Moroney and T. M. Walker (1966) found that between 1949 and 1957 the relatively labor-rich and low-wage Southeast tended to attract relatively labor-intensive industries. However, tests about the factor intensity of industry already located in the region proved inconclusive.

Summary and Conclusions

What can be concluded from all these studies? The results are clearly mixed, with perhaps a slight dominance of results consistent with or not completely in conflict with the basic Heckscher-Ohlin model. At this time it does not appear to be particularly promising to engage in future studies in order to accumulate more of the Leontief-type information. Chances are that more mixed results of the sort already reported would be found. Instead, the greater payoff seems to lie in studies which attempt to confirm or reject explanations of the Leontief paradox directly. Discussion of explanations of the Leontief paradox produced since the 1950s follows.

II. THE LEONTIEF PARADOX AND EXTENSIONS OF THE HECKSCHER-OHLIN MODEL

Leontief's own explanation of his findings was that U.S. labor was "more effective" than foreign labor, so that U.S. imports which showed up in U.S. production statistics as capital-intensive goods would be produced abroad with labor-intensive methods. Since Leontief's work, economists have rediscovered and analyzed carefully the concepts of human and knowledge capital, which have made the notion of "more effective" U.S. labor more precise and which generally support Leontief's proposition.

The idea of human and knowledge capital is based on the simple notion that a type of capital is formed when a person spends a certain time in such activities as building a machine, going to school, or doing research. In each case resources are being used up in current production which is not being consumed. Recall from national income analysis that by definition society's savings and investment in a given time period are equal to the nonconsumed part of production.

More specifically, research and development lead to the improvement of machinery and technological processes used in actual manufacture, of the quality of goods and services produced and of the managerial techniques utilized in the organization of business, governments, and other social processes. The stock of knowledge which results in an increased value of output from a given stock of resources is known as knowledge capital. Human capital formation takes place through formal education, on-the-job training, and health care, all of which raise the quality of the services performed and decisions made by labor, management, professionals, and bureaucrats.

Research based on these notions by T. W. Schultz, Gary Becker, Mark Blaug, and others has revealed that in competitive markets individual decision makers have the incentive to equalize marginal rates of return to investment in all three types of capital. Empirical studies by and large have confirmed the validity of these theoretical considerations.

Applications of the human and knowledge capital concepts to the explanation of U.S. trade patterns by Peter Kenen (1965), Donald Keesing (1966) and (1967), and William Gruber, D. Mehta, and R. Vernon (1967) showed that U.S. export performance, as measured by industries' ratios of export to total U.S. production, is an increasing function of the proportion of the industries' labor forces in highly skilled categories and of the research and development expenditures expressed as a percentage of the industries' sales. Generally, these findings support the Heckscher-Ohlin theory that countries export goods produced intensively with factors of production they possess in relative abundance. There is a presumption that if human and knowledge capital services were included properly in a U.S. input-output table, a repetition of Leontief's calculations would show that the United States exports capital-intensive and imports labor-intensive products. However, this type of study still must be undertaken.

Taste Conditions

The analysis of Chapter 3 was carefully designed so that country A was shown to have a relative abundance of capital, good Y was produced with capital-intensive techniques, and the opening up of world trade made the price of Y in country A relatively more expensive than it was under autarchy. As a result, country A specialized in the production of good Y and exported it. Accordingly, our example produced a trade pattern consistent with the Heckscher-Ohlin theorem that a country exports the good produced intensively with the factor in which it is abundantly endowed. Our example is, of course, also inconsistent with Leontief's findings.

One of the simplest ways to remedy this inconsistency between theory and empirical findings is to change an assumption about tastes underlying the analysis of Figure 3–5 in Chapter 3. As the theoretical economist Ronald Jones first pointed out, if country A had a great preference for the consumption of the capital-intensive good, the pretrade relative price in

Figure 3–5 might have been more like the world price WW' shown, and production and consumption would have taken place in the upper left section of the production frontier. Under these conditions the opening of trade would have been likely to have resulted in a relative cheapening of the capital-intensive good and adjustment of production toward the labor-intensive good. Trade would then show the pattern found by Leontief, the export of labor-intensive and import of capital-intensive goods.

However, this explanation of the Leontief paradox suffers from the problem that it is valid only under the assumption of internationally different tastes. Consider that if tastes were the same in all countries, then before trade the rest of the world would also be specialized heavily in the production of the capital-intensive good, and the opening up of trade would not necessarily result in a decreased relative price for that good and the pattern of trade predicted above. Empirical evidence presented by Hendrik Houthakker (1957) on household consumption patterns in many different countries suggests that the income elasticities of demand for classes of goods, such as food, clothing, housing, and others, are very similar. Consequently, the explanation of the Leontief paradox based on the assumption of international differences in tastes should be rejected on the basis of available empirical evidence.

U.S. Tariff Structure

Tariffs and their structure will be discussed at length in the next part of this book. Here it is only necessary to indicate that the government of the United States collects at its borders a tax on the importation of certain products. This tax raises the price of the imported goods in the United States, so it encourages domestic production, and discourages imports. Now consider the hypothesis that U.S. tariffs protect most heavily those U.S. industries that use labor-intensive technology. Under these conditions Leontief's paradox could be explained by the relative absence of U.S. imports of labor-intensive products in the statistics on which his calculations are based. In theory, of course, the Heckscher-Ohlin theorem holds only if there is complete freedom of trade.

Empirical evidence on the labor-protective structure of U.S. tariffs is quite strong, according to the studies of Stefan Valavanis-Vail and William Travis, while Georgio Basevi found some evidence to the contrary.

Natural Resources

Let us assume that the United States is relatively poorly endowed with natural resources and that the production of these resources in the United States is very capital intensive. Under these conditions, U.S. imports would tend to consist of natural resources or products embodying them which, if they were produced domestically, would require capital-intensive technology. Jaroslav Vanek (1959), examining U.S. imports and production from this point of view, found that on the average U.S. exports embodied only half the value of natural resources as U.S. imports did. At the same time, it is quite well known that mining operations and first-stage processing of natural resources tend to be very capital intensive in the United States. Consequently, Leontief's calculations do not reveal a paradox; rather, they are consistent with the Heckscher-Ohlin theorem that countries import goods embodying the relatively scarcer factor of production, which in the case of the United States is natural resources.

Factor Intensity Reversals

In our discussion of production functions surrounding Figure 3–1 in Chapter 3, we stated explicitly the assumption that the two isoquants for goods X and Y intersect only once and have identical marginal rates of substitution. As a result of this assumption, the relative factor intensity of the two products is the same at all relative input prices. Now consider the possibility that the two isoquants intersect more than once, have different curvatures to their isoquants, or both. The latter condition is shown in Figure 4–2. At the input price ratio R_1R_1' the expansion ray OY_1 is steeper than the ray OX_1, indicating that Y is the relatively capital-intensive product. However, at the different factor price R_2R_2', product Y is the relatively labor-intensive product.

The application of the theoretical possibility of factor intensity reversals of this sort to the explanation of the Leontief paradox is straightforward. If U.S. factor prices imply relatively cheap capital, as shown with the ratio line R_1R_1', but the relatively cheap labor situation shown as R_2R_2' prevails in the rest of the world, then it is possible to find the United States importing goods which would have been produced by capital-intensive methods at home but in fact were produced abroad by labor-intensive methods.

To find out whether such factor intensity reversals do take place in the real world, it is necessary to collect data on production techniques used in different countries. B. S. Minhas (1962) collected such statistics for 24 industries and 19 different countries and found factor reversals in 5 of the industries. Furthermore, he found a low correlation of $+0.328$ between the capital/labor ratios of 20 industries existing in both the United States and Japan. Leontief and Moroney have raised some questions about how great the probability is that factor intensity reversals do take place in the real world by analyzing Minhas's statistics somewhat more closely. From these studies we can conclude that factor intensity reversals do take place, but they are not frequent enough to serve as a major, empirically relevant explanation of the Leontief paradox.

FIGURE 4-2
Factor Intensity Reversals

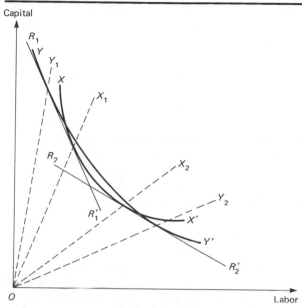

The isoquants XX' and YY' intersect twice. As a result, industry X is relatively labor intensive when the factor price ratio is R_1R_1' and relatively capital intensive when the factor price ratio is R_2R_2'. The different relative factor intensities at different relative factor prices are shown by the fact that Y_1 is steeper than X_1, and X_2 is steeper than Y_2.

Identical Production Functions

In our discussion of production functions in Chapter 3 we introduced the explicit assumption that given proportions of capital and labor are being combined in all countries to produce the same value of output; in other words, production functions are the same in all countries. We modified this analysis above by the consideration of human and knowledge capital, which permits us to explain the real-world phenomenon that in some countries given inputs of physical capital and ''labor'' are combined to produce different quantities of the same output than in other countries. However, we retained the assumption that otherwise production functions are identical, so that if some countries could acquire the human and knowledge capital they now lack, their labor and physical capital would be as productive as that in other countries possessing such human and knowledge capital.

Let us now consider the possibility that there are differences in the physical environment of countries, the physiological and mental capabilities of the population, and the culturally determined organization of society. The physical environment influences the productivity of labor and capital by requiring different expenditures on plant construction and transportation facilities, to deal with climate and geographic characteristics. There is no way in which knowledge or human capital can substitute for the requirement to heat plants in some countries and air-condition them in others or to transport goods over many different kinds of topography. Human beings may differ in their ability to do heavy physical or mental work in individual countries even after they have had equal amounts of schooling and other forms of training. Differences in attitudes towards work, competition, and technology grounded in religion and long-standing cultural traditions tend to affect the efficiency with which factors of production are combined in different countries.

We now assume that all of these influences result in making production functions unequal throughout the world. As a result, the Leontief paradox can be explained simply as the result of the fact that U.S. trade is produced with other input proportions abroad than it is domestically, much as in the case of the factor intensity reversals.

There are no theoretical or empirical studies which could be cited to support the notion that production functions are different and that such differences can explain the Leontief paradox. The reason for the absence of such studies is that explanations of real-world phenomena which are based on the special circumstances of each case, such as environmental conditions or the human and social characteristics of each country, tend to become tautological. In the extreme, "explanations" consist of listings of all of the determinants of trade, and there are no hypotheses or theorems to test. The essence of economic theorizing is simplification, and to consider all of the factors we have discussed as causing different production functions would so complicate the analysis that it would be unmanageable.

Summary and Conclusions

We found in this section that the Leontief paradox can be explained, and the basic Heckscher-Ohlin model can be made consistent with empirical evidence on the relative factor intensity of U.S. trade, by several modifications and extensions of the model. Each of these explanations taken alone is theoretically capable of explaining the paradox, though in several instances empirical studies aimed specifically at examining the relevance of the explanations showed them to be of only limited validity. Bhagwati has written a paper (1959) in which he shows schematically the complexity of the Heckscher-Ohlin model and the validity of some theorems under one or a number of combined empirically supported changes in assumptions. We will not produce such a scheme here, but it is obvious how complex it must be and how many qualifications must be attached to the simple factor proportions and factor price equilization theorems we developed in the preceding chapter.

The payoff from all of the theoretical and empirical work prompted by the Leontief paradox is that we have provided for greater understanding of the determinants of international trade and the structure of the Heckscher-Ohlin system. In so doing we have made international trade theory more useful for the evaluation of government policies concerning economic relations among nations. In the next section we will continue this process of modification and extension of the basic Heckscher-Ohlin model by considering a new set of empirical evidence that is inconsistent with this model and by searching for changes in assumptions that are capable of explaining the empirical paradoxes.

III. INTRAINDUSTRY TRADE AND EXTENSIONS OF THE HECKSCHER-OHLIN MODEL

In applications of the Heckscher-Ohlin model to the analysis of policy questions, it is often necessary to estimate trade and changes in trade by individual industries. For example, preceding the agreement to form the European Economic Community (the Common Market) which was reached in 1957, analysis of the effects of economic integration in Western Europe had to be estimated by considering how much trade would increase as a result of the removal of tariffs and other barriers, and which industries would grow or diminish in each country as comparative advantage asserted itself in the region of free trade. Answers to these questions were sought eagerly by governments in the 1950s as the advantages and disadvantages of joining the union were discussed publicly. There was especially widespread fear that market forces would lead countries to lose entire industries in which they had no comparative advantage. For example, France was concerned about its automobile industry in competition with German manufacturers, who had enjoyed superior export performance in third countries. At the same time German wine growers were concerned about the competition from France's famous vineyards.

Predictions made by economists about the increases in the level of trade among nations of the European Economic Community turned out to be much too low, and public fears about the decline of certain industries were almost completely unfounded. Some years after integration had taken place Verdoorn, Balassa, and Grubel all found that the expansion of trade in the Economic Community did not take the form the Heckscher-Ohlin model had predicted (for example, exchange of German cars for French wines) but instead took the form of German cars for French cars, German wines for French wines, and so on. While the basic Heckscher-Ohlin model explains trade between industries, which we can call interindustry trade, the studies of economic integration in Europe revealed the importance of trade involving commodities belonging to the same industry, which is known as intraindustry trade.

In a subsequent study Grubel and Lloyd (1975) found that intraindustry trade is strong not only among countries of the European Economic Community, but among all industrial nations. Willmore (1972) found it important also in trade among developing countries in the Central American Common Market. In an effort to measure the phenomenon precisely, the following index was developed:

$$B = 1.0 - \frac{X - M}{X + M} \qquad (4-1)$$

It implies that for a given industry the index of intraindustry trade, B, is at its maximum of 1.0 when exports exactly equal imports and the ratio in Equation (4-1) is zero. On the other extreme, when an industry either has exports but no imports or vice versa, the index becomes zero because the ratio is 1.0.

Grubel and Lloyd calculated weighted averages of this index for ten industrialized countries—the United States, Canada, Japan, Belgium–Luxembourg, Netherlands, Germany, France, Italy, United Kingdom, and Australia using the three digit Standard Industrial Trade Classification (SITC) level of aggregation to represent "industries." At this widely used level of aggregation are descriptions of industry categories such as Office Machines, Railway Vehicles, Road Motor Vehicles, Aircraft, Ships and Boats, Furniture, and Footwear. Average intraindustry trade of the countries listed above in 1967 is shown in Table 4-1, by broad industry classes. As can be seen, almost one half of international trade among these highly industrialized nations consists of the exchange of commodities be-

TABLE 4–1
Average Intraindustry Trade, 1967 (in 10 industrialized countries)

SITC Class		Level
5	Chemicals	0.66
7	Machinery and transport equipment	.59
9	Other commodities and transactions	.55
8	Miscellaneous manufactured articles	.52
6	Manufactured goods classified by material	.59
1	Beverages and tobacco	.49
4	Animal and vegetable oils and fats	.40
0	Food and live animals	.37
2	Crude materials, inedible, except fuel	.30
3	Mineral fuels, lubricants and related materials	.30
	Weighted average	0.48

Source: Herbert Grubel and P. J. Lloyd *Intra-Industry Trade: The Theory and Measurement of International Trade in Differential Products* (New York: Halstead Press, 1975).

longing to the same industry. The table also shows that the index is higher for manufactured goods than for raw materials and agricultural products.

The index has risen in recent years from an average for these 10 countries of 0.36 in 1959 to 0.42 in 1964 and 0.48 in 1967. Trade among countries of the European Economic Community alone averaged 0.54 in 1959 and 0.67 in 1967. Willmore found that trade in manufactures among countries of the Central American Common Market showed an intraindustry index of 0.22 in 1961 and 0.40 in 1967.

It is tempting to dismiss all of these calculations of intraindustry trade and its growth as simply involving the theoretically inappropriate level of statistical aggregation. According to this argument, all we need is a level of aggregation where there are either exports or imports, but not both. There must be such a level because, under competition, entrepreneurs will not find it profitable to import and export *identical* products. Once we have found these data, we can then apply the basic Heckscher-Ohlin model to analyze trade. Grubel and Lloyd analyzed Australian trade statistics from this point of view, drawing on data which showed the lowest level of aggregation at which most governments keep their records. For example, these data showed the seven-digit commodities Skiboots, Sand Shoes Rubber Soled, and Sand Shoes with other Soles. These items were part of the five-digit group Footwear with Leather Uppers and Soles of Rubber or Plastic, which in turn were part of the three-digit class of trade called Shoes, the two-digit class Footwear and the one-digit class Miscellaneous Manufactured Articles.

Averaging Australia's trade statistics at each level of aggregation, Grubel and Lloyd found that in 1968–69 intraindustry trade was 0.43, 0.26, 0.20, 0.15, and 0.06 at one- through seven-digit levels. In other words, even at the level of record keeping showing the most detailed breakdown of commodities available, there still was an average 0.06 index of intraindustry trade. Thus, it is not technically feasible to restrict empirical studies based on simple Heckscher-Ohlin theorems to statistics at the theoretically appropriate level of aggregation, where a country has exports or imports, but not both.

Generally, economists engaged in empirical research have not dealt with the problems of choosing an appropriate level of aggregation, and we will not discuss it here any further. Instead, we draw the conclusion that the existence of intraindustry trade represents a phenomenon that is not just a statistical artifact but reveals an inconsistency between the real world and the basic Heckscher-Ohlin model. In the remainder of this chapter we will modify and extend this basic model by considering the causes of intraindustry trade, first in goods that are undifferentiated in their functions and second in goods that are differentiated according to style, quality, or some performance characteristic.

Functionally Homogeneous Products

We can define domestically and foreign produced goods as being functionally homogeneous if, when they are placed on a store shelf next to each other and carry an identical price, consumers are indifferent as to a choice between them. If one is more expensive than the other, consumers will only buy the cheapest. Examples of functionally homogeneous goods are raw materials such as copper and aluminum, agricultural products such as flour and eggs, and simple manufactures such as nails and cotton white goods. At first thought it seems almost impossible that any country could be on record as simultaneously exporting and importing products of this sort. However, statistics show that countries do this, and the analytical reasons are related to the costs of transportation, storage, selling, and packaging and the indivisibilities in production facilities, all of which were assumed away in the basic Heckscher-Ohlin model.

Transportation Costs.   The reasons transportation costs can give rise to intraindustry trade in a commodity such as gravel are easily understood with the help of Figure 4–3, where the points A_1, A_2 and B_1, B_2 are assumed to be locations in countries A and B, respectively, where gravel can be mined at equal unit costs. The circles around each gravel pit delimit the marketing area accessible to each under the assumption that the costs of transportation are the same for every firm. Of interest to our analysis are areas where the circles are overlapping, such as between circles around A_2 and B_2. In Figure 4–3 the marketing area enclosed by the two circles is divided between the two firms by the line MN, which represents the locus of equal distance from A_2 and B_2. Under the assumption of proportionality between distance and transport cost, consumers resident in the area to the right of MN are supplied most cheaply from B_2, and those to the left of MN, from A_2. By analogous reasoning we can find the precise marketing areas for every point of production.

Now consider that the region shown in Figure 4–3 is divided by the historically determined border, at which trade records are kept, but otherwise trade is free. Under these conditions and competition among producers, country A imports gravel from gravel pit B_2 to supply gravel at least cost to residents living in the area marked by horizontal lines. At the same time country A exports gravel from pits A_1 and A_2 to residents in country B, in the areas marked by vertical lines.

In this simple model of international trade we have shown how the existence of transportation costs and minimization of delivered product prices give rise to international trade in functionally homogeneous products. Thus we have found one explanation of intraindustry trade. Our simple model, however, can readily be used to demonstrate how the basic Heckscher-Ohlin model can be made more consistent with reality, in a more general way, by the introduction of transportation costs. Thus, we

FIGURE 4–3
Trade and Transportation Costs

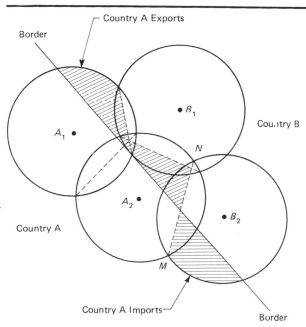

Source: Adapted from Herbert G. Grubel and P. J. Lloyd, *Intra-Industry Trade* (New York: Halstead Press, 1975), p. 74.

The centers of the circles in Figure 4–3 represent points of production of gravel, and the circumferences of the circles are the limits to which gravel is shipped. When circles overlap, shipping limits are demarcated by straight lines connecting intersections of circles. A political border bisecting the production and market areas for gravel can lead to shipments of gravel from country A to country B, and simultaneously from B to A. The shaded areas represent territories which are supplied from the other country.

might generalize that the size of circles limiting market areas around points of production is a decreasing function of the ratio of transportation costs to the price of a product. For example, in the case of haircuts, this ratio is very high, the circle is very small, and international trade in this service does not exist. On the other hand, in the case of high-value, low-weight manufactures such as optical instruments, the circle is very large and tends to span the globe. German and Japanese cameras and lenses are sold throughout the world.

Returning to the basic Heckscher-Ohlin model, in Figure 3–5 (Chapter 3) the existence of transportation costs for one country would be shown by the fact that the opening up of trade brings about a smaller price change than it does in the absence of transportation costs. The world price ratio, WW', including transportation costs, is somewhere between the pretrade ratio and the one assumed to prevail in the absence of these costs. The higher transport costs are, the smaller are the gains from trade and specialization. In the extreme of nontraded goods such as haircuts, there are no gains from trade at all.

Storage Costs. Storage costs give rise to intraindustry trade in functionally homogeneous products which are manufactured at least cost and at a time that is different from when they are consumed. Most important in this group of goods are perishable agricultural products such as fruits and vegetables. In analogy with our basic two-country model, we can make the case rigorously by assuming that demand for a specific good, say strawberries, is constant throughout the year in both countries. Now if seasons for growing this good differ in the two countries, each will export the functionally identical product in one season and import it in another, because the costs of transportation are smaller than the costs of storing the products in the producing country between the time of concentrated production and continuous consumption in each country. Most frequently trade of this type takes place between northern and southern countries of continents or hemispheres.

Storage costs also enter into the trade of electricity, which can be produced at low marginal cost up to a capacity limit. Peak-load demand for electricity is determined by daylight hours and moves across continents from east to west. Electricity is exported by countries when domestic demand is below its peak and imported at times of peak demand. In the case of electricity, the phenomenon of intraindustry trade is due to both the high cost of storing the product, which in fact is near infinity, and the indivisibilities of the production process, which require large, capital-intensive generating plants operating at low marginal cost.

Selling Costs. Selling costs are responsible for the appearance of intraindustry trade in the form of what is known as "entrepôt trade," which involves the packaging, storing, sorting, cleaning, and blending of goods that remain essentially unchanged in the process. Countries may thus report the import and export of functionally homogeneous products which have been prepared for further distribution among wholesalers or retailers. This kind of intraindustry trade is often shown separately in national statistics, especially for small countries such as Hong Kong and Singapore, where it plays an important role. In other countries, however, this type of intraindustry trade is difficult to distinguish from rapidly growing trade in a wide range of differentiated products which have been transformed, often only marginally, by highly labor-intensive processes of assembly or finishing. We will further analyze this form of trade, often carried on by multinational corporations, below.

Information Costs. An important role in the provision of brokerage, insurance, banking, and shipping services in international trade is played by insurance costs. Firms providing these kinds of services regularly to domestic clients possess a comparative advantage in competition with foreign firms through their knowledge about the credit worthiness and reliability of their customers. Therefore, exporters and importers in every country often purchase these services from domestic firms, and statistics showing trade in these services tend to reveal the existence of intraindustry trade.

Generally, intraindustry trade in functionally homogeneous products differentiated by location, time of existence, or associated information is probably quantitatively not significant, though reliable information on this is not available. The main purposes of the preceding analysis have been to show how the simple Heckscher-Ohlin model can be enriched and made consistent with real-world phenomena, and to increase understanding of the nature and determinants of international trade.

Differentiated Products: Scale Economies

Goods traded internationally are grouped in the same statistical class for reporting because they are close substitutes in either production or consumption, or both. To illustrate this classification scheme, consider Figure 4–4, in which the vertical and horizontal axes measure the degree of substitutability of products in use and similarity of input requirements, respectively.

FIGURE 4–4
Causes of Product Differentiation

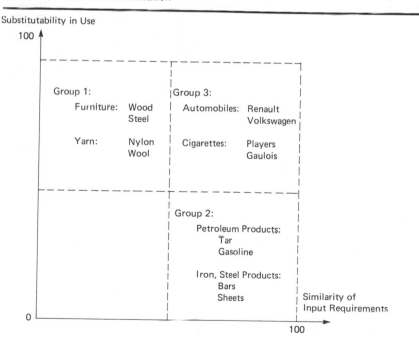

The industries in which intraindustry trade takes place can be classed conveniently into three groups. Group 1 consists of industries in which goods are close substitutes in use but have rather dissimilar input requirements, such as furniture made of wood or steel and yarn made of nylon or wool. The explanation of intraindustry trade in this group is readily undertaken within the framework of the basic Heckscher-Ohlin model, because input requirements are sufficiently dissimilar so that the factor proportions theory can explain comparative advantage.

Group 2 commodities are poor substitutes in use, such as tar and gasoline or iron bars and iron sheets, but they have very similar input requirements. It is useful to distinguish two subsets of goods in this group. The first consists of goods which are produced jointly in technologically determined proportions; examples are petroleum products of different volatility and coking coal and gas. It is easy to see that in the case of such products, one country may end up with an excess supply of one of the joint products, say tar, in meeting some of its domestic demand for gasoline. We would then observe intraindustry trade in petroleum products, which is explained by the amendment of the basic Heckscher-Ohlin model which accounts for the existence of joint products.

The second subclass of Group 2 products, such as iron bars and sheets, has characteristics resembling closely those of goods in Group 3, and we will discuss them together. Goods in Group 3 are typically very close substitutes in the basic functions they perform for consumers, but they are differentiated by style, quality, minor variations in the combination of performance characteristics, or often just by brand name. Most importantly, for our purposes of analysis the manufacturing input requirements of the products are extremely similar. Examples of Group 3 goods are automobiles, distinguishable primarily by brand name and styling, such as Volkswagen and Renault, and cigarettes, say the British Players brand and the French Gaulois brand. In the same manner, iron and steel products representing the second subclass of Group 2 have very similar input requirements.

Why cannot international trade in these goods be explained by the basic Heckscher-Ohlin model presented in Chapter 3? To answer this question let us use the tools of analysis developed there and consider the production frontier for two kinds of cigarettes, identical in every respect except for brand names. Under the assumption of constant returns to scale, the production frontier for these two goods must be a straight line with a 45-degree slope, implying a one for one tradeoff in production over the entire range of output. This same production frontier for different brand cigarettes exists in countries A and B, regardless of the relative factor endowments of the two countries. If under autarchy each country produced two different brands, exchanging at the price ratio of 1 to 1, the opening of trading opportunities will not result in trade, because the price ratios in the two countries are identical. In terms of the cigarette or car examples, there should be no incentives for profitable specialization and exchange of Players for Gaulois cigarettes and Volkswagen for Renault automobiles we actually can observe.

Now even if we assume that the production of differentiated goods of Group 3 requires some dissimilar inputs, we must still face the fact that trade in these goods takes place primarily among countries which have very similar factor endowments. Our examples of trade in cars and cigarettes involved the very similar England, France, and Germany. Consequently, the production frontiers of these countries concerning these types of products tend to be very similar, so that pretrade price ratios would give rise to little opportunity for gains from specialization and trade.

The solution to the inconsistency between the real world and the basic Heckscher-Ohlin model is to drop the assumption of constant returns to scale. In Figure 4–5 we show a production frontier based on the assumption that the production of each brand of cigarette is subject to increasing returns to scale. These production conditions imply that the average cost

FIGURE 4–5
Increasing Returns to Scale

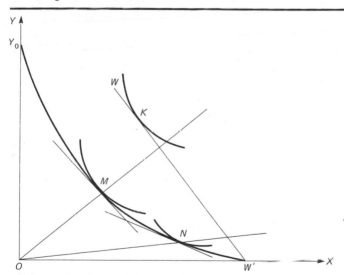

The production frontier, Y_0W', is convex from below, indicating that output is subject to economies of scale. Before trade, equilibrium is at point M, which is stable because of the assumed existence of oligopolistic market structures, differentiated products, and economies of scale due to the length of runs. Free trade establishes world price WW' and leads country A to specialize in the production of X and consumption at point K, for welfare gains equal to the move from the indifference curve going through M to that going through K.

per unit of output is smaller the larger the output is. For example, when the country produces, at point M, roughly equal amounts of brands X and Y, the relative price ratio is near 1 to 1. On the other hand, at point N production involves more of X than Y, and because of the scale economies X is relatively much cheaper than Y.

Economies of scale in production traditionally were considered to arise from the operation of increasingly larger plants, especially in the chemical industry or when production involves assembly-line processes. The larger plants result in lower costs per unit of output, because of labor specialization, and the operation of the physical principle that the carrying capacity of pipes and vessels increases more rapidly than the cost of manufacturing them. Empirical studies have shown that these kinds of economies of scale are not as important as theorists had made them out to be. Individual countries in Europe before integration already had optimal size plants in most industries, judging by the standards of U.S. plants, which presumably had been built to exploit all scale economies.

However, in recent years researchers have discovered a second source of scale economies, the length of run in the production of differentiated goods within the same plant. Before European economic integration, the European plants tended to have much higher unit costs than U.S. plants producing the same goods, according to industrial statistics. It has now become apparent that this difference in costs was due to the fact that the average European plant produced many more varieties, styles, and sizes of the same commodity than did the corresponding U.S. plants. The fewer the number of differentiated products manufactured in each plant, the lower are per unit costs, because of savings in inventories of intermediate inputs and outputs, downtime of machines, and stoppages in work as dies and other tools are changed. Furthermore, machines can be constructed specifically for long high-speed runs, and labor has to learn fewer tasks. The importance of reductions in the cost of output due to the increased length of runs has been documented by Armen Alchian and Jack Hirschleifer in industry studies and found for Canada in studies by Ron and Paul Wonnacott and by Donald Daly, B. A. Keys, and E. J. Spence.

Let us return now to Figure 4–5 and consider country A before trade at point M, producing two varieties of a certain good, say a small car well suited for short-distance driving and a large, roomy one for driving great distances. At this mix of output, domestic producers are maximizing profits and satisfying genuine consumer needs, and there are no incentives to move from this particular output mix. In the real world, of course, oligopolistic industries producing such differentiated goods typically cover a whole spectrum of needs by marketing many varieties and styles, but to keep the analysis simple we consider only the convenient two-goods case.

When trade is opened up, country A will move to complete specialization in the production of one of the two varieties. In the example of Figure 4–5, country A is assumed to specialize in the production of good X, the car more suited for long-distance driving, trading at the world price WW' to reach the indifference curve at point K. It is obvious that consumption at K brings country A to a higher indifference curve than the one it had reached under autarchy at point M, and thus we have the analytical equivalent of the gains from trade and specialization under the basic Heckscher-Ohlin model. Consumers continue to enjoy the availability of cars differentiated in their functions, even though country A is completely specialized in production.

One of the important insights of the basic Heckscher-Ohlin model developed in Chapter 3 was that we could predict on which of the two products country A would specialize in production. Recall that country A specialized in the good requiring most intensively the factor of production with which it was relatively well endowed. The analytical equivalent of this theorem in a world of differentiated commodities produced under increasing returns to scale is much more complex, and it is necessary to draw on a variety of underlying conditions.

Physical Environment. To pursue the automobile example, we can consider country A to be the United States. This country is characterized by relatively large driving distances, between and even within cities, for which large automobiles are better suited than small ones. The U.S. manufacture before trade therefore can be assumed to have been in the neighborhood of point N in Figure 4–5, where the output mix and relative price favored large cars before the opening of trade. In the rest of the world, on the other hand, conditions were most suited for the smaller cars, and at the resultant output mix the relative price favored small cars, as is shown with the price ratio WW' in Figure 4–5. As trade opened up through the lowering of tariff barriers and transportation and communications costs, the existing relative prices in the United States and the rest of the world favored U.S. specialization in the production and export of larger cars and the importation of smaller ones.

History and Culture. We will now introduce historical and cultural factors into our discussion of scale economies. For example, Germany historically had political, economic, and military ties with Turkey, and these are responsible for the German public's preference for Turkish blend cigarettes. For well-known historic reasons, the English public developed a taste for Virginia blend cigarettes. Yet in both countries there are some people who prefer the blend that is not used by the majority. Because of the economies of scale in production it is more economical to supply this minority demand through imports rather than through domestic production. Another example in this class of explanations is trade in furniture. Sweden has had the most developed program of publicly subsidized housing. However, this housing has involved small apartments, and it led to the development of the Scandinavian style of furniture, which is particularly suited for these conditions. It is now exported throughout the world, including to the United States, where during the pioneer development of the country a particularly heavy style of furniture came into use. This American furniture, now known as colonial style, is in turn being exported to Scandinavia to meet the demand from a minority of consumers who prefer this style.

The development of national styles and characteristics in a wide range of consumer goods is the result of so many historic and cultural influences that it is difficult to theorize about them. For many purposes of analysis we simply must take as exogenously determined the characteristics of the models of automobiles, clothing, shoes, consumer durables, alcoholic beverages, prepared foods, and so on, with which individual countries are identified.

Recently, Jacques Dreze of Belgium found that in his small native country the shelves of retail stores are filled with goods of foreign design, and there are few if any associated with particular Belgian tastes and traditions. He hypothesized that this is due to the fact that the size of the market for native Belgian designs is too small to permit exploitation of scale economies which are available to producers in other, larger countries. He found that the only way Belgian consumer goods industries can survive, without the protection of tariffs and in the presence of low costs of transportation and communication in the European Economic Community, is to specialize in the production of standardized, neutral designs used in all countries. Thus he found that Belgium produces and exports large quantities of heavy china and glassware used in the majority of restaurants throughout the world and specializes in the production of standardized sports equipment.

Quality of Products. The quality of goods is one characteristic which transcends the kinds of design features originating with the cultural and environmental heritage of nations. Staffan Linder (1961) argued that a country tends to specialize in the production and export of that quality of products which is demanded by the majority of its population, while it imports the qualities demanded by both the richest and the poorest segments of its population. Linder found support for his hypothesis in the case of his native country Sweden, but efforts to replicate his results for other nations generally have not been successful.

One problem associated with testing Linder's hypothesis is the difficulty of finding a reliable empirical proxy for the quality of goods. The value of a unit or ton of a commodity seems a good proxy for quality, but at the levels of aggregation at which trade statistics are available, many other variables influence unit values. For example, in the item "Shoes" there tend to be men's, women's, and children's shoes and a whole range of styles, from ordinary walking shoes to sandals and ski boots. Observed differences in the unit value of shoes traded by nations would be relevant for a test of Linder's hypothesis only if the mix of the varieties of shoes were the same for each country, which of course it is not. For this reason Linder's thesis should be tested only at a very low level of aggregation in trade statistics, which unfortunately is not available in published form.

Technical Market Size.   Our preceding discussion of trade in differentiated products concentrated on consumer goods. However, an important proportion of world trade is in the form of producers' capital equipment and intermediate inputs. In a fundamental study of prices and characteristics of U.S. goods in these categories, Irving Kravis and Robert E. Lipsey (1971) found that the U.S. domestic market is large enough to warrant the production of a number of highly specialized machines and components which could then be exported successfully, even though the United States is a significant importer of other goods in the same industry.

For example, these economists found that the United States produces roller bearings with special heat, pressure, and corrosion resistance required in only relatively few applications. Yet, in the large U.S. market these applications come to a sufficiently high number that the producers of these bearings reap the benefits of economies of scale which permit successful exports, while at the same time the United States is a very heavy importer of standard roller bearings. Similarly, the relatively large U.S. market demands offset printing machines capable of producing economically large runs. In meeting this domestic demand, U.S. producers enjoy scale economies which permit exports of these types of printing machines to the relatively few users in the rest of the world. On the other hand, the United States imports printing machines specifically designed for shorter runs and frequent changes in mats, such as are called for by typical foreign demand conditions.

Differentiated Products: Product Cycles

All of the preceding analysis about trade in differentiated products has relied for explanation on the existence of scale economies in the form of length of runs. It did not involve any reference to processes of technical change involving time. Recently, Raymond Vernon and a number of his associates at the Harvard Graduate School of Business have developed a dynamic theory of comparative advantage which fits into our discussion of intraindustry trade because it involves, in part, differentiated products. As will soon become obvious, it explores some aspects of the nature of scale economies and length of runs that the preceding discussion neglected.

The problem with the preceding analysis, to which Vernon's dynamic theory is relevant, concerns this question: If, for example, the rest of the world has a comparative advantage in the manufacture of roller bearings generally, why cannot they also produce more cheaply the special heat- and corrosion-resistant bearings the United States now produces and exports? Presumably, the input requirements for all roller bearings are very similar, and economies of scale can be exploited by either U.S. producers or those in the rest of the world. The answer to this question is that the U.S. producers possess a certain input into the production process of these specialized roller bearings which is not accessible to the foreign manufacturers.

The input, usually not available to foreigners is knowledge about how to produce, market, or service a particular good. It may be unavailable to non-U.S. producers for two analytically distinct reasons. First, the knowledge may be protected by government-regulated patent and copyright systems. This government protection of innovators is designed to encourage research and the development of new processes and products by firms through assuring them a temporary excess profit sufficient, on average, to recoup their investment before competitors can imitate their innovations.

Second, and perhaps more important, there is a form of natural protection enjoyed by many producers who have "learned by doing" and thus acquired a form of knowledge which is not accessible to others except through an expensive period of experimentation and learning on their own. This natural protection is especially prevalent in industries whose technology is still evolving and changing. It has been observed widely that in such industries costs per unit of output fall with the passage of time and the quantity of output.

Outstanding examples of the protection of knowlege by patents and copyrights are found in the pharmaceutical and chemical industries. Once the secret of producing new goods in these industries is known, it is usually fairly easy for highly trained scientists and engineers to initiate production, and patent or copyright regulations are required to protect investors' rights. Examples of natural protection are found in the electronic and computer industries, where only actual production experience, often involving many small innovations, can show producers how to bring down the cost per unit of output.

The important characteristic of this knowledge about production processes or products is that it tends to depreciate. Patents and copyrights terminate after 15 years, and as technology settles down and industries mature, imitation becomes possible without the need to incur high costs of learning by doing. At such times, the comparative advantage principles stressed by the basic Heckscher-Ohlin model assert themselves.

Vernon combined individual elements of the preceding analysis into an explanation of U.S. exports based on product cycles. He found that the development of new processes or products in the United States provides U.S. manufacturers with a temporary comparative advantage, based on the knowledge input in the production process. As these products or technologies mature and the knowledge becomes obsolete, production for some of them is shifted abroad, and the previously exported goods are then imported into the United States. In the meantime, however, further innovations have resulted in the export of new U.S. products in the same industry. Also, some products may be produced with technologies in which the United States has a comparative advantage, and they continue to be manufactured in the United States even after the technology has settled down.

An outstanding example of such product cycles involves the manufacture of radio receivers since the end of World War II. Early in the period U.S. producers dominated the world market for radios built with vacuum tubes. Japan took over a large share of this market, exploiting her comparative advantage in low labor costs which is relevant to the process of assembling the radios. Then U.S. industry developed the transistor, and for a number of years the U.S. radio industry competed successfully with Japanese radios based on the old technology. However, after a few years Japanese producers again took advantage of low labor costs in making the wire connections between transistors, which had become available in standard specifications at low prices throughout the world. The next cycle of temporary U.S. advantage was based on printed circuits to replace wires connecting transistors. The latest technology involves integrated circuits, silicone chips, and other forms of miniaturization which dominate transistor-based methods in many applications, both in performance and cost. This also has been developed in the United States and provides U.S. producers with a comparative advantage. It remains to be seen whether the cycle of the past will be repeated or whether technology in electronics has finally settled down. If it has matured, the next interesting and unresolved question is whether the new technology is relatively capital or labor intensive.

This dynamic theory of international trade, based on the existence of knowledge as an essential input into the production process, is applicable to markets for differentiated and homogeneous products, though in the latter case product cycles are less dramatic and frequent. They would typically involve production process innovations in the chemical and metals industries.

Intraindustry trade, which we have attempted to explain in this section of Chapter 4, arises in the context of product cycles as new goods or processes are introduced. Thus it is possible to have in the United States simultaneous exports of U.S. transistor radios and imports of vacuum tube radios. Intraindustry trade in product cycle goods takes place also among countries which engage in research and product development in the same industry. A good example is the pharmaceutical industry, in which there is a large amount of trade in European- and U.S.-developed drugs and medicines.

As an extension of the basic Heckscher-Ohlin model, Vernon's product cycle analysis has two essential ingredients. First, it involves time in a fundamental way, and therefore it is genuinely dynamic. Second, it introduces the notion that the U.S. comparative advantage in international trade may to a large extent be based on its stock of knowledge capital. If we consider that the production of this knowledge, through research and development, is very human and also capital intensive, then the factor proportions theory of the basic Heckscher-Ohlin model is reconfirmed by Vernon's approach. Through the human and knowledge capital aspects, this theory is linked to the extensions of the basic Heckscher-Ohlin model discussed above as responses to the Leontief paradox.

Labor Value-Added Processes

One final important source of intraindustry trade involves the shipment of intermediate products from the United States and Europe to low-wage countries for assembly or finishing and the subsequent reimportation of these goods. Gerald Helleiner (1973) has documented the phenomenal increase in international trade based in this category since about 1967. He cites some examples which provide a flavor of the kinds of labor-intensive value-added processes on which this trade is based. For example tuners are assembled in Mexico for U.S. electronics manufacturers, baseballs are sewn together from U.S. components in Caribbean islands, automobile wire harnesses are assembled in Taiwan for Japanese automobile manufacturers, and German cameras are assembled in Singapore.

International trade designed to exploit low labor costs abroad is most frequently undertaken by large, multinational firms, and we shall discuss this trade further in a later chapter devoted to the analysis of multinational firms. However, we should note here that these firms, through their multinational activities, have excellent information about costs of production in different countries and are capable of moving knowledge capital between countries at very low cost. They are thus in a uniquely favorable position to exploit classical sources of comparative advantage, and this may well lead to a diminution of the volume of international trade in product cycle goods. They are also likely to assist in the development of countries that now have little industry, as we will note in the next chapter. Intraindustry trade due to labor value-added processes clearly is consistent with the basic Heckscher-Ohlin model, under the assumption of constant returns to scale. According to the model, the phenomenon appears only because of the aggregation of international trade statistics.

Summary and Conclusions

In this section we have shown that intraindustry trade is an empirically significant phenomenon which in part is consistent with the basic Heckscher-Ohlin model and, according to the model, due only to the fact that statistical reports of trade require the aggregation of individual commodities. To a significant degree, however, intraindustry trade also appears to be due to some real-world conditions which have been assumed away in the construction of the basic Heckscher-Ohlin model.

In attempting to explain intraindustry trade we have brought together in this section a number of analytical refinements and extension of the basic model. Thus we have discussed the role of transportation, storage, and information costs and of production indivisibilities in the determination of international trade in functionally homogeneous products. We have also presented a number of recent contributions to the theory of trade in differentiated products which were based on the assumed existence of economies of scale in production due to length of runs, on the creation and depreciation of knowledge capital, and on the exploitation of low labor costs in developing countries, particularly in labor-intensive processes of assembly or finishing. Of special interest were attempts to explain the determination of trade in differentiated consumer and producers' goods on the basis of the characteristics of the physical environments of nations, cultural and historic traditions, technical market size, and the quality of products in relation to various countries' per capita incomes.

All of these modifications and extensions of the basic Heckscher-Ohlin model used in the explanations of the Leontief paradox and of the intraindustry trade phenomenon increase our understanding of the determinants of international trade. Unfortunately, however, through these modifications and extensions international trade theory has also become much more complex, aestetically less pleasing, and theoretically less powerful than the basic Heckscher-Ohlin model. As economists have come to know as an immutable law, however, all benefits are acquired at some cost, or "there is no such thing as a free lunch." Future developments of international trade theory are likely to be acquired only by further sacrifices in the simplicity of already existing theory.

BIBLIOGRAPHICAL NOTES

Empirical studies of the Ricardian trade model are by MacDougall (1951, 1952), Stern (1962) and Balassa (1963). The original Leontief (1953) findings led to a large number of studies covering different countries: Tatemoto and Ichimura (1959) for Japan, Bharadwaj (1962) for India, Wahl (1961) for Canada, and Stolper and Roskamp (1961) for East Germany. Vanek (1959) and Naya (1957) considered the role of natural resources in trade patterns. Leonticf (1956) and Baldwin (1971) refined the original Leontief approach and used different data basis. Tarshis (1954),

MacDougall (1951, 1952), Kravis (1956), Moroney and Walker (1966), and Moroney (1972) tested the Heckscher-Ohlin model in ways different from Leontief.

The role of human capital as a third factor of production has been applied to international trade theory at a theoretically rigorous level by Kenen (1965). Johnson (1968) applies the ideas more generally to commercial policy theory. The concept and measurement of human capital is discussed in a book of readings edited by Blaug (1970). Empirical studies about the role of human and knowledge capital in international trade are by Gruber, Mehta, and Vernon (1967) and Keesing (1966, 1967).

Jones (1956–57) discusses theoretically the explanation of the Leontief paradox due to taste differences. Empirical evidence on price and income elasticities in different countries is presented by Houthakker (1957) and Prais and Houthakker (1955). The effect of tariffs on trade and the explanation of the Leontief paradox are studied theoretically and empirically by Valavanis-Vail (1954, 1958), Basevi (1966), and, in a difficult book, by Travis (1964). Minhas (1962) gives a theoretical explanation of the Leontief paradox based on factor intensity reversals and supports it with empirical data. Bhagwati (1959) provides a clear survey of the modifications of the Heckscher-Ohlin model suggested by the theoretical and empirical work which followed the discovery of the Leontief paradox.

The section in this chapter dealing with intraindustry trade and theories of differentiated products is based on Grubel and Lloyd (1975). A review of studies applying imperfect competition theory to international trade theory has been published by Johnson (1967b). The important concept of economies of scale due to the length of run is discussed generally by Alchian (1959) and Hirschleifer (1962) and applied to problems of trade liberalization theoretically and empirically by Daly et al. (1962) and Wonnacott and Wonnacott (1967). Posner (1961) provided an early exposition of the product cycle theory of trade, which was refined and expanded by Vernon (1966). Hufbauer's book (1966) is an in-depth study of the chemical industry characterized by frequent product cycles. Explanations of trade in products differentiated by quality and design are given by Linder (1961) and Dreze (1960), respectively. Kravis and Lipsey (1971) discuss product differentiation in capital goods. The practice of sourcing is discussed and documented by Helleiner (1973).

CONCEPTS FOR REVIEW

Leontief paradox

Human capital

Knowledge capital

Factor intensity reversal

Intraindustry trade

Functional homogeneity of goods

Economies of scale in production
due to:
    Plant size
    Firm size
    Length of runs
Product cycle

POINTS FOR FURTHER STUDY AND DISCUSSION

1. Interview producers in your town to find out which lines of products they sell abroad and to which countries. Try to establish the characteristics of imported

substitutes for goods manufactured by this producer and ask him why he cannot compete with these imports.

2. What happens to the factor price equilization theorem if the Heckscher-Ohlin model is extended formally to consider more than two factors of production and goods? (See chapter in Bhagwati et al., 1971, for a guide to the literature on this subject.)

3. On a simpler level of analysis, try to employ the concept of comparative advantage to a set of commodities, all of which have different labor-capital input requirements. For help on this subject see Haberler (1950).

4. When there are economies of scale in production, does the market necessarily lead to maximum world output?

5. Draw different sets of isoquants with zero-, one-, two-, and three factor intensity reversals over the full range of relative factor prices.

6. Discuss the welfare implications of product differentiation and relate your discussion to the arguments over the merits of free trade.

5 Economic Growth and International Trade

IN THE TWO PRECEDING CHAPTERS, the Heckscher-Ohlin model was used to show the effects of international trade on welfare, income distribution, and so on, under the assumption that the countries concerned had a given stock of capital and labor. Section I of this chapter considers a country in international trade equilibrium and then analyzes the implications of exogenously given growth in the factors of production on welfare, the pattern of trade, and factor prices. Section II considers modifications of the analysis necessary if the growth of factors is not exogenously given but is influenced by international trade itself.

Section I consists of three subsections. In the first we analyze the effect of factor growth on conditions in a small country for which the world price of goods is unchanged as a result of its own trade. The entire analysis involves a careful taxonomy of possible effects of growth and yields the widely cited Rybczynski theorem. The second subsection relaxes the small-country assumption and considers the possibility that domestic factor growth worsens a country's terms of trade. One interesting possibility in such a world is that the welfare of the growing country is actually reduced, a phenomenon which Jagdish Bhagwati has called "immiserizing growth." The final subsection deals with the growth of knowledge capital and imperfections in its distribution. The analysis enlarges upon Raymond Vernon's product cycle concept which we mentioned in our analysis of intraindustry trade in Chapter 4. It represents an extension of the basic Heckscher-Ohlin model in a world of technical change and product innovations.

The second section of this chapter presents the theory and controversy about the influence international trade has on economic development. We discuss first the relationship in the basic model involving comparative statics and the normal gains from trade. This section contains theoretical arguments and empirical evidence designed to show that trade harms growth. The validity of these arguments is examined both theoretically and on the basis of empirical evidence accumulated in recent years. The chapter concludes with a subsection giving theoretical arguments and empirical evidence in support of the notion that greater reliance on international trade leads to accelerated economic development.

I. GROWTH AND WELFARE IN THE HECKSCHER-OHLIN MODEL

Factor Growth in a Small Country

Consider small country A in international trade equilibrium, as shown in Figure 3–5 in Chapter 3. An increase in productive capacity results in an outward shift of the production possibilities locus, the precise ways of which will be discussed below. It can readily be seen from Figure 3–5 that as long as country A produces both goods initially, any outward shift of the production frontier must shift upward the world price line, which is assumed here to be unaffected by this growth in country A. Any such outward shift of the world price line in turn implies that country A can reach a higher level of community welfare. It thus follows that economic growth must always raise the welfare of a small trading nation.

This conclusion is most important and follows so readily from the basic Heckscher-Ohlin model that it is often overlooked. It is also pushed into the background by a set of elaborate classification schemes of effects of growth on the proportionate increase in consumption, production, and consumption and production combined. We now turn to this taxonomy, whose main virtue is that it further increases understanding of the basic Heckscher-Ohlin model and relates it to some other widely used concepts of economic analysis.

Consumption Effects. In Figure 5–1 we show the highest world price line, Y_0X_0, country A can attain with its initial resource endowments and the implicit production frontier, which is not shown to keep the analysis simple. Point C shows the initial point of consumption and the ray OS represents the ratio in which X and Y are consumed.

Now assume that economic growth pushes outward country A's production frontier by so much that it can trade along the world price ratio Y_1X_1 shown in Figure 5–1. It is clear that the combination of X and Y actually chosen for consumption by the residents of country A depends on the indifference map. We do not show this map because in principle it could lead to a tangency anywhere along the price line Y_1X_1. In the absence of any useful a priori information about the consumption map of any

FIGURE 5–1
Growth and Consumption

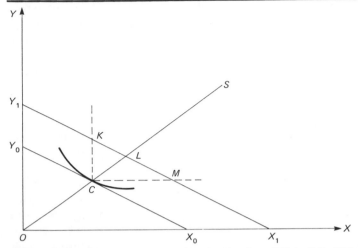

Growth shifts outward the attainable price line from Y_0X_0 to Y_1X_1. With good X assumed to be country A's import good, if tastes are such that at the higher income the new consumption point is between Y_1 and K, growth is ultra antitrade biased; between K and L, growth is antitrade biased; on L, growth is neutral; between L and M, growth is protrade biased; and between M and L, growth is ultra protrade biased.

country, we are forced to limit our analysis to a taxonomic classification scheme of possible outcomes.

The taxonomy can best be explained on the basis of Table 5–1. Assuming that good Y is the export good, if the new point of consumption lies on the price ratio section Y_1K shown in Figure 5–1, country A has a strong preference to consume its own export good and a very strong preference against the consumption of the import good X. As can be seen, along the Y_1K segment absolutely less of X is consumed than at the lower income level. Under these conditions growth is said to be ultra antitrade biased.

TABLE 5–1
The Effects of Growth and Consumption on Trade

Consumption Region	Characteristic	Bias
Y_1K	Absolute decrease in consumption of X	Ultra Antitrade
KL	Absolute increase, but less than proportionate increase in consumption of X	Antitrade
L	Equi-proportionate increase in consumption of X and Y	Neutral
LM	Less than proportionate but absolute decrease in consumption of Y	Protrade
MX_1	Absolute decrease in consumption of Y	Ultra Protrade

Along the segment KL, consumption of X increases absolutely, but proportionately the quantity of X relative to Y consumed at the higher income is less than at the lower income. This situation is known as antitrade bias. If growth leads to consumption at point L on the Y_1X_1 price line and OS ray, growth is known as having a "neutral" effect on trade because X and Y are consumed in unchanged relative proportions. By analogy the terms "protrade bias" and "ultra protrade bias" were derived; they can be seen to be applicable to segments LM and MX_1, respectively, in Figure 5-1.

The 19th-century Prussian statistician Ernst Engel (not Karl Marx's friend Friedrich Engels) compiled information on individuals' demand for particular goods as a function of income. His research and subsequent studies showed that there exist fairly consistent patterns in the income elasticity of demand for certain classes of goods. Food, for example, tends to represent an increasingly smaller proportion of budgets as income rises. Some food items, such as potatoes and bread, actually tend to be consumed in smaller quantities at higher than at lower income levels. Luxury goods, on the other hand, tend to be consumed in absolutely and proportionately larger amounts as income increases.

Empirical information of this sort can be used to predict the development of a small country's trade levels as its productive capacity increases. For example, if in Figure 5-1 the export good Y is a luxury good, then we can expect that economic growth is antitrade or perhaps even ultra antitrade biased. On the other hand, if Y is a staple food, growth will be protrade or ultra protrade biased. The characteristics of countries' export goods from this point of view are of some importance for the strategies of economic development to be discussed below.

Production. In our analysis of the Edgeworth Box diagram and its relation to the production possibilities frontier of Chapter 3, we showed that the relative endowments of individual countries with capital and labor determine the shapes of the countries' production frontiers, given the factor intensities of the two goods. We now use the same analytical tools to consider the production frontiers of a given country, A, before and after growth in factor supplies. Because of the importance of relative factor supplies, we will examine three polar cases of growth, maintaining the assumption that Y is the capital intensive good.

1. Growth of One Factor Only. In Figure 5-2, the top panel shows the familiar Edgeworth Box diagram with a given stock of labor and capital, the production function origins X and Y_0, and the initial equilibrium with trade at point A. The units of measurement of goods X and Y have been chosen arbitrarily so that the maximum output of good X shown in the bottom panel of Figure 5-2 equals that of the initial labor endowment XL_0. On the production frontier initial output is at point A'.

Now consider an increase in the supply of labor shown as a horizontal

FIGURE 5–2

Increase in Labor and the Production Frontier

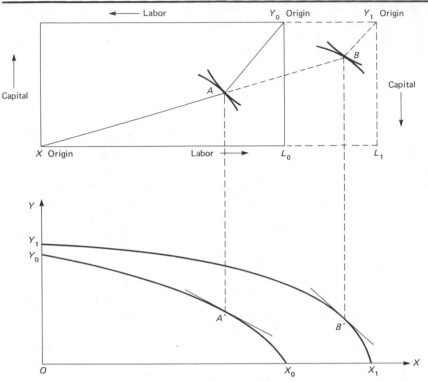

In Figure 5–2, country A under free trade experiences a growth in only its labor force, which expands the Edgeworth Box only horizontally from XL_0 to XL_1. Since factor intensities remain unchanged under free trade, the XA ray is extended to XB, while the Y_0A and Y_1B rays are parallel, but the latter is shorter than the former. In the bottom panel this fact is reflected in the absolute decrease of output of Y in spite of growth. The situation illustrated follows from the Rybszynski theorem, which says that in the H.-O. model growth leads to an absolute reduction in the output of the good which uses intensively the factor whose supply is increased.

expansion of the Edgeworth Box from XL_0 to XL_1, with the origin of the Y production function moving from Y_0 to Y_1. Retaining our initial scaling units, the maximum output of X increases proportionately less than the increase in labor, since at this maximum output the full employment of all resources requires a higher capital/labor ratio, and under the assumption of linearly homogeneous production functions there are diminishing returns to labor. Consequently the ratio L_0L_1/XL_0 is greater than X_0X_1/OX_0. The maximum output of the capital-intensive good Y is increased somewhat because even though good Y is capital intensive, labor can be substituted in the production process. However, because of the capital intensity of the production function for Y, diminishing returns to labor are stronger and the maximum increase in Y output is proportionately less than for X; that is, $X_0 X_1 / OX_0 > Y_1 Y_0 / OY_0$. Given these explanations for the maximum output levels for X and Y, it follows from our arguments about the shape of the production frontier made in Chapter 3 that the new frontier must bulge out more towards X than Y, as shown in Figure 5–2.

Of particular interest is the equilibrium output mix before and after growth at the given world commodity price ratio. For reasons we established in Chapter 3, in equilibrium relative factor prices and intensities must be the same in all countries having identical production functions. For these same reasons, prices and intensities must be the same for a country with different factor endowments, and the new equilibrium output in the enlarged Edgeworth Box in Figure 5–2 is at point B, where the factor intensity ray for X is the same as at A and the ray for Y is parallel to that at A. The relative lengths of the rays at A and B show clearly that, after growth, output of X must be larger and that of Y must be smaller than they were initially. This fact is also reflected in the bottom panel of Figure 5–2, showing an absolute decrease in output of Y between the initial and the new equilibrium points, A' and B'. This observation has led to a celebrated theorem named after its discoverer, T. M. Rybczynski.

This Rybczynski theorem states generally that the growth of one factor of production must always lead to the absolute decrease in the output of the good using intensively the nongrowing factor. Our diagrammatic analysis reveals readily the validity of this theorem. The intersection of the unchanged X ray with the parallel Y ray must necessarily be closer to the Y origin when the box is expanded horizontally. More intuitively, the result is caused by the requirement of full employment of all resources, which can be achieved after the increase in labor only if capital is released from the initial production mix. But since factor intensities must remain unchanged, for reasons already discussed, only reductions in the output of Y and increases in X set free net quantities of capital, which are then available for employment with the additions to labor and some further labor released in the switch from Y to X.

The Rybczynski theorem is an implication of the Heckscher-Ohlin model in the context of growing factor supplies. It embodies a prediction which has not been obvious before development of the formal apparatus of the model and which to some degree runs against intuition. More advanced formal theorizing in international economics embodying refinements or extensions of the basic Heckscher-Ohlin model frequently considers it an important check on the validity of the logical structure and reasoning of these models if they imply the Rybczynski theorem results. For this reason, more than its real-world importance, the Rybczynski theorem is mentioned frequently in the advanced international economics literature.

2. *Equiproportionate Growth of Both Factors.* In Figure 5–3 we show again the Edgeworth Box and production frontier of country A, in equilibrium with a given stock of capital and labor. An equiproportionate increase in capital and labor is shown geometrically by the expansion of the box along the extended diagonal, as is done in Figure 5–3.

FIGURE 5–3
Equiproportionate Increase in Capital and Labor

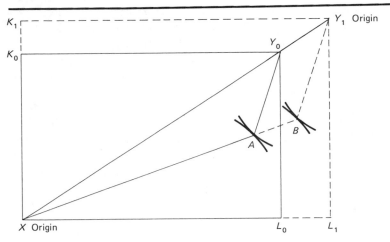

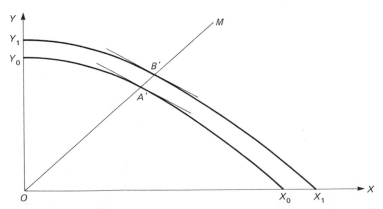

Equiproportionate growth of both factor supplies leads to equiproportionate expansions of the Edgeworth Box in Figure 5–3, from XK_0 to XK_1 and XL_0 to XL_1, where $K_1K_0/K_0X = L_0L_1/XL_0$. With unchanged traded goods prices, factor intensities remain the same, which is shown by the facts that XY_0 and XY_1 are on a straight line and that Y_0A and Y_1B are parallel. Because of the equiproportionate expansion of the rays $XA/XB = XY_0/XY_1$ the expansion ray OM in the bottom panel is a straight line.

The most interesting implications of equiproportionate factor growth are on the production frontier and the equilibrium output at unchanged world output prices. As can be seen from the diagram, the production frontier is expanded outward equiproportionately along its entire range, including the initial output combination A'. Therefore, the new output B' lies along the ray OM from the origin through A'.

Why does the production frontier shift outward by the same proportionate distance equal to the proportionate increase in factor supplies over its entire range? To answer this question consider the maximum output of X before and after growth. The technology used in both instances requires the use of capital and labor in exactly the same proportion in which it is available in the country as a whole. Under the assumption of constant returns to scale, therefore, the increase in output must be equiproportionate to the increase in the length of the production ray, which in turn is equal to the proportionate increase in the factor supplies. The argument can be repeated for complete specialization in Y and for other points along the production frontier, except that at less than complete specialization the sum of capital/labor ratios in each industry, weighted by their respective absolute capital and labor uses, must equal the country's overall capital/labor ratio. Since after growth the overall ratio and the individual industries' ratios are unchanged, the equilibrium condition can be met only if the weights change equiproportionately, which in turn implies equiproportionate increase in the output of each commodity.

3. *Growth in Factor Proportion Equal to Use in One Industry.* Now consider the case where capital and labor grow in a proportion just equal to the one in which they are used in the production of Y. In Figure 5–4 we show this condition by placing the upper right-hand corner of the Edgeworth Box on the extension of the Y production ray. As can be seen in Figure 5–4, factor growth of this type leaves unchanged the length of the X ray and, by moving the Y origin further away from the point of efficient production, lengthens the Y ray. This lengthening of the Y ray necessitates relabeling the Y isoquant at point A,B and implies an increase in the output of Y. Output of X remains unchanged. These changes are reflected also in the bottom panel of Figure 5–4, where the expanded production frontier's tangency with the world price ratio at point B' indicates higher output of Y and unchanged output of X.

The intuitive explanation of this result is that under the assumed proportionate growth in factors they are used completely and without the generation of excess demands or supplies in the manufacture of Y. To maintain full employment of all resources, the output of X cannot and should not be increased.

It is not very difficult to generalize from the preceding examples of growth in factor supplies to any combinations of growth, though we will not do so here. The main purposes of the preceding analysis were to show

FIGURE 5–4

Growth Equal to Capital/Labor Ratio in Y Industry

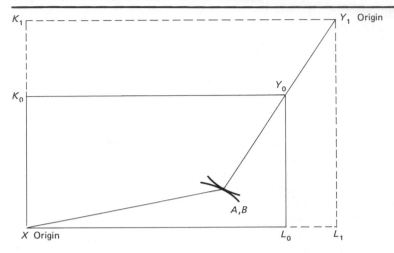

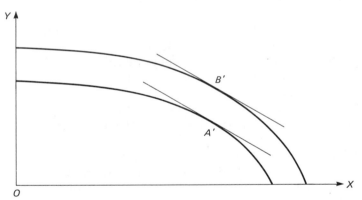

The expansion of factor supplies in country A by L_0L_1 of labor and K_0K_1 of capital takes place in the same ratio at which capital and labor are used under free trade in industry Y. Therefore the line $A,B–Y_1$ is a straight line. In the new equilibrium only the output of good Y has increased. For this reason in the bottom panel point B' is vertically above A', implying zero growth of production of good X.

that the character of the growth in factors determines the manner in which the production frontier is expanded and to lead to another taxonomy of effects.

The terminology and approach to the classification of the effects of growth on production are identical to those underlying the consumption effects discussed in connection with Figure 5–1. For example, in the case where only the supply of labor is increased, the output of the capital-intensive good Y must decrease absolutely, as we discussed above and showed in Figure 5–2. In this case, if Y is the export good, growth is considered to have an ultra antitrade bias because there is an absolutely smaller output of the good sold abroad. In the case of equiproportionate growth shown in Figure 5–3, growth is neutral. In the case underlying Figure 5–4 growth is right at the line between being ultra protrade and protrade biased. It should be noted, however, that in the classification scheme of Figure 5–1 and Table 5–1, with Y the export good, the effects under the production case are exactly the opposite of those under the consumption case. For example, the segment MX_1 implies an absolute decrease in the domestic *consumption* of the export good Y, ceteris paribus making available more of Y for export. Hence, the effect is trade creating, or ultra *pro*trade biased. On the other hand, growth in segment MX_1 *production* means an absolute decrease in the availability of the export good Y and therefore an ultra *anti*trade bias.

Combined Effects. After the analysis of the effects of growth on (first) consumption and trade and (second) production and trade, we can conclude the taxonomy by combining the production and consumption effects. In Figure 5–5 we show the polar case where both production and consumption effects are neutral and the before and after equilibrium

FIGURE 5–5
Consumption and Production Effects Combined

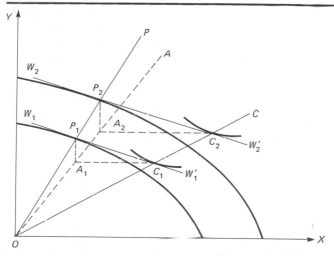

The outward shift of the production frontier, together with the consumption preferences of country A, determine the nature of the bias in growth. It is possible to draw trade triangles such as $P_2A_2C_2$ at any resultant combination of P and C (except when $C = P$, there is no trade). If the corner of the triangle lies to the left of the ray OP, growth and trade are ultra antitrade biased; if it is between OP_1 and OA_1, they are antitrade biased; on OA_1 they are neutral; between A_1 and C_1 they are protrade biased; to the right of C_1 they are ultra protrade biased.

points are on the respective rays OP and OC. Under these conditions the combined effects on trade are also neutral, with equiproportionate growth in exports and imports, $P_1A_1/P_2A_2 = A_1C_1/A_2C_2$, and the origins A_1 and A_2 of the trade triangles on the ray OA.

Of course, again, anything is possible, and in the absence of specific information we can only classify possible combined effects. In this case we concentrate on the location of alternative points A_2 along a line analogous to that in Figure 5–1. For example, with Y the export good, if the production effect is neutral (as shown in Figure 5–5) but consumption is biased and therefore to the right of the OC ray on the world price line W_2W_2', then the corresponding point A lies to the right of the OA ray. In Figure 5–1, A would be on the LM segment of the Y_1X_1 line. The combined effect of growth on trade in this case is protrade biased. As can readily be envisioned by considering Figure 5–5, both the export PA and import AC segments of the trade triangle must be longer than they are when under conditions of neutrality in both production and trade. Lengthening of these trade triangle segments signifies increased trade. Other combinations of biases in production and growth can result in net effects ranging from ultra protrade to ultra antitrade bias. With Y as the export good the former is on the bottom and the latter is on the top segments of the Y_1X_1 line in Figure 5–1, as in the case of consumption effects.

Technical Change.   Gains in productive capacity represented by outward shifts in the production frontier can be caused by increases in factor supplies (discussed above), technical innovations, or both. The subject of technical improvements is an important component of microeconomic theory and production function analysis. It involves a fairly formidable taxonomy for the classification and naming of particular effects which, like the taxonomy of trade effects just concluded, is useful for efficient discussions among experts and serves to deepen the understanding of underlying determinants of trade.

However, a full development of the terminology and effects of technical change and its subsequent superimposition upon the already complicated taxonomy of growth, consumption, and trade is not warranted here. Therefore we will simply outline different types of technical change and indicate broadly how they affect the production frontier. First, it is necessary to realize that technical improvement can affect productivity of capital and labor in either of our assumed two industries or only in one. Furthermore, the technical change may increase the productivity of one factor more than the other, either equally in both industries or differently in each.

Given all of these possible sets of changes, the simplest case involves equal productivity gains in both industries and for both factors. Under these conditions the country's production frontier is expanded equiproportionately along its entire range, and with unchanged world product prices, production expands neutrally along the original production ray. In every important analytical respect, technical progress of this sort is identical to the equiproportionate factor growth discussed in connection with Figure 5–3.

A second polar case involves savings in capital and labor such that the maintenance of a given output of one industry, say Y, at initial relative factor prices can be attained through equiproportionate reductions in the use of physical units of both factors. This condition, which is known as neutral technical progress, is equivalent to the increase in factor supplies in proportion equal to their use in industry Y. As can be recalled from our analysis surrounding Figure 5–4, such growth leads to an increase only in the output of product Y.

The analysis becomes very complex and difficult to carry out in general terms if technical change is biased in its effect on the input requirements of the two factors, even in the case of only one industry and savings in input requirements of only one factor. The fundamental reason for this is that as a result of biased technical change we encounter changes in equilibrium capital/labor ratios, which in the analysis of factor growth provided an essential ingredient in finding new equilibrium positions. For example, consider a reduction in the capital input requirement of industry Y at the initial factor prices. Entrepreneurs in industry Y are induced to hire more labor relative to capital and expand output, since initially the cost of production is lowered and the final product prices are unchanged. However, as labor is demanded for these purposes, its price relative to that of capital rises. We now get a substitution of capital for labor in both industries. In the new full-employment equilibrium, both industries will use more capital-intensive technologies, and the output of both is increased. However, the precise relative increases can be known only after mathematical specification of the production function, product price ratio, initial-factor supplies, and degree of technical innovation. Geometric analysis cannot handle this problem.

Large Countries and Growth

In the preceding discussion of economic growth and its effects on trade and welfare, one of the key assumptions was that country A is so small that its growth does not alter the world price ratio. We will now relax this assumption.

Figure 5–6 presents in solid lines the initial offer curves of countries A and B, which we developed in Chapter 3 and used to demonstrate the determination of the world price ratio OT. Now consider growth in productive capacity in country A, while country B stays at its original level of development. Depending on the nature of the production functions for goods X and Y and the relative proportions in which capital and labor

FIGURE 5-6
World Price Ratio and Growth

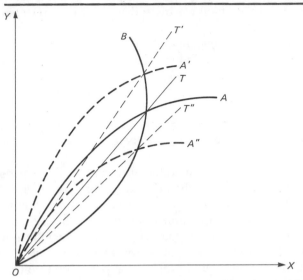

Countries A and B are in equilibrium initially at the world price ratio *OT,* marking the intersection between offer curves *OA* and *OB*. Depending on taste and growth biases, growth of country A's production capacity may either shift the offer curve outward or shrink it inward. In the former case the world price deteriorates to *OT'*, in the latter case it improves to *OT''*.

grow, a given set of indifference curves in country A can yield a new offer curve lying either inside or outside of the original one. We show these two possibilities in Figure 5-6 as offer curves *A''* and *A'*, respectively. With the unchanged offer curve of country B, in the latter case, the terms of trade for country A improve, and in the new equilibrium it can obtain more of the import good *X* for a given amount of the good *Y* than it did before growth. In the former case, however, the terms of trade deteriorate.

It is worth recalling, from our derivation of the offer curves in Chapter 3, that their contours are determined by the particular shapes of the community indifference curves and the production frontiers. Also recall, from earlier parts of this chapter, that the shape of the production functions and the relative growth of factor supplies or the nature of technological advance exogenously determine the production frontier. For these reasons we cannot rule out logically either of the two outcomes, and we conclude that growth may either improve or worsen the terms of trade of a large, growing country.

The preceding analysis can readily be adapted to a world in which both countries A and B are growing. In this situation we must consider shifts in both countries' offer curves. Again, on a purely logical basis, the net result of these shifts may be either an improvement or a deterioration of country A's terms of trade.

Let us now turn to the case where country A's growth results in the worsening of its terms of trade, to such an extent that welfare in country A actually declines. This case has been made famous in an article by the Indian-born economist Jagdish Bhagwati, now teaching at the Massachusetts Institute of Technology, who described the phenomenon as immiserizing growth. Following Bhagwati's approach, we show, in Figure 5–7, country A in initial equilibrium at production point P_1 on the frontier

FIGURE 5–7
Immiserizing Growth

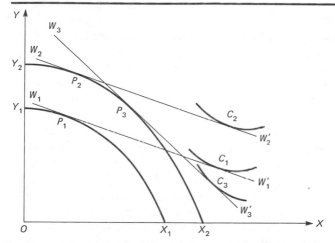

Country A is shown to experience growth in physical output capacity from X_1Y_1 to X_2Y_2. If the world price ratio remained unchanged after growth, $W_1W_1' = W_2W_2'$, an improvement in welfare, such as from C_1 to C_2, must always take place. However, it is possible that the deterioration of the world price accompanying growth, as from W_1W_1' to W_3W_3', leads to lower welfare, as at point C_3.

X_1Y_1, and consumption at C_1 where the indifference curve is tangent to the world price at W_1W_1'. Growth is assumed to expand the production frontier to X_2Y_2. We can see readily that at the initial world price, $W_2W_2' = W_1W_1'$, growth necessarily increases welfare, as we argued above. With production at P_2 the consumption indifference curve tangent to the world price line at C_2 must be above the pregrowth curve.

The deterioration of the terms of trade in our model means a lowering of the relative price of country A's export good Y. This is shown by the steepening of the world price line to W_3W_3'. At this price production moves to P_3 and consumption to C_3. As can be seen, in the particular circumstances country A is at a lower level of welfare after growth in factor supplies than it was before such growth.

The preceding analysis brings out the point that it may be misleading to consider growth in welfare to be synonymous with growth in the capacity to produce more physical units of output, either through increased availability of factors of production or through improved technology. In order to move from physical units of output to welfare, we need to consider prices, as was done here.

However, the case of deteriorating welfare in the presence of physical growth should be kept separate analytically from the case where externalities accompanying growth reduce welfare. This latter case has been receiving a great deal of attention in recent years as public concern about pollution, congestion, and other negative by-products of growth affecting the "quality of life" has manifested itself widely. In our analytical framework of Figure 5–7 we would represent the welfare effects of production externalities by redrawing a new production frontier inside the existing one. The distance between the old and new frontiers is determined by the cost of eliminating the externalities through the installation of pollution-control equipment required by law for the maintenance of publicly chosen standards of environmental quality. Since this additional manufacturing equipment requires real resources which have to be diverted from the production of consumption goods, the total capacity to produce these goods is reduced accordingly. This is shown by a shrinkage of the frontier. We can draw the market price of the two products tangent to the new frontier and find the new consumption point just as we did before. Of necessity the shrunken frontier must bring the consumption point to a lower indifference curve and reduced welfare. We conclude from this exercise that if growth results in both negative production externalities and deteriorating terms of trade, it is more likely to reduce welfare than if only the latter effect takes place.

In the preceding paragraph we discussed only externalities arising from the production process. It is well known that consumption itself gives rise to externalities in the forms of litter, noise and smoke pollution for automobiles or the disturbance of neighbors by hi-fi equipment, to mention just a few instances. These effects are more difficult to incorporate into the model surrounding Figure 5–7 than were the production externalities. However, in principle it is clear that the social value of a bundle of goods should be reduced to reflect the loss of welfare their consumption by one person brings about for others. Presumably this should lead to a redrawing or relabeling of the consumption indifference map, which cannot be undertaken in a graphically convenient and analytically rigorous manner. The main point for our purposes of analysis is that the existence of negative consumption externalities tends to increase further the likelihood that growth may lead to a deterioration of welfare above what it is when only negative production externalities and terms of trade effects are present.

What are the chances that in the real world immiserizing growth will take place in any country? As we will discuss in the next part of this chapter, there has been some evidence that the terms of trade of developing countries, exporting mostly staple agricultural and mining products, have been deteriorating during the past 50 years. However, the deterioration has not been severe, and the growth in productive capacity has been sufficiently rapid to avoid actual immiserization in terms of physical goods adjusted for relative price changes. On the effects of externalities, the final word is not yet in. Generally, pollution is not a severe problem in developing countries, simply because they have few industries. Evidence on the more general problem of "quality of life" involves difficult value judgments and may never become solid. All indications are that people want more goods, and concern about other aspects of the quality of life become important only after people have reached a certain minimum standard of living based on the supply of physical goods.

In considering problems of the real world in this context of immiserizing growth, it is worth remembering that in many developing countries per capita incomes have remained relatively stagnant for long periods. This is primarily because of rapid population growth, which has been overwhelmingly more important than whatever deterioration of the terms of trade has taken place. In other sections of this book we will examine commercial policies governments can use to avoid the deleterious effects of falling world prices for their exports.

Growth in Knowledge Capital

In the preceding analysis we have considered some effects of growth in factors of production, strictly in the tradition of the simple Heckscher-Ohlin model developed in Chapter 3. We now turn to the analysis of the effects of growth that follows from one of the most important of the modifications of the simple model that were undertaken in Chapter 4. This modification concerns the existence of differentiated products which are improved through continuous changes in design and performance. Also, we will consider the effects of improvements in manufacturing technology or processes for production of a given product.

This analysis fits into the context of growth and trade because the driving force of the improvements is knowledge capital formation. According to Irving Fisher and the recent formalization of his ideas by Harry G. Johnson, this is one of the alternatives to capital formation in the form of physical and human capital, the effects of which were discussed in Chapter 4. All three forms of capital require for their creation the use of

FIGURE 5–8

Technological Gap and Product Cycle Trade

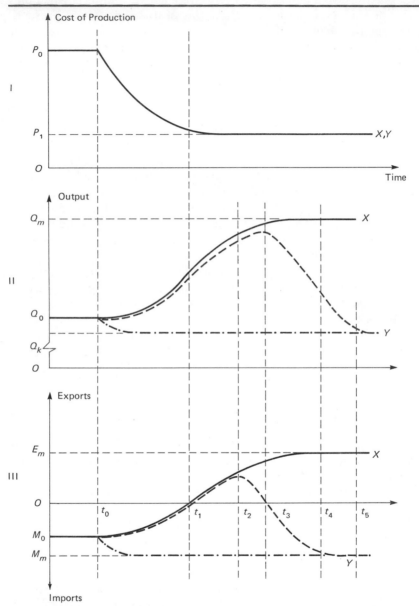

Note: Solid line in Panels II and III represents good X; broken line represents good Y. Both goods are represented by the solid line in Panel I. The broken line with dots represents good Y if the technical innovation in country A were not protected.

Panel I of Figure 5–8 shows the cost of production for both goods X and Y at P_0, until at time t_0 an innovation of the product or technology lowers production costs, which ultimately settle down at price P_1 after a period of learning.

In Panel II total output of good X, in which country A has developed a permanent currently produced output which cannot be consumed, and thus they conform to the Keynesian definition of equilibrium savings and investment. Both knowledge and human capital raise the output otherwise flowing from a given stock of labor and physical capital. Human capital is formed through the education of labor, while knowledge capital is raised through expenditures on research and development and through "learning by doing."

Knowledge capital has one particular characteristic not shared by human or physical capital. This characteristic is that it can be copied by other producers who study new goods or processes on the market. While such copying does not reduce the social usefulness of the knowledge capital to society as a whole, it could eliminate all returns for innovators to their investment in research and development. To compensate for this characteristic of knowledge capital, and to assure continued private investment in this form, governments have created patent and copyright laws to protect innovators from their competitors for a limited time. In the case of pure, nonpatentable knowledge, governments subsidize the production of this form outright through the financing of laboratories and independent researchers in universities and institutes. As a result of this legislation and government expenditure, there exists a tendency for marginal rates of return to be equalized for all three forms of capital. This implies the existence of the necessary conditions for the socially optimal allocation of savings.

With this background of understanding of the nature of knowledge capital, we can turn to the problem of how growth in this factor of production affects international trade patterns. We do so by drawing on the work of Raymond Vernon and his associates at the Harvard Graduate School of Business. The essence of their analysis is incorporated in Figure 5–8 and can be summarized as follows.

In all three panels of Figure 5–8 we show time along the horizontal axis. First we consider the case where two homogeneous goods, X and Y, are initially produced in country A at a price shown as OP_0 in Panel I, and in a quantity represented as OQ_0 in Panel II. The same goods are imported from abroad in a quantity OM_0 shown in Panel III. There is static equilib-

---

comparative advantage, is shown to rise until it reaches a maximum of Q_m. If the technological innovations cause country A to have a comparative disadvantage in producing good Y, and if the technology is freely available, output drops quickly to Q_k. If the technology is protected by patents, then output of good Y rises until time t_3, when the production knowledge becomes available to the rest of the world. Thereafter, output falls to Q_m.

Panel III shows the development of trade for good X, which shows maximum exports of E_m. The trade in good Y goes from imports to exports and, at time t_2, back to imports, if knowledge is protected for a time. If production knowledge for Y is not protected, then imports increase quickly to their maximum at M_m.

rium in the demand for, price, and import of these goods, until at time t_0 research and development in country A leads to the lowering of their cost of production. The true pattern of production cost is shown in Panel I as involving a gradual falling as bugs are worked out of the new system and workers and managers learn by doing. Ultimately the cost settles down at OP_1.

We now distinguish goods X and Y and trace their pattern of production and export through time. First consider good X, the output of which exhibits a pattern frequently encountered in the real world and shown as the S-shaped curve in Panel II. At first output rises slowly, as the innovation has not yet lowered production costs very much and delays are encountered in making users switch from old sources of supply to the new one. But eventually, as costs and prices fall more drastically, output accelerates more rapidly. Before the market is fully saturated at output OQ_m, however, the rate of increase in output slows down again, because of difficulties encountered in persuading the last buyers to switch to the new source of supply. At time t_4 costs and output have settled down and remain at this level in our assumedly otherwise static world.

In Panel III we show the development of foreign trade in good X, which exhibits an S-shaped time pattern analogous to that found for output, and for the same reasons. After time t_0, imports diminish slowly and become zero at time t_1. Exports begin at t_1 and reach their peak at t_4. In this case of good X, a technological innovation resulting from the growth in knowledge capital has turned comparative advantage principles in favor of country A. Thus, if country A is relatively well endowed with capital, our specific example implies that good X initially was produced with labor-intensive methods and after the innovation with capital-intensive methods. We conclude, therefore, that comparative advantage based only on the existence of labor and human and physical capital may be changed permanently by competitively determined research and development. If we look at country A's exports and imports at any given time, we can find evidence in support of the basic Heckscher-Ohlin model. Our analysis of the role of knowledge capital, however, brings out the fact that at two different points in time comparative advantage patterns can have switched, even though the relative factor endowments and tastes of the separate countries have remained unchanged.

The emphasis of Vernon's original analysis, however, is not on good X but on good Y. Returning to Panels II and III of Figure 5–8, notice the broken line representing good Y following the output and export pattern of good X until time t_2, when (by assumption) patent protection for the cost-reducing production process has ended. At this point foreign competitors begin to take advantage of the technical innovation, and they regain the comparative advantage in the manufacture of Y which they had lost temporarily. Panel III shows that at t_2 exports of Y from country A fall, and at t_3 they cease altogether and the country again becomes an importer, as before the innovation. We show that the long-run equilibrium level of imports reached at t_4 is OM_m, below the original one of OM_0. This indicates that the innovation has strengthened foreign comparative advantage in equilibrium relative to its previous level. This is not necessarily so, however, and OM_m could be above OM_0. Panel II shows the development of total output of Y in Country A that is logically analogous to the development of the trade pattern just discussed. In the new equilibrium, country A's output of Y is at OQ_k, below the original OQ_0. However, there is no reason why OQ_k could not be above OQ_0. If it were, the preceding analysis would be unchanged in its fundamental points. The broken line with dots between the dashes shown in Figure 5–8 represents the time pattern of trade and output of good Y that would have taken place if the technical innovation in country A had not been protected by patents. Trade and output would have fallen quickly to their long-run equilibrium levels.

The main conclusion to be drawn from the preceding analysis is that knowledge capital formation can cause a country to enjoy a temporary comparative advantage in the manufacture of a particular good for which, in the absence of restrictions on the availability of knowledge, it would have a comparative disadvantage. Then, the analysis of trade patterns at any given time can reveal that country A exports labor-intensive products while it is relatively well endowed with capital. The particular pattern of trade ceases once the knowledge capital depreciates, either naturally, through further technical innovations, or after the expiration of patent protection. It should be noted, however, that if a country has a strong program of research and development in particular industries, it is possible that a continuous flow of innovations maintains the comparative advantage in goods produced intensively with the factor in which it is relatively poorly endowed. In such situations it may be useful to return to the models of international trade discussed in Chapter 4, in which stocks of human and knowledge capital, along with labor and real capital, are treated in a different way and are used to explain patterns of trade in the framework of the more basic two-factor Heckscher-Ohlin model.

Our analysis of Figure 5–8 was based on the assumption that innovation had affected the cost of producing the homogeneous goods X and Y. However, according to the evidence presented in Chapter 4, a large proportion of world trade consists of differentiated products sold in oligopolistic markets, where competition takes the form of improved design of goods to give them better performance characteristics or appearance, rather than the lowering of price. Analytically, we can think of these improvements as leading to a lowering of the price per unit of a service provided by a given product, and it matters little whether the improvements merely exploit a frivolous consumer demand created, perhaps, by heavy advertising expenditures. The main concern here is that the improvements lead to increased sales and output, the reduction of the importation of close substitute products, and the eventual export of the good in patterns like those shown in Panels II and III of Figure 5–8. If the innovations have this kind of effect, all of the preceding analysis concerning the lowering of the cost of producing a given good can be applied to the case of innovation of differentiated products.

In the real world, there is probably a large amount of international trade in differentiated products in which given countries have a temporary competitive advantage which erodes with time, as improved substitutes come on the market. Examples of such goods are electronic equipment, automobiles, household appliances, furniture, and minor consumer products such as food, clothing, and detergents. Innovative product differentiation is widespread in the pharmaceutical, machine tool, and computer industries, though it is not as noticeable to ordinary consumers as is the innovation process in consumer goods.

Generally, the available literature in international economics dealing with the modifications of the Heckscher-Ohlin model that are required by the existence of differentiated products and research and development is of very recent origin, and, in comparison with the literature concerning the Heckscher-Ohlin model, it appears to suffer from lack of rigor. Perhaps greater rigor cannot be achieved because of the nature of the problems under consideration. However, in spite of this fact, it appears that further theoretical and empirical work in this field will add greatly to our understanding of what countries trade and why they do so in a dynamically changing world in which oligopolistic market structures and product differentiation play an important role.

II. INTERNATIONAL TRADE AND ECONOMIC DEVELOPMENT

In Section I of this chapter we considered the effects which exogenously given growth in labor and different forms of capital have on welfare and the pattern of world trade. Now we turn to the analysis of problems arising from the possibility that a causal relationship runs from international trade to the growth in factors and through it to welfare. In so doing we touch briefly upon many problems central to the body of a relatively new branch of economics which concerns itself with the theories and policies of economic development. However, this body of knowledge is so large that we cannot treat it satisfactorily here. It should be remembered that besides foreign trade, policies concerning agriculture, finance, education, monetary and fiscal matters, and so on are of great importance to economic development.

Our plan of analysis is first, to present the classical arguments about the effects of trade on growth; second, to outline uncritically the arguments and empirical evidence presented against the classical arguments, and third, to evaluate the merit of the anticlassical position, both theoretically and by the consideration of available empirical evidence. In all of the following discussion it is important to remember that the essential argument is over the level of welfare a given developing country enjoys, either by letting market forces determine its level and composition of international trade or, alternatively, by interfering with this market result through government policies, the nature of which will be discussed at the appropriate point in the analysis. By considering this question as the central one for our discussion, we disregard the fact that all domestic policies have foreign trade repercussions. This is undesirable, but it has to be done to keep the exposition manageable within a text on international economics.

A final, general note of clarification is required. We will deal with the causal relationship between trade and growth in the context of developing countries because the topic has been discussed most intensively in recent years by economists concerned with these countries. However, in principle, the analysis is applicable to countries at all stages of development, not just those that euphemistically have become known as developing. In fact, the countries of the world can be arranged along a number of continuous scales, according to a number of objectively observable characteristics of the degree of development, such as per capita incomes; the proportion of industrial goods in total output; the availability of roads, telephones, and railroads; the level of educational attainment; and the rate of growth of output. We will deal with countries which are at the bottom of the scale with respect to most of such indices of development, but it should be remembered that the issues to be discussed apply with different degrees of validity to all countries.

The Classical Arguments

The basic classical argument for free trade was made in Chapters 2 and 3 above in the context of the comparative static analysis of the Ricardian and Heckscher-Ohlin trade models. These gains from trade relate to growth in two ways. First, the gains in welfare themselves are equivalent to a growth in factors under autarky, as follows directly and easily from the Heckscher-Ohlin models presented above. Second, the higher level of welfare brings about higher savings and therefore investment, under the usual Keynesian assumption that savings are a constant proportion of income.

These two effects of trade on growth are based on comparative static analysis and the large number of simplifying assumptions discussed above. More realistic (but also much more complicated and less rigorous) models of economic processes introduce considerations about dynamic changes accompanying growth and movements between static equilibria. Many economists, such as Alexander Cairncross and Gottfried Haberler, have argued that very important dynamic forces are released as foreign trade develops. Thus, trade brings increased competition and forces domestic business to become more efficient, often by the adoption of new technology. Through trade, countries can obtain capital goods embodying the latest technology, which domestic industry cannot produce. Foreign traders are led to the discovery of profitable areas for lending and investment, and the resultant capital flows represent additions to factor supplies and lead to growth which the comparative static analysis does not predict.

The historic development of the United States and Canada lends a great deal of support to the view that "trade is an engine of growth," using Cairncross's terminology. Export industries, especially agriculture and mining, expanded rapidly in the 19th century and attracted foreign investment in transportation facilities and the manufacture of farm equipment. The growth of these industries in turn had important feedback effects on the demand for steel and other inputs.

However, the development of North America may have been a special case, as it involved a continent rich in natural resources and a small population culturally attuned to the conditions of industrialization, free competition, and trade. The case of developing countries in the 20th century certainly is different in many ways, as we can see from the following arguments.

The Case for Foreign Trade Restrictions

Gunnar Myrdal, a well-known Swedish humanist and liberal economist, argues that foreign trade brings into traditional societies cheap manufactured products which compete successfully with the output of master craftsmen, destroying cultural values and skills developed over a long period of time. To pay for the imports of these manufactured goods, new industries are developed which draw on the abundant supply of low-skilled labor and which involve the manufacture and mining of primary goods for which the world demand is relatively unstable and inelastic. Free foreign trade, therefore, according to Myrdal, produces negative externalities through fostering the disappearance of skilled artisans and cultural values and the growth of industries. causing economic instabilities and the creation of a mass of impoverished, unskilled workers. For these reasons governments in developing countries are justified in interfering with free trade.

Raul Prebisch (1964) and Hans W. Singer (1950) begin their analysis of the harmful effects of free trade by considering the consequences of the fact that the developing countries tend to specialize in the production and export of primary and agricultural commodities. These goods have the following undesirable characteristics.

First, the demand for and supply of these goods are rather price inelastic and subject to relatively large cyclical and random shifts. Consequently, price fluctuations tend to be relatively large, and they cause harmful instabilities in the incomes of producers and the foreign exchange earnings of the developing countries.

Second, the income elasticity of demand for primary and agricultural products is low because these products tend to be necessities and because technological innovations have yielded many manufactured substitutes in the developed countries. Furthermore, because producers in the developing countries are numerous and can draw on large stocks of unemployed labor, improvements in productivity in agriculture and primary-product industries tend to result in lower prices rather than higher returns to factors of production. While these characteristics exert downward pressures on the prices of the goods exported by the developing countries, analogous forces are at work to raise the prices of imported goods. Thus, the income elasticity of demand for manufactured goods tends to be high, and the strong organization of industries and labor in developed countries is responsible for the fact that productivity increases lead to higher factor payments and constant product prices. The combined effect of these trends causes a secular deterioration of the terms of trade of developing countries. In terms of the theoretical analysis above, the welfare-increasing effects of growth in the production frontier are offset in part by adverse changes in the relative world price of imported and exported goods for the developing countries.

Third, problems with domestic overproduction of agricultural products have led many developed countries to protective measures, such as tariffs, quotas, and the barriers on imported substitutes. These policies have directly reduced world prices and the exports of wheat and other temperate-zone agricultural products which have been the traditional exports of a number of temperate-zone developing countries in Latin America and the Mediterranean. Developing countries in the tropics experienced reduced exports and lower prices for rice, coconuts, fruits, and cane sugar, which are close substitutes for the wheat, oil seeds, fruits, and sugar beets produced at artificially high levels behind protective tariff walls in the developed countries. Moreover, traditionally, in many developed countries several tropical agricultural products, such as coffee, tea, and cocoa, have been considered to be luxuries and therefore have been burdened with heavy domestic excise taxes. These taxes have had the effect of reducing consumption of these goods in the developed countries and thus lowering world prices and exports from the developing nations.

The first of these three characteristics of the export goods of developing countries has led to recommendations for the establishment of price stabilization boards to even out fluctuations in demand and supply. All three have been used to justify the recommendation that developing countries should adopt policies to reduce their dependence on foreign trade. This aim is to be achieved through "import substitution policies," which consist of tariffs, quotas, and other restrictions on imports. In order to obtain the resources needed for the production of the formerly imported goods, the output of export goods has to be reduced. As a result, import substitution policies lower the overall level of trade of the developing countries below the level free market conditions would have yielded.

Not only were the import substitution policies based on the considerations just presented, but they also received substantial support from a particular view of the development process which was articulated most persuasively by Albert O. Hirschman. According to this view, once an industry had been established behind a tariff wall, say the shoe industry, its demand for leather, shoelaces, and yarn would stimulate domestic production of these formerly imported inputs into the shoe-manufacturing process. The argument is that many of the goods imported by developing countries possess such "linkages" to other industries, and therefore their domestic production induced by protection would lead to a dynamic, self-sustaining process of development.

It should also be mentioned that import substitution policies found strong intellectual support from the idea of "infant industry" protection. This idea will be discussed at greater length in the next part of this book. Suffice it here to say that the idea has a respectable history, and it served as the rationale for the adoption of tariffs by the United States and the newly formed Germany in the 19th century. According to this view, domestic industry needs protection from foreign competition during its infancy and until, as a mature industry, it has achieved economies of scale and accumulated experience in manufacturing so that it can compete without further support from government.

Evaluation of Arguments against Trade

Myrdal's criticism of free trade involves an implicit value judgment about the merit and significance of production by skilled handicraftsmen. During the Middle Ages in Europe, when craft guilds were widespread, society in general was well ordered, and many artistic achievements of lasting value were produced. At the same time, however, society was also quite rigid: there was little social and economic mobility, guilds restricted output, there were limited technical improvements, and per capita incomes were low and stagnant. But even if one prefers the package of good and bad aspects of the artisan economy over that of the modern industrial society, most countries today do not have the opportunity to opt for the former. The introduction of modern hygiene has lowered death rates dramatically, and because birth rates continue at high levels, populations increase at rapid rates. The traditional social organization cannot increase output sufficiently to take care of these greater populations. Furthermore, inevitable contacts with other cultures, fostered by modern means of transportation and communication, have called forth demands for greater social mobility and economic change, and these are inconsistent with the preservation of output patterns and organizations necessary for the flourishing of traditional artisans.

The thesis that the primary products exported by the developing countries are subject to particularly large fluctuations in demand, supply, and prices has been challenged by a number of empirical studies, most notably those by J. D. Coppock (1962), Alistair MacBean (1966), and Benton Massell. Objective tests simply do not permit the generalization that prices and incomes of the producers of primary and agricultural products are more unstable than those of producers of industrial goods.

Furthermore, we need to realize that, theoretically, foreign trade may either aggravate or reduce disturbances of domestic origin, such as harvest failures, bumper crops, natural disasters affecting output of industry, civil disturbances, strikes, regional wars, and ordinary business cycles. It all depends on whether or not variations in demand and supply in the rest of the world tend to be correlated with domestic disturbances. The law of large numbers suggests that, on average, an individual country's disturbances should be offset by disturbances of the opposite sort in the rest of the world. It is indeed very rare that wheat harvests are below average in all parts of the world and much more likely that bad harvests in one part are balanced by bumper crops in another part of the world. Ronald McKinnon has shown more generally and through empirical data that countries can stabilize domestic prices and incomes through foreign trade. We will return to this idea in our discussion of optimum currency areas in Part Four.

The Prebisch-Singer evidence on the deterioration of the terms of trade of developing countries in recent decades has been challenged by a number of researchers on grounds of statistical inadequacies. Thus, Charles Kindleberger has argued that the evidence is based on data from Britain which report U.K. imports as including the costs of insurance and freight, (known as c.i.f.) and U.K. exports as excluding these charges (known as f.o.b., free on board). During the period studied by Prebisch, transportation and insurance costs fell significantly, and it is certain that the data used overstate the extent of the deterioration of the developing countries' terms of trade. It may even be that these costs fell sufficiently to have produced an improvement of relative prices of the goods evaluated at the point of loading and unloading in the developing countries.

Another statistical defect of the data used to support the Prebisch-

Singer evidence is that the data do not reflect changes in the quality of products. They consist of unit price indices, and these can indicate a rise in the price of a good even though the economically relevant price per unit of service attached to the good has fallen. For example, steel-belted radial tires cost more per unit than tires produced with previously known technology, yet it is well known that the superior performance of radial tires has actually led to a reduction in the price per mile driven. Quality improvements of this sort have been more frequent in the manufactured exports of the developed countries than in the primary and agricultural products exported by the developing countries. Consequently, the data used to support the Prebisch-Singer arguments have overstated the extent of the deterioration of the developing countries' terms of trade. However, we can note that this analysis leaves out the fact that frequently the quality of manufactured goods also deteriorates, and in the United States it has been shown that on balance improvements and reductions in the quality of goods probably have been equal in recent decades, so that unit price indices adequately reflect cost changes on average. For this reason the developing countries' deteriorating terms of trade probably recorded correctly what Prebisch intended them to show.

More fundamental, however, is the point of criticism of the Prebisch-Singer arguments which rests on a proper understanding of the relationships between welfare and two important definitions of the terms of trade. The first, which we have used until now, refers to the relative prices of traded goods. It is known as the net barter terms of trade and is the appropriate measure in comparative static analysis of the type we developed in Chapter 3. In this analysis international trade is equivalent to barter, and the stocks and productivity of the factors of production are assumed to be constant. Changes in welfare under free trade for country A can be brought about only through exogenously given changes in the terms of trade. In this analytical framework it is legitimate to conclude that the deterioration in the terms of trade must always lead to reduced welfare.

Now we need to expand this analysis to account for technological improvements. For this purpose consider the export industry in country A, consisting of a large number of small firms producing the homogeneous export good X. Industry equilibrium is disturbed by an improvement in the technology for producing good X, discovered in some publicly owned research laboratory and made available free of charge to all firms. Competition among producers using this superior technology leads to reduction in the price of good X, until returns to all factors of production are at a competitive, normal level. In a closed economy, the lower price of X means that, ceteris paribus, the factors of production can purchase more of good X than before the technical innovation, and the country's overall standard of living will be raised. In an open economy we can discover the welfare change accompanying the technical change and the deterioration in the net barter terms of trade by considering what happens to the terms at which physical units of labor and capital embodied in the export and import goods are exchanged through trade. The rate at which these factors exchange, known as the factoral terms of trade, may better or worsen, depending on a whole host of taste, technical, and endowment conditions which we discussed in connection with the Heckscher-Ohlin model in Chapter 3. For our purposes of analysis it is important to note that between two periods of time when technology has affected factor productivity, welfare changes are a function of factoral terms of trade, since they indicate the social gains to be had from the international exchange of the unchanged basic units of production, labor and capital. Proper consideration of this measure of welfare thus gives rise to the possibility that a country's net barter terms of trade have fallen while its factoral terms of trade have remained unchanged or improved.

In more common-sense terms, our analysis, applied to the case of developing countries, implies that it is illegitimate to infer from a fall in export relative to import prices that welfare also falls, since the lower export prices may have been caused by increased productivity. Depending on the extent of the productivity gains and the extent of the price reductions, it is possible that a given stock of productive resources purchases more foreign goods than it did before the productivity gains, and in this sense a country's welfare will increase in spite of lower prices for its exports. Of course, this conclusion does not mean that a country's welfare gains would not have been greater if it could enjoy a productivity increase in its export industries *and* the maintenance of existing relative prices of exports and imports. However, elementary economic analysis shows that these two events cannot operate together, except in the case of quantitatively unimportant world suppliers holding an exclusive patent on a new production process. Higher productivity leads to increased output, which in turn can be sold only by inducing consumers to buy through a lower price.

Evaluation of Import Substitution Policies

In spite of the objections raised to the Prebisch-Singer arguments in favor of import substitution policies, practically all developing countries adopted these policies after World War II. The imposition of tariffs and other protectionist devices most often occurred in response to balance-of-payments problems, but there is little doubt that the Prebisch-Singer view of the problems facing developing countries provided a substantial rationale for governments to adopt this method for getting out of balance-of-payments problems rather than using more conventional tools such as devaluations and income adjustments, which we will discuss in Part IV below.

In the late 1960s and 1970s it became increasingly evident that import substitution policies had not achieved what was expected of them. Balance-of-payments problems were alleviated only temporarily and very often became worse within a short time. Linkages provided no powerful incentives for sustained development. Unemployment problems were not solved, and the growth in per capita incomes remained low.

Penetrating analyses by John Power (1966), Santiago Macario (1965), Anne Krueger (1966) and others indicated some reasons why these policies demonstrated such small success. As inefficient industries were brought into existence behind tariff walls, they attracted scarce factors of production away from previously efficient and competitive industries. The exchange rate rose as imports were reduced, lowering prices received by exporters. Efficient export industries were thus forced out of business by the dual taxes of higher factor costs and lower product prices. In a sense, import substitution policies had led to the creation of inefficient, high-cost industries for the manufacture of previously imported goods and the destruction of efficient export industries, without any net gain in employment and with a decrease in the value of output evaluated at world prices.

A certain reaction has set in in response to the unhappy experiences with import substitution policies. Many countries have begun to pay greater attention to their actual and potential export industries and are helping agriculture, which under import substitution policies suffered from rising prices for their manufactured inputs and the maintenance of low output prices. These lower prices, mainly for food products, were justified to keep down the cost of living of the population in urban centers.

It is difficult to know how strong will be the ultimate reaction to the widespread failure of import substitution policies. Economic analysis of the gains from trade discussed in Part One of this book implies that a return to greater reliance on international trade and specialization will yield higher standards of living and should stimulate growth. As we will discuss in Part Two, existing distortions in the domestic economies of the developing countries, which cause inefficiencies and represent barriers to growth, should be combatted with policies aimed at their fundamental causes. The indirect elimination of these causes through the interference with trade is highly inefficient.

BIBLIOGRAPHICAL NOTES

The taxonomy of the effects of growth on trade is developed in Johnson (1961), ch. 3 and 4; 1962, ch. 4; Meier (1963), and Corden (1956). Rybczinski (1955) contains his theorem. Immiserizing growth is found in Bhagwati (1958). Findlay and Grubert (1959) consider the role of technical change. The references to the human and knowledge capital approach are Johnson (1968), Arrow (1962), and the original contribution by Fisher (1930).

A hardnosed economist's view on development and trade is found in Johnson (1967a). At a simpler level of exposition, in inexpensive paperback form, is Helleiner (1972). Meier (1970) has collected in abbreviated form and analyzed most of the following original contributions mentioned in the text, and he provides an extensive bibliography: Cairncross (1962), Haberler (1959), Myrdal (1956), Prebisch (1964), Singer (1950), Hirschman (1958), Kindleberger (1961), Power (1966), Macario (1965) and Krueger (1966). The question of instability of prices of and demand for primary products has been analyzed by Coppock (1962), MacBean (1966), and Massell (1964, 1970). A case study of Indian development efforts is Bhagwati and Desai (1970). A more general evaluation of development programs undertaken for the OECD is Little, Scitovsky, and Scott (1970). Corden (1971a) considers the effects of trade on the rate of economic growth.

CONCEPTS FOR REVIEW

Rybczinski theorem

Immiserizing growth

Ultra protrade bias

Antitrade bias

Fisher's approach to the nature of capital

Trade as an engine of growth

Import substitution policies

Development linkages

Factoral terms of trade

POINTS FOR FURTHER STUDY AND DISCUSSION

1. Assume that the production of luxury automobiles is subject to constant returns to scale and very labor intensive, while demand for them is highly income elastic in the United States. What kind of trade bias for automobiles would you expect to observe for the United States?

2. Consider wheat and steel production and trade for the United States through time. What has happened to wheat exports as a proportion of total output and steel imports as a proportion of total consumption?

3. Attempt to find out from a drugstore how long brands of antibiotics on its shelves have been available and what proportion is produced abroad or made domestically under foreign license.

4. Assume that the income elasticity of demand for country A's export good in country A is very high. Under these conditions, is it more or less likely that growth leads to immiserization than if the income elasticity for the good is low?

5. Show diagrammatically the effect of an increase in both factors of production in the same proportion in which they are used in the production of good X. What must happen to the output of good Y?

6 Some Data on the Importance and Growth of World Trade

IN THIS CHAPTER we bring together a few data which permit us to put into perspective the relative importance of international trade for individual countries, the growth of this trade through time, the share of trade contributed by some key countries, and the composition of trade by some important categories of commodities. The presentation of these statistics permits us also to introduce some useful information about the sources and nature of data on international trade used by governments, business and academic researchers.

I. THE NATURE AND SOURCES OF DATA

The data are presented in four tables, at the bottom of which sources of the data are indicated. These general statistics on world trade can be found in the publications of the United Nations (*Statistical Yearbooks*), of the International Monetary Fund (*International Financial Statistics*), and of the World Bank and International Monetary Fund, jointly (*Direction of Trade*). The statistics published by these international organizations are secondary in the sense that they do not represent information collected on the spot or from the agents involved in particular transactions. Only the governments of individual countries collect and publish such primary data. For greater detail on the level, sources, and composition of trade of individual countries and precise definitions, coverage, and methods of collection, it is necessary to go to the national sources directly. The statistical offices of the developed countries publish a number of series on trade, and national statistical yearbooks often provide convenient annual summaries.

The publications by international organizations from which our data have been drawn, aside from the convenience of providing a single source, have a great advantage over national sources. To the fullest extent possible, national differences in coverage and definitions have been reconciled and adjusted, so that comparisons among countries are meaningful.

In the tables we have provided it can be seen that a number of more or less arbitrary decisions about coverage and presentation had to be made. First, the years 1938, 1948, 1958, and 1968 were chosen because 1938 was the last year of trade undistorted by World War II, which began in September 1939. The year 1948 was a decade later, and it can also be considered to have been the first year of normalcy after the war. Germany's currency reform took place in 1948, signaling the start of a long period of rapid development. The other dates are each a decade after 1948, but 1958 also marks the year when Western European nations removed most of the restrictions on the use and exchange of their currencies imposed after the war.

Second, it is impossible to produce a table of manageable size in which all countries of the world would be shown individually. For this reason, we have shown separately only the trade of the major industrialized countries of North America, Western Europe, the Soviet Union, Japan, and Australia, as well as India, which is one of the most important developing countries of Asia. All other countries have been aggregated in conventional major regional groupings.

Third, in order to provide comparability of national statistics, which are normally published in national currencies, there must be a convenient world numeraire. Since the end of World War II, this numeraire has been the U.S. dollar, while before then it was the British pound sterling. The reasons for this choice will become more obvious in our later analysis of the international monetary system. Suffice it here to say that in 1968 the U.S. share of international trade was 13.7 percent of total world trade, a larger share than that of any other country. In the earlier part of this century and in the 19th century Britain similarly held the largest share of world trade, so statistics were then denominated primarily in sterling.

Fourth, we expressed world trade volume as the sum of exports plus imports. For the world as a whole all exports must necessarily equal imports, but for individual countries in any given year the two do not have to be equal, as we shall note in following parts of this book. For this reason the sum of exports and imports tends to reflect more accurately the trends and magnitudes we are interested in than do data on exports or imports alone.

Fifth, we used subgroupings of international trade statistics which have been agreed upon internationally in a code known as the Standard International Trade Classification (SITC). This code has been adopted by all countries of the world and has aided greatly in making national statistics comparable. The code has 10 major classes, running from 0 to 9, such as Food and Live Animals (0), Beverages and Tobacco (1), Crude Materials (2), Mineral Fuels (3), and so on. Subdivisions in each major class codify more detailed classes of goods, such as Butter (0.23) and Eggs (0.25), Silk (2.61) and Jute (2.64). Only few purposes of analysis require subdivisions to the level of five digits, which involve such categories as Prepared or Preserved Crustaceans and Mollusks (0.32.02) and Prepared Foods Obtained by Swelling or Roasting Cereal Grains (0.48.12).

Sixth, we should note that it has been a long-standing tradition for international trade statistics to report a given country's exports free on board (f.o.b.) and imports cost, insurance, freight (c.i.f.). One significant exception to this rule is the United States, which reports both exports and imports as f.o.b. The differences in these two types of statistics are readily apparent from these descriptive titles. In Table 6–1, which makes inter-country comparisons, the fact that the trade of all countries is consistently reported as exports plus imports leaves only minor biases resulting from the f.o.b.–c.i.f. problem. In Tables 6–2 and 6–3 we consider global trade by subclasses through time. Here exports at f.o.b. provide unbiased information. The trade matrix of Table 6–4 uses only exports f.o.b., as reported by individual countries. It is clear that all figures in the matrix would be larger if the imports c.i.f. had been employed. Under either approach, however, the basic nature of the world trade matrix would be the same.

With this introductory information about the sources, practices, and conventions of international trade statistics in mind, we can turn to analysis of the tables from several different points of view.

II. THE GROWTH AND COMPOSITION OF TRADE

The upper portion of Table 6–1 shows the level of world trade in current dollars (the first five columns) and as a percentage change by decades (the next five columns). It can be seen that world trade total value grew from $48.9 billion in 1938 to $1,157.8 billion in 1973, for a 24-fold increase in 35 years. This growth is equal to a compound rate of 9.5 percent per year. The rate was largest during the decade 1938–48, when the world economy was recovering from the Great Depression of the 1930s, and during the five-year period 1968–73, when the world economy experienced a superboom.

These statistics on the growth of trade in current dollars can be very misleading, however, because of the effects of general world inflation. What really counts for welfare is the growth of the volume, not the dollar value, of trade. In the last three rows of Table 6–1 we show indexes of the volume of world trade by decades, with 1963 = 100. According to these data the volume rose from 40 in 1938 to 240 in 1973, for a 600 percent

TABLE 6-1

Growth and Importance of World Trade

Region or Country	Exports Plus Imports (billions of U.S. dollars)					Percent Change					World Share		1968 Trade	
	1938	1948	1958	1968	1973	1938–48	1948–58	1958–68	1968–73	1938–73	1938	1973	% GNP	Per Capita (dollars)
North America	$ 7.2	$ 26.7	$ 43.2	$ 94.0	$ 194.9	370%	162%	217%	207%	2,706%	14.9%	16.8%		$ 303
Canada	1.6	5.7	10.2	24.0	48.6	356	179	235	203	3,038	3.3	4.2	36%	1,154
United States	5.3	19.7	31.1	67.3	138.9	372	158	216	206	2,621	10.8	12.0	8	335
Latin America	3.9	14.9	20.1	29.0	58.9	382	135	144	203	1,510	7.9	5.1		390
Europe: Market economies	21.5	44.2	88.1	211.6	534.0	206	199	240	252	2,484	44.0	46.1		
France	2.2	5.6	11.3	26.6	72.6	255	202	235	273	3,300	4.5	6.3	21	533
Germany (Federal Republic)	—	2.5	16.9	45.0	124.1	—	676	266	276	—	—	10.7	33	776
Italy	1.2	2.6	5.8	20.5	50.0	217	223	353	243	4,167	2.4	4.3	27	388
United Kingdom	6.7	14.4	19.4	33.2	69.3	214	135	168	209	1,034	13.2	6.0	33	600
Europe: Planned economies	3.1	6.2	20.6	49.8	109.1	200	332	242	219	3,519	6.3	9.4		
U.S.S.R.	0.6	2.5	8.7	20.0	42.6	416	350	230	213	7,100	1.2	3.7		85
Africa	2.7	8.6	13.3	23.1	46.7	319	155	173	202	1,730	5.5	4.0		71
Asia: Developing, market economies	5.7	13.9	21.4	41.4	105.2	244	154	193	254	1,846	1.2	9.1		
India	1.2	3.1	3.0	4.3	5.9	258	96	143	137	492	2.5	0.5	11	8
Asia: Planned economies	1.0	1.2	4.0	4.6	10.5	20	333	115	228	1,050	2.0	0.9		
Japan	2.2	1.0	5.9	26.0	75.2	45	590	440	289	3,418	4.5	6.5	18	257
Oceania	1.6	4.0	5.4	10.3	23.3	250	135	190	226	1,456	3.3	2.0		554
Australia	1.0	2.9	3.5	7.3	16.2	290	121	209	222	1,620	2.0	1.4	34	608
World total value	$48.9	$120.7	$222.0	$489.8	$1,157.8	248%	184%	221%	236%	2,368%				
Compound rate/year						9.5	6.25	8.25	18.75	9.5				
World total quantity (1963 = 100)	40	39	71	151	240	98%	182%	213%	159%	600%				
Compound rate/year						–0.0	6.2	7.9	9.8	5.3				
Developed countries	35	35	70	155	250	100	200	221	161	714				
Developing countries	55	50	75	136	207	91	150	181	152	376				

Note: See sources for definitions and precise coverage. Regional value data do not sum to world total data for a number of reasons.

Source: United Nations, *Statistical Yearbook, 1971*, Tables 143, 144, 15 for trade value and volume; for 1973 data, *1974 Yearbook*, Tables 148, 15; International Monetary Fund, *International Financial Statistics, 1971 Supplement*: country statistics—GNP, line 99A; exchange rate, line A; population, line 99Z.

increase, or a compound rate of growth of 5.3 percent per year. Since the value of trade grew at 9.5 percent, it follows that prices rose at the rate of 4.2 percent per year. The volume figures show most dramatic differences between decades. The period 1938–48, which includes World War II and recovery from the Great Depression, saw a zero real rate of growth in trade. All of the 9.5 percent per year growth during that decade (as noted above), therefore, was due to price increases. The decade 1958–68 had a 7.9 percent annual rate of real growth and the inflationary period of 1968–73 produced a real growth rate of 9.8 percent annually.

Growth by Countries

The greatest growth rates in current dollar value of trade were enjoyed by the Soviet Union during the period 1938–73. The 71-fold increase of Soviet trade is by far the largest of all nations and regions. However, this statistic is somewhat misleading, as the base of trade on which this development took place was extremely small in 1938. Of the market economies, the largest growth rates were enjoyed during the entire period by Italy, Japan, France, Canada, and the United States with between 42- and 27-fold increases. Because of Germany's separation into two countries after World War II it is not possible to calculate comparable figures for the Federal Republic of Germany, though subperiod averages show that this country's trade grew at extremely high rates. During the boom period 1968–73 Japan enjoyed the largest growth (increased 2.9 times), followed by Germany (2.8 times) and France (2.7 times). Of the industrial countries the slowest growth of trade during the full period was experienced by the United Kingdom.

Recalling (from our discussion of Chapter 5) the role of international trade in economic development, we can note the differences in the growth in volume of trade of the developed and developing countries, as shown in the last two rows of Table 6–1. While during the full period 1938–73 trade of the developed countries grew 7.1 times, that of the developing countries grew only 3.8 times. Similar relationships obtain in each of the subperiods.

One convenient measure of the importance of a country or region in total world trade is its share in this trade. The world share, 1973, column of Table 6–1 shows that the United States, with 12 percent, held the largest world trade share of any nation. Germany (10.7%), Japan (6.5%), France (6.3%), the United Kingdom (6.0%), Italy (4.3%), and Canada (4.2%) followed, in that order. The market economies of Western Europe together accounted for 46.1 percent of world trade.

Noteworthy are the small shares of world trade held by the planned economies of Europe and Asia, 10.3 percent together, and by the developing countries of Latin America (5.1%), Africa, including the Union of South Africa (4.0%), and Asia, including the oil countries of the Mideast (9.1%). The largest developing country with a market economy, India, has a share of world trade of only 0.5 percent.

In the last two columns of Table 6–1 we have assembled two types of statistics which permit us to make some inferences about the importance of foreign trade in the economies of individual countries. The first of these shows the value of international trade as a percentage of gross national product (GNP) in 1968. There is a clustering of countries around the one-third mark, with Canada leading at 36 percent, followed by Australia at 34 percent and Germany and the United Kingdom, both at 33 percent. The United States, the largest trading nation in the world, has overall trade representing only 8 percent of its GNP. For the developing country of India, trade represents 11 percent of GNP.

The second measure of the importance of trade for a country is trade per capita. Here Canada leads the countries on the list by a very large margin ($1,154), followed by Germany ($776), Australia ($608), and the United Kingdom ($600). By this measure India ($8), Africa ($71), and the Soviet Union ($85) show a very low involvement in international trade, while the United States ($335) and Japan ($257) are in the middle range.

Composition by Commodities

It is a well-known fact that national economic development involves the relative growth of manufacturing and service industries at the expense of the production of food, raw materials, and fuels. This pattern of development is also reflected in the growth of international trade.

In Table 6–2 we show that in the period 1938–73 food and raw materials represented a fairly steadily declining proportion of world trade, 44.4 percent in 1938 and 23.8 percent in 1973. Fuel, mostly petroleum since 1948, held steady at about 10 percent. The share of manufactures rose by a quarter, from 44.7 percent in 1948 to 64.9 percent in 1973.

The composition of trade among market economies during the period 1953–73 is shown in Table 6–3. The categories of trade are finer than in Table 6–2, but the pattern is the same as revealed there. Even in the relatively short span of 20 years, the share of food in total trade fell from 22.3 percent in 1953 to 13.2 percent in 1973. The raw materials share similarly fell from 17.7 to 10.1 percent. On the other hand, the importance of chemical products nearly doubled, from 4.4 to 7.3 percent, as did the share of trade in machinery and transportation equipment, from 15.5 to 28.9 percent. The largest share of trade was in "other manufactures," which represented 23.8 percent in 1953 and 27.8 percent in 1968. The rapid increase in trade in machinery and transportation equipment is to a sub-

TABLE 6-2
Composition of World Trade

Commodity Group Exports (f.o.b.)	1938		1948		1958		1968		1973	
	Billions of U.S. $	%	Billions of U.S. $	%	Billions of U.S. $	%	Billions of U.S. $	%	Billions of U.S. $	%
Food and raw materials	$ 9.2	44.4%	$24.5	46.0%	$33.6	35.6%	$ 54.6	26.1%	$120.9	23.8%
Fuel	1.7	8.2	5.0	9.3	10.9	11.5	20.5	9.8	57.2	11.3
Manufactured goods	9.8	47.3	23.8	44.7	49.9	52.9	134.2	64.1	330.0	64.9
Total	$20.7	100.0%	$53.3	100.0%	$94.4	100.0%	$209.3	100.0%	$508.1	100.0%

Source: United Nations, *Statistical Yearbook, 1974*, Table 14.

TABLE 6–3
Composition of Trade among Market Economies, 1953–1973

SITC Classes, Exports (f.o.b.)	SITC Numbers*	1953 Billions of U.S. $	1953 %	1958 Billions of U.S. $	1958 %	1963 Billions of U.S. $	1963 %	1968 Billions of U.S. $	1968 %	1973 Billions of U.S. $	1973 %
Food	0 + 1	$16.1	22.3%	$18.3	19.9%	$ 23.0	17.8%	$ 28.7	14.2%	$ 64.4	13.2%
Raw materials	2 + 4	12.8	17.7	13.6	14.8	18.1	14.0	22.3	11.0	49.6	10.1
Fuels	3	6.9	9.5	10.4	11.3	13.1	10.2	19.8	9.8	55.5	11.4
Chemical products .	5	3.2	4.4	5.1	5.5	8.1	6.3	14.7	7.3	35.5	7.3
Machinery and transport equipment ..	7	11.2	15.5	18.3	19.9	29.0	15.3	55.1	27.3	140.7	28.9
Other manufactures .	6 + 8	17.2	23.8	23.1	25.1	34.1	26.4	58.2	28.8	135.4	27.8
Total	0–9	$72.3	100.0%	$92.0	100.0%	$129.0	100.0%	$202.0	100.0%	$487.4	100.0%

* SITC numbers: 0, 1, 2, . . . , 9.
Source: United Nations, *Statistical Yearbook, 1974*, Table 15.

stantial degree accounted for by the growth in trade in automobiles and capital goods, the nature of which was discussed in Chapter 4 under the topic of intraindustry trade.

Matrix of World Trade

In Table 6–4 we show the 1968 matrix of trade among a group of selected countries and regions, which permits us to bring out some interesting interdependencies that the global data presented earlier hid.

In order to understand the nature of a trade matrix, note that the vertical columns, such as the first column for the United States, show the exports of the respective country to every other country and region. Analogously, the first row shows U.S. imports from every other source. The totals in the bottom row and in the last column indicate the sums of every country's exports and imports, respectively. Individual countries, of course, do not trade with themselves, so that the diagonal cells of the matrix for them are empty. However, regional groupings of countries do trade with each other, and for these the entries along the diagonal represent intraregional trade.

The sums of the last row and last column must be equal, and they represent the value of total world trade, $220.1 billion in 1968. This figure represents exports *or* imports measured f.o.b. Doubling this figure to $440.2 billion to make it comparable to the exports plus imports presented in Table 6–1 yields an estimate of trade $49.6 billion short of the figure presented there for world total value of 1968 trade. This difference probably for the largest part represents the insurance and freight charges mentioned above, which are thus seen to amount to about 10 percent of world trade. In addition, the difference may be due to some minor discrepancies in statistical coverage and definitions, which often arise when different sources are consulted (United Nations for Table 6–1, International Monetary Fund for Table 6–4), and which cannot be discussed here.

In considering some of the regional patterns, we might note that in 1968 the largest U.S. trading partner was Canada, followed by industrial Europe (excluding the United Kingdom), Latin America, and Japan. The overwhelming importance of the United States in Canada's trade is apparent from the fact that of a total of $12.4 billion exports, $8.5 billion, or 71 percent, went to its southern neighbor. Industrial Europe as a whole received fewer exports from Canada than did the United Kingdom, with which Canada has historic political and economic ties through the Commonwealth. On the other hand, industrial Europe was the most important trading partner of the United Kingdom, with the United States following in second place.

Trade among countries of industrial Europe was $44.4 billion in 1968, or 56 percent of the group of countries' total exports of $79.2 billion. This

TABLE 6–4

Matrix of World Trade, 1968 (billions of U.S. dollars, f.o.b.)

Exports to \ Exports from	United States	Canada	United King-dom	Japan	Indus-trial Europe	Other Europe	Latin America	Middle East	Asia	Africa	Australia and New Zealand	Soviet Area	Total
United States	—	8.5	2.2	4.1	7.0	0.8	4.7	0.3	2.4	0.8	0.6	0.2	31.6
Canada	8.1	—	0.6	0.3	0.8	0.1	0.5	0.1	0.2	0.1	0.1	0.1	11.0
United Kingdom	2.3	1.1	—	0.4	5.2	1.3	0.9	1.1	0.9	2.0	1.0	0.8	17.0
Japan	3.0	0.6	0.2	—	0.8	0.1	0.6	1.4	1.6	0.6	0.9	0.8	10.6
Industrial Europe	7.6	0.9	4.9	1.1	44.4	0.3	2.8	2.9	1.2	5.1	0.3	2.9	74.4
Other Europe	1.3	0.1	1.6	0.2	5.0	0.3	0.5	0.4	0.1	0.5	0.1	1.1	11.2
Latin America	5.3	0.4	0.8	0.7	3.2	0.3	3.0	0.1	0.1	0.1	0.1	0.1	14.2
Middle East	1.1	0.0	0.9	0.5	2.2	0.2	0.1	0.6	0.3	0.1	0.1	0.7	6.8
Asia	3.6	0.2	1.0	3.6	2.0	0.1	0.1	0.7	2.7	0.1	0.5	1.2	15.8
Africa	1.2	0.1	1.5	0.5	4.2	0.3	2.9	0.3	0.3	0.5	0.1	0.4	12.3
Australia and New Zealand	1.0	0.2	1.0	0.5	0.7	0.0	2.6	0.1	0.3	0.0	0.3	0.1	6.8
Soviet Area	0.2	0.3	0.6	0.6	3.7	1.0	0.3	0.5	0.7	0.3	0.2	?	8.4
Total	34.7	12.4	15.3	12.5	79.2	4.8	19.0	8.5	10.8	10.2	4.3	8.4	220.1

Note: For countries included in different categories, see source. For regions, entries in diagonal of matrix represent intraregional trade. Soviet area intraregional trade is not public knowledge. Totals may not agree with those in other tables due to different definitions and coverage. 0.0 indicates less than $0.05 billion.

Source: International Monetary Fund, *Direction of Trade*, annual. 1968–72.

fact shows the overwhelming importance of international trade among neighboring industrial countries at similar levels of development and with similar cultural backgrounds and resource endowments, though Europe's trade was stimulated especially by the formation of the European Economic Community in 1958. At the same time it should be noted that the intraregional trade of developing regions, such as Latin America, Africa, and Asia, represents a much smaller proportion of their total exports, 15.7, 5.0, and 25.0 percent, respectively.

A general feature of the matrix worth noting is the fact that only 3 cells of a total of 140 have a zero entry (trade below $5 million). This shows that trade takes place between all major regions of the world, and the interdependencies are pervasive and complex. This multinational character of world trade tends to be forgotten in theoretical analysis of the patterns and gains from trade such as that we presented in the preceding chapters, where we adopted the analytically most useful assumption that the world consists only of two countries, A and B, where B is "all of the other countries." The matrix of Table 6–4 should be a reminder that for many practical purposes of analysis, the simple two-country model needs to be modified to account for the complexities of the real world.

Summary and Conclusions

The data on the growth and importance of world trade presented in this chapter show that between 1938 and 1973 world trade volume grew at a compound annual rate of 5.3 percent in real terms and 9.5 percent, in value terms. For most of the important industrial countries the level of trade represented about one third of the value of their GNP in 1968, though for the United States it represents only 8 percent of GNP. Industrial countries in 1968 traded between $300 and $1,150 per inhabitant. The developing countries contributed only a relatively small amount to the value of world trade, and during the period 1938–73 their share in the value and volume of total trade declined substantially.

The analysis of the composition of world trade from 1938 to 1973 showed that food and raw materials represented a continuously smaller share of total trade, while large gains were registered by trade in chemicals and machinery and transportation equipment. The matrix of world trade in 1968 revealed that most trade took place among the industrialized regions and countries of the world, especially those with great physical proximity and cultural similarities. On the other hand, trade of the developing nations tended to be with developed countries rather than with other developing countries.

These data indicate that international trade played an important (and growing) role in the economic activities of most market economies. The fact of this growth can be interpreted as evidence of the existence of the gains from trade analyzed in preceding chapters of this book.

BIBLIOGRAPHICAL NOTES

International Financial Statistics, a monthly bulletin published by the International Monetary Fund, contains a most useful set of statistics for individual countries and the world as a whole. The data are available on electronic tape (monthly update). It has the virtue that every effort has been made to assure international comparability of national statistics. The United Nations publishes a wealth of statistics in a number of different bulletins and yearbooks, too numerous to list here. The Bank for International Settlements in Basel, Switzerland, publishes an *Annual Report,* with an authoritative review of economic developments in the industrial countries. The Organization for Economic Cooperation and Development in Paris has a publication program for statistics and economic analysis almost as large as that of the United Nations. It limits coverage to about 20 Western industrial nations, however, and in some areas goes into greater depth. Almost every major country's central bank and treasury publishes statistics on national economic magnitudes, and for many studies it is necessary to consult these publications. For example, for the United States, see the *Federal Reserve Bulletin* (monthly); for Britain, *Bank of England Quarterly Review;* for Germany, *Monthly Statistical Review.*

CONCEPTS FOR REVIEW

Standard Industrial Trade Classification

Free on board

Cost, insurance, freight

Trade matrix

POINTS FOR FURTHER STUDY AND DISCUSSION

1. Construct trade matrices for automobiles and petroleum for the major industrial countries and oil producers. Compare the number of cells in the two matrices with low or zero entries. If there is a difference, how do you explain it? Can you find any interesting patterns by rearranging countries in the matrix, as for example putting all oil-producing nations next to each other and arranging automobile-producing countries in descending order of GNP size?

2. Compare the values of exports from country I to country J reported by country I with imports from country I into country J as reported by country J for a number of products. Is there a difference? How can you explain the difference?

3. Measure for some major industrial countries recent growth rates in the imports and exports of raw materials, petroleum, and manufactures. Compare this with the same measures for some developing countries. Are there any interesting patterns? Interpret their causes and welfare implications.

part two

COMMERCIAL POLICIES

7 The Nature and Effects of Protection

A GOVERNMENT imposes a tariff on the import of a good by requiring that a payment be made to its customs agents when the good enters its territory. The size of this payment is determined by law; it may either be a specified percentage of the foreign price of the good or an absolute value per unit of the good. Normally, the tariff revenue is used by the government to provide public goods and services, as from any other revenue. The most evident effect of tariffs is that the domestic relative prices of goods differ from those prevailing in the rest of the world and, therefore (as we discussed in Part One), from what they would have been in the country under free trade.

In Chapter 7 we analyze the changes in production, consumption, tariff, and welfare associated with the imposition of a tariff on good X by country A within the two-commodity general equilibrium framework developed in Part One. We then discuss these same effects within a partial equilibrium setting which permits us to develop some further concepts, such as losses of consumer surplus and effective protection. The chapter closes with a brief analysis of the equivalence of tariffs, subsidies, quotas, and other nontariff barriers to trade, such as health, safety, and labeling laws. All of these government interferences with free trade have as a result the creation of a wedge between the domestic and world price of a traded good to producers, consumers, or both, which is also one of the most important effects of tariffs.

In Chapter 8 we use the analytical tools developed in Chapter 7 to discuss the reasons for the imposition of tariffs, which include arguments about the exploitation of monopoly power, the raising of revenue, the changing of domestic income distribution, the elimination of distortions, the assurance of national economic and military independence, and the development of industry. Chapter 8 closes with the argument that whenever an economy is encumbered by any of the market failures or distortions commonly used as a justification for the imposition of tariffs, the optimum strategy is the direct attack of the problem, which avoids the introduction of further distortions in the foreign trade sector.

In Chapter 9, the last one of this part on commercial policies, we summarize empirical studies on the cost of protection and present a brief review of the history and likely future development of movements toward greater freedom of trade.

I. GENERAL EQUILIBRIUM EFFECTS OF A TARIFF IN A SMALL COUNTRY

In Figure 7–1 we show the production possibilities locus of country A and its production (P_0) and consumption (C_0) in the initial free trade equilibrium at the exogenously given world price, W_0W_0'. This part of the graph reproduces the conditions originally analyzed in Figure 3–5 (in Chapter 3), in the context of demonstrating the gains from trade. Now we consider the effects of the imposition of a tariff at the rate t on the importa-

FIGURE 7–1
Import Tariff on X in a Small Country

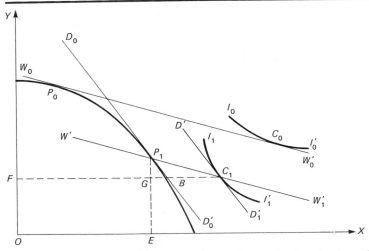

Under free trade and at the world price W_0W_0', equilibrium is at production P_0 and consumption at C_0. Under protection production is at P_1 and consumption at C_1. Domestic producers and consumers allocate their expenditures on the basis of the domestic price ratio $D_0D_0' = D_1D_1'$, while trade takes place at the initial world price W_1W_1', with GP_1 trading for GB domestically and for GC_1 internationally. Therefore, BC_1 represents government tariff revenue, which is distributed to the public to reach point C_1. Protection lowers welfare from I_0I_0' to I_1I_1'.

tion of good X. The tariff raises the relative price of good X in country A; in Figure 7–1 it steepens the price line to $D_0D_0' = D_1D_1'$, where the difference in the two price slopes is equal to the tariff rate. Producers react to this new price ratio by shifting output to P_1. As can readily be seen by comparison with Figure 3–5, the new output involves a higher amount of the import good X and a lower amount of the country's export good Y.

The new equilibrium conditions at P_1 and C_1 indicate that country A exports P_1G of good Y for GC_1 of good X at the world price line W_1W_1', parallel to W_0W_0'. This unchanged world price results from the small-country assumption. However, domestic consumers, like producers, trade at the tariff-inclusive domestic price D_1D_1' and therefore exchange P_1G of Y for a GB of X. The remaining amount, BC_1, of X is collected by the government in the form of tariff revenue. In our model we have assumed that this tariff revenue is returned to consumers and enters their spending decisions. This is why at point C_1 the indifference curve I_1I_1' is tangent to the domestic relative price line D_1D_1', which is parallel to D_0D_0'. Consequently, the point of consumption, C_1, must be characterized by the fact that it lies on the world price line W_1W_1', going through the production point P_1, and that it represents a point of tangency between the domestic price line D_1D_1' and the community indifference curve. The simultaneous determination of points P_1 and C_1 assures that there must always be a set of points satisfying the above relationships, which may be summarized as shown in Table 7–1.

TABLE 7–1
Conditions in the Presence of a Tariff

	Import Good X	Export Good Y
Production	FG	P_1E
Consumption	FC_1	GE
Trade at world price	GC_1	P_1G
Trade at domestic price	GB	P_1G
Tariff revenue	$GC_1 - GB = BC_1$	—

The most important conclusion following from the preceding analysis is that the level of welfare of country A with the tariff must always be below the level under free trade, as we have shown in Figure 7–1. This must be so in the present model because the tariff always shifts the point of production towards the tariff-protected import good. Since the world price is assumed to be unchanged by this policy, the world price line going through the new production point is necessarily below its free trade position. Consequently, only an indifference curve lower than I_0I_0' can intersect this new line. In more intuitive terms, this result is based on the fact that if free trade results in welfare maximization, as we argued above it does under clearly specified conditions, then any government-induced change in production and consumption must lower welfare in a country in which these conditions hold.

II. GENERAL EQUILIBRIUM EFFECTS OF A TARIFF IN A LARGE COUNTRY

By assumption, a large country can affect relative prices of goods in the world by changes in domestic economic conditions. In the context of tariff theory this assumption implies the simple, but also most important, point that a tariff can actually increase welfare rather than having always to decrease it, as we have argued in the case of the small country. This favorable outcome occurs from the combination of particular domestic and foreign demand and supply elasticities which have the net effect of causing a fall in the relative world price of country A's imported good. Under the circumstances, the tariff-imposing country can reach the position where it gets so much more of the import good for its exports that it ends up better off with than without the tariff.

This intuitive explanation of the positive welfare effect of a tariff is central to much theorizing and has given rise to the concept of the optimum tariff. As we will show in the next chapter, this theoretical interest derives from the fact that it provides the most widely accepted justification for the imposition of tariffs by countries.

In terms of more rigorous analysis, the effect can be shown readily within the analytical framework of Figure 7-1. If the tariff lowers the world price of the imported good, then the new world price line is flatter than the original one. It is easy to visualize how such a new line, going through P_1, extends far enough and yields tariff revenue sufficient for the country to reach a community indifference above the free trade I_0I_0'. We have not drawn in such a line, to keep Figure 7-1 simple and because the model employed there does not lend itself to the analysis of how the new world price ratio is determined.

A simple model capable of showing the general equilibrium effects of a tariff in a two-country world is presented in Figure 7-2, and a more complete, but also rather complicated geometric analysis of the same subject matter can be found in the Appendix to this chapter. In Figure 7-2 we show the offer curves OA and OB of the two countries, A and B, respectively, resulting in a free trade equilibrium of E_0 according to the analysis presented in Chapter 3, especially that surrounding Figure 3-10. The imposition of a tariff by country A results in an equiproportionate shrinkage of the OA schedule to OA' which is also known as the tariff-distorted offer curve. The nature of this shrinkage can best be understood by considering that under free trade country A was willing to trade OK of its

FIGURE 7–2
Effects of Tariff on a Large Country

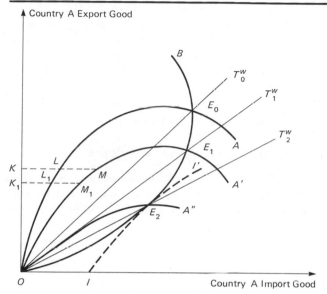

The pretrade offer curve, *OA*, is distorted by a tariff to *OA'* and by a still higher tariff to *OA''*, causing improvements in the terms of trade from OT_0^w to OT_1^w and OT_2^w, respectively. The tariff rate for *OA'* is $LM/KL = L_1M_1/K_1L_1$, since under free trade country A would have required *KL* of its import good *X* for the export of *OL* of good *Y*. Under protection, the country insists on receiving an extra *LM* units of import good *X* for its exports of *Y*, with *LM* representing the duty paid to the government. At point E_2 and with offer curve *OA''*, country A has reached its highest attainable trade indifference curve, *II'*, given B's offer curve, *OB*. At E_2 country A enjoys the benefits of its optimum tariff.

export good for *KL* of its import good. As Chapter 3 showed, this fact follows directly from the definition of the offer curve. The imposition of the tariff now means that country A is willing to give up *OK* of its export good only if it receives *KM* of the import good, *LM* of which is collected at the border in the form of tariff revenue. The tariff rate (*t*) is defined as the extra imports demanded over the free trade imports, $t = LM/KL$. For example, if $KL = 2$ units of good *X* and $LM = 1$ unit of good *X*, then the tariff rate is 50 percent. We find other points of the tariff-distorted offer curve *OA'* by applying the analogous reasoning. Thus, in Figure 7–2 point M_1 on *OA'* is found by virtue of the fact that $LM/KL = L_1M_1/K_1L_1$ with the only unknown in the equation being L_1M_1.

After the imposition of the tariff the new world equilibrium is found at point E_1 where the offer curve *OA'* intersects the original offer curve *OB* of country B. In this new equilibrium the world price has moved in favor of country A, implying that country A, for a given amount of its export good, receives more of the import good than it did before the tariff was imposed. Recall from our derivation of the offer curves in Chapter 3 that the more favorable the world price ratio is for country A, the higher the level of welfare it reaches. Therefore, the imposition of the tariff causes an improvement in country A's welfare. By the same reasoning, however, it is also easy to see that country A's improvement in welfare must lead to a deterioration of country B's welfare. In the next chapter we will discuss the implications of this fact, especially that country B could react to A's tariff by imposing one of its own. We defer also until the next chapter discussion of the offer curve OA'' in Figure 7–2, which is assumed to represent the outcome of the adoption of the optimum tariff by country A.

III. PARTIAL EQUILIBRIUM EFFECTS OF A TARIFF

For many purposes of analysis it is useful to consider the production and trade effects of a tariff on an industry which is so small that changes in output and price have only negligible repercussions on other industries and therefore can be assumed to be zero.

In Figure 7–3 we show the normally sloped industry demand and sup-

FIGURE 7–3
Partial Equilibrium Effects of a Tariff

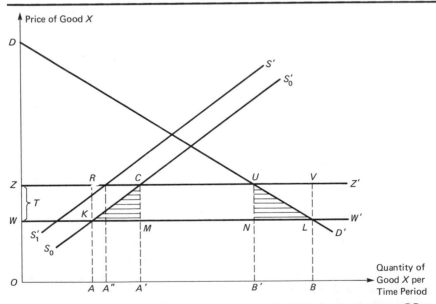

The partial equilibrium demand and supply curves of an industry are shown as DD and S_0S_0' respectively. Under free trade and at the world price OW, domestic production is OA, consumption is OB, and imports are AB. The imposition of T dollars tariff on the importation of good X raises the domestic price to OZ, increases output to OA', reduces consumption to OB', creates $MNUC$ tariff revenue, and causes a welfare loss equal to the shaded triangles $KMC + NLU$.

ply curves for such a small industry producing good X as a function of the domestic price. In the absence of trade the equilibrium price and quantity traded would be at the intersection of the demand and supply curves. However, let us now consider that country A can import from the rest of the world any desired quantities of good X at a certain price, which can be converted into a domestic currency price, OW, by methods to be discussed in detail in Part Three. Under these assumptions the line WW' represents the world supply curve and in free trade equilibrium there will be OA domestic output, AB imports and $OB = OA + AB$ consumption.

Let us now assume the imposition of a tariff at the rate of t, resulting in an increase in the domestic price of X by $T = OW \cdot t$. At the new domestic price of $OZ = OW + T = OW(1 + t)$, again, any desired quantities of X can be imported, which is shown by the perfectly elastic world supply schedule ZZ'. In equilibrium we find the following effects of this tariff:

1. The production effect: The increase in output of AA', the value of which at the new price is $ARCA'$.
2. The subsidy effect: The total increased revenue of producers is equal to the area $WKRZ$ plus $ARCA'$, but according to the definition of the supply curve the area $AKCA'$ is increased factor cost, so that the net subsidy to producers is equal to $WZCK$, which is also equal to a redistribution of income from consumers to producers.
3. The consumption effect: The decrease of consumption of $B'B$, which has a value of $B'UVB$ at the new domestic price.
4. The balance-of-payments effect: The reduction in imports of AA' plus BB' has a world price value of $AKMA'$ plus $B'NLB$.
5. The tariff revenue effect: Remaining imports of $A'B'$ yield a government revenue of $MCUN$.
6. Consumption tax effect: The increased cost to consumers is equal to $WZUN$.
7. Welfare effects: The losses in welfare consist of the deadweight loss of producers' and consumers' surplus equal to the shaded triangles KMC and NLU, respectively.

We find these losses of producer's and consumer's surplus by consideration of the following facts. Initially at the price OW the welfare of consumers was equal to the entire area $ODLB$ under the demand curve. At the new price, OZ, total consumer surplus is $ODUB'$. Let us first consider the area $B'ULB$ no more part of the welfare triangle in the new situation. It is accounted for by the world value $B'NLB$ of goods no longer purchased, plus the shaded triangle NUL. Consumers, of course, can allocate the money $B'NLB$ not spent on X to the purchase of other goods, which may be assumed to yield at the margin equal utility to what the consumption of X would have. The net loss, therefore, is only the triangle NUL.

Next, consider the area $WZUN$, which under the initial conditions represented consumer surplus and for which payment now has to be made to the government and producers. From the point of view of the economy as a whole, the tariff receipts $MCUN$ and the net subsidy to producers $WKCZ$ are transfer payments which redistribute income but by themselves do not represent a social loss. For example, if the government owned the production facilities for X it could return the extra net producers and tariff revenue to the consumers by provision of a public good or reduction in other taxes paid. However, such payments would not exhaust the full consumption tax effect, leaving the second shaded triangle KMC in Figure 7–3. It represents the inefficiency in production brought about by the tariff-induced use of resources in an industry in which their marginal productivity, evaluated at world product prices, is below that in their previous use.

For economists the welfare effects represented by the two triangles NUL and KMC are of greatest interest. In recent years increasing attention is being given by economists to the income redistribution effect, $WZCK$. In Chapter 10 we will consider the result of attempts to measure the size of triangles from information about demand and supply elasticities of products and tariff rates on industries. Producers are, of course, most interested in the size of the production and net subsidy effects. Governments often are most concerned about the balance-of-payments effects of tariffs, as we shall discuss in Part Four. Before the development of sophisticated industrial economies and bureaucracies, the revenue effect was still important for governments, since tariffs can be collected efficiently at nations' borders. The consumer tax effect should be of greatest concern to the consumers. However, since in the real world and in most countries tariff *changes* are small, the tax effect also tends to be small, and it either goes unnoticed or is of insufficient magnitude to the individual consumer to deserve his attention. We will deal with the concerns of affected parties in the theory of tariff determination in the next chapter.

IV. THE THEORY OF TARIFF STRUCTURE

We now extend the partial equilibrium analysis of the preceding section to consider the effects of imposing tariffs on intermediate inputs into the manufacture of good X, as well as on good X itself. This analysis is known as the theory of tariff structure or of effective protection. It was developed during the 1960s, largely through the efforts of the Australian National University's W. M. Corden and Harry G. Johnson of the University of Chicago. Massive empirical work was carried out by Bela Balassa of Johns Hopkins University and under his direction.

The concept of effective protection is based on the important fact that tariffs on intermediate products increase prices of these products for domestic users, thus raising the costs of manufacture and reducing what otherwise would have been the production-increasing effect of a tariff on a manufacturer's final good X. From the point of view of the user of any intermediate input, a tariff on it is equivalent to a tax on production.

These general notions can easily be represented in Figure 7–3 by the upward shift of the supply curve to S_1S_1', in response to the imposition of tariffs on the imported goods used in the manufacture of good X. This shift does not affect the domestic price of X, which stays at OZ, or the demand curve. Consequently, the consumption effect and loss of consumer surplus are unaffected by the tariffs on inputs. The main consequence of the upward shift of the supply curve is a reduction in domestic production from OA' to OA''. As can be seen from Figure 7–3, it is possible that the upward shift of the supply curve is so great that production is reduced below the free trade level, in spite of a tariff on product X. In such an instance it is said that the tariff structure imparts negative effective protection to the process of producing good X.

The change in the production effect brought about by the tariffs on inputs implies corresponding changes in the level of imports, balance of payments, tariff revenue, income redistribution, and producers' surplus. This can be specified easily by analogy with the definitions provided above in the case of a tariff only on the good X. But we do not provide such specifications here, since traditionally the main concern of the theory of tariff structure is not with these effects but with the changes in value added in the manufacture of X under protection and under free trade.

Value added in a manufacturing process is defined as the expenditure on primary factors of production, labor, land, capital, and profits. Thus, if the market price of a unit of good X is \$10, and all intermediate inputs cost \$8, then value added is \$2. Assuming that the preceding prices are those prevailing under free trade, let us now consider the implication of imposing a 10 percent tariff on the import of good X. As a result, the price of X rises domestically to \$11 and value added rises from \$2 to \$3 per unit, since nothing has happened to the \$8 cost of intermediate inputs. Consequently, the nominal tariff of 10 percent on the final good X has raised value added under protection (V') 50 percent above what it was under free trade (V). By definition, therefore, the rate of effective protection (g) for the process of producing X is 50 percent:

$$g = \frac{V' - V}{V} = \frac{3 - 2}{2} = .50. \qquad (7–1)$$

Now let us amend the preceding example by considering the imposition of a tariff on the intermediate inputs into the manufacture of X at an average rate of 5 percent. As a result, the costs of intermediate inputs rises to \$8.40, and, with the tariff-inclusive price of X at \$11, the value added under protection is only \$2.60. The effective rate of protection under the assumed structure of tariffs on intermediate inputs and the output of good X, therefore, is 30 percent:

$$g = \frac{V' - V}{V} = \frac{2.60 - 2.00}{2.00} = .30. \tag{7-2}$$

Given the definition of effective protection, the precise formula for the calculation of effective protection is

$$g = \frac{t - \Sigma a_i t_i}{1 - \Sigma a_i} \tag{7-3}$$

where t is the tariff rate on the final good X, a_i is the coefficient measuring the input of the intermediate product i per unit of output of X, and t_i is the tariff rate on the input i. Free trade value added is $V = 1 - \Sigma a_i$, and protected value added is $V' = (1 + t) - \Sigma a_i(1 + t_i)$. After insertion into equation 7–1 and simplification, this becomes equation 7–3.

The theory and measurement of effective protection developed rapidly during the 1960s because the rate of effective protection reflects more accurately than the nominal tariff rate how much advantage a domestic operator of a production process is given, relative to operators in the rest of the world. It has been found that in industrial countries, seemingly very low nominal rates on such processes as making cocoa butter, instant coffee, and aspirins provide domestic producers with extremly high effective protection, which makes it impossible for producers in developing countries to enter such industries and sell their output in the protected markets of the industrial countries. On the other hand, the very complicated tariff structures of developing countries have been found to provide extremely low or in some instances even negative effective protection for some industries. These insights and others we cannot discuss here have been derived through the analytical tool of effective protection and can be used to revise tariff structures so that they serve the objectives of individual countries or the world economy as a whole better. It may be that at some time in the future international negotiations about tariff changes will be conducted entirely in terms of effective protection rather than the traditional nominal tariff rates.

V. ON THE EQUIVALENCE OF TARIFFS AND OTHER TRADE BARRIERS

In the preceding sections of this chapter we analyzed the partial and general equilibrium effects of tariffs. However, tariffs are only one of several different methods used by governments to restrict imports. We will now discuss how quotas, subsidies, multiple exchange rates, border tax adjustments, and health and safety rules operate, and in what important ways they produce equivalent or different effects as compared to tariffs.

Quotas

Recall that in Figure 7–3 the tariff T per unit of good X had the effect of reducing imports from AB under free trade to $A'B'$ under protection. Let us now return to the initial free trade situation shown in this figure and consider that the government does not impose a tariff but instead prohibits the importation of good X by anyone except holders of a license entitling them to bring into the country exactly $A'B'$ units of good X. This imported quantity, which is known as the quota, added to domestic supply is consistent with domestic equilibrium only if the domestic price of X rises to OZ, as under the tariff regime. As can be seen from Figure 7–3, at this price domestic supply, plus the quota imports, just equals domestic demand. In this situation, the consumption, production, balance-of-payments effects, and so on are the same as under the tariff regime, except for a problem concerning the tariff revenue. If the import licenses are auctioned off to the highest bidders, then under competition they produce a government revenue just equal to $MNUC$, which is the same as under the tariff regime. If, on the other hand, the government gives away the licenses free of charge to importers on the basis of some criteria, such as political merit, then all of this revenue accrues to the importers. As a consequence, the quota produces an income redistribution effect not encountered with the use of a tariff. In the United States during the 1950s and 1960s crude oil import quotas were severely criticized as resulting in heavy subsidies to giant U.S. oil companies.

As a further point in our analysis of the effects of quotas, we should note the nature of voluntary quotas, which were used by the United States and some Western European countries to restrict the importation of textiles, steel, meat, and some other commodities during the 1950s and 1960s. Under this system of trade restriction, foreign governments are asked to limit *exports* by their own domestic producers, through licensing or some other device, to a certain quantity, such as $A'B'$ in the preceding example. This method has the important effect that the foreign producers can sell their goods at the domestic equilibrium price, OZ, and thus acquire revenue equal to $MNUC$ above what they would have earned in the absence of the voluntary quotas. For importing countries, therefore, voluntary quotas are more costly than tariffs or normal import quotas, since they produce identical welfare losses and other effects, but in addition they lead to the loss of the tariff revenue (or income to quota holders, as the case may be) and a correspondingly smaller improvement in the balance of payments.

Voluntary quotas were used by the United States and some Western European countries because the trade restrictions on the particular commodities tended to affect primarily low-income, developing countries, and the loss of revenue was considered to represent a form of foreign aid. As we shall see below, the main objectives of these trade restrictions were to avoid excessive contraction, or in some cases even total loss, of the particular domestic industries, with accompanying politically costly unemployment and financial bankruptcies. To achieve these objectives, while at the same time creating the appearance of adherence to the principles of free trade and aid to developing nations, voluntary quotas were considered to represent a suitable instrument of policy. Exporting countries accepted voluntary quotas, since they knew that the disruptions in the importing countries under free trade might otherwise have resulted in the imposition of tariffs or import quotas which would have been even less desirable than the "voluntary" export quotas.

In closing this section on the equivalence of tariffs and quotas we will analyze briefly the case where the production of good X is undertaken by a monopolist rather than the perfectly competitive firms we assumed gave rise to the industry supply curve in Figure 7–3 above. Under a tariff regime, the monopolist maximizes profits by producing the quantity of output at which the world price plus tariff equals his long-run marginal cost. In effect, the supply curve is equal to his long-run marginal cost curve. However, under the quota system the monopolist has the power to influence the domestic price, since after exhaustion of the quota further imports are impossible at any price. In effect, under these conditions he faces a segment of the less than perfectly elastic domestic demand curve, and profit-maximizing output is where marginal revenue equals marginal cost. Since the marginal revenue curve is below the demand curve and the marginal cost curve is the same under the tariff and quota regimes, the monopolist's output must be smaller, and the domestic price must be higher under the quota than the tariff regime. Space limitations prevent us from working through this case in Figure 7–3 to show the precise differences, but the preceding conclusions represent a qualitatively unambiguous result which may be of some real world importance when governments face a choice between the use of a quota or tariff.

The preceding analysis provides us with a clue why domestic producers, who often have some degree of monopoly power, prefer to receive quota rather than tariff protection. But besides giving rise to the opportunity to exploit monopoly power, quotas have an added advantage for producers which arises from the fact that governments change quotas only at infrequent intervals. Therefore, when domestic demand grows while production costs and the world price remain constant, a quota keeps imports at the same quantity, and domestic output is increased. Under a tariff, increased demand automatically would lead to increased imports at the world price. Similarly, when world prices are falling or domestic costs are rising, or both, while demand is constant, under a tariff regime imports increase automatically, but a quota keeps imports constant. Under these dynamic conditions, unless the government continuously adjusts the quota to maintain its equivalence with a tariff, producers are better off with quotas than tariffs. Correspondingly, society incurs greater welfare and income redistribution costs under the former than the latter form of protection.

In the real world the cost of gathering information about changing cost and demand conditions is very high, bureaucratic responses to these changes tend to be sluggish, and quotas rarely are auctioned off in a perfect market. For these reasons most economists believe that tariffs are superior to quotas.

Subsidies

Subsidies to producers have the effect of shifting the supply curve S_0S_0' in Figure 7–3 outward and to the right (shift is not shown in Figure 7–3). The amount of the subsidy is determined by the desired effect. For example, if the objective of the policy is to increase output from OA to OA', as under the tariff T, then the subsidy must be just large enough to bring about an intersection between the new supply curve and the world price line WW' at point M. It is clear that under these conditions imports are $A'B'$ plus $B'B$, since the domestic price of good X stays at WW'. The welfare costs of consumers, NLU, incurred with a tariff are absent, and balance of payments, income redistribution, revenue, and other effects are also different from what they would have been under tariff T, giving rise to the same output effect.

If the policy objective of the subsidy is to reduce imports to $A'B'$, as with the tariff T, then the subsidy would have to be large enough to increase domestic production by AA' plus $B'B'$ units. We will not discuss here the many differences and similarities between subsidies and tariffs under the different sizes of subsidies. The most important points about subsidies are given below.

First, if a government's objective is to increase domestic output or to restrict imports by a given amount, then a subsidy appears to be superior to a tariff, since consumers continue to enjoy the low world price and do not suffer the loss of consumer surplus characteristic of tariffs. Similarly, there is no deadweight loss of producers' surplus. However, since the money paid as subsidy to producers has to be raised by a tax, in all cases except a head or poll tax, which cannot be avoided and leaves all marginal allocation decisions unchanged, analogous welfare costs are incurred. Therefore, the superiority of the subsidy over the tariff is not necessarily equal to the avoided loss of consumer and producer surplus.

Second, subsidies require a periodic appropriation in government budgets. Their social merit is therefore subject to periodic review, in the light of changing economic conditions and needs of society. Tariffs, on the other hand, are reviewed only infrequently, and they give rise to government revenue. The government budget process therefore tends to produce pressures for retention rather than elimination of tariffs. For these reasons—lack of periodic review of social merit and budgetary bias in favor of retention—economists favor subsidies over tariffs.

Multiple Exchange Rates

Many developing countries use exchange controls to influence the level and composition of their foreign trade. To see how this system operates, let us assume that a government permits the free export and import of all goods except one, which, in continuity with our preceding analysis, may be considered to be good X in Figure 7–3. The free market equilibrium exchange rate is equal to $K = 1$, or more conventionally $1 equals 1 £ sterling, and the government buys relatively small quantities of foreign exchange at this price. Furthermore, assume that at this exchange rate the price of the good X domestically would be OW, say $2, if we assume the world price in sterling (WS) to be £2, and since the domestic price is equal to the world price times the exchange rate, i.e., $OW = WS(K) = \$2$.

Now consider that the government sells the foreign exchange at a price of $K + T$ sterling, where $T = 0.5$ to importers who are permitted to use this currency to purchase good X abroad. The domestic price of this good must be $OW = WS(K + T) = \$3$. In effect, the government extracts from importers of good X a tax per unit, which in our example is exactly equal to the per unit tariff discussed above in the original analysis surrounding Figure 7–3. The difference between the multiple exchange rate and the tariff is that in the former case the government makes a profit from the exchange transaction, while in the latter it raises an equivalent tariff revenue. All other effects of tariffs and multiple exchange rates are the same.

Multiple exchange rates have often been used by governments as parts of sets of pervasive controls of all aspects of foreign trade. They can be administered with great flexibility by central banks responsible for exchange rate policy, and therefore they often are out of control of the legislatures, which typically have tariff-making authority. Furthermore, while tariffs have to be published and therefore are known by all countries and subject to international criticism, multiple exchange rates can be administered in greater secrecy. Therefore, they tend to give bureaucrats more protection from internal and foreign scrutiny. For all of these reasons, multiple exchange rates are desirable to some governments, and economists, who believe in rational, open decision making and in achieving the necessary protection at the lowest cost, prefer tariffs over multiple exchange rates.

Miscellaneous Nontariff Barriers

As we shall discuss in Chapter 9, after World War II great progress was made in the lowering of tariffs and quotas of all countries through international agreements. During the 1960s it became apparent that at the low tariff levels achieved by then, other nontariff barriers to trade may be as important as tariffs in distorting and lowering international trade.

In the theoretical framework of the Heckscher-Ohlin model discussed in Part One, any government regulation which changes domestic relative factor or goods prices must lead to patterns of domestic production, consumption, and trade different from those which would have prevailed in their absence. In this sense, all government rules and regulations represent barriers to free trade. However, economists have limited the concept of nontariff barriers to particular sets of government laws which result in different costs of production to foreign and domestic producers. We will analyze the nature of some of these barriers to provide a "flavor" rather than an exhaustive list, which would be too long for this text.

Government Expenditures. Most major industrial countries of the world grant preferences to domestic suppliers of goods by at least four methods. First, invitations for tenders on certain types of contracts, such as military supplies and weapons, may be sent only to domestic suppliers. Second, tenders for more general merchandise contracts may be publicized inadequately and late to potential foreign suppliers. Third, tenders may be in technical dimensions, which mean extra costs of working out contracts for foreign suppliers. Fourth, governments may accept higher priced domestic contracts rather than foreign contracts, as stipulated by law or more generally when it is considered to be in the public interest.

Border Taxes. Under international agreements countries are permitted to rebate to exporters excise and sales taxes paid during earlier stages of production of the exported goods. At the same time, importers are required to pay tariffs plus excise and sales taxes applicable to any particular import goods. Since the United States raises only a very small fraction of government revenue through excise and sales taxes and Europe raises a large fraction thereby, U.S. exporters argue that they are at a competitive disadvantage against European exporters in third countries, in the United States, and in their efforts to compete in Europe. Thus, in Europe and third countries, U.S. exporters receive practically no government rebates and must charge the full U.S. price. European producers, on the other hand, can sell at prices much below those in effect domestically when exporting to the United States or to third countries.

Technical and Administrative Hindrances. The U.S. tariff law has two peculiarities which create distortions in trade. The first relates to the fact that the tariff rate on any benzenoid chemical is applied to its world price when it is not produced in the United States but to the U.S. wholesale price when U.S. manufacture exists. Since the U.S. wholesale price is often above the world price, two very similar products in the same broad tariff category may be assessed a different effective tariff rate if one is not produced in the United States and the other is. The result is a distortion of relative prices. Second, all whiskey sold in the United States is assessed an excise tax of $10.50 per gallon of 100 percent or less proof (50 percent alcohol content) whiskey. Since whiskey bottled for consumption is 86 proof, the excise tax on bottled, imported whiskey falls on 14 percent water, and foreign producers in effect pay an excise tax rate of $(100/86) \times \$10.50 = \$12.21$ per gallon of 100 percent proof whiskey. U.S. producers pay their tax when the whiskey is at 100 percent proof, and thus they pay a lower rate than do importers of bottled whiskey. One of the effects of this particular U.S. law has been the encouragement of imports of whiskey for bottling in the United States. To the extent that bottling represents an activity in which the rest of the world has a comparative advantage, the whiskey tax law creates a distortion of free trade patterns which in principle could be caused by tariffs of the appropriate size and on the appropriate activity.

Most countries have consumer protection laws governing specifications of electrical appliances and of vehicles; sanitary rules to be followed in packing meat, fruits, and so on; and rules governing the labeling of contents and origins of packages. These standards of specification are not the same in all countries; for example, the maximum permissible speed for tractors is 17, 13, and 10 mph, respectively, in France, Germany, and the Netherlands. Exporters of tractors from France and the Netherlands into Germany have to incur different extra costs of adjustment not encountered by their German competitors, to make their tractors conform to German law. This extra cost represents an impediment to trade and causes distortions in trade patterns which in principle are equivalent to those created by tariffs.

Summary and Conclusions

Most acts of government which influence the relative domestic prices of goods or factors have trade-distorting effects. Tariffs have been historically the most important and most widely used instrument for directly reducing countries' imports. For this reason the analysis of Sections I–IV in this chapter considered the effects of tariffs. However, in this last section of the chapter we have analyzed a number of other instruments governments are using to influence the pattern of trade deliberately, such as subsidies, quotas, and multiple exchange rates, and often unintentionally, such as border tax adjustments and health and safety regulations. All of these instruments have effects which could have been brought about instead by tariffs of a certain magnitude, on particular activities. All of the social costs and income redistribution effects of tariffs are generated also by these nontariff barriers to trade. In the next chapter we will therefore return to the principle of exposition of analyzing only the specific problems surrounding the use of tariffs.

APPENDIX

A Complete General Equilibrium Model of a Tariff

The general equilibrium model of the effects of a tariff on a large country in this Appendix expands on the discussion presented in the main part of the text. It centers on Figure 7A–1 and reproduces the offer curves of countries A and B derived above in connection with Figure 3–10. We show country A's production block in free trade equilibrium with its origin at E_0. The world price is OT_0^w, which also prevails domestically at point $C_0 = P_0$. The initial level of welfare is I_0I_0'.

Now consider that country A imposes a tariff, t. The world price changes, and we assume that it comes to rest in overall equilibrium at OT_1^w. (We will defer until the next chapter discussion of country A's choice of t and country B's likely response to the imposition of the tariff.) The new world price line intersects B's offer curve at point E_1, where we have placed the origin of country A's production block in the new equilibrium. Recall from the construction of Figure 3–9 that through point E_1 must go a country A trade indifference curve, a segment of which is shown as the broken line TI. This trade indifference curve of country A is not tangent to the world price line OT_1^w, because otherwise E_1 would have to be on A's offer curve. However, at E_1 we can find the domestic price line LT_1^d tangent to the trade indifference curve. This domestic price line prevails also at the point of domestic consumption and production, $C_1 = P_1$, and its slope differs from that of the world price line OT_1^w by the tariff rate t. The simultaneous determination of the world and domestic price lines guarantees that there must always be a point like E_1 where a domestic price line is tangent to the trade indifference curve and with a slope different from the world price by the tariff rate.

The line OT_2^d is parallel to LT_1^d, whose slope we have just determined, but it goes through the origin O. It allows us to show that in equilibrium OK units of export good Y are exchanged domestically for KM of the import good X. But since at the world price the same OK units of Y bring KE_1 of X, the amount ME_1 must represent the tariff revenue in the form of X, and the tariff rate is equal to ME_1/KM. Under the assumption that this revenue is distributed to consumers and enters their purchasing decisions, we find that in equilibrium the following relationships hold:

	Import Good X	Export Good Y
Production	RC_1	E_1R
Consumption	QC_1	SR
Trade at world prices	QR	E_1S
Trade at domestic price	QN	E_1S
Tariff revenue	NR	—

FIGURE 7A–1

Import Tariff on Good *X* in a Large Country

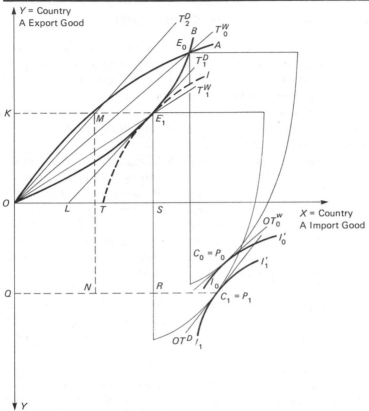

Under free trade, the origin of country A's production block in Figure 7A–1 is at E_0, and it reaches point $C_0 = P_0$ for consumption and production. C_0 quantities are measured along the *Y* and *X* coordinates, with zero as the origin. P_0 quantities are measured relative to the production block. At $C_0 = P_0$ and E_0, the world and domestic price ratios OT_0^w are identical.

After the imposition of the optimum tariff, the origin of the production block is at E_1, and consumption and production are at point $C_1 = P_1$. At this point country A reaches the indifference curve I_1I_1', which is above I_0I_0', reached under free trade. The trade indifference curve *TI* is tangent to B's offer curve at E_1, implying that country A has imposed its optimum tariff. At E_1 and $C_1 = P_1$, the parallel domestic price ratios LT_1^d and OT^d are tangent.

In equilibrium the world price line is OT_1^w, the domestic price LT_1^d, so that the tariff revenue in terms of good *X* is ME_1, and the tariff rate is ME_1/KM.

    The most important conclusion following from the preceding analysis is that country A improved its welfare from I_0I_0' to I_1I_1' through the imposition of a tariff on imports. In common-sense terms, the tariff improved the country's terms of trade sufficiently to leave a net welfare gain, even after adjustment for the inefficiencies which accompanied the tariff imposition.

It should be noted, however, that country A's gains come at the expense of country B, which at E_1 is at a lower level of welfare than at the free trade E_0.

BIBLIOGRAPHICAL NOTES

Anyone interested in an in-depth study of the theory and policy implications of protection will find a most careful exposition and all needed references to the existing literature in Corden (1971b, 1974). Johnson (1971a) has a convenient collection of his contributions to tariff theory.

The concept of effective protection had been in the economics literature for some time before its systematic exposition and empirical application in the 1960s. Corden (1971a), in an appendix to the book, details this history. The key articles in the field are Barber (1955), Johnson (1965c), and Corden (1966). Balassa (1965, 1971) has contributed a wealth of empirical estimates. A conference volume on problems in the theory and measurement of effective protection is Grubel and Johnson (1971).

The equivalence of tariffs and other forms of protection has been discussed in the classic by Lerner (1968) and by Holzman (1969). Different forms of nontariff barriers and their importance in recent years are analyzed by Baldwin (1970) and the Curzons (1971) and are reviewed by Stern (1973b).

CONCEPTS FOR REVIEW

Effects of a tariff
   Terms of trade
   Production
   Subsidy
   Consumption
   Balance of payments
   Revenue
   Consumption tax
Consumer surplus

Producer surplus
Effective protection
Value added
Negative effective protection
Quota
Voluntary quota
Multiple exchange rates
Border taxes

POINTS FOR FURTHER STUDY AND DISCUSSION

1. Explain how, in Figure 7–1, country A can reach the same production and consumption points P_1 and C_1 through payment of an export subsidy on good Y rather than an import tax on good X. Indicate the amount of subsidy, equivalent to the tariff revenue, needed to be paid in equilibrium.

2. Can you specify which part of the loss in welfare due to a tariff imposition in Figure 7–1 can be attributed to lost output (negative production effect) and which part to trade at the world price (positive trade effect)? Hint: Refer to the analysis surrounding Figure 3–7.

3. What happens to the partial equilibrium effects of tariffs if, in Figure 7–3, either the domestic demand or supply curve is perfectly inelastic?

4. Discuss the case where, in Figure 7-3, the tariff T is so large that the new line ZZ' is above the intersection between the demand and supply curves.

5. Give an economic interpretation of the empirical finding that some industries have negative rates of effective protection.

6. It has been observed that in many countries tariff rates tend to be an increasing function of the protected industry's position along the spectrum from raw materials to semifinished and final products. Is this phenomenon, known as cascading of tariffs, consistent with the theory of effective protection?

8 Reasons for Tariff Protection

As WE HAVE NOTED, tariffs tend to reduce national and world welfare, except in the case where improvements in the terms of trade of one country outweigh losses in efficiency. Why, therefore, do countries impose tariffs?

The answers to this question we consider in this chapter are derived from arguments which have been developed by governments and interested groups in the economy and presented before legislative hearings, where national tariff policies are determined. These arguments can be classified into four broad categories. The first involves the exploitation of monopoly power and the attainment of more favorable terms of trade. It yields the optimum tariff argument.

The second category of arguments is based on the notion that some of the assumptions which are made to prove the optimality of free trade are not met in the real world. Consequently, free trade leads to less than optimal conditions, and tariffs are alleged to raise rather than lower welfare. Invalid assumptions of the Heckscher-Ohlin model are said to include the absence of scale economies in production, the free availability of knowledge, efficiently operating factor markets, and the absence of external effects.

The third category of arguments for tariffs is based on the extension of social welfare functions to include not only the basic income of goods and services, but also income distribution and government revenue for the provision of public services.

The fourth category of arguments for tariffs rests on the existence of uncertainty and economic fluctuations which result in temporary and frequently large swings in demand, supply, or prices of particular commodities. Under these conditions temporary tariffs can stabilize prices and employment in industries and avoid the incurrence of unnecessary real adjustment costs by producers and consumers.

In the fifth section of this chapter we present general arguments against the use of tariffs and demonstrate the important principle that if there are domestic market failures or social welfare targets requiring government intervention, the policies to correct them should always be aimed directly at the source of the market failure or target of the welfare objective, rather than being made to operate through the foreign trade sector. We also argue that market institutions have a tendency to internalize externalities, obviating the need for tariffs. To avoid repetition we will not present this argument against tariffs when analyzing the specific and traditional reasons for tariffs in Sections II and III below.

Until very recently the domestic political processes underlying the determination of national tariff structures have received little attention. However, in recent years studies by Jonathan Pincus (1973) of 19th-century tariffs and J. H. Cheh (1974) of current U.S. tariffs have provided strong evidence that the protection of labor-intensive industries in politically important regions is the dominant motivating force of U.S. tariff legislation. While the empirical evidence thus suggests that maintenance or redistribution of income to labor is the most important determinant of U.S. tariffs, the arguments used in public justification of the policies rarely have involved the narrow self-interest of labor. Instead, they have used socially more respectable arguments, such as the national interest, market failures, equity considerations, and others. We now turn to the analysis of these arguments for tariff protection.

I. THE OPTIMUM TARIFF

If a country is large enough so that its policies can affect the relative prices of commodities in the world, it faces in effect demand and supply curves for its tradable goods which are less than perfectly elastic. As is well known from price theory, whenever a buyer or seller is confronted with such imperfectly competitive market conditions, profits are maximized by trading at prices and quantities where marginal revenue and marginal cost are equalized. In essence, the optimum tariff argument is based on a strictly analogous exploitation of market power by a large country, and the tariff is the instrument whereby it attains a welfare-maximizing position above that which the unmitigated market forces would have produced.

However, in the case of the optimum tariff we are dealing with a general equilibrium model and cannot use the conventional partial equilibrium models familiar from price theory. The model we employ was developed above in connection with Figure 7-2 and Figure 7A-1 in Chapter 7, and it now is simple to explain the optimum tariff in this framework.

The optimum tariff argument says that if country A wishes to reach the highest level of welfare possible, it should pick the tariff rate that produces a world price and a corresponding point on country B's offer curve that is tangent to country A's highest trade indifference curve. In Figure 7-2 such an optimum is represented at point E_2 by the tangency of the indifference curve II' with country B's offer curve. Therefore, the tariff rate which results in the world price OT_2^w is the optimum tariff. Of course, Figure 7-2 was constructed to fulfill these conditions, and it is clear that other tariff rates would have resulted in different world prices and corresponding equilibrium points on country B's offer curve, either above or below the optimum point E_2. But as can readily be seen from the inspection of Figure 7-2, none of these points could have been on, or tangent to, a higher trade indifference curve than II'. Therefore no tariff other than the optimum yields a higher level of welfare.

For many students this analysis of the optimum tariff argument provides sufficient insights for understanding the most important principles. However, students who are interested in the algebraic formulation of the optimum tariff condition are referred to the first section in the Appendix to this chapter.

Optimum Tariff and Retaliation

A question which we raised but did not answer in the preceding chapter was why country B would accept the deterioration in her terms of trade resulting from country A's unilateral imposition of a tariff. The answer is that in all likelihood country B would retaliate by imposing a tariff of its own. However, country A, in turn, may retaliate with a new tariff, and so on. What is the likely outcome of such a process of successive rounds of retaliatory tariff impositions?

To analyze this problem, consider Figure 8-1, in which we have drawn the free trade offer curves OA and OB with an equilibrium point E, on grounds justified in connection with the analysis of Figures 3-9 and 3-10. Point E, on country B's free trade offer curve, represents the corresponding point F_0 in our analysis of the optimum tariff in Figure 7-2. Now consider that country B finds itself at E_1 and faces country A's tariff-distorted offer curve. Assuming that there will be no retaliation, country B improves and maximizes its welfare by imposing an optimum tariff of its own, distorting its offer curve to OB' and choosing equilibrium point E_2. In Figure 8-1 we show a further step in this process of retaliation, where country A distorts its offer curve to A'' and reaches trade indifference curve T_aT_a tangent to OB' at E_3. It seems clear that such behavior repeated

FIGURE 8–1
Tariffs and Retaliation

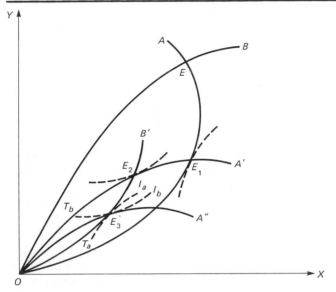

After free trade equilibrium at point E, country A imposes an optimum tariff and moves to E_1. Now country B retaliates by finding its optimum tariff position at E_2 on country A's distorted offer curve, OA'. The process of retaliation may come to an end before the cessation of trade if by chance one country's highest trade indifference is tangent to the other country's optimally distorted offer curve. Such a situation is shown at point E_3, where neither country can improve its welfare by the further imposition of a tariff.

by each country in turn leads to continuously lower levels and ultimately to complete cessation of world trade, with the corresponding losses of welfare for each country and the whole world.

However, this outcome of the analysis depends crucially on our assumption that each country acts as if it believed that the other would not retaliate. In the real world, of course, countries do expect that others will not permit a reduction in their welfare to take place without some policy response. Therefore, it seems reasonable to conclude that countries will not start tariff wars by unilateral attempts to improve their own welfare through the imposition of a tariff, except in circumstances where lack of knowledge or domestic political problems in trading partners are considered to prevent retaliation.

From the analysis thus far we reach the important conclusion that, while the exploitation of monopoly power through the imposition of a tariff can in principle lead to the improvement of the welfare of one country, the threat of retaliation effectively prevents employment of this tool by individual countries.

However, this conclusion has been challenged by Harry G. Johnson of the University of Chicago who introduced the following possibility. Consider in Figure 8–1 the stage in the tariff war where country A's offer curve is OA'' and country B's is OB'. By assumption, point E_3 involves A's optimum tariff. But now consider that, as we have shown in Figure 8–1, country B's highest trade indifference curve, T_bI_b, attainable with the given offer curve OA'' coincidentally is tangent to it at E_3. Under this special condition country B has no incentives to distort its offer curve by the imposition of another tariff, and E_3 is a point of stable equilibrium.

This result changes the conclusion reached for the case where we disregarded the possibility that countries can be at their optimum points simultaneously. According to the amended analysis it is possible that one country can improve its welfare at the expense of the other without inviting retaliation. Incentives therefore exist for one country to try to find such a point, even though the new equilibrium must lower total welfare, since only free trade is optimal.

Optimum Export Tax

It is difficult to find empirical evidence that countries have imposed import tariffs consciously to exploit positions of inelastic supply for their imports generally, or even for some particular products. The explanation of this fact is that monopsony positions are very rare. Typically, traded goods are required by all nations, as our trade matrix of Chapter 6 has shown, and very seldom is one nation a big enough buyer of one particular good to affect its world price. As we shall see in the next sections of this chapter, countries generally have used arguments other than the optimum tariff to justify the use of trade restrictions. In spite of this fact, however, tariffs may have the effect of improving a country's terms of trade, and the optimum tariff argument therefore is relevant for the analysis of unintentioned consequences.

While import monopsony conditions are rare, export monopoly positions for particular commodities are more frequent because countries may have exclusive patents, raw materials, or human skills. When countries enjoy such monopolies as suppliers they can improve their terms of trade by the use not of *import* tariffs but of export taxes on the relevant products. During the 1930s Hitler's Germany, under its economics minister Hjalmar Schacht, imposed export taxes on certain chemical products, drugs, and optical instruments for which Germany was the only supplier and for which substitutes were not readily available. Similarly, the oil-producing nations in 1973 and the Central American producers of bananas in 1974 imposed export taxes to exploit their monopoly positions. It is clear that the changes in relative world prices of commodities brought about by the export taxes have analytically equivalent effects as import tariffs do, since they raise the price of a country's exports relative to imports charged to the rest of the world. The most important conscious real-world use of the optimum tariff argument may thus be found in the justification of export taxes on goods in which countries have a monopoly position.

II. TARIFFS TO CORRECT MARKET FAILURES

In price theory we define "market failures" as economic processes which cause the allocation of resources in the economy to be inefficient, or in more technical terms, to be not Pareto-optimal. Therefore, when such market failures exist, government intervention through the imposition of tariffs, in principle, can make the economy operate efficiently and can increase one person's welfare without decreasing that of another person.

Our analysis of market failures is divided into three subsections. The first contains the traditional infant-industry argument. The second deals with a modern argument analogous to the infant-industry argument and concerns a "labor-surplus economy." The final subsection presents arguments for protection based on genuine externalities in production and consumption.

Infant-Industry Argument

The best known and most widely used justification for tariffs historically has been the infant-industry argument. It was used persuasively in the last century by Friedrich List of Germany and Alexander Hamilton of the United States, when these two countries attempted to industrialize and catch up with Great Britain, the leading industrial power in the world at the time. It has been used in the 20th century by developing countries trying to acquire their own industries.

The power of the infant-industry argument for tariffs derives from the fact that it implies only a temporary use of tariffs, to protect a newly created industry from allegedly unfair competition of established firms abroad until it is a strong and vigorous adult. At such a time the tariffs can be removed, and the country will possess an industry in which it has a comparative advantage in the conventional sense of the Heckscher-Ohlin model we developed in Part One. The tariff-imposing country and the world thus can enjoy gains from trade which would have been absent if the government had not interfered temporarily with the free forces of the market.

The mechanism whereby one industry or an entire industrial sector moves from infancy to adulthood can best be described by assuming the existence of a country in which, initially, the entire population is engaged in traditional agriculture and artisan occupations. The work force has no experience working in factories, has little work "discipline," and is un-familiar with modern machines, and entrepreneurs and managers know little industrial technology and cannot organize large quantities of capital and many workers. As a result, the costs of producing industrial goods initially would be very high and not competitive in world markets. How-ever, once production gets underway behind tariff walls, the workers, managers, and entrepreneurs "learn by doing" and acquire all of the skills and work habits that lead to lower costs of production.

The most important characteristic of this learning by doing is that it cannot be acquired in any other way, as through the purchase of knowl-edge in world markets or through a traditional apprenticeship in which the learner pays a master. All of the cost-reducing benefits accrue to the economy as a whole and cannot be appropriated by particular industries or workers. If they were appropriable, the capital market could be as-sumed to advance funds for the period of learning which could be repaid with appropriate interest upon the industry's maturity, once the factors of production have attained their maximum productivity.

Another source of cost reduction is the development of technological economies of scale internal to the industry but external to firms. For example, the market for steel created by the domestic growth of steel-using firms may lead to economies of scale in the production of steel. As a result, the cost of production of the industry using steel as an input falls. But existing market organization does not permit steel users to anticipate these lower steel prices and incorporate them in their rate-of-return calcu-lations. Privately, therefore, the individual firm may not be profitable and the investment would not be undertaken, though socially the entire group of firms would be profitable. The imposition of tariffs allows realization of these social benefits of the industries.

While this theoretical case for infant-industry tariffs sounds very con-vincing, in the real world there are three important problems. First is the difficulty encountered in identifying industries that have a good chance of becoming a genuine source of comparative advantage to the country. We have discussed (in Chapter 5) the difficulties developing countries of the 20th century have met in attempting to overcome the problem of identify-ing infant-industry candidates. They tried to induce import substitution through the indiscriminate application of tariffs to all industries. But these countries cannot have a comparative advantage in all industries, and pro-tection of all industries has lead only to a reduction of overall trade. Furthermore, once an industry has developed behind tariffs, it becomes most difficult politically to remove the protection. Demands then change from the need for infant-industry protection to adolescent-industry pro-tection. All the time, however, the protection of the industry represents an inefficiency and a costly drag on the economy.

Second, even if an industry grows up and matures into one having comparative advantage in the world economy, it becomes very difficult to recognize when this has taken place and to bring about the political agreement for the removal of the tariff. This is so because, except in the most competitive industries with free entry, and so on, genuine reductions in the cost of production become capitalized as rents to labor, management, or capital. These rents are lost once the tariffs are removed, which thus becomes equivalent to a wealth redistribution policy. Consequently, the beneficiaries of this rent oppose strongly the removal of the tariffs, and often they have great financial resources at their command.

Third, even if comparative advantage in an industry develops at some time and tariffs are reduced, there remains the problem of comparing the social costs during infancy to the benefits of the future, all properly related to each other at the social rate of discount. These kinds of calculations, of course, are difficult to carry out in practice, since the relevant information is unavailable. They do point to the fact that the development of comparative advantage is a necessary but not sufficient condition justifying the use of a temporary tariff for the protection of an infant industry.

In recent years Johnson has raised a further, most fundamental objection to the infant-industry argument for protection. This objection represents the application of a principle developed by Ronald Coase and a group of other economists at the University of Chicago Law School. According to the Coase theorem, traditional economic analysis has been paying insufficient attention to the fact that business and social organizations tend to change in order to internalize what under the assumptions of comparative static analysis are externalities. Thus, according to this argument, economies of scale external to the firm but internal to the industry would generate incentives for firms in the industry to amalgamate, which would enable them to internalize and benefit from the externalities. For this reason, if there are such externalities, the market would respond to them and there would be no need for tariff protection. If the market does not react in the manner indicated, there is a prima facie case that the externalities are either nonexistent or too small to warrant exploitation, so that an infant-industry tariff would also not be justified on economic grounds. If the government believes that the reason for the absence of the change in institutions is that the market has imperfect information, then the first-best solution to this problem is the publication of the relevant information.

The Coase theorem can be shown to predict correctly the elimination of all externalities only in the absence of costs of transaction, such as information and legal incorporation. Its empirical validity has been questioned by many economists, and the final evaluation is not yet available. However, regardless of how powerful the theoretical case against infant-industry protection along these lines of argument may be, the fact remains that, historically, infant-industry tariff arguments have been used widely for the justification of protection of industry in the United States, Germany, Canada, Japan, Australia, and several other countries. Furthermore, the success of these countries is often cited as justification for the use of tariffs to induce industrial growth in developing countries. However, we should be skeptical about the use of these countries' experience as a justification for tariffs, because it is not evident at what cost the industries were acquired and whether or not alternative policies could have been used to attain the same objectives.

A curious variant of the infant-industry argument for protection has become fashionable in recent years and has been formalized by H. Peter Gray of Rutgers University. The argument, known as the senescent industry argument, is used to defend tariff protection for industries which operate with obsolete and inefficient machinery and equipment and which are in danger of extinction because they cannot compete with producers using the most modern manufacturing facilities. In parallel with the infant-industry argument, the temporary protection of the senescent industry permits it to earn sufficiently high profits to obtain the modern equipment. Thereafter, tariff protection can be dropped and comparative advantage again comes into operation, leaving the world economy at a higher level of efficiency than would have existed in the absence of the temporary tariff. The criticism of this argument parallels that in the case of the infant-industry argument. If there are such economies to be had from modernization, the private capital market would lend the necessary funds. If the private market is inefficient, then the existence of senescent industries lends further support to efforts at making the capital market more efficient. If such efficiency cannot be achieved, then the government should provide a direct subsidy for the modernization of the senescent industry.

Labor-Surplus Economy

Students of development economics are familiar with Arthur Lewis's model of the labor-surplus, or dual, economy. According to this model, in many developing nations there exists a surplus of labor in the agricultural sector which has resulted in an extremely low, or zero, marginal productivity of labor there. Yet there is a positive wage rate in the industrial sector of the developing countries. Consequently, entrepreneurs have to pay a wage which exceeds the opportunity cost of labor in agriculture, and they hire less than the socially optimal quantity of labor. Under these circumstances, as Everett Hagen of the Massachusetts Institute of Technology has argued, a tariff induces higher industrial output, which requires labor withdrawn from agriculture, where it has zero productivity, for a net social gain in output. As in the infant-industry case, after economic development has progressed sufficiently and the causes of zero productivity in agriculture have been eliminated, the tariff can be removed.

The heart of the dual-economy argument has been criticized for not recognizing the positive productivity of labor in agriculture during peak harvesting periods and for neglecting the added social cost of providing for labor in the industrial urban setting, as compared to life in rural areas. To the extent that these considerations invalidate the dual-economy argument, they also invalidate the argument that tariff protection yields net social gains. Unfortunately, economists have not reached agreement on the empirical validity of the dual-economy model, and therefore a final judgment on the merit of the argument for protection based on it cannot be made.

Externalities

The purest case of market failures exists when the production or consumption of a good affects the welfare of the public and the price of the good does not reflect these external benefits or costs. In the case of positive externalities, overall social welfare can be raised by increasing domestic production, while negative externalities require decreased output. As we have shown (in Chapter 7), tariffs can be used to change domestic relative prices which induce the desired increases and decreases in the output of particular commodities.

Historically, arguments for the protection of the entire industrial sector have been built on the view that industry permits urbanization and increased specialization among workers, which tend to stimulate growth of productivity, science, and cultural pursuits such as literature, music, and other fine arts. In some countries at other times it has been argued that agriculture deserves protection because farmers carry on valuable social traditions, and the rural population, strong and healthy from work in the fields, represents a valuable supply of manpower for the military in case of war. Also related to national defense is the argument that protection of certain key industries is required to keep them producing at levels sufficiently high to support a country's needs when war stops all foreign trade.

The biggest problem with these types of arguments for protection is that they involve unquantifiable value judgments about the merit of the externalities. Therefore, they can be used in principle to support any level of protection, depending on the proponent's evaluation of the benefits.

Two important arguments for protection based on externalities have become prominent in recent years. The first arises from increased public consciousness about the costs of pollution and congestion of the environment. In the framework of our basic general equilibrium trade model, we may consider that the production of export good Y results in pollution, while that of X does not. A tariff on the importation of good X would draw resources into industry X and out of industry Y, with the conventional changes in the level of trade and consumption. The lower output of Y reduces pollution for the desired social gain. However, there are some social losses from reduced gains from trade, along the lines discussed in Part One. An optimum tariff and resource shift is attained when marginal benefits from the reduction in pollution equal the marginal cost of reduced income from the lower level of trade.

The second argument arises from the situation where a country suffers from immiserizing growth because individual entrepreneurs are drawn into the privately profitable activity of producing the good Y, which can be sold abroad in increasing quantities only if terms of trade deteriorate. Since the privately profitable actions of some individuals lower the welfare of other people in the country, we are dealing with the case of an externality. As in the case of pollution, a tariff on the import of good X increases its domestic production and causes a decline in the output of Y, with a corresponding (desired) lowering of the negative externalities.

The preceding examples involve production externalities. The case of consumption externalities can be analyzed analogously. If good Y, say automobiles, results in negative externalities through pollution or congestion, then a tariff would raise its relative price for consumers, who would be induced to consume less and lower the magnitude of the negative externalities.

The most important objection to the use of tariffs in dealing with externalities is that they are inefficient, as we will discuss in Section V of this chapter. Anticipating somewhat the contents of this section, the argument simply is that if there are externalities, they should be corrected by the use of taxes or subsidies aimed at the market failure directly, as a tax on the emission of pollutants, and not through tariffs, which could introduce added costs of consumption or force the country into giving up some of the benefits of international trade and specialization.

III. SOCIAL WELFARE FUNCTION

The government sector of the major Western market economies has grown dramatically in recent decades, to where in 1970 the receipts of the governments of Sweden, the United Kingdom, Canada, and the United States represented 41, 33, 29, and 29 percent of GNP, respectively, of these countries. As is well known, these government expenditures are undertaken to redistribute income and provide public goods. The imposition of tariffs has also been defended on the grounds that they redistribute income and raise revenue out of which public goods or income redistribution is financed. While the need to provide public goods is often considered to arise from a market failure, we prefer here to use the analytical approach that both income redistribution and the provision of public goods are undertaken by governments to maximize a social welfare function, in which income distribution and public goods are arguments.

Income Redistribution

The income redistribution effect of a tariff has been shown rigorously, first by Wolfgang Stolper and Paul Samuelson within the framework of the Heckscher-Ohlin model. Recall that the Stolper-Samuelson theorem states that a tariff raises the relative income of the factor of production that is used intensively by the protected good. The theorem can be understood most readily by considering the bottom panel of Figure 3–2 in Chapter 3, where we assume point E' represents the original output combination under free trade, with Y being the capital-intensive export good. The imposition of a tariff on import good X increases the domestic relative price of X and creates a new production equilibrium at D'. The top panel of Figure 3–2 shows that this shift in production involves moving along the contract curve from point E to point D. Recall that this movement is accompanied by increased capital intensity of the production technique in both industries. Such greater capital intensity can be achieved only by raising the relative price of labor. Since good X is the protected, labor-intensive product, we have shown that in this simple model the Stolper-Samuelson theorem must always hold.

However, in a celebrated paper Lloyd Metzler of the University of Chicago (1949) has shown that for a large country which affects its terms of trade through the imposition of a tariff, this theorem does not necessarily hold. Metzler's argument is based on the possibility that the elasticities of the domestic and foreign offer curves are such that a tariff causes the *domestic* price of the imported good to fall rather than to rise, as is assumed in the standard case analyzed in the context of Figure 7–2. An intuitive explanation of the Metzler results goes as follows. Country B has a rather inelastic demand curve for country A's export good Y, so that an increase in the relative price of that good caused by the tariff brings about only a small decrease in B's imports. But at the higher relative price of Y, country A now receives a greater supply of good X than under free trade. To induce consumption of this larger quantity of X and to reduce its domestic production, therefore, the *domestic* relative price of X has to fall from its free trade level, even though the tariff has raised its external world level. We thus have the result that the protection of the labor-intensive good X brings about a decrease in its output and therefore a fall in the relative price of labor.

The income redistribution argument for protection is used frequently, though rarely in the form of an appeal for higher wages and a larger share of income for labor, at the expense of capital. Mostly the argument is couched in terms of the need for protection from foreign competition, which is alleged to pay its labor "unfair," low wages and therefore to be able to sell products at prices which force domestic producers out of business and lower the wages paid in the particular industry. From our study in Part One we know, of course, that such seemingly "unfair" competition from cheap foreign labor is the necessary consequence of the operation of the principles of comparative advantage, without which there can be no gains from trade. Yet, governments often have accepted these kinds of arguments for protection because in Western industrialized countries in recent decades, the free importation of very labor-intensive products (such as textiles) from the developing countries would have resulted in very low wage rates in these industries. Thus it was deemed to have been in the public interest to protect the wage rates of workers in these industries through the imposition of import tariffs, on the grounds that the income distribution which would have resulted from free trade was inconsistent with society's welfare function.

The main objections to this argument for protection are rather obvious. In a dynamic world there will always be shifting patterns of comparative advantage, and if factors of production in all countries are protected from developing foreign competition, the world will forego potentially large gains from trade. The proper policy of government, in the face of the declining competitiveness of an industry, is to assist retraining and relocation of its factors of production in other industries which are gaining in competitiveness. Under these conditions, income redistribution does not result. If, however, income redistribution is a desirable goal for its own sake, it should be accomplished directly through appropriate tax and expenditure policies which do not involve the foreign sector. We will discuss this point more rigorously in Section V of this chapter.

Revenue Tariffs

At the early stages of economic development, governments have few sources from which to collect revenue equitably and at low cost, since the largest part of the economy operates on a subsistence basis, the monetary sector is small, and the government bureaucracy is small and inefficient. Under these conditions the foreign trade sector tends to be one of the most important sources of taxation. Foreign trade flows conveniently through a few border towns or harbors, where it is often transhipped onto long-distance modes of transportation. Even at early stages of economic development, specialized international banking houses carry on financing and foreign exchange transactions. Consequently it is relatively easy for governments to monitor and tax foreign trade flows. S. R. Lewis has shown in a regression analysis that the proportion of government revenue collected from foreign trade is a decreasing function of economic development.

The use of tariffs to raise revenue brings conflicts in the use of tariffs to attain other objectives. For example, if a tariff is designed to prevent all imports of a particular good, tariff revenue is zero. At the other extreme, to raise revenue it may be necessary to have a tariff on a good which should not be protected for any other reason. A conflict of special interest is shown in Figure 8–2. Following the model developed around Figure

FIGURE 8–2
Maximum Revenue Tariff

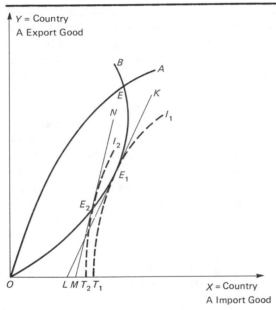

At point E_1 in Figure 8–2 country A enjoys the benefits from the imposition of the optimum tariff, reaching $T_1 I_1$ welfare at the tariff-inclusive domestic price ratio LK. The tariff revenue is OL in terms of good X. If country A imposes a tariff higher than the optimum, such as is represented by the slope of the line MN, then it reaches a nonoptimum level of welfare, on $T_2 I_2$. However, at this tariff level revenue is OM, which is greater than the optimum tariff revenue MN.

7–2, we show country A's optimum tariff position at E_1 on country B's offer curve. Recall from the analysis of Chapter 7 that the domestic price line, KL, tangent to A's trade indifference curve, $T_1 I_1$, at E_1, measures tariff revenue in terms of the import good X by the distance OL. Now consider a tariff higher than the optimum which reduces trade further and results in equilibrium point E_2. Country A's trade indifference curve, $T_2 I_2$, going through this point obviously indicates a lower level of welfare than the optimum $T_1 I_1$. But the domestic price line MN tangent to $T_2 I_2$ at E_2 shows that at this higher tariff level, revenue is OM, greater than OL at the optimum tariff. Because A's trade indifference curves are sloping downward and B's offer curve is rising as shown, the maximum revenue tariff must always be above the optimum tariff.

In general, the revenue tariff argument is sound under conditions where the social cost of raising revenue in any other way is higher, as may be the case in developing countries. Even though the tariff creates social costs and reduces the gains from trade, these costs are worth incurring if the social productivity of the government expenditures exceeds the opportunity cost of the resources plus the cost of collection. The real-world difficulties in the use of this argument arise from the need to know the value of these costs and benefits.

Industry as a Consumption Good

The public discussions on programs for the creation of industry in developing countries can easily be interpreted as implying that industry is considered to be a symbol of progress and development worth having as such, rather than for the traditional reasons of import substitution or the creation of comparative advantage. Johnson has argued that if industry is considered to have these public-good characteristics and as such enters into a country's social welfare function, then conventional criteria of efficiency and corollaries such as the infant-industry argument are inapplicable. In their place we must put considerations of the true social cost of such projects of public consumption in relation to other uses of the resources involved. Again we have a case where benefits cannot be measured objectively. The only constraint on politicians wanting to use potentially vast amounts of public resources to meet what they consider to be demand for a public consumption good is the democratic political process itself, which assures that in the long run the government undertakes only projects desired by the public.

IV. ECONOMIC INSTABILITY

In the analysis presented in this book thus far we have very rarely needed to refer to costs of adjustment, information gathering, and unforeseen changes in production conditions, or demand and supply at home and abroad. In Part Four we will deal at length with problems arising from economic instability and uncertainty and the existence of adjustment costs. Here we need mention these conditions only briefly, because they are often used as arguments for temporary tariff protection.

Assume that in country A resources are fully employed and trade is balanced, as in the pure-theory models presented above. Now consider that in the rest of the world a depression or bumper crop temporarily lowers the relative price of country A's import good. In terms of comparative static analysis, country A would benefit from such an improvement in its terms of trade, and there would be no justification for any government intervention. However, let us now introduce into the analysis two elements of realism.

First, let us assume that society puts a value on keeping stable the incomes of individual groups in the economy. It is clear from the analysis presented above that the change in country A's terms of trade lowers the relative income of the factor of production used intensively in the imported good. Consequently, taking advantage of the temporarily lower relative world price of the imported good causes a temporary decrease in the relative income of one of the two factors of production. Since under our assumption this relative income change causes a loss of welfare, a temporary tariff which prevents a change in the relative world price of the good from being transmitted to the domestic economy increases welfare. However, the tariff involves the cost of reduced gains from trade in the conventional comparative static sense. The temporary tariff should therefore be used only when the gains from reduced instability of incomes exceeds the costs of reduced gains from trade.

Second, as world and domestic product prices change in the manner hypothesized above, factors of production are induced to move from import into export industries, only to be faced by the opposite incentives once the assumed temporary price change has been reversed. Factors of production working in industries subject to these sorts of shifts are compensated for their moving costs by higher wages, but from a social point of view these adjustment costs are a waste which can be eliminated by the use of a temporary tariff which prevents the domestic relative price changes. As in the case of the income stability argument, these benefits must be weighted against the costs of tariff-reduced gains from trade.

Variants of these arguments about income distribution and adjustment costs are based on the concept of optimum rates of adjustment, according to which temporary tariffs are used to cushion the impact of sudden, dramatic changes in demand or supply of an industry, without preventing the free forces of the market from ultimately asserting themselves. Optimum adjustment rates take account of the normal rates of attrition of an industry's labor force and depreciation of its capital stock. The idea is that at the proper rate of decrease of demand, an industry's output is allowed to shrink without requiring the reallocation of labor or losses in the value of the existing capital stock. More generally, this argument has been used to defend the imposition of tariffs as part of an overall program to correct a balance-of-payments disequilibrium, as we shall discuss further in Part Four of this book. Devaluations and income adjustments require time to become operative, while tariffs tend to reduce imports more promptly.

These arguments for temporary tariff protection are popular and have been used successfully in many countries and under many circumstances.

The problem with these arguments is that they assume the absence or improper functioning of futures markets and speculation. As is well known, these markets and activities provide the economic function of evening out fluctuations in demand, supply, and prices, to the extent that it is efficient, given the cost of storage and information and the opportunity cost of capital. In free market economies, therefore, the use of temporary tariffs to avoid social costs of adjustment and income instability must be based on the notion that futures markets and speculation are operating inefficiently, and either the government knows better than speculators what future prices will be, or fluctuations involve externalities which require public subsidization of the free market stabilization process. The notion that government bureaucrats can predict the future better than speculators is considered unrealistic by most economists. The notion that economic fluctuations involve externalities will be discussed at length below, in connection with arguments about flexible versus fixed exchange rates.

Historically one of the most important uses of temporary tariffs has been as a complement to or substitute for monetary and fiscal policies aimed at the maintenance of full employment. During the Great Depression of the 1930s, almost all of the Western free enterprise economies did not know how or were unwilling to use monetary and fiscal policies with the intensity needed to attain full employment. Tariffs switched demand from foreign to domestic products and thus aided domestic employment.

During the 1930s countries learned that such policies tended to invite retaliation by trading partners, so that export sales were lost and there was corresponding unemployment. As a result, total world trade declined or failed to grow, and world welfare was decreased through foregone gains from trade and specialization. This experience of the 1930s has led to international agreements (to be discussed in the next chapter) which have outlawed the use of tariffs as an aid to employment. Fortunately, the Keynesian revolution in economic analysis after World War II has increased the ability of governments to maintain full employment more efficiently, with the help of monetary and fiscal policies. Therefore, the use of tariffs for this purpose is primarily of historic interest.

We conclude this section on motives for the use of tariffs based on the existence of uncertainty by discussing bargaining tariffs. As we shall show in the next chapter, historically there have been many bilateral and multinational efforts to reduce tariff barriers. Curiously enough, some nations have imposed tariffs or refused to lower some of them in order to put themselves in a stronger position to demand reciprocal concessions from trade partners. These policies fortunately have not been used after World War II. However, in 1971 the United States set a dangerous precedent when a "temporary" import tariff surcharge of 10 percent was imposed as part of a package of policies designed to alleviate persistent U.S.

172 International Economics

balance-of-payments deficits. We will discuss the cause and solution to these U.S. payments difficulties later, in Part Four. Here it is important only to note that this U.S. tariff increase was initiated for the express purpose of obtaining a tool for bargaining with other countries about exchange rate changes and other adjustment policies.

V. THE ARGUMENT FOR THE COMBINED USE OF TARIFFS AND SUBSIDIES

A review of the argument for tariff protection made in the preceding parts of this chapter reveals that, except in the case of the optimum tariff, the justification for protection arises from an alleged divergence between the free market price and social value of a good, as for example when the price of good does not reflect its value in defense, its cost of pollution, or its use as a revenue source. In the general equilibrium, two-commodity analytical framework, this condition has been shown by Jagdish Bhagwati, in a generalization of earlier work by Johnson and others, to involve the need to adjust the relative price applicable to either producers or consumers, never to both. Therefore, it is socially optimal to change the relative price of the two goods in the required manner only in the market in which the divergence between private and social values is found, and to leave the other market at the world price ratio. This enables producers or consumers to reap the benefits from international specialization and trade.

The argument can be put differently. If there is an inefficiency in the economy because of a divergence between private and social cost of production or consumption, then the efficient approach is to eliminate the cause of the distortion directly and not by the introduction of a further distortion involving the foreign trade sector.

These ideas can be presented more precisely with the help of Figures 8–3 and 8–4, which in all essentials repeat Figure 7–1. In Figure 8–3 the tariff is used to move production from P_0 to P_1, for example to increase the output of good X which has a social value during a war which is not reflected in its private price. The conventional and inefficient way is for consumers and producers to find equilibrium at the tariff-distorted domestic price, $DD' = D_1D_1'$. As we showed earlier, under these conditions welfare falls from I_0I_0' to I_1I_1'. The efficient solution is, however, to let consumers allocate their purchases on the basis of the world price ratio W_1W_1', enabling them to reach equilibrium at point C_2 and a welfare level indicated by the indifference curve I_2I_2'. As can be seen from Figure 8–3, being on I_2I_2' must always involve a smaller welfare loss than being on I_1I_1'. In practice the efficient solution can be attained by creation of the domestic price ratio D_1D_1', through a tariff on the importation of X, while at the same time a subsidy on X is paid on the domestic market for consumers to maintain the world price W_1W_1' for them.

FIGURE 8–3

Efficient Attainment of Desired Production Effect

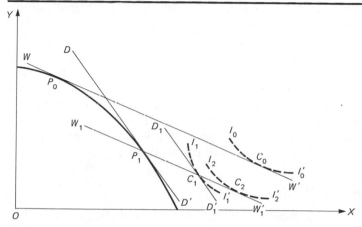

The socially desirable output point P_1 can be attained by the creation of a domestic price DD' different from the world price WW'. However, then it is better to permit consumption at the world price such as W_1W_1' and reach C_2 rather than to charge consumers the same price as producers and reach only the lower welfare point C_1.

FIGURE 8–4

Efficient Attainment of a Desired Consumption Effect

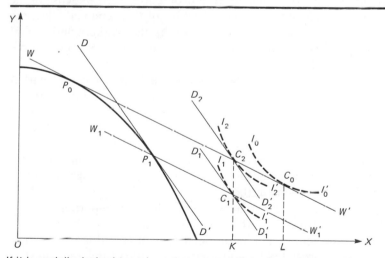

If it is socially desired to reduce the consumption of good X from OL to OK, it can be achieved either by establishing the same distorted domestic price for consumers and producers $(DD' = D_1D_1')$ and consuming at point C_1, or by permitting free trade to continue at the world price WW' and establishing a domestic price such as D_2D_2' to attain the desired consumption point C_2. The latter method achieves the same objective as the former, but at a lower cost of welfare.

The analysis of Figure 8–4 is strictly analogous to that of Figure 8–3 with the exception that the distortion assumed to exist requires a reduction in the consumption of X from OL to OK. With the conventional use of a tariff, this objective is achieved by creation of the domestic price, DD', and movement of production to P_1 and consumption to C_1. The efficient solution of the problem requires maintenance of the world price for domestic producers at WW' and production remaining at P_0. The imposition of an excise tax on good X is then used to establish the price $D_2D_2' = D_1D_1'$ for consumers and to move them to consumption point C_2 and welfare level I_2I_2'. From Figure 8–4 it is apparent that this solution must always permit a greater consumption of Y with the given consumption of OK units of X_1, so that it is superior to the use of a tariff.

VI. SUMMARY AND CONCLUSIONS

A review of the arguments for protection presented above reveals that, except for the optimum tariff argument, all are based on one of three false notions or a combination of the three.

First, the arguments may be based on a false conception of the real world, as in the case where it is believed that the free market cannot internalize the externalities of infant industries or that the net marginal social productivity of labor in industry is higher than in agriculture.

Second, the arguments may represent the self-interest of certain groups in the economy which would benefit from protection at the expense of the rest of the country. The most outstanding case of this type is the income redistribution argument, which has been used by the workers and capital owners of many industries threatened by dynamic losses of comparative advantage and rising imports.

Third, the arguments may involve the use of tariffs in correcting market failures (defense, pollution problems), taking account of elements in the country's social welfare function (public goods, income distribution), or dealing with economic uncertainty and instability (balance-of-payments deficits, bargaining). We have shown that in all of these cases, the objectives can be attained more efficiently by policies aimed at eliminating their cause directly through taxes or subsidies, rather than through the introduction of further distortions in the foreign sector.

As a result of these considerations we reach the very important conclusion that the case for free trade which was made in Part One of this book remains intact. The importance and social role of this doctrine of free trade can best be appreciated by considering the role of the economist in government. The former U.S. Secretary of the Treasury and of Labor George P. Shultz, an economist, compared the economic policy making of government with the task of sailing a ship. The ship's ultimate target is reached by following a compass setting. Economists using the principle of efficiency and its corollary, free trade, must constantly provide this compass setting for government policy makers. The arguments for protection presented in this chapter are used by politicians and their constituents to influence the direction the ship takes. Economic policy makers cannot ignore these political forces and must adjust their policies in the short run, much as a sailing ship must change course and tack to take advantage of winds if it is to reach its ultimate destination. However, the ship's compass and the economists' principles of efficiency assure that during these tacks and politically necessary deviations from the set course, sight is not lost of the final policy.

APPENDIX

Optimum Tariff Formula Derived

The optimum tariff (t) expressed as a function of the elasticity of the foreign offer curve (E_b) is

$$t = \frac{1}{E_b - 1} \qquad (8A\text{-}1)$$

and can be derived as follows.

Assuming that competition exists in factor and goods markets in Country A, the domestic price (d) is equal to the world price (W) plus the tariff:

$$d = W(1 + t) \qquad (8A\text{-}2)$$

which can be written as

$$t = \frac{d}{W} - 1 \qquad (8A\text{-}3)$$

In Figure 7A–1 we can see that the prices of Y in terms of X are

$$d = \frac{E_1 S}{LS} \qquad (8A\text{-}4)$$

$$W = \frac{E_1 S}{OS} \qquad (8A\text{-}5)$$

Substitution of 8A–4 and 8A–5 in 8A–3 yields

$$t = \frac{\dfrac{E_1 S}{LS}}{\dfrac{E_1 S}{OS}} - 1 \qquad (8A\text{-}6)$$

$$t = \frac{OS}{LS} - 1 = \frac{OS - LS}{LS} \qquad (8A\text{-}7)$$

But since $OS\text{-}LS$ in Figure 7A–1 is OL

$$t = \frac{OL}{LS} \qquad (8A\text{–}8)$$

The definition of the elasticity of country B's offer curve is

$$E_b = -\frac{\dfrac{dY}{Y}}{d\left(\dfrac{Y}{X}\right)\left(\dfrac{X}{Y}\right)} \qquad (8A\text{–}9)$$

remembering that X is B's export good and serves as the numeraire in its price definition of foreign demand, consistent with the definition employed in Equations 8A–4 and 8A–5. By simple rules of differentiation we can rewrite the denominator of 8A–9

$$\frac{d\left(\dfrac{Y}{X}\right)}{\dfrac{Y}{X}} = \frac{dX}{X} - \frac{dY}{Y} \qquad (8A\text{–}10)$$

and obtain

$$E_b = -\frac{\left(\dfrac{dY}{Y}\right)}{\dfrac{dX}{X} - \dfrac{dY}{Y}} \qquad (8A\text{–}11)$$

Let us simplify the right hand side of Equation 8A–11 by dividing numerator and denominator by $-dY/Y$:

$$E_b = \frac{1}{1 - \left(\dfrac{dX}{dY}\right)\left(\dfrac{Y}{X}\right)} \qquad (8A\text{–}12)$$

But we know from Figure 7A–1 that

$$\frac{dX}{dY} = \frac{LS}{E_1 S} \qquad (8A\text{–}13)$$

$$\frac{Y}{X} = \frac{E_1 S}{OS} \qquad (8A\text{–}14)$$

which can be substituted into Equation 8A–12:

$$E_b = \frac{1}{1 - \dfrac{LS}{OS}} \qquad (8A\text{–}15)$$

Writing $1 = (OL + LS)/(OL + LS)$ and $OS = OL + LS$ we get:

$$E_b = \cfrac{1}{\cfrac{OL + LS - LS}{OL + LS}} \tag{8A-16}$$

$$= \cfrac{1}{\cfrac{OL}{OL + LS}} = \frac{OL + LS}{OL} \tag{8A-17}$$

$$= 1 + \frac{LS}{OL} \tag{8A-18}$$

Therefore, by transposing 8A–18:

$$\frac{OL}{LS} = \frac{1}{E_b - 1} \tag{8A-19}$$

Which after substitution in equation 8A–8 becomes the optimum tariff equation

$$t = \frac{1}{E_b - 1} \tag{8A-1}$$

It is possible to check simply and intuitively on the correctness of this formula by considering the case where country B's offer curve is a straight line. In such a case country B is willing to exchange any quantities of X and Y at the given price, which we remember is the definition of an infinitely elastic demand curve. In terms of the preceding algebraic derivation the straight-line offer curve implies that the ratio LS/OS in equation 8A–15 in the limit approaches one so that the denominator becomes zero and the elasticity is infinity. Entering $E_b = \infty$ into Equation 8A–1, we find that the optimum tariff is 0, as it should be in the case where a country has no monopoly power and faces perfectly elastic demand curves.

On the Equivalence of Export and Import Tariffs

The purpose of this section of the Appendix to Chapter 8 is to show that there is an equivalence between tariffs on imports and exports. For this purpose consider Figure 8A–1, in which we show country A's free trade offer curve OA and tariff-distorted offer curve OA'. As discussed in Chapter 7, under free trade country A was willing to export ON of Y for NP of X, but with a tariff on the import good equal to PL, it is willing to sell ON of Y only if it obtains NL of X, PL of which is collected as tariff revenue. Thus PL/NP is the tariff rate in terms of the import good. Other points on the OA' offer curve are found by measuring the horizontal distance from the Y axis to the free trade offer curve and adding horizontally the value required to attain the constant import tariff ratio.

FIGURE 8A–1
Export and Import Tariffs

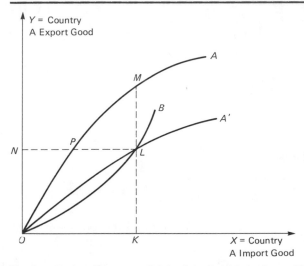

The free trade offer curve OA is distorted by the imposition of a 100 percent *import* tariff. As a result, the distances PL and NP are equal, and the ratio $PL/NP = 1$; PL is the import tariff revenue. Points other than L on OA' have been found by making equal the horizontal distances between the Y axis and OA on the one hand, and OA and OA' on the other. At point L the *export* tariff revenue is ML and the export tariff rate is ML/LK. The export tariff rate is different from the import tariff rate and, under the assumption that the distorted offer curve represents a constant import tariff rate, the export tariff rate varies over the entire length of the offer curve.

The government can also specify collection of the tariff revenue in terms of the export good. For example, point L on OA' is attained by specifying that, whereas under free trade country A was willing to surrender KM of its export good for OK of the import good, under protection it is willing to give up only KL of Y for the same amount of X. The tariff rate is MB/LK. In an analogous manner, equivalent export tariff rates can be found for all points on OA', which was drawn for a constant import tariff rate. However, along this OA' offer curve the export tariff rate is not a constant, since equality of the ratio of import duty over free trade imports does not assure equality of the ratio of the export duty over exports at all points of the offer curve.

The Metzler Case

In this section of the Appendix to Chapter 8 we present the conditions under which the imposition of a tariff lowers the income of the factor of production used intensively by the product protected by a tariff. This condition can arise only if the relative *domestic* price of the imported product is lowered by the tariff. To study this possibility, first consider the "normal" case shown in the left panel of Figure 8A–2.

Under free trade equilibrium at E, the domestic and world price ratio is

FIGURE 8A–2
The Metzler Case

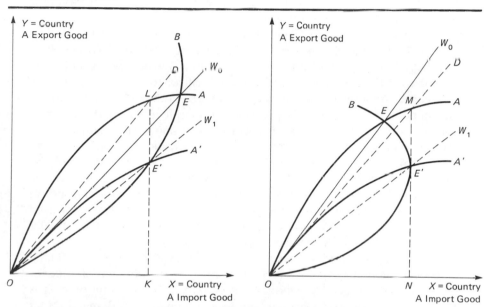

The left panel shows the "normal" effect of an export tariff on good Y; the world price of X falls from OW_0 to OW_1, but the domestic price rises. Under these conditions output of X goes up and the factor demanded intensively in the production of X enjoys an increase in pay. The right panel shows a case where the imposition of an export tariff causes both the domestic and foreign prices of X to fall, causing a contraction of the output of X and a drop in the income of the factor of production used intensively. In this, the Metzler case, the Stolper-Samuelson theorem does not hold.

OW_0. The imposition of an export tariff shrinks country A's offer curve from A to A' equiproportionately toward the horizontal axis, such that at any vertical line, such as KL, the ratio $LE'/E'K$, which is the tariff rate, is a constant. Under protection, the world price is OW_1, at which OK of good X is imported in return for the export of $E'K$ of good Y. Upon transacting their foreign business, the domestic producers of good Y must surrender LE' of good Y to the government as the tariff, which the government distributes as a "public good." As a result, the domestic price ratio under protection is OD, or LK/OK. As can readily be seen from the left panel of Figure 8A–2, after the tariff is in effect at the *world* price a given amount of the import good can be purchased for less of the export good than under free trade, but at the *domestic* price the given amount of the import good can be obtained only through the exchange of more of the export good than under free trade. In other words, protection has raised the domestic relative price of the import good, induced increased domestic production, and raised demand for, and the price, of the factor of production used intensively in the manufacture of good X. This is the normal Stolper-Samuelson result presented above in the text. If X is labor intensive, the tariff raises the income of labor.

Now consider the right panel of Figure 8A–2, which in all essentials repeats the left panel. The crucial difference between the two panels is that the right one has an offer curve for country B which shows an inelastic part over the segment affected by the tariff distortion of country A's offer curve. As a result, the new equilibrium E' in the right panel is to the right of point E, whereas in the preceeding example E' was to the left of E. For our purposes of analysis, this fact has the important result that the imposition of the tariff has lowered both the domestic (OD) and the world prices (OW_1) relative to the free trade price ratio (OW_0), as can readily be seen from an inspection of the right panel of Figure 8A–2. Under the conditions of a lowered domestic relative price for the import good X, output of X is decreased, and the demand for and price of the factor used intensively in the production of good X decreases. This is the Metzler case, and the Stolper-Samuelson theorem does not hold.

Intuitively, this result comes about when the price elasticity of demand for good Y in country B is low so that in spite of the higher world price for Y, demand is reduced by only a small quantity. At the same time, it is necessary that country A have a high income elasticity of demand for its own export good Y. Since the tariff increases income in country A, world and domestic demand for good Y may be increased relative to that for good X by so much that the relative price of good Y rises domestically, whereas under "normal" conditions it would fall.

BIBLIOGRAPHICAL NOTES

A thorough review of the literature with references to the subject of this chapter is found in Corden (1974). The determinants of tariff structures have been studied by Pincus (1975) and Cheh (1974). The classics on the optimum tariff literature are Scitovsky (1941–42) and Graaf (1957), ch. 9. The reference to the tariff retaliation analysis is Johnson (1953–54).

A traditional exposition of the infant-industry argument for protection, with further references to earlier literature, can be found in Grubel (1967a). Two original formulations of the infant-industry argument are List (1904) and Hagen (1958). The argument employing the Coase (1966) model is in Johnson (1970a). The social welfare arguments about income effects are in Stolper and Samuelson (1941) and elaborated on in Metzler (1949). The empirical importance of the revenue tariff is found in Lewis (1963). Johnson (1965a) presents the case for industry as a consumption good. The argument that it is optimal to correct distortions directly was first set out incisively by Johnson (1965b) and generalized elegantly by Bhagwati (1971a).

CONCEPTS FOR REVIEW

Optimum tariff

Optimum export tax

Infant-industry argument tor protection

Learning by doing

Coase theorem

Labor-surplus economy

Stolper-Samuelson theorem

Metzler effect

Revenue tariff

Tariff and subsidy argument for efficiency

POINTS FOR FURTHER STUDY AND DISCUSSION

1. Give and explain a list of characteristics of industries which, in your view, increase the probability that an industry receives a high level of tariff protection. How does your list compare with those of Cheh and Pincus?

2. Consult international trade statistics to discover products or industries in which one country or a small group of countries has an export monopoly. Are these goods or industries candidates for export taxes?

3. Assume that a country has identified a genuine infant industry which, if protected for a period, would yield long-run benefits to the country. Now argue the case against a tariff for the industry and in favor of a subsidy. Distinguish the case of a subsidy to the producers and to labor.

4. Analyze the economic effects of a tariff on an industry producing a revenue which is always used to pay a subsidy to producers in that same industry.

5. Find out the cases where major industrial countries since 1960 have used general tariffs or quotas on a temporary basis. What were their alleged motives? For how long have these general tariffs and quotas been in effect, on average?

6. Discuss the use of the tariff cum subsidy principle in the case where a country suffers from domestic distortions simultaneously in production and consumption.

9 The History, Future, and Cost of Protection

ACCORDING TO ECONOMIC ANALYSIS, as we noted in the preceding chapter, there remains a strong case for free international trade, in spite of the many sophisticated arguments for protection used in the past. In Section I of this chapter we present a brief history of the struggle for free trade, showing how the powerful, noneconomic forces of liberalism, nationalism, and international cooperation have produced cycles of protectionism and free trade. In this discussion we cannot draw on formal models, and most of our analysis will be descriptive and suggestive rather than providing causal explanations.

In Section II we analyze the nature of a few of the most important issues which have arisen in past movements towards free trade and which continue to haunt present efforts to reduce protectionism. We conclude this chapter with a review of some studies of the cost of protection in recent years and attempt to provide an answer to the question of why countries do not adopt free trade unilaterally.

I. A SKETCH OF HISTORIC TRENDS

Western Europe emerged from the Middle Ages dominated by despotic monarchs who used their sovereign power to regulate foreign trade. Their aim was to create favorable balances of payments and accumulate gold for their own treasuries and supposedly to ensure the well-being of their people. This policy, known as mercantilism, and the absolute monarchs who promulgated it came under attack in the 18th and 19th centuries from the rising middle class and its articulate spokesmen like the liberal philosopher John Locke and economists like Adam Smith and David Hume.

The cornerstone of liberal philosophy was freedom of the individual, and for liberal economists it was laissez-faire in domestic and foreign economic affairs. In the first half of the 19th century, as Great Britain industrialized rapidly, it adhered to this liberal philosophy in domestic affairs. World trade also grew substantially and became relatively free from government interference.

However, during the last third of the 19th century, this movement toward free trade began to be reversed, as two other ambitious nations, Germany and the United States, attempted to develop their own industries and imposed infant-industry tariffs. Other smaller countries followed, and fierce competition for world export markets developed. Protection of home markets through tariffs became an accepted practice. Accompanying these economic trends was a growing militant nationalism which culminated in World War I. After this war, attempts were made to return the world to the era of 19th-century liberalism, but in the face of a number of economic difficulties besetting the major countries during the 1920s (such as Britain's balance-of-payments-deficits and unemployment and Germany's overwhelming burden of war reparation payments), economic nationalism again dominated, and trade restrictions continued to grow. In the United States protectionism reached its peak with the passage of the Smoot-Hawley Act in 1930, under which the average duty on imports reached 53 percent.

The unemployment and economic chaos of the Great Depression, starting in 1930, led to a fundamental change in U.S. attitudes toward free trade. Under the leadership of President Franklin D. Roosevelt, the Trade Agreements Act of 1934 was passed. This act withdrew direct tariff-making authority from the highly partisan and political arena of Congress and gave it to the President. He was authorized to cut tariffs up to 50 percent below the rates set under the Smoot-Hawley Act. The basic principle guiding actual tariff cuts was bilateral reciprocity of concessions. According to this principle, the United States negotiated cuts in the tariffs of a given country and the United States only on commodities that were important in the bilateral trade of the two countries and represented balanced trade. In order to avoid the administrative nightmares and inefficiencies of having many different tariff rates on every imported good, according to national origin, the bilaterally agreed-upon tariff cuts were then applied to all trading partners. The use of only the lowest tariff rate for all countries was pushed strongly by Roosevelt's Secretary of State Cordell Hull, and this became known as the most-favored-nation principle of tariff setting.

By 1940 the United States had concluded bilateral tariff agreements with 20 countries. However, the bilateral approach, combined with the most-favored-nation principle, suffered from the defect that for most commodities there were many free-loader countries which benefitted from the lower tariffs negotiated between the United States and its trading partners. Consequently, bilateral negotiators faced the dilemma of limiting cuts to the few commodities that typically dominated bilateral trade, or cutting tariffs on a wider range of goods, which permitted increased imports from third countries from which no corresponding concessions were received. The way out of this dilemma was the substitution of multilateral for bilateral tariff-bargaining sessions.

Even while World War II hostilities were still being pursued, diplomatic efforts were underway to create an efficient international machinery for the reconstruction and liberalization of the international economic system. The outcome of these attempts in the field of international trade was the establishment of an organization known as the General Agreement on Tariff and Trade (GATT), headquartered in Geneva, Switzerland. In this agreement practically all market economies committed themselves to abide by rules which ended or restricted severely two of the most costly and undesirable features of the protectionist period before the war, the use of trade controls which discriminated among nations and the use of quotas. Furthermore, the agreement provided a system for arbitrating commercial disputes among nations and created a forum for a number of multilateral negotiations for the reduction of tariff barriers. The provisions against discrimination and for multilateral negotiations were the cornerstone of the U.S. position in the conference leading to GATT. They had evolved as the main principles of U.S. foreign trade policy after the passage of the Trade Agreements Act of 1934.

In the postwar years, GATT was a great success. Most nations adopted the most-favored nation principle in setting tariffs, and quotas were largely replaced by tariffs. Few commercial disputes had to be settled through GATT intermediation, probably because Geneva provided a ready and continuous forum for consultation and the exchange of information. Most significant, however, were the successes achieved in multilateral negotiations for tariff cuts in 1947, 1949, 1951, 1956, 1962, and 1967. The proportion of U.S. imports subject to reductions and the trade-weighted average cuts were highest at the initial conference in 1947 and in 1967—the proportions subject to cuts was 44 and 67 percent of all dutiable imports, respectively, in those years, and in both instances the cuts averaged 35 percent. During this period the real protective effect of the U.S. tariff system declined further, since a significant proportion of U.S. tariffs are specific rates, expressed as a certain number of dollars per unit of an imported item, and inflation automatically decreased the ad valorem rates on these commodities. As a result of negotiated reductions and inflation, U.S. rates dropped from a high average of 46.7 percent in 1934 to about 12 percent in 1962.

This record of U.S. tariff reductions in the postwar years up to 1962 was similar to that of all other major industrial countries. However, the record was marred by the existence of an escape-clause provision in the U.S. Trade Agreements Act, under which the U.S. President was granted special authority to enter GATT negotiations. According to this escape clause, a U.S. industry which believed that it had been injured by foreign competition as a result of tariff concessions made under the agreement had the right to petition the U.S. Tariff Commission for relief. If such injury was found to have taken place, the President could rescind the tariff-lowering commitment made by treaty.

The concept of "injury" was interpreted as having taken place when foreign imports as a share of U.S. consumption of a particular good rose. This provision was more controversial in principle than it was important in practice. Between 1948 and 1962 the U.S. Tariff Commission investigated 113 alleged cases of injury and recommended relief in 41. The President rescinded tariff concessions in only 15 of these cases. At the same time, such nontariff barriers as the "Buy American" act and the national defense amendment to the Trade Agreements Act provided protection for domestic producers selling to the U.S. government and those involved in the manufacture of defense-related goods.

In order to remove the major shortcomings of postwar U.S. trade policy, in 1962, under the leadership of President John F. Kennedy, the Trade Expansion Act was passed. It had several new features, the most important of which are as follows. First, it permitted across-the-board tariff reductions, replacing the tedious commodity-by-commodity negotiations that had characterized earlier rounds. Second, the concept of injury was redefined to make it more difficult for the U.S. Tariff Commission to find in favor of an industry. Third, the President was not obliged to grant tariff protection to an industry which the Tariff Commission had found injured.

Fourth, and from the economist's point of view most significant, the act provided for adjustment assistance to firms or workers injured by imports due to tariff reductions. This policy explicitly recognized the fact that the *imposition* of a tariff may lead to higher profits in the protected industry. If it does, the owners of assets in the industry enjoy a once-and-for-all increase in the market value of their assets; subsequent buyers of these assets earn only normal profits. Now when the government *reduces* tariffs and profits in the industry fall, current owners, for analogous reasons, suffer a loss in the value of their assets. Tariffs have similar effects on the human capital value of some workers in an industry. Because the capital losses of owners and workers in these situations are caused by deliberate and unavoidable government actions, in the name of overall public welfare, economists believe that it is appropriate that the general public, through the government, pay compensation to those who lose from the tariff reduction.

The tariff negotiations based on the 1962 Trade Expansion Act, known as the Kennedy round, were completed in 1967 after the President's death. They succeeded in reducing tariffs to such low levels among the major industrial market economies that their economic effect now is very small. The very success of these rounds of mutual tariff reductions has brought into prominence the importance of other trade barriers, such as the border tax adjustments and health and safety regulations discussed in Chapter 7. Consequently, the Nixon round of GATT negotiations in 1974 was concerned primarily with the removal of these nontariff barriers to trade.

The postwar record of trade liberalization was marred not only by U.S. policies such as the operation of the escape clauses and the Buy American act, but also by the policies of some of the European countries. In 1958 Belgium, France, Germany, Italy, and the Netherlands formed the European Economic Community (EEC), one of the main features of which was the ultimate complete removal of all barriers for trade within the community, while a common tariff schedule was put into effect for trade with the rest of the world. The EEC also adopted a very protectionist policy toward agricultural products which, except in some feed grains and tropical products, assured European autarchy. Former French colonies in Africa were given discriminatory low tariffs or free trade access to the entire EEC market. In our analysis of problems of economic development and foreign trade in Part One of this book, we discussed the heavy use of tariffs and other trade barriers by the developing countries of the world.

In spite of these remaining trade restrictions in the world, however, the record of liberalization since the depression of the 1930s has been very substantial. This same period of history has been characterized by rapid and sustained increases in per capita incomes in the industrial countries and, as we showed in Chapter 6, by dramatic growth in international trade. In modern history, therefore, the two periods of most sustained and significant growth in world income and trade, the mid-19th century and the postdepression era, also were periods of movement toward free trade. The theoretical models we have presented above suggest strongly that the freeing of international trade is likely to have contributed importantly to this world prosperity.

II. CONTINUING ISSUES IN TRADE LIBERALIZATION

One of the most important principles underlying the trade liberalization efforts under GATT in the postwar era has been nondiscrimination of tariffs in the form of the most-favored-nation principle. This principle has come under attack, with charges that it in fact discriminates against developing countries and it is violated by economic integration agreements.

Discrimination against Developing Countries

The developing countries have argued that in the multilateral trade negotiations under GATT, the developed countries chose to cut tariffs only on items that were important in trade among themselves. They left significant barriers on the products that have been the traditional exports of the developing countries, such as agricultural products and simple manufactures, most notably textiles. There is some merit to these arguments, in support of which we can cite a specific clause of the 1962 U.S. Trade Expansion Act. Under this act the U.S. President was authorized to *eliminate* duties on any category of goods in which the EEC and the United States together accounted for 80 percent or more of world trade, while tariffs on all other goods could be cut to a maximum of 50 percent only. The Kennedy round thus in principle could have led to unrestricted EEC-U.S. trade in a number of important, high-technology goods, while it would have retained barriers on trade in important export goods of the developing countries.

This de facto discrimination inherent in the GATT approach to trade liberalization and some other problems of the international economic system to be discussed below led the developing countries in 1964 to form their own association, known as the United Nations Conference on Trade and Development (UNCTAD), which is located with a staff of 200 in Geneva. As the name implies, this conference took place under the auspices of the United Nations, which the developing countries consider to be one of their most important forums for the discussion of matters concerning their interest. The first UNCTAD report was published in 1964, and it was followed by several other conferences and reports thereafter.

One of the main demands of the UNCTAD conferences has been for preferential and unilateral tariff concessions by the industrial countries on exports of simple manufactures and consumer goods from the developing countries. In the views of the developing countries, such preferences would correct the de facto discrimination inherent in the GATT trade liberalization moves. It was argued that the preferences would be temporary, lasting only until industry in the developing countries had grown sufficiently. The resemblance of this reasoning to the infant-industry argument presented in Chapter 8 is apparent. But preferences have another important implication. Economic analysis suggests that they would have the effect of transferring to the developing countries all of the tariff revenue otherwise collected by the industrial countries. This is so because the domestic price of textiles in the United States, for example, would remain at the world price, plus the tariff. The developing countries' imports into the United States would sell at marginally below that domestic price, and the difference between the domestic and world price would accrue to the developing countries' producers, in the form of extra profits or rent to factors of production.

The proposal for preferences had great appeal to the developing countries, which expected them to assist their development efforts and to lead to a transfer of resources free from the odium and alleged strings attached to the foreign aid grants of industrial nations. The slogan "Trade, not Aid" summarized well the attitudes of the developing countries on this issue. The industrial countries were generally sympathetic toward the demand for preferences, but domestic political problems prevented them from making any really major concessions. For example, the threat to the prosperity or even the existence of the U.S. textile industry which results from free trade is not altered, and the domestic political implications are not changed by virtue of the arguments about equity and efficiency made by UNCTAD. Australia has granted tariff preferences on a list of goods imported from the developing countries which is larger than that of any other industrial nation. However, as Peter J. Lloyd of the Australian National University has shown, these preferences apply only to carefully selected goods for which no close domestic substitutes are being produced and which therefore do not threaten any Australian industries.

Regional Trade Associations

The formation of the EEC, as noted above, had as major provisions the removal of all tariffs on trade within the community and an equalization of all tariffs toward the rest of the world. Similar provisions were made by the Central American Common Market (CACM) founded in 1963, which consists of Costa Rica, El Salvadore, Guatemala, Honduras, Nicaragua, and Panama. The European Free Trade Association (EFTA), created in 1959 and consisting of Austria, Denmark, Great Britain, Norway, Portugal, Sweden, and Switzerland, and the Latin American Free Trade Association (LAFTA), created in 1961 and consisting of Argentina, Brazil, Chile, Colombia, Ecuador, Mexico, Paraguay, Peru, Uruguay, and Venezuela also have as their goals the removal of tariffs on trade among association members. While common-market countries harmonize external tariffs, the free trade association members retain their own tariffs for trade with the rest of the world.

These important efforts towards regional free trade are clearly in violation of the most-favored-nation principle for tariff setting, since they involve different rates for members than for nonmembers. However, the policies have never been challenged officially before GATT by any injured member. The United States, which probably has suffered most from the discriminatory effects of regional trade associations, did not protest the formation of the EEC in this manner because the development of a strong and united Western Europe has been the target of U.S. foreign policy since the end of World War II, for political and military reasons considered to be worth some economic costs. The Latin American association and market promised to strengthen their members' economies and aid their development, which also was a U.S. policy objective whose attainment was worth some cost to the United States.

While the discriminatory policies of regional trade associations have never been the subject of official complaints lodged with GATT, they have been and continue to be discussed in bilateral negotiations, especially between the EEC and the United States. In these negotiations other matters of mutual interest are discussed continuously, such as exchange rate policies, military alliances, and capital flows, so that we can presume that the costs of tariff discrimination have been settled in the overall process of political bargaining on all of these matters.

The discriminatory trade concessions discussed above are just one element of the larger process of economic integration, the nature of which will be treated with greater analytical rigor in the final part of this book.

Agriculture

From the very beginning of multilateral efforts directed toward trade liberalization, agriculture has been granted a special status and generally has been exempted from tariff cuts. There are two reasons for this special status of agriculture. First, historically, in democratic Western countries, regional election districts were determined when the population was predominantly rural. The migration into cities and decline in relative rural population density has not been accompanied by completely corresponding changes in voting districts. Thus agricultural districts have been left with disproportionate power in legislatures, which they have used to assure protection of agriculture from foreign competition.

Second, historically, in times of war, self-sufficiency in food has been crucial for national survival. This defense argument for the protection of agriculture has undoubtedly helped rural legislators to attain passage of protectionist laws which have also served the interests of their constituents.

The protection of agriculture has led to self-sufficiency in nearly all nontropical basic food products in the EEC and the United States. It has thus prevented the development of international specialization, which probably would have resulted in large food exports to Europe from the United States, Canada, and a number of developing countries.

The protection of agriculture has a particular difficulty not common to other industries. In the EEC and the United States, domestic price support programs high enough to maintain agricultural incomes at the politically desired levels during the 1950s and 1960s have caused the accumulation of vast stocks of wheat, feed grains, powdered milk, eggs, cheese, butter, meat, and so on. To dispose of stocks of these commodities, they were frequently donated to developing countries as foreign aid, ruining what under free trade might have been the export markets of countries with a comparative advantage in the production of agricultural products. As we discussed above in connection with the role of international trade in development, a number of the countries that have lost export markets in this manner probably were developing countries themselves. Developing countries in tropical regions were hurt further by the practices of some of the developed countries which taxed heavily the consumption of tropical fruits and beverages such as cocoa and coffee, since they were considered to be luxury goods and competitive substitutes for some domestic fruits and beverages of agricultural origin.

The problem of agricultural protectionism may well disappear in the 1980s and thereafter, as the predicted rapid growth of world population and income will result in excess demand for food and, as a result of higher product prices, high levels of incomes of the rural population in industrial countries.

Miscellaneous Issues

Several of the problems which haunted efforts for trade liberalization in the past are likely to continue in the future. Escape clauses could come into frequent use if and when major economic crises such as a deep recession or depression overcome the world. Nontariff barriers to trade are likely to increase as consumerism and concerns about ecology and pollution lead to a proliferation of pollution-, health-, and safety-standard legislation by national governments. A renewal of the Cold War or the development of new military rivalries can bring forth defense tariffs.

A new problem of the future may be the exploitation of monopsony power by countries or groups of countries which are major suppliers of key raw materials or industrial products. The oil embargo of 1973–74 imposed by the Arab countries and the resultant increase in petroleum prices and export revenues of oil-producing nations may be the model for action by producers of copper, natural rubber, aluminum, zinc, and many other products. It is difficult to know how strong monopsonies in these products can become and how elastic the world demand for them, and therefore the scope for the raising of prices, is. However, it is not inconceivable that new initiatives for multilateral agreements will be necessary to prevent the world from sliding back into an international economic system which is dominated by nationalist policies detrimental to world welfare as a whole.

III. THE COST OF PROTECTION AND ARGUMENTS AGAINST UNILATERAL FREE TRADE POLICIES

After our discussion of the history of protection and of the most important remaining issues, it seems safe to conclude that in all likelihood national protective policies will continue to impede international trade in the future. If the past is a guide for the future, we may well find that the strength and intensity of protectionism will go in cycles, much as it did during the past 200 years analyzed above. From this perspective of history and our understanding of the principles of gains from trade, two questions suggest themselves. First, how costly in terms of welfare are current levels of protection, and therefore how important is it to continue to press for further trade liberalization? Second, since most of the difficulties in free trade movements appear to arise from the need to reach agreement on mutual concessions, why don't countries move to free trade unilaterally, and thus achieve the kinds of gains in welfare which our theoretical analysis suggests they can attain? We will attempt to answer these two questions.

The Cost of Protection

Attempts to measure the cost of protection are of recent origin and involve a large number of simplifying assumptions, many of which are of questionable validity. We can discuss here only the general approach to the measurement problems and present the results.

The major and most innovative measurement of the cost of protection has been undertaken by Harry G. Johnson for the United Kingdom and by Robert Stern of the University of Michigan and Georgio Basevi of the Catholic University of Louvain for the United States. All of these studies are based on the model of the partial equilibrium effects of tariffs discussed above in connection with Figure 7–3, and all involve measurement of the size of the triangles of consumer and producer surplus. Recall from the analysis of Figure 7–3 that for the measurement of the size of these triangles we need information on prices and quantities of a good produced, consumed, and imported under free trade and under protection. In the real world we can observe directly only data relating to the state of protection, such as data on the domestic price, production, and imports. However, we also know the tariff rate, and therefore we can infer the world price under the normal assumption that it is competitively determined and differs from the domestic price by the value of the tariff. In terms of Figure 7–3, therefore, we know the size of the vertical part of the two triangles from the domestic price and tariff rate, and we know the distances of the triangles from the origin as represented by domestic consumption and production. The most difficult information to obtain is the slopes or elasticities of the demand and supply curves, from which it is possible to estimate the changes in consumption and production—that is, the horizontal base of the triangle, induced by the tariff.

Studies of the cost of protection have handled the problem of elasticities in two different ways. The first involves assuming "plausible" values for the elasticities, drawing on knowledge compiled in specialized econometric studies of elasticities. This approach lends itself well for estimates based on very aggregate trade statistics. It provides ranges of cost and insights into the sensitivity of the results to the assumptions about the elasticities. The second way requires researchers to make their own estimates of elasticities for disaggregated import classes.

The results of both approaches have been that the welfare costs of protection in industrialized countries have a dollar-value equivalent of 0.05 to 0.1 percent of U.S. gross national product (GNP). At the end of 1970, when GNP was about $1,000 billion per year, the welfare cost of protection, according to these estimates, therefore would have been equal to between $0.5 billion and $1 billion.

Basevi (1968) introduced two important refinements into the calculation of costs of protection. First, he estimated the net protective effect of the entire U.S. tariff *structure,* giving explicit recognition to the fact that tariffs on inputs have the effect of reducing the protection of processes afforded by tariffs on final goods alone, as we noted in Chapter 7 above. For this purpose he used the concept of a uniform tariff equivalent first developed by W. M. Corden, calculating what uniform tariff on all imports would have the same restrictive effect as the existing U.S. structure on final and intermediate input goods. It turned out that the U.S. uniform tariff equivalent in 1960 was higher than the trade-weighted mean of all nominal tariffs used in other studies not concerned with tariff structure. Second, Basevi took account of the general equilibrium repercussion of unilateral tariff removals, which, according to our analysis of the optimum tariff, should cause a deterioration of the terms of trade of a country as large as the United States. The results of Basevi's estimates did not differ significantly from those derived by others. While he found somewhat greater efficiency losses by the imposition of U.S. tariffs in the form of the triangles of producer and consumer surplus, he also found that these losses were offset by the improvements in the terms of trade enjoyed by the United States through the imposition of the tariffs. It appears to be quite clear, from all of the studies of the cost of protection which used the basic approach sketched above, that refinements of the estimates by disaggregation, better data on elasticities, or the introduction of general equilibrium effects will have little effect on the results. Even if cost estimates were to more than double, they would still come to less than 1 percent of GNP.

Most economists, when confronted with the results of these empirical studies of the cost of protection, find the estimates disturbingly low in the light of the theoretical analysis of the gains from trade and the manner in which, typically, the graphs representing these ideas are drawn. According to these estimates, the case for free trade, however powerful it may be theoretically, apparently is not very strong in the real world. As a result, governments ought to be more willing to give in to interest groups demanding protection from foreign competition, for any of the reasons discussed in Chapter 8. How then can we reconcile these findings of low cost of tariffs with the notion that international trade affects our welfare importantly, a notion which many people hold, as a result of personal experiences as the consumers of wide ranges of imported goods and as students of the theory of international trade? There are a number of answers to this question.

First, we can consider whether the $1 billion welfare effect for the United States in 1970 really is a small one. For this purpose we should remember that this is a flow effect, repeated and growing every year, along with GNP. In an absolute sense $1 billion is such a large sum that its magnitude is difficult to comprehend by standards of personal finance and income. It is small only as a percentage of GNP, but then any one government policy or natural or man-made catastrophe, such as a flood or strike, is known to have only a very small effect on the GNP of a large, modern industrial country such as the United States.

Second, as we showed in Chapter 6, the United States differs from the rest of the world significantly by having only a very small segment of her economy dependent on foreign trade. The U.S. markets are large enough to permit exploitation of the gains possible from specializing in production and from having regional rather than international trade. For this reason we would expect much larger costs of protection for smaller countries, though actual empirical evidence in the tradition of the studies discussed above is not available for smaller countries.

Third, the studies of the cost of protection neglect the effects of non-tariff barriers to trade. When we discussed the nature of these nontariff barriers in Chapter 7, we mentioned that in the views of some experts in the 1970s they may restrict trade more than the remaining tariffs.

Fourth, the studies neglect such costs as those for administering tariffs, which consist of public expenditures for customs officers and the guarding of borders and, what is often forgotten by governments, the private costs business and individuals incur in filling out customs declarations and suffering through border control efforts. While these administrative costs are not in the pure model of the gains from trade and can therefore not be used to explain the empirical findings of low costs of protection in terms of this model, we should realistically include them in a more general assessment of the overall welfare cost of government intervention in free trade.

Fifth, the model underlying the studies is unrealistic in ways stressed by our analysis of the intraindustry trade phenomenon in Chapter 4. As we argued there, in modern market economies most major consumer- and capital-good industries are characterized by the existence of product differentiation, whereby each product is subject to scale economies in production due to the length of runs. Given the pattern of product differentiation, the industry supply curve is upward sloping, as is assumed in the cost-of-protection studies. However, according to the intraindustry trade model, lowering of tariffs leads not only to a movement along these industry supply curves but also to downward shifts, because free trade causes product differentiation patterns to change and the particular length-of-run economies of scale to be exploited. The traditional model underlying the estimates of the cost of protection does not take account of these changes in national patterns of product differentiation and the resultant scale economies and downward shifts in aggregate industry supply curves, thus leading to an underestimate of the gains from free trade.

Sixth, the theoretical model underlying the estimates of the cost of protection essentially involves comparative static analysis. As we discussed in Chapter 5 in connection with the issue of the role of international trade in economic development, many economists believe that significant welfare gains from foreign trade are associated with dynamic processes outside the conventional comparative static analytical framework. Thus, foreign trade introduces powerful competition into the economy, which increases the efficiency of firms in production and distribution and forces them to adopt the best technology and to produce the best goods. Furthermore, contact with foreign competition is likely to lead to capital inflows and outflows and to make it possible to reap benefits from domestic and foreign production of knowledge capital brought along by direct foreign investment, as we shall discuss in greater detail in Part Five.

The preceding six answers to the question of how we might reconcile the inconsistency between our theoretical prediction and empirical findings about the cost of protection are logically rigorous but impossible to evaluate with precision. However, in total, these six points make a rather convincing case that the empirical studies of the cost of protection involving the measurement of producer and consumer surplus triangles have resulted in serious underestimates of the real cost of protection. We conclude, therefore, that it remains in the public interest to continue to pursue vigorously the ideal of free international trade.

Why Not Unilateral Free Trade Policies?

Our review of the history of protection has shown that countries generally have been willing to lower their tariff barriers only if other countries were willing to make reciprocal concessions. Yet, our analysis of the gains from trade has never involved the need to make an assumption about the behavior of trading partners. The gains from trade accrue to any one country willing to enter the world market. In the light of the difficulties encountered in negotiating international agreements on mutual trade liberalization, the question arises why countries do not engage unilaterally in tariff reductions, in order to obtain the benefits from international specialization and trade for themselves. There are a number of answers to this question.

First, a large country, through a unilateral tariff reduction, is likely to experience a deterioration in its terms of trade, for reasons explained in Chapters 7 and 8. Most countries of the world are too small for this argument to apply to them. But even for large countries we need to weigh the terms-of-trade effects against the efficiency losses. As Basevi showed in the study mentioned above, for the United States the elimination of all tariffs would lead to a net welfare gain, because the positive efficiency effect exceeds the negative terms-of-trade effect.

In popular arguments over tariff reduction, the ideas about adverse terms-of-trade effects tend to be posed in somewhat simpler terms. For example, the argument might be that the original imposition of the tariff involved a gain to the domestic country at the expense of the rest of the world, since domestic interests proposed the tariff and foreigners generally opposed it. Therefore, it must follow that reducing the tariff gives up something to the rest of the world for which compensation is due. This popular argument may be interpreted as the more sophisticated terms-of-trade argument.

Second, the benefits of trade liberalization accrue to society as a whole, but the burden of adjustment to free trade falls upon a clearly identifiable group of workers and owners of capital. The interests injured by trade liberalization tend to be organized and to be well represented in the legislatures of market economies by lobbyists and by their elected representatives. Generally, the political theory of democracy suggests that lobbyists and legislators cannot consistently and successfully pursue the interests of their clients against those of the general public unless they have a good case on grounds of efficiency or equity. As we mentioned above in connection with the need for adjustment assistance, the workers and owners of capital in an industry under protection typically earn only normal rates of return, since all of the rent due to the tariff accrued to workers and owners at the time the tariff was imposed. Consequently, the workers and owners of capital in an industry whose tariffs are reduced tend to suffer losses of wealth and income purely as a result of the government's actions, and the government is responsible for an inequity. This serves as the basis of the arguments made by the injured parties' lobbyists and representatives, who tend to be successful unless there is public adjustment assistance, or political bargaining leads to compensation.

No country has developed a program of adjustment assistance for victims of unilateral trade liberalization policies, and in most countries the political bargaining process on large and wide-ranging programs of tariff reductions works only imperfectly. For these reasons potential victims of trade liberalization have historically been able to block major unilateral tariff reduction programs.

Third, as we shall discuss in Part Four of this book, under the system of the fixed exchange rates which has characterized the international monetary system until 1973, unilateral tariff reductions tend to lead to balance-of-payments deficits, losses of reserves, and the need to make socially costly adjustments. Under reciprocal tariff reductions, these adjustment costs can be avoided.

Summary and Conclusions

We have discussed in this section the estimates of the cost of protection made on the basis of the partial equilibrium model and involving the concepts of consumer and producer surplus. These estimates of the cost of protection have been low and have contradicted the notion developed earlier that gains from free trade are important. We gave a number of reasons why these estimates may have a downward bias and concluded that there remains a strong case for free trade.

The analysis of reasons why countries do not move unilaterally to remove their trade barriers and enjoy the gains from trade involved terms-of-trade effects, considerations of equity for the interests injured by tariff reductions, and balance-of-payments adjustment costs. All of these reasons are valid, and they point to the need for programs of public education about the gains from trade, for programs of public compensation for interests injured by trade liberalization, and for greater flexibility of exchange rates and other policies designed to reduce adjustment costs. Without these policies it has been impossible in the past to achieve unilateral tariff reductions in Western market economies, and there is little hope that it will be possible to do so in the future.

BIBLIOGRAPHICAL NOTES

On past and current problems of commercial policy, see Curzon (1965, 1971). Meier (1973) reprints and analyses key documents relating to commercial policy issues. The U.S. Commission on International Trade and Investment Policy, the Williams Commission Report (1971) contains a collection of essays which consider the options and problems of future U.S. foreign economic policies.

The large literature on estimates of the cost of protection is reviewed by Corden (1975), who also provides an extensive set of references. The works mentioned in the text are Lloyd (1971) on preferences, Johnson (1958a), Stern (1964), and Basevi (1968) on the cost of protection.

CONCEPTS FOR REVIEW

Mercantilism

Most-favored-nation principle

Multilateral negotiations

Escape clause

Injury from imports

Buy-American provisions

Tariff preferences

Adjustment assistance

Cost of protection

POINTS FOR FURTHER STUDY AND DISCUSSION

1. From U.S. Tariff Commission documents, try to find out the number of instances that adjustment assistance has been provided since 1965 and what dollar sums were involved. What proportion of applications was denied? Which industries made the largest numbers of applications?

2. Using newspaper and magazine reports, gather information on the negotiations for further trade liberalization under the Nixon round.

3. Explain why a developing country would be better off if the United States granted it a tariff preference than if the United States went to completely free trade in a given industry.

4. Compile a list of regional trade associations in existence presently, giving their dates of formation, membership, and general provisions.

5. Using data on industrial countries' imports of petroleum in one or more recent years, calculate the income redistribution and welfare losses due to the rise of petroleum prices from $3 to $10 per barrel. Assume that $3 is the cost of production, including delivery, distribution, and exploration, and that both demand and supply elasticities are 1. Redo the calculations assuming different elasticities.

part three

FOREIGN EXCHANGE MARKETS AND BALANCE-OF-PAYMENTS STATISTICS

10 The Foreign Exchange Markets

THE ANALYSIS presented in Parts One and Two was undertaken basically without any reference to money or prices of goods and services expressed in any currency. Instead, welfare was considered to be a function of absolute quantities of goods consumed and prices were relative, such as so many units of X for a unit of Y. In Part Three we introduce into the analysis money and the prices of commodities, expressed in domestic and foreign currency units.

The most important analytical task to be accomplished in Part Three is to show (in Chapter 11) that under reasonable assumptions about the real world, the existence of different currencies in individual countries does not alter the conclusions about gains from trade that were derived in Part One. As in price-theoretic analysis of the closed economy, money in principle is nothing but a veil around real economic processes which makes them more efficient by permitting the existence of an exchange rather than a pure barter economy. For this purpose we shall derive, in Chapter 11, the relative prices of goods X and Y in domestic currency units, first under autarchy and then with free trade, in complete analogy with the procedure employed in the pure theory presented in Part One. We then expand this basic model to accommodate other sources of foreign exchange demand and supply, such as capital flows, government transfers, and speculation, and show how they affect the determination of the foreign exchange rate and international flows of real goods and services.

However, before we begin these analytical exercises, in this chapter we introduce information about the institutions of the foreign exchange market which involves a number of concepts and conventions that are not part of common public knowledge. One way we do so is by presenting for study foreign exchange quotations from a daily newspaper.

In Chapter 12 we analyze the determinants of the price of foreign exchange agreed upon between a buyer and seller on a certain date and at a certain time before the actual delivery of the foreign exchange. This market for forward exchange, as it is known, has considerable fascination for many because it gives rise to the opportunity to gamble legitimately and at relatively low cost for potentially high gains, and to pit one's own skill in forecasting a price against that of other market participants.

Chapter 13 presents principles of accounting for a nation's balance of payments as a record of how it is doing in its economic relations with the rest of the world and as a diagnostic tool for revealing the need for adjustment policies of the type to be discussed in Part Four. Chapter 13 also presents a brief history of the exchange rates and balance of payments of some major industrial market economies.

Some Foreign Exchange Market Customs

On the business pages of most daily newspapers in the major cities of the Western world can be found foreign exchange quotations, alongside tables of stock market prices and interest rates. Table 10–1 reproduces in fascimile a foreign exchange quotation from one of these papers, *The Wall Street Journal* for April 10, 1974.

The caption of the table headed "Foreign Exchange" states that it lists selling prices in dollars. This means that all of the quotations represent the price of a foreign currency unit in terms of dollars. For example, the quotation Argentina (Peso) for Tuesday, .1020, means that on that day it took $0.1020 to buy one Argentinian peso. This method of stating the required number of domestic currency units to buy one foreign unit is followed in nearly all major Western market economies, with the notable exception of Britain, where quotations are always in terms of the number of foreign currency units required to buy one pound sterling. It is important to remember this peculiarity of the British foreign exchange market when reading U.K. newspapers. However, we shall carry out all of our analysis in this book using the definition of the foreign exchange rate as the price of a foreign unit of exchange in terms of domestic currency units. As a convention we adopt the notation that $R(\$ \cdot \pounds)$ is the symbol for the exchange rate expressed as the dollar (domestic currency) price of sterling (the foreign currency).

The term "selling price" in the caption of the table says that the quotation refers to the price at which a large customer could have bought the currency. The price at which foreign currency could have been sold normally is 0.125 percent below the selling price. For example, according to the table, 1 million Austrian shillings on Tuesday would have cost U.S. $52,800, but it could have been sold for only U.S. $52,734. The spread of $66 represents the foreign exchange dealer's or bank's commission. The

TABLE 10–1
Foreign Exchange Quotation from *The Wall Street Journal*

Foreign Exchange

Tuesday, April 9, 1974

Selling prices for bank transfers in the U.S. for payment abroad, as quoted at 4 p.m. Eastern Time (in dollars).

Country	Tuesday	Monday
Argentina (Peso)	.1020	.1020
Australia (Dollar)	1.4925	1.4925
Austria (Schilling)	.0528	.0533
Belgium (Franc)		
Commercial rate	.025490	.025625
Financial rate	.024330	.024652
Brazil (Cruzeiro)	.1570	.1570
Britain (Pound)	2.3760	2.3950
30-Day Futures	2.3640	2.3830
90-Day Futures	2.3345	2.3500
180-Day Futures	2.2920	2.3025
Canada (Dollar)	1.0296	1.0294
Colombia (Peso)	.0400	.0400
Denmark (Krone)	.1619	.1635
Ecuador (Sucre)	.041	.041
Finland (Markka)	.2657	.2669
France (Franc)	.2049	.2064
Greece (Drachma)	.0338	.0338
Hong Kong (Dollar)	.1972	.1974
India (Rupee)	.1285	.1285
Iraq (Dinar)	3.4925	3.4925
Israel (Pound)	.2385	.2385
Italy (Lira)	.001572	.001572
Japan (Yen)	.003585	.003596
30-Day Futures	.003525	.003555
90-Day Futures	.003440	.003475
180-Day Futures	.003410	.003446
Lebanon (Pound)	.4310	.4280
Mexico (Peso)	.08006	.08006
Netherlands (Guilder)	.3672	.3713
New Zealand (Dollar)	1.4675	1.4675
Norway (Krone)	.1795	.1804
Pakistan (Rupee)	.1020	.1020
Peru (Sol)	.0234	.0234
Philippines (Peso)	.1490	.1490
Portugal (Escudo)	.0400	.0402
Singapore (Dollar)	.4114	.4124
South Africa (Rand)	1.4950	1.4950
Spain (Peseta)	.01703	.01703
Sweden (Krona)	.2233	.2257
Switzerland (Franc)	.3245	.3265
Uruguay (Peso)	.00097	.00097
Venezuela (Bolivar)	.2337	.2338
West Germany (Mark)	.3875	.3923
30-Day Futures	.3885	.3931
90-Day Futures	.3893	.3936
180-Day Futures	.3906	.3946

Supplied by Bankers Trust Co., New York.

Prices for foreign banknotes, as quoted on the last business day (in dollars):

	Buying	Selling
Argentina (Peso)	.075	.095
Australia (Dollar)	1.40	1.48
Austria (Schilling)	.05	.057
Belgium (Franc)	.023	.028
Brazil (Cruzeiro)	.13	.1550
Britain (Pound)	2.34	2.43
Canada (Dollar)	1.01	1.04
China-Taiwan (Dollar)	.021	.0285
Colombia (Peso)	.035	.04
Denmark (Krone)	.15	.1750
Egypt (Pound)	1.45	1.65
Finland (Markka)	.26	.28
France (Franc)	.20	.22
Greece (Drachma)	.03	.036
Hong Kong (Dollar)	.1950	.21
India (Rupee)	.08	.10
Italy (Lira)	.0013	.0015
Japan (Yen)	.0035	.0037
Malaysia (Dollar)	.37	.43
Mexico (Peso)	.078	.082
Netherlands (Guilder)	.36	.38
New Zealand (Dollar)	1.25	1.40
Norway (Krone)	.17	.19
Pakistan (Rupee)	z	z
Philippines (Peso)	.12	.1350
Portugal (Escudo)	.037	.043
Singapore (Dollar)	.36	.43
South Korea (Won)	.0018	.0025
Spain (Peseta)	.016	.018
Sweden (Krona)	.21	.24
Switzerland (Franc)	.32	.34
Turkey (Lira)	.064	.0725
Uruguay (Peso)	.0007	.00125
Venezuela (Bolivar)	.2275	.2340
West Germany (Mark)	.38	.4050

Supplied by one major New York bank.
z-Not available.

Currency Futures

Tuesday, April 9, 1974

Closing futures prices, in dollars, for actively traded currencies on the International Monetary Market of the Chicago Mercantile Exchange, compared with the previous session (in parentheses):

BRITAIN, POUND—Sept. 2.29 (2.309).

CANADA, DOLLAR—Sept. 1.029 (1.0295); Dec. 1.0288 (1.0305).

WEST GERMANY, MARK—June .3886 (.3936); Sept. .3895 (.3945); Dec. .390 (.395).

SWITZERLAND, FRANC—June .3245 (.3265); Sept. .3244 (.327); Dec. .3243b (.327); March '75, .325 (.32715); June .326 (.328).

JAPAN, YEN—June .003453 (.003502); Sept. .003395 (.003432).

MEXICO, PESO — Dec. .07745a (.07735); March '75, .0766b (.07681); June .076 (.076).

a-Asked. b-Bid.

Source: *The Wall Street Journal,* April 10, 1974.

spread between buying and selling rates often is the only charge imposed by foreign exchange dealers and banks in this business, though in transactions involving only small sums an additional service charge may be added. The spread may be higher than 0.125 percent in foreign exchange markets other than New York and London, and during an exchange crisis or in the case of rarely traded currencies, it may be higher even in these two deepest and most active of the world's foreign exchange markets. Because market participants know the customary spread between buying and selling rates, usually both are not published.

The prices quoted are for large foreign exchange customers. It is the tendency for buyers and sellers trading in small quantities and who are unknown to banks or foreign exchange dealers to have to pay slightly higher prices or to sell at lower prices. On the other hand, very large regular customers may be able to negotiate better than these quoted prices.

The caption of the table states that the quotations are for bank transfers in the United States for payment abroad. This phrase means that a buyer of foreign exchange receives it on deposit with a foreign bank or branch of a U.S. bank abroad, to be drawn on with a check or payment order. At the same time the buyer transfers to the U.S. bank the corresponding dollar value of the foreign exchange. By analogy, a sale of foreign exchange involves a foreign deposit turned over to a U.S. bank, which transfers to the seller a U.S. dollar bank deposit in settlement. Funds in these transactions become available for payment 2 "clear," or working, days after the purchase or sale. Thus, if one owes 1 million Argentinian pesos payable on Thursday, April 11, in Buenos Aires, it is necessary to buy the pesos no later than Tuesday, April 9. At the present virtually all foreign exchange transactions are settled in this brief period through the use of cables. Before the age of telecommunications settlements sometimes took weeks; for example, in London–New York transactions it was the length of time required for a ship to cross the Atlantic.

It is still usual for firms or persons importing or exporting goods to possess bank deposits or take out loans only in domestic currency. Therefore they must go through "transfers abroad" to settle their obligations. However, since the middle 1960s increasingly large numbers of firms in international business have accounts with their domestic banks which are denominated in foreign currencies. This practice is part of the phenomenon known as Eurodollar or, more generally, Eurocurrency markets. The origin and characteristics of these markets will be analyzed below. Here we only need to note that a firm possessing such a foreign currency deposit with its own domestic bank typically wishes to have purchases of foreign exchange transferred not abroad but to be kept on deposit with its local bank. A regular check drawn on the firm's account but denominated in foreign currency can then be used to settle a debt abroad.

The caption in the table indicates that the foreign exchange rates were quoted at 4 P.M. Eastern time. In all major foreign exchange markets, demand and supply change throughout the day, causing fluctuations in the prices of currencies. For this reason it is normally an arbitrary decision which of the prices prevailing during the day is quoted in the newspapers.

Some give opening day, noon day, or closing day rates. Others give the range of prices during the day at which transactions have taken place. It is clear that intrinsically no one price quotation is superior to another. If analysts have a choice they pick a price according to the use to which it is to be put. If one were interested in analyzing the interdependence of the London–New York markets, it would be wise to use closing day prices in London and opening day prices in New York, since because of the differences in time zones only during this period are both markets open for business simultaneously. On the other hand, *The Wall Street Journal* reaches U.S. businessmen early in the morning of every working day, and the preceding day's 4 P.M. quotations are most useful to them in planning their activities for the day.

Prices can move quickly in the foreign exchange market, and when a broker or bank quotes a price on the telephone he can be held to it for only one minute. But even this short time period involves some risk for the foreign exchange dealer. For example, if the buyer or seller, upon receiving the quotation, tenders a large sum which cannot be resold or bought at the same price, the dealer nevertheless is obligated by the convention of the market on the price he has quoted. For this reason dealers may quote different prices to different customers, depending on the level of the transaction in which they expect to be involved. As Paul Einzig describes vividly in a book on the London foreign exchange market, customers know of this habit of dealers and therefore may engage in acts of bluff and counterbluff. For example, in an instance when a large amount of foreign exchange is to be placed by a firm, one of its lower level employees may deal with the broker, rather than the usual senior employee.

The Organization of the Market

At the bottom of the table from *The Wall Street Journal* (Table 10–1), we find the information that the quotations have been supplied by the Bankers Trust Company of New York. The quotation of this bank should be representative of the market price, because it is part of the New York market, which is organized in a manner most easily understood by considering Figure 10–1. At the base of the pyramid is the large number of firms and individuals whose normal business activity gives rise to demand for or supply of foreign currencies. We have here the traders in goods and services, capital exporters and importers, tourists, and so on. Let us consider, for example, Firm 1 in New York, which has just bought some goods from a firm in Britain and owes it £1,000. It goes to one of the two banks with which it is doing regular business, as indicated by the lines going from Firm 1 to Banks 1 and 2 in Figure 10–1. The foreign exchange department of that bank is in touch with all other banks and a set of brokers through the telephone, and thus it knows the price of pound

FIGURE 10–1

The Foreign Exchange Market

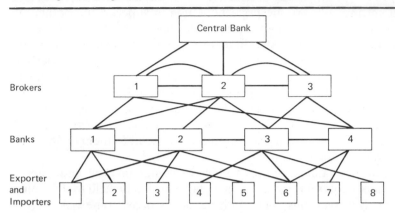

Boxes represent participants in the foreign exchange markets and the lines connecting them symbolize business connections. The boxes in the bottom row represent exporters and importers who turn to banks, shown in the next row above, when they wish to sell or buy foreign exchange. Banks try to match this demand and supply among their own customers, but if this is not possible they turn to other banks and brokers. These brokers, shown in the next row above, tend to specialize in certain currencies. The foreign exchange market is dominated by the central bank, which occasionally buys or sells foreign exchange to influence rates. It deals mostly through brokers.

sterling being quoted in the market at the time Firm 1 wishes to make its purchase. Because of the efficient operation of this market (as analyzed in the last section of this chapter), it typically does not pay the average customer to get quotations from more than one bank. We assume, therefore, that Firm 1 enters a verbal agreement to buy £1,000 at the quoted price. Written confirmation of the order from the bank follows in the next day's mail, and the sterling funds are available to the British exporter in a U.K. bank two clear days later, as we discussed above. The New York bank either receives a check or debits the account of Firm 1 for the dollars required to pay for the sterling, $2,376 on April 9, 1974, according to Table 10–1.

The bank owing these £1,000, ceteris paribus, would typically now have what is known as an open position. That is, the bank owes payment in a currency that it does not possess. Therefore, it is subject to the risk of financial loss if the price of sterling in dollars rises by the time it actually acquires the pound sterling, although of course it may also profit if the price falls. Traditionally banks in such a situation would attempt immediately to close their open position by buying £1,000 from another of its customers in the export business, from another bank, or from a broker. In recent years, however, conservative operation of the business in this manner has given way to greater willingness of banks and brokers to engage in some speculation by keeping open positions for periods of varying length.

Brokers in foreign currencies play an important role in the market by specializing in the handling of certain currencies for which the market is not deep and active enough to find matches of demand and supply readily by just dealing within or between banks. Brokers are also the channel through which governments buy and sell foreign exchange, for reasons to be discussed below. In most countries the central bank is responsible for carrying out official exchange transactions, and it must have a special relation of trust with foreign exchange brokers, since knowledge about the government's activities in the market can result in large gains from private speculation by informed parties.

Banks and brokers are interconnected with each other through telephones within the same city and country, thus creating a nationwide foreign exchange market. Some banks and brokers also stay in communication with analogous foreign exchange markets abroad, matching demand and supply and determining equilibrium prices on a worldwide basis. As a result, foreign exchange rates at any given moment tend to be identical in all parts of the world, except for differences in transactions costs. The New York bank which provided the quotations in Table 10–1 is plugged into this global market, which is interconnected by telephones and provides an efficient and reliable source of information about the prices at which foreign currencies are traded.

In some countries of Western Europe, notably Germany and France, the informal national market for foreign exchange described above with the help of Figure 10–1 has superimposed on it a formal market. Thus, in Frankfurt, every day between 12 and 13 hours in a small room above the Stock Exchange, representatives of the Frankfurt banks, brokers, and a representative of the Bundesbank, the German central bank, meet and trade in foreign exchange. This Frankfurt meeting is connected through telephones to similar meetings of bankers and brokers in other major cities in Germany, such as Munich, Berlin, Hamburg, Duesseldorf, and Cologne. This physical market for foreign exchange is a relic of the times before telephones created instant communications and foreign exchange traders required an opportunity of this sort to buy or sell excess quantities of currencies for which they could not find a match among their own customers. Today, the meetings primarily serve the function of setting an "official" exchange rate for the day, which is the one at which a transaction takes place during the hour or otherwise is the preceding day's rate. This official rate is used by German banks to settle minor transactions and by offices selling or buying bank notes, and it is applicable to certain types of transactions for legal purposes, such as the reporting of foreign income for tax authorities. However, interbank business and trades with large domestic and foreign customers are often executed at negotiated or current market prices which are different from the official price throughout the day.

Futures and Forward Markets

Under the selling prices for the British pound, the Japanese Yen, and the German mark in Table 10–1, there are quotations in New York for 30- 90- and 180-day futures, in addition to the prices applicable to the spot market, which, as we have noted, involves delivery two clear days hence. Futures prices are for currency to be delivered 30, 90 or 180 days later at the price given on any particular day. Futures contracts are entered into by exporters and importers of goods and services whose foreign exchange receipts or payments are at these future dates and who wish to make certain of the domestic currency (dollar) value of their foreign income or obligations as of a particular day. Similar motives underlie the purchase of futures contracts by the exporters and importers of short-term capital, while speculators enter the market expecting to gain from favorable spot prices at the time the contracts are due. We will discuss the determinants of these currency futures prices in detail in Chapter 12.

As regards futures contracts, one other important institutional peculiarity is apparent from Table 10–1. In the main table, under the heading "Foreign Exchange," futures are quoted for the three currencies noted above for delivery 30, 90, or 180 days from the date given in the table head. Traditionally this kind of quotation was referred to as the forward exchange market. Under the separate heading "Currency Futures" in Table 10–1 there are quotations for contracts applicable to a specified date in the future, such as June, September, and December, for example, in the case of the West German mark. This manner of quotation for futures was instituted in 1972 by the International Monetary Market of the Chicago Mercantile Exchange. Thus the kind of futures contracts which long has been used in the trade of wheat, eggs, silver, and so on at this market began to be provided for currencies. Dealing in contracts of fixed size, such as DM 10,000, for example, and in certain dates important for dividend, interest, or tax payments, the Chicago futures currency market supplements the services provided by the New York forward market and facilitates speculation.

The Market for Bank Notes

We should note that in the description of the foreign exchange markets above, all references were to transactions involving checks or bank transfers. Demand and supply were equal in the market at the given price, including purchases or sales of central banks designed to achieve this equality at a price of their choice. Most important is the implication of this market analysis that foreign trade and capital flows going through these currency markets do not lead to any physical transfer of foreign bank notes or coins across international borders. Only tourism and illegal activities such as smuggling or tax evasion give rise to trade in this form of currency.

The bottom half of the list headed "Foreign Exchange" in Table 10–1 gives buying and selling rates for bank notes (no coins) in New York on April 9, 1974. Several things are worth noting about these quotations. First, the prices are for the full day. They do not change throughout the day in response to changes in demand and supply, as they do in the other currency market discussed above. Second, selling prices for bank notes may be higher or lower than selling prices for bank transfers. In other words, if a U.S. tourist goes to Australia and wishes to take along Australian $1,000, he can buy the bank notes for U.S. $1,480, according to Table 10–1. If, on the other hand, he wants to obtain the cash by withdrawing it upon his arrival from an Australian bank to which he has had it transferred by a U.S. bank, he has to pay $1,492.50. A comparison of the prices for Swedish Krona on that same day according to Table 10–1 shows that the acquisition of 1,000 krona bank notes requires $240, while an equivalent amount transferred through a bank requires only $225.70. These price differences of bank notes and bank transfers are explained primarily by the cost of holding, protecting, and transporting notes and bank deposits and the influences of demand and supply. In countries of northern Europe, for example, the price of Italian lira notes is above that of transfers at the beginning of the summer, when tourists planning to vacation in the south have a great demand for that currency. When these tourists return from their vacations at the end of the summer, increased supplies of lira depress their price below that of bank transfers. Transaction costs and the loss of interest prevent complete arbitrage of prices through the purchase of cheap lira in the fall and sale of expensive lira in the spring. Transaction costs limit arbitrage between Italy and other countries at all times.

Third, the spread between buying and selling prices for bank notes is much larger than the 0.125 percent in the market for bank transfers. For the Australian dollar, for example, the spread is 8 cents, or about 5.4 percent of the selling rate of $1.48. This large margin represents compensation for the cost of holding inventories of bank notes which are not interest bearing and the risk of theft, both of which are higher in the case of bank notes than of bank deposits.

Some Effects of an Efficient Foreign Exchange Market

The foreign exchange market, whose main organizational features were described above, is one of the most efficient markets in existence for the following four important reasons. First, information about demand, supply, and prices travels quickly and cheaply through the telephone network. Second, the market participants, especially the banks and brokers, have developed many conventions for the rapid, inexpensive transaction of business. For example, buying and selling orders are executed by verbal but legally binding agreements over the telephone. As Paul Einzig notes in his book about the London foreign exchange market (1966), a large number of unwritten but well known rules in existence for many decades regulate the behavior of market participants. For example, if the clerk of a currency broker makes an obvious error in quoting a price, such as inverting the sequence of two figures, it is not proper business ethics to take advantage of this error by placing a profitable large buy or sell order at this price. A broker or bank which would engage in such an act would be ostracized by the rest of the London exchange market, even though existing ethics specify that the firm whose clerk made the error must make good at the quoted price.

Third, foreign exchange is a perfectly homogeneous commodity requiring no grading as to quality or any other characteristic. In contrast with, for example, extremely heterogeneous used automobiles, buyers and sellers know exactly and immediately all of the relevant characteristics of the currency in which they are dealing. Fourth, foreign currencies (other than bank notes) have a very low cost of storage, since the owner can always invest them in foreign short-term money markets and earn interest which may not be lower than the rate equivalent domestic funds could earn in the domestic money market.

Arbitrage

In the foreign exchange market with the characteristics, described above, prices for the same currency in different locations in the world tend to be equal because of a market activity known as arbitrage. Arbitrage involves the simultaneous purchase and sale of a currency to take advantage of a difference in price in two locations. For example, if the price of a French franc in terms of German marks $R(FF \cdot DM)$ quoted in Paris were $R(FF \cdot DM) = 2.0$ while in Frankfurt the quote for francs were $R(DM \cdot FF) = 0.60$, an arbitrager could buy a million francs in Paris at the cost of DM 500,000 and sell them in Frankfurt for DM 600,000. Following the principle of buying low and selling high, the above arbitrage operation yields a profit of DM 100,000 and requires no capital investment, since the mark required to buy the franc in the initial step is repaid immediately upon resale of the franc. The entire operation takes only a telephone call between Paris and Frankfurt and one call in either the Paris or Frankfurt market. For banks and brokers who have leased telephone or teletype lines between major financial centers, the marginal cost of communication in the arbitrage operation is near zero. The arbitrage just described tends to put upward and downward pressure on the franc price in Paris and Frankfurt, respectively, until arbitrage ceases to be profitable and in equilibrium the following condition holds:

$$R(\text{DM} \cdot \text{FF}) = 1.0/R(\text{FF} \cdot \text{DM})$$
$$= 1.0/2.0 = 0.5$$

As a result of these characteristics of arbitrage operations, economists often make the assumption that prices of foreign exchange are completely equalized through arbitrage by dealers and brokers who watch prices continuously in two countries. A study of exchange rates quoted in two countries often suggests that arbitrage is not operating as the theory predicts, however. Exchange rate quotations of this sort suffer from the fact that nearly always they are taken at different points in time, when the prices may be different even though arbitrage equalizes prices perfectly at any given moment in time.

It should be noted, as an interesting extension of the preceding discussion of currency arbitrage, that analogous forces tend to equalize prices of homogeneous commodities, such as silver, wheat, or cocoa beans quoted for future delivery in markets as far apart as Winnipeg, Canada, and Milan, Italy. In the case of these commodities for spot delivery, however, prices in two locations may diverge by as much as the cost of transportation, which is near zero for currencies. The arbitrage of commodity prices between countries involves going through the foreign exchange markets, spot or forward as the case may be.

Next, we discuss a form of arbitrage which involves three different currencies. To understand the function of this form of arbitrage, assume that market forces have created equality between the spot rates for sterling dollar $R(\pounds \cdot \$)$ in London and New York $R(\$ \cdot \pounds)$, so that $R(\$ \cdot \pounds) = 1/R(\pounds \cdot \$)$. The analogous relationships hold with respect to the dollar-mark $R(\$ \cdot \text{DM})$ and the mark-sterling $R(\text{DM} \cdot \pounds)$.

The point of triangular arbitrage is that, if two of the above three rates are known, the third one, also often referred to as the cross-rate, is implicit. Thus, $R(\$ \cdot \pounds) = R(\$ \cdot \text{DM}) \cdot R(\text{DM} \cdot \pounds)$ in equilibrium. For a numerical example, $2.50 = .25 \cdot 10.00$. Profitable opportunities for triangular arbitrage exist whenever this equation does not hold, as for example when the $R(\$ \cdot \text{DM})$ rate is 0.30 rather than 0.25, with the other two rates at 2.50 and 10.00, as above. In such a situation an arbitrager can purchase $2.50 to buy one pound sterling in New York, obtain DM 10 for the pound in Frankfurt, and resell the DM 10 for $3 in New York, for a net profit of $0.50 from this set of transactions. From our previous analysis of the low cost and instantaneous operation of arbitrage, it follows that market forces can be assumed to maintain consistency of cross-rates in the sense of the above equation at all points in time.

We should note that it is possible in principle to engage in arbitrage involving more than three currencies simultaneously. However, market participants rarely do so, because an equation like the one constructed above for the triangle New York–London–Frankfurt also exists for New York–London–Paris and all other combinations of rates. As long as all of these combinations of cross-rates are consistent, no opportunities for profitable arbitrage going through more than three currencies exist.

The preceding analysis can be illustrated by consideration of Table 10–2

TABLE 10–2
Exchange Cross-Rate Quotations

July 31	Frankfurt	New York	Paris	Brussels	London	A'sterdam	Zurich
Frankf't..	—	2.572-574	58.84-93	6.69-70	5.52-53	96.92-97.06	95.15-.34
N. York...	38.90-94	—	22.87-90	2.603-608	2.1560-1570	37.78-80	37.10-15
Paris	169.70-70.1	4.37-38	—	11.375-400	9.378-403	164.52-.92	161.375-775
Brussels ..	14.86-95	38.37-42	8.75-80	—	82.18-82.51	14.42-51	14.12-22
London....	5.52½-53½	2.1530-45	9.39-41	82.55-85	—	5.69-70	5.80½-82
Am'erdam	103.10-15	2.6532-57	60.665-715	6.906-911	5.6905-55	—	98.005-.055
Zurich.....	105.03-22	2.699-703	61.76.88	7.025-040	5.801-8105	101.77-95	—

Source: *The Financial Times* (London), August 1, 1975.

representing foreign exchange cross-rates published by the British newspaper *The Financial Times*. A similar table is published daily in the *Herald Tribune,* a newspaper favored by North American visitors to Europe. Using such a table of cross-rates, tourists and businessmen can find very readily the value of foreign exchange in terms of their domestic currencies for each of the countries they are visiting. It is also easy to estimate the value of foreign exchange from one country in terms of a third country's currency. For example, an American owner of Dutch guilders would look at the row labeled Amsterdam and find how many guilders it takes to purchase 100 deutsche marks (103.10–15), one U.S. dollar (2.6532–57), 100 French francs (60.665–715) and so on, though the exact price he would have to pay would tend to be somewhat higher, for reasons discussed above. The two figures shown for every exchange rate, typically involving only the last two or three digits of the quotation, indicate the daily range of the transactions observed. The table permits testing the proposition that cross-rates should be consistent. For example the price of the deutsche mark quoted in Zurich (95.15–34) should be equal to 1 divided by the price of the Swiss franc in Frankfurt (105.03–22), except for the differences in timing of the quotations and charges mentioned above. Similarly, arbitrage operations at these quotations involving more than two currencies tend to show the absence of profit opportunities. Anyone making such calculations, however, should be aware of the fact that in the table the row of London quotations shows the price of sterling in terms of foreign currency, while all of the other row quotations show the unit price of foreign exchange in terms of domestic currency.

We close the current chapter on foreign exchange markets by noting one more institutional convention. In newspapers reference is often made to the value of individual currencies, say the pound sterling, in terms of a trade-weighted average. Such a quotation is useful for policy makers who wish to know, in one single figure, what has happened to the value of a country's currency relative to all other currencies in the world. For this purpose it would be meaningless, for example, to take a simple average of all sterling exchange rates in the world, since the resulting index would give equal weight to small and large countries and important and unimportant trading partners. Therefore the decision has been made to calculate the average by weighting with a country's bilateral trade with each foreign partner. Since relative trade patterns change only slowly, a comparison of the index number at different points in time gives useful indication of the changes in the value of one country's currency in the rest of the world.

BIBLIOGRAPHICAL NOTES

Institutional descriptions of the foreign exchange markets are found in Einzig (1961, 1966) and Holmes and Schott (1965). Good combinations of institutional material and analysis are provided by Yeager (1975) and Aliber (1969, 1973). The novel by Erdman (1973) conveys an excellent flavor of foreign exchange market operations, and in the process of telling an entertaining story, it passes on much useful information about these markets. The *Federal Reserve Bulletin* periodically gives a record of its involvement in foreign exchange markets. Grassman (1973) reports on a unique survey of Swedish firms concerning their foreign exchange billing, payment, and holding practices.

CONCEPTS FOR REVIEW

Spot exchange rate   Official exchange rate
Forward exchange rate   Arbitrage
Futures exchange rate   Triangular arbitrage
Eurodollars

POINTS FOR FURTHER STUDY AND DISCUSSION

1. Calculate the returns of arbitrage operations involving two, three, or more currencies by using spot and forward exchange rate quotations from daily U.S. and various foreign papers. Are the profit opportunities larger in operations involving some currencies than others? Are there differences in returns during the 1960s and the 1970s? If there are, try to explain the differences. Is arbitrage more profitable involving spot or forward rates?
2. Calculate returns from arbitrage operations involving copper, gold, and wheat in London and U.S. markets, using daily U.S. and U.K. newspapers.

3. Find out from your local bank the cost of taking to Australia $1,000 Australian in bank notes as against acquiring these from a bank after your arrival.

4. Call a bank in your town four times during a day and find out the exchange rate for sterling, German marks, and Brazilian cruzeiros. Call two or three banks simultaneously to obtain quotations for the same currency. Are the answers you received consistent with theoretical expectations? If they are not, try to discover the source of divergence.

5. Make inquiries in your town to find out how and at what price you could obtain Malaysian dollars. Is it more difficult to get a quotation and delivery on the Malaysian dollar than the German mark or British sterling? Explain why.

11 The Determinants of the Spot Exchange Rate

THE DETERMINANTS of the spot exchange rate are analyzed in this chapter, under the assumption that the world consists only of two countries, the United States and Britain. The United States (or country A) will be assumed to be the home country, with the dollar as the domestic currency. Britain (or country B) represents "the rest of the world" and has the pound sterling as its domestic currency. We furthermore assume in the first part of this chapter that the two countries produce and trade only two goods, X and Y, which are the U.S. import and export good, respectively. The basic analytical framework of this chapter thus is identical to that underlying Part One of this book. Using the procedure followed there, we consider the effect of opening up trade on the domestic production and consumption existing under autarchy. We show that the existence of foreign exchange does not alter the basic conclusions reached in Part One.

In the Section II of this chapter we analyze the influences which speculation in foreign exchange, capital flows, and government activities have on the determination of the spot exchange rate. These activities were not considered in the pure model of Part One because they originate in financial transactions that are not part of that model. The objective of our analysis here is to show how these financial activities have real effects which lead to imbalances in trade in goods and services. We also use the basic model to make the point that in the absence of government intervention in the foreign exchange market there are never any balance-of-payments deficits, since the exchange rate always serves as a mechanism to equalize the market's foreign exchange demand and supply. This point is of great importance for the understanding of the international adjustment mechanism to be discussed in Part Four. Throughout this chapter we assume that the home country, A, is small relative to the rest of the world, or country B, so that its actions do not affect existing relative world prices of goods or the return on capital.

We conclude this chapter by discussing the concept of purchasing power parity, which for many years has attracted the interest of economists as a practical way of determining equilibrium exchange rates after periods when market forces had been suppressed, as during periods of war or severe domestic crises. The insights derived from this section have interesting implications for those who are contemplating working and living abroad or visiting foreign countries as tourists.

I. TRADE IN GOODS

The analysis in this section involves two different approaches, use of a numerical example and use of graphs. An algebraic model presented in the Appendix to this chapter underlies the numerical example. Before we begin the analysis, however, it is useful to set out clearly, for convenient reference, the notation to be used in this and the following chapters. This notation is necessary because in our analysis we have to distinguish clearly between quantities and prices of both commodities and foreign exchange, where the prices of commodities in turn may be given in either domestic or foreign currency.

Commodities
   Prices: $X(\$)$ is the price of good X in terms of dollars.
           $Y(\$)$ is the price of good Y in terms of dollars.
           $X(\pounds)$ is the price of good X in terms of sterling.
           $Y(\pounds)$ is the price of good Y in terms of sterling.
           And so on for other currencies, given in parentheses after the symbol for the commodity.
   Quantities: X, Y, Z stand for the physical quantities of goods X, Y, and Z.

Foreign exchange
   Prices: R is the symbol for the exchange rate, or the price of foreign exchange in terms of domestic currency units. Whenever the analysis concerns only two countries, R is the exchange rate between the dollar and sterling, with the dollar treated as the home currency.
           In some discussions below we need exchange rates between more than two countries. Under these circumstances we place in parentheses after the letter R the symbols of the two currencies involved, always placing the home currency first.
           Thus $R(\$\cdot\pounds)$ is the price of sterling in terms of dollars.
           $R(\$\cdot DM)$ is the price of Deutsche marks (DM) in terms of dollars.

$R(\pounds \cdot FF)$ is the price of French francs (FF) in terms of sterling.

Quantities: $, £, DM, and FF are the quantities of dollars, sterling, Deutsche marks, and French francs, respectively.

Spot versus forward exchange: In the next chapter it becomes necessary to distinguish spot and forward exchange rates. We retain the spot–exchange rate notation and introduce the symbol FR for the forward–exchange rate dollar-sterling in two-country models. Whenever more than two currencies are involved, we put the two relevant currency symbols into parentheses after the FR, following the same principles as in the spot-market notation: $FR(\$ \cdot \pounds)$, $FR(\$ \cdot DM)$ stand for the dollar-sterling and dollar-DM forward rates, quoted from the United States as the home country.

Actual versus expected exchange rates: In the analysis of speculation we also distinguish between actual and expected exchange rates. We retain the notation for actual spot and forward rates and place an E before the expected rate. For example, $E(R)$ and $E(FR)$ represent the values of the spot and forward dollar-sterling exchange rates, respectively, expected to prevail at a certain date in the future, the date to be specified in the analysis. Whenever more than two currencies are involved we specify them according to the principles set out above. For example, $E[R(\pounds \cdot FF)]$ is the expected sterling–French franc spot exchange rate.

Fortunately, the more complicated symbols need to be used on only rare occasions, and in these instances they will be defined again. Therefore there is no need to commit the notation to memory, though in moments of confusion it may be useful to refer to the outline above.

Theoretical Model

Table 11–1 gives a numerical example of the relationships among domestic demand and supply for both the import good X and the export good Y which give rise to the demand for and supply of foreign exchange. Consider for the moment only the upper half of Table 11–1, dealing with the import good (or service) X. It can be seen that Column (1) gives a set of prices and Columns (2) and (3) give the quantities demanded and supplied at these prices, respectively. For reasons well understood from price theory, the quantity demanded is a decreasing function of price, and the quantity supplied is an increasing function. The general shape of these functional relationships is assumed to be linear for expositional ease. It is reflected in the demand (DD') and supply (SS') curves in Panel A1 of Figure 11–1, where we measure the price of X in dollars $[X(\$)]$ on the vertical axis and the quantity of X on the horizontal axis.

A new concept not commonly used in general price theory underlies the numbers in Column (4) of Table 11–1. These numbers reflect the excess

FIGURE 11–1
Exchange Rate Determination: Trade in Goods

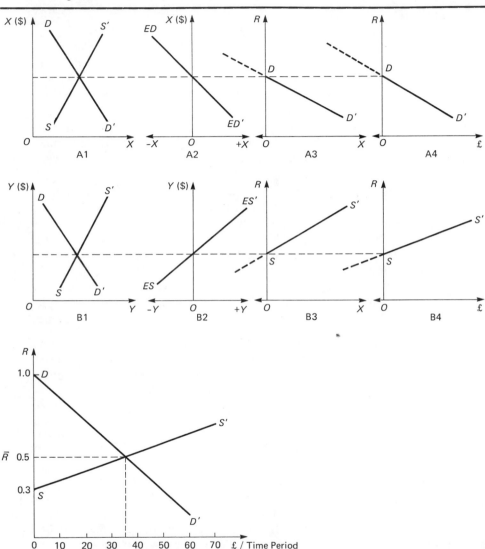

Panel A1 of Figure 11–1 shows country A's industry demand and supply curves for its import good X as a function of the domestic dollar price. Panel A2 represents the net of industry demand minus supply, which is zero at the equilibrium price, negative above, and positive below the equilibrium price. In Panel A3 zero excess demand for X in terms of the exchange rate is found by multiplying the given world sterling price of good X by the exchange rate and selecting that exchange rate at which the resultant dollar price gives rise to zero excess demand. The schedule DD' shows the positive excess quantities of good X demanded for import as a function of the dollar-sterling exchange rate. In Panel A4 the schedule DD' represents the demand for sterling as a function of the

TABLE 11–1
Derivation of Demand and Supply Schedules for Sterling

A. Import Good X

(1)	(2)	(3)	(4)	(5)	(6)	(7)
			Excess			
Price of			Quantity	Price of	Exchange	
X in	Quantity	Quantity	of X	X in	Rate	Quantity of
Dollars	Demanded	Supplied	Demanded	Sterling	R($ · £)	Demanded
1.0	11.5	5.2	6.3	10	0.10	63
2.0	11.0	5.4	5.6	10	0.20	56
5.0	9.5	6.0	3.5	10	0.50	35
7.0	8.5	6.4	2.1	10	0.70	21
10.0	7.0	7.0	0	10	1.00	0
15.0	4.5	8.0	−3.5	10	1.50	−35
20.0	2.0	9.0	−7.0	10	2.00	−70

B. Export Good Y

(1)	(2)	(3)	(4)	(5)	(6)	(7)
			Excess			
Price of			Quantity	Price of	Exchange	
Y in	Quantity	Quantity	of X	Y in	Rate	Quantity of
Dollars	Demanded	Supplied	Supplied	Sterling	R($ · £)	£ Supplied
.50	14.5	7.5	−7.0	5	0.10	−35
1.00	14.0	10.5	−3.5	5	0.20	−17.5
1.50	13.5	13.5	0	5	0.30	0
2.50	12.5	19.5	7.0	5	0.50	35.0
3.50	11.5	25.5	14.0	5	0.70	70.0
5.00	10.0	34.5	24.5	5	1.00	122.5
7.50	7.5	45.0	37.5	5	1.50	187.5

quantity of good X demanded domestically at the different prices shown in Column (1). They are derived by subtracting the number of units of good X supplied at every price from the number of units demanded. For example, at the price of X equal to 2, the public in the home country demands 11 units, but country A's industry supplies only 5.4, leaving an excess de-

---

exchange rate, which is derived by multiplication of the physical quantities shown in Panel A3 by the world sterling price of good X.

Panels B1–B4 represent the export-good industry of country A and are constructed in the same way as Panels A1–A4, with the exception that the domestic schedule in Panel B2 represents excess supply. Thus the supply schedules in Panels B3 and B4 are of positive magnitudes.

In Panel C the demand and supply curves are combined to represent equilibrium in the foreign exchange market. The vertical axis measures the dollar-sterling exchange rate, and the horizontal axis shows the quantity of sterling traded per time period. In equilibrium at $\bar{R} = 0.5$, domestic excess demand X is satisfied by the importation units of good X worth £35. The excess supply of good Y exported is also worth £35.

mand of 5.6 units. As can be seen from a comparison of Columns (1) through (4), at low prices excess demand is positive, at high prices it is negative. At the price of $10, excess demand is zero. Under autarchy this price and the accompanying equal quantities (7) demanded and supplied represent domestic equilibrium in industry X. Panel A2 in Figure 11–1 shows an excess demand curve ($EDED'$) which crosses the zero quantity line at the equilibrium price, $X(\$) = \bar{X}(\$)$, and which has the typical downward slope of demand curves for normal goods. The excess demand is shown to be negative and positive at prices above and below $\bar{X}(\$)$, respectively.

Now consider Column (5) in Table 11–1. It shows that the world price of X is £10, regardless of what the domestic price or excess demand for this good is in country A. This invariability of the world price of X follows from our assumption that country A is so small relative to the rest of the world that its demand or supply does not affect the world price. In Column (6) we introduce certain dollar-sterling, $R(\$ \cdot \pounds) = R$, exchange rate values which were chosen deliberately in such a manner that when applied to the sterling price of good X, they yield a domestic dollar price for X just equal to that found in Column (1). For example, in the second row the exchange rate is 0.20, at which the sterling price of X equal to 10 is turned into the dollar price of 2 shown in Column (1), i.e., $X(\$) = X(\pounds) \cdot R$, or $2 = 10 \cdot (0.20)$. For our purposes of analysis, the precise units of the exchange rate shown in Column (6) are of no particular importance. What is important is the fact, clearly apparent from Columns (4) through (6) in Table 11–1, that the excess quantities of good X demanded in country A at the exogenously given world price of good X in sterling are a decreasing function of the price of foreign exchange. Thus when the dollar price of sterling is 0.20, country A has an excess demand for X of 5.6 units. At an exchange rate of $1.50, excess demand is a negative 3.5 units of X, which means that good X is so expensive in terms of dollars that domestic supply exceeds demand, and it becomes an export good at these prices. In the graphical analysis and discussion of equilibrium exchange rate determination we shall consider the exchange rate only in the range where excess demand for good X is positive.

Let us now turn to Column (7) and the last step in the analysis of the functional relationship between the price of foreign exchange and the quantity of foreign exchange demanded. Column (7) is derived by multiplying Column (4), the excess quantity of X demanded, by Column (5), the sterling price of good X. Column (7) thus shows the number of pounds sterling demanded for payment of the import good X. Inspection of the last two columns of Part A of Table 11–1 indicates that the quantity of sterling demanded for the import of good X is a decreasing function of the price of foreign exchange.

The preceding relationship between Columns (4) and (6) is plotted in panel A3 of Figure 11–1, and the relationship of Columns (6) and (7) is plotted in Panel A4. Both graphs show a downward-sloping demand curve, which over the positive range is drawn as a solid line and in the negative range as a broken line. According to our numerical example, the intercept of the demand curves in Panels A3 and A4 is at $1, though for the graphical representation this particular value is of no importance. What we have shown is that, given normally sloped domestic industry demand and supply curves and a fixed sterling price for good X, the excess-demand curve for sterling is a decreasing function of the exchange rate, though henceforth we shall refer to it as a demand rather than the excess-demand curve.

We now turn to the derivation of the supply curve for sterling as a function of the exchange rate, in a manner strictly analogous to that used in the derivation of the demand curve. In Part B of Table 11–1 we show, in Columns (1) through (4), the functional relationships between the dollar price of the export good Y, domestic demand and supply, and the excess supply schedule. The latter is defined as the value of Column (3) minus Column (2). The numerical values were chosen in such a way that at the range of the exchange rate where excess demand for good X is positive, the excess supply for good Y is also positive, so that the two functions can be plotted in the same positive sterling space as in Panels A4 and B4. In every other way the derivation of Part B follows that of Part A in Table 11–1, and Panels B1 through B4 are analogous to Panels A1 through A4. We find that according to the numerical example, the domestic equilibrium price of good Y under autarchy $\overline{Y}(\$)$ is $1.50, and that the intercept of the supply curve in Panels B3 and B4 is at $0.30.

We are now in a position to determine the equilibrium exchange rate for country A by finding in Table 11–1 that exchange rate at which excess quantities of sterling demanded and supplied are equal. As can be seen from the last two columns of Table 11–1, this condition holds at the exchange rate of 0.50 and a quantity of £35 traded per time period. In Panel C of Figure 11–1 we have plotted these relationships, knowing the value of the intercepts for the demand and supply curves at 1.0 and 0.3, respectively, and knowing also the equilibrium exchange rate $\overline{R} = 0.5$ and the equilibrium quantity of £35 traded. Because of the assumed linear functions, the slopes in Panel C reflect accurately the numerical example of Table 11–1.

Given our knowledge of the equilibrium exchange rate, we can now determine the dollar prices of X and Y prevailing in country A after the opening of trade. As can be seen from Table 11–1, at the exchange rate of 0.5 the price of X is $5 and of Y it is $2.50. The ratio of these two prices is $Y(\$)/X(\$) = 0.5$, the same as the ratio of these two goods in pounds, or $Y(\pounds)/X(\pounds) = 5/10 = 0.5$. This must be so because to find the ratio in dollars from the ratio in sterling we have to multiply the denominator and numerator of the sterling price ratio by the same equilibrium exchange rate, or the entire fraction by factor of 1.0. The equality of the domestic and foreign price ratios in this model is the same as the equality of these in the pure model developed in Part One.

We can note the following additional similarities between the pure model and the partial equilibrium model with foreign exchange. First, the domestic price ratio under autarchy is $Y(\$)/X(\$) = 1.50/10.0 = 0.15$, while under free trade it is 0.5. This means that trade leads to an increase in the relative price of the export good Y, which is necessary to induce increased domestic production and which is the same found in the pure trade model. Second, under autarchy country A consumes 7.0 and 13.5 units of goods X and Y, respectively, while under free trade the corresponding quantities are 9.5 and 12.5. There is a gross gain in consumption of X equal to 2.5 units and a reduction in consumption of Y equal to 1.0 unit. But since at the free trade equilibrium prices one unit of X (\$5) exchanges for two units of Y (\$2.50), the net gain from trade is equal to \$10, or the equivalent of two units of X or four units of Y.

From this simple model of the foreign exchange market we can reach the following important conclusions. As in the pure trade model without money or foreign exchange rates, under autarchy domestic production and consumption are equalized at a certain relative price for the two goods produced in the economy. The opening up of trade at a given world price ratio in terms of a foreign currency price different from the domestic price under autarchy leads to an increase in the domestic relative price of the export good, increased output of Y, and decreased output of X. Trade permits increased consumption, and the gains from trade can be measured either in terms of good X, good Y, or domestic currency. Therefore, in all important respects the foreign exchange market model yields qualitatively the same results as does the pure trade model. In addition, it provides us with some useful insights about functional relationships between the exchange rate and the demand and supply for foreign exchange, bringing out clearly also that the equilibrium exchange rate is dependent on all of the forces which underlie the positions of the domestic demand and supply curves in both industries, as well as on the foreign prices of the traded goods.

In closing this section on the determinants of the equilibrium exchange rate, we can briefly analyze the effects some changes in domestic conditions and world prices have on the equilibrium exchange rate. For this purpose it is most useful to employ Figure 11–1 because we are interested only in qualitative rather than precise quantitative predictions. As a first case consider that technological change leads to an outward shift in the supply curve of industry X shown in Panel A1. This change is reflected in Panel A2 in a shift of the excess-demand schedule downward and to the left, since at any given domestic price the increased supply combined with a given demand reduces excess demand. In Panels A3, A4, and C the demand curves shift downward and to the left correspondingly. As a result we find in Panel C that the exchange rate and level of trade must fall, as long as the supply curve is neither vertical nor horizontal. This result makes intuitive sense, since the assumed improvement in productivity is in country A's import industry, and this makes imports less necessary.

As a second case consider the exogenous increase in the world price of country A's import good X. In our construction of Table 11–1 and Figure 11–1, we found the domestic price of X by multiplying the sterling price of X by the exchange rate. For any given exchange rate in Column (6) of Table 11–1, Part A, therefore, the domestic price is higher. But since at this higher price the quantities demanded and supplied are smaller and larger, respectively, the excess demand is reduced. In Panel A3 of Figure 11–1 the demand curve is unambiguously shifted down and to the left. However, now we must take account of the fact that for these fewer imported units of X, at every exchange rate more pounds sterling must be paid. As a result, the new demand curve for sterling shown in Panels A4 and C of Figure 11–1 may be to the right or left of the original one, depending on the elasticities of the functions involved. Consequently, the effect of an increase in the world price of a country's import good may either raise or lower its exchange rate and level of trade.

In the Appendix to this chapter we analyze simple equations underlying our numerical examples. This makes it possible to see with greater precision how and why certain assumed changes in basic determinants of the exchange rate influence its equilibrium level.

II. CAPITAL FLOWS, SPECULATION, AND GOVERNMENT

In this section we extend the model of the foreign exchange market presented above by introducing sources of demand for and supply of foreign exchange other than that arising from the import and export of goods. We do so by considering different classes of foreign exchange market participants according to their motives of behavior, such as international trade in assets; speculation; the international, unilateral transfer of income or wealth; and stabilization of the exchange rate by the government. We defer to following chapters the analysis of the welfare effects and other ramifications of the activities of these market participants.

Capital Flows

The simplest model of international capital flows is the classical one, based on a set of assumptions designed to bring out the most elementary aspects of the savings and investment process. These assumptions are that only firms hold real capital, the construction of which is financed by the issuance of long-term bonds. These bonds yield an interest rate equal to the marginal productivity of real capital. The general public does all of the saving and holds only bonds.

Now consider that before the opening up of trade, the two countries described above, A and B, are in equilibrium in domestic goods markets and in the capital market. At the existing domestic equilibrium interest rates in the two countries under autarchy, there exists an international interest rate differential in favor of country B. When autarchy ends and trade in goods and assets is permitted, the residents of country A are assumed to wish to acquire a certain number of country B bonds. We defer until later chapters the rigorous analysis of the precise determinants of this number of bonds and the general equilibrium repercussions of these purchases, especially on interest rates in the two countries. In this chapter we are interested only in the general effect of capital flows on the foreign exchange market. Therefore we consider that in the period after the opening up of international economic relations between countries A and B, the residents of country A wish to acquire an exogenously given number of country B bonds valued at OM sterling.

FIGURE 11–2
Capital Flows and the Exchange Rate

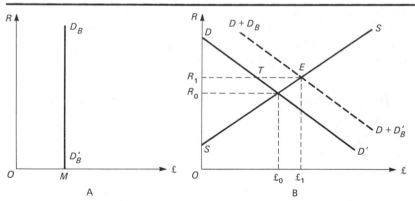

In Panel A the demand curve $D_B D_B'$ represents the perfectly inelastic demand of country A's residents for country B's bonds, worth OM units of sterling. In Panel B this sterling demand due to the import of bonds is added to the demand and supply schedules derived from the trade in goods. In the new equilibrium the price of foreign exchange is raised to OR_1, and the turnover of sterling is increased to $O\pounds_1$.

In Panel A of Figure 11–2 we show this value of bonds in terms of sterling along the horizontal axis, while the vertical axis measures the price of foreign exchange, R, in the tradition of the model developed above. It can be seen from the figure that the demand curve for bonds, $D_B D_B'$, is independent of the exchange rate. We will defend this treatment of the demand for long-term assets in our analysis of speculation in the next section of this chapter.

In Panel B of Figure 11–2, which has the same axis as Panel A, we show the foreign exchange demand and supply curves which we derived above from country A's trade in goods. The equilibrium exchange rate and quantity of sterling traded are shown as R_0 and $£_0$, respectively. The demand for country B bonds by country A's buyers leads to a parallel outward shift of the demand curve for foreign exchange from DD' to $D + D_B - D + D_B'$ by the amount OM, which is equal to TE in Panel B. The equilibrium exchange rate and amounts of exchange traded during the period are OR_1 and $O£_1$, respectively.

As can readily be seen, the new equilibrium exchange rate is above the old one at which trade is balanced. Since all of the conditions underlying the drawing of the foreign exchange demand and supply curves in Panel B of Figure 11–2 remain unchanged by the purchase of the foreign bonds, the effect of the exchange rate change on trade can be detected by moving along these curves. Thus, at the higher exchange rate, demand for sterling for the import of good X is decreased and supply of sterling from the export of Y is increased. These effects take place for reasons which should be clear from the model presented in Section I of this chapter. At the higher price for foreign exchange the domestic prices for X and Y are raised, causing domestic demand and supply for both commodities to be decreased and increased, respectively, which in turn leads to smaller imports of X and larger exports of Y. As a result, country A has a surplus in the value of exports over imports, which in equilibrium is just equal to the value of the bonds acquired abroad, or in Panel B, the distance TE between the original demand and supply curves at the exchange rate OR_1.

This simple model leads to the fundamental and important conclusions that the desire by the residents of country A to export capital and acquire foreign assets leads to an increased demand for foreign exchange, a rise in the price of foreign exchange, and a trade surplus just large enough to pay for the bonds through the transfer of real goods of equal value. In other words, the change in the exchange rate leads to the net export of real resources to pay for the import of financial assets. These real resources are used in country B to add to its capital stock. The effects of this addition on welfare and rates of return to capital in both countries and consequent capital flows in other periods will be analyzed in Chapter 25.

The preceding analysis can readily be amended to account for the fact that in the real world international capital flows involve not only the purchase of bonds but also the purchase of equities and real estate and the direct ownership of business firms. In all acquisitions of foreign assets the residents of the capital-exporting country have to enter the foreign exchange market to obtain the currency with which to compensate the owners of the assets abroad. The resultant effects on the exchange rate and trade balance are the same as in the case of bonds, as analyzed above.

Speculation

Speculation in the spot exchange market involves the sale or purchase of a foreign asset at today's price, R_0, and its repurchase or sale at time t in the future at a price R_t, in the hope that a profit is realized. While a speculator knows today's price with certainty, the future price is only expected, $E(R)_t$. This decision to buy or sell can be formulated as follows, dropping the £ and $ subscripts:

If $R_0 > E(R)_t$: Sell.
If $R_0 < E(R)_t$: Buy.
If $R_0 = E(R)_t$: Enter no transaction.

For example, if today the price of one pound sterling is $1 and it is expected to be $0.9 dollars a week later, then the speculator sells sterling, expecting to profit at the rate of $0.1 dollar per pound.

The rate of return from speculation is a function of the length of time of the investment of the speculative funds. In the above example, the 10 percent reduction in the price of foreign exchange which was assumed to have taken place in one week involves a 520 percent rate of return per year, abstracting from compounding of interest and the difference in yields obtainable on the one-week holding of funds in country A rather than country B. It is clear that for any given expected difference between the buying and selling prices of foreign exchange, the annual rate of return from speculation is a decreasing function of the investment period.

Long-term foreign investments typically are made without regard to expectation about future exchange rates, as in our analysis of the demand for bonds above, for two reasons. First, exchange rate changes over the longer run are very difficult to predict. Second, as we shall discuss in Part Four of this book, in the long run relative exchange rate changes are nearly perfectly correlated with relative price level changes in the relevant countries, so that, for example, capital gains in the foreign currency value of an asset in a rapidly inflating country tend to be offset by losses from the accompanying depreciation of that country's exchange rate. In the case of bonds, the nominal rate of interest tends to reflect the return on real capital, plus a premium for expected inflation. In this case the inflation premium in the interest rate tends to compensate investors for changes in the country's exchange rate. Because of these theoretical relationships between a country's rate of inflation, interest rate, and exchange rate, in the long run we are justified in drawing the demand curve for long-term foreign assets as a vertical line, as in Figure 11–2, Panel A, above.

For short-term investments to be held speculatively for a time period of t days, in which the expectation of capital value changes from exchange rate fluctuations are important, we show the demand for foreign exchange as in Panel A of Figure 11–3, where the vertical and horizontal axes

FIGURE 11–3
Speculation and the Exchange Rate

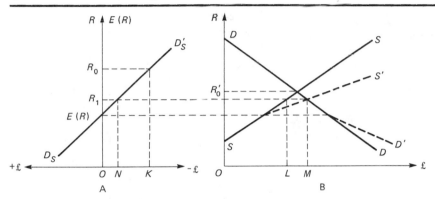

The demand curve $D_S D_S'$ in Panel A of Figure 11–3 shows the quantities of sterling demanded ($+£$) and supplied ($-£$) as a function of the exchange rate and the expectation that the future spot rate is $OE(R)$. For example, if the spot rate is OR_1, speculators sell ON sterling in expectation of repurchasing it at the lower price $OE(R)$ in the future.

In Panel B the foreign exchange demand and supply schedules DD' and SS' arising from trade in goods only are modified to include the effects of speculation. At exchange rates above $OE(R)$, speculators add to supply (SS''). In Panel B speculators expecting a fall in the exchange rate in the future to $OE(R)$ lower the previously existing equilibrium rate from OR_0' to OR_1. At this price the traders' excess demand, LM, is met by speculators.

measure the exchange rate and the quantity of foreign exchange demanded or supplied, respectively. The schedule $D_S D_S'$ shows a zero demand or supply at a spot exchange rate equal to the expected spot rate at time t, assuming that the interest rate differential on short-term investment in the two countries, A and B, is zero. When the actual spot rate is above the expected spot rate, the schedule shows a sale or negative quantity of sterling demanded, for reasons discussed above. On the other hand, if the actual spot rate is below the expected spot rate, speculators add to the demand for foreign exchange.

We assume that the schedule shown is that for the market as a whole and consists of many speculators, all of whom hold the same views on the value of the expected spot exchange rate in the future. One could assume alternatively that the market schedule is net, after speculators with different views on the future exchange rate (and therefore different views on the merit of sales or purchases) have concluded transactions with each other.

But for reasons to become obvious shortly, it is more convenient to assume here that all speculators hold the same expectations.

The essence of speculation is the assumption of risk. However, risk comes in differing degrees of intensity, the nature of which can be explained with the help of Figure 11–4. In the two graphs presented in

FIGURE 11–4
Probability Distribution of Future Exchange Rate

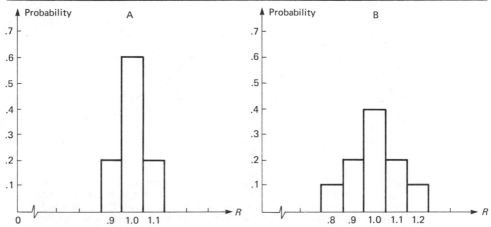

Both Panels A and B in Figure 11–4 show the probability distributions of prices of assets held for a specified length of time. Both distributions have a mean of 1.0, indicating that the best guess is that each of them will be worth 1.0 in the future. However, the asset shown in Panel A has a smaller variance of expected returns than does the asset shown in Panel B. The former asset is considered to be less risky than the latter and is preferred by risk avoiders.

Panels A and B, we measure along the horizontal axis the price of foreign exchange and along the vertical axis probabilities. Panel A shows an individual speculator's perception of the price of sterling at a certain time in the future. Typically, he has a best guess as to the most likely price, such as 1.0 in Panel A. He believes that this price has a probability of .6 of being realized. On the other hand, he believes that the price may also be .9 or 1.1, each with a probability of .2. Panel B shows another perception of the likely future spot exchange rate. Again the best guess is that the rate will be 1.0, but in this case only with a probability of .4. Other outcomes, with the perceived probabilities, show a wider range of possible outcomes in this than in the preceding situation. It should be noted that in both cases the probabilities shown add to 1.0, and the characteristics of the two probability distributions can be summarized conveniently by their mean, also known as the expected price $E(R)$ and standard deviation (or variance).

Economists have developed a large body of rigorous analytical models based on the notions that the variance of the probability distribution about future prices is a measure of risk and that speculators and investors typically are risk avoiders in the sense that, ceteris paribus, they prefer to speculate or invest in one situation rather than another because the probability distribution in the first situation has a smaller variance and therefore less risk than in the second situation. We cannot develop formal models of speculation and investment under conditions of risk here, so we introduce the notion of risk into our analysis of currency speculation in the following way. The riskier a situation, the fewer speculators are tempted to enter the market, and the smaller the amount of money that will be invested by every speculator in the market. Consequently, if the D_SD_S' schedule in Figure 11–3, Panel A, shows the functional relationship between the quantity of sterling demanded or supplied for speculative purposes and the spot exchange rate, under conditions depicted in Figure 11–4, Panel B, then if conditions were to change to those shown in Panel A, the D_SD_S' schedule would be flatter. Under the less risky conditions, but with the same expected price, speculators would be demanding or supplying more sterling at any given spot rate. In the extreme, if the future spot rate were certain to be equal to 1, speculators would be willing to demand or supply so much foreign currency that the D_SD_S' schedule is perfectly elastic at the expected price.

The speculators' schedule in Figure 11–3, Panel A, shifts in response to changes in the expected future spot rate such that the intercept with the vertical axis always is at the expected spot rate, given a zero interest rate differential. The schedule also shifts in response to changes in the interest rate differential on short-term investment in countries A and B. This is so because the spot funds shifted for speculative purposes can earn some interest in the money markets of the two countries, and the difference in interest should be considered as adding to the cost or expected gains from the speculation proper. In the derivation of the speculative schedule in Figure 11–3, Panel A, we assumed a zero interest rate differential. Now if, ceteris paribus, a differential in favor of the sterling market were to develop, then the entire schedule would shift upward because the purchase of sterling at a rate above the expected future spot rate and its later sale at that expected rate involves a capital loss. The intercept will be above the expected spot rate by an amount which, if converted into an annual rate of return, is just large enough to be made up by the interest rate differential in favor of the sterling money market. In other words, a speculative investment at the intercept exchange rate invested in the foreign money market is expected to yield a zero net gain from the higher foreign interest advantage, because of an equal-sized expected exchange rate loss. As a result, there are no incentives for speculation at the intercept rate. By analogy, the development of an interest rate differential in favor of the dollar money market results in a downward shift of the $D_S D_S'$ schedule in Figure 11–3.

Let us now integrate the speculative schedule into the model of the foreign exchange market in which only traders in goods and services are active. For this purpose we show in Figure 11–3, Panel B, the demand and supply curves derived above in Section I of this chapter. In the absence of speculation, the equilibrium exchange rate is R_0'. In the presence of speculative market expectations, as represented by the schedule $D_S D_S'$ in Panel A, the equilibrium exchange rate is R_1, which represents the point of intersection between the horizontal addition of the trader supply schedule and the speculators schedule, SS'', in Panel B. As can be seen, at R_1 the supply of sterling by exporters of goods is OL and by speculators, LM, for a total of OM, which is equal to the quantity demanded by importers. The schedule SS'' is drawn in such a way that of necessity at R_1 the quantity of sterling supplied by speculators, according to Panel A, is ON, which in turn is just equal to LM in Panel B.

As can be seen from Panel B in Figure 11–3, at rates below the expected spot rate, $E(R)$, speculators add to the demand for foreign exchange and change the demand schedule from DD' to DD''. Under the conditions assumed to exist in Figure 11–3, the speculators expect a lowering of the exchange rate in the future from R_0' to $E(R)$ and their market sales of currency push the current spot rate in this direction, to R_1. For this reason the equilibrium exchange is determined by the intersection of the trader demand schedule with the supply schedule, including speculators. If expectations are for a rise in the exchange rate above that determined by traders, then the segment of the demand schedule including speculators enters into the determination of the exchange rate.

The model of speculative behavior developed above is based on the activities of owners of spot funds. Thus, residents of country A, where the dollar is the native currency, typically need to sell dollar assets in order to buy sterling if they expect an increase in the price of sterling. However, if the residents of country A expect a depreciation of sterling, they typically do not have in their portfolios sterling assets to sell. We can consider that in these conditions the residents of country B, whose portfolios tend to be denominated in sterling, enter into the market by selling them for dollars. Of course, the demand for dollars in the market implies the supply of sterling. According to this analysis, therefore, the speculative schedule of Figure 11–3, Panel A, involves residents of both countries A and B, just as the demand and supply schedules for goods involve traders in both countries, since exporters of one country necessarily have as their counterparts importers in the other country, and vice versa for importers.

Now we consider forms of speculation in foreign exchange which do not require the ownership of spot funds but instead are based on borrowing or the timing of payments or purchases. Speculation through borrowing represents a ready extension of the procedure discussed above. A resident in country A whose asset portfolio is denominated in dollars can speculate on the lowering of the price of sterling by borrowing today in country B, selling the sterling proceeds for dollars, and expecting to repurchase the sterling and repay the loan in the future when the price of sterling has fallen. This form of speculation is motivated by the same considerations discussed above in connection with speculation with owned funds, and it permits retention of the analytical tool of the speculative schedule as before. Multinational enterprises which have ready sources of credit in many countries are known to take advantage of this form of speculation frequently, while lenders of short-term funds, often also the multinational enterprises, tend to hold certain proportions of their asset portfolios in foreign currencies expected to appreciate in value.

According to some analysts, however, one of the most important forms of speculation involves traders in goods who change the timing of their basic transactions or payments in order to reap extra profits from expected changes in the price of foreign exchange. How this speculation takes place can be understood most readily within the analytical framework developed above, where country A is assumed to be small relative to country B, the rest of the world. This assumption implies that a change in the external value of country B's currency, the pound sterling, does not affect the domestic sterling price of any goods. Furthermore, such a relationship may conveniently be assumed to produce the custom that all bills in B's foreign trade are denominated in sterling.

Now consider that an exporter in country A expects the value of sterling to go from $1 to $1.10 within the near future, so that his export good, worth £2 abroad, will increase in value from $2 to $2.20 domestically. It is obvious that this exporter has a strong incentive to delay turning his sterling receipts into dollars. For this reason the supply curve for foreign exchange depicted in Figure 11–1, Panel C, is shifted upward and to the left during the time period when exporters expect an appreciation of sterling.

Now consider the behavior of importers into country A. They face the prospect that as a result of the expected increase in the price of sterling from $1 to $1.10, the dollar value of an import good worth £3 will go from $3 to $3.30. Consequently, importers have strong incentives to speed up the placement of orders and the payment of sterling obligations. These actions of importers tend to shift upward and to the right the demand curve for sterling shown in Figure 11–1, Panel C. It can readily be envisaged (therefore we do not show it in a diagram) that the shifts in the demand and supply curves for foreign exchange just explained lead to an equilibrium price for foreign exchange in the current period which is higher than it would have been, ceteris paribus, in the absence of the expected appreciation of sterling. The activities of traders engaging in speculation thus result in what is known as leads and lags in payments and purchases, which tend to justify the expectations of the speculators.

The economic and welfare effects of speculation in foreign exchange are as beneficial as they are in other markets if speculators forecast prices correctly. As is well known from the theory of speculation, if today's price of wheat is $1 per bushel, but speculators expect that next year's price will be $1.50 because of a bad harvest or increased demand, they buy wheat today to resell next year at the higher price. In so doing they raise today's price above $1 and lower next year's price below $1.50. They raise welfare by inducing consumers through the higher price to use less wheat during the current period of relatively abundant supply and by relieving the relative shortage next year. If speculators forecast correctly the forces influencing future demand, supply, and equilibrium prices, their actions even out the fluctuations in prices and reduce the hardships which would have befallen consumers otherwise in the future, because of shortages due to fundamental developments in the economy beyond the control of producers, governments, or speculators.

Speculation in foreign exchange plays an analogously beneficial role in that it leads to an evening out of exchange rate fluctuations which would have taken place otherwise for fundamental reasons, such as shifts in the demand and supply curves in domestic industries (as we discussed in connection with Figure 11–1) or changes in commodity prices in the rest of the world, all of which are exogenously determined and take place in the presence or absence of speculators.

Speculation in foreign exchange and all markets affects welfare adversely if it is based on false expectations about future developments. Under these conditions speculators add to price fluctuations and aggravate shortages and surpluses in goods markets. It is not known whether speculators on balance forecast developments correctly or incorrectly. There is evidence from the analysis of major periods of speculation that expectations feed on themselves, and psychological influences are more dominant than the careful analysis of real factors in the determination of speculative activities. On the other hand, theory suggests that speculators who cannot forecast real developments accurately tend to lose money, until they are forced to cease speculation. Thus, we would expect to see speculative activities dominated by persons who have a consistently good record in forecasting fundamental trends in demand and supply. However, it is quite conceivable that speculation attracts continuously a large group of persons who forecast badly, lose their money, and drop out, only to be replaced by new entrants into the market. If this floating population of bad speculators is large enough, destabilizing speculation can persist for a long period of time.

Solid empirical evidence on the ability of speculators to forecast prices accurately is not available. If forced to pass a judgment, we might conclude, from the theoretical arguments just presented and from the fragmentary empirical evidence available, that probably in "normal" periods speculation is beneficial and stabilizing, but during periods of great fundamental changes in the world, masses of speculators are often wrong, and they are influenced by psychological factors of their own making.

Government

National governments enter foreign exchange markets for two fundamental reasons. First, they make unilateral transfers of funds abroad for which the motivation typically is noneconomic. Examples of such transfers are foreign aid and military expenditures. Normally such payments are appropriated by governments in their own currency. As an example, consider that country A wishes to provide a $1 million grant of aid to the government and population of country B. Country A's government treasury thus sends a check for $1 million to the government of country B, which in turn sells these dollars in the foreign exchange market to obtain sterling for distribution among its population. In the analytical framework of Panel C Figure 11–1, this supply of dollars is equivalent to an increase in the demand for sterling in the foreign exchange market and is represented by an outward shift of the demand curve. Of necessity, therefore, the new equilibrium exchange rate must be above the old one at which trade was balanced. At this higher rate country A runs a $1 million trade surplus, for reasons analyzed above in Figure 11–2, in connection with capital flows. In effect then the donation of $1 million in the form of a check leads to the transfer from A to B of real goods worth that amount. For purposes of later analysis it is important to note here that foreign aid and other such government transfers, as well as capital exports, must lead to a depreciation of the exporting country's exchange rate and the development of a trade surplus. If it does not, because of government interferences, the aid- or capital-receiving country does not obtain the real goods necessary to benefit from these transfers.

A minor point worth noting is that the outward shift of the demand curve for sterling in response to the sale of $1 million by the government of country A is not parallel. Instead, the extent of the shift is determined by the value of the exchange rate itself. For example, when the rate is $1, the demand curve at this rate is £1 million to the right of the one based on the importation of goods. On the other hand, if the rate is $2 or $0.5, the demand curve at these rates is moved out by £0.5 million or £2 million, respectively. The resultant nonlinear demand curve affects the precise equilibrium exchange rate change attained from any given sized dollar government transfer abroad, but it does not affect the most important qualitative conclusions we reached above about the direction of the exchange rate change.

The second reason for government participation in the foreign exchange market is to stabilize the exchange rate. In Figure 11–5 we show the demand and supply curves for foreign exchange which are assumed to reflect the actions of traders, speculators, and movers of capital. The

FIGURE 11–5
Government Stabilization of Exchange Rates

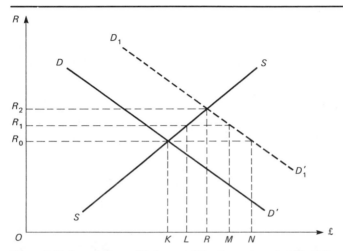

Given initial market equilibrium at OR_0, the outward shift of the demand curve from DD' to D_1D_1' leads to an excess demand of KN sterling, if the government pegs the rate at its initial level. If the exchange rate is permitted to adjust completely to OR_2, excess demand is zero. If the exchange rate is permitted to adjust somewhat, such as to OR_1, then the excess demand is reduced from its extreme, KN, to LM. Generally, excess demand or supply quantities for any given exchange market disturbance are a decreasing function of the exchange rate changes permitted by the government.

equilibrium exchange rate is R_0. Now consider that, for some reason, the demand curve for sterling shifts upward and to the right, to D_1D_1'. In Part Four of this book we will analyze in some detail the causes and nature of these shifts in foreign exchange demand and supply. Here we are interested primarily in explaining the stabilization policies of governments and focusing on the effects of the exogenously given shift in demand, which in the absence of government intervention results in an equilibrium exchange rate of R_2.

In most Western market economies, governments have charged either their central banks or their treasuries, or both in cooperation, to hold international reserves consisting of foreign exchange, gold, or other assets which can readily be converted abroad into foreign exchange. These reserves are used to intervene in the foreign exchange market in order to prevent or dampen the exchange rate changes which the free operation of the market tends to produce, such as the change from R_0 to R_2 in Figure 11–5. If the government wishes to maintain the original equilibrium exchange rate, R_0, in face of the disturbance which resulted in the new demand curve D_1D_1', then, according to Figure 11–5, it needs to sell KN sterling to meet the market's excess demand at the old exchange rate. If, on the other hand, the government wishes merely to reduce the magnitude of the exchange rate change which would have resulted in the free market, say to R_1 rather than R_2, then the required amount of official sale of foreign exchange is only LM, less than the KN required for complete stabilization. From these two discrete cases we can readily generate a generalization of extreme importance for our analysis to come in Part Four. The need to supply foreign exchange in the private market from international reserves in the face of any given excess-demand situation is a decreasing function of the amount of exchange rate change permitted. In the example of Figure 11–5, the total prevention of an exchange rate change requires KN sale of sterling. Permitting the maximum change to the new equilibrium exchange rate requires zero sale of sterling. A change in between these two extremes of zero and maximum, such as to R_1, requires a positive quantity of sterling to be sold, but less than when the rate is kept completely fixed.

We should note a few interesting and important aspects of government stabilization policies in the foreign exchange market. First, if the disturbances which give rise to the excess-demand situation persist, then foreign exchange sales have to be repeated every period. For example, the relationships shown in Figure 11–5 indicate flow demand and supply per time period, say a year. If the demand curve stays at its D_1D_1' position for two years before returning to DD', the government has to sell a total of two KN sterling if it wants to keep the exchange rate at R_0 during the entire period. Second, if the disturbance in the exchange market involves shifts in either the demand or supply curve, or both, in such a manner that at the initial equilibrium rate there is an excess supply of foreign exchange, then stabilization requires the government to buy, and it ends up adding to its holdings of foreign exchange. Third, in our model of the market consisting of only two countries, only one of them needs to intervene in order to reduce or eliminate the fluctuations caused by the free market, since when the sterling-dollar rate is fixed the dollar-sterling rate is fixed also.

The economic significance of foreign exchange market stabilization policies by governments will be one of the central topics to be discussed in Part Four, but the most important points of this analysis can be anticipated here briefly. They are that, in principle, the well-known balance-of-payments problems which have haunted all countries repeatedly in the past century are due to their efforts to maintain fixed exchange rates or to let them move only by inadequate amounts, in the face of persistent excess demand for foreign exchange at these rates. As a result, countries often ran out of foreign exchange to supply in the private market, and "crises" tended to develop. Typically, they were resolved by policies designed to shift the demand and supply curves for foreign exchange, by raising the supported price of foreign exchange, or both. In order to clarify the terminology to be used in the remainder of this book we define devaluation of a currency as the official act of raising the price at which the government purchases foreign currencies and at which, therefore, private transactions take place. As we will discuss at length in Part Four, such devaluations are characteristic of an international monetary system in which governments have committed themselves to maintain "fixed" or "parity" exchange rates. The official decision to lower the price at which foreign currency is traded by the government under such regimes is known as an upward valuation, or more simply as revaluation. On the other hand, when the price of foreign currencies rises or falls without an official announcement, the events are commonly referred to as currency depreciations and appreciations, respectively. Depreciations or appreciations may or may not be accompanied or even caused by government intervention. The essence of the distinction between devaluations and revaluations on the one hand and depreciations and appreciations on the other rests with the presence in the former case and the absence in the latter of an official commitment to the maintenance of a certain exchange rate in the market through government intervention.

The question arises why countries bother to intervene in the foreign exchange market, if it leads to these kinds of crises. The answer is that governments believe that the stabilization of the exchange rates reduces uncertainty and encourages international specialization, trade, and capital flows, and they also believe that the resultant benefits exceed the costs associated with occasional balance-of-payments crises. We will examine the validity of these arguments in Part Four.

III. PURCHASING-POWER PARITY

In the first part of this chapter we showed that at the freely determined equilibrium exchange rate, trade of country A is balanced, and the prices of all traded goods are equalized in the sense that their domestic price equals the world price times the exchange rate. As a result of this fact it should be possible to do two things. First, it should be possible to live as well in country B on an income of £1,000 as in country A on an income of $2,000, if the dollar-sterling exchange rate is 2 and we abstract from income and excise taxes. Second, if for some reason, such as a war, trade between countries A and B has been interrupted and price levels in the two countries have moved at different rates during the period, then it should be possible to calculate an equilibrium exchange rate for the two countries from information on the domestic currency prices of goods to be traded internationally.

Following the terminology developed by the Swedish economist Gustav Cassell, we can calculate the absolute purchasing-power parity exchange rate $PP(\$ \cdot \pounds) = PP$ as being 2, from knowing, for example, that a bushel of wheat (W) in country A sells for $4 W($)$ and in country B for 2 $W(\pounds)$: $PP = W($)/W(\pounds) = 4/2 = 2$. By analogy, the relative purchasing-power parity exchange rate at time t, PP_t, is equal to the ratio of the price of wheat in countries A and B at time t, $W($)_t/W(\pounds)_t$, over the ratio of these prices at time 0, multiplied by the exchange rate at time 0,

$$PP_t = R_t = \frac{\dfrac{W($)_t}{W(\pounds)_t}}{\dfrac{W($)_0}{W(\pounds)_0}} \cdot R_0$$

For example, if at time zero the price of a bushel of wheat were $2 and £2 and the exchange rate were 1, then at time t, with the dollar price of wheat doubled at $4 and that of sterling at £2, the purchasing power parity exchange rate should be 2.

However, as tourists and those who have lived in other countries know well, the purchasing power of a given domestic sum of money converted into foreign currency rarely permits the purchase of equal bundles of goods abroad and domestically. Similarly, attempts to calculate purchasing-power parity exchange rates from national price data have yielded nonsensical results. They show, for example, that the market exchange rates of developing low-income countries are too low and should be appreciated to become equal to the calculated purchasing-power parity rates. Yet we know that nearly all developing countries have chronic excess market demand for foreign exchange, which would only be aggravated by a further increase in the foreign value of their currencies. The failure of purchasing-power parity calculations to yield correct information in these two uses have to be attributed to the fact that the model of exchange rate determination which was presented in Section I of this chapter, and which suggests the uses of these calculations, neglects the existence of nontraded goods and services.

Every country produces a number of goods and services which are not traded internationally because transportation costs relative to their value are too high, as we argued in Chapter 4. Because there is no trade in these goods and services, their prices are not equalized at existing exchange rates. This is why a tourist from country A may find that at the market exchange rate the prices of food, clothing, automobiles, and other traded products are the same in country B as in A, abstracting from different rates of sales and excise taxes, while at the same time he may find that his dollars buy more haircuts, restaurant services, household help, and so on in country B than in country A.

We can illustrate the problems which arise from the existence of non-traded goods for the interpretation of purchasing-power parity exchange rates by the use of Table 11–2, in which we show the prices and budgets of

TABLE 11–2
Prices and Quantities in Consumer Baskets

	Country A		Country B	
	Unit Price in $	Quantities/Period	Unit Price in £	Quantities/Period
Bread	2	5	1	4
Wine	6	4	3	2
Haircut	6	1	1	3

an "average" consumer in countries A and B. As can be seen from this table, at the exchange rate of 2 for sterling-dollars, the prices of the two traded goods, bread and wine, are equalized. However, in country A the nontraded haircuts are more expensive relative to the traded goods than they are in country B. As a result of these relative goods prices, consumers in country A favor the consumption of traded goods, as compared with country B consumers, who purchase proportionately more of the non-traded good.

In the hypothetical world represented in Table 11–2, what is the purchasing power of the dollar relative to the pound sterling? The answer to this question can be approached in two ways. First, we can find out the ratio of the dollar and sterling value of the baskets of goods bought by the "average" consumers in their native countries. This calculation is done simply by adding up the sums of money spent on individual goods, given the quantities and prices shown in Table 11–2:

$$VA(\$) = \Sigma P_i(\$) \cdot Q_i(\$),$$

where $VA(\$)$ is the dollar value of the average country A consumer basket, and $P_i(\$)$ and $Q_i(\$)$ are the dollar prices and quantities of commodities i and $i = 1, 2, 3$ in the basket. The value of $VA(\$)$, from Table 11–2, is $40. The analogous value of a country B average consumer basket $VB(£)$ is £13. The purchasing-power parity ratio using these data is:

$$K_1 = VA(\$)/VA(£) = 40/13 = 3.08$$

Second, we can find out the ratio of the value of country A's average consumer basket in dollars and in sterling. The value of a country A basket in sterling $VA(\pounds)$ is found by calculating the sum of the product of country A quantities with country B prices:

$$VA(\pounds) = \Sigma P_i(\pounds) \cdot Q_i(\$)$$

Using Table 11–2 figures, this comes to £18. The purchasing-power parity ratio calculated in this manner is:

$$K_2 = VA(\$)/VA(\pounds) = 40/18 = 2.22$$

These two purchasing-power parity indices convey different information. The first one shows that if a person with average country A tastes and the normal consumption expenditure of $40 moves to country B and lives like the average consumers there do, he can convert his $40 into £20 at the assumed market exchange rate of 2 and purchase 20/13 ≈ 1.5 average country B market baskets. A given income or wealth in dollars thus allows him to increase his standard of living by about 50 percent. This same implication of a 50 percent income increase can also be derived by forming the ratio of the purchasing power parity index, K_1, over the market exchange rate, $K_1/R = 3.08/2.00 ≈ 1.5$. The second ratio indicates that an average consumer from country A who wants to buy the same basket of goods in country B that he is used to consuming in country A can buy only $K_2/R = 2.22/2.00 ≈ 1.1$ baskets by exchanging his dollars into sterling at the market exchange rate.

The preceding illustration agrees well with the experience of many tourists from high-income countries like the United States, Canada, and Britain, where services and other nontraded goods are relatively expensive, who vacation or live temporarily in low-income countries like Mexico, Spain, Portugal or India, where nontraded goods and services are relatively cheap. If they are willing to live like the native people, their vacation money goes much further than if they insist on maintaining their customary consumption patterns. Most tourists and others who change domiciles for longer periods make adjustments in their expenditure patterns which put them somewhere in between the two extremes, living like the local residents or retaining completely their original consumption habits. For this reason, purchasing-power parity indexes calculated and published by the German Statistical Office arbitrarily are made equal to the mean of the two extreme ratios:

$$K^* = \frac{K_1 + K_2}{2} = \frac{3.08 + 2.22}{2} = 2.65$$

Purchasing-power parity indexes such as this are used by multinational enterprises, international organizations such as the United Nations and the International Monetary Fund, and national governments to determine equitable pay levels in new employment locations for employees hired in one country and transferred into others. In some countries courts of law determine alimony and other payments in support of persons made by a resident of one country to a resident of another, taking into account these purchasing-power parity indexes. For tourists and persons contemplating migration after retirement or the taking up of permanent residence and employment in another country, these purchasing-power parity calculations provide valuable information which is not implicit in the market exchange rates.

As already mentioned, purchasing-power parity indexes have been used to estimate whether a country's market exchange rate is appropriate for the attainment of an international payments balance. The calculations of relative purchasing-power parity made by Cassel during the interwar period and by Hendrik Houthakker of Harvard University for the U.S. dollar during the 1960s generally were considered to be of little value for the intended purpose of finding an equilibrium exchange rate, for several reasons. They did not take account of structural changes in various countries' economies during the period over which the relative purchasing powers of currencies were calculated. For example, the discovery of a major oil deposit tends to alter a country's entire pattern of comparative advantage, and therefore calculations of purchasing-power parity which are based on different consumer baskets and different proportions of nontraded goods at two points in time in that country are invalidated. Similarly, changes in several countries' domestic taxation patterns, net foreign investment, and government expenditures abroad enter into the determination of equilibrium exchange rates, along with price level changes measured by the purchasing-power parity indexes. Very important also is the fact already mentioned that in the case of purchasing-power parity calculations involving industrial and developing countries, the results imply the undervaluation of the developing countries' currencies, which is totally inconsistent with other evidence.

However, recently Bela Balassa of Johns Hopkins University provided an important analysis (1964) of the cause of this finding of the apparent undervaluation of developing countries' currencies. He argued that in individual countries the ratio of prices of nontraded goods and services over the prices of traded goods is an increasing function of per capita incomes in these countries. The reason given for this functional relationship is that most of the nontraded goods and services are characterized by zero or very small international differences in production technology, and therefore labor input requirements. For example, cutting hair is done in much the same way in all countries of the world, by a barber using standard tools. However, the local currency wages of workers in these nontraded goods and service industries are determined by their opportunity cost in the sectors of the economy producing tradable goods. Since this opportunity cost is higher in high-income than in low-income countries, the wages and therefore the prices of nontraded goods and services, relative to those of traded goods, are an increasing function of average labor productivity in the traded-goods sector, and therefore of average per capita incomes of countries.

This argument can be illustrated with the help of the following example. Assume that the average worker in country A is highly productive and manufactures a ton of steel a day, worth $50 in world prices. His wage is related to this productivity for simplicity, and can be assumed to be $50 a day. In order to prevent barbers in country A from leaving their jobs and working in steel mills, barbers have to be paid a competitive wage, which again for the sake of simplicity we assume to be $50 a day. Now if a barber can handle 25 haircuts a day on average, he must charge $2 per haircut to reach his $50-a-day income. By contrast, in low-income country B a steel worker produces only one half ton of steel a day, and at the market exchange rate his wage is $25 a day. By the same argument as above, a barber in country B earns $25 a day. The key point of Balassa's analysis is that while there are significant differences in the productivity of labor in the manufacture of traded goods, the very source of international differences in income, the productivity of labor in a service industry such as barbering is very similar in all countries. Under the extreme assumption that the productivity of barbers is the same in countries A and B, the price of a haircut in country B under the other assumed conditions must be $1. As a result, we find the ratio of the prices of haircuts to steel to be higher in country A, the high-income country, than in B, the low-income country.

Given this functional relationship, we can readily understand why purchasing-power parity calculations involving two countries with different income levels will always show the low-income country to have low prices and an overvalued currency. At the market exchange rate, the traded goods entering into the market baskets in both countries cost the same, but the nontraded goods and services in the baskets cost less in the low-income than in the high-income country. This result of Balassa's analysis also deepens understanding of the numerical example underlying Table 11–2 above, where we assumed, without explanation of causes, that haircuts were relatively cheaper in country A than in B, in relation to traded goods.

Balassa used regression analysis to support his theoretical arguments and found that, indeed, the degree of apparent currency overvaluation of a country relative to the dollar was an increasing function of the proportionate difference between the per capita incomes in that country and in the United States.

These insights into the nature and shortcomings of purchasing-power parity calculations can in principle be used to adjust estimates of the equilibrium exchange rate for the bias introduced by the existence of nontraded goods and services. However, much more analysis is necessary to also incorporate into such calculations the effects of structural changes in countries' economies, tax systems, and balance-of-payments composition, in order to bring purchasing-power parity calculations to the level of usefulness suggested by the simple model of exchange rate determination presented in preceding parts of this chapter.

Our analysis of purchasing-power parity calculations should make us suspicious of international comparisons of standards of living which use national estimates of income per capita in domestic currency converted into U.S. dollars at market exchange rates. These estimates tend to bias downward the value of income in low-income countries, because the non-traded goods and services in the representative market basket of consumers in these countries enter at a low price relative to the one at which they enter the consumers' basket in developed countries. As Balassa and Paul David of Stanford University have shown in independent studies, a proper adjustment of per capita income figures of the developing countries for this fact tends to lead to about 40 percent higher incomes for them than are suggested by estimates based on the conversion of national currency income estimates at the market exchange rate. This adjustment does not alter the basic proposition that the standard of living in most developing countries is substantially below that in industrial countries, but it does change somewhat our estimate of how low it is in developing countries when we consider the quantity of goods and services this income can purchase.

APPENDIX

Algebraic Model of the Foreign Exchange Market

The numerical example and geometric model of the foreign exchange market presented in the text have as their basis the following equations:

$$\text{Demand function for } X: \quad D_X = 12 - .5X(\$) \qquad (11\text{A--}1)$$
$$\text{Supply function for } X: \quad S_X = 5 + .2X(\$) \qquad (11\text{A--}2)$$
$$\text{Demand function for } Y: \quad D_Y = 15 - 1.0Y(\$) \qquad (11\text{A--}3)$$
$$\text{Supply function for } Y: \quad S_Y = 4.5 + 6Y(\$) \qquad (11\text{A--}4)$$

where D and S denote physical quantities demanded and supplied per time period, respectively, and the symbols $X(\$)$ and $Y(\$)$ refer to the prices of the two traded goods in dollars. Columns (2) and (3) in both parts of Table 11–1 are derived from the above equations by inserting the dollar prices found in Column (1).

The before-trade domestic equilibrium price, $\overline{X}(\$)$, is found by setting equal Equations (11A–1) and (11A–2) and solving for the price of X:

$$D_X = S_X = 12 - .5X(\$) = 5 + .2X(\$) \qquad (11\text{A--}5)$$

$$\overline{X}(\$) = 10.0 \qquad (11\text{A--}6)$$

By analogy, the before-trade domestic equilibrium price, $\overline{Y}(\$)$, is found from Equations (11A–3) and (11A–4):

$$\overline{Y}(\$) = 1.50 \tag{11A-7}$$

Therefore, the pretrade domestic price ratio is $Y(\$)/X(\$) = .15$.

Column (3) in Table 11–1, Part A, can be derived by inserting the prices from Column (1) into the following equation for excess demand (ED_X) which is equal to $D_X - S_X$, or Equations (11A–1) minus (11A–2).

$$ED_X = D_X - S_X = 12 - .5X(\$) - (5 + .2X(\$)) \tag{11A-8}$$

$$ED_X = 7 - .7X(\$) \tag{11A-9}$$

By analogy, excess supply is

$$ES_Y = S_Y - D_Y = 4.5 + 6Y(\$) - (15 - 1.0Y(\$)) \tag{11A-10}$$

$$ES_Y = -10.5 + 7Y(\$) \tag{11A-11}$$

The quantity of sterling demanded $D(\pounds)$ in Column (7) is a function of the excess domestic demand—Equation (11A–11)—times the sterling price of X, $X(\pounds)$, but with the domestic price of X expressed as a function of both the foreign price and the exchange rate. That is, under free trade the domestic price of X is given by Equation (11A–12)

$$X(\$) = X(\pounds) \cdot R \tag{11A-12}$$

Therefore,

$$D_\pounds = [7 - .7(R \cdot X(\pounds))] \cdot X(\pounds) \tag{11A-13}$$

$$D_\pounds = 7(X(\pounds)) - .7[R \cdot (X(\pounds))^2] \tag{11A-14}$$

By analogy, the quantity of pounds $(\pounds)$ supplied $(S_\pounds)$ is

$$S_\pounds = -10.5(Y(\pounds)) + 7[R \cdot (Y(\pounds))^2] \tag{11A-15}$$

The equlibrium exchange rate $\overline{R}$ is found by setting equal demand and supply and solving for the exchange rate:

$$D_\pounds = S_\pounds = 7(X(\pounds)) - .7[R \cdot (X(\pounds))^2]$$
$$= -10.5(Y(\pounds)) + 7[R \cdot (Y(\pounds))^2] \tag{11A-16}$$

$$\overline{R} = [7(X(\pounds)) + 10.5(Y(\pounds))]/[.7(X(\pounds))^2 + 7(Y(\pounds))^2] \tag{11A-17}$$

Inserting into Equation (11A–17) the values of 10 and 5 for $X(\pounds)$ and $Y(\pounds)$, respectively, assumed in the construction of Table 11–1, we find the equilibrium exchange rate to be 0.5.

At this exchange rate, the free trade domestic relative price $\overline{\overline{Y}}(\$)/\overline{\overline{X}}(\$)$ is equal to the ratio of the world prices in sterling converted into the domestic price at the equilibrium exchange rate:

$$\overline{\overline{Y}}(\$)/\overline{\overline{X}}(\$) = Y(\pounds) \cdot \overline{R}/X(\pounds) \cdot \overline{R} \tag{11A-18}$$

But since in equilibrium the exchange rate applied to both exports and imports must be the same, it follows from Equation (11A–18) that the free trade domestic and world price ratios must always be the same, as we argued also in the pure-theory model.

It is instructive now to check on the accuracy of our reasoning and algebraic manipulations by considering levels of domestic production and consumption and exports and imports. At the equilibrium exchange rate of $\bar{R} = 0.5$, given $X(\pounds) = 10$, $Y(\pounds) = 5$, and Equations (11A–1) through (11A–4):

	X	Y
Domestic prices in dollars	5	2.5
Quantities demanded domestically	9.5	12.5
Quantities supplied domestically	6.0	19.5
Excess quantities demanded	3.5	−7.0
Value of excess demand in sterling	35.0	−35.0

From the preceding example of a set of specific equations reflecting domestic demand and supply conditions and foreign prices, it can be seen that the equilibrium exchange rate is determined by the elasticities of the domestic demand and supply curves and the foreign prices. In reference to the problem of the effect of a foreign price change on the exchange rate prices raised above in the context of Table 11–1, we can note that according to Equation (11A–17) foreign prices enter into the determination of the equilibrium exchange rate both in linear form and squared. Moreover, the weights of the prices in this form in the numerator and denominator are determined by the sums of the intercepts and slopes of the basic demand and supply equations. For these reasons it is difficult to generalize about the effects of a change in world prices on a country's exchange rate. However, given a basic system of equations and values for the intercepts and slopes of the functions, such as in Equations (11A–1) through (11A–4) above it is always possible to solve Equation (11A–17) and obtain unambiguous results for each special case.

The problems of generalizing about the effects of certain changes in the determinants of the equilibrium exchange rate encountered in the context of a numerical example and specific equations point to the shortcoming of these techniques of analysis, which was already mentioned in Chapter 1. Valid generalizations can be derived efficiently only by the use of general mathematical specifications of the functions set out in the above equations. However, such a mathematical model of the foreign exchange market involves techniques considered unsuitable for this text. Students who are interested in a mathematical model of the foreign exchange market are referred to the references given at the end of this chapter and to the derivation of the Marshall-Lerner condition in Chapter 16 below, which involves a well-known model of the foreign exchange market in the analysis of the effects of official changes in currency values.

BIBLIOGRAPHICAL NOTES

The classics in the theory of foreign exchange rate determination are Machlup (1964), Haberler (1949) and Robinson (1947). The general theory of portfolio choice is developed by Sharpe (1970), and students in international economics can obtain a good overview by reading ch. 1. Levin (1970) integrates foreign exchange market theory into portfolio-choice theory.

The purchasing-power parity classic is Cassell (1923). A recent article in the Cassell tradition is by Houthakker (1967). Balassa (1964) has made a fundamental contribution to the theory and empirical evidence of purchasing-power parity. A scholarly review of the entire literature on purchasing-power parity is in Officer (1976). The reference to David is 1972.

CONCEPTS FOR REVIEW

Excess demand
Excess supply
Speculation
Purchasing-power parity
Nontraded goods

Devaluation
Depreciation
Revaluation
Appreciation

POINTS FOR FURTHER STUDY AND DISCUSSION

1. Use the functional relationships shown in Columns (1) through (4) of Table 11–1 and recalculate Columns (6) and (7) in Part B of Table 11–1 under the assumption that $Y = 10$ sterling instead of 5. Find the new equilibrium exchange rate using Table 11–1, the graphical approach of Figure 11–1, and the algebra of Equations (11A–1) through (11A–17).

2. Repeat the preceding exercise but make the price of $Y = 1$ sterling. What happens to the trade pattern of country A? Be careful about the signs of equations and excess demand and supply schedules.

3. Using the functional relationship in Table 11–1, find the equilibrium exchange rate under the assumption that residents of country A wish to acquire 10 to purchase foreign assets.

4. Find in the *Financial Times* for July 1 (or nearest date if it is a weekend) in every year 1960–75 the sterling price of a share of Unilever quoted on the London stock exchange. Calculate the year-to-year changes in capital value and take their mean and variance. Now redo the calculation but introduce the dollar-sterling exchange rate, assuming that you bought $1,000 worth of sterling stock on July 1, 1960, and resold it at the price and exchange rate prevailing on July 1, 1961. Repeat the process, using $1,000 to purchase Unilever stock on July 1, 1961, at the prevailing price and exchange rate, and so on for all 15 years. Now calculate the annual capital value changes in dollars experienced and estimate the mean and variance. Are the means and variances calculated in sterling and dollars different? What do you infer from this result for the influence of the exchange rate on foreign asset values?

5. In statistical yearbooks of Britain and the United States, find for the period
    1955–75 annual consumer price indices. Calculate ratios of U.K. to U.S. price
    indices and the sterling-dollar exchange rate. Plot the two series on a time
    series graph. In another graph measure the price ratio and exchange rate ratio
    on the vertical and horizontal axes, respectively, and plot the observations for
    every year. Interpret the results in the light of the purchasing-power parity
    hypothesis and the theory of spot–exchange rate determination.

6. Find a one-year time series of daily exchange rates for some currency. As-
    sume that a speculator believes that tomorrow's exchange rate is always going
    to be equal to the moving average of the 10 days preceding today. If today's
    rate is above that average, sell $100 of the foreign currency at today's rate and
    repurchase it at tomorrow's rate, and vice versa if today's rate is below the
    last 10 days' average. Calculate the cumulative losses or gains during the year.
    Try some other trading rules that appeal to you to find out whether any give
    you consistent profits from such currency speculation. How do you handle the
    opportunity cost of the funds used in speculation?

12 The Forward Exchange and Eurocurrency Markets

Two MARKETS which generally may be considered to be part of the foreign exchange market discussed in the preceding two chapters, but which have sufficiently distinct characteristics and functions to warrant separate treatment, are considered in this chapter. Both the forward exchange and the Eurocurrency markets have been analyzed in detail in a number of books, but there is continued disagreement about some operational aspects and economic effects of these markets and the legal and institutional framework in which their functions continuously change. Consequently, the analysis to be presented in this chapter is only a summary of some selected issues. Students whose interest in these subjects has been awakened are referred to the citations at the end of this chapter for further readings.

I. THE FORWARD EXCHANGE MARKET

As in our analysis of the spot exchange market in Chapter 11, it is useful to distinguish in the forward exchange market classes of market participants by their motives: interest arbitragers, speculators, traders, and hedgers. In discussing the motives of these market participants in detail, we will derive functional relationships between the forward rate and quantities of forward currency demanded and supplied. We will also use the two-country model introduced in Chapter 11, in which the United States is the home country, with dollars as its domestic currency, and Britain is the rest of the world, with sterling as its domestic currency.

Interest Arbitragers

Traditionally, it has been considered that one of the most important sources of demand and supply of forward exchange emanates from wealth holders, such as banks and manufacturing and trading firms, which habitually invest or borrow in the short-term money markets of the world. To keep the exposition simple, let us consider a U.S. firm which has K dollars available for a 90-day investment in a high-quality instrument, such as treasury bills. It invests in the United States or Britain, depending on the outcome of the following calculation:

$$K (1 + I \text{ (U.S.)}/4) \gtreqless K(1/R)(1 + I \text{ (U.K.)}/4) FR \qquad (12\text{--}1)$$

where $I(\text{U.S.})$ and $I(\text{U.K.})$ are the 90-day interest rates on U.S. and U.K. treasury bills, respectively, and R and FR are the dollar-sterling spot and 90-day forward rates, respectively. The left-hand side of Equation (12–1) gives the value of the investment in the United States at the end of the 90-day period. The division of the interest rate by 4 is necessary, since $I(\text{U.S.})$ is the annual rate of return in which all interest rates are quoted, but the investment considered here is only for one quarter of a year. However, to simplify exposition in subsequent equations, we will assume that the interest rate has been adjusted for the appropriate length of the forward exchange contract, and therefore we will drop the division by 4 and simply show the interest rate.

The right-hand side of Expression (12–1) gives us first the value of the K dollars in sterling (K/R) converted at the spot rate and then the value including the foreign interest $(K/R)(1 + I(\text{U.K.})/4)$. This sum is then multiplied at the presently prevailing forward exchange rate to ascertain the dollar value of the investment in Britain at the time of its maturity. The forward sale of the sterling investment for dollars thus assures the comparability of the investment return in the two centers for the U.S. wealth holder, and in effect it eliminates all risk from foreign exchange changes during the period of investment in Britain. If the left-hand side of Expression (12–1) is greater than the right, the U.S. firm is assumed to invest in U.S. treasury bills, if the right side is larger than the left, it invests in U.K. treasury bills. If the two sides are equal, the firm is indifferent about the location of its investment.

Though we will not do so here, it is not difficult to show rigorously that whenever the pattern of interest and exchange rates creates incentives for a U.S. investor to move funds to Britain, this same pattern of rates induces British investors to keep their funds at home or to return assets previously held in the United States. Similarly, since borrowers are just the counterpart of lenders, whenever, for example, incentives are for U.S. investors to buy U.K. bills, British borrowers are induced to sell these bills to Americans to obtain loans. For these reasons it is convenient to continue our analysis by reference to the behavior of investors in the United States, but it should be remembered that investors and borrowers in both countries are motivated analogously.

Concerning the motives of investors presented in connection with Expression (12–1), it is worth elaborating on investors' motives to purchase forward exchange. This act is known as buying forward "cover" for the foreign asset holdings against the risk of exchange rate changes which affects the capital value of the foreign assets. In 90 days, historically and on the average, exchange rates do not tend to move very much in absolute values, except during the relatively rare occasions when, under regimes of fixed exchange rates, devaluations of 5, 10 or more percent take place. However, the problem faced by short-term investors is that when they experience devaluations or depreciations of this magnitude while they hold foreign bills and are not covered, they tend to suffer a substantial loss, expressed as an annual rate of return. For example, a 10 percent devaluation or depreciation of sterling during a 90-day investment period involves a loss of about 40 percent per annum on the capital, disregarding problems of compounding interest. Even when there is no official devaluation or market depreciation, "normal" exchange rate changes of small absolute size can turn into large losses expressed as an annual rate of return on investment, which can easily exceed the interest advantage from the foreign investment. Of course, for analogous reasons foreign investment can lead to large rates of return from favorable exchange rate revaluations or appreciations. However, observers of international short-term investment markets report that a large quantity of funds is potentially available for covered interest arbitrage in the manner just described. These movements of funds which give rise to the demand for or supply of forward exchange are of interest to us here. Investors who buy foreign assets and leave them exposed to the exchange risk are speculators in spot exchange. Their motives and effects have been analyzed in Chapter 11.

Interest Parity Theory

Using Expression (12–1) as a starting point, we can now readily develop the interest arbitrage theory of forward exchange, whose most prominent exponent has been J. M. Keynes. For this purpose, let us assume that the spot exchange rate and the short-term interest rates shown in Expression (12–1) are determined exogenously. Then it follows that in response to capital flows only the forward rate can change. The theory is that it will adjust until Expression (12–1) is an equality. For example, when the right side of the expression is greater than the left, U.S. investors buy British bills and sell forward sterling. Ceteris paribus, these forward sales of sterling put downward pressure on the rate, which continues until all incentives for further arbitrage are eliminated, and the two sides of Expression (12–1) are equal.

Let us now assume that Expression (12–1) is an equation, as Keynes's theory suggests, and develop the concept of the parity forward rate, which is central to his theory. Through simple algebraic manipulation and by dropping the division by 4, for reasons discussed above, we can derive the equation:

$$FR^* = [(I(\text{U.S.}) - I(\text{U.K.})/(1 + I(\text{U.K.}))]R + R \qquad (12–2)$$

where FR^* is defined as the parity forward rate. It represents that forward rate at which, given the U.S. and U.K. interest rate and the spot rate shown on the right side of Equation (12–2), incentives for covered interest arbitrage are zero. Keynes's theory suggests that the market forward exchange rate has a tendency to be equal to this parity forward rate. In other words, if the forward rate is at "parity," then interest arbitrage incentives are zero.

Another useful way of looking at Keynes's theory is to consider the covered arbitrage margin (CAM), which is defined as the interest advantage of domestic over foreign investment, net of any capital gain or loss from the exchange transaction:

$$\text{CAM} = (I(\text{U.S.}) - I(\text{U.K.}))/(1 + I(\text{U.K.})) - (FR - R)/R \quad (12–3)$$

The first part of the right-hand side of the equation gives the interest rate differential on the two treasury-bill rates. It is positive when the U.S. rate exceeds the U.K. rate, zero when both are equal, and negative when the U.K. rate exceeds the U.S. rate. The division of the simple differential by $1 + I(\text{U.K.})$ follows from algebraic necessity and represents a discount factor which in practice tends to be very small and may be neglected. The second term of the equation represents the difference between the forward and spot rate and therefore the capital gain or loss from the exchange transaction, expressed as a percent of the spot exchange rate. Since both terms are percentages, they can be subtracted from each other and the net represents the CAM in terms of a percentage rate of return.

Financial publications, such as the *Federal Reserve Bulletin* of the United States, regularly publish data on the covered arbitrage margin using Equation (12–3) and market observations of interest and exchange rates. According to Keynes, the covered arbitrage margin in equilibrium is zero, and the market should push the forward rate toward such an equilibrium. However, inspection of actual data on covered arbitrage margins reveals that it is very rarely zero. Closer consideration of interest and exchange rate data reveals that it may be positive or negative, depending on the relative sizes of the interest differential, i.e., $(I(\text{U.S.}) - I(\text{U.K.}))/(1 + I(\text{U.K.}))$ and the exchange rate adjustment, i.e., $(FR -$

$R)/R$. Of particular importance for forward exchange policy by the government is the case where a country's money market interest rate exceeds that in the rest of the world, i.e., $(I(\text{U.S.}) - I(\text{U.K.}))/(1 + I(\text{U.K.})) > 0$, but the exchange rates are such that $(FR - R)/R > (I(\text{U.S.}) - I(\text{U.K.}))/(1 + I(\text{U.K.}))$, so that CAM < 0. In other words, it is possible that the market forward exchange rate relative to the spot rate leads to such a large capital loss on the exchange transaction accompanying covered interest arbitrage that the covered arbitrage margin for the United States is negative, and capital moves to the United Kingdom in spite of the U.S. advantage in the simple market rate of interest. We will return to this case below.

The actually observed persistence of positive and negative covered arbitrage margins of substantial size for often-long periods has led to the development of the so-called modern theory of forward exchange. This introduces, explicitly and systematically, sources of demand for and supply of forward exchange other than the one emanating from interest arbitragers. The modern theory will be developed with the help of demand and supply curves as the primary expositional device. However, it retains Keynes's interest arbitrage theory as an integral part of the model.

Geometric Model

In Figure 12–1 the vertical and horizontal axes measure exchange rates, spot and forward, and the quantity of forward exchange, respectively. The AA' line or schedule represents the functional relationship between the quantity of forward exchange demanded or supplied by interest arbitragers, under the assumption that the spot-rate and interest rate advantages in favor of the United States are given exogenously. According to Equation (12–2), when the interest advantage lies with the United States, the parity forward rate must be above the current spot rate. The AA' schedule is seen to cross the vertical axis at the parity forward rate, indicating that if the actual forward rate is at parity, there are no incentives for covered interest arbitrage flows. Therefore, demand or supply of forward exchange is zero.

The shape of the AA' schedule indicates that at forward rates other than parity, positive amounts of forward exchange are traded. When the rate is below parity, arbitragers buy forward sterling, and when it is above parity they sell. This proposition follows from Equation (12–3) and the assumed U.S. interest advantage. It can be understood most readily by considering the fact that when the forward rate equals the parity rate, $FR = FR^*$, CAM in Equation (12–3) is zero. Therefore, if the forward rate is below the parity rate, $FR < FR^*$, CAM is positive, and the assumed simple interest advantage in favor of the United States is preserved. Consequently, interest arbitragers move sterling funds into the United States

FIGURE 12–1
Covered Interest Arbitrage: No Expected Devaluation

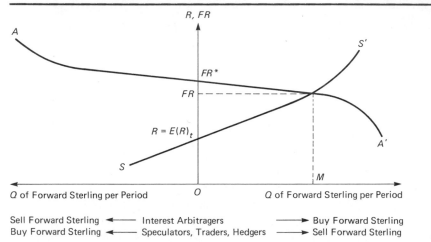

Sell Forward Sterling ◄――― Interest Arbitragers   ――► Buy Forward Sterling
Buy Forward Sterling ◄――― Speculators, Traders, Hedgers ――► Sell Forward Sterling

The AA' line or schedule in Figure 12–1 reflects the functional relationship between the forward exchange rate and the quantities of forward sterling sold (left of vertical line) and purchased (right of vertical line) by interest arbitragers. Given the spot exchange rate and the interest rate differential between New York and London, the parity forward rate, FR^*, can be calculated according to the interest parity theory. If the actual forward rate is equal to the parity rate, then interest arbitrage is zero. Therefore, the AA' schedule intersects the zero axis at FR^*. The elasticity of the AA' schedule is determined institutionally, with the inelastic sections arising from diminishing returns to foreign asset holdings.

The speculator line or schedule, SS', reflects the quantities of forward sterling sold (right) and bought (left) by speculators who expect the spot rate to be $E(R)_t$ in the future. The equilibrium is at the intersection of the arbitrager and speculator schedules, resulting in a market foward rate, $0FR$, and the holding of $0M$ forward sterling by arbitragers who have shifted $0M$ funds into New York.

and offer to buy forward sterling to cover the exchange risk. The right-hand side of the AA' schedule in Figure 12–1, therefore, is equivalent to a demand schedule for forward sterling: at R, $0M$ sterling is demanded. By strictly analogous reasoning it follows that at the given U.S. interest advantage, forward rates above parity provide net incentives for covered arbitrage flows to Britain. Therefore, the left side of the AA' schedule represents a supply curve of forward sterling, due to the desire of investors to return their funds into dollars upon maturity.

The elasticity of the AA' schedule reflects the willingness of individual wealth holders to increase the share of their portfolios held abroad and of new wealth holders to enter the market. Diminishing returns to the general benefits of portfolio diversification and the increasing marginal "inconvenience" of having funds abroad lead to the shape of the AA' schedule, indicating that the quantity of arbitrage funds moved is an increasing function, but at a decreasing rate, of the covered arbitrage margin. At either end of the schedule the elasticity diminishes, as the shares of portfolios consisting of foreign assets are large, and only increasingly larger returns can persuade wealth holders to suffer the added diminishing returns from diversification and from holding assets abroad. The AA' schedule shifts parallel upward or downward as, at a given spot rate, the interest rate advantage in favor of the United States increases or decreases, respectively, and therefore the parity forward rate and the intercept of the AA' schedule changes according to Equation (12–2). If the simple interest advantage is in favor of Britain, the parity forward rate and therefore the intercept of the AA' schedule is below the spot rate.

Speculators, Traders, and Hedgers

Following the derivation of the demand (or supply) curve of forward sterling arising from the activities of covered interest arbitragers, we can now derive the corresponding supply (or demand) schedules and then find the market equilibrium forward exchange rate at the point of intersection between these two schedules.

Speculators. Forward exchange speculators behave much like the spot exchange speculators we analyzed in connection with Figure 11–3 in Chapter 11. They form an expectation about the likely future spot rate, such as $E(R)_t$ in Figure 12–1. If the forward rate for 90 days hence is equal to the expected spot rate at that time, expected profits are zero, and speculators neither buy nor sell forward exchange. On the other hand, if the forward rate is above the expected spot rate, speculators sell forward sterling, expecting to profit in 90 days by buying sterling spot at the lower rate and delivering it under the terms of the forward contract at the higher price. For this reason, the SS' schedule in Figure 12–1 is sloping upward from the left to the right and has an intercept with the vertical axis at $R = E(R)_t$. The elasticity of the speculators' schedule is determined by the shape of the probability distribution of expected returns, as we noted in connection with spot speculation and Figure 11–4. Generally, the greater the certainty about the expected spot rate in the future, the more elastic is the schedule. In the analytically extreme case of certainty, the speculative schedule would be perfectly elastic.

There is one important difference between speculation in spot and forward exchange which is often important in speculators' decisions to operate in the spot or forward markets. While the former requires the outright ownership or borrowing of the full amount used in speculation, the latter requires ownership or borrowing of only a fraction, normally 10 percent, of the face amount of the forward commitment. Banks and foreign exchange dealers are willing to accept forward exchange commitments on this kind of margin because the difference between spot and forward rates tends to be less than 10 percent. Therefore, a speculator's commitment can nearly always be covered at the time of forward contract maturity by buying (or selling) spot and making up the difference from the margin held by the bank or dealer. As a result of this low margin requirement, speculators can leverage their assets substantially. Thus forward exchange speculation amounts to a legitimate form of gambling which gives rise to the possibility of very high rates of return but also, of course, very large losses, as evidenced by a number of bank failures in Europe during 1974. Because of this possibility of leverage, it is believed that the speculators' schedule (SS') shown in Figure 12–1 tends to be quite elastic during "normal" times and very elastic when economic crises lead to the expectation of major currency revaluations.

Traders. Traders, that is exporters and importers of goods and services, often enter the forward exchange market because in normal business deal-ings they tend to commit themselves to a price denominated in foreign currency units, and this leads to an actual exchange transaction at some time in the future. For example, a U.S. wheat exporter may sell wheat at 2 pounds sterling per bushel today, with the payment due 90 days hence upon delivery of the wheat in Britain. In order to ascertain the dollar value of the wheat sale, the U.S. exporter typically would sell forward the contracted-for sterling. In fact, in some industries with narrow profit margins, the sales price quoted in foreign currency often is based on the competitive domestic price converted at the current forward exchange rate applicable to the time of expected payment. It is clear that traders who have commitments to receive or make payments in foreign currency at a future date and do not cover them are really speculators, because they create and maintain an exchange risk. In fact it is reported by informed observers that a certain proportion of traders always cover themselves, while some of them form and act on speculative expectations before they decide whether or not to cover their exchange risk.

The effect traders and traders-speculators have on the forward exchange rate can be analyzed most easily by assuming, in the first instance, that all U.S. traders, exporters and importers, whose business involves open foreign exchange commitments automatically and always buy forward exchange cover, and that the level of exports and imports is a function of the forward exchange rate. Under these assumptions traders give rise to demand and supply curves for forward exchange in strict analogy to those developed in the context of the spot market. An excess *supply* curve for forward exchange can be derived from these, and it will be upward sloping from left to right, intersecting the vertical axis of Figure 12–1 at the rate where trade is balanced. For example, if in Figure 12–1 trade is balanced at R, then at FR the net excess supply of forward sterling is $0M$, considering for the moment the SS' schedule as if it stood for the functional relationship between traders' net excess supply of forward exchange and the forward rate. The speculators' and traders' demand for and supply of forward exchange can be combined by adding the two schedules horizontally. As a result, the new schedule is more elastic than either alone, and the intercept shifts up or down depending on whether trade is balanced at a rate above or below the expected spot rate.

Now we can relax the assumption that all traders cover themselves automatically and consider that instead they decide upon forward cover, according to their views of the forward rate at the time of contract maturity relative to the expected spot rate in the future. We rule out from consideration behavior which involves borrowing and speeding-up payment or lengthening the payment period as involving spot exchange speculation, which we noted in Chapter 11 results in "leads and lags" in the balance of payments. Our typical importer is assumed to owe a payment of sterling 90 days hence and to compare only the alternatives of buying the sterling forward or not doing so. If he expects the price of spot sterling to be below the current forward rate, he requires fewer dollars to meet his sterling obligations by not buying forward than by buying it. The more importers tend to behave in this way, the larger the expected gain and the more certain the expectations about the lower spot rate in the future. But now consider a typical U.S. exporter who has contracted to receive sterling in the future. If he expects the spot rate at that time to be below the current forward rate, he is motivated always to sell sterling forward.

As a result of this asymmetrical behavior of importers and exporters, we find that where at a given forward rate and under the assumption of automatic coverage there was a certain excess supply of forward sterling, the speculation by traders causes a larger excess supply. By analogous reasoning there is greater net excess demand whenever the spot rate in the future is expected to be above the current forward rate. Therefore we reach the important conclusion that speculation by traders on their future receipts or payments in sterling increases the elasticity of the functional relationship between the forward exchange rate and the excess quantity of forward sterling originating with traders. This relationship could be plotted in Figure 12–1; it would look much like the SS' schedule shown there, with the intercept being somewhere between the expected spot rate and the forward rate at which trade is balanced. Horizontal addition of the pure speculators' and traders-turned-speculators' schedules causes the new schedule to be more elastic than either alone and more elastic than it is when traders do not speculate.

Hedgers. Let us now analyze another source of demand for and supply of forward exchange, known as hedgers. Holders of foreign assets such as inventories, accounts receivable, and plant and equipment, which are part of a longer term foreign business venture or investment, and holders of long-term liabilities denominated in foreign currency, such as bonds, are subject to exchange risks. This is because accounting conventions require that foreign subsidiaries or wholly owned enterprises be consolidated into domestic profit and loss statements and balance sheets, by conversion of the foreign assets and liabilities at the current spot exchange rate. Currency revaluations can lead to large losses or gains under this common accounting method, so incentives are created to offset them systematically. The forward exchange market creates such an opportunity for eliminating exchange risk. Thus, for example, a U.S. firm holding long-term sterling assets would tend to sell forward sterling, so that at all times the sterling assets are covered by an offsetting sterling obligation, and vice versa for sterling obligations. When a revaluation takes place, gains or losses from the exchange conversion of the assets or liabilities tend to be matched by the losses or gains from the forward exchange contract. Such an activity of continuously covering long-term foreign assets or liabilities is known technically as hedging. It is undertaken by a substantial proportion of the holders of foreign assets and liabilities, and it tends to be insensitive to expected exchange rate changes.

The activities of hedgers can be incorporated into the preceding model which includes interest arbitragers, speculators, and traders by assuming that all U.S. holders of long-term sterling assets and liabilities and all U.K. holders of dollar assets and liabilities hedge them continuously, regardless of the forward exchange rate. We can then imagine that the forward sterling sales by U.S. hedgers are matched by purchases of forward sterling by U.K. hedgers, leaving a certain net excess supply of sterling, under the assumption that the net U.S. long-term asset position exceeds the net U.K. asset position in Figure 12–1. This net excess supply would be added horizontally to the schedule SS', shifting it downward but leaving the shape unchanged.

Market Equilibrium

We can now see that the activities of speculators, traders, and hedgers in the forward exchange market can be summed and represented by a function such as SS' between the forward exchange rate and the quantity of forward sterling sales or purchases. Since we are interested here only in qualitative rather than precise quantitative conclusions, we can assume that the SS' schedule shown in Figure 12–1 represents the combined behavior of speculators, traders, and hedgers. As a result, the forward exchange rate, FR, represents market equilibrium where the demand for forward exchange of $0M$ sterling by arbitragers who have moved funds into the United States is just equal to the $0M$ forward exchange supplied by speculators, traders, and hedgers.

As can be seen in Figure 12–1, unless the arbitrage schedule AA' is perfectly elastic, the equilibrium forward exchange rate is not equal to the parity forward rate, as the simple interest parity theory of forward exchange suggested. However under "normal" conditions, when the SS' schedule is not too elastic and its intercept is close to the parity rate, the intersection between the AA' and SS' schedules is at the elastic part of the AA' schedule, and the covered arbitrage margin is small. Keynes considered small covered arbitrage margins of plus or minus 0.5 percent per annum as reflecting transactions costs and therefore as being consistent with his parity theory. However, it seems unreasonable to attribute small observed covered arbitrage margins to transaction costs, because these tend to be very small and therefore to be swamped by the data imperfections discussed in Chapter 10. According to the modern theory of forward exchange observed, nonzero covered arbitrage margins are consistent with equilibrium and infinitesimally small transaction costs.

Expected Dollar Devaluation

In Figure 12–2 we show a "speculative" condition in the forward exchange market which permits us to illustrate the cause of much interest in forward exchange policy held by governments and to show the effects of government intervention in this market. The actual spot rate is R and the

FIGURE 12–2
Covered Interest Arbitrage: Expected Dollar Devaluation

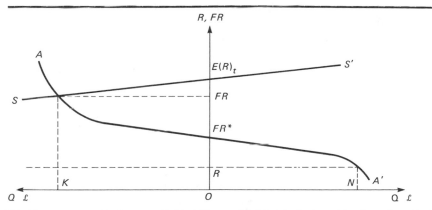

This diagram repeats the essentials of Figure 12–1 but is designed to show the effects of speculative expectations for an increase in the price of foreign exchange (a dollar depreciation) from the current rate, OR, to $OE(R)_t$. As in Figure 12–1, $FR^* > R$, which according to the parity theory implies an interest advantage in favor of New York. Under these conditions the market forward rate induces arbitragers to shift OK funds to London and places them on the inelastic part of their schedule. As a result, in market equilibrium there is a large gap between the market and parity forward rates, revealing the existence of unexploited covered interest arbitrage margins. Forward exchange policy can peg the exchange rate at OR and induce $KO + ON$ covered short-term capital to move from London to New York.

interest rate advantage is in favor of the United States, so that the parity forward rate FR^*, and therefore the intercept of the AA' schedule, are both above the spot rate. These conditions are the same as those underlying Figure 12–1. The difference between the two figures arises from the assumed expectation of a devaluation of the dollar, or increase in the price of sterling, in the future to $E(R)_t$ in Figure 12–2. Furthermore, we show the SS' schedule going through $E(R)_t$ to be very elastic, which indicates a firm belief in the likelihood of this dollar devaluation.

Given these expectations, the SS' schedule intersects the AA' schedule in the left half of the diagram and in the inelastic part of the AA' schedule, which gives rise to an equilibrium forward exchange rate a considerable distance from the interest parity rate. The intersection of the schedule in the left half of the diagram indicates that interest arbitragers are induced at this forward rate to move funds from the United States to Britain and sell sterling forward to speculators. This result is very important for government policies, because it shows that speculators in forward exchange, who have great leverage on their investments through the 10 percent margin requirement discussed above, can cause capital to flow out of the country with the higher interest rate. This in turn implies increased demand for *spot* sterling and upward pressures on the dollar-sterling spot exchange rate in the sense of an outward shift of the demand curve in Figure 11–1, Panel C. In this manner, forward exchange speculators can add to a *current* U.S. balance-of-payments deficit and increase the probability that the expected devaluation of the dollar does take place, ceteris paribus.

However, the U.S. government in this situation can intervene in the forward exchange market by buying or selling any amount of forward sterling offered at a chosen price. For example, in Figure 12–2 we show intervention at the current spot rate, R. The result of this policy is that the $0K$ capital held in Britain is repatriated to the United States, and furthermore $0N$ new capital is drawn into the United States, giving rise to a swing of $0K + 0N$ spot sterling in favor of the U.S. balance of payments. Such an improvement could be sufficiently large to finance a balance-of-payments deficit from trade or other causes until other remedial government policies to correct these causes can become effective. Forward exchange policy under these circumstances can help to prevent a devaluation which otherwise forward exchange speculators could have brought about. It also obviates the need to change the domestic interest rate from its preferred level to attract foreign capital.

However, such government policy is not without its risks and costs. When, in Figure 12–2, the government sells, at R, $0N$ sterling forward to interest arbitragers, it must also sell to speculators. In our diagram we cannot show how much forward sterling speculators are willing to buy from the government, since the SS' schedule intersects with the government supply schedule at R, at a great distance from the origin of the graph. The government, of course, has no difficulties in writing obligations for the delivery of sterling in the future, but the policy may turn out to be very costly. If in spite of the induced short-term capital inflow the dollar has to be devalued, the government has to deliver sterling at the low price to speculators and interest arbitragers at the time of the contract maturity, which it has to purchase at the higher price in the spot market. The government thus faces the potential of very large financial losses from forward exchange policy. Peter Oppenheimer of Oxford University has argued that in 1964–65 forward commitments of the Bank of England could easily have reached £2,000 million at their peak. A 20 percent devaluation would have brought a loss of £400 million. In 1967 and 1968 the Bank of England reported actual losses on forward commitments of £105 and £251 million, respectively. While many other considerations, which we cannot discuss here, enter into the decision of governments to intervene in the forward exchange market, these potential losses are important, and they set limits to the use of an otherwise attractive policy for dealing with currency speculators.

Summary and Conclusions

We have shown that the forward exchange market permits wealth holders to eliminate the foreign exchange risk resulting from their dealings abroad. At the same time, the forward exchange market also permits outright speculators to leverage their assets and traders to turn speculators by covering or not covering future foreign exchange receipts or payments arising from their regular foreign trade activities. The demand for and supply of forward exchange emanating from these sources is determined by interest rates at home and abroad, the spot rate, and level of international long-term indebtedness, and expectations about spot rates in the future. In this part of Chapter 12 we have shown how these forces interact to determine the forward exchange rate in the market and how they can create excess demand or supply in the spot exchange market. Thus they give rise to official government forward exchange policy.

II. THE EUROCURRENCY MARKETS

In Chapters 10 and 11 we described the behavior of traders and investors with foreign business dealings. To some extent this description has become incomplete, as a result of the development of the Eurocurrency markets of the 1960s and 1970s. Recall that in the traditional model traders and investors purchase foreign exchange only as they need it, to make payments abroad, and sell it after receipt from abroad. Banks and foreign exchange brokers hold only working balances of foreign currencies. The public holds demand deposits with, and owes liabilities to, the domestic banking system, denominated only in the currency of the given country. Thus, a British bank in the traditional model would accept deposits and make loans only in sterling and restrict its assets and liabilities in foreign currency to amounts sufficient to carry on the foreign exchange brokerage business.

The development of the Eurodollar and more generally the Eurocurrency markets has changed all that. We now find that European banks accept deposits and make loans in dollars and European currencies other than their domestic currencies. During the 1970s banks in Singapore and Hong Kong began to engage in analogous practices, and we saw the development of an ''Asia-currency market.'' In order to simplify exposition, we will from now on refer only to the Eurodollar market, though it should be remembered that the principles to be developed in this context are applicable to all European and Asian currency markets.

From the above description it follows that Eurodollars are simply short-term deposit obligations of banks in Europe, denominated in dollars. Interest is paid on these dollar deposits, the rates of which are published regularly in the financial press alongside the interest rates prevailing in the domestic money markets of the European countries. In order to earn income with which to pay this interest on the deposits, and in order to eliminate the exchange risk of the dollar obligations, these banks make loans in dollars and match the amount of dollar liabilities and assets in their portfolios.

Multiple Expansion

European banks as a system can give rise to a multiple expansion of deposits, starting from a given initial deposit. The principle underlying this expansion is the same as that known from the domestic banking system multiplier, and it can be explained briefly, as follows. Consider a British exporter who has been paid for merchandise by a check for $1 million drawn on a U.S. bank. He deposits the check with a U.K. bank, with the stipulation that he receives these dollars back in 90 days and that a certain interest be paid. As a result, the British bank has a 90-day dollar obligation and owns a deposit with a U.S. bank. Typically it now lends out a fraction of these dollars for 90 days, say $900,000, in the Eurodollar market, retaining only $100,000 as a highly liquid deposit in its own name with the U.S. bank, to protect itself against unforeseen withdrawal contingencies. Let us now assume that the borrower of these dollars from the U.K. bank writes a check against them and uses it to pay a dollar debt to another European firm, say one in Germany, which wishes to invest the $900,000 for 90 days. For this purpose it deposits the check drawn on the U.K. bank with its own German bank, which in turn is paid by the U.K.

bank through a check drawn on the U.S. bank deposit it owns. As a result of these activities the U.S. bank continues to show only a $1 million deposit obligation to European banks, $900,000 to the German bank and $100,000 to the U.K. bank. The British bank has a $1 million deposit obligation matched by a $900,000 asset in the form of a loan to the initial European borrower and a $100,000 deposit with the U.S. bank. Presumably, it is in portfolio equilibrium until the 90-day maturity of its deposit and loan.

However, it is clear, and easily understood by analogy with the domestic multiplier analysis, that the German bank in our example now is in the analytically identical position as is the U.K. bank at the beginning of our analysis. The German bank is in disequilibrium and has the incentive to make a loan, retaining a fraction of available funds as a margin of safety. This loan in turn leads to a deposit with another European bank, and so on. The main conclusion is that, ultimately, the sum of dollars on deposit with European banks exceeds the inital "base" of $1 million by a multiple, the size of which is determined by the fraction of every deposit retained by each bank as a liquid safety margin. In principle, when this margin is 10 percent, the total Eurodollar deposits, based on the initial $1 million deposit, can reach $10 million.

However, as in the domestic banking system, the Eurodollar system is subject to leakages which tend to prevent this multiplier maximum from being reached. In the Eurodollar market there exists a particularly powerful leakage in the form of deposits with a U.S. bank. For example, if the initial $900,000 loan by the U.K. bank in our example had been used to pay an American firm which deposited the receipts with a bank in the United States, then the multiple expansion would have been short-circuited, because dollars deposited with a bank in the United States, of course, do not count as Eurodollars. Also, if the $900,000 had been bought by a European central bank, as a result of its exchange rate stabilization program, the multiplier process would have been short-circuited, since European central banks tend to hold their dollar assets in the form of deposits with U.S. banks or U.S. treasury bills. As a side note it may be worth relating here that during the 1960s some European central banks deposited their dollar holdings with the Bank for International Settlements in Basel, Switzerland, which paid a higher interest rate than U.S. banks. In order to earn the interest it was paying on these deposits, this Basel bank, representing an official agency of central banks (as we shall discuss below), invested the dollars in the Eurodollar market and thus contributed to the multiple expansion of Eurodollars.

The magnitude of the multiplier operating in the Eurodollar market is not known with certainty, because of severe data problems (to be discussed below). John Makin of the University of Washington in Seattle has estimated it to have been between 7 and 20, though a number of informed observers, such as Fred Klopstock of the Federal Reserve Bank of New York, argue that leakages are so great as to make it near zero, while Alexander Swoboda of the Graduate Institute of the University of Geneva suggests that it is between 1.5 and 1.75.

The preceding description of the nature of the Eurodollar market and of the operation of the multiplier has provided the necessary institutional information to make it possible to appreciate the two main analytical problems surrounding the Eurodollar phenomenon. These are as follows: First, what caused the development of the market? Second, what are the implications of the market's existence for international capital markets generally and for the question of national monetary policy?

Some Data

Before we turn to our analysis of the causes of the development of the Eurodollar market, it is useful to consider briefly the size and growth of this market. For this purpose let us consider Figure 12–3, which shows that the external liabilities in foreign currencies of banks in the eight reporting European countries grew rather constantly between 1967 and 1973. In 1967 the total was about $22.5 billion, and by December, 1973, it

FIGURE 12–3
External Liabilities in Foreign Currencies of Banks of Eight Reporting European Countries (in 1,000 millions of U.S. dollars)

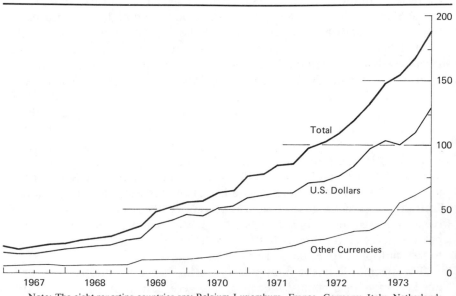

Note: The eight reporting countries are: Belgium-Luxemburg, France, Germany, Italy, Netherlands, Sweden, Switzerland, and the United Kingdom.
Source: Bank for International Settlements, Annual Report, 1974, p. 158.

had reached $191.4 billion. While at the beginning of the period dollars represented 80 percent of the total, in 1973 they represented only 68 percent.

Other statistics provided by the same source as Table 12–1 show that, at the end of 1973, of the $61 billion Eurocurrencies other than the dollar, $32 billion were Deutsche marks, $17 billion Swiss francs, $5 billion sterling, and about $2 billion each were guilders and French francs, and about $3 billion was in other currencies. In terms of individual countries, at the end of 1973 banks in the United Kingdom had about $91 billion in foreign currency liabilities, or about 48 percent of the total. Banks in France, Belgium, and Italy had liabilities of $27, $24, and $24 billion, respectively. The banks in other reporting countries—Germany, Netherlands, Sweden, and Switzerland—had much smaller liabilities, summing to the remaining $25 billion.

The World Bank provided some interesting figures about the borrowers whose Eurocurrency loans were publicized in 1973. In Table 12–1 we

TABLE 12–1
Publicized Eurocurrency Credits in 1973 (millions of U.S. dollars)

Industrial Countries		Developing Countries	
Denmark	$ 243	Algeria	$1,352
Finland	424	Brazil	718
Italy	4,713	Greece	600
Netherlands	252	Indonesia	478
South Africa	498	Iran	712
United Kingdom	3,069	Mexico	1,572
United States	1,247	Panama	251
Others	—	Peru	734
Total	$11,125	Spain	467
		Un. Arab Emirates	330
		Yugoslavia	235
		Zaire	287
		Others	—
		Total	$9,117

Source: *IMF Survey*, August 1974, p. 266; compiled by World Bank.

provide a selected list of countries in which the borrowers reside. As can be seen, the heaviest borrowers in 1973 were located in the industrial countries of Italy, the United Kingdom, and the United States, plus the developing countries of Algeria and Mexico. Not included in the totals shown in Table 12–1 are countries of the Communist bloc, such as Poland, Bulgaria, and the Soviet Union, which also borrowed $420, $115, and $50 million, respectively.

Referring to the types of borrowers in the first half of 1974, the following characteristics are noted by the World Bank. Over 80 percent of the lending was to governments or to agencies with a government guarantee, and 61 percent went directly to governments and public financial institutions, such as central banks and development banks. Lending to public utilities amounted to 14.3 percent of all loans to industrial countries and 8.1 percent of loans to developing countries. We can assume that the above figures are roughly representative of the types of publicized borrowers in other years, though of course changes do take place all the time.

However, these characteristics of publicized borrowers may be misleading, since more loans are made to private firms and are not published. Thus, while the publicized Eurocurrency credits covered by the World Bank data totalled $22 billion in 1973, the Bank for International Settlements showed a net increase in outstanding Eurocurrency loans of $60 billion in the same year. Considering that a certain proportion of the loans outstanding at the end of 1972 matured in 1973, it is obvious that new unpublicized loans made that year exceeded the publicized loans by well over $38 billion.

These statistics on Eurocurrency lending and borrowing are impressive as absolute figures and as a fraction of total bank lending in individual countries. Thus, for example, at the end of 1973 the French deposit money banks had a total of demand plus time deposits of about $90 billion, which must be compared with their $27 billion foreign currency obligations. For Italy's commercial and savings banks, the corresponding figures were $115 billion and $24 billion, respectively. For Germany, on the other hand, the deposit money banks' time and demand deposit liabilities of $180 billion compared with only $6 billion in foreign currency obligations. In England, where the Eurocurrency markets had their start and which has a tradition of banking and well equipped institutions, at the end of 1973 current and deposit accounts of all banks amounted to £95 billion, of which more than half, or £51 billion, were denominated in currencies other than sterling. We conclude that for Britain, at least, Eurocurrencies represent a significant part of total bank deposits.

Causes of the Eurodollar Market Development

In our analysis of the causes of the development of the Eurodollar market, we focus on the question of why lenders and borrowers in a given European country, say Britain, do not behave in the manner postulated in the traditional model developed in Chapters 10 and 11. More specifically, the problem concerning British lenders is why they find it more profitable to lend dollars to a bank in Europe rather than in the United States, and, furthermore, why they find it more profitable to lend dollars rather than their home currency, sterling. By analogy, the question concerning borrowers is why they find it profitable to borrow dollars from a bank in

Europe rather than the United States, why they borrow dollars rather than sterling. There are two analytically distinct causes of this behavior: first, government regulations and other noneconomic factors, and second, real economies.

Noneconomic Causes. The Eurodollar market is believed to have had its start during the early 1960s when the Soviet Union sold gold in the London bullion market and bought U.S. wheat for domestic consumption. In the course of this business the Soviet Union occasionally was the temporary owner of large sums of money realized from the sale of gold before it was needed to make payments in dollars for the imported wheat. The question was in what form the funds should be held. There was no market for rubles, and therefore investment in them was not possible. The Russians had to hold their money in some Western currency. The pound sterling and other major European currencies had a history of devaluation and exchange controls which left the dollar as the safest currency. Moreover, because the payment for the wheat ultimately was to be made in dollars, transaction costs were saved by selling the gold for dollars and keeping the proceeds invested temporarily in dollars.

However, placing money in dollar investments had two disadvantages for the Soviets. Because of the Cold War they perceived a risk of confiscation, and ideologically it was uncomfortable to be lending money to "imperialist" U.S. banks. The solution to this problem consisted of persuading a British bank paying an interest rate which was at least competitive with that prevailing in the United States, to accept a temporary dollar deposit from Russia. In fact, later on it turned out that frequently the interest rate on such deposits was higher than that obtainable on U.S. investments. As a result of this transaction, the Soviet-owned U.S. dollars on deposit with a U.S. bank were transferred to the ownership of a British bank, and the problem of the risk of confiscation and the uncomfortable ideology was eliminated. The Russians continued to hold dollars, but they were on deposit with a "safe" British bank. In effect, even if the interest rate paid by the British bank to the Russians had been lower than that available from a U.S. investment, the implicit return in terms of safety and ideological purity clearly created the basic condition: The Eurodollar investment was more profitable than either the dollar investment in the United States or investment in the domestic currency.

Government regulations and noneconomic causes also motivated borrowers to go to the banks in Britain that had to lend out these dollars deposited by the Russians. In European countries and, especially, Japan, tight monetary policy and the direct allocation of credit left many firms unable to obtain loans, even though they were willing and able to pay very high rates of interest. These firms were ready borrowers of Eurodollars, which they sold in their foreign exchange market to obtain the local funds necessary for their real investment. Normally these firms covered themselves against the exchange risk implicit in their owing dollars at the maturity of their loan by buying forward dollars. The spot and forward exchange transactions required in connection with the Eurodollar loans may have added to or subtracted from the interest cost of the loan itself, as we discussed above in our analysis of the forward exchange market. But clearly, the actions of these firms revealed that the Eurodollar loan, inclusive of all transactions and other costs, was cheaper than a domestic currency loan, the cost of which may be considered to have been infinity in the case of firms which, through credit rationing, were unable to obtain loans at any cost.

A U.S. government regulation known as Regulation Q of the Federal Reserve System stipulates the maximum interest rate a U.S. bank can pay on deposits. This regulation was responsible for the growth of the Eurodollar market, because during periods of high world and U.S. interest rates early in the 1960s and 1970s, British banks would offer yields on dollar deposits in England exceeding those permitted under Regulation Q. These British banks attracted large deposits away from banks in the United States, which in turn found themselves short of funds to make loans. Potential borrowers from U.S. banks, thus unable to obtain loans in the United States, borrowed from British banks. Of course, it did not take long for U.S. banks to realize the loss of business which this shift of lending and borrowing abroad implied, and they reacted by opening up branches in Europe which soon were major participants in the Eurodollar markets. Again it is clear that in this case the U.S. lenders found it more profitable to lend in Europe than in the domestic market, and borrowers, who could not obtain funds in the United States at any cost during periods of tight credit, benefited from borrowing abroad.

From these examples of motives underlying the entry into the Eurodollar market by the Soviets and firms subject to credit rationing or reacting to regulations about maximum interest rates, we can generalize that the Eurodollar market represents a response of the free enterprise system in dealing with efforts of governments to regulate and control the economy. As such a response, the Eurodollar market has caused an erosion of national economic sovereignty which is being resented and resisted by many countries; we will discuss this later. However, even if governments did not attempt to regulate and control economies, the Eurodollar market would still exist, for a number of reasons to be discussed next.

Economic Causes.   Generally, international trade and capital flows can be carried out more efficiently if there exists one currency serving for all countries as a convenient standard and store of value. After World War II the U.S. dollar served in this capacity, and before that it was the British pound sterling. As we shall argue at greater length in the part of this book dealing with international monetary organization, the economies of having such a "key" currency arise from the savings of transaction and information costs. International travelers encounter some of these economies when, at airports, they find price quotations in local currency and dollars. The dollar quotations are not only for U.S. travelers but also for those from other countries. Thus, a Brazilian tourist landing in Greece can readily figure out the cost of a good by knowing only the Brasilian cruzeiro–U.S. dollar exchange rate. He does not have to know the rate of the cruzeiro with the Greek drachma or the currency of any other country he visits during his travels. Furthermore, he can pay for his merchandise in dollars at all airports and does not have to change cruzeiros into local currency each time he makes a purchase. For this reason, Brazilian travelers are more likely to be carrying U.S. dollars than any other currency. These economies arising from the existence of one key currency in the world are much like those stemming from having one language which all peoples of the world learn as their foreign language. At present this language is English; readers of this book in non-English speaking countries are implicitly enjoying the benefits of these economies.

Because of the role of the dollar as a key currency, much of international trade is denominated and settled in dollars. Richard Caves and Ronald Jones (1973) state that over 40 percent of the foreign trade of France is carried on in dollars. The fact that dollars have such a great use in commerce and finance has contributed to the growth of the Eurodollar market, because firms engaged in foreign trade tend to find that they receive payments and have to make payments in dollars, but often not on the same date. By keeping their funds in dollars in between receipt and disbursement rather than in a domestic currency, these firms save transactions costs, even if the interest rates on Eurodollars and local currency deposits are identical. For strictly analogous reasons, firms in temporary need of funds profit from borrowing dollars to make a payment and repay the loan from an expected receipt in dollars in the future. Thus a Eurodollar market might exist even if lending and borrowing rates in all money markets were the same.

But there are also economic reasons why the spread between lending and borrowing rates in the Eurodollar market is smaller than that in the national markets of the United States and European countries. One is that banks which are not branches of U.S. banks in Europe are not required to keep minimum deposits with their central banks on Eurodollar deposits. As is well known from banking theory, these minimum required deposits with the central banks represent a tax on banking operations. They cannot serve as a liquidity buffer as originally believed when the modern banking legislation was passed, since they have to be maintained under penalty of law. But these minimum deposits have evolved as one of the main instruments through which monetary policy is carried out. Now, since this tax is absent from the deposit-loan business in Eurodollars, banks in competition and pricing at marginal cost can operate their Eurodollar business at a smaller profit margin than their domestic deposit-loan business, which is subject to these minimum deposit requirements. In 1972 branches of U.S. banks in Europe were obligated by the Federal Reserve System to maintain minimum deposits on all Eurodollar deposits, and in 1974 rumors began to circulate in European countries that the United States would require its banks also to maintain minimum deposits on all foreign currency deposit obligations. The economic reasons for these requirements will be discussed below. The main point to note here is that the absence of these requirements on Eurocurrencies in the past has undoubtedly contributed to the relative profitability and therefore the expansion of the Eurodollar market. However, as the continued participation in the market of U.S. branch banks in Europe since 1972 suggests, the elimination of this advantage will not spell an end to the market, because of the existence of the other real factors discussed here.

Another reason the spread between lending and borrowing rates in the Eurodollar market is smaller is that the privately owned commercial banking systems in European and other Western free enterprise economies have, over the past century, developed into rather closely knit domestic oligopolies, which are protected by government legislation from domestic and, until the recent revolution in communication and travel technology, from foreign competition. As is typical of such oligopolistic industries, competition takes many forms, such as through the opening of many branches or the provision of fancy services and buildings, other than price, which in the case of banking is reflected in the spread between lending and borrowing rates. As a result, the spread tends to be so large that foreign banks and radically new types of business, such as the Eurodollar business, which are not covered by the traditional domestic oligopoly agreements can expand and through competitive marginal cost pricing can fit the spread between lending and borrowing rates inside that of the existing domestic business. Furthermore, since Eurodollar loans and deposits are of interest typically only to large firms and institutional borrowers, the average size of transactions is much above the banks' overall average, and the cost of administering this particular department of the banking business is lower than average. Marginal cost pricing in this branch of business, applied under pressure from foreign competition outside the traditional domestic oligopoly, therefore results in a spread between lending and borrowing rates which probably would be smaller than that for the average domestic business, even in the presence of perfect competition among banks.

The reason why this new form of competition in financial markets has developed in the 1960s rather than earlier is due to the revolution in communications and transportation which was brought about by jet airplanes, computers, and communication satellites and which in turn made possible the unprecedented growth in world trade, as we have shown in Chapter 6, and of multinational operations, as we will argue in Chapter 22. This growth in trade and multinational enterprises increased the opportunity for the exploitation of the economies of a key currency, which in turn was reinforced by the favorable competitive price in dealing in this international market for dollars.

A third reason for a smaller lending-borrowing spread in the Eurodollar market is that this market provides the opportunity for large borrowers, such as public utilities, multinational corporations, and even national governments, to obtain loans which are too large to be handled by banks within one country. During the past decade such borrowers have been able to obtain loans of a size unprecedented in European history through banking consortia which lend dollars. The advantages of such loans to the borrowers are savings in legal and placement costs, since they avoid dealing with banks in different countries and in different currencies. They also avoid the assumption of different exchange risks resulting from repayment and debt-service obligations in different currencies. The lenders benefit since, by keeping the share of each Eurodollar loan they make small, they spread their default risk among many borrowers. The lending banks' exchange risks are nil, since they tend to match dollar assets and liabilities, as was mentioned above. Once established, institutions for lending through international consortia operate at a low marginal cost.

Summary and Conclusions.   We have shown that the development of the Eurodollar market is due in part to the free enterprise response to national efforts to control and regulate the banking system and some political, noneconomic considerations. More fundamentally, however, the market exists because of the real economies enjoyed by the users of dollars as a key currency, the absence of minimum deposit requirements on Eurodollar deposits for non–U.S. branches of European banks, and the economies of scale and risk diversification inherent in multinational Eurodollar loan consortia. The oligopolistic market behavior of national banking systems, developed during the past century of industrialization and under the umbrella of government legislation, has resulted in inflated costs and large spreads between borrowing and lending rates. These permit competitors and types of business not covered by the oligopoly to engage in a profitable Eurodollar business, with a spread of lending and borrowing rates which fits comfortably inside that of the domestic business.

It is impossible to know the relative importance of the factors contributing to the growth of the Eurodollar market, either in the past or in the future. Furthermore, as institutions change and government regulations are imposed, the nature of the Eurodollar market is likely to change. It is even conceivable that at some time in the future it may disappear. But if the data indicated above are any guide for the future, the Eurodollar market may be with us for a long time.

Economic Effects of Eurocurrency Markets

From our analysis of the causes of the development of Eurocurrency markets in the preceding section, we can readily imply its beneficial effects. The market increases the overall efficiency of the international capital market by lowering the cost of operation through the breaking down of oligopolistic market structures, the exploitation of economies of scale, better diversification of risk for lenders and borrowers, and increased arbitrage opportunities between individual countries' markets. Competitive pressures on domestic capital markets and banking structures emanating from the Eurocurrency markets tend to produce institutional changes and induce greater efficiency, and these tend to benefit the local population of every country. The increased use of dollars provides the world with external benefits from the widespread use of a key currency, for reasons already discussed.

Counterbalancing these gains are certain losses in welfare. As we noted in our analysis of causes, the Eurocurrency markets permit private entrepreneurs to escape their countries' systems of regulation and control. As a result, nations tend to lose a portion of their sovereignty over their national economic affairs to the forces of international markets. If one is inclined to believe that national governments on average impose controls and regulations which increase a country's welfare, then Eurocurrency markets are harmful. On the other hand, if one believes that government controls and regulations on average fail to increase welfare because of incompetence, special-interest power, or simply corruption, then the fact that the Eurocurrency market makes inoperative many of these controls and regulations is welcomed. A balanced view is probably that some of the forms of government control circumvented by the Eurocurrency markets were bad, and it is good that they are becoming inoperative. Others, however, it would be desirable to retain.

The most important classes of government regulations of the economy which have been threatened by the Eurocurrency markets have to do with cyclical demand stabilization through monetary policy and avoidance of bank failures through provisions for deposit insurance and a lender of last resort. Cyclical demand stabilization has been made more difficult through the fact that firms can circumvent restrictive domestic monetary policy. For example, during the 1960s and 1970s Germany attempted to control domestic inflation through a tight monetary and fiscal policy. However, German banks and ultimate borrowers were able to obtain funds in the Eurocurrency markets, mostly by dealing through banks in other countries. The dollars which they thus obtained were used to add to the real demand for goods and services in Germany directly, to the extent that some other German entrepreneurs were willing to accept dollars in payment. The dollars in effect added to the stock of money in Germany. More important, probably, was the effect resulting from borrowers' sales of the dollars in the open market. Under fixed exchange rates the German authorities were obliged to purchase these dollars, since Germany during that period experienced an excess supply of dollars at the prevailing exchange rate. In payment for these dollars bought in the exchange market, the German central bank had to make available Deutsche marks, which could serve as a high-powered reserve for the multiple expansion of credit and a consequent, undesired easing of monetary policy. Depending on the elasticity of demand for Eurocurrency loans, given the German interest rate, this easing could be so great as to defeat all stabilization efforts.

There is no full understanding of how serious the loss of national monetary sovereignty has been in individual countries, or about the overall inflationary impact of Eurocurrency markets in the world as a whole. As we have seen above, for most countries, Eurocurrency deposits represent a sizable but manageable fraction of total bank deposits, and presumably the inflationary impact of these added deposits could have been offset by correspondingly tighter domestic policies. The normal noninflationary growth of the money supply necessitated increases in the reserves of commercial banks with the central banks of European countries, and these increases exceeded those necessitated by foreign exchange purchases in connection with the sale of Eurocurrencies by domestic borrowers. These sales of Eurocurrencies should not be confused with speculative sales of foreign exchange in expectation of a currency appreciation, which haunted Germany and the Netherlands on several occasions during the 1960s and 1970s. The increases in commercial bank reserves accompanying these speculative episodes were very large and exerted undue upward pressures on the money supply of these countries. We conclude that in principle the Eurocurrency markets add to the money supply of nations and the world, but their precise impact is unknown and probably small enough to be offset by proper national monetary policies if this is so desired.

The second function of monetary authorities in modern Western countries, besides regulating the money supply, has been the prevention of bank panics and depressions, which were the bane of capitalism in the 19th and early 20th centuries. These bank panics tended to occur when a general cyclical business downturn produced bankruptcies of manufacturing and trading firms. Banks which had made loans to such firms in turn faced financial troubles that were aggravated by the run of depositors on the banks to obtain their funds before the bank became bankrupt. Since no bank can have in its portfolio enough liquid assets to satisfy all depositors, they were forced into the liquidation of longer term assets, often at a loss.

Frequently, because of these runs on their deposits, banks failed that otherwise would have been financially sound. Financial troubles of this sort tended to spread throughout the banking system and brought about widespread unemployment and losses in the real sector of the economy. Central monetary authorities have succeeded in practically eliminating bank panics and depressions of this sort through deposit insurance and the provision of discounting facilities. At present, when a bank does go bankrupt through mismanagement or fraud, depositors are assured of receiving their money through both the insurance and the willingness of the authorities to accept the banks' long-term assets in collateral for cash with which to pay depositors.

In the Eurocurrency markets there are no such insurance schemes and lenders of last resort. Consequently, some financial analysts fear that a worldwide recession may lead to defaults on loans, with the kinds of repercussions that characterized 19th-century bank panics. It is difficult to assess the likelihood of such events. Banks in the Eurocurrency business still are covered by their national banking systems, and it is questionable whether these authorities will permit bank panics to develop, since the Eurocurrency business is an integral part of the overall business of banks. Yet, just because they are involved in the Eurocurrency business in this way, it is likely that in the future the authorities will develop a program of regulation and control to prevent the development of bad lending practices, fraud, and so on. Such a program will probably be instituted after the authorities have been forced to bail out a number of institutions in financial difficulties. The resultant regulations and control will come at the cost of efficiency and dynamism in the market. Very likely it will eventually lead to the strengthening of national oligopolies and the formation of international oligopolies. These developments appear to be the inevitable cost of the attempts of governments to prevent the instabilities which freely working markets tend to produce.

Some financial analysts have voiced fears that the Eurodollar market would collapse if the United States began to run balance-of-payments surpluses, which would in effect rob the market of the base on which the multiple deposit expansion takes place. These fears appear to be unfounded. They are based on a confusion between different kinds of balance-of-payments surpluses, the nature of which will be discussed in the next chapter. The main point is that if dollars were threatened to be withdrawn from the market, interest rates would rise sufficiently to keep them there. In other words, market forces would induce U.S. short-term capital outflows sufficiently large to counteract any dollar withdrawals resulting from other payments surpluses. That this analysis is correct may be seen from the fact that there exists a large business in Euro-Deutsch marks, even though Germany has been in heavy balance-of-payments surplus throughout the period.

Summary and Conclusions

In this section we have argued that the benefits of the Eurocurrency markets stem from the increases in the efficiency of international and domestic capital markets and the increased use of key currencies in the world. Costs of these markets stem from the potential loss of national monetary sovereignty and increased financial instabilities. Until the middle 1970s, these costs have not been great, and they remain a threat rather than a fact. Consequently, benefits outweigh costs. However, in the future these costs may well become significant. They are certain to be combatted by national legislation and international agreements. Unfortunately, these curbs on Eurocurrency markets are likely to reduce simultaneously their efficiency and flexibility.

BIBLIOGRAPHICAL NOTES

Einzig (1961) gives much useful institutional information on the question of forward exchange markets. Analytically rigorous models of forward exchange rate determination are found in Grubel (1966), Sohmen (1969) and, using dominantly mathematics, Levin (1970). A classic in the field is Tsiang (1959). A collection of papers on recent forward exchange intervention by the Bank of England, including the one by Oppenheimer cited in the text, is Chalmers (1971).

Institutional information about the Eurodollar market is provided by Einzig (1973) and in the book of readings edited by Prochnow (1970). Swoboda (1968) and Mayer (1970) present theoretical models of the determinants and effects of the Eurodollar market, interest rates, and multipliers. Focusing on the nature and magnitude of the multiplier are the articles by Friedman (1971), Klopstock (1970) and Makin (1973).

CONCEPTS FOR REVIEW

Interest arbitragers
Hodgers
Interest arbitrage theory of forward
  exchange
Parity forward rate

Covered arbitrage margin
Eurodollar multiplier
Regulation Q
Key currency

POINTS FOR FURTHER STUDY AND DISCUSSION

1. Make up buying and selling rules for forward exchange analogous to those suggested at the end of the preceding chapter for spot exchange rates and discover whether any one of them would have been profitable over a period of a number of years. In the case of forward exchange the calculation of profits and losses and formation of expectations involve the comparison of today's 90-day forward rate with the spot rate 90 days later.

2. Assume that you, as an American, had a £1 million asset in Britain on January 1, 1965. Consider the dollar value of that asset on that day. Now calculate the cost or net profit of hedging this asset through the sale of forward sterling every three months at the prevailing forward rate until a day around January 1, 1975, when the last forward contract matures and you have the equivalent of your investment in dollars. Compare the cost of this hedging strategy with the cost of converting the £1 million into dollars at the spot exchange rate on the day your last forward contract matures. Would hedging have been more profitable than not hedging? Would hedging have given any other benefits if there had been uncertainty about the date on which you wanted the foreign sterling asset turned into dollars?

3. Calculate covered arbitrage margins for 30-, 60-, and 90-day maturity securities and forward contracts for the London–New York markets for a number of years. Are there any consistent differences in these margins at the same points in time? Calculate the annual rate of return implicit above in the forward discount or premium at these different exchange rate maturities. Are there any systematic patterns among these rates? Can you develop any theoretical views about these patterns?

4. Find interest rates on 90-day short-term Eurodollar deposits and compare them with New York and London interest rates of the same maturity. Is there any systematic relationship? Now calculate the rate of return on Eurodollar deposits at this maturity from the point of view of an English lender who sells the dollars at the spot-dollar starting rate and repurchases them at the 90-day forward rate prevailing on the day of the spot transaction, taking into account the rate at which he could have lent out his sterling funds. What is the average size of the covered arbitrage margin involving this 90 day Eurodollar and London bill rate and the sterling dollar spot and forward exchange rates?

5. Consider what would happen to the Eurodollar market if European commercial banks were required to keep minimum deposits with their central banks on dollar deposits, as they are required to do with domestic currency deposits.

13 Balance-of-Payments Statistics and Postwar History

THE TERM "balance of payments" appears frequently in the business pages of newspapers and magazines. On occasion it even gives rise to headline stories and editorials in the press. In these stories the news about the balance of payments almost always seems to be bad and to be accompanied by proposals for government policies which would affect adversely the daily lives of the public, such as proposals for higher taxes, interest rates, and unemployment; for restrictions on travel, imports, and capital flows. What is the balance of payments which warrants so much attention and leads to these unpopular government policies? In this chapter we present first a brief definition and description of the usefulness and importance of balance-of-payments statistics. Then we provide some information about how the statistics are collected and presented for analysis. In the concluding part we discuss the recent history of the balance of payments of the United States, Britain, Canada, and Germany.

I. THE NATURE, COLLECTION, AND PRESENTATION OF STATISTICS

A widely used definition of the balance of payments is that it is a statistical record of all economic transactions which have taken place during a given time period between a country's residents and the rest of the world. The balance-of-payments statistics of the United States are collected and published by the Department of Commerce. In other countries analogous government agencies, sometimes special statistical offices, are in charge of balance-of-payments data collection and processing. The methods and principles underlying the collection of balance-of-payments

275

data for the United States are typical of those of other countries. We will discuss them briefly because students, who may be referring to these data at various points in their working lives, can benefit from knowing something about the limitations of coverage and sources of errors in them.

The basic problem faced by any statistics-gathering agency is that the ideal coverage of all transactions is possible only at very great cost in the form of outlays by the agency itself and, perhaps even more important, in the form of work required by firms and individuals in completing statistical questionnaires. In the light of these problems, all statistics-gathering agencies of governments, including the balance-of-payments division of the U.S. Department of Commerce, adhere to the principle of pushing data collection only to the point where at the margin costs and benefits are equal. Wherever possible, they employ data already collected or compiled for other purposes. In practice, the application of this principle means often a rather less than complete coverage of transactions and consequently the possibility of sizable errors in the estimates.

Let us now turn to some information about the collection of data in some specific categories of balance-of-payments data. First, quantitatively most important is information on the level of trade in goods and services. This information is passed on to the U.S. Department of Commerce primarily by the customs agents of the U.S. Treasury, which is in charge of administering the tariff laws. Consequently, as international travelers know from first-hand experience, all U.S. land, air, and sea ports of entry and exit are guarded carefully, and all commercial imports and exports are registered. Coverage of commercial trade in goods and most services sold in connection with goods, therefore, is rather complete. There are some gaps in coverage, such as exports and imports by private individuals using parcel post or moving goods in tourists' suitcases, but these gaps are not important in total value. Some categories of trade in services, such as income from capital abroad, royalties on movies, patents and copyrights, require special surveys of and regular reports from trade associations and often are covered rather incompletely and inaccurately. Expenditures by tourists are estimated from questionnaires handed out to a small sample of all travelers and returned voluntarily. Information on pension checks sent abroad to former U.S. workers, a balance-of-payments account known as unilateral transfers, is gathered from banks and private and government pension funds. Data on long- and short-term capital flows are obtained through questionnaires from a relatively small number of banks, multinational enterprises, and investment firms which carry on the bulk of capital flows. Very accurate information and almost complete coverage is available on government transactions, except those involving some military and intelligence activities.

Generally, when the data collection depends on sampling, efforts are made to obtain representative coverage and, very importantly, at certain lengthy time intervals careful in-depth studies of the entire universe of transactions are made. On these occasions, for example, an entire planeload of tourists may be interviewed individually to obtain accurate information on expenditures abroad. The estimates thus obtained are then used to adjust normally received questionnaire replies for misreporting and the tendency of some groups of tourists to report more frequently than others. In spite of these efforts to use scientific methods for the elimination of biases inherent in sampling, incomplete but regular coverage, and voluntary compliance, there remain some sources of errors in the data which cannot be eliminated readily.

For example, one important and well-known source of inaccuracies in balance-of-payments data arises from the valuation procedures employed in recording the transactions. Normally the invoices used in merchandise trade reflect true value, but in trade with some countries and at certain times firms have strong incentives to falsify the value of the merchandise in order to reduce tariff obligations or circumvent exchange restrictions, as we will discuss further in Chapter 16. Gifts present special difficulties, since market value may not be known readily. For example, the "gift" of services provided by the United States through the activities of U.S. Peace Corps volunteers abroad should be reflected in the U.S. balance of payments, given the basic definition of this document. But what value should be given to this credit in the accounts? It was decided that the value should be equal to the stipends of the volunteers plus the cost of administering the program, though from the economist's point of view it would have been more meaningful to include also the opportunity cost minus the stipends of the volunteers. The decision on valuation in this case, as in others, is made on the basis of practical and political considerations. In the case of the Peace Corps it would have been difficult to establish with any degree of reliability the opportunity cost of the volunteers, and it was deemed politically safer to underestimate rather than overestimate the dollar value of the services provided by the Peace Corps. On the other hand, foreign aid in the form of wheat exports under Public Law 480 during the 1950s and 1960s was valued consistently at domestic U.S. prices rather than lower world prices, leading to an overstatement of the value of U.S. aid and exports in this category.

Let us now turn to the problem of what the U.S. Department of Commerce and analogous statistical offices in other countries do with the information obtained through the channels just discussed. Formerly in books and now with the help of computers, running totals are kept of transactions with the rest of the world in large numbers of accounts distinguished by many different characteristics. For example, merchandise trade is categorized according to the country of transaction and the type of goods. The latter occurs according to the scheme known as Standard Industrial Trade Classification (SITC), which we discussed above in

Chapter 4. Balance-of-payments statistics in this fine detail are of interest only to specialists in governments, academia, and trade associations. For general public use the detailed accounts are aggregated into categories (which will be discussed shortly) and published quarterly in the U.S. *Survey of Current Business* and analogous national publications of other countries. International agencies, such as the International Monetary Fund and the United Nations, use the primary government publications to issue balance-of-payments statistics arranged differently, to suit particular groups of analysts and to facilitate international comparisons.

Some Accounting Principles

After the description of balance-of-payments data collection and handling procedures, we must now turn to the more involved analysis of the accounting principles used in the decision to enter a given transaction on the credit or debit side of the balance sheet. In general, balance-of-payments statistics are constructed by the use of the principles of double-entry bookkeeping. While these principles are not difficult to understand, their full exposition is lengthy and involved. Therefore, we sketch them here only briefly and ask students who want to know more about them to turn to an elementary accounting textbook.

The basic tool of the double-entry bookkeeping process are the T-accounts, which have the credit entries on the left side and the debit entries on the right side. Every transaction must enter into one account with a credit and into another with a debit. The actual accounting procedures can best be understood with the help of an example in a highly simplified accounting system.

Thus, let us assume that a country's transactions during a given period consist only of a merchandise export of $10 and an import of $7, both of which are paid for through the extension of credit from the seller to the buyer, actual payment to be received in the next accounting period. In Figure 13–1 we show an account labeled "Merchandise," into which the exports are entered as a credit and the imports as a debit. The entry corresponding to the exports necessary under the double-entry bookkeeping principle is on the debit side of the account in Figure 13–1 named "Short-Term Capital." The entry is labeled "Import of trade credit bill" because of our assumption that payment is received through the exporter's acceptance of a certificate of indebtedness by the foreign buyer. Under this assumption, therefore, the merchandise transaction gives rise to the simultaneous trade in short-term assets. By analogy, the merchandise import leads to the export of a trade credit bill, which is entered on the credit side of the Short-Term Capital account.

Now we close the books and calculate different balances. In the Merchandise account the closing entry is for $3 on the debit side and is labeled

FIGURE 13–1
A Simplified T-Account System

Merchandise

Credit		Debit	
Exports	$10	Imports	$ 7
		Merchandise balance	3
	$10		$10

Short-Term Capital

Credit		Debit	
Export of trade credit bill	$ 7	Import of trade credit bill	$10
Balance on short-term indebtedness	3		
	$10		$10

Balance of Payments

Credit		Debit	
Merchandise balance	$ 3	Balance on short-term indebtedness	$ 3

"Merchandise balance." The corresponding entry is in the Balance-of-Payments account on the credit side, with the same sum and label. Since the balance is on the credit side in the Balance-of-Payments account, it can be inferred that the country during the period had an excess of exports over imports and therefore what is known as a surplus in merchandise trade. The second step of closing the books requires balancing of the short-term capital account with a credit labeled balance on short-term indebtedness, which has a counterentry on the debit side of the balance of payments account. As can be seen, after every complete accounting entry and after closing of the books both sides of the T-accounts together must always be equal. Yet, the accounts provide useful information for analysis of the following sort used by analysts and policy makers.

In the final balance the crucial item is what we have called the "Balance on short-term indebtedness." This item relates the current period's balance of payments to the country's state of private short-term debts and assets and, in a more complete model to be developed below, to official short-term asset holdings known as international reserves. International reserves are exchangeable for foreign exchange which is usable in foreign exchange rate stabilization operations. These stocks of private and public short-term foreign assets and liabilities can be netted out to derive the country's net short-term foreign asset position. This position of a country is in an important sense equivalent to the cash and short-term asset holdings of firms and individuals. The funds are used to meet temporary payments imbalances caused by business cycles or random shocks to stability, as we shall discuss at greater length in the next part of this book. Without such financing, countries, just like firms and individuals, would have to make drastic changes in their production and consumption patterns or risk capital losses from the forced, quick realization of long-term assets whenever imbalances arise. The import or export of foreign short-term assets in the balance of payments which affect the stock of the assets available for these purposes, therefore, is the key item in the balance of payments. If there is a net import or net export of these short-term assets in common usage, the balance of payments is known as being in surplus or in deficit, respectively.

The other side of the final simplified balance-of-payments account in Figure 13–1 shows that the imbalance is attributable to the Merchandise account balance, which shows a surplus of exports over imports. As we shall see in the next section of this chapter, in practice balance-of-payments statistics consider many different accounts, and several final balances, both surpluses and deficits, are presented for analytical and policy purposes.

Students may wish to learn about a simple rule of thumb according to which they can decide whether any given transaction, ceteris paribus, has a positive or negative influence on the change in net indebtedness toward the rest of the world; that is, whether a transaction improves or worsens the balance of payments. This rule helps in understanding analysis and in evaluating the effects which trends in trade and capital flows have on the future balance of payments. The rule is that all economic transactions giving rise to demand for foreign exchange result in debit entries in original accounts and, therefore, worsen the balance of payments. By analogy, transactions increasing the supply of foreign exchange result in credit entries and improve the balance of payments. Recall from our analysis of Chapters 10 and 11 that imports of goods, services, and assets cause demand for foreign exchange, while exports in these categories cause supply of foreign exchange. Therefore imports worsen and exports improve the balance of payments.

From experience it is known that most students encounter a small semantic problem in the use of this simple rule. While the export of goods increases the supply of foreign exchange, the export of capital increases demand for it, and vice versa for the import of goods and capital. The confusion which can arise from this fact can readily be avoided by thinking of capital flows as representing trade in assets and by remembering the rule (as stated above) that the import and export of assets lead to demand for and supply of foreign exchange, respectively.

The preceding rule is not applicable to two categories of transactions which are of some analytical interest but which, for the average balance-of-payments user, are of little practical importance. First, there are gifts in kind made by private individuals and governments. For example, the gift of $1 million of wheat by the U.S. government to a foreign country is reported as a $1 million merchandise export. Now if this export of Merchandise account entry were matched by a corresponding debit entry in the Short-Term Capital account, as in the case of ordinary commercial merchandise exports, at the end of the accounting period there would be evidence of increasing holdings of foreign short-term assets which in fact did not take place, since the transaction involved a gift. For this reason, a special account known as Government Grants Abroad has been created, and the gift transaction leads to a debit entry in it. When the books are closed, the closing credit entry in the Grants account is matched by a debit entry in the final Balance-of-Payments account. This takes the place of what in the case of a commercial merchandise export would have been an increase in foreign short-term asset holdings. We thus end up with an accurate record of merchandise exports and changes in net foreign short-term indebtedness. The same principles of accounting are used in the case of merchandise gifts by private persons, except that these are recorded in an original account labeled "Private Remittances Abroad."

The second category to which the rule regarding effects of exports and imports on the balance of payments does not apply concerns monetary gold held by the U.S. Treasury. Historically, this has been considered to be part of the country's foreign net short-term asset position, since the gold can be exchanged so readily and without risk of capital loss into other forms of assets useful for financing temporary international payments imbalances. Now when the Treasury buys gold in private U.S. markets and there is no balance-of-payments record, there could be a change in the U.S. foreign net short-term asset position which could not be explained by the normal balance-of-payments surplus. For this reason, U.S. Treasury purchases of domestic gold are shown as a credit in the Merchandise account and as a debit in a government foreign short-term asset account which is officially known as the International Reserve Asset account.

Individual Accounts and Balances

After the preceding consideration of more or less abstract accounting procedures and conventions, we now turn to the discussion of actual U.S. balance-of-payments data, which are found in Table 13–1. This table has been compiled especially for the purposes of this book, but in its basic

TABLE 13–1

Balance of Payments of the United States for 1973 (billions of U.S. dollars)

	Credit	Debit	Balance
1. Merchandise exports	75.5		
2. Merchandise imports		77.4	
3. Balance on Merchandise account: (1) − (2)			−1.9
4. Invisible exports, total	28.4		
4a. Foreign tourist expenditures in U.S.	3.3		
4b. Transportation income	5.3		
4c. Other services income	5.8		
4d. Investment income	14.0		
5. Invisible imports, total		21.9	
5a. U.S. tourist expenditures abroad		5.4	
5b. Transportation expenditures		5.8	
5c. Other service expenditures		2.2	
5d. Payments on foreign investment in U.S.		8.7	
6. Balance on Invisible account: (4) − (5)			+6.5
7. Balance on Trade account: (3) − (6)			+4.6
8. Unilateral Transfers received, total	0.0		
9. Unilateral Transfer paid (excl. military), total		3.9	
9a. U.S. government grants		1.9	
9b. U.S. pensions		0.7	
9c. Private remittances		1.3	
10. Balance on Unilateral Transfer account: (8) − (9)			−3.9
11. Balance on Current account: (3) + (6) + (10)			+0.7
12. Long-term capital inflows	7.9		
12a. U.S. government with private foreign agencies	1.1		
12b. Private direct investment	2.5		
12c. Private long-term securities	4.3		
13. Long-term capital outflows		9.7	
13a. U.S. government		2.7	
13b. Private direct investment		4.9	
13c. Private long-term securities		2.1	
14. Balance on Long-term Capital account: (12) − (13)			−1.8
15. Basic Balance: (11) + (14)			−1.1
16. Short-term Capital inflows	10.7		
16a. Held by private foreigners	5.6		
16b. Held by foreign monetary authorities	5.1		
17. Short-term Capital outflows		7.0	
17a. Held by private U.S. residents		7.0	
18. Balance on Short-term Capital account: (16) − (17)			+3.7
19. Balance on Capital account: (14) + (18)			+1.9
20. Balance on Autonomous account: (15) + (18)			+2.6
21. Transactions in official reserve assets, total	0.2		
21a. Gold	0.0		
21b. Convertible currencies	0.2		
21c. Assets with the International Monetary Fund	0.0		

TABLE 13–1 (continued)

	Credit	Debit	Balance
22. Errors and Omissions		2.8	
23. Liquidity balance: (15) + (17a) + (22)			−10.9
24. Official settlements balance: (15) + (18) − (16b) + (22)			−5.3
Total of underlined items	122.7	122.7	

Note: This table is a modified version of the one published in the source, in which many notes concerning precise definitions and coverage may be found.
Source: *Survey of Current Business,* June 1974, p. 34.

design it resembles closely the balance-of-payments statistics of the United States and other countries published in a number of sources mentioned at the end of Chapter 6. However, even within a country, the presentation of balance-of-payments statistics is not uniform, and it differs according to the needs of the audience to which the publication addresses itself.

In Table 13–1 we show the most important accounts of the balance of payments without underlining. Among these are accounts for exports and imports of merchandise; invisibles, which is the official name of what above we have called loosely "services," long-term and short-term capital, and unilateral transfers. Some of the accounts have subaccounts, such as the invisibles, which consist of tourist, transportation, and other service expenditures and income on investments. In the first and second columns, entries on these accounts are shown under the headings "credit" or "debit," according to the accounting principles developed above. Underlined items represent the sums of subaccounts and, as can be seen from the last line of the table, the sums of the underlined items in both columns are equal. This arises from the use of the double-entry bookkeeping principles discussed above.

The individual accounts are of some interest to analysts, especially when they involve the comparison of different years, as is possible with the data presented in Table 13–3 below. For example, it is interesting to note that merchandise exports and imports represent over one half of the total credits and debits in the U.S. balance of payments, while trade in invisibles and long-term capital flows represent about 25 and 9 percent of this total, respectively. Noteworthy also are the relatively large credit entries under investment income ($14 billion) and short-term capital inflows ($10.7 billion). One important account is shown in Line 22, Errors and Omissions, with a debit of $2.8 billion. This entry is believed to reflect to a large extent, unrecorded short-term capital flows induced by leads and lags in commercial payments, as discussed in Chapter 11. The figure is formed when the sums of the credit and debit entries, derived independently and from many different sources, fail to be equal in the final closing of the books. Another important original account is shown in Line 21 as Transactions in Offical Reserve Assets, with three different subaccounts, gold, convertible currencies, and assets with the International Monetary Fund. This account reflects the purchases or sales of foreign exchange under-

TABLE 13–2
Key Balances for Balance-of-Payments Analysis

I. BASIC BALANCE

      1. Balance on Current account
\+ 2. Balance on Long-term Capital account
\= 3. Basic Balance

    which is financed by

      4. Balance on Short-term Capital account
\+ 5. Transactions in Official Reserve Assets
\+ 6. Errors and Omissions

II. BALANCE ON AUTONOMOUS ACCOUNT

      1. Basic Balance
\+ 2. Balance on Short-term Capital account
\= 3. Balance on Autonomous account

    which is financed by

      4. Transactions in Official Reserve Assets
      5. Errors and Omissions

III. LIQUIDITY BALANCE

      1. Basic Balance
\+ 2. Short-term Capital held by U.S. residents
\+ 3. Errors and Omissions
\= 4. Liquidity Balance

    which is financed by

      5. U.S. Short-term Capital held by foreigners
      6. Transactions in Official Reserve Assets

IV. OFFICIAL RESERVE SETTLEMENTS BALANCE

      1. Basic Balance
\+ 2. Balance on Short-Term Capital account
\− 3. Short-term Capital held by foreign monetary institutions
\+ 4. Errors and Omissions
\= 5. Official Reserve Settlements Balance

    which is financed by

      6. Transactions in Official Reserve Assets
      7. Short-term Capital held by foreign monetary institutions

---

taken by the U.S. government in order to stabilize the exchange rate, as we discussed in Chapter 10. This is one of the most important ways in which changes in a country's net foreign short-term asset position take place.

From our theoretical discussions it is clear that for each account the credit and debit entries can be added, with the debit entry as a negative number, to derive a balance for that account. For example, we could find the Balance on Transportation account, which is reported by Line 4b income of $5.3 billion and by Line 5b expenditures abroad of $5.8 billion, giving a negative balance of $0.5 billion. However, balances of such sub-accounts are of relatively little interest to most analysts, and we do not show them in Table 13–1. Instead, we show underlined only the balances on the major accounts, the Merchandise (Row 3), Invisibles (Row 6), Unilateral Transfers (Row 10), Long-Term Capital (Row 14) and Short-Term Capital (Row 18) accounts. In each case, it can be seen how the balances were derived by considering the figures given after each name, which indicate the rows which were summed to obtain the balance. The value of the balance is shown in the third column of the table. A summing of these five accounts plus the Transactions in Official Reserve Assets and the Errors and Omissions accounts must net to zero, since each of these balances is the net of some credit and debit entries, the sum of which we know to be equal.

In Table 13–1 we also show a number of balances which are not derived by the simple netting of the accounts but which involve the complex summing of certain balances and accounts. These balances are the basic balance (line 15), balance on autonomous account (line 20), the liquidity balance (line 23) and the official reserve settlements balance (line 24). Following each of these balances in Table 13–1 we show how they are derived by the summing of different accounts. These balances are central to balance-of-payments analysis. In Table 13–2 we set out schematically and for easier comprehension the key features of their composition. We now turn to a discussion of the rationale for their construction and use in balance-of-payments analysis.

Different Balances for Analysis

We stated in our discussion of principles above that the central concern of balance-of payments analysis is with the question of how a country's economic transactions with the rest of the world affect its net short-term foreign asset position. It is now necessary to elaborate on this basic idea and introduce a number of real-world complications.

Foremost of these complications is the problem of defining more accurately economic transactions with the rest of the world which have to be financed. There are different definitions which underlie the four different concepts of the balance of payments shown in Table 13–2. Thus, the basic balance adds up the balances on current and long-term capital accounts, under the assumption that these types of transactions tend to be a function of fundamental economic conditions, such as domestic and foreign prices, the exchange rate, income levels, growth rates, and savings propensities, which change only slowly and are relatively stable. According to this view, short-term capital flows and errors and omissions are volatile elements in the balance of payments which tend to average to zero over the business cycle or random economic disequilibrium. The basic balance thus conveys information about the net effects which very fundamental economic forces have on the balance of payments and which policy makers need to watch if they are concerned about the changes in the country's net short-term foreign asset position. According to this view, in the long run a country's basic balance should average to zero unless it is desired to deliberately increase or decrease its holdings or its indebtedness on short-term capital accounts. As can be seen from Table 13–2, under the basic balance the financing of imbalances is through changes in official reserve holdings, the private and foreign government short-term asset position, and errors and omissions, which are assumed to be either random or unrecorded short-term capital flows due to leads and lags in payments averaging to zero in the long run.

The balance on autonomous account shown in Section II of Table 13–2 is defined as the basic balance plus the balance on short-term capital account. Policy makers should be concerned about this balance rather than the basic balance if international short-term capital flows are not just transitory phenomena netting to zero in the long run but are the result of fundamental economic forces. For example, U.S.–owned multinational corporations may be increasing their holdings of foreign short-term assets as part of their natural growth. As another example, foreign firms and governments may be increasing their short-term dollar holdings, along with their growth in income and wealth, because dollars can be used very readily in international transactions. If the changes in the net U.S. short-term asset position accompanying these trends are permanent, then policy makers should attempt to achieve a long-run zero balance on autonomous account, unless it is desired to change deliberately the stock of official reserve assets. Under the autonomous-account definition of the balance of payments, imbalances are financed through the official reserve account and errors and omissions, the latter assumed to average to zero in the long run.

The liquidity balance-of-payments concept was developed in the postwar years by Walther Lederer of the U.S. Department of Commerce. Until the middle of the 1960s, it was the official (and privately the most widely used) measure of the health of the U.S. balance of payments. The difference between the liquidity and autonomous-account concepts lies in the treatment of errors and omissions and, most importantly, U.S. short-term assets held by foreigners and foreign assets held by U.S. residents. The argument is that U.S. residents' holdings of foreign assets should be considered as contributing to the balance-of-payments imbalance, as a regular matter which has to be financed in the long run. Therefore, these holdings by U.S. residents are shown in Table 13–2 as determining, together with the basic balance and errors and omissions, the payments imbalance. Foreign lending through purchase of U.S. assets, on the other hand, may be only a temporary phenomenon and can be reversed easily at the will of private foreign investors and governments. Therefore, such lending should not enter into the determination of the balance which has to be financed in the long run, but should properly be considered a source of financing the imbalance, as can be seen from Table 13–2, Section III, Line 5.

This asymmetric treatment of short-term capital flows according to the residency of their holders embodies a conservative philosophy concerning appropriate balance-of-payments policies, for the following reasons. In the postwar years the rest of the world accumulated large amounts of U.S. dollars in both private and official portfolios at a rapid rate, because there was a great need to replenish war-depleted stocks of private internationally acceptable means of payment and stocks of officially held reserves. By taking these exports of U.S. assets out of the category of accounts making up the balance of payments under the liquidity definition, the United States showed greater deficits than under the autonomous-account definition. The liquidity definition during this period therefore tended conservatively to overstate the U.S. balance-of-payments deficit and to induce sometimes costly measures to reduce the deficit and protect the net foreign short-term asset position of the country, according to this definition.

During the 1960s a professional economists' opinion developed which argued that the liquidity definition of the balance of payments was too conservative, overstated the U.S. deficits, and therefore led to unnecessary restrictions on the U.S. domestic monetary and fiscal policies aimed at the achievement of full employment and growth. In 1965 a presidential task force of economists, under the leadership of E. M. Bernstein, published a report recommending the use of a further balance-of-payments concept in U.S. statistics. This is known as the official reserve settlements concept, shown in Section IV of Table 13–2. As can be seen, under this concept the balance of payments consists of the sum of the basic balance, errors and omissions, and short-term capital account balance, the latter adjusted for the short-term capital held by foreign monetary institutions. Financing of the imbalance occurs through official reserve transactions and the holdings of U.S. assets by foreign monetary institutions. The rationale for this balance-of-payments concept is that foreign private holdings of U.S. dollars should be regarded as permanent, just like the U.S. holdings of foreign assets, since those balances are needed to carry on the growing transactions in international trade. The dollar holdings by foreign monetary authorities, on the other hand, tend to be induced by the state of the U.S. balance of payments and may be accumulated or decumulated by the rest of the world in response to its payments imbalances. According to this view, policy makers who do not wish to change their reserve holdings and net indebtedness to foreign monetary authorities therefore should attempt to average the official reserve settlements balance to zero.

Problems of Balance-of-Payments Analysis

Publications of the U.S. balance of payments tend to show all of the four balances just discussed, and the nonspecialist has great difficulty in deciding which of these balances is most relevant for decisions of policy makers, the analysis of trends, and the making of forecasts. The problem is that none of the four balances is ideally suited for either of these purposes. Each balance reveals a different aspect of a potential problem, just as all of the measurements of bodily functions made by medical doctors are used in the diagnosis of many different aspects of a person's state of health. The experienced balance-of-payments analyst takes into consideration a country's balance-of-payments records according to all four basic definitions. In further diagnostic work, the other accounts and balances presented in Table 13-1 are also considered.

It is difficult to present abstract guidelines for how analysts can best understand the implications of balance-of-payments data and trends. The difficulty is due to the fact that the purposes of balance-of-payments analysis are very diverse, and at the same time these purposes determine the nature of the analysis. At one extreme the purpose of balance-of-payments analysis is to plan government policies to assure that a country's net foreign short-term asset position is what it should be. This type of analysis is undertaken typically by civil servants in many departments of central governments. It involves the analysis of trends in many original accounts, tempered by forecasts of changes in domestic and foreign economic conditions. Coming up with correct diagnosis and policy recommendations is as much an art as a science. Other government uses of balance-of-payments data may occur in the estimation of effects of specific programs or events, such as the official aid program or foreign direct investment, on the balance of payments. In these applications sophisticated econometric analysis of payments data, backed by theoretical modeling of processes, is required.

At the other extreme balance-of-payments data may be used by a firm's economist to analyze individual merchandise accounts in order to plan its marketing and production strategies. It is clear that the firm's type of output and past business connections determine directly what and how data are used. Another set of information obtainable from balance-of-payments statistics which is used as an input into many business decisions concerns likely changes in exchange rates prompted by imbalances. These exchange rate changes are important for many business decisions, since they determine the price at which goods are imported or can be sold abroad, as we have shown in Chapters 10 and 11 above. This sort of analysis also is more of an art than a science, since it involves many judgments about trends and behavior of governments in the future. Yet, in this, as in all balance-of-payments analysis objectives, the quality of decisions and judgments is improved by the careful study of the current and historical balance-of-payments statistics.

While it is not possible to generalize usefully about balance-of-payments analysis techniques, we can discuss a few pitfalls of analysis which are easily fallen into and can be discovered occasionally in government reports and newspaper stories.

First, it is often believed that positive merchandise trade, current account, and overall payments, which lead to a growth in reserves, are good, while any negative balances are bad. Such conclusions are unwarranted. Surpluses on current account imply that a country is sending to the rest of the world a net amount of real goods and services which therefore are not available for domestic consumption or investment. In return the country receives claims on private assets abroad, and so on. Under certain conditions, which will be appreciated more fully after studying the analysis in Part Four of this book, it may be in the interest of a country's population to run a deficit in the overall balance of payments or current account. It should also be noted that the world's balance of payments is a zero-sum game in which one country's surplus necessarily implies an equal-sized deficit for the rest of the world. Therefore there would be inevitable conflicts if all countries tried to run payments surpluses and none were willing to accept deficits.

A second pitfall of balance-of-payments analysis is that balance-of-payments statistics are published every quarter, both adjusted and unadjusted for seasonal variations. A common mistake made in the interpretation of balance-of-payments data is to pay too much attention to short-term fluctuations. There are many random elements in international trade and finance, and normally it takes a number of quarters, sometimes years, before significant, important trends can be discerned. In fact, official statistics themselves are revised for a number of years after initial publication, as statistical offices obtain more complete and more reliable data.

A third pitfall is that it is often tempting to assign causal interdependencies to changes or levels of accounts which are correlated with levels or changes in other accounts. For example, in a year a country's overall balance of payments may have deteriorated by $100, while at the same time there was an equal deterioration in the long-term capital account. Under such circumstances it is tempting to argue that the $100 increase in the overall deficit was caused by increased long-term capital outflows, and therefore the increase in the deficit could be eliminated by a reduction in capital outflows. Such reasoning is fallacious and neglects the interdependence of the entire economy. Thus, it is entirely possible that domestic demand conditions in the period under consideration were such that exports of merchandise would have fallen by $300 had it not been for the export of $300 worth of machinery and certain other goods used by a certain business firm abroad, which was acquired in that year with the $100 capital outflow. In other words, the long-term capital export actually improved the overall balance of payments from what it would have been otherwise. Consequently, the reversal of the $100 capital flow would improve the capital account by that sum but worsen the overall balance of payments by $200.

Other examples of fallacious assignment of cause and effect are as follows. Foreign official aid has been a consistently large negative item in the U.S. balance of payments. Cutting or eliminating this aid would not result in a correspondingly large improvement in the U.S. balance of payments, however, since the recipient countries, now without the means of payment, would reduce their merchandise purchases from the United States and other countries, which in turn would also be likely to reduce spending in the United States. Another example is that if the United States reduced tourist expenditures abroad through the imposition of taxes on foreign travel, the resultant improvement in its balance of payments would tend to be mitigated or even offset by reduced U.S. exports of aircraft to foreign carriers and of goods which are consumed by U.S. tourists abroad. Another example is that balance-of-payments statistics are often available which show relations between two countries. These statistics may reveal that there are certain trade partners with which a given country is in consistent and sizable deficit or surplus. It makes little sense to attempt improvement in one country's overall balance of payments by eliminating the deficit with one particular other country. To see that this is so, consider a world consisting of three countries, A, B and C. A has a surplus with B and a deficit with C, while B has a surplus with C. Now if A restricts trade with C and eliminates its deficit with that country, C will be without the means to run a deficit with B and has to eliminate it. But now B cannot sustain its deficit with A and has to balance its trade with A. Thus, in the end, A has experienced an improvement in its formerly negative trade balance with C but has suffered an equal-sized deterioration in its formerly positive balance with B, for a zero net improvement.

The lessons to be learned from these examples of fallacious conclusions drawn from the inspection of balance-of-payments data are that solid policy implications can be reached only after careful and intensive analysis which takes into consideration as many as possible of the complex interrelationships of activites in the domestic and international economies. In the real world, these purely economic considerations have to be supplemented by judgments about lags, imperfections in the operation of economic incentives, and political motives. As a result, balance-of-payments analysis is an art as well as a science, mastery of which is achieved by few.

II. BALANCE OF PAYMENTS OF THE UNITED KINGDOM, THE UNITED STATES, CANADA, AND GERMANY

Table 13–3 presents the balance of payments of four major Western countries since the end of the Korean War and the early 1970s. The information contained in these data is useful as a record of recent economic history, a knowledge of which helps students to put into perspective current and future events. The developments of the period also serve as a background to the theoretical analysis of the international adjustment mechanism and international factor movements in Parts Four and Six. The data for recent years were taken from the latest publications available at the time of writing. Because of the revisions of data taking place for a number of years after initial publication, the statistics for the latest years may have become obsolete. However, because revisions rarely involve major changes, the analysis to be presented here is not likely to become false. In preparing the balance-of-payments data for this book it was necessary to manipulate published statistics to obtain a format consistent with our theoretical analysis, since every country publishes many more detailed and special data than are useful for our purposes here. The resultant data may not be perfectly consistent either as between countries or through time. For details on coverage and definitions, readers have to consult the official sources for each country.

The United Kingdom

For Britain the foreign sector has had important influences on domestic economic policies during the period covered. As can be seen from Table 13–3, the overall balance financed through official reserve transactions was positive 10 years and negative 13 years, with positive and negative runs of 2 to 5 years. International reserve holdings rose and fell together with these surpluses and deficits but stayed within a fairly narrow range of $1.958 billion in 1952 and $3.719 billion in 1960, until a doubling of these reserves took place in 1971 as a result of a massive overall payments surplus. The exchange rate was stable around 2.80 dollars per pound sterling until the devaluation to 2.40 in 1967. In 1971 the currency ap-

TABLE 13–3. Balance of payments accounts of United Kingdom, United States, Canada, and Germany, 1952–1974 (balance in millions of U.S. dollars)

	1952	1953	1954	1955	1956	1957	1958	1959	1960	1961
UNITED KINGDOM										
1. Goods and services	319	221	350	−367	753	801	1,114	594	−468	300
2. Unilateral transfers	156	202	−11	−73	−168	−196	−191	−224	−255	−310
3. Capital flows	−374	−543	−535	−341	−524	−297	−540	−703	−537	190
4. Errors and omissions	165	73	198	344	115	272	218	−42	818	−71
5. Balance financed officially	+266	−47	−48	−437	+176	+580	+602	−375	−442	+109
6. Reserve holdings ($ billion)	1.958	2.670	3.034	2.392	2.276	2.274	3.068	2.800	3.719	3.318
7. Exchange rate = R($ £)	2.810	2.811	2.795	2.804	2.786	2.859	2.803	2.800	2.804	2.808
UNITED STATES										
1. Goods and services		2,799	4,288	4,710	6,755	8,570	5,341	2,852	6,705	8,053
2. Military expenditures		−2,423	−2,460	−2,701	−2,788	−2,841	−3,135	−2,805	−2,734	−2,596
3. Unilateral transfers		−2,471	−2,280	−2,498	−2,423	−2,345	−2,361	−2,348	−2,331	−2,577
4. Capital flows		−391	−1,281	−1,082	−2,217	−3,154	−3,171	−405	−3,821	−3,380
5. Errors and omissions		366	191	515	568	1,184	511	423	−922	−847
6. Balance financed officially		−2,120	−1,542	−1,056	−105	1,414	−2,815	−2,283	−3,103	−1,347
7. Change in reserve holdings		1,256	516	182	−869	−1,225	2,292	1,035	1,845	606
8. Change in liability to foreign official monetary authorities		864	1,026	874	974	−249	523	1,248	1,258	741
9. Balance on liquidity definition									−3,677	−2,252
10. Reserve holdings ($ billion)		23.46	22.98	22.80	23.67	24.83	22.54	21.51	19.36	18.75
11. Of which gold		22.09	21.79	21.75	22.06	22.86	20.58	19.51	17.80	16.95
12. Liquid external liabilities		11.36	12.45	13.52	14.90	15.83	16.85	19.43	21.03	22.94
13a. Of which due to foreign official		6.47	7.52	8.26	9.15	9.14	9.65	10.12	11.09	11.83
13b. Of which due to private sector		4.89	4.93	5.26	5.75	6.69	7.20	9.31	9.94	11.11
CANADA										
1. Goods and services	467	−183	−143	−337	−954	−987	−604	−925	−643	−345
2. Investment income	−274	−243	−284	−327	−387	−454	−457	−510	−495	−445
3. Unilateral transfers	−25	−25	−16	−43	−46	−76	−104	−133	−144	−126
4. Capital flows	−130	412	571	663	1,437	1,408	1,278	1,557	1,242	1,203
5. Balance financed officially	38	−39	127	−45	49	−110	112	−11	40	286
6. Reserve holdings ($ billion)	1.94	1.91	2.04	1.99	2.04	1.94	2.05	2.04	2.00	2.29
7. Exchange rate = R(C.$ · U.S.$)	0.971	0.974	0.966	0.999	0.960	0.985	0.964	0.953	0.996	1.043
GERMANY										
1. Goods and services					1,355	1,841	1,894	1,781	1,930	1,847
2. Unilateral transfers					−287	−441	−450	−773	−822	−1,112
3. Capital flows					31	−586	−508	−1,328	486	−777
4. Errors and omissions					114	406	−112	−50	573	102
5. Balance financed officially					1,211	1,220	824	−371	1,966	60
6. Reserve holdings ($ billion)	0.96	1.77	2.80	3.02	4.20	5.20	5.88	4.79	7.03	7.17
7. Exchange rate = R(DM · $)	4.20	4.20	4.20	4.22	4.20	4.20	4.18	4.17	4.17	4.00

Notes: Balance financed officially is shown with sign which indicates + = surplus; − = deficit. U.S. balance on liquidity from *Report of the President,* 1975, p. 351. 1974 figures are preliminary.

Sources: *International Financial Statistics,* 1972 Supplement, August 1974 and February 1976, individual country statistics. See original source for coverage.

1962	1963	1964	1965	1966	1967	1968	1969	1970	1971	1972	1973	1974
652	731	−585	377	802	−148	−88	1,610	2,130	3,098	870	−2,533	−7,612
−339	−384	−485	−514	−566	−889	−1,164	−543	−495	−513	−661	−1,056	−962
−274	−615	−800	−539	−1,602	−727	−1,427	−1,046	868	2,890	2,080	2,616	3,153
210	−232	−22	78	−159	510	−316	972	141	731	−1,450	1,177	1,063
+249	−500	−1,892	−598	−1,525	−1,254	−2,995	+993	+3,054	+6,467	−3,000	203	−4,355
3.308	3.148	2.315	3.004	2.099	2.695	2.422	2.527	2.827	6.582	5.647	6.476	6.939
2.803	2.797	2.790	2.803	2.790	2.407	2.384	2.401	2.394	2.552	2.348	2.323	2.349
7,599	8,291	10,733	9,253	8,235	8,357	5,629	5,352	6,964	3,601	−1,021	8,797	4,043
−2,449	−2,304	−2,133	2,122	−2,935	−3,138	−3,140	−3,341	−3,371	−2,864	−3,558	−2,180	4,043
−2,614	−2,742	−2,754	−2,836	−2,890	−3,080	−2,875	−2,910	−3,149	−3,526	−3,773	−3,622	−7,405
−3,993	−4,694	−6,299	−5,075	−1,758	−1,574	2,518	6,204	−10,027	−16,717	414	−3,817	−9,741
−1,245	−485	−1,080	−507	−431	−985	−493	−2,603	−1,104	−10,982	−3,129	−4,925	4,704
−2,702	−1,934	−1,534	−1,289	219	−3,418	1,641	2,702	−9,821	−29,766	−10,297	−5,744	−8,398
1,533	1,377	171	1,222	568	52	−880	−1,187	2,477	2,348	32	209	−2,095
1,169	1,557	1,363	67	−187	3,366	−761	−1,515	7,344	27,418	10,322	5,095	7,176
−2,864	−2,713	−2,626	−2,478	−2,151	−4,683	−1,611	−6,081	−3,851	−21,965	−13,882	−7,606	−15,655
17.22	16.84	16.57	15.45	14.58	14.83	15.71	16.96	14.49	13.19	13.15	14.38	16.06
16.06	15.60	15.47	14.07	13.24	12.07	10.89	11.86	11.07	11.08	10.49	11.65	11.83
24.27	26.39	29.36	29.57	31.02	35.67	38.47	45.91	46.96	67.81	82.88	92.57	119.10
12.71	14.42	15.79	15.83	14.90	18.19	17.34	16.00	23.33	50.65	61.52	66.78	76.66
11.56	11.97	13.57	13.74	16.12	17.48	21.13	29.91	23.63	17.16	21.36	25.79	39.12
−151	193	328	−257	−226	446	806	85	2,168	1,365	621	873	2,229
−544	−583	−627	−707	−760	−847	−887	−847	−955	−1,058	−1,433	−1,566	2,229
−82	−91	−94	−81	−89	−61	26	−84	−111	−82	228	338	556
922	616	729	1,190	743	479	378	906	350	550	784	−107	1,699
145	135	336	145	−332	17	323	60	1,575	892	−327	463	+26
2.56	2.61	2.89	3.04	2.70	2.72	3.05	3.11	4.68	5.70	6.05	5.77	5.82
1.078	1.081	1.074	1.077	1.083	1.082	1.074	1.073	1.011	1.001	0.996	0.996	0.996
864	1,459	1,324	−86	1,593	3,970	4,554	3,780	3,205	3,155	4,520	10,184	16,159
−1,299	−1,273	−1,328	−1,605	−1,581	−1,609	−1,828	−2,171	−2,425	−3,026	−4,122	−5,734	−6,483
−74	566	−444	586	209	−2,511	−1,878	−5,016	2,986	2,085	1,738	3,835	−9,501
282	−46	555	780	255	109	855	370	2,250	1,878	2,181	1,070	−641
−226	686	107	−325	476	−41	1,703	−3,037	6,168	4,263	5,106	9,364	−466
6.96	7.65	7.88	7.43	8.03	8.15	9.95	7.13	13.61	18.39	23.80	33.10	32.40
4.00	3.98	3.98	4.01	3.98	4.00	4.00	3.69	3.65	3.27	3.20	2.70	2.41

preciated to 2.55 but fell again in 1972 and reached an all-time low of 2.32 in 1973. It remained at this level throughout 1974. Not shown in the table is a dramatic fall of the pound sterling's rate to below $2 in 1976.

The periods of balance-of-payments deficits which tended to follow periods of surpluses necessitated restrictive domestic monetary and fiscal policies, which led to unemployment and reduced economic growth. For reasons to be discussed in the next part of this book, these policies eventually produced surpluses and permitted more expansionary monetary and fiscal policies and a return to full employment and greater growth. These British policies of economic expansion and payment deficits, alternating with contraction and surpluses, became known as "stop-go." They are often used as an example of how adherence to fixed exchange rates and resultant payments imbalances have undesirable consequences for the stability and growth of a country's real economic sector, which is the prime determinant of economic welfare.

An examination of the components of Britain's balance of payments reveals that the balance on goods and services has been negative in only 7 out of the 23 years. On the other hand, unilateral transfers, representing to a large extent foreign aid to developing countries, have been negative and growing since 1954. Similarly, the capital balance has been negative and large except in 1961 and 1970–74, the latter period being one of very large short-term capital inflows caused by the increases in liabilities of British banks in connection with the growth of the Eurocurrency business. Because of these large unilateral transfers and capital exports during the 1950s and 1960s, Britain needed to attain a substantial surplus on goods and services accounts if she wanted her overall payments to be positive.

It may be interesting to note that errors and omissions in the balance of payments have been fairly large throughout the period and were negative in 7 out of the 22 years. During the period 1972–74, which was characterized by widespread currency speculation, the errors and omissions became very large relative to both the trade and overall balances.

In our analysis of the adjustment mechanism we will discuss in detail the theoretical effects of a currency devaluation on the trade balance. We can see from Britain's data that the 1967 devaluation of sterling did not lead to an improvement in the trade balance until 1969, suggesting that a devaluation is neither a sufficient nor a necessary condition for the improvement of a country's trade balance.

The United States

The overall balance of payments of the United States was positive only in 1957, 1966, 1968, and 1969. It was negative, but never by more than $3.5 billion per year, in the remaining years, except during 1970–74. The massive deficits of 1970, $9.8 billion, and 1971, $29.8 billion, led to a major change in the international monetary system and the 1971 dollar devaluation, which we will discuss in later chapters.

One of the outstanding characteristics of the U.S. balance of payments during the period has been the persistent large surplus on the goods and services account balance, which was negative only in 1972. However, these surpluses were insufficient to compensate for the large U.S. military expenditures, unilateral transfers, and capital outflows. The military expenditures are such an important item in the U.S. balance of payments that they are shown separately in the statistics, even though theoretically they should be simply a part of the goods and services balance. The unilateral transfers represent primarily foreign aid to developing countries. The military expenditures and unilateral transfers fluctuated only little throughout the period and rose slowly each year, from about $2.5 billion in 1953 to about $3.5 billion in 1972. The capital balance exhibited large fluctuations and was negative most years, with net inflows taking place only in 1968, 1969, and 1972. The years 1970 and 1971 saw very great capital outflows of $10 billion and $16.7 billion, respectively, which contributed substantially to the dollar devaluation in 1971. We can note again that in 1972, the year following the dollar devaluation, the U.S. trade balance worsened rather than improved, as had been implied by some simple price-theoretic considerations. Moreover, in 1972 the trade balance reacted powerfully and registered a $8.8 billion surplus.

In rows 7 and 8 of the U.S. part of Table 13–3 we show how the United States has financed the payments deficits during the period. Row 7 reflects changes in reserve holdings defined in the conventional way and consisting of changes in the stock of gold, foreign exchange, and assets with the International Monetary Fund. For reasons discussed above in the context of accounting principles, the positive entries in these compensating accounts signify reserve reductions, and the negative ones represent increases. As can be seen, during the 22 years under consideration reserves decreased in all but four. Since the United States started the period holding almost all the reserves in the form of gold, these reserve drains showed up almost exclusively as reductions in gold holdings. These trends can be seen readily by considering total holdings of U.S. reserves in line 10 and reserves of gold in line 11. Most significant for later purposes of analysis is the gradual but persistent decline in gold holdings from $22 billion in 1952–57 to $10.5 billion in 1972. The increase to $11.7 billion in 1973 was caused almost completely by a revaluation of the gold stock from $38 to $42.22 per ounce, which took place in February 1973.

Until 1971 U.S. dollars were legally convertible into gold if presented to the U.S. Treasury by a foreign monetary authority. This feature, combined with great confidence in the strength and stability of the U.S. economy and the accompanying acceptability of the dollar as a private and intergovernmental means of payment and store of value, led to a situation in which foreign governments were happy to accept short-term U.S. dollar obligations rather than gold as a settlement of U.S. payments deficits. For this reason we show in Line 8 the change in U.S. short-term liabilities to foreign official monetary authorities as a second method of official compensatory financing of the U.S. deficit. As can be seen, these U.S. liabilities grew in all but 4 of the 22 years and amounted to the extraordinarily large sums of $27.4 and $10.3 billion in 1971 and 1972, respectively. Line 13a shows the aggregate of these liabilities. They rose from a modest $6.5 billion in 1953 to $76.7 billion in 1974.

The U.S. dollar during this period was held not only by foreign monetary authorities but also by private individuals, as we discussed above in the context of the Eurodollar market developments. On Line 13b we record the stock of dollars held by the foreign private sector. This stock grew from $4.9 billion in 1953 to $39.1 billion in 1974, with an intermediate peak of $29.9 billion in 1969 and a low of $17.2 billion in the crisis year 1971. If we add changes in this private holding of dollars to the officially financed overall balance, we arrive approximately at the U.S. balance of payments under the liquidity definition shown on Line 9.

The relationship between U.S. gold holdings and overall liquid liabilities on the one hand and legal requirements for U.S. domestic monetary purposes on the other marks two important dates in U.S. foreign economic relations. First, in 1960, for the first time since the 1920s, U.S. external liabilities of $21.0 billion (line 12) exceeded U.S. holdings of gold of $17.8 billion (line 11). This relationship of assets to liabilities raised questions about the ability of the United States to convert its obligation into gold on demand and led to speculation against the dollar and a conversion of $1.7 billion of obligations into gold. Both of these events appear minor in retrospect, but they were a major shock at the time which led to a fundamental reexamination of the nature of a international monetary system which uses dollars as a major form of reserve holding. They set into motion efforts for reform of the system which we will discuss in Chapter 23 and which were implemented to some extent in 1970–74.

Second, in 1971 the U.S. gold holdings reached $11.0 billion, which represented an amount just necessary to meet existing legal requirements, which stipulate that U.S. currency in circulation must be backed by a certain amount of gold. While this legal requirement could have been circumvented by some technical adjustments in the U.S. Treasury and emergency legislation could have been passed, the domestic U.S. inflation and the trend in the U.S. trade and capital balances, which had led up to this point, were interpreted by many observers as demanding drastic action. As a result, speculation in the form of short-term capital outflows and changes in payments patterns reflected in errors and omissions in the balance of payments reached the unprecedented figures of $16.7 and $11.0 billion, respectively, in 1971. In the face of these pressures on the dollar,

President Richard Nixon announced on August 15, 1971, a suspension of the gold convertibility of the dollar, a 10 percent import surcharge, and a number of drastic domestic economic policies aimed at stopping inflation. Since this period several of the major industrial nations have abandoned their commitment to the maintenance of fixed parity exchange rates, and several significant realignments of currency values have taken place. We can thus conclude that the international reserve and debt position of the United States in 1971, which is reflected in the data in Table 13–3, triggered fundamental changes in the international monetary system and economic relations, the ultimate form of which was and is only dimly perceived.

We close our discussion of recent U.S. balance-of-payments history by a brief analysis of the relationship between the balance of payments under the liquidity definition (line 9) and the official reserve settlements definition (line 8). As can be seen from these statistics, in all years except 1970 and 1971 the liquidity balance-of-payments deficit was larger than that under the official reserve settlements definition. This fact reflects simply the growth of U.S. dollar holdings by the private sector abroad, which was interrupted and actually became negative during the episodes of speculation against the dollar in 1970 and 1971. The sales of dollars by private wealth holders expecting a depreciation of its value necessitated equivalent purchases by foreign monetary authorities who were committed to the maintenance of fixed exchange rates. Thus these sales contributed to the recorded larger deficits under the official reserve settlements definition.

Canada

Relative to Britain and the United States, Canada is a small country. It has vast natural resources and a rapidly growing population, a large share of which consists of immigrants. A ready market for Canada's resources is provided by the United States. At the same time, Canada depends heavily on the importation of manufactures from the United States. In order to reduce her dependence on raw-materials exports and manufactured imports, tariffs were imposed to encourage development of a native industry after World War II.

These basic characteristics of the Canadian economy give rise to the need for large amounts of capital imports, especially since most natural-resource industries require large quantities of capital per unit of output. As a result, the Canadian balance-of-payments statistics are dominated by a substantial, fairly constant inflow of capital throughout the period and an analogous, steadily growing outflow on goods and services, representing payments to the foreign owners of this capital. As a comparison of lines 2 and 4 in the Canadian part of Table 13–3 shows, until about 1965 capital imports exceeded the value of the payments to the foreign owners of the capital, but since then the situation has been reversed. As a result, during the earlier years Canada ran a deficit on goods and services other than investment income, which, as we have seen in Chapter 12, is necessary to transfer effectively the real resources counterpart of the capital inflows. For analogous reasons, in the later years, when capital inflows were smaller than debt-service payments, Canada needed to run trade surpluses and did so successfully.

From September 30, 1950, to May 1, 1962, Canada was the only major industrialized country in the world to have a floating exchange rate. This did not mean a complete absence of official intervention in the foreign exchange market but, as can be seen from Line 5, during that period Canada was able to limit its intervention to very small amounts, alternately buying and selling foreign exchange. During these years the exchange rate was remarkably stable, with a low of $0.953 Canadian per U.S. dollar in 1959 and a high of 0.999 in 1955. However, because of problems with domestic employment, the nature of which cannot be discussed here, the Canadian government in 1962 decided to commit itself to the maintenance of the Canadian dollar at a discount of about 7.5 percent, relative to the U.S. dollar. In the two years following this pegging, the balance on goods and services other than investment income and the overall payments balance moved into substantial surplus, suggesting that perhaps the Canadian dollar had been undervalued. In the remaining years of the sixties, under the fixed exchange rate regime, these two important balances exhibited fluctuations related to the business cycle. The turbulent period 1970–74 is reflected in unprecedently large surpluses and fluctuation in these two accounts, even though Canada, along with a number of the other major industrial countries, abandoned its commitment to a fixed parity in 1972. In 1972 and 1973 the Canadian dollar went to a premium relative to the U.S. dollar and international reserves rose to a peak of $6 billion in 1972, after they had been around $2 billion until 1960 and had risen to a new plateau of about $3 billion during the period 1961–74.

Germany

We include this country in our analysis since it was one of the few countries of the world which during this period experienced persistent and heavy surpluses on goods and services and after 1969, on the overall balance. Furthermore, the Deutsche mark experienced the most dramatic increase in value relative to the dollar. After it had been at $4.20 between 1952 and 1960, it moved to $4 between 1961 and 1968 and from then on enjoyed a steady increase, to $2.41 in 1974. As a result of these exchange rate changes, a dollar invested in German marks in 1960 would have risen by about 36 percent in capital value by 1970. This sort of experience was in part responsible for the large capital inflows Germany recorded after

1970, which were both recorded overtly and reflected in errors and omissions. These capital inflows themselves led to further increases in the value of the German currency, further inflows, and so on, on a cycle feeding on itself. The rise in the value of the mark would have been even greater after 1969 if the German authorities had not purchased vast quantities of foreign exchange in the market, as a result of which Germany's reserve holdings rose from $7.1 billion at the end of 1969 to $32.4 billion at the end of 1974.

However, even before the dramatic events in the period 1970–74, Germany had persistent large surpluses on the goods and services balance, which was negative only during the year 1965. These trade surpluses are especially remarkable since they went on even after currency appreciations which had increased the cost of German goods in the rest of the world and decreased the cost of imports in Germany. The trade surpluses were offset to only a small degree by unilateral transfers, which grew steadily throughout the period and consisted of war reparations, foreign aid, and, increasingly, remittances of foreign "guest" workers in Germany to their families in native countries. Until 1969 net capital outflows dominated over net capital inflows, in total sum and in the number of years. After 1969 came four years of large net capital inflows, which, according to statistics not presented here, consisted mainly of short-term capital. During the period 1956–69 the overall balance of payments was negative only in 5 of 14 years, and this permitted Germany to increase its reserve holdings from $4.2 billion to $7.1 billion.

Summary and Conclusions

In this section we have analyzed very briefly the balance-of-payments experiences of four major industrial countries between 1952 and 1974. We have noted that each country is characterized by a special and different set of problems. The United States did not run a sufficiently large surplus in private goods and services to pay for its military expenditures abroad, foreign aid payments, and capital exports. As a result, it suffered large and persistent balance-of-payments deficits, losses of gold, and increased indebtedness to foreign monetary authorities. This process culminated in the suspension of gold convertibility and a devaluation of the dollar in 1971. Britain's experience was dominated by a perpetual series of alternating deficits and surpluses, associated with a downward trend of the value of sterling and a steady level of reserve holdings. Canada's experience resembles closely that of Britain, except that the value of her currency was the same at the beginning and end of the period. Germany's overall balance of payments exhibited some fluctuations and was negative for a number of years during the period, but cumulatively it was strongly positive, in spite of sizable increases in the value of the mark.

The one feature all of these countries' balance of payments have in common is the instability of the accounts for goods and services and capital flows. Intercountry differences in this instability are in magnitude rather than kind. The countries discussed here as well as all other countries in the world suffer from these instabilities, in spite of efforts to avoid them and to modify domestic policies aimed at full employment, price stability, and growth, in order to attain stable international payments balances. The next section of this book deals with the causes of the payments instabilities and analyses methods for dealing with them.

BIBLIOGRAPHICAL NOTES

An important document of the U.S. procedures for collecting, presenting, and interpreting balance-of-payments statistics is the Bernstein Report (1965), incorporating the work of a committee of distinguished economists appointed by President Lyndon Johnson. Cooper (1966) analyses the report in a review. Lederer (1963) explains his views on balance-of-payments accounting. An original and very useful analysis of the basic theoretical problems of balance-of-payments accounting is Mundell (1968).

CONCEPTS FOR REVIEW

Balance of payments
Trade in invisibles
Current accounts
Unilateral transfers
Capital accounts
Errors and omissions

Official reserve transactions
Liquidity balance of payments
Official reserve settlement
   accounts
Net foreign short-term asset
   position

POINTS FOR FURTHER STUDY AND DISCUSSION

1. Write a report on U.S. gold production, industrial use, and monetary use. Attempt to reconcile these data with the annual balance-of-payments entries concerning the change in U.S. gold holdings.

2. Read periodic balance-of-payments reports of different countries and analyze differences in their methods of reporting imbalances and in the emphasis placed on subcategories.

3. For a number of industrial countries, consider the relationship between the quarterly size of errors and omissions in the balance of payments and current or lagged subbalances such as merchandise, short-term capital, or current accounts. Are there any correlations? Try to explain the phenomena theoretically.

4. To gain familiarity with balance-of-payments statistics, compile and compare tourist and merchandise expenditures and receipts for a number of developed and developing countries. What percentage of merchandise trade are the tourist expenditures and receipts, gross and net? Is there a tendency for large net tourist receipts to be matched by corresponding imbalances on merchandise balances? Explain the phenomenon theoretically.

part four

THE INTERNATIONAL
ADJUSTMENT
MECHANISM

14

Overview of Adjustment Problems and International Monetary Systems and an Analysis of Adjustment through Exchange Rate Changes

To THIS POINT our discussion has been disassociated almost completely from the problem of uncertainty. We assumed that we knew the factor endowments, production, and welfare functions of the countries we were considering and that these would be either stable or subject to known changes through time. The model of the world built on such assumptions is very useful and yields many important and interesting conclusions. It also gives a reasonably realistic description of relationships and magnitudes prevailing in the long run. The decisions of countries about trade, capital flows, and commercial policy are best made within such an analytical framework of certainty.

However, in the real world nothing is certain; nature and the activities of men and governments continuously introduce disturbances into the basic magnitudes, interdependencies, and the welfare and production functions we have assumed to be known and stable in our analysis. In fact, these random disturbances tend to be so powerful and to have such important effects on the welfare of people that the overwhelmingly largest share of the time and effort of economic analysts and government policy makers is taken up in dealing with these disturbances. This is often at the expense of concern over the fundamental policy issues of international economic relations which were raised in the first two parts of this book.

In Part Four we will develop analytical models capable of enhancing understanding of how countries can deal with the problems raised by the existence of uncertainty and instability. Unfortunately, this body of knowledge is not as neat and systematic as that about the pure theory of international trade discussed above. Moreover, this body of knowledge is continuously evolving, and in the 1970s it is caught in the middle of the agonizing reappraisal of the validity of some theorems of Keynesian analysis as compared to views of the greater importance of money. Moreover, the issues are confused by changing institutions, such as the abandonment by many major countries of the maintenance of fixed parity exchange rates; the uncertain role of gold in the system, caused by an end to official U.S. dollar gold convertibility in 1971; and the formation of regional monetary and trading associations like the European Economic Community and of producers' cartels like the Organization of Oil Producing and Exporting Countries. A review of textbooks in international economics reveals no one approach to an exposition of the body of knowledge about the mechanism of adjustment to international disturbances. In this book we develop our own novel approach in the hope that it will permit students to learn the subject with the least confusion and greatest ease.

In this chapter we present a brief description of how disturbances manifest themselves in the foreign exchange market, how individual countries can deal with payments imbalances, and what methods characterize specific organizations of the international monetary systems for the world as a whole. This description of methods for dealing with payments imbalances and systems for their use permits us to indicate the chapters in which they are discussed in detail, thus providing the student with an overview of the material to be presented in Part Four of this book. The concluding sections of this chapter are devoted to a careful analysis of the advantages and risks of using exchange rate changes as a method for dealing with payments imbalances.

I. METHODS AND SYSTEMS FOR DEALING WITH PAYMENTS IMBALANCES

The need for international adjustment arises from the basic fact that disturbances emanating from nature, developments within the private sector of economies, and government activities originating domestically or abroad bring about shifts in demand and supply curves of foreign exchange. In Figure 14-1, which reproduces the essentials of Figure 11-5, we show a typical situation where the initial equilibrium of the economy, at an exchange rate OR_0 and with a turnover of $O\pounds_0$ of foreign exchange per time period, is disturbed by an upward shift of the demand curve from D_0D_0' to D_1D_1'. In the real world it is common that, from one period to the next, both the demand and supply curves shift upward or downward, but to keep the exposition simple we restrict our analysis to the case shown, which incorporates all of the features essential for discussing the types of adjustment to the disturbances available to a small country.

The exhaustive list of methods available for dealing with the assumed

FIGURE 14–1

Foreign Exchange Market Disequilibrium

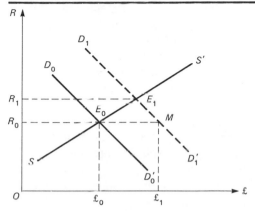

Initial exchange market equilibrium at the rate OR_0 is disturbed by an upward shift of the demand curve from D_0D_0' to D_1D_1'. The government can either let equilibrium be restored by an increase in the exchange rate to OR_1, or it can finance the excess demand of E_0M at the initial exchange rate OR_0 by the sale of exchange from its reserves or it can use domestic policies to cause shifts in the demand and supply curves.

shift of the demand curve for foreign exchange shown in Figure 14–1 is as follows. The country can:

1. Let the market exchange rate rise to OR_1.
2. Finance the excess demand for foreign exchange E_0M at the previous period's exchange rate OR_0 by drawing down its stock of international reserves.
3. Impose direct controls on private-sector foreign exchange transactions which shift the demand or supply curve, or both, such that the excess demand for foreign exchange is eliminated at the previous period's exchange rate, OR_0.
4. Change domestic prices and costs of production through appropriate deflationary measures for the purpose of shifting the demand and supply curves of foreign exchange downward and upward, respectively, such that the excess demand for foreign exchange is eliminated at OR_0.
5. Reduce aggregate demand and income so that the demand for imports is reduced, the demand curve is shifted downward, and excess demand for foreign exchange is eliminated at OR_0.

These different methods of adjustment are often used in combination. One analytically important combination involves letting the exchange rate adjust part of the way toward its natural market equilibrium, while financing or adjusting by the use of methods 3 through 5 to the remaining, smaller excess demand for foreign exchange. This pattern of behavior was discussed in Chapter 11 in connection with Figure 11–5.

In Sections II and III of this chapter we will deal in greater detail with the basic rationale for, and the possible difficulties arising from, the use of exchange rate depreciation as a method for dealing with the payments disequilibrium. The use of direct controls for this purpose is discussed in Chapter 15. The next two chapters, 16 and 17, deal with the use of income and price adjustments in the absence and the presence of money and short-term capital, respectively. The targets of full employment, known as internal balance, and of the balance of payments, known as external balance, give rise to a set of special difficulties as governments try to achieve both policy targets simultaneously. These difficulties are discussed in Chapter 18. A novel approach to the explanation of balance-of-payments imbalances, known as the monetarist approach to the balance of payments, is presented in Chapter 19. In the concluding Chapter 20 of Part Four the entire analysis of the preceding 5 chapters is integrated and reviewed.

Which of the methods for dealing with payments imbalance listed above an individual country uses is determined in principle by the international monetary system in existence. In Table 14–1 we list three prototypes of

TABLE 14–1
International Monetary Systems and Methods of Adjustment

Name of Monetary System	Characteristic Adjustment Methods
I. Freely floating exchange rates (have never been tried as a system)	Automatic exchange rate changes
II. Gold standard (about 1890–1914)	Automatic price and income adjustments
III. Managed exchange rates	
A. Parity Exchange Rates (1946 to about 1971)	Financing Price and income adjustments
1. IMF system	Controls
2. Dollar gold exchange standard	Discrete, large exchange rate revaluations
B. Managed float (about 1971 to present)	Financing Price and income adjustments
1. IMF system to be renegotiated	Controls Continuous, small exchange rate adjustments

international monetary systems which have either existed historically or which have been proposed for adoption by economists. As can be seen from the table, the first of these systems, freely floating exchange rates, has never existed. This system uses automatic exchange rate changes as the only method of adjustment to payments imbalances, and its advantages and disadvantages are discussed in Chapter 22, in Part Five. The second international monetary system listed in Table 14-1 is the gold standard, which actually guided individual countries' adjustment behavior from about 1890 to 1914. Under this system adjustments to payments imbalances also took place automatically and involved price and income changes, as we shall discuss in detail in Chapter 21, in Part Five.

The international monetary system of managed exchange rates, the third item listed in Table 14-1, is characterized by the fact that in this system countries use all five methods for dealing with payments imbalances. However, as we shall see in Chapters 23 and 24, it is useful to distinguish two subclasses of managed exchange rate systems. The first of these is known as the parity exchange rate system and the second one as the managed float system. The distinguishing feature between the two is that under the parity system, which existed between 1946 and about 1971, exchange rate changes were undertaken by international agreement only in large, discrete steps, while under the managed float system, in operation since about 1971, exchange rate changes have been continuous and small. In Chapter 24, the final chapter in Part Five, we will discuss the likely shape of a future international monetary system from the points of view of both theoretical desirability and political feasibility. We will also attempt to provide in Chapter 24 an integrated model of how individual countries use all methods for dealing with payments imbalances efficiently in an international system of managed exchange rates.

II. EXCHANGE RATE ADJUSTMENT AND POSSIBLE PROBLEMS

We now turn to a careful, detailed analysis of the first method for dealing with payment imbalances, letting the exchange rate adjust. For this purpose we return to the model employed in Part Three in which we analyzed the foreign exchange market of country A, with trade only in goods and services. There are assumed to be no capital flows or government transactions.

The process of adjustment to a balance-of-payments disequilibrium through an exchange rate change is extremely simple and straightforward. In terms of the example of a disequilibrium situation shown in Figure 14-1, the excess demand for foreign exchange caused by the upward shift of the demand curve from D_0D_0' to D_1D_1' is eliminated simply by a change in the exchange rate from OR_0 to OR_1. In an important sense, this argument is the disappointingly uncomplicated case of international adjustment through exchange rate changes. This story is not affected fundamentally by the introduction of considerations about the role of the government in the foreign exchange market. Thus, it matters little to the basic argument whether the equilibrium is restored through a discrete change in the exchange rate, as under the parity exchange rate system; whether the rate moves there slowly, as under a system of managed float; or whether it moves there completely without government intervention, as under the system of freely floating exchange rates.

Given these facts about exchange rate adjustment, students may be tempted to ask why this method is not used exclusively by countries and why there is so much discussion about it by the public and in the economics literature. The answer to this question is that there are two problems associated with the use of exchange rate adjustment to payments disequilibrium. First, there is the problem that exchange rate changes involve real costs of adjustment in the production and consumption sectors of economies. Therefore, if the exchange rate change is only temporary and may be reversed in a later period, then it imposes a cost on society which can be avoided by its prevention. This argument against exchange rate adjustment to disequilibrium has to be made in an analytical framework in which the sources of disturbances are considered carefully, and uncertainty and randomness in economic variables are introduced explicitly. We will develop such an analytical framework, and within it the theoretical case against the dominant use of exchange rate adjustment to disequilibrium, in Chapter 22.

Second, even within the analytical framework of comparative statics used hitherto in this book, there is the problem that exchange rate depreciation may not eliminate the excess demand for foreign exchange but may actually worsen it. The analysis of this problem occupies the remainder of this chapter. We approach the topic in three ways. First, we develop a verbal description of the problem, and then we show its existence in terms of the foreign exchange market diagram and some analytical processes underlying it. The third approach is presented in an appendix to this chapter and involves the mathematical derivation of the so-called Marshall-Lerner condition, which specifies precisely when raising the price of foreign exchange fails to improve the balance of trade of a country.

The analysis of the remainder of this chapter is necessary because of the historical fact that during the 1930s and now in the 1970s it has been observed on several occasions that countries with balance-of-trade deficits devaluing their currencies experienced not a reduction, but actually an enlargement in their balance-of-trade deficits. An outstanding example of such an occurence is the worsening of the U.S. trade balance in 1971 and 1972 after the large devaluation of the dollar in the middle of 1971, though most of the existing literature on this subject is based on the experience of the 1930s. The cause of such a perverse effect of currency devaluation on the trade balance can be understood quite readily at an intuitive level by remembering the typical adjustments of exports and imports discussed above in Chapter 11. Thus, the depreciation increases the domestic price of the importable good X, inducing consumers to buy fewer of it and producers to manufacture more of it, and thereby reducing the excess demand for it and the implicit quantity of foreign exchange demanded. At the same time the exchange rate increase raises the domestic proce of the export good Y, inducing increased production and increased consumption. This permits greater exports to take place and results in a greater supply of foreign exchange. All of these adjustments, under the normal assumptions underlying the foreign exchange market analysis of Chapter 11, lead to the result that an increase in the price of foreign exchange eliminates the excess demand for foreign exchange.

However, let us now consider what happens typically when a devaluation fails to eliminate the excess demand for foreign exchange. First, the quantity of good X imported is reduced only very little, because the elasticity of the domestic industry demand and supply curves is low, causing the demand curve for foreign exchange to be also very inelastic. As a result, the quantity of foreign exchange required to pay for the import of good X is reduced by only a small amount. Second, the demand for country A's export good Y is also very inelastic abroad, so that at the lower price after the currency depreciation only a small number of additional goods is exported. Under these conditions it is possible that the increased foreign exchange revenue due to the greater number of units sold abroad is smaller than the loss of revenue on all of the previously sold units at the lower price. As a result, the total quantity of foreign exchange supplied is smaller at the higher than at the lower price of foreign exchange. If we now combine the assumed effects of reduced demand and supply of foreign exchange accompanying the currency depreciation, then it is possible to find that this depreciation increases rather than eliminates the existing excess demand for foreign exchange.

To supplement this verbal analysis with a diagram, we use Figure 14–2. This figure represents the foreign exchange market, with the quantity of foreign exchange on the horizontal axis and the exchange rate on the vertical axis. The demand curve shown is rather inelastic, but it has the normal negative slope. On the other hand, the supply curve shown is unusually sloped in the same direction as the demand curve and, what is very important, the slope of the supply curve is flatter than that of the demand curve. Now let us consider that country A, characterized by a foreign exchange market with such demand and supply curves, is initially at the exchange rate R_0. It notices the existence of an excess demand for foreign exchange which is being met by supplies from the government's stock of reserves. Following the principles developed above for the normal case, this government decides to raise the exchange rate to R_1 to eliminate the excess demand. But, as can be seen from Figure 14–2, at R_1 the excess demand for forcign exchange is increased, not reduced.

FIGURE 14–2
Unstable Foreign Exchange Market

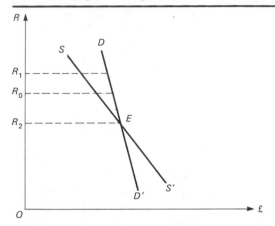

The foreign exchange market shown in this graph is unstable. Any initial displacement from equilibrium, such as to OR_0 from E leads to excess demand, which, however, is not eliminated but is increased through a rise in the exchange rate. By analogy, excess supply increases with falling exchange rates at prices below equilibrium. The instability is found whenever both demand and supply curves are sloped negatively and the demand curve is steeper than the supply curve.

Another consequence of conditions as depicted in Figure 14–2 is that if country A is initially in equilibrium at the exchange rate R_2, then the development of any excess demand for foreign exchange in the absence of government intervention leads to an explosive and unbounded appreciation of the exchange rate. Such instability of the foreign exchange market therefore requires pegging of the exchange rate at the equilibrium level.

Derivation of Demand and Supply Schedules

From Figure 14–2 and the preceding analysis, it is obvious that the problem of the worsening of the excess demand for foreign exchange after an increase in the exchange rate depends crucially on the elasticities of the demand and supply curves. We now turn to the theoretical analysis of the determinants of the elasticities of these curves and to the statement of conditions necessary if exchange rate depreciation is to improve the trade balance. For this purpose we use first Figure 14–3, in which in two separate panels we show the markets for imports and exports of country A, measuring along the horizontal axis the physical quantities of the goods traded and along the vertical axis their prices in foreign currency. Under the assumption that country A is small, the supply curve $X(\pounds)S$ for the import good X is perfectly elastic at the world price $X(\pounds)$. The demand curve D_0D_0' is the excess-demand function for good X derived from the

FIGURE 14–3
Devaluation and Trade Balance: Small Country

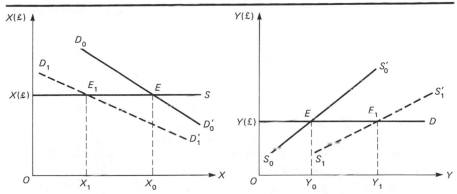

In Figure 14–3, country A is a small country, so that the supply curve for imports it faces, $X(£) - S$ in the left panel, and the demand curve for its export good, $Y(£) - D$ in the right panel, are both perfectly elastic. In initial equilibrium and with the demand curve D_0D_0' for imports, the quantity of sterling spent on imports is equal to $OX_0EX(£)$. Devaluation of the dollar increases domestic prices of good X at all foreign prices in sterling, thus inducing reduced domestic demand, increased supply, and the resultant reduced excess demand, which is shown by a shift of the demand curve to D_1D_1'. Total sterling expenditure on imports falls to $OX_1E_1X(£)$.

The right panel shows that foreign exchange earnings at the initial supply curve S_0S_0' for good Y are $OY_0EY(£)$. Devaluation of the dollar raises sterling prices of good Y at all dollar prices, inducing reduced domestic demand, increased supply, and the resultant excess supply, which is reflected in the shift of the supply schedule to S_1S_1'. The sterling earnings from the exports rise to $OY_1E_1Y(£)$. We conclude that a small country's devaluation must always lower demand for and increase supply of foreign exchange, improving the balance of trade.

domestic industry demand and supply curves, as in Chapter 11, but with the difference that in the present context we assume that the exchange rate is fixed, and the functional relationship shown is between the foreign price of the good and the excess quantity demanded domestically. With the exchange rate given, a decrease in the world price of the good lowers the domestic price equiproportionately and with the assumed normal domestic industry demand and supply curves the excess demand curve must slope downward, as is shown. We should note that in equilibrium the quantity of sterling foreign exchange demanded for imports is equal to the quantity of good X imported (OX_0), times the sterling price per unit, $OX(£)$, that is, the area $OX_0EX(£)$.

Now comes a crucial new step in the analysis not found in Chapter 11. Let us assume that for some reason the dollar price of sterling is raised, that is, the exchange rate of country A is depreciated. Such an event does not alter the world supply curve, and it remains at $X(£)S$, but the demand curve is shifted downward and to the left, to D_1D_1'. This shift of the demand curve results from the fact that at any given starting world price for good X, the higher foreign exchange rate implies a greater domestic dollar price in country A, and therefore a smaller excess quantity demanded. Importantly, this shift is smaller the less elastic are the domestic industry demand and supply curves underlying the excess-demand function, since such lack of elasticity implies that at a higher price consumers reduce their purchases only little, and producers respond by only a small increase in output. The shift of the demand curve D_0D_0' to D_1D_1', under the assumption of linear industry demand and supply curves, is greater at high than at low starting prices. This is so because change in the exchange rate raises the dollar prices of the good equi-proportionately and therefore by a greater absolute amount at the high than the low prices.

With these facts about the effects of a currency depreciation established, we now can note that in the new equilibrium the total volume of foreign exchange demanded, $OX_1E_1X(\pounds)$, is smaller than that at the lower price of foreign exchange. The decrease in the quantity of foreign exchange demanded for any given exchange rate change is smaller the less elastic the domestic industry demand and supply curves are. The functional relationship between the price of foreign exchange and the demand for it is reflected in the slope of the demand curve for foreign exchange in Figures 14–1 and 14–2, where these two arguments in the function are plotted along the two axes, and R_0 and R_1 are the lower and higher exchange rates, respectively. As is apparent from inspection of Figure 14–3, a currency depreciation can never result in an increase in the quantity of foreign exchange demanded as long as the supply curve is either perfectly elastic or has the normal upward slope. Therefore, the demand curve for foreign exchange must also always have the normal downward slope.

Let us now turn to the right-hand panel of Figure 14–3, which shows the world demand curve for country A's export good Y as a function of the world sterling price. The small-country assumption justifies drawing this curve, $Y(\pounds)D$, perfectly elastic at the world price, $OY(\pounds)$. The supply curve for good Y at a given exchange rate, R_0, is shown as S_0S_0', with an upward slope for reasons strictly analogous to those developed above in the derivation of the demand curve for good X. In the initial equilibrium the supply of sterling arising from the export of Y is equal to the area $OY_0EY(\pounds)$. Further, by analogy with the good X analysis, a rise in the exchange rate increases the domestic dollar price of good Y at all given world prices in sterling, causing decreased quantities demanded and increased quantities supplied and resulting in the nonparallel shift of the supply curve outward and to the right to S_1S_1'. This shift is smaller the smaller are the elasticities of the industry demand and supply curves. A glance at Figure 14–3 reveals that at the new equilibrium and under our assumptions the depreciation of the exchange rate must always lead to an increase in the quantity of foreign exchange supplied. The conditions shown in Figure 14–3 thus must always lead to a foreign exchange market diagram such as Figure 14–1, with an upward-sloping supply and a downward-sloping demand curve. The assumption which gave us this result is that of the small country, which causes the perfect elasticity of the foreign supply and demand curves. The preceding analysis thus leads us to the important conclusion that, all else remaining unchanged, a small country can always improve its trade balance and eliminate all excess demand for foreign exchange by a rise in its exchange rate.

The tools of analysis developed in the context of Figure 14–3 now permit us to demonstrate readily the conditions under which a rise in the exchange rate leads to a reduction in the quantity of foreign exchange supplied. For this purpose, consider the right-hand panel of Figure 14–4,

FIGURE 14–4
Devaluation and Trade Balance: Marshall-Lerner Condition

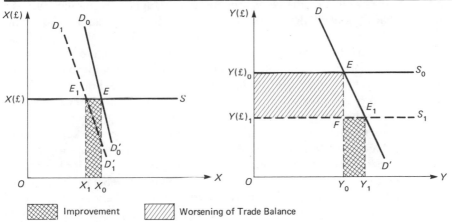

The Marshall-Lerner condition is illustrated by assuming a perfectly elastic world supply schedule for country A's import good X, $X(\pounds)S$ in the left panel, and a perfectly elastic domestic supply schedule for the country's export good Y, $Y(\pounds)_0S_0$ in the right panel. Devaluation shifts the demand curve for imports to D_1D_1' and the supply curve for exports to $Y(\pounds)_1S_1$. The graph shows a relatively small reduction in sterling expenditures on imports because of the low elasticity of the domestic demand for imports. At the same time, total revenue from exports has fallen, since, because of the low elasticity of the demand curve, the revenue lost on the previously sold units, $Y(\pounds)_1FEY(\pounds)_0$, is greater than revenue gained from the sale of additional units ($Y_0Y_1E_1F$). The illustration thus demonstrates the possibility that the existence of low demand elasticities can cause a devaluation to result in the worsening of a country's trade balance.

which shows the conditions in country A's market for the export good Y. Note that the difference between the two panels depicting good Y's position in Figures 14–3 and 14–4 is the assumed slopes of the demand and supply curves. In the second figure we abandon the small-country assumption and make the foreign demand for good Y a decreasing function of its price, implying that if the country wishes to sell more of good Y abroad it can do so only by lowering its price. For convenience in a further analytical step below, the supply curves have been drawn perfectly elastic, though the main point to be made here does not depend on this assumption.

In Figure 14–4 we can see that the total quantity of foreign exchange supplied through the export of good Y at the initial exchange rate is $OY_0EY(\text{£})_0$, while at the higher exchange rate it is $OY_1E_1Y(\text{£})_1$. Whether the new rectangle is larger or smaller than the old one depends on the elasticity of the demand curve over the relevant range of the shift. As is well known, when the elasticity is greater than 1, then the revenue increases; if it is smaller than 1 it decreases, and it remains unchanged at a level of 1. The preceding reasoning implies that if the demand curve for country A's export good Y has an elasticity smaller than 1, then the total quantity of foreign exchange supplied at the higher exchange rate is smaller than it is at the lower exchange rate. This functional relationship shows up as the negatively sloped supply curve for foreign exchange shown in Figure 14–2. With the preceding arguments we have thus established that it is logically possible and cannot be ruled out empirically that a large country faces an inelastic demand curve for its export goods and therefore has a negatively sloped foreign exchange supply curve.

However, the existence of a downward-sloping foreign exchange supply curve alone does not necessarily lead to the exchange market instability which has prompted the current analysis. For the instability to exist it is also necessary that the demand curve be steeper than the supply curve. It can readily be visualized and need not be shown in a separate graph that even if both the demand and supply curves are negatively sloped, if the demand curve is flatter than the supply curve the equilibrium is stable, and currency depreciation eliminates excess demand for foreign exchange.

The Marshall-Lerner Condition

The preceding analysis has served to point to the crucial determinants of the condition of instability in the foreign exchange market shown in Figure 14–2: The elasticities of demand for foreign imports into country A and for exports from country A. In Section III of this chapter we analyze the determinants of these elasticities in the real world and consider some problems encountered in measuring them empirically. However, before we turn to this topic we need to develop a well-known formal condition necessary for the improvement of a country's trade balance after an increase in the exchange rate. This condition, known as the Marshall-Lerner condition, is derived generally in mathematical form in the appendix to this chapter. As a study of this appendix reveals, even in mathematical form the perfectly general formulation of the condition leads to a very complex expression and it is necessary to make simplifying assumptions about elasticities. In principle, to achieve the expositional simplification one can assume that some of the demand and supply curves in Figure 14–3 are either zero or infinity.

Figure 14–4 shows one set of assumptions popular in the literature and used in the appendix. It is that the elasticities of supply in the export sectors of country A and the rest of the world are infinity, which implies that there are constant costs of production in both. In Figure 14–4, which is to be used to illustrate the Marshall-Lerner condition, the elasticity of the supply curve for the imported good X into country A is shown as perfectly elastic. However, the shift of the demand curve accompanying exchange rate depreciation is assumed to be very small, implying a low elasticity of excess demand for imports. As a result of these conditions, the reduction in the demand for foreign exchange caused by the depreciation is very small. It is marked with plus signs. The elasticity of supply for the export good Y in panel two of Figure 14–4 is also shown as being perfectly elastic while the elasticity of demand for country A's exports is less than one, as can be seen from the relatively much larger size of the area representing decreased foreign exchange earnings $(Y(\pounds)_1 FEY(\pounds)_0)$ marked with plus signs following the exchange rate change. The situation shown in Figure 14–4 clearly is one in which exchange rate depreciation leads to a worsening of the trade balance. The value of Figure 14–4 conditions for our purposes of analysis is that it permits us to describe what we may call the simple Marshall-Lerner condition. This condition, the derivation of which is given in the appendix to this chapter, can be stated as follows: A country's trade balance is improved by the depreciation of the exchange rate if the elasticities of the country's demand for imports and of the demand of the rest of the world for its exports sum to greater than 1. Clearly, in Figure 14–4 both demand elasticities are low, and a comparison of the negative and positive rectangles representing gains and losses in the foreign exchange balance shows that the devaluation causes a net increase in the excess demand for foreign exchange. From this it follows that the sum of the demand elasticities is smaller than 1.

One set of elasticities illustrates well the validity of the Marshall-Lerner condition. Assume that the demand curve for the import good X is perfectly inelastic, so that an exchange rate depreciation fails to shift the curve altogether, leaving the total demand for sterling unchanged. Under these conditions the elasticity of foreign demand clearly and unambiguously determines whether or not the trade balance improves. The depreciation raises the excess demand for foreign exchange if the elasticity is smaller than 1 and lowers it if the elasticity is greater than 1.

In conclusion we should note that the preceding analysis can be undertaken for the case of a decrease in the price of foreign exchange and in terms of domestic currency. Because of space limitations, to keep the exposition simple, and because no fundamental new insights can thereby be obtained, we do not repeat the analysis here for exchange rate appreciations and in terms of domestic currency. However, students may find that such exercises deepen their understanding of the basic arguments, and they may wish to consider working through the analysis from these points of view.

III. ELASTICITIES IN THE REAL WORLD

The overwhelmingly most important implication of the analysis in the preceding section concerns the crucial role of elasticities of demand and supply for traded goods in the determination of exchange market instability. In both our verbal and diagrammatic analyses, this point has been stressed. In the remainder of this chapter we turn to the examination of empirical evidence on the size of price elasticities.

The first measurements of price elasticities in international trade, undertaken during the 1930s and 1940s, often yielded estimates of low elasticities. A combination of this fact and the observation mentioned earlier in this chapter, that on some occasions countries that devalued their currencies experienced deterioration in their trade balances, led to what is known as "elasticity pessimism" among economists and officials of governments and international organizations. This pessimism had some influence on the organization of the international monetary system after World War II (as we shall discuss in Chapter 23) and on the attitudes of governments toward currency revaluations in recent decades. However, elasticity measurements undertaken since the 1950s revealed that elasticities in fact were high enough to assure foreign exchange market stability. They also showed that the findings of the earlier studies had been based on the incorrect use of econometric techniques and insufficient data, the neglect of important changes in ceteris paribus conditions accompanying currency revaluations, and a disregard of the fact that elasticities change through time. These errors point out three ways the estimation of trade elasticities can be improved.

Econometric and Data Problems

In Figure 14–5 we measure the price of country A's export good in sterling on the vertical axes and the quantity of the good exported per time period on the horizontal axis. In the initial equilibrium, with a given exchange rate, R_0, the world price of good Y is $Y(£)_0$, and OY_0 of good Y is exported. For purposes of econometric estimation we observe only this price and quantity. Now assume that country A's exchange rate is devalued by K percent to R_1. We know from the analysis of Section II in

FIGURE 14–5
The Identification Problem

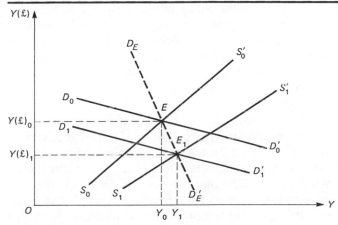

Empirical observation produces only points E and E_1. If it is assumed that the two observations were produced by the shift of the supply curve only from S_0S_0' to S_1S_1', then it is inferred that the demand curve is very inelastic. Such an inference would be false, and demand would be highly elastic if in fact the empirical observation had been brought about by the simultaneous shift of the demand and supply curves, as is shown.

this chapter that such a devaluation causes the domestic supply curve for good Y to shift downward and to the right, as shown in Figure 14–5, from S_0S_0' to S_1S_1'. Observations about prices and quantities required for econometric estimates are limited to the one new equilibrium point E_1 in Figure 14–5. Our theory tells us that the observed change in quantities and prices is due to the shift in the supply curve, with the world demand curve having remained stationary. By comparing the two points of observation, E and E_1, we can calculate the elasticity of the demand curve, D_ED_E', from the equation defining the elasticity, $\epsilon = |(\Delta Y/Y)/[\Delta Y(\pounds)/Y(\pounds)]|$. In the way in which Figure 14–5 was drawn, such an estimate would reveal the existence of a low elasticity.

However, let us now analyze the implications of the assumption that the world demand curve is very elastic. In the initial period it goes through point E as D_0D_0' does in Figure 14–5, and, at the same time, when country A devalues its exchange rate some event in the rest of the world causes the demand curve to shift downward to D_1D_1', producing the equilibrium point E. The econometric problem is that the observation of prices and quantities at points E and E_1 alone does not permit a distinction to be made between the two cases where the demand curve remains stationary and where it shifts. Yet, from Figure 14–5 it is obvious that if the demand curve actually does shift, then the estimate of its elasticity is seriously biased downward.

The problem of ignorance about the shifts of the demand and supply curves is known as the identification problem. Theoretically, and in econometric techniques, the problem can be handled by the use of further information; for example, about changes in world income which shift the demand curve. We will discuss the nature of this other information in the next section. However, it is clear from the preceding example that the naive estimates of trade elasticities, such as those done during the 1930s and 1940s and those based on only price and quantity information, were bound to produce misleading results.

Another important source of bias in the econometric estimation of trade elasticities arises from the need to use price indices of traded goods, since countries import and export large numbers of different goods. In this context the most outstanding problem is due to the fact that the price indices typically are unit price indices and therefore do not reflect properly changes in the composition or quality of the bundle of goods. For example, when in the early 1970s the United States began to export jumbo jet aircraft with a much higher unit value than that of earlier planes, the price index of U.S. airplane exports showed a substantial rise in prices. Yet, what is economically relevant is, of course, the per person cost of air transportation facilities embodied in the planes, which is lower in the case of jumbo than normal-sized jets. Thus, while the price index showed a rise, it actually should have shown a fall. Similarly, as Irving Kravis of the University of Pennsylvania and Robert Lipsey of the National Bureau of Economic Research have shown in a careful study based on sample questionnaires (1971), prices of capital goods often rise at the same time that the cost per useful service unit produced by them falls. Yet, prices of goods can remain unchanged or even fall while quality deterioration actually increases costs per unit of service. Unit price indexes fail to reflect these difficult-to-measure characteristics of goods which determine demand for the goods. Therefore the use of unit price indexes can bias measurements of price elasticities in international trade, especially in industries and countries where technological advances are strong.

Neglect of Other Conditions

It is a well-known proposition from demand theory that the relationship between the price of a good and its quantity demanded is partial, and it assumes that other determinants of demand remain constant. This is an important and theoretically useful assumption, but it is rarely fulfilled in the real world. In the context of the identification problem we noted how the neglect of these other conditions leads to biased econometric estimates and showed that income changes are one such condition which needs to be quantified. Other important determinants of the demand for and supply of country A's exports which often change along with prices are the cost and availability of trade credit, delivery times, exchange restrictions, the availability of substitute goods, taxes, and subsidies. Some of these changes shift the demand curve and others shift the supply curve of foreign exchange, independently of the shifts caused by the exchange rate change.

In recent years several researchers have attempted to estimate price elasticities of international trade by quantifying changes in these ceteris paribus conditions. Most notable among these are Hendrik Houthakker and Stephen Magee whose study (1969) estimated simultaneously price and income elasticities of international trade in several countries, and Robert Gregory of the Australian National University, who considered (1971) the importance of the order backlogs and speed of delivery of firms as determinants of trade elasticities. These studies tended to produce higher estimates of price elasticities than earlier ones which had neglected these ceteris paribus conditions.

Change of Elasticities through Time

One of the most important of the characteristics of price elasticities of demand and supply in international trade which were neglected in earlier studies is that they change through time. In a theoretical and empirical paper (1973), Helen Junz of the Federal Reserve Board of Governors and Rudolf Rhomberg of the International Monetary Fund suggested that it is useful to distinguish five different sorts of lags between changes in relative prices and actual increases or decreases in quantities traded. First, there is the recognition lag, which arises because information about new prices is not known to buyers and sellers immediately after an exchange rate change. This lag may be rather short, though in international trade involving long distances and problems in communication it is longer than in domestic markets. Second, there is the decision lag, which is due to the fact that businessmen need time to assess the importance of price changes, form opinions on the likelihood of their persistence, and place new orders. Third, there is a delivery lag, which arises because it takes time for newly ordered goods to arrive at the border of the country, where they are recorded as imports or exports. Fourth, there is a replacement lag. In some industries producers may use up inventories and wear out existing machinery before placing new orders. Finally, there is the production lag; it takes time to increase output of goods for which demand has increased. Production of some goods may be profitable in the short run as long as the price covers variable cost, but in the long run it is terminated as fixed investment wears out.

It may be useful to illustrate the nature of these lags with the help of the stylized example of imports of automobiles into the United States. Upon a devaluation of the U.S. dollar, in the short run shipments of automobiles are already contracted for and on trains and ships heading for the United States. If the invoice for them is written in dollars, U.S. statistics show, for a certain period after the devaluation, import prices and quantities unchanged. If the invoice is in foreign currency units, then the dollar value of imports will have risen, but import quantities are unchanged. We would conclude from this "short run" evidence, based possibly on observation of one or two quarters, that U.S. demand for imported automobiles is perfectly inelastic. However, in the intermediate run, the higher prices of the imported cars relative to domestic cars decrease their sales, and imports are reduced. The magnitude of the reduction in imports depends on the extent of the price rise, which is determined in the intermediate run by the following sorts of considerations. Foreign producers may not pass on the full proportionate increase in the price due to the exchange rate change, accepting a lower domestic price as long as it covers marginal costs of production. Similarly, U.S. dealers of imported cars may lower their mark-up covering variable but not fixed costs. Such pricing strategies are most likely if a dollar appreciation or U.S. car price increases are expected to take place in the foreseeable future. But if such events do not take place and relative production costs remain the same in the longer run, the foreign producers and domestic dealers have to cover fixed costs, and prices have to be raised to reflect the true costs of production and distribution. After this happens, sales to the United States decline still further, as American consumers switch to the relatively cheaper domestic substitutes which the U.S. producers have been able to manufacture after the time-consuming expansion of facilities. Foreign production declines, U.S. dealers of imported cars go out of business, and a decrease in imported automobiles is noted.

In their econometric studies of price elasticities and lags, Junz and Rhomberg found that following price changes, 50 percent of the ultimate full effect of changes in quantities of goods traded takes place in the first three years following the price change, and about 90 percent in the first five years. It is therefore not surprising that estimates of price elasticities of demand and supply in international trade which are undertaken without regard to lags should underestimate the true longer run effects of relative price changes.

One important determinant of the trade balance in the very short run, specifically, is the extent to which invoices are written in domestic or foreign currency. William Branson of Princeton University and Stephen Magee of the University of Chicago have developed the following line of argument. Consider that U.S. exporters, for reasons of market strength, are able to have their invoices denominated in dollars, thus protecting themselves from exchange risks. For analogous reasons, all U.S. imports are invoiced in foreign currencies. Now consider that the U.S. dollar is devalued and that for a certain quarter all goods crossing borders have been ordered and invoiced before the devaluation. Under these conditions, U.S. statistics will show during this quarter a dramatic worsening of the deficit, because the value of the reported imports in foreign currency is the same, but the value of the exports converted from their dollar value into foreign currency at the new exchange rate is decreased by the full proportional amount of the devaluation.

The preceding model can readily be modified to take account of differences between the assumed and actual invoicing behavior of U.S. traders. However, the assumed behavior is consistent with the actual dramatic worsening of the U.S. trade balance following several quarters after the 1971 devaluation of the U.S. dollar. It undoubtedly explains what in a more naive theoretical model would have been interpreted as extreme price inelasticity in international trade.

Summary and Conclusions for Sections II and III

Section II presented the "normal" and simple case of currency devaluation, which was the basis of our analysis of the foreign exchange market in Chapter 11. When country A lets the price of foreign exchange rise, the change in relative prices of domestic and foreign products induces country A residents to buy less from abroad and the rest of the world to buy more. The value of country A's exports increases and that of its imports decreases, causing an improvement in the balance of trade. However, because historically on occasion it has been the experience of countries that devaluation does not improve but worsens their trade balances, it was necessary to analyze, more carefully than in Chapter 11, what determines the elasticity of demand for and supply of foreign exchange.

In theoretical terms, we showed the importance of the elasticities of domestic demand for and supply of internationally traded goods in country A and the rest of the world. We provided a geometric explanation of the simple Marshall-Lerner condition for elasticities, whose fulfilment assures that devaluation will improve the trade balance. In Section III we provided an analysis of the determinants of elasticities through time and indicated conceptual econometric and data problems encountered in the measurement of price elasticities in international trade.

We can conclude from all this analysis that price elasticities of demand and supply in international trade are high enough in the longer run to permit countries to improve their trade balance by devaluation and worsen it through currency appreciation. The foreign exchange market model of Chapter 11 is representative of the real world. Where results expected from this model do not materialize and econometric results support the notion of elasticity pessimism, we must remain skeptical as to the proper use of econometric techniques, data, information about other changes in the determinants of trade, and the length of period chosen for observation.

APPENDIX

The Marshall-Lerner Condition

The mathematical derivation of the Marshall-Lerner condition in this appendix may be skipped without loss of continuity in the argument of the book. The following exposition follows closely that of Egon Sohmen of the University of Heidelberg presented in an appendix to Charles Kindleberger's text before the fifth edition (1973).

We use the following symbols, which are defined as:

Q_y, Q_x: Physical quantity of country A's exports and imports, respectively.

V_y, V_x: Foreign currency value of Country A's exports and imports, respectively.

$Y(\pounds), X(\pounds)$:   Foreign prices of exports and imports, respectively.

$Y(\$), X(\$)$:   Domestic prices of exports and imports, respectively.

R: Exchange rate expressed as the number of domestic currency units (dollars) required to acquire one unit of foreign currency (sterling).

E_y: Foreign elasticity of demand for exports.

E_x: Domestic elasticity of demand for imports.

The balance of payments is defined as

$$B = V_y - V_x \tag{14A-1}$$

According to our theoretical analysis above, the quantity of exports is a function of domestic prices in dollars divided by the exchange rate, i.e., $Q_y[Y(\$)/R]$ where the square bracket indicates a functional relationship. Multiplying the quantity of exports by the foreign currency price of the exports gives the value of exports in foreign currency

$$V_y = Q_y \left[\frac{Y(\$)}{R} \right] \cdot \left(\frac{Y(\$)}{R} \right) \tag{14A-2}$$

By analogy, the imports quantity is a function of their sterling price adjusted for the exchange rate $Q_x[X(\pounds) \cdot R]$ and the value is found by multiplying the quantity by the foreign price:

$$V_x = Q_x \left[\frac{X(\pounds)}{R} \right] \cdot X(\pounds) \tag{14A-3}$$

Substituting the last two equations into the first we get

$$B = Q_y \left[\frac{Y(\$)}{R} \right] \cdot \left(\frac{Y(\$)}{R} \right) - Q_x \left[\frac{X(\pounds)}{R} \right] \cdot X(\pounds) \tag{14A-4}$$

What above we have called the simple Marshall-Lerner condition is derived by assuming that the supply elasticities in country A and the rest of the world are infinity, so that in effect the prices of country A's export good Y and the rest of the world's export good X are constants, i.e., $Y(\$) = \overline{Y(\$)}$ and $X(\pounds) = \overline{X(\pounds)}$. As a result of this assumption, the trade balance becomes a function of the exchange rate and we can find the effect of an exchange rate change by differentiating B with respect to R:

$$\frac{dB}{dR} = \frac{d\,Q_y}{d\left(\frac{Y(\$)}{R}\right)} \cdot -\frac{Y(\$)}{R^2} \cdot \frac{Y(\$)}{R} + Q_y\left(-\frac{Y(\$)}{R^2}\right) - \frac{d\,Q_x}{d(X(\pounds) \cdot R)} \cdot (X(\pounds))^2$$

$$(14A-5)$$

Here we have made use of the rule for differentiation of a product, $d(u \cdot v)/dr = (du/dx) \cdot v + u(dv/dx)$ and of a fraction $(d(c/x))/dx = -c//x^2$, where c is a constant.

Equation 14A–5 can be rewritten as

$$\frac{dB}{dR} = Q_y\left(\frac{Y(\$)}{R^2}\right) \cdot \left[\frac{d\,Q_y}{d\left(\frac{Y(\$)}{R}\right)} \cdot \frac{\frac{Y(\$)}{R}}{Q_y} - 1\right]$$

$$+ Q_x \frac{X(\pounds)}{R} \cdot \left[\frac{d\,Q_x}{Q_x} \cdot \frac{X(\pounds) \cdot R}{d(X(\pounds) \cdot R)}\right] \qquad (14A-6)$$

The first expression in braces is the price elasticity of foreign demand for exports E_y, which is defined as the proportionate change in the quantity of exports, dQ_y/Q_y, divided by the proportionate change in the price of exports, $(d(Y(\$)/R)/(Y(\$)/R)$:

$$E_y = -\frac{dQ_y}{Q_y}\bigg/\frac{d\left(\frac{Y(\$)}{R}\right)}{\frac{Y(\$)}{R}} \qquad (14A-7)$$

The second expression in braces represents the analogously defined elasticity of import demand, E_x. We can therefore rewrite 14A–6 as

$$\frac{dB}{dR} = Q_y\left(\frac{Y(\$)}{R^2}\right)(E_y - 1) + Q_x\left(\frac{X(\pounds)}{R}\right) \cdot E_x \qquad (14A-8)$$

A devaluation raises R and it leads to an improvement in the trade balance only if

$$dB/R > 0 \qquad (14A-9)$$

which in terms of equation 14A–8 implies

$$\left[Q_y \left(\frac{Y(\$)}{R} \right) \Big/ Q_x(X(\pounds)) \right] \cdot E_y + E_x < 1 \qquad (14A–10)$$

Since $Q_y(Y(\$)/R)$ is the value of exports and $Q_x(X(\pounds))$ is the value of imports, equation 14A–10 is to be interpreted as implying that if trade is initially balanced, a devaluation improves the trade balance if the sum of the two demand elasticities exceeds one:

$$E_y + E_x > 1 \qquad (14A–11)$$

It is intuitively obvious from Equation (14A–10) that if trade is in surplus initially, there is some value of the elasticities which assures trade balance improvement from devaluation, even if the sum of the elasticities is smaller than one. By analogy, if the balance is initially in deficit, then a sum of elasticities exceeding 1 is required to obtain improvement through devaluation.

We conclude this mathematical analysis of the Marshall-Lerner condition by presenting simply and without derivation the conditions necessary for trade balance improvement when supply elasticities are less than infinite:

$$Q_y \left(\frac{Y(\$)}{R} \right) \Big/ Q_x(X(\pounds)) \cdot \left(\frac{E_y(1 + e_y)}{E_y + e_y} \right) - \frac{e_x(1 - E_x)}{(e_x + E_x)} > 0 \quad (14A–12)$$

where e_y and e_x are the price elasticities of supply of exports and imports, respectively. The derivation of this condition is explained in the article by Joan Robinson of Cambridge University (1974) and in the more advanced textbooks of Robert Stern (1973a) and Richard Caves and Ronald Jones (1973).

BIBLIOGRAPHICAL NOTES

The Marshall-Lerner condition derives its name from the original writings by Marshall (1923) and Lerner (1944). More rigorous specifications are found in Robinson (1947), Haberler (1949) and Machlup (1964). Relevant to the problem of exchange market stability also are the papers by Tsiang (1961) and Johnson (1956), though their main concern is the integration of exchange rate and income adjustments.

A review of the elasticity pessimism controversy is provided in Harberger (1957). Leamer and Stern (1970), ch. 3, discuss problems of elasticity measurement. Kravis and Lipsey (1971) analyze the theoretical and empirical difficulties encountered in the construction of international trade price indexes. Recent empirical estimates of price elasticities taking account of simultaneous income and other changes are Houthakker and Magee (1969) and Gregory (1971). The changes of price elasticities through time are discussed and measured by Junz and Rhomberg (1973), Dunn (1970), Branson (1968), and Magee (1973).

CONCEPTS FOR REVIEW

Marshall-Lerner condition
Elasticity pessimism
Unit price indexes
Identification problem

Lags in exchange rates and trade
  levels
Ceteris paribus conditions

POINTS FOR FURTHER STUDY AND DISCUSSION

1. Find out from a local car dealer who imports from Germany, Japan, or France how long it took after major currency revaluations during the 1960s and early 1970s for the prices of cars in the showroom to reflect these new exchange rates. Try to find out where billing for cars is done—at the manufacturer's foreign headquarters or by the domestic wholesale importer? Find out whether any expected imports were covered by the forward purchase of currency, and how long it takes for a car to be moved from the place of manufacture to the showroom. Can these facts explain the lag of price changes after currency revaluations? What are the implications of your findings for the measurement of price elasticities?

2. Find out unit price indexes for U.S. exports of commercial airplanes from U.S. trade statistics. From other sources, such as manufacturers' reports or journals, gather data on the types and prices of airplanes exported. From this information you should be able to work out the extent to which increases in unit price indexes of U.S. airplanes were due to the sale of bigger planes and to what extent they indicated genuine increases in price.

3. Survey studies attempting to measure price elasticities of demand and supply in international trade and make a list of independent variables and lag structures introduced to explain these elasticities.

4. Repeat the analysis underlying Figures 14–3 and 14–4 in terms of domestic currency, so that you have along the vertical axis the domestic currency dollar rather than sterling. Note the differences between the two approaches of specifying the Marshall-Lerner condition.

15 Direct Controls on International Trade

ONE OF THE METHODS for dealing with payments imbalances described in Chapter 14 is direct controls on international trade. In the analytical framework of Figure 14–1, the effects of controls are to shift the demand and supply curves in the foreign exchange market such that excess demand or supply conditions at any chosen exchange rate are eliminated. In this chapter we present the cases for and against the use of direct controls. Then we describe in detail methods of direct controls used primarily to affect relative prices between foreign and domestic goods and to influence traded quantities directly. The description of control methods is followed by an analysis of how private markets tend to circumvent these government controls.

I. THE CASE FOR AND AGAINST DIRECT CONTROLS

The most fundamental case for the use of direct controls must be made in an analytical framework in which the source and nature of disequilibrium is examined in a model of uncertainty. In Chapter 22 we develop such a model to explain how the use of direct controls, income adjustments, and financing can increase the efficiency of an economy and can avoid the social costs of exchange rate instability which tend to result from letting all adjustment take the form of exchange rate changes. The fundamental justification for the use of direct controls must therefore await Chapter 22. In the meantime we simply assume that countries are unwilling to let exchange rates adjust freely to eliminate all payments disequilibria and that instead they attempt to keep exchange rates fixed or permit only gradual changes. The primary method for attaining these objectives is the financing of imbalances. Direct controls are used as a supplement to or substitute for financing under conditions when a country runs out of reserves, wants fast and predictable balance-of-payments effects, and wishes to achieve other policy objectives simultaneously. In almost all cases policy makers consider the use of direct controls as temporary measures, to be abandoned once the sources of the payments imbalance cease to operate.

More precisely, as a supplement or substitute for financing, controls can affect payment disequilibria quickly because they reduce imports immediately after they are put into effect. If the controls are specified in terms of physical quantities of imports, the quantity and value of import reductions are precise, except for the problems of evasion to be discussed below. Controls can also be specified according to commodities, and therefore they can influence the composition of imports precisely. This aspect of import reduction implies an advantage for governments which, for other social or economic reasons, wish to influence patterns of expenditures in the economy. For example, a developing country may consider undesirable the import of what its leaders believe to be items of frivolous consumption, such as cosmetics and soft drinks. Under these conditions, direct import controls limiting quantities or prohibiting certain types of cosmetics and beverages relieve a balance-of-payments deficit and achieve other social objectives simultaneously. In the preceding chapter we noted that price elasticities in international trade may be low in the short run but tend to increase with the passage of time. Direct controls on the quantity of imports, in principle, can be imposed simultaneously with an exchange rate depreciation. This will affect the level of trade both immediately and during the period when economic and technical substitutions to relative price changes take place and increase the price elasticities, in the manner discussed in Chapter 14. When the elasticities have reached a certain level, controls can be removed and the improvement in the balance of payments remains permanent.

The arguments against the use of direct controls in dealing with balance-of-payments imbalances are based on the price-theoretic models of comparative statics. At the highest level of abstraction, controls interfere with the free market and distort what otherwise would be efficient relative prices of individual commodities or, in the case where the exchange rate is distorted, price differences between domestically and foreign produced goods. As a result, there are the well-known losses of efficiency in the form of consumer and producer surpluses. Additional costs of direct control arise from the government's use of resources in their administration and in attempts by the private sector to circumvent the controls, legally or illegally.

The efficiency costs of controls depend on whether or not they discriminate between individual commodities and between individual countries of export or import. Generally, costs are lower the smaller is the discrimination in these senses. For example, a temporary tariff at a uniform rate on all imports affects all traded goods by an equal degree, and in a sense it is equivalent to the devaluation of a currency restricted to imports only. It does not distort the relative profitability of different import-competing products or imports from different countries, and thus it avoids the costs incurred by drawing factors of production into some temporarily favored industries or by opening up trade channels with certain favored countries which then have to be reversed again as the controls are removed. At the other extreme of the degree of neutrality is the system of multiple exchange rates, which deliberately distorts relative prices of import-competing and exportable goods and of bilateral trade agreements which favor one country or a group of countries. The use of these systems for purposes of short-term balance-of-payments policies is much more inefficient than using uniform tariffs.

Before we turn to the discussion of specific control methods, we need to discuss briefly some necessary steps which are required before any controls can be instituted. First, there have to be guarded border crossing points at which all imports and exports can be recorded and officials can ascertain that traders have complied with all of the relevant control regulations. Most countries have such border crossing points where custom officials are employed to assure compliance with tariff regulations, the purpose of which is other than balance-of-payments control, as we discussed in Part Two of this book. The marginal cost of using the existing customs bureaucracy for the administration of balance-of-payments control measures is relatively small.

Second, most methods for balance-of-payments control involve foreign exchange receipts and disbursements. For this reason, exporters and importers have to produce documents concerning the prices, methods of payment, and foreign banking arrangements associated with the commercial transactions. The production of this information, often in large numbers of copies for different government agencies, represents a substantial social cost of using direct controls which is passed on to the general public in the form of higher costs of products. The government itself has to create agencies or departments within existing agencies, such as the central bank or the ministries of trade, to gather information relevant for decision making by executives, to administer the central programs, and to administer justice in case of disputes. When there are different jurisdictions among government agencies over different control programs or aspects of the same programs, there arises the need for coordination among them. All of these government activities require real resources paid for by the public through taxation, the magnitude of which depends on the general efficiency of the bureaucrats and the size of the control program. However, it is worth noting that in general when a country already has a substantial bureaucracy attending to the administration and regulation of the private sector and the provision of defense, economic information, justice, and other public goods, the marginal cost of control administration is lower than if a country has a small public sector. In modern Western industrial nations in the 1970s, the marginal cost of administering temporary control programs and gathering, interpreting, and acting on information is probably quite low, since relevant skills and information channels between the private and public sectors already exist.

A final point worth noting about the methods of control on international trade to be discussed in the next section of this chapter is that they are illegal under the international agreements reached after the end of World War II. In spite of this fact they have been used widely during the postwar years, mostly by developing countries but on occasion also by industrialized nations. While the postwar agreements outlawed the use of direct controls on trade in goods and services for balance-of-payments purposes, they permitted countries to use controls over short-term capital flows. Methods for control in this category will be discussed below in Chapter 17 in the context of the broader topic of how countries can deal with disequilibrating short-term capital flows.

II. METHODS OF CONTROL

The most widely used methods of control and market techniques for avoiding them are discussed under the following headings: exchange controls, including trade licensing and multiple exchange rates; payments agreements; tariffs and subsidies; and quantitative restrictions, such as embargoes and quotas.

Exchange Controls: Trade Licensing and Multiple Exchange Rates

Trade licensing and multiple exchange rates are part of the general system of exchange controls under which every foreign trade transaction must be registered with the authorities, and no bank can make or accept payment of foreign currencies without official approval. There are restrictions on the transportation of foreign exchange by tourists. When the authorities have information on every potential foreign trade transaction, they can issue specific licenses for imports, using a whole range of possible criteria. Thus they may grant import licenses automatically for basic food stuffs and raw materials but be more reluctant to do so if the good has luxury characteristics. Such general principles may be mitigated by the desire to encourage certain domestic industries because of the externalities they provide or to increase the welfare of certain groups of the population who have great political power. However, a pure system of licensing applies the same exchange rate to all transactions and thus assures neutrality in the imported price, though unless the importation of all goods is reduced equiproportionately, there tend to be domestic relative price effects.

Most programs of import licensing, especially in developing countries, are combined with the use of different exchange rates for different classes of imports. Furthermore, exports also are subject to different exchange rates. We discussed the economic effects of such multiple exchange rate systems in Part Two, in connection with commercial policies considered more generally. Multiple exchange rates can be used to encourage or discourage certain domestic activities, using a wide variety of social criteria, in addition to dealing with balance-of-payments problems. Therein lies their attraction in practice for development ministries, as well as their economic costs if the authorities are incompetent or dominated by corrupt bureaucrats and legislators.

The most important way in which market forces tend to circumvent import-licensing schemes is through bribery and corruption of officials. When licensing restricts the importation of a certain good, its domestic price rises above the world price times the exchange rate. A license to import the good at the world price then brings the importer an extra profit (or rent, in technical economic terms) which is equal to the difference between the imported and domestic prices. In order to obtain this rent importers are willing and able to spend a certain amount to influence bureaucrats to give them rather than anyone else the license or to increase the number of licenses given. Bribes of this sort may be relatively open and an accepted way of life, or they may be hidden and subtle, as in the form of a guaranty of a lush job with a private company in the future. The longer and the more restrictive licensing programs are in operation, the greater is the amount of rent available for bribery and corruption.

Multiple exchange rates have similar effects as import licenses do in creating rent for importers. In addition, they can lead to subsidies for exporters. Private business therefore also tends to use part of the rent and subsidies to influence the pattern of multiple exchange rates imposed by the government. However, the effectiveness of the program is also jeopardized by a technique known as under- or overinvoicing. For example consider that country A wishes to tax the export of good Y, worth £10 per unit, by requiring that all foreign currency proceeds be surrendered to the government, which then pays the exporter in domestic currency at an arbitrarily unfavorable exchange rate, say one dollar per pound sterling rather than the "equilibrium" rate of two dollars per pound sterling, so that he receives only $10 rather than $20. Under these conditions exporters tend to take refuge in the practice of writing a bill to the foreigner understating the value of the export shipment by misrepresenting the quantity of exports, the quality of the product, or the foreign unit price received. At the same time the exporter makes a confidential deal with the foreign buyer, who is normally willing to do so for a price, that he be paid the true value of the shipment in a clandestine account abroad. Customs officials typically are not capable of discovering the misrepresentations of quantity, quality, or true foreign price, and the exporter can use the sterling held abroad for personal consumption on trips or for sale in black markets for currencies which are usually developing when exchange controls exist.

One group of potential buyers of such currency tends to be importers into country A who are penalized by taxation through an unfavorable exchange rate. They would pay the original exporter dollars in a purely domestic transaction outside of the exchange control system and use the sterling funds abroad to pay for a part of their imports. Then they would induce their supplier to bill them at a price below the true one. As a consequence they have to purchase only a smaller amount of sterling at the penalty dollar exchange rate, and they obtain the product at a lower dollar cost than if they went through official channels only.

Payments Agreements

In the immediate postwar years, when Western market economies had not restored their productive capacities and markets were not functioning properly because of past rationing and war-distorted relative prices, various countries made large numbers of bilateral trade and payments agreements. These agreements stipulated that country A would export certain goods, specified in quantity and domestic currency value, to country B, in return for imports from that country, specified also in terms of quantity and domestic currency value. An implicit exchange rate was used to reach agreement on what represented equal values of the two bundles of goods exchanged. In some agreements goods were not specified, but the governments agreed to issue import or export licenses as demanded by the private sector only up to certain limits, and under the condition that trade be balanced. Presently similar trade and payments agreements are in operation between some countries of the Soviet bloc and the rest of the world.

Networks of such payments agreements assured that countries did not suffer from payments imbalances, but they also came at the cost of limited international specialization and rigidities in trade patterns. Much of international trade involves multilateral rather than bilateral balancing. For example, in the 19th century very profitable trade patterns involved a British export surplus of manufactures for the sugar and rum of the West Indies, which balanced its deficit by exports of sugar and rum to the United States. The U.S. trade deficit with the West Indies in turn was balanced by a net surplus of food exports to Britain. As a result, each of the three countries had overall balance in their payments but imbalanced trade with each partner. If trade during this period had been guided by bilateral agreements, its total volume would have been lower, and world welfare would have been at a level below the one actually experienced. Another disadvantage of bilateral agreements is that changes in economic and technical conditions which cause comparative advantage, and therefore the optimal pattern of trade, to change can sometimes be incorporated in such agreements only at a substantial cost of negotiation and delays in time.

Private market reactions to the institution of bilateral trade agreements mostly takes the form of nondelivery of exports or purchase of imports which are noneconomic. For this reason, many trade and payments agreements never were carried out to the full extent, and all agreements had certain safeguards to prevent the accumulation of large net indebtedness for either country. In recent years, since bilateral trade agreements between Western and Eastern bloc countries have proliferated, the governments on both sides have occasionally found themselves burdened with goods and raw materials they wanted to sell but could not, because they lacked the necessary technical expertise. Private firms have been founded to specialize in the disposal of such goods.

Tariffs and Subsidies

We have already discussed, in Part Two, the nature and effects of tariffs and subsidies imposed to deal with externalities and to achieve certain social objectives. Tariffs and subsidies used for the attainment of a trade balance are identical in their effects to those discussed earlier. The big difference between them is that the former are expected to be used only for relatively short times, while the latter tend to be in place for longer periods.

Temporary tariff surcharges on imports have been used in recent years by the United States and Britain. They have caused the least inefficiency because they have tended to apply uniformly to all goods and have been of short duration. In developing countries in the postwar years, tariffs originally imposed for temporary balance-of-payments reasons have often become permanent and indistinguishable from protective tariffs.

An important justification for temporary tariffs and subsidies arises from the fact (discussed above) that elasticities in international trade increase through time. Thus, if balance-of-payments conditions require a quick improvement, currency devaluation and the temporary tariffs and subsidies change relative prices of domestic and foreign goods more than is necessary in the long run. Even relatively low elasticities in the short run will bring a significant improvement in the trade balance. As elasticities increase through time, it then is possible to remove the tariffs and subsidies and retain the improved trade balance, because of the effects of the exchange rate changes alone.

Whenever tariffs and subsidies are in existence for only short time periods, markets have insufficient incentives to develop methods for evading them, though it is likely that under- and overinvoicing takes place in order to lower the tariff duties based on a fixed tariff rate. Also to the extent that tariffs and subsidies are temporary, incentives are created for importers to delay shipments and exporters to speed them up, in order to avoid or take advantage of the programs. However, such actions are consistent with the objectives of the policies and reinforce the pure price effect of the tariffs and subsidies.

Quantitative Restrictions: Embargoes and Quotas

The most effective method for curtailing imports in balance-of-payments crises is through the imposition of embargoes or quotas, which can be applied to all imports or to only selected categories of goods. Embargoes which stop imports altogether must be of limited duration and can be made to reduce payments deficits over any arbitrary accounting period. However, temporarily suppressed demand is likely to reappear again soon after removal of the embargo unless more fundamental changes, such as a currency depreciation, are combined with the embargo and reduce real demand for imports. As in the case of tariffs and subsidies, an embargo can reduce imports during the period when time changes elasticities. Embargoes are such drastic measures that they are used rather infrequently.

Quotas are somewhat less drastic than embargoes. They can be used to reduce imports directly and reliably by any desired amount and in any category of goods by limiting the physical quantities or value of imports totally or only those from certain countries. These features have made quotas a favorite tool of balance-of-payments policy, and they have been employed frequently by devloping countries in the postwar years. Like import licensing, quotas give rise to opportunities for corruption and bribery of officials who allocate the quotas to private entrepreneurs and can permit markets to avoid or circumvent the control policies. Another important market response to quotas is the illegal smuggling of goods, though it tends to be less profitable if quotas are used only for short periods.

Summary and Conclusions

Controls on imports and exports can be used to eliminate imbalances in a country's international payments. In the analytical framework adopted in this book, the effects of such controls are to shift the foreign exchange demand and supply curves such that they intersect at the exchange rate a country wishes to maintain. The arguments in favour of using controls are that they permit the quick and certain reduction in payments imbalances. In a world in which price elasticities of demand and supply increase through time, controls on trade can be used in combination with a devaluation to achieve quick and certain improvements in the trade balance in the short run. In the longer run the controls can be removed and the favorable trade balance is retained because of the results of the devaluation and the high price elasticities.

The arguments against the use of controls to deal with payment imbalances is that they involve costs of economic inefficiency, since they distort relative prices and invite market responses for their circumvention through corruption, bribery, smuggling, and the falsifying of trade and payments documents. Moreover, controls create vested interests which oppose their removal. Finally, there are administrative costs of controls which fall on both the private and public sectors. These costs tend to be lowered by provisions for private accounting systems and having existing government bureaucracies take on the administration of the controls as a marginal job. This fact is especially relevant if controls are imposed only for short duration.

We can conclude that there may be a case for the use of controls for short periods, but in practice it is difficult to envisage many instances where the benefits in terms of desired exchange rate stability outweigh the short-run costs of administration and inefficiency in operation, adverse influence on public honesty, and the likelihood that vested interests will succeed in turning short-run into long-run controls, with an accompanying increase in inefficiency. Direct controls for balance-of-payments purposes remain popular, especially with developing countries, perhaps because in these countries intervention in economic affairs is an accepted norm of behavior, and the controls for balance-of-payments purposes are considered to be an extension of overall development programs. In Western industrial countries, controls over trade have been used mostly in situations of extreme economic crisis, such as during the 1930s and in the immediate postwar era, or when fundamental changes in the economic system take place, as in 1971 when the U.S. dollar was devalued for the first time in over 30 years and major efforts were launched to reform the international monetary system. In Western countries, controls on trade for balance-of-payments purposes are considerably less important than controls on capital flows, which we will discuss in Chapter 17.

BIBLIOGRAPHICAL NOTES

The use of direct controls for balance-of-payments purposes is discussed in the literature on nontariff barriers to trade, such as Baldwin (1970), Curzon (1971), and

Stern (1973b). Gutowski (1972) gives an interesting account of German experiences with direct controls during the 1960s. Krueger (1966) discusses the cost of controls in a case study of Turkey.

CONCEPTS FOR REVIEW

Exchange controls
Trade licensing
Multiple exchange rates
Quantitative restrictions

Quotas
Embargoes
Payments agreements

POINTS FOR FURTHER STUDY AND DISCUSSION

1. Attempt a classification of direct-control methods according to their dominant direct effect on either relative domestic and foreign prices, with quantities free to adjust, or on the supply of quantities imported, letting the rent on import licenses reflect the difference in the domestic and foreign prices at the market exchange rate.

2. Read newspaper and government reports issued on the occasions of the imposition of direct controls on trade by Britain during the 1960s and by the United States in 1971. What has been the official justification for their use, how discriminatory were the methods, how long did they exist, and what were official reasons for their abandonment?

3. Attempt to compile lists of direct controls on trade in effect presently in India, Pakistan, and Brazil. Write up a report about them which would be needed by a firm doing business with these countries. Start your research with library resources but also attempt to obtain information from relevant foreign embassies.

Income Effects Combined with
Exchange Rate Changes for
Internal and External Balance

A SIMPLE KEYNESIAN MODEL of income determination for a small country, A, with managed exchange rates in a world without money, international short-term capital flows, and government spending or taxes is presented in the first part of this chapter. We assume that students are familiar with basic concepts of national income accounting, the consumption function, equilibrium income, and so on. The emphasis of the analysis is on ways in which the conventional basic model found in introductory textbooks is modified by the existence of a foreign sector. We develop our analysis using algebra, a numerical example, and, finally, geometry.

In Section II of this chapter we combine into one model the effects of income and exchange rate changes on both equilibrium income and the balance of payments. The model uses a specific initial disequilibrium condition to illustrate the problem of finding simultaneously balance in foreign trade and full-employment income. In the final part of this section the Swan diagram is presented to show more generally the problem of attaining these equilibrium conditions simultaneously.

I. A SIMPLE MODEL OF INCOME DETERMINATION

A typical Keynesian model of income determination in a closed economy and without a government sector is given by the following four equations:

$$Y = C + I \qquad (16\text{--}1)$$
$$C = a + bY \qquad (16\text{--}2)$$
$$I = \bar{I} \qquad (16\text{--}3)$$
$$S = I \qquad (16\text{--}4)$$

The first equation is definitional; it states that income and production (Y) in equilibrium are equal to the sum of expenditures on consumption (C) and investment (I). The second and third equations reflect measurable behavioral characteristic of the economy. Thus, consumption is at a when income is zero and increases with income at the rate b, where b is also known as the marginal propensity to consume, which has to be a number smaller than 1 if the system of equations is to have an economically meaningful solution. Equation (16–3) indicates that investment is an exogenously given magnitude independent of the level of income. Equation (16–4) gives the condition that in equilibrium savings (S) equal investment.

A few fundamental properties of this model of income determination for country A are as follows. First, there are three parameters and four variables in the equation system; the three parameters, a, b, $\bar{I}$, are given exogenously through measurement, and the four variables, Y, C, I, and S, are determined endogenously. The equality between the number of unknowns and equations assures that the system is determinate. Second, by algebraic substitution, we can find solution values for any of the endogenous variables, leaving on the right-hand side only the exogenously given values of a, b, and $\bar{I}$. For example, the solution value, or equilibrium level, of income (Y^*) is

$$Y^* = (a + \bar{I})/(1 - b) \qquad (16\text{–}5)$$

Third, the income multiplier, k, is defined as the multiple by which income changes as a result of an exogenous change in expenditure, in the form of either consumption (da) or investment (dI). The multiplier can be found most directly by differentiating Equation (16–5) with respect to expenditure,

$$dY^*/d\bar{I} = 1/(1 - b) = 1/\text{MPS} = k, \qquad (16\text{–}6)$$

where the marginal propensity to save (MPS) is equal to $(1 - b)$. Therefore, the change in equilibrium income associated with a change in expenditure $d\bar{I}$ is

$$dY^* = (1/(1 - b)) \cdot d\bar{I} = k \cdot d\bar{I} \qquad (16\text{–}7)$$

Fourth, we should note that the system of equations assures the most fundamental economic proposition of Keynesian analysis, that in equilibrium so-called leakages from the income stream in the form of savings are just equal to the injection into the income stream in the form of investment. Consequently it is assured that all of the production, for which the public has received an income of equal value, is bought for consumption and investment, even though the public has saved some fraction of its income independently of the decision to invest. Finally, for purposes of later analysis it is useful to point out that Equations (16–1), (16–2), and

(16–4) can be combined to find the savings function:

$$S = Y - C = -a + Y(1 - b),\tag{16–8}$$

where $(1 - b)$ is the marginal propensity to save.

After this review of national income determination in a closed economy, we can readily expand this model to include a foreign sector, for the sake of simplicity again leaving out a government sector. We do so in the following set of equations:

$$Y = C + I\tag{16–9}$$
$$C = a + bY\tag{16–10}$$
$$I = I_d + I_f\tag{16–11}$$
$$I_d = \bar{I}_d\tag{16–12}$$
$$I_f = X - M\tag{16–13}$$
$$X = \bar{X}\tag{16–14}$$
$$M = e + fY\tag{16–15}$$
$$S = I_d + I_f\tag{16–16}$$

The first two equations of the system are the same as in the closed-economy model, but Equation (16–11) shows that in an open economy investment expenditure has two components, domestic (I_d) and foreign (I_f). In analogy with the closed-economy model, we assume that I_d is given exogenously and independently of income, as $\bar{I}_d$, in Equation (16–12). However, foreign investment is defined in Equation (16–13) as being the difference between exports (X) and imports (M) of goods and services. Therefore foreign investment, or the trade balance, is equivalent to the injections into the income, such as consumption and domestic investment. For this reason, it may be useful to rewrite the fundamental income-expenditure identity of Equation (16–9) by substitution of Equations (16–11) and (16–13):

$$Y = C + I_d + (X - M)\tag{16–9a}$$

Either Equation, (16–9) or (16–9a), can be used in further analysis. We show them both here in order to bring out the basic analogy between the closed- and open-economy systems of income determination.

Equation (16–14) shows that we assume exports to be given exogenously as $\bar{X}$, in parallel with domestic investment expenditures. Equation (16–15) gives the import demand function and shows that imports are at the level of e when income is zero and increase at the rate f with income. The parameter f is known as the marginal propensity to import and is always less than 1. Equation (16–6), the equilibrium condition of equality between savings and investment, the latter consisting of domestic plus foreign investments, is the last equation of our model of income determination in an open economy.

We can now note a few interesting properties of this model, most of which come into play when we discuss in the last part of this chapter the policy problems countries encounter in trying to maintain full employment and balance in trade in the face of random disturbances.

First, it is worth checking to see that the new system of equations is determinate. There are six parameters, a, b, e, f, $\overline{X}$, and $\overline{I}_d$, and eight variables determined by the eight equations in the system, Y, C, I, X, M, I_d, I_f, and S.

Second, again by substitution of equations we can find the solution value for income:

$$Y^* = (a - c + \overline{I}_d + \overline{X})/((1 - b) + f) \tag{16–17}$$

and from it, by differentiation, the open-economy multiplier k'

$$dY^*/d\overline{I} = 1/((1 - b) + f) = k' \tag{16–18}$$

or

$$k' = 1/(MPS + MPM) \tag{16–19}$$

where MPM is the marginal propensity to import. The analogy between equations (16–6) and (16–18), representing the closed and open-economy multipliers, is straightforward. The denominators contain the leakage parameters for both domestic behavior and foreign sector relations and determine the sizes of the multipliers. The open-economy multiplier is necessarily smaller than that for the closed economy, since the marginal propensity to import is a positive number which is added to the positive denominator.

Third, income and the foreign sector are interrelated in a number of ways. For example, an increase in exports raises income in the same way as an increase in domestic investment, as can readily be seen by differentiation of Equation (16–17) with respect to exports. As another example, consider that an increase in imports, as reflected in an increase in the parameter e, decreases equilibrium income because differentiation of Equation (16–17) with respect to e yields $-k$. More generally, as Equation (16–15) shows, imports are a function of income. Since changes in the propensity to consume or invest change the level of equilibrium income, they also have indirect repercussions on imports.

Fourth, the basic model of income determination in an open economy has led Sidney Alexander to point to a fundamental aspect of any balance-of-payments problem. This aspect will be central to our analysis in the next section, and disregard of it has caused many countries to suffer from perpetual payments deficits. Alexander introduces into the analysis the concept of absorption, A, which is defined as:

$$A = C + I_d + G, \tag{16–20}$$

or the total domestic expenditure on goods and services by consumers, investors, and the government (G). We can substitute Equation (16–20) into Equation (16–9a) and find:

$$X - M = Y - A \tag{16–21}$$

This simple identity has the very important interpretation that if a country's output, Y, is given by full employment of resources, the trade balance, $X - M$, can be influenced only by policies of the government leading to changes in absorption, A. For example, if a country's expenditures on consumption, domestic investment, and government services, A, exceeds its output of goods and services, Y, then the trade balance must be negative, and according to Equation (16–13), foreign investment, I_f, is also negative. Such a decumulation of foreign assets or credit cannot continue indefinitely, and sooner or later every country must bring into equality the size of its domestic output and absorption. Alexander's formulation of the problem has the great advantage of showing clearly that such a reduction in absorption requires governmental policies designed to reduce consumption, investment, or government expenditures, or all of them. We shall see later how monetary and fiscal policies, currency revaluation, and direct controls can achieve such changes in absorption.

Some students may find it useful to visualize the operation of the equation system just presented through a numerical example and geometry. The geometric exposition, which has a long tradition in Keynesian income determination analysis, is given in the final part of this section. Next we give a numerical example.

Numerical Example

Assume the following values for the exogenously given parameters characterising the economy of country A.

$$a = 20 \tag{16–22}$$
$$b = .8 \tag{16–23}$$
$$\bar{I}_d = 25 \tag{16–24}$$
$$\bar{X} = 30 \tag{16–25}$$
$$e = 10 \tag{16–26}$$
$$f = .3 \tag{16–27}$$

Substituting in Equation (16–17) gives as the equilibrium level of income:

$$Y^* = (20 - 10 + 25 + 30)/(.2 + .3) = 65/.5 = 130 \tag{16–28}$$

Other solution values of interest in the system are:

$$C = 20 + .8 \times 130 = 124 \tag{16–29}$$
$$M = 10 + .3 \times 130 = 49 \tag{16–30}$$
$$I_f = X - M = 30 - 49 = -19 \tag{16–31}$$
$$I = \bar{I}_d + I_f = 25 + (-19) = 6 \tag{16–32}$$
$$S = Y - C = 130 - 124 = 6 \tag{16–33}$$
$$S = I = 6 \tag{16–34}$$

The final equality between savings and investment at 6 is, of course, the condition for equilibrium. It assures that leakages from the income stream through savings and imports equal the injections through domestic investment plus net exports.

We can now use this numerical example to illustrate the characteristics of the model noted verbally above. First, the multiplier is

$$k' = 1/(.2 + .3) = 2 \qquad (16\text{--}35)$$

As an application of the multiplier consider

$$dY = k' \times d\bar{I}_a = 2 \times 10 = 20, \qquad (16\text{--}36)$$

which says that an increase in investment of 10 results in an increase of equilibrium income of 20. This fact can also be verified and the correctness of the income multiplier established by solving Equation 16–17 for the higher level of investment.

$$Y^* = (20 - 10 + 35 + 30)/(.2 + .3) = 75/.5 = 150, \qquad (16\text{--}37)$$

which is indeed 20 above the equilibrium level of 130 for income found in Equation (16–28), under the assumption that domestic investment is 25.

Second, we can note the interdependence of the foreign trade sector with domestic conditions. Thus, the hypothesized increase in domestic investment to 35 raises imports to

$$M = 10 + .3 \times 150 = 55 \qquad (16\text{--}38)$$

and thus raises the trade deficit to

$$I_f = X - M = 30 - 55 = -25 \qquad (16\text{--}39)$$

Third, returning to the case where $\bar{I}_d = 25$, let us now consider a decrease in imports through a change in the value of the constant e in the import function from 10 to 5, that is, $de = -5$. The value of the multiplier is $dY/de = k'$:

$$k' = -1/(.2 + .3) = -2 \qquad (16\text{--}40)$$
$$dY = k \cdot de = 2 \times 5 = +10, \qquad (16\text{--}41)$$

implying increase in income of 10, which is verified by

$$Y^* = (20 - 5 + 25 + 30)/(.2 + .3) = 70/.5 = 140 \qquad (16\text{--}42)$$

Geometric Representation

The Keynesian model of income determination presented algebraically above can also be developed with the help of geometry. In doing this, we will elaborate upon and extend points made earlier. Importantly, however, the geometric technique will also provide us with a most suitable tool for the analysis in Section II of this chapter, where we discuss the difficult problem of internal and external balance through the use of both interdependent exchange rate and income adjustment policies.

In Figure 16–1 we measure expenditures and leakages along the verti-

FIGURE 16–1
Income Determination in an Open Economy

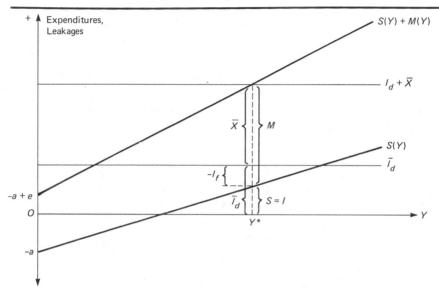

Savings are shown as a function of income, $S(Y)$. The schedule $S(Y) + M(Y)$ sums the savings and the import function. Domestic investment $(\bar{I}_d)$ and exports $(\bar{X})$ are shown as functions independent of income. At equilibrium income, Y^*, leakages from the income stream in the form of savings (S) and imports (M) are equal to injection exports $(\bar{X})$ plus domestic investment $(\bar{I}_d)$. However, since imports exceed exports, foreign investment (I_f) is negative, and total investment $(I = I_d + I_f)$ is smaller than domestic investment. Total savings is equal to total investment.

cal axis and income along the horizontal axis. We plot the injections of expenditure through domestic investment and exports as horizontal lines, indicating that they are independent of income in country A. The line $\bar{X} + \bar{I}_d$ is the total of expenditure injections which in equilibrium must just be equal to the leakages of expenditures due to savings and imports. We find this point of equality between injections and leakages by plotting the functional relationships between income and savings on the one hand and imports on the other. According to Equation (16–8), the intercept of the savings function is $-a$ and the slope is $(1 - b)$. Added vertically to this line shown in Figure 16–1 is the import function, so that the total leakage function, $S(Y) + M(Y)$, has an intercept of $(-a + e)$ and a slope of $(1 - b + f)$.

We can see that the total leakage function intersects the total expenditure function at Y^*, the equilibrium level of income in Figure 16–1, equivalent to the algebraic solution in Equation (16–17). At this equilibrium income level, the savings function shows domestic savings to be S and the import function shows imports to be M, while exports are $\overline{X}$ and domestic investment is $\overline{I}_d$. The difference between exports and imports is negative, representing a trade deficit and negative foreign investment of I_f. Because this foreign investment is negative, total savings of country A are smaller than domestic investment. This is possible only because of a net reduction in foreign asset holdings or credits abroad equal to the payments deficit.

It should be noted here that this deficit is equal to the excess demand for foreign exchange at the fixed exchange rate we discussed above in connection with Figure 11–4. This deficit is also equal to the amount of foreign exchange country A has to supply to satisfy the excess demand at the fixed exchange rate. The foreign exchange used for this purpose is acquired (as we have already noted) by running down holdings of international reserve assets or by borrowing abroad.

The geometric representation of the Keynesian income-determination model in Figure 16–1 can readily be used to show the effects different kinds of exogenous disturbances have on the equilibrium level of income and how changes in absorption are necessary to eliminate a payments deficit. For this purpose we have drawn Figures 16–2 and 16–3, which

FIGURE 16–2
Income and Rise in Expenditures

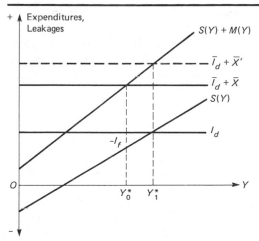

Repeating the essentials of Figure 16–1, in Figure 16–2 initial equilibrium is at Y_0^*, with a negative level of foreign investment equal to the excess of imports over exports. Under the assumption of an exogenous increase in exports, the expenditure schedule becomes $I_d + \overline{X}'$, equilibrium income is established at Y_1^*, and the trade imbalance and foreign investment are eliminated. Domestic investment equals savings.

FIGURE 16–3

Income and Rise in Imports

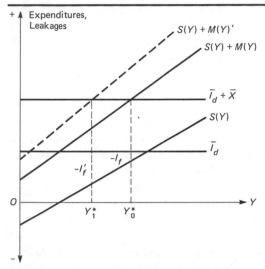

Again repeating the essentials of Figure 16–1, in Figure 16–3 initial equilibrium is at Y_0^*, with the trade deficit equal to negative foreign investment ($-I_f$). An assumed increase in the propensity to import shifts upward the leakages schedule to $S(Y) + M(Y)'$ and results in the new income, Y_1^*, and the worsened trade balance and negative foreign investment (I_f').

repeat in all essentials Figure 16–1. At the initial equilibrium Y_0^*, the sum of expenditure injection, $\bar{I}_d + \bar{X}$, equals the sum of leakages, and there is a trade deficit of $-I_f$ in both graphs.

Now consider, as a first case of a disturbance, the upward shift of the expenditure function to $\bar{I}_d + \bar{X}'$ in Figure 16–2, due to some exogenous increase in demand for country A's exports which result perhaps from a bad harvest abroad or a subsidy to exporters in country A. The new equilibrium level of income is Y_1^*, which is above Y_0^* by an amount determined by the multiplier. Recall that the magnitude of this multiplier depends on the marginal propensities to save and import, which in Figures 16–1 and 16–2 are reflected in the slope of the leakage function. In the particular case drawn, the multiplier is a little greater than 1. At the new income level, Y_1^*, the exogenous increase in exports is just big enough to succeed in the elimination of the trade imbalance. Therefore exports exactly equal imports, and savings equal domestic investment, as can be seen in Figure 16–2.

As we shall note again in the next section of this chapter, the elimination of the trade deficit through the hypothesized increase in exports is successful only if the original level of income Y_0^* does not represent capacity output. If output cannot be increased beyond Y_0^*, then the higher demand for goods and services causes prices to rise in country A and leads to reduced exports and higher imports. This is the point stressed by Alexander's absorption analysis discussed above. In terms of Figure 16–2, the rise in prices resulting from excess demand at Y_1^* can be represented as resulting in a downward shift of the expenditure and leakage schedules, to where equilibrium is restored at full capacity in Y_0^*. If all characteristics of the economy are still the same as they were before the institution of a subsidy to exporters, then the deficit in the new equilibrium will be the same as it was before the subsidy, and the original trade deficit will be restored. We will return to this point below.

Now we consider a second case of exogenous changes to the functional relationships shown in Figure 16–3 and assumed to result in the initial equilibrium, Y_0^*. Assume that country A experiences an increased propensity to import, causing an upward shift of the leakage schedule to $S(Y) + M(Y)'$. Such a shift may be prompted by the elimination of import restrictions in existence previously or the granting of subsidies by a foreign government to its exporters. The particular shift of the leakage schedule shown in Figure 16–3 leads to an equilibrium income of Y_1^* and a trade deficit of I_f', which is greater than the deficit at the initial equilibrium. The increased leakages due to the higher import propensity have the effect of lowering the equilibrium level of income to Y_1^*, which is below the initial equilibrium income level, Y_0^*. If Y_0^* is full employment income, then it can be restored only if the assumed increase in imports is compensated by an increase in expenditures through lowering of the domestic savings propensity, increased exports, or higher domestic investment.

For many purposes of analysis in international economics, the graphic representation of the Keynesian model used in Figures 16–1 through 16–3 is not as useful as one which focuses more specifically on the trade balance. In Figure 16–4 we develop such a graph. In Panel A we measure income along the horizontal axis and savings and domestic investment along the vertical axis. In the upper section of Panel A we graph the familiar increasing functional relationship between income and savings, $S(Y)$, and the level of investment, I_d, assumed to be independent of income. In the lower part of Panel A we introduce the novelty of the present representation, the functional relationship between income and savings minus domestic investment. As can be seen in Panel A, when income is zero savings are negative, and the sum of savings minus investment is negative, since investment is positive. However, at higher income levels savings are higher, while investment is unchanged. Generally, the higher the level of income the smaller is the sum of savings minus investment, until at Y_1 the two are equal. At Y_1 the line $S(Y) - \bar{I}_d$ intersects the income axis and at higher levels of Y it is positive. In a closed economy Y_1 would represent equilibrium, since only at it do the intended savings equal actual investment.

FIGURE 16–4
Keynesian Income Model with Focus on Trade Balance

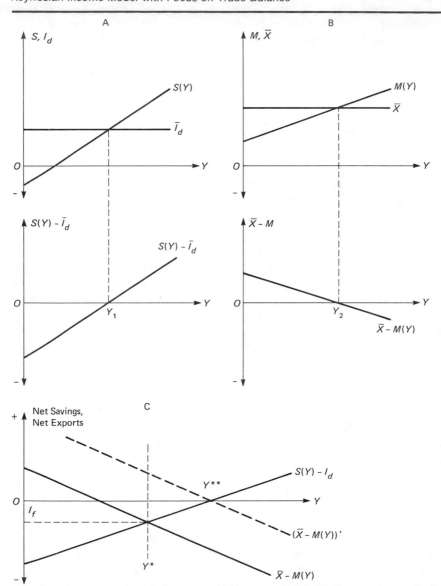

Panel A in Figure 16–4 shows the derivation of the net domestic leakage schedule, $S(Y) - I_d$ in the lower section, from the savings, $S(Y)$ and investment, I_d, schedules in the upper section. Panel B shows the derivation of the net export schedule, $\bar{X} - M(Y)$, in the lower section from the import, $M(Y)$ and export, $\bar{X}$, schedules in the upper section.

In Panel C the net savings and net export schedules are combined to determine equilibrium income at Y^*, which is associated with a trade deficit, $\bar{X} - M(Y) < 0$; $I_f < 0$; and negative net savings, $S(Y) - I_d < 0$. A currency devaluation shifts the net export schedule to $(\bar{X} - M(Y))'$ and produces the new equilibrium income at Y^{**}, which is associated with trade balance, zero foreign investment, and equality between domestic savings and investment. Y^{**} is genuine equilibrium only if it is equal to or below full employment.

In the top section of Panel B of Figure 16–4 we present the functional relationships between income and exports and imports, which is netted out to $\overline{X} - M(Y)$ in the lower section of Panel B, where all functions are derived in a fashion strictly analogous to that employed in Panel A. Since at zero income, exports exceed imports and both are positive, the intercept $\overline{X} - M(Y)$ is positive, and since imports are an increasing function of income and exports are a constant, the line $\overline{X} - M(Y)$ is downward sloping, intersecting the income axis at Y_2 where $\overline{X} = M(Y)$.

In Panel C we plot the net savings and net export functions in one graph. As can be seen, the two functions intersect at Y^*, which analytically is the same equilibrium level of income as that shown as Y^* in Figure 16–1. The characteristics of this equilibrium are that both net savings and net exports are negative, and the surplus of imports over exports equals the excess of domestic investment over savings, which we saw above to be equal to foreign investment, I_f. The usefulness of Figure 16–4 in the analysis of some important problems in international adjustment will become obvious in the next section.

II. THE PROBLEM OF INTERNAL AND EXTERNAL BALANCE

We are now in a position to combine and integrate the three elements of international adjustment analyzed separately above: exchange rate changes, controls on trade, and income changes. We do so by using Figure 16–4 and considering the problem of attaining simultaneously full employment and balance in external payments, which is also known simply as the problem of internal and external balance.

Recall that in Panel C of Figure 16–4, at the equilibrium income, Y^*, country A has a balance-of-payments deficit. Now assume that this country wishes to eliminate this deficit by reducing imports and increasing exports, through what is known as expenditure-switching policies, involving exchange rate depreciation, controls on trade, or both. For our purposes of analysis the important effects of these policies are a downward shift of the import schedules and an upward shift of the export schedules in Panel B of Figure 16–4, resulting in an upward shift of the $\overline{X} - M(Y)$ schedule. To keep Figure 16–4 simple, we show the effect of the balance-of-payments policies only in Panel C, as the shift of the net export schedule to $(\overline{X} - M(Y))'$, which leads to the new equilibrium level of income, Y^{**}, at which trade is balanced and net foreign investment is zero. However, whether country A's trade deficit problem has been solved permanently depends on whether the new equilibrium level of income, Y^{**}, is above or below full employment. In order to simplify the following analysis, let us distinguish two possibilities: one, that Y^{**} is full employment, and two, that Y^* is full employment. Let us assume furthermore that up to full employment prices fall, at full employment they are stable, and above that level they rise. We also assume that the world price level is stable.

Case 1

In this case the initial equilibrium income is one of less than full-capacity use of resources; especially, there is an undesirably high level of unemployment. In the language of the literature concerned with the problem under discussion here, country A suffers from both internal and external imbalance, that is unemployment and a trade deficit. The upward shift of the net trade schedule leads to full-employment equilibrium income of Y^{**}, and the trade deficit is eliminated. There are no further problems. The net increase of country A's domestic output caused by the balance-of-payments policies is the same in principle as that achieved by expansionary monetary and fiscal policy in a closed economy. The policies produce equality between leakages through savings and imports, and expenditure injection through domestic investment and exports, at just the sustainable level of income and capacity output.

Case 2

The more difficult problem arises when country A is at full employment at the initial equilibrium level of income, Y^*, and has the trade deficit I_f. Under these conditions the expenditure-switching policies lead to excess aggregate demand for goods and services and consequent increases in domestic prices and wages. The entire increase in output between Y^* and Y^{**} shown in Panel C, Figure 16–4, represents only an increase in the nominal value of national output. But when prices and wages rise in country A while those in the rest of the world remain stable, as we assumed above, foreigners buy fewer of country A's goods, and the export schedule shifts downward. At the same time, country A's residents buy more foreign goods, and the import schedule is shifted upward. These influences manifest themselves as downward shifts of the $(\overline{X} - M(Y))'$ schedule in Panel C, and they continue as long as there is excess demand in country A and inflation persists. The entire process comes to an end only after the net export schedule is back in its initial position and equilibrium income is returned to Y^*. At this point country A is again in perfect domestic balance, but its payments deficit is back at the original level of I_f. The essential difference between the situation at the outset and in the new equilibrium are that the domestic price level is higher and the external value of the currency is lower.

If country A again attempts to improve its foreign trade deficit by depreciating its currency, it runs into the same process of inflation and ultimate return to the same position where the deficit reappears at a higher level of prices and lower currency value. In order to eliminate the deficit permanently and retain its internal balance, country A has to combine currency devaluation with what is known as policies for reduced absorption. In our simplified model without a government, these policies cause a reduction in consumption and investment expenditures or a rise in savings. In a more complete and realistic model, importantly, absorption can also be reduced by the lowering of government expenditures and the raising of taxes. Such absorption-reducing policies produce an upward shift of the net savings schedule in Panel C, Figure 16-4, so that in the new equilibrium the upward shifts of both the net savings and net export schedules result in an intersection exactly at Y^* and the point of zero foreign trade imbalance. In Panel C this intersection of the net savings and net export schedules would occur on the Y axis and at Y^*, though to keep the graph simple we do not show this equilibrium condition.

The lowering of absorption which is necessary if a country at full employment and with a trade deficit wishes to restore trade balance can be achieved either through deliberate policies or through the automatic processes which accompany inflation. Deliberate policies in the fuller model require the tightening of monetary and fiscal policies which, through higher interest rates and taxes, will reduce consumption and domestic investment. In the absence of deliberate policies, the inflation reduces absorption automatically through three different processes. First, there may be income redistribution away from pensioners and some wage earners whose incomes fail to rise as quickly as prices, and to other wage earners and profits. To the extent that the former group has a higher propensity to consume than the latter, the inflation-induced income redistribution causes a decrease in total consumption. Second, the price increases lower the value of money balances held by the public. In order to restore the real value of these balances so as to maintain them at a constant fraction of wealth or of income, the public has to reduce consumption. Third, if the government's income and corporate taxation schedule is progressive, then as prices increase the real share of income taken as taxes is raised. The higher share of public income going to the government forces reductions in consumption and investment expenditures and thus reduces absorption.

The functioning of all of the automatic processes for the reduction of absorption operating through the inflationary process is unreliable in speed and effect. For example, income redistribution may be redressed by government policies such as the indexing of government transfer payments, and increases in government tax revenue may be anticipated and spent immediately so that reductions in consumption expenditures are matched by corresponding rises in government spending. The automatic processes have the added disadvantage that they may lead to forced cuts in spending by groups in the economy who are least able to afford them. For these reasons, it is socially undesirable for governments to rely on automatic reductions in absorption for the attainment of both internal and external balance, in situations where there is a trade deficit at full employment. From this analysis we reach the important conclusion that countries wishing to attain both internal and external balance reliably and at least social cost need explicitly designed policies for the reduction as well as the switching of expenditures. In recent decades a number of countries in Western Europe, especially Britain and Italy, have been unwilling or unable to combine expenditure reduction with devaluation. Consequently they have suffered periodic recurrences of their balance-of-payments deficits and continuous price inflation.

The Role of Money

The income-determination model presented in this chapter excludes any consideration of the role of the money supply. We will remedy this deficiency in the next chapter, but it is instructive to use the present model to anticipate one of the main conclusions to be reached in this chapter, both because the point is important and because the present analytical framework can be adjusted readily for the task.

Let us assume that we are at the initial situation of internal balance in country A at Y^*, with an external deficit of $\bar{I}_d$ as shown in Figure 16–4, Panel C. As we know from Chapter 11, the trade deficit is matched by an excess demand for foreign exchange, which the government meets by selling foreign currency from its reserves. In return it receives from the public domestic money balances of equivalent value. Therefore the money holdings of the public are reduced, interest rates rise, and consumption and investment expenditures are curtailed. In our geometric analysis, the $S(Y) - \bar{I}_d$ schedule shifts upward. With the net export schedule unchanged, a new equilibrium income level is established below that of full employment, and, according to our assumptions, prices fall. The fall in prices in turn shifts upward the net export schedule, for reasons discussed above. This process of adjustment continues until equilibrium is established at Y^*.

From the preceding analysis we conclude that if a country experiences a prolonged period of full employment and external deficits, it is because the government neutralizes the automatic effect the deficit has on the money supply by corresponding open-market operations. In an important sense, therefore, it is true that any trade deficit of a country is due to the excessive creation of money. This conclusion is consistent with a point brought out by the absorption approach: The deficit persists because aggregate expenditures are not reduced through appropriately restrictive monetary policy. The same conclusion is also reached by the monetarist critics of Keynesian income analysis though, as we shall see in Chapter 19, they focus their analysis on another aspect of the mechanism of domestic and international adjustment.

The Phillips Curve Modification

One of the most serious problems associated with the simple Keynesian income-determination model presented in this chapter is the definition and operational concept of full-capacity or full-employment income. It is easy enough to define full-employment income as the one at which, in equilibrium, prices are stable and above and below which prices rise and fall, respectively, and to develop logically consistent models providing many useful insights around this definition. However, during the late 1950s public dissatisfaction grew with this definition of full employment, as it was discovered that price stability could be achieved only at relatively high levels of unemployment: in the United States, for example, at about 6 percent. At the same time empirical studies by A. W. Phillips of the London School of Economics showed that historically in Britain there had been periods of different unemployment levels and price changes which suggested a functional relationship between unemployment and inflation like the one shown in Figure 16–5 as PP'. This became known as the Phillips curve; it was found simply by connecting series of points, like A and B, which represented the experience of Year 1, 2 percent inflation and 4 percent unemployment (point A), and of Year 2, zero inflation and 6 percent unemployment (point B).

Similar relationships were found for other Western countries besides Britain, and it was assumed that countries had a choice to aim for any level of unemployment as long as they were willing to bear the consequences of the inflation rates implied by the empirically found Phillips curve. In the United States, for example, public discussions and economic analysis led to the view that U.S. welfare, on balance, would be increased if the full-employment target were set at 4 percent and inflation of 2 percent were accepted. In 1961 President John F. Kennedy announced officially that the U.S. government considered 4 percent unemployment as the target of "full employment" for monetary and fiscal policies, and later other major Western countries defined full-employment similarly.

Let us now assume that in fact countries have the option to redefine full employment in this manner and that they have the tradeoff with inflation suggested by the Phillips curve. What difference does this new concept of full employment make for the model of internal and external balance presented above? To answer this question it is useful to consider two different cases: In the first, country A and the rest of the world have chosen targets implying equal rates of inflation, and the second country A's target implies a different rate of inflation than that in the rest of the

FIGURE 16–5
The Phillips Curve Tradeoff

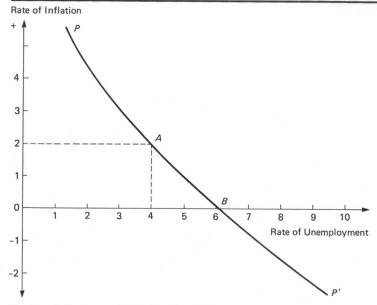

The line *PP'* represents the functional relationship alleged to exist between the rate of unemployment at which an economy is operating and the rate of inflation it experiences. For example, according to the Phillips curve model, a country has the option of operating either at point *B*, where the unemployment rate is 6 percent and there is no inflation, or at point *A*, where the unemployment rate is at 4 percent and inflation at 2 percent.

world. In the first case our analysis of internal and external balance needs to be modified only very slightly. We simply have to remember that the price increase accompanying country A's devaluation is added to the normal inflation, and what counts is the relatively greater rate of price increase in country A and the rest of the world. Otherwise in equilibrium all prices are rising at the same rate, export and import functions are not shifted, and the basic lines of argument remain unchanged.

In the second case, consider that country A is at the point of internal balance Y^*, newly defined as, say, 4 percent unemployment and entailing 2 percent inflation. It also has the trade deficit I_d shown in Panel C of Figure 16–4. Now if the rest of the world maintains price stability, then in each time period country A's import and export functions shift upward and downward, respectively, because of the change in relative prices of domestic and foreign goods. Consequently, excess demand appears, and the external trade imbalance worsens. Country A can offset both of these influences by depreciating its currency at the same rate at which its inflation exceeds that in the rest of the world, 3 percent in our example. Such a policy ensures that the import and export functions stay fixed through time. Under these conditions we are at the analytically equivalent problem as in the previous case.

We conclude from this discussion that the basic implications of our analysis concerning the need for a proper mix of policies for switching and reducing expenditures to attain simultaneous internal and external balance remain unchanged by the redefinition of full employment in the Phillips curve framework. However, we should note in closing this discussion that the existence of a tradeoff between unemployment and inflation has been questioned by theoretical analysis of underlying microeconomic processes and challenged by the experiences of the late 1960s and early 1970s, when the full-employment targets could be maintained only at the expense of accelerating inflation. As a result of these developments, it may well be that in the future countries will return to the use of monetary and fiscal policy for the maintenance of price stability, and employ other policies, such as labor retraining and labor relocation assistance, to reduce the level of unemployment which otherwise would result at price stability. If this happens, the simple version of our model will again be relevant for the analysis of problems concerning the simultaneous attainment of internal and external balance.

The Swan Diagram

The analysis of the required mix of policies for expenditure reducing and switching presented above in the context of Figure 16-4 was based on a specific disequilibrium situation of initial internal balance and external deficit. This facilitated exposition but is of limited generality. From the model of Figure 16-4 it is possible in principle to analyze what policy mixes are needed in different initial situations, such as domestic excess demand combined with a trade surplus, but only through tedious consideration of special circumstances. Fortunately we have available an analytical model which permits us to consider all possible combinations of imbalances and balances and to find directly in each case what combination of expenditure switching and reducing is required to attain internal and external balance. This analytical apparatus has been developed by Trevor Swan of the Australian National University. It is presented in Figure 16-6 in slightly modified form to facilitate relating it to the models presented earlier in this chapter.

Along the vertical axis of Figure 16-6 we measure country A's exchange rate, R, defined in the normal way as the price of a unit of foreign exchange. Along the horizontal axis we measure domestic absorption expenditures. The line EE' shows points at which external balance is maintained through the combination of the exchange rate and absorption. The EE' line slopes upward and to the right because at a low level of absorp-

FIGURE 16–6

The Swan Diagram for Finding Internal and External Balance

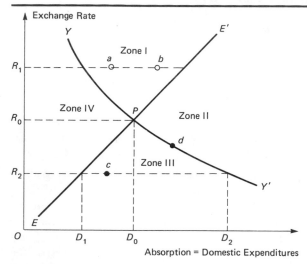

Absorption = Domestic Expenditures

The line YY' in Figure 16–6 represents the combination of domestic absorption expenditures and the exchange rate at which a country's economy is in internal balance, that is, enjoys full employment. The YY' function slopes downward because, to assure internal balance, the high net exports at high exchange rates must be combined with low domestic absorption rates, while low exchange rates and low absorption go together.

The line EE' represents the combination of absorption expenditures and the exchange rate at which a country enjoys external balance, that is, balanced trade. The EE' function slopes upward since at low exchange rates exports are discouraged but imports are kept down by low absorption expenditures while at high exchange rates exports are encouraged but high domestic absorption expenditures raise imports.

Internal and external balance are attained simultaneously only at point P. If the country finds itself in Zone I, it has an external surplus and internal excess demand; in Zone II external deficit, internal excess demand; in Zone III external deficit internal underemployment; and in Zone IV external surplus and internal underemployment.

tion expenditures, such as D_1, the equilibrium level of income is low, and, with a given exchange rate and import demand schedule as a function of income, imports are also low. Therefore, if external balance is to exist and imports equal exports, the price of foreign exchange may be low, such as R_2. However, at a higher level of absorption such, as D_0, equilibrium income and imports are higher. External balance then requires a rise in the price of foreign exchange, which raises exports and lowers imports. At some exchange rate above R_2, such as R_0, external balance is achieved, given the level of absorption D_0.

The preceding arguments about the slope of the EE' line imply that if, for some reason irrelevant for our purposes of analysis, a country finds itself at a point like b, which is the left of EE', it must have an external surplus.

This conclusion follows readily from the fact that if at the exchange rate, R_1, associated with point b it is possible to increase absorption and thereby also increase imports and yet attain external balance, then at the lower absorption level imports must have been smaller than exports. For analogous reasons, any points to the right of the EE' schedule represent a foreign trade deficit.

The line YY' represents a combination of exchange rates and absorption at which internal balance, or more precisely, full-employment income, is attained. The line slopes downward and to the right because at a high level of absorption, such as D_2, the exchange rate must be low and induce only a low level of injection into the expenditure stream in the form of net exports, perhaps even a trade deficit, in order to maintain equality of injections and leakages at full employment. On the other hand, at a lower level of domestic absorption, such as D_0, internal balance is attained by having an exchange rate above R_2, such as R_0, at which exports are greater and imports are smaller, giving a greater net injection into the income stream.

Any point to the right of the YY' line represents a point of excess demand or inflationary pressures, because if we find a country at a point such as a in Figure 16–6, a reduction in domestic expenditures at a constant exchange rate, R_1, leads to internal balance on the line YY'. For analogous reasons any point to the left of the YY' line represents deficient aggregate demand and therefore underemployment.

We are now in the position to consider the two schedules YY' and EE' together. We find that only at the point of intersection, P, and an exchange rate R_0 and absorption of D_0 does country A enjoy both internal and external balance. If the country finds itself at any point off the two schedules, it suffers from internal and external imbalances in the following combinations, in the different zones shown in Figure 16–6:

Zone I. External surplus, internal excess demand.
   II. External deficit, internal excess demand.
   III. External deficit, internal underemployment.
   IV. External surplus, internal underemployment.

The analysis above surrounding Figure 16–4 can be represented in Figure 16–6. In Case 1 we had assumed that Y^{**} in Figure 16–4 was full employment, so that the initial equilibrium at Y^* implied the existence of unemployment and a trade deficit. In the Swan diagram this particular set of conditions is found at a point in Zone III, such as c. Point c in relation to equilibrium suggests that country A must both devalue its currency from R_2 to R_0 and raise absorption expenditures to D_0.

In Case 2 above the initial equilibrium position at Y^* was assumed to imply full employment and an external deficit. In Figure 16–6 this condition is shown by point d on YY' but to the right of the EE' schedule. The position of d implies the necessity of reduced absorption plus a devaluation if internal and external balance are to be achieved, as we concluded in Case 2 above.

A set of disequilibrium conditions of some special interest is found at point a in Zone I, where there is an external surplus and excess demand. Generally, the excess-demand condition implies that the country needs to reduce domestic absorption. However, as the Swan diagram shows clearly, under the particular set of circumstances represented by point a, the attainment of external balance requires a currency appreciation. This appreciation is so large that exports fall and imports rise by so much as to create a condition of underemployment, which in turn can be remedied only by an increase in absorption. By analogy there are sets of external balance conditions combined with underemployment which require reduced domestic absorption for the attainment of internal and external balance. We do not show such a set of conditions in Figure 16–6, and students may wish to test their understanding of the Swan diagram analysis by locating such a point for themselves.

BIBLIOGRAPHICAL NOTES

One of the earliest applications of Keynesian income determination models to the foreign trade sector is Machlup (1943). The classic in the field is Meade (1951), ch. 1–7. The absorption concept was developed by Alexander (1951, 1952). The geometric exposition in the text follows Kindleberger (1973), ch. 20.

The problem of internal and external balance has been argued most clearly in the classic by Johnson (1958b). Corden (1960) uses and refines Swan's (1963) contribution, which had been presented in 1955 at an Australian conference of economists and circulated as a mimeographed paper. Fleming (1971) and Corden (1973) contain analytical tools relevant to the problems raised by the Phillips curve tradeoff for the maintenance of internal and external balance.

CONCEPTS FOR REVIEW

Marginal propensity to import

Foreign investment or domestic investment

Open-economy multiplier

Absorption

Internal and external balance

POINTS FOR FURTHER STUDY AND DISCUSSION

1. See Machlup (1965) and other textbooks for extension of the multiplier analysis, including repercussions of changes in country A's income on imports from other countries and their incomes and resultant demand for country A's exports.

2. Using the equation system underlying the numerical example in the text, find equilibrium income by assuming a rise in the marginal propensity to import from $f = .3$ to $f = .4$ (Equation 16–27). By how much does the marginal

propensity to consume have to change if the increase in the marginal propensity to import is to be compensated for, leaving equilibrium income unchanged?

3. Using the numerical example in the text resulting in the equilibrium level of income at 130, calculate what increase in exports is necessary to achieve an equilibrium income of 160. What is the level of foreign investment at this income?

4. Using the numerical example in the text, find the level of domestic investment expenditure and exports to move the economy to an equilibrium level of income of 140 and simultaneously zero foreign investment, which is attained when exports and imports are equal.

5. Using the Swan diagram, discuss conditions when an economy can move to equilibrium using only an exchange rate change, even though it is in internal and external disequilibrium. Repeat the exercise for the case where only absorption changes are necessary.

6. Analyze what happens to the curves in the Swan diagram if country A chooses to accept an annual inflation rate of 4 percent per year, while the rest of the world has absolute price stability. What happens to the curves as a result of economic growth?

17 Adjustment with Money, Short-Term Capital Flows, and Speculation

THE MODELS of international adjustment presented in the preceding chapters have lacked important elements of realism by omitting any formal consideration of the roles of money, interest rates, and international short-term capital flows. The models without money have the great advantages of relative simplicity and concentration on the real adjustments behind the veil of financial changes. As such they are a great aid in understanding some aspects of the process of international adjustment to disturbances of internal and external equilibriums. However, in the real world monetary policy questions and international short-term capital flows greatly complicate the management of the economy and make it more difficult to attain internal and external balance. Furthermore, in recent years there has developed a school of thought, known as the monetarist approach to the balance of payments, which claims that monetary policy is the only key to international adjustment. We will discuss the reasoning behind this approach in Chapter 19.

In Section I of this chapter we present an analysis of the role of short-term capital flows in a world of laissez-faire policies adhering either to the gold standard or freely floating exchange rates. We then examine the problems caused by short-term capital flows under systems of managed exchange rates, and in Section III we discuss methods which have been developed for their control.

I. THE ROLE OF SHORT-TERM CAPITAL FLOWS IN ADJUSTMENT

In the following analysis we consider that small-country A is initially in equilibrium at full employment with balanced trade, no capital flows, and

358

an interest rate on short-term capital equal to that in the rest of the world. Now let us assume that the external balance is disturbed by the development of a trade deficit, caused either by a reversible bad harvest or the destruction of a large stock of capital, the restoration of which requires a long time. The analysis is undertaken first by assuming that country A has fixed exchange rates and then by assuming that exchange rates float freely.

Fixed Exchange Rate Case

The payments deficit of country A under the fixed exchange rate causes a reduction in its money supply. Under the gold standard the reduction is directly through the outflow of gold, and under a managed exchange rate system it is due to the fact that when the government meets the excess demand for foreign exchange through the sale of reserves, it acquires domestic currency and thereby reduces the stock of money held by the public. The reduction in country A's money supply leads to an increase in its domestic interest rate, which in turn leads to an inflow of short-term capital from abroad. How much the interest rate rises upon the appearance of the deficit and how much capital flows into the country depend on the interest elasticity of the capital flows. For example, if the elasticity is very high, then only a small increase in the domestic interest rate attracts large amounts of capital, and the more these capital flows succeed in eliminating the deficit, the smaller are the losses in money and further upward pressures on the interest rate. In the extreme case of nearly perfect interest elasticity of supply of capital, the rise in the interest rate in country A is infinitesimally small. We need not concern ourselves here with the determinants of this interest elasticity; we simply assume that for country A it is institutionally given and somewhere between zero and infinity.

Whatever the level of the capital inflow it can be used to finance imports and maintain the country's standard of living at a higher level than otherwise would have been possible. However, ultimately the loan from the rest of the world to country A has to be repaid. Such repayment occurs after a future above-average bumper harvest or the reconstruction of the capital stock. In the latter case the existence of a higher than normal interest rate induces greater than normal savings and leads to a capital stock above that which was destroyed. The effects of the bumper harvest and capital formation are excess supplies and a fall of agricultural product and manufactured good prices below their normal averages. This leads to an export surplus and repayment of the loan and interest on it by a mechanism analogous to that discussed in the context of the initial deficit.

The important welfare implications of this process of short-term capital inflows and outflows is that country A can deal with the calamities of a bad harvest or capital stock destruction over a longer period of time, and through a less drastic cutback in consumption, than would be necessary in the absence of the capital flows. Under the assumption of the decreasing marginal utility of income, the smaller income reductions, even though they have to be maintained for a longer period, result in a smaller loss of welfare than do the drastic but short-lived reductions. These welfare gains from international short-term capital flows in the classical model are akin to those enjoyed by a family which, beset by the calamity of an accident or illness, borrows money to stretch out payments for the bills and to provide an income while the family head is out of work. Since all countries can benefit from international short-term capital flows in this manner, the international monetary system can be considered to operate like an insurance scheme, under which countries lend to each other in periods of emergency and in consequence suffer less from the kinds of adversities afflicting all of them at certain times.

Freely Floating Rates Case

Let us now assume that country A has freely floating rates, is in initial internal and external balance, and then experiences a bad harvest or the destruction of some domestic capital stock. The result is the development of a trade deficit and the depreciation of the exchange rate, while there is upward pressure on the interest rate. Speculators, expecting a bumper harvest at some time in the future or the restoration of the capital stock within a certain time, know that after these events the exchange rate will appreciate again, and they purchase quantities of country A's currency. This speculative capital inflow limits the extent of the initial exchange rate depreciation and interest rate increase in the analogous manner in which capital flows in the fixed exchange rate case limit the increase in the interest rate. Because of the smaller exchange rate change, country A's shift of resources into export industries is reduced, and adjustment costs are saved. The reduction in real income accompanying the deterioration of the terms of trade implied in the currency devaluation is smaller as a result of the speculative capital flows. In the presence of money, interest rates, and capital flows, therefore, international adjustment to payments disturbances under freely floating exchange rates involves lower real costs than it does in the absence of the capital flows. Since the benefits we showed accruing to country A are available to all countries, we can conclude that under both the gold standard and freely floating exchange rate systems, international capital flows are the vehicle by which all countries of the world are linked efficiently in an anonymous, automatic scheme of insurance. Under this scheme countries afflicted by payments imbalances lend financial capital among themselves to even out fluctuations in real income which are otherwise necessitated.

II. SHORT-TERM CAPITAL FLOWS IN MANAGED ECONOMIES

If governments manage economies according to Keynesian principles and maintain fixed exchange rates for long periods of time, as under the International Monetary Fund (IMF) parity rate system (discussed in Chapter 23), international short-term capital movements can be an aid to adjustment, as in the laissez-faire world. However, they are also potentially a very serious constraint on the maintenance of internal and external balance. We will analyze the circumstances under which these favorable and unfavorable conditions prevail, drawing on a presentation made by James Meade of Cambridge University. Underlying this model is the assumption that over the relevant time horizon, exchange rates remain fixed, so that there are no short-term capital flows by speculators expecting to make a profit from exchange rate changes. All capital movements are in the form of interest arbitrage and take advantage of observable interest rate differentials between countries. After completion of this analysis we turn to the case of speculative short-term capital flows based on expected gains from exchange rate changes.

Meade's analysis centers on Table 17–1, where on the left side four

TABLE 17–1
Meade's Model of Internal and External Balance

		In Country A, with External Deficit		In Country B, with External Surplus	
Given Domestic Conditions of:		\multicolumn{4}{c}{*Interest Rate Needs to be Adjusted*}			
Case	*For:*	*External Balance*	*Internal Balance*	*External Balance*	*Internal Balance*
1. Excess demand in both countries		up	up	down	up
2. Deficient demand in both countries		up	down	down	down
3. Excess demand in country B and deficient demand in country A		up	down	down	up
4. Excess demand in country A and deficient demand in country B		up	up	down	down

possible cases of internal imbalance in two large countries, A and B, are shown. Case 1 is where both countries suffer from excess aggregate demand, Case 2 where they both suffer from deficient aggregate demand. The remaining two cases involve combinations of excess and deficient demand in the two countries. The interest adjustment required for the attainment of external and internal balances in each country and case is shown on the right-hand side of Table 17–1, under the assumption that country A has an external deficit and country B has an external surplus.

Case 4 gives no problems to policy makers. In country A both internal and external balance require the raising of the interest rate, and in country B, analogously, the interest rate has to be lowered to achieve both balances. The interest rate differential resulting from these policies causes short-term capital to flow to the country with the trade deficit, so that the adjustment process is aided, as in the laissez-faire model presented above.

Case 1 requires that country A raise the interest rate for the attainment of both external and internal balances, while country B needs a higher interest rate for internal and a lower rate for external balance. If the two countries cooperate and country A raises its rate by a certain amount, country B can raise its rate as well, but not by as much as country A. Thus it creates an interest rate advantage in favor of country A. Under these conditions the classical benefits of international short-term capital flows can be enjoyed, though there is the cost of either or both countries adopting a change in the interest rate by an amount constrained by the need to create the proper international interest rate differential. Therefore, while the direction of interest rate changes is correct for the attainment of balances, the speed of adjustment is likely to be different from ideal. Case 2 is the mirror image of Case 1 and requires no further comment.

Case 3 represents the situation in which a genuine conflict exists between the interest rate changes required for internal and external balance in both countries. If country A lowers the interest rate to increase domestic aggregate demand, and country B raises the interest rate to curtail demand, the interest rate differential created favors country B, which is in balance of payments surplus, and the resultant capital flows aggravate rather than improve international adjustment problems. In a managed economy with fixed exchange rates, therefore, international short-term capital flows are a potential source of instability rather than a tool to aid adjustment. It is important to note that this conflict arises even if, as assumed, capital flows are motivated only by interest arbitrage opportunities and not by speculation.

Speculation

Let us now extend the preceding analysis to include the consideration of international short-term capital flows motivated by the expectation of gains or the avoidance of losses from exchange rate changes, as characterized the 1930s and the IMF parity exchange rate system of the postwar years. Under these conditions it is possible that short-term capital flows do not facilitate but make more difficult the process of dealing with payments imbalances, even in cases where in the preceding analysis they did so, as for example in Case 1 in Table 17–1. In such a situation country A raises its interest rate to constrain excess aggregate demand and simultaneously to attract short-term capital to reduce the payments deficit. However, the higher interest rate may fail to attract the short-term capital if speculators believe that the country will have to devalue its currency in the future because it is low on reserves. In fact, there have been many historic instances where speculators have evidently interpreted the act of raising the interest rate as a signal that a government considers its reserves to be low and in need of support by capital inflows. According to the implied probability of a coming devaluation, speculators then moved funds out of rather than into the country which had raised its interest rate. Under these circumstances, on occasion countries have been forced by the speculation into an exchange rate change which would not have been necessary if the higher interest rate would have had a chance to reduce aggregate demand and the balance of trade deficit, through a time-consuming process of domestic adjustment to the higher cost of borrowing. Countries into which the speculative capital flows moved sometimes found that their purchases of foreign exchange for the maintenance of the exchange rate led to excessively large increases in the money supply and the threat of undesired inflation. Consequently, these surplus countries could be forced by short-term capital flows into an appreciation of their exchange rates which was not warranted by basic balance-of-trade conditions.

Currency revaluations caused by speculative capital flows are inefficient economically, since they require compensating adjustments after the capital flows have been reversed. They are also politically costly, since they affect adversely the welfare of some important segments of the economy, such as workers for whom the prices of imported goods have risen through a devaluation and exporters whose competitive position abroad is reduced by a currency appreciation. Because of these problems arising from short-term capital flows, in the case of conflict as analyzed by Meade as well as under conditions of speculation, most countries have instituted measures to combat undesired international short-term capital flows.

III. METHODS FOR DEALING WITH UNDESIRED SHORT-TERM CAPITAL FLOWS

After World War II agreements were reached to liberalize international trade and free long-term capital flows from the restrictions which had been imposed during the catastrophic economic crises of the 1930s, as individual nations sought to minimize their effects. However, the agreements which led to the establishment of the International Monetary Fund and the reorganization of the international monetary system, to be discussed in Chapter 23, explicitly permitted countries to retain the policies they had developed for dealing with short-term capital flows, even though they involved direct controls and discriminatory interferences with market processes.

The most important of the instruments of control over short-term capital flows can be classed into four groups: foreign exchange control, control over rates of return, forward exchange policy, and international cooperation.

Foreign Exchange Control

A natural by-product of the existence of control systems for all foreign transactions is foreign exchange control over short-term capital flows. When all traders of merchandise, services, and assets are required to report their transactions with the rest of the world to government authorities, it is administratively easy to regulate the purchase or sale of foreign assets for short-term investment. However, even when there are general foreign exchange controls, markets tend to develop methods for avoiding such restrictions. We have already discussed the practice of speeding up or delaying payments and making changes in domestic goods inventories. Furthermore, there are methods of overinvoicing or underinvoicing. Firms and individuals resort to arrangements avoiding use of the foreign exchange market. For example, a U.S. professor who spends a sabbatical year in England may be paid rent on his house in the United States in pound sterling by his tenant, who has sterling assets in England which are subject to exchange control. Authorities cannot keep track of airline tickets bought from a worldwide company in one country with controlled local currency for an international trip and subsequently sold abroad for a currency not subject to such control.

In the late 1960s and early 1970s France and Belgium created two foreign exchange markets, one for the "commercial franc," in which at an officially pegged rate traders in goods and services and long-term assets transact their business, and one for the "financial franc," in which foreign exchange arising from short-term capital transactions was traded at a market-determined rate. Excess demand for foreign exchange from short-term capital exporters tends to appreciate quickly the financial franc rate and therefore to choke off further capital outflows. This two-tier system works when the spread in the rates is not very large. Under these conditions, of course, it is also not needed. When the two markets have widely separate rates, then it becomes profitable to disguise short-term capital flows as commercial or long-term capital transactions. The methods used to exploit such profitability have already been indicated.

Controls over Rates of Return

Controls over rates of return can be employed in the absence of overall foreign exchange registration procedures. They have been used by Germany, Japan, and Switzerland during periods when the currencies of these countries were expected to be appreciated. The governments of Germany, Japan, and Switzerland prohibited banks from accepting deposits by foreigners, required that they pay lower than market interest rates, or actually taxed foreign deposits, depending on the specific circumstances of the times. These regulations generally were not very successful. It is simply too easy to find intermediaries other than banks in these countries who will either channel the funds directly to the banks or who, more legally, will borrow abroad and invest the proceeds in their own name in banks which are unable to accommodate foreigners directly. Furthermore, financial and manufacturing enterprises in the countries which had these regulations tended to vastly expand their own borrowing abroad, which had the same effect on the foreign exchange market as deposits by foreigners. In response to this loophole, laws were passed to restrict borrowing abroad by residents in surplus countries. These laws, in turn, were circumvented by new market responses, as Armin Gutowski of the University of Frankfurt has shown in a case study (1972) of German attempts to control capital inflows.

Forward Exchange Policy

A number of central banks have used forward exchange policy to influence the magnitude and direction of short-term capital flows. The methods of operation and the associated costs of this policy have been discussed in Chapter 12 and need not be developed here. An evaluation of postwar experience of the use of this policy suggests that generally it has the desired effect, and it is a useful weapon in the arsenal of central banks. However, during periods of very strong expectations of a pending currency revaluation, the capital flows affected by the forward exchange policy tend to be a relatively small proportion of spot funds moving without cover, and the troubles for governments arising from the speculator are relieved only marginally by the forward exchange policy.

International Cooperation

In the postwar years, international cooperation has been one of the most effective methods for dealing with international short-term capital movements. This cooperation took the form of official agreements among the major Western countries to extend credit to one another, in case any one country or a group of countries lost excessively large quantities of reserves as a result of foreign exchange market intervention necessitated by short-term capital flows. These agreements were reached within two different international financial associations. During the 1950s the International Monetary Fund (IMF) made available some of its resources to countries whose currencies were under speculative attack. However, these measures were inadequate, and in response to speculative episodes involving the German mark and Dutch guilder in 1961, the countries belonging to the Bank for International Settlements (BIS) in Basel, Switzerland, signed the Basel Agreement. The BIS had been founded after World War I as part of the more general drive toward international cooperation which also saw the creation of the League of Nations. During the wave of nationalism in the 1930s the BIS lost power and influence, but it remained intact as a legal entity and retained a bureaucracy. After World War II it attained new prominence because it permitted more confidential, effective consultation among the large, important industrial nations than did the IMF, with its more than 100 member countries. Nevertheless, the big countries thought it in their own interests, as well as the world's, to strengthen the IMF's ability to deal with short-term capital flows. Thus, in the fall of 1961, the IMF Articles of Agreement were amended by the General Agreement to Borrow. Under it $6 billion were made available by the Group of Ten—Belgium, Canada, France, Germany, Italy, Japan, the Netherlands, Sweden, the United Kingdom, and the United States—to any countries in this group requiring assistance in dealing with short-term capital outflows.

The theory behind this international cooperation is the same as that underlying central bank discounting facilities and deposit insurance programs in individual countries. Bank panics involving deposit withdrawals caused by expected bank failure or liquidity crises often brought about widespread bank failures, which could have been avoided if the public had not lost their confidence in the system. Consequently, central banks, toward the end of the 19th and the beginning of the 20th century, began to make available to banks large quantities of cash through the rediscounting of bills and to protect depositors through insurance against failures by individual banks. Public panic leading to deposit withdrawals soon died out, once it became known publicly that all demands for cash could be met by the banks. The cash withdrawn earlier was redeposited with the banks, which then in turn could repay the advances they had received from the central bank. Under the Basel Agreement and the International Agreement to Borrow, participating nations can draw on very large resources to meet the demands for foreign exchange arising from speculative capital outflows. After a time, when devaluation does not take place, speculative expectations are reversed and the capital returns, and with it the means is provided to repay the loan received from other countries which are members of the agreements.

This method of cooperation for dealing with speculative short-term capital flows works only if the participating countries are in fact willing and able to engage in necessary monetary and fiscal policies to eliminate basic payments deficits after they have run out of the normal means to finance them. After all, the advance of liquidity to a bank cannot save it from bankruptcy if its liabilities exceed its assets and equity. Speculators who note that countries are in persistent basic payments deficits and that they are unwilling or unable to engage in the necessary expenditure-reducing and expenditure-switching policies, therefore, may not be persuaded that a devaluation can be avoided in the longer run, even though the speculative outflows are financed by the funds authorized by the international agreements. Such speculators will not return their money to the country deemed to be facing devaluation, especially if the interest advantage of doing so is small or even negative, and the "temporary" financing may have to be turned into a long-term loan. At this point the purpose of the agreements is perverted, and they lose credibility. In practice, of course, it is difficult to know whether or not policies for expenditure reducing or switching have been initiated with sufficient strength and when they are likely to become effective in eliminating the basic imbalances. Thus, bureaucrats administering the agreements and safeguarding them against abuse are in a difficult position to know when credit should be extended to a given country under speculative attack which is in continued basic external imbalance.

In spite of these difficulties of administering cooperative efforts for dealing with the effects of speculative international capital flows, cooperation and the expansion of the equivalent of rediscounting facilities for countries through the IMF holds the greatest promise for giving countries the freedom to manage their domestic economies and foreign balances, without the constraints imposed by international capital flows motivated by speculative expectations or simple interest rate differentials.

BIBLIOGRAPHICAL NOTES

The classic statement of the problem raised by short-term capital flows for internal and external balance is Meade (1951). Nurkse (1944) and Bloomfield (1950) are major works which analyze the effects of short-term capital flows during the 1930s. Gutowski (1972) reports on the German experience with programs of control on short-term capital inflows.

CONCEPTS FOR REVIEW

Financial franc versus commercial franc

Meade's case of conflict

Welfare-raising versus welfare-reducing short-term capital flows

Methods for controlling short-term capital flows

POINTS FOR FURTHER STUDY AND DISCUSSION

1. Collect quarterly averages of short-term interest rates prevailing during the 1950s, 1960s and 1970s in the United States, Britain, Germany, Canada,

Australia, and Italy. Compute the means and variances of these rates for five-year periods. Has there been a narrowing of the variance? Does this imply increased interdependencies and difficulties in dealing with short-term capital flows?

2. For some major countries find the size of quarterly short-term capital flows through time and express them as fractions of these countries' holdings of reserves, domestic money stocks, and the level of merchandise trade. Do the statistics reveal that the short-term capital flows have become an increasingly more important problem?

3. Compare Germany's regular quarterly increases in its domestic monetary base and its short-term capital inflows between 1965 and 1975. Do the data reveal that foreign exchange market opeations caused by capital flows have resulted in Germany's loss of control over its money supply?

18

Internal and External Balance through the Mix of Monetary and Fiscal Policy

IN THE KEYNESIAN MODEL of income determination presented in Chapter 16, there were assumed to be no money, interest rate, foreign exchange market, and international short-term capital flows. In the present chapter we amend this basic Keynesian model to include all four of these important influences on income. To do so we draw on the well-known Keynesian *LM–IS* curve analysis and amend it through the incorporation of a foreign exchange market. This model is presented in detail and with the help of some simple equations and four-sector diagrams in the Appendix to this chapter. In the main body of the text we present only verbal arguments to explain the slopes and shifts of the *LM–IS–FE* curves and the nature of equilibrium.

The main applications of this Keynesian model of income determination demonstrate first how automatic adjustments tend to return the system to equilibrium after it has been disturbed; second, how monetary and fiscal policy can be mixed to attain simultaneously internal and external balance (even in Meade's problem Case 3 discussed in the preceding chapter), and third, how a small country has to deal with the problems raised by the existence of a perfectly elastic supply curve of foreign short-term capital. The chapter concludes with a number of criticisms which have been made of the monetary-fiscal policy mix models.

The analysis to be presented in this chapter is central to an understanding of much of the foreign economic policy discussion in the postwar years. The governments of many countries often have sacrificed full-employment objectives in order to restore balance-of-payments equilibrium, while maintaining a fixed exchange rate, and academic economists have argued, on the basis of the *LM–IS–FE* model, that a proper mix of monetary and fiscal policy would make it unnecessary to accept anything less than full employment. By presenting the essence of the Keynesian postwar policy prescription, this chapter helps set the stage for the revolutionary criticism of Keynesian economics in the international sphere which has emanated from the so-called monetarist interpretation of the balance of payments. This position will be presented in the next chapter.

I. UNDERSTANDING THE *LM–IS–FE* MODEL

The discussion to follow is based on the more rigorous analysis found in the Appendix to this chapter, which students may wish to consult for a really thorough understanding of the *LM–IS–FE* model. The model is best considered in the context of Figure 18–1, in which income and the interest rate in the large country, A, are measured along the horizontal and vertical

FIGURE 18–1
Income Determination with *LM, IS,* and *FE* Curves

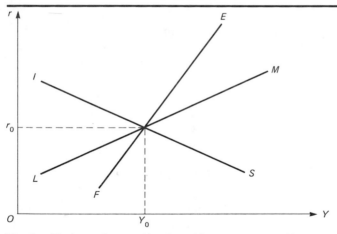

The line *IS* shows the combination of interest rates and income at which savings and investment are equal. The function is sloped negatively because investment and savings are low at high interest rates and low incomes, while they are high at low interest rates and high incomes.

The line *LM* shows the combination of interest rates and income at which the money market is in equilibrium. This condition requires that the supply of money equal the sum of demand for liquidity and transactions purposes. The function slopes upward because, given the supply of money, high speculative demand for money at low interest rates requires low transactions demand at low income; when interest rates are high, speculative demand is low, and income and transactions demand can be high.

The line *FE* shows the combination of interest rates and income at which the foreign exchange market is in balance. The function is sloped positively because at low income, net imports are low and the small amount of short-term capital required for balance can be attracted at low interest rates. High income levels lead to large net imports and require high interest rates and capital inflows.

Equilibrium in all three markets is found where all three schedules intersect at one point (r_0, Y_0).

axes, respectively. We will explain the nature and slopes of the three curves shown and analyze how exchange rate changes affect their positions in the graph.

The *IS* curve shown in Figure 18–1 reflects the combinations of income and the interest rate at which the goods market in country A is in equilibrium. The curve slopes downward because at high interest rates, investment is low and is equal to savings only at a low level of income, while at low interest rates investment is high and equals savings at high income levels. In a model with a foreign and a government sector, such as we are using here, this familiar functional relationship needs to be expanded, and investment is considered more generally to reflect injections into the income stream consisting of domestic investment, exports, and government spending for stabilization purposes. In such an expanded model, savings reflect leakages from the income stream in the form of savings and imports. Exports and imports are assumed to be determined by the exchange rate, given costs of production in country A and the rest of the world, for reasons discussed in preceding chapters. A devaluation increases exports and therefore injections and decreases imports and therefore leakages, leading to a shift of the *IS* curve upward and to the right. Fiscal policy stimulation through an increase in government spending also shifts the *IS* curve upward and to the right.

The *LM* curve in Figure 18–1 shows the combination of interest rates and income at which the financial market of country A is in equilibrium. The *LM* curve slopes upward and to the right for several reasons. First, at a high interest rate, the opportunity cost of holding money balances for speculative and precautionary purposes is high, and the public demands less money for these purposes than at a lower interest rate. Second, the demand for transactions balances is an increasing function of income. Therefore, the given money supply and the demand for money for speculative-precautionary purposes and transactions balances are equal only when income is high and the interest rate is high or when income is low and the interest rate is low. An exchange rate devaluation shifts the *LM* curve upward and to the left, on the grounds that the devaluation causes an increase in the price level through higher prices of tradable goods. At the higher price level the public demands more money for transactions purposes, which can be obtained from speculative-precautionary money holdings only through a higher interest rate. Therefore, after a devaluation equality in the demand for and supply of money can be achieved only if at any given level of income the interest rate is higher than it was before the devaluation. An increase in the money supply causes a shift downward and to the right of the *LM* curve, because at any given interest rate and demand for speculative balances, more money is available to finance transactions demand balances and a higher level of income.

The *FE* curve in Figure 18–1 indicates the combination of interest rates and income at which excess demand for foreign exchange is zero because an imbalance on trade account is matched by an imbalance of the opposite sign on the capital account. This curve slopes upward and to the right because at a given exchange rate, imports and the difference between imports and exports are an increasing function of income, while short-term capital inflows are an increasing function of the interest rate. Therefore, overall excess demand for foreign exchange is zero only when the interest rate and income are both low or when they are both high. The *FE* curve shifts downward and to the right when the currency is devalued because at any given level of income the trade balance is more positive or less negative, and the foreign exchange market balance requires a lower interest rate to induce the needed greater outflow of capital if the balance is positive or smaller inflow if it is negative. The *FE* schedule is not shifted by either monetary or fiscal policy.

In Figure 18–1 we have drawn the *FE* schedule with a steeper slope than the *LM* curve. There are some theoretical justifications for this, but to develop them here would lead us too far from our main purposes of analysis. The principal reason for assuming the *FE* curve is steeper than the *LM* curve is pragmatic, because only under these conditions does the system give economically meaningful results. As we have noted, a devaluation causes the *FE* curve to shift downward and to the right and the *LM* curve, to shift upward and to the left. Under the assumed relative slopes of the *LM* and *FE* curves, the new intersection between the two curves is to the right and above the original one. If the slopes were reversed, the new intersection would be to the left and below the original one. But we know as a general proposition from simpler Keynesian models that a devaluation increases net injections and drives the system toward a higher level of income and, with a given money supply, to a higher interest rate. Therefore only the assumed relative slopes of the *LM* and *FE* curves yield economically meaningful results. In a sense this restriction imposed on the relative slopes of the two curves is analogous to the one well known from closed-economy model building, which postulates that the marginal propensity to consume out of income must be less than 1. Without this restriction the entire Keynesian model of income determination produces economically meaningless results.

In the *LM–IS–FE* framework of analysis, complete equilibrium exists only if all three schedules intersect at the same point, as in Figure 18–1, resulting in r_0 and Y_0 equilibrium values. If such an equilibrium condition does not exist, there must be three intersections of the three linear functions. In the following analysis we shall assume that if total equilibrium does not exist and there are three intersections of the curves, the level of income and the interest rate in country A are determined in the domestic goods and money markets, that is, through the intersection of the *LM* and

IS curves. Consequently, it is always the foreign exchange market that is in disequilibrium and adjusts or causes adjustment, through a mechanism to be discussed next.

II. AUTOMATIC ADJUSTMENT MECHANISMS

The objective of our analysis in this section is to explain the way in which, according to the *LM–IS–FE* model, the economy has an automatic tendency to move toward complete equilibrium in all three markets if the foreign exchange market is out of equilibrium. The insights from this exercise are important for understanding the causes of perpetual balance-of-payment disequilibria in the real world, because if the system has a tendency toward such automatic adjustment and equilibrium is not being reached, then some government policies must be preventing it. The mechanism of the model permits us to show precisely which policy actions prevent the economy from reaching equilibrium. Finally, the exercises of this section prepare us for an appreciation of the next section, in which we show how monetary and fiscal policy can be used to maintain internal and external equilibrium in a world of first, fixed exchange rates and second, perfectly elastic capital flows.

Let us assume that in Figure 18–2 the economy is in equilibrium initially at point A, with income Y_0 and the interest rate r_0. Now consider that at Y_0 there is unemployment and that it is the desire of the government to use monetary policy to move to full employment at Y_1. Alternatively, we could assume that some change in public preference for holding money has taken place. In either case, the *LM* curve is shifted to $L'M'$. According to our assumption above, the domestic goods and money markets move into equilibrium quickly at point B, with Y_1 and r_1, but the foreign exchange market is in disequilibrium of the following type.

If at r_0 and Y_0 there is zero excess demand for foreign exchange, then at the lower interest rate less capital is attracted into country A (or more flows out), and at the higher income the trade deficit is worsened (or surplus is reduced). Therefore, with *FE* remaining in its initial position, there is a balance-of-payments deficit if the domestic economy is at point B. This deficit leads to excess demand for foreign exchange, and if the government lets the exchange rate depreciate, the *FE* schedule is shifted downward and the right, to $F'E'$; the *LM* schedule is shifted upward and left, to $L''M''$; and the *IS* schedule is shifted upward and right, to $I'S'$, for reasons discussed above. The new complete equilibrium point C shown in Figure 18–2 is at Y_2 and, for expositional simplicity, at the initial interest rate r_0.

The main point of the analysis is that exchange rate adjustment must bring about equilibrium in all three markets, because unless the balance of payments is zero, an excess demand for foreign exchange continues to

FIGURE 18–2

Automatic Adjustment Mechanism

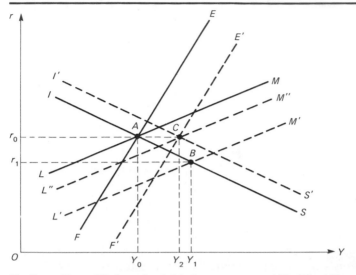

Starting with equilibrium at point A, the exogenous shift of the LM curve to L'M' moves the system to point B, under the assumption that in disequilibrium the intersection of the LM and IS curves always determines the system's location. At the new income and interest rate (Y_1 and r_1) there must be a balance-of-payments deficit, since payments were balanced at the initial equilibrium (Y_0 and r_0). If the payments imbalance is allowed to force a depreciation of the exchange rate, then the FE curve shifts to F'E' (due to smaller net imports); the IS curve is shifted upward to I'S' (due to smaller net leakages in the foreign trade sector); and the LM curve is shifted upward and to the left to L"M" (due to an increase in the price level induced by the exchange rate depreciation, which in turn increases the transactions demand for money). Point C is equilibrium only if the foreign exchange market is balanced. Persistent foreign exchange market disequilibria are possible only if the exchange rate is not permitted to change.

lead to exchange rate depreciation and shifts in the LM and IS curves until the payments deficit is eliminated. The complete equilibrium attained by this process need not be one of full employment, and the attainment of this objective may require further doses of monetary policy expansion. However, it is intuitively obvious that through appropriate changes in monetary policy and exchange rate adjustments, complete equilibrium can be reached at full employment. If, in the face of the initial payments deficit at point B, the government maintains the exchange rate at its initial level and meets the excess demand for foreign exchange in the market by selling exchange from its reserves, country A's money supply in the hands of the private sector is reduced automatically. Accordingly, the LM curve is shifted upward and to the left until the original equilibrium position at r_0 and Y_0 is reestablished.

From this analysis we can reach two important conclusions. First, if a given deficit persists, it does so because the government prevents either the exchange rate from depreciating, the money supply from being reduced, or both. In all instances, therefore, the government policies prevent adjustment through deliberate action. Second, the analysis implies that a country in external balance but internal imbalance through underemployment, as at Y_0, generally needs to engage in expenditure switching through devaluation and expenditure changing through monetary policy if it wishes to attain simultaneously internal and external balance, assuming that expenditure changing can be undertaken only through monetary policy. The conclusion reached in Chapter 16 with the help of the Swan diagram and the Keynesian model without money therefore carries over into the model with money, though the next section is devoted to the analysis of the problem when both monetary and fiscal policy can be used for expenditure changing.

All of the preceding analysis can be applied with slight modifications to disequilibrium situations caused by random or policy-induced shifts in the IS or FE curve. We will not present such exercises here in order to save space, though students may find it a useful test of their understanding of the model by working through a graph and specifying the shifts of the curves accompanying automatic pressures on the exchange rates and the money supply in the different disequilibrium situations. By analogy, the same results can also be produced by postulating initial payments surpluses rather than deficits.

III. MONETARY AND FISCAL POLICY WITH FIXED EXCHANGE RATES

We now come to one of the best known applications of the *LM–IS–FE* model. Pioneered by Marcus Fleming of the International Monetary Fund and stated most elegantly by Robert Mundell of Columbia University, this analysis created much interest among policy makers during the 1960s, and it has led to a large body of academic writings expanding and refining the basic model. The main point of our brief summary of the arguments will be to demonstrate that countries can maintain a fixed exchange rate and attain simultaneously internal and external balance by applying monetary and fiscal policy in a proper mix.

To undertake this demonstration, let us consider that country A is originally in equilibrium at point A with r_0 and Y_0 in Figure 18–3, but that full employment is at Y_1, above Y_0. In the preceding section we showed that using monetary policy alone required an exchange rate change to reach full employment and external balance. Now we assume that the exchange rate is fixed, leaving the FE curve in its initial position in Figure 18–3. Under these conditions, internal and external balance can be attained by moving the system to point B, which is on the original FE curve

FIGURE 18–3
Mix of Monetary and Fiscal Policy

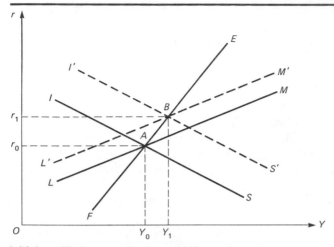

Initial equilibrium at point A (r_0 and Y_0) is assumed to represent underemployment. The economy can be moved to full employment, Y_1, without a change in the exchange rate by expansionary fiscal and restrictive monetary policies, which shift the IS and LM curves to $I'S'$ and $L'M'$, respectively. The new point of equilibrium, B, is on the FE curve, which has not been shifted, and produces full employment (Y_1) at the higher interest rate (r_1).

and is associated with full employment. Monetary and fiscal policy must then be used to shift the LM and IS curves and force them to go through point B. As can be seen from Figure 18–3, in the situation drawn there monetary policy needs to be restrictive and fiscal policy expansionary to reach $L'M'$ and $I'S'$. At point B internal and external equilibria are attained, and short-term capital flows, instead of giving rise to a policy dilemma, are used explicitly to achieve these two objectives.

We can illustrate an important principle of the theory of economic policy with the help of the internal-external balance and monetary fiscal policy model. This principle, developed first by Jan Tinbergen of the Netherlands, states that if governments wish to attain a given set of policy objectives it is necessary that the number of policy instruments equal the number of policy targets. In the last formulation of the internal-external balance problem, the two policies, of course, are monetary and fiscal policy. In the formulation of the internal-external balance problem in the preceding chapter without short-term capital flows, the two policies were expenditure switching and expenditure changing. By distinguishing monetary and fiscal policy as two different methods for changing expenditures, it is possible to relinquish the use of the policy instrument of expenditure switching. The same principle can be seen to operate under the assumptions that the level of the interest rate in a country affects its growth rate and that the growth rate is added as a third policy target to internal and external balance. Under these conditions it is necessary to add exchange rate changes to monetary and fiscal policy to be able to achieve all three targets simultaneously.

In the advanced literature on the monetary-fiscal policy mix we can find discussions of what Robert Mundell has called the assignment problem. It elaborates on the preceding analysis by considering a world in which the two government authorities responsible for carrying on monetary and fiscal policy do not communicate with each other and pursue in successive discrete steps only one of the two specific targets assigned to them in advance. For example, fiscal policy is used to attain internal balance only and does not take into consideration the state of the external balance, and vice versa for monetary policy. It turns out that under this code of behavior the economy may not be moved toward but away from internal and external balance, depending on the interest elasticity of capital flows and a host of other conditions. Students interested in this problem are referred to readings suggested at the end of this chapter. We can note, however, that the practical relevance of the assignment problem is not very great, because in most countries there are continuous consultations between treasurers responsible for fiscal policy and central banks responsible for monetary policy. At the very least, central banks which can vary monetary policy smoothly and continuously try to do so, keeping in mind both internal and external balance and the effect on aggregate demand generated by existing or anticipated fiscal policy actions.

IV. PROBLEMS OF THE SMALL COUNTRY

In the preceding model we have assumed that a country faces a given supply elasticity of short term capital, so that at the prevailing world interest rate a certain difference in the domestic and world rates causes a determinate, finite capital flow which can be used to maintain external balance in the manner analyzed. However, in the postwar world technological improvements and falling costs in communication and travel have induced the growth of institutions which have brought many of the smaller countries of Western Europe and of other parts of the world to the point where the demand and supply elasticities they face are extremely high. Mundell has used the *LM–IS–FE* model to analyze the problem of attaining internal and external balance in a country in which, in the extreme, the elasticity of supply of and demand for short-term capital is infinity, at the rate prevailing in the world. In Figure 18–4 we show a country in such a situation, with the *FE* curve horizontal at r_0. Let us now consider that initial equilibrium is at point A, with income at Y_0, which is below full employment, and that the country wishes to move to full em-

FIGURE 18–4
The Small-Country Problem

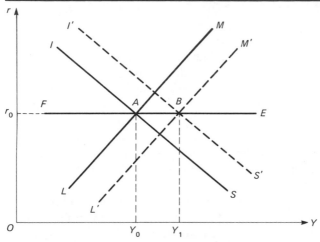

A small country has a perfectly elastic *FE* schedule, as shown, because at the world interest rate Or_0, infinite quantities of capital can be imported or exported. Such a country can move from Y_0 to Y_1 only by fiscal policy if it has a fixed exchange rate and only by monetary policy if it has a freely floating exchange rate.

ployment at Y_1. The analysis proceeds under the assumptions first, that exchange rates are fixed, and second, that they are floating freely.

Fixed Exchange Rates Case

Monetary policy shifts the *LM* curve in Figure 18–4 to $L'M'$ and, according to the intersection between the *IS* and $L'M'$ curves, causes downward pressures on the interest rate which, because of the perfect elasticity of the foreign short-term capital demand-supply curve, cannot be realized. Instead, short-term capital leaves the country and causes an excess demand for foreign exchange, which under the commitment to the fixed exchange rate is met by government sales of foreign exchange. But, since the sale of the foreign exchange causes a reduction in the domestic money supply, the *LM* curve is shifted upward and to the left. This process of excess demand for foreign exchange, government intervention, and money supply reduction continues until the *LM* curve is returned to its initial position. In the new equilibrium the small country finds that the net effect of its expansionary monetary policy is that its loss of official reserves is precisely matched by private holdings of short-term assets abroad. If the monetary authorities attempt to maintain the increased money stock through sterilization of the effects of the foreign exchange market intervention on the money supply, the capital outflows continue until the country runs out of reserves, at which point it has to give up the fixed exchange rate, sterilization policy, or expansionary monetary policy.

Let us now consider that the small country committed to a fixed exchange rate decides to use fiscal policy for the attainment of full employment, Y_1. In terms of Figure 18–4, the fiscal policy shifts up and to the right the IS curve, to $I'S'$, and according to its intersection with the LM curve causes an upward pressure on the interest rate. But because the supply elasticity of foreign short-term capital is infinite, the interest rate cannot rise, and instead capital flows into the country. This capital inflow at the fixed exchange rate requires the official purchase of foreign exchange to absorb the excess supply and leads to a corresponding increase in the domestic money supply. As a result, the LM curve is shifted outward until it is at the intersection point B. The new equilibrium in all three markets is at full employment income, Y_1. We therefore reach the important conclusion that a small country which is facing a perfectly elastic demand and supply curve for foreign short-term capital and which maintains a fixed exchange rate can use fiscal policy only to affect its level of income.

Freely Floating Rates Case

If a small country with a perfectly elastic capital demand-supply schedule and freely floating exchange rates uses expansionary monetary policy, the LM curve is shifted outward and to the right, to $L'M'$, and downward pressure is created on the interest rate. The result is short-term capital outflows and depreciation of the exchange rate. Remember from the preceding sections of this chapter that the exchange rate depreciation shifts the IS curve outward. The process of downward pressure on the interest rate, capital outflows, and exchange rate depreciation ceases only when the intersection between the IS and LM curves is on the FE schedule. In earlier analysis we have seen that the exchange rate change also leads to a shift of the LM curve upward and to the left. Overall equilibrium therefore tends to take place at an income level below that reached by the initial intersection between the shifted LM and the stationary FE curves. However, further changes in the money supply can be undertaken to reach complete equilibrium at any desired level of income. In practice, there may be difficulties encountered in finding the proper level of monetary policy, but the preceding analysis shows clearly that a small country with freely floating exchange rates can reach full employment through the use of monetary policy.

On the other hand, if such a country uses fiscal expansion in an attempt to shift the IS curve in Figure 18–4 to $I'S'$, the result is upward pressure on the interest rate, capital inflows, and an appreciation of the exchange rate which shifts the IS curve back until it is in its original equilibrium position. Fiscal policy cannot achieve a permanent increase in equilibrium income.

The preceding analysis leads us to the conclusion that a small country facing a perfectly elastic demand-supply schedule for foreign short-term capital to achieve full employment can use only fiscal policy if it maintains a fixed exchange rate and monetary policy under freely floating exchange rates. If it uses the false policies under the two different exchange rate regimes, market processes are generated to offset the initial effects of the monetary or fiscal policy.

V. CRITICISMS OF THE MONETARY-FISCAL POLICY MIX MODELS

The use of the monetary-fiscal policy mix models just presented in the real world during the 1960s has been constrained by a special characteristic of fiscal policy. In democratic countries of the West, fiscal policy changes are slow and hampered by the need to ask legislatures to enact changes in tax rates and government expenditures. Since the tax changes and government expenditures affect different interest groups in the economy differentially, the political process is used to assure equity and efficiency. This political process works slowly and unreliably. Consequently, it has been and is difficult to obtain the level of fiscal ease or restraint required theoretically, at the time and intensity when needed to achieve the benefits attainable by the proper use of monetary and fiscal policy in combination.

On a more technical level, the idea of dealing with the conflict between internal and external balance through the proper mix of monetary and fiscal policy has come under criticism on two basic grounds. The first of these will be discussed in Chapter 19; it centers more generally on the validity of the Keynesian income-determination models in the longer run. The second basic criticism applies only to the monetary-fiscal policy mix problem and focuses on the fact that the balance of payments is a flow, while capital flows lead to changes in the size of stocks of assets and to correspondingly changing costs of interest payments.

More precisely, the analysis of the adjustment mechanism in a world with money and short-term capital flows just discussed implies that in any given position where all three markets are in equilibrium, the flows of income, investment, exports, imports, and so are repeated period after period. When there is an equilibrium which equalizes the value of exports and imports, there is no reason why it cannot be maintained for an indefinite length of time. In terms of concepts developed in earlier parts of this book, under these conditions country A's absorption of real goods and services just matches its full-capacity output. However, let us now consider a case where, according to the *LM–IS–FE* analysis, there is equilibrium in all three markets, but the country runs a deficit on current account which is just matched by an inflow of capital. The country absorbs more real goods and services than it can produce. Such a condition cannot be sustained in the long run because period after period the deficit is matched by an increase in short-term obligations toward the rest of the world. Long before these obligations have reached infinity, two processes assert themselves.

First, the rest of the world's own stock of short-term capital will be run down, and diminishing returns to lending to country A will set in. The larger the stock of capital already borrowed, the greater is the interest differential required to attract the capital required to match a given-sized current account deficit. In the real world, of course, there are institutional limits on the interest rate which can be generated domestically, without causing serious problems for domestic investment and housing and ultimately for the growth rate. For these reasons, it is misleading to consider the intersection of the *LM*, *IS*, and *FE* curves, even at full employment, to be necessarily a genuine equilibrium. Except when trade is balanced, the flow equilibrium of the *LM*, *IS*, and *FE* curves implies a stock disequilibrium and it is therefore not sustainable.

Second, as the stock of foreign capital held by country A increases, the interest payments to be made abroad grow rapidly, even if the interest rate remains unchanged. For example, consider that one country has a trade deficit requiring a capital inflow of $100 per year and that the interest rate is 10 percent per year. In the second period already the interest payments are $10, and it is necessary to attract $110 to meet the excess demand for foreign exchange. In the third period the obligations to foreigners are $210, the interest payments required are $21, and it is necessary to attract $121 rather than just $100, as the simple model implies. Most students are familiar with the properties of compound interest, which we see at work here in the rapid increase in the debt-service obligation and stock of indebtedness. In the analytical framework of this chapter (especially Figure 18–1), this interest payment requirement implies a shift upward and to the left of the *FE* curve through time. The intersection of the *LM*, *IS*, and *FE* curves in Figure 18–1 is only a flow, not a stock equilibrium.

We conclude from the preceding criticism of the monetary-fiscal policy mix model for the resolution of the internal-external balance problem that the policy prescriptions resulting from this model are valid only in the short run. In the longer run we return to the fundamental proposition of our analysis in the preceding chapter, that every country must match its domestic absorption expenditures to its productive capacity. Money, interest rates, and short-term capital flows make it possible for an individual country to disregard this fundamental truth in the short run only.

APPENDIX

Derivation of the *LM*, *IS*, and *FE* Curves

In Figure 18A–1 we show a diagram consisting of four sectors labeled A–D. It is used to derive the functional relationship between income (Y) and the interest rate (r) at which the goods market in small-country A is in equilibrium, in the sense that the withdrawals from the income stream through domestic savings and imports are equal to the injections into the expenditure stream, consisting of domestic investment, government expenditures, and exports.

FIGURE 18A–1
Derivation of the *IS* Curve

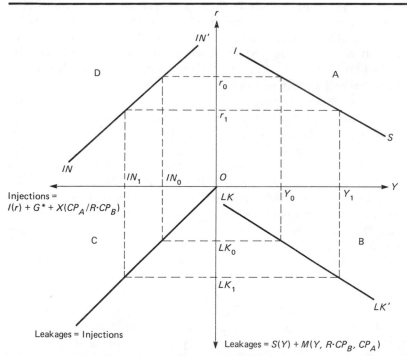

In Sector B the *LKLK'* schedule shows the functional relationship between income and total leakages, consisting of savings and imports, which is positive because both savings and imports are an increasing function of income. Sector C shows the equilibrium condition that leakages equal injections. In Sector D the *ININ'* schedule shows that injections are a decreasing function of the interest rate. The *IS* schedule in Sector A gives the combination of interest rates and income at which goods markets are in equilibrium, or in other words, injections equal leakages. The equations showing the determinants of leakages and injections indicate that both are a function of the exchange rate. A depreciation shifts upward the leakage and injection schedules and therefore the *IS* schedule.

In Sector B we plot the positive functional relationship between income and leakages (LK), given by the equation:

$$LK = S(Y) + M(\overset{+}{Y}, \overset{-}{R \cdot CP_B}, \overset{+}{CP_A}) \qquad (18A–1)$$

where S and M represent savings and imports, respectively; the symbols in parentheses denote functional dependence; Y is income; $R \cdot CP_B$ is the exchange rate times the cost of production in country B; and CP_A is the cost of production in country A. The signs above the symbols indicate the sign of the partial derivative and should be interpreted as in the following example. The equation shows that imports are an increasing function of income and of the cost of production in country A and a decreasing function of the foreign cost of production times the exchange rate. A rise in R means a devaluation of country A's currency and a decrease in imports, which is consistent with earlier analysis in this book. In principle the leakage function can be measured for every country.

In Sector D of Figure 18A–1 we show that injections into the income stream (IN) decrease with the interest rate, where the injections are the sum of domestic investment (I), government expenditures for purposes of fiscal stabilization (G), and exports (X):

$$IN = I(\overset{-}{r}) + G + X(\overset{-}{CP_A/R}, \overset{+}{CP_B}) \qquad (18A–2)$$

According to Equation (18–2), domestic investment is a decreasing function of the interest rate, and exports are an increasing function of the foreign cost of production and a decreasing function of the ratio of the domestic cost of production over the exchange rate. The latter relationship implies that if costs of production in countries A and B are unchanged but the exchange rate is depreciated (that is, R increases), then the ratio decreases in value and exports rise, which is consistent with our earlier analysis. The level of G in Equation (18–2) is determined by policy, which may be represented as:

$$G = G^*, \qquad (18A–3)$$

where the asterisk indicates the level of government expenditures incurred for fiscal policy purposes. By introducing government expenditures and fiscal policy in this manner, we simplify the analysis as compared with what it would have to be if there were government expenditures matched to some extent by tax receipts. Starting from any level of G in this model, an increase in G means fiscal stimulus and a decrease means fiscal ease. When the government runs a deficit or surplus in its budget through the fiscal policy, we assume that it sells or buys securities in the private market. The effect of these security transactions on the rate of interest is assumed to be offset completely and automatically by required changes in the money supply.

The equilibrium condition in the goods market is given by the familiar equation:

$$Y = C + I + G + (X - M), \qquad (18A-4)$$

which can be rewritten as implying the equality between leakages and injections into the income stream:

$$I + G + X = S + M \qquad (18A-5)$$

This rewriting uses the fact that by definition

$$S = Y - C, \qquad (18A-6)$$

and substitutes this expression in Equation (18A–4) to derive (18A–5). Sector C in Figure 18A–1 contains a 45-degree line which assures equality in the values of leakages and injections.

We are now ready to derive the IS function in Sector A of Figure 18A–1, which represents the combination of interest rates and income at which the goods market is in equilibrium, in the sense that the income received by the public in country A and matched by an equal value of production is used up for consumption, investment, government expenditures, and net exports, as indicated in Equation (18–4). We call this function the IS curve in regard for the tradition developed in the derivation of the closed-economy model that the equilibrium condition requires only equality between savings and investments, even though in the open-economy model it requires equality between total injections into, and leakages out of, the expenditure stream. The derivation of the IS curve can be started by considering, in Figure 18A–1, that at the income OY_0, the sum of leakages is OLK_0. In order to have an equal amount of injections, we move horizontally to the 45-degree line from OLK_0 and vertically up from there to the injections axis. There we note that the equilibrium amount of injections, OIN_0, is forthcoming only at an interest rate Or_0. Therefore, the interest rate consistent with OY_0 income is Or_0. The preceding analysis can be repeated for other income levels, such as OY_1. The conclusion emerges that the IS curve is sloping downward and to the right, as the one shown in Figure 18A–1, Sector A. Under the simplifying assumption that the leakage and injection functions are linear, the IS curve is linear also, and therefore its entire length can be found by plotting just two points, as we have done.

The LM Curve. In Figure 18A–2 the LM curve represents equilibrium in the monetary sector of country A. In Sector B we plot the demand for money as an increasing function of income, KK', on the grounds that the public on average holds a sum of money for transaction purposes which is a constant fraction of real income:

$$MT = MT(\overset{+}{Y/P_A}), \qquad (18A-7)$$

FIGURE 18A–2
Derivation of the *LM* Curve

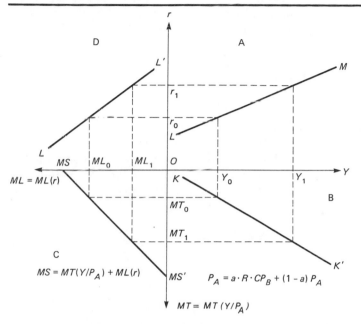

In Sector B the *KK'* schedule shows the demand for transactions balances as an increasing function of income. In Sector C the line *MSMS'* indicates the combinations of money used for transactions and liquidity purposes which adds up to the total money supply, *OMS = OMS'*. The schedule *LL'* in Sector D shows that the liquidity demand for money is a decreasing function of the interest rate. The *LM* curve in Sector A plots the combination of interest rates and income at which the given supply of money equals the sum of the liquidity and transactions demand. The equations in Sectors C and D show that the link between the *LM* curve and the exchange rate runs from the effect of the exchange rate on country A's price level and through the price level on the transactions demand for money. A depreciation shifts the *LM* curve upward and to the left.

where MT is the quantity of money demanded for transactions and P_A is the price level in country A. The price level is related to the cost of production in countries A and B through the equation

$$P_A = a \cdot R \cdot CP_B + (1 - a)(P_A), \qquad (18A–8)$$

where a is the proportion of total goods in the price index represented by traded goods. For example, assume that initially costs of production in both countries are at 100, $a = 20$, and the exchange rate is 1, given $P_A = 100$. Now assume that country A devalues its currency by 10 percent, making $R = 1.1$, all else remaining unchanged, including a. Under these conditions the price level in country A rises to 102 because the prices of traded goods have gone up by 10 percent, but since the traded goods represent only one fifth of the total in country A's price-determining market of goods, the increase in the price level is only one fifth of 10 percent, namely 2 percent. The relationships between the price level in country A, the costs of production in countries A and B, and the exchange rate presented here play an important role in understanding the operation of the adjustment mechanism in the *LM–IS–FE* framework and in some recent controversies over the role of money to be discussed in the next chapter. The formulation presented here captures the essence of the analysis, even though it is unrealistic to assume that a is a constant.

Returning to Figure 18A–2, in Sector D we plot the demand for money for liquidity purposes as a decreasing function of the interest rate, LL', on the grounds that the holding of money for speculation on future interest rate changes and as a precaution against unforeseen contingencies is increasingly more expensive, the higher the interest rate. Rationally, therefore, the public demands smaller money balances for speculation and precaution, the higher is their opportunity cost. The equation representing this function is

$$ML = ML(\overset{-}{r}), \tag{18A–9}$$

where *ML* is the demand for money for speculation and precautionary purposes. In Sector C the line labeled $MSMS'$ represents the total quantity of money in existence in the economy which can be used either for transactions or speculative precautionary purposes, as is implied by the equation

$$MS = MT(\overset{+}{Y/P_A}) + ML(\overset{-}{r}), \tag{18A–10}$$

where *MS* is the money supply. The money supply is assumed to be determined by government policy,

$$MS = MS^* \tag{18A–10a}$$

We find the relationship between the interest rate and income at which the money market is in equilibrium by considering that at the income level OY_0 transactions demand for money is OMT_0, leaving at the given money supply OML_0 for speculative-precautionary purposes, which in turn is demanded only at interest rate Or_0. Equilibrium therefore is at income OY_0 and the interest rate Or_0. By analogy we can derive other points on the *LM* curve, such as by starting with OY_1. We find that the points of equilibrium in the money market lie on the line *LM*, representing an increasing functional relationship between income and the interest rate.

The FE Curve. In Figure 18A–3 the FE curve represents equilibrium in the foreign exchange market in the sense that the excess demand for foreign exchange arising from trade is just matched by the supply of foreign exchange accruing through the inflow of short-term capital. In cases where there is excess supply of foreign exchange arising from a positive trade balance, there are capital outflows, and the resultant demand for exchange creates balance in the exchange market. We derive this

FIGURE 18A–3
Derivation of the *FE* Curve

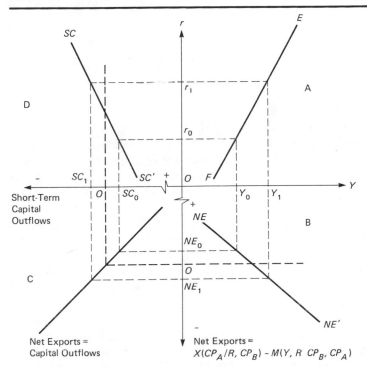

The line *NENE'* in Sector B shows that net exports are a decreasing function of income, while the line *SCSC'* in Sector D shows that short-term capital outflows are a decreasing function of the country's interest rate. The 45-degree line in Sector C indicates the equilibrium condition of equality between net exports and capital outflows. Foreign exchange market equilibrium is shown in Sector A by the increasing functional relationship between the interest rate and income. The exchange rate enters the net exports schedule through its effects on exports and imports, as can be seen from the equation in Sector B. A depreciation shifts downward and to the right the *FE* schedule.

equilibrium condition by considering that net exports, *NENE'*, are a decreasing function of income, for reasons discussed in the preceding chapter and in connection with Equations 18A–1 and 18–12 and formalized in the equation:

$$NE = X(\overset{-}{CP_A/R}, \overset{+}{CP_B}) - M(\overset{+}{Y}, \overset{-}{R \cdot CP_B}, \overset{+}{CP_A}) \qquad (18A\text{–}11)$$

The innovation in drawing Sector B of Figure 18A–3 is that, in contrast with the other four-sector diagrams presented above, there are negative and positive values of the net export function, necessitating the drawing of a dotted reference line at zero net exports. For analogous reasons there are such zero reference lines in Sectors C and D of Figure 18A–3. Now in

Sector D we plot the increasing functional relationship between the interest rate and short-term capital outflows, $SCSC'$, which reflects the equation

$$SC = SC(\bar{r}) \tag{18A-12}$$

where SC is the short-term capital outflows. As can be seen from Figure 18A–3, Sector D, these outflows are positive at a low interest rate and negative at a high interest rate, where the latter case, of course, represents a capital inflow. The slope of this schedule reflects the interest elasticity of short-term capital, which is determined by institutional factors.

The FE schedule is derived simply now by considering that at an income of OY_0, net exports are ONE_0, which are matched by OSC_0 capital outflows at an interest rate Or_0. Repeating the same process for OY, we find the FE curve in Sector A as an increasing function between income and the interest rate.

In the specification of the FE curve above we stipulated the equilibrium condition that there be no excess demand for foreign exchange, so that $SC = NE$. It is worth mentioning here that it is possible instead to define a payments balance function (B) which may be either positive or negative, depending on whether the country wishes to accumulate or decumulate international reserves. Under these conditions, equilibrium is $B = SC - NE$, and the function in Figure 18A–3, Sector A, would be called the BB' curve. However, to keep the present analysis simple and make it relevant directly to the question of internal-external balance through the proper mix of monetary and fiscal policy, we retain the definition of foreign exchange market balance as one where private excess demand for foreign exchange is zero.

Shifts of the Curves.   Shifts of the curves can be explained most readily by summarizing the equilibrium conditions in the three markets, as follows. In the goods market the equilibrium condition is equality between Equations (18A–1) and (18A–2), that is leakages and injections:

$$S(Y) + M(Y, R \cdot CP_B, CP_A) = I(r) + G + X(CP_A/R, CP_B) \tag{18A-13}$$

For the money market the analogous condition is that the money supply equals the demand for money, from Equations (18A–9) and (18A–10):

$$MS = ML(r) + MT[Y/(a \cdot R \cdot CP_B + (1 - a)(P_A)] \tag{18A-14}$$

and for the foreign exchange market from Equations (18A–11) and (18A–12):

$$SC(r) = X(CP_A/R, CP_B) - M(Y, R \cdot CP_B, CP_A) \tag{18A-15}$$

In these last three equations all of the functional relationships indicated by the parentheses are assumed to be known. The cost of production levels

CP_A and CP_B and the traded goods share, a, are given exogenously, and the monetary and fiscal policy variables, MS and G, are determined by government decisions. As a result there are only the three endogenous variables, r, Y and R (the interest rate, income, and exchange rate) for the three equations, thus providing a necessary condition for the solution of the system. In the derivation of the LM, IS, and FE curves in Figures 18A–1 through 18A–3, we assumed that the exchange rate is constant so that the curves could be plotted in the r and Y space. The properties of this system of equations and their graphical representation which are of greatest interest to us are how the three curves shift in response to changes in the exchange rate, the money supply, and government expenditures.

A change in the exchange rate, say a devaluation which raises the value of R, affects the goods market through a decrease in imports and an increase in exports. These facts are familiar from the analysis in preceding chapters but can be seen by inspection of Equation (18A–13), where R appears in the parentheses following both imports and exports. We do not show the shifts of schedules in these three figures to keep them unstructtered, but we will indicate the direction of the shifts, referring to up and down strictly in relation to the location of the curves in the four-sector diagrams. Thus, a devaluation shifts upward both the $LKLK'$ and the $ININ'$ functions, so that the IS curve is shifted upward and to the right.

The devaluation affects the LM curve by causing an increase in country A's price level and a resultant shortage of money for the maintenance of a constant relation between transactions balances and income, as is clear from Equation (18A–14) and its derivation. In Figure 18A–2 the devaluation causes a downward shift in the KK' curve, indicating that for any given level of real output, Y more money for transactions is required. This shift in the KK' curve, in turn, all else remaining the same, causes the LM curve to shift upward and to the left. Finally, the devaluation affects the FE curve by decreasing imports and increasing exports, as can be seen from Equation (18A–15). In Figure 18A–2 the devaluation shifts the $NENE'$ curve upward, implying that at every given level of income the net exports are higher than before the devaluation.

A change in monetary policy, say an increase in the money supply, affects only the money market, since the variable MS appears only in Equation (18–14) representing this market. In Figure 18A–2, the increase in the money supply leads to an outward shift of the MS schedule in Sector C, which in turn implies that the LM curve is shifted downward and to the right. A change in government expenditures, say an increase in G, affects only the IS curve, since the variable G appears only in the goods market equation, (18A–13). The increase in G shifts upward the $ININ'$ curve in Figure 18A–1, Sector D, and upward and to the right the IS curve.

BIBLIOGRAPHICAL NOTES

The analysis of internal and external balance in a world with money draws heavily on Stern (1973a), ch. 10. The classics in the field of the appropriate use of monetary and fiscal policy are Mundell (1962) and Fleming (1962). The best known formulation of the problem of equal numbers of targets and instruments is in Tinbergen (1952a, 1952b). Criticisms and extensions of the monetary-fiscal policy mix approach are very numerous, and the following references can help students to appreciate the issues involved: Floyd (1969), Niehans (1968), Prachowny (1973), Swoboda (1972), Tower (1972), and Whitman (1970).

CONCEPTS FOR REVIEW

Movements along and shifts of the
   LM, IS, FE curves
Complete equilibrium
Monetary-fiscal policy mix

Problem of matching numbers of
   instruments and targets
Assignment problem

POINTS FOR FURTHER STUDY AND DISCUSSION

1. Analyze what happens to the market adjustment mechanism under the assumption that the LM, IS, and FE curves in Figure 18–1 are all sloped upward and to the right, but the order of steepness is as follows: First, FE, LM, IS; second, FE, IS, LM; third, LM, FE, IS.

2. Show that if the government of country A adds growth as a third target to balance-of-payments equilibrium and full employment, it needs to add another policy instrument to monetary and fiscal policy. What policy instrument might be useful for this purpose?

3. Analyze institutional arrangements and practices of the U.S., German and British governments by which monetary and fiscal policies are coordinated to attain both internal and external balance.

4. Work through the monetary-fiscal policy mix model, assuming that prices in country A fall, remain constant, and rise at points below, at, and above full employment, respectively.

19 The Monetarist Approach to Balance-of-Payments Adjustment

DURING THE LATE 1960s and early 1970s, a number of economists then at the University of Chicago, most notably Robert Mundell and Harry G. Johnson, launched a barrage of criticism against the Keynesian model of income determination in an open economy which we presented in the preceding three chapters. This criticism is difficult to present in an analytically rigorous manner since it has not resulted in a comprehensive model equivalent to the *LM–IS–FE* type. Instead, there exist a number of individual papers, each of which focuses on a particular problem of international adjustment brought to the foreground by a number of assumptions. The realism of some of these assumptions is in doubt, and the analytical importance of them is not fully understood. Moreover, the assumptions made in the separate papers are not consistently the same in all. However, the main monetarist criticisms of the Keynesian balance-of-payments adjustment models appear to be that they focus on the short run, and because of this defect they fail to recognize that in the long run the only cause and cure of international payments disequilibria lies in the use of monetary policy. The monetarists hold that fiscal policy and exchange rate adjustments do not cause and cannot alter payments disequilibria, a view which indeed is in striking contrast with that emerging from the Keynesian models, in which fiscal and exchange rate changes are considered two of the key policy instruments, of at least equal value to monetary policy.

Our purpose in this chapter is to set out verbally and at a relatively nonrigorous level of analysis the conditions under which, in the long run,

Source: Copyright © 1976, by International Finance Section, Department of Economics, Princeton University.

only monetary policy determines the balance of payments of a country. For this purpose we start by presenting the basic critique of the Keynesian closed-economy model which has been formulated by the so-called monetarists, the most notable of whom is Milton Friedman of the University of Chicago. Once we understand this criticism, the international implications of the monetarist view of the economy follow with relative ease. Needless to say, the monetarist approach to national and international economic policy making is not accepted universally, and the Keynesian models presented above still constitute the orthodox view held by most economists. At the same time, however, the problems of inflation and unemployment haunting Western countries during the late 1960s and early 1970s have pointed to the need to amend, refine, or replace the Keynesian model. The monetarists present an interesting and in many ways persuasive substitute for the Keynesian model.

I. MONETARIST CRITIQUE OF THE KEYNESIAN CLOSED-ECONOMY MODEL

It is useful to distinguish two different phases in the evolution of Keynesian macroeconomic analysis. During the first phase the focus of analysis was on how monetary and fiscal policies could be made to combat the traditional business cycles which have haunted free enterprise economies throughout modern history, in an especially virulent form during the Great Depression of the 1930s. The second phase began during the late 1950s and early 1960s, when the focus of analysis shifted to the problem of how to lower the average rate of unemployment experienced over the complete cycles of boom and recession. This shift was brought about by the experience of the immediate postwar decade, during which the amplitude of business cycle fluctuations was very small by historic standards, but the average rate of unemployment in the United States was between 5 and 6 percent. The shift was achieved by the introduction of the analytical concept of the Phillips curve tradeoff between unemployment and inflation, which we explained above in Chapter 16. The conclusion of the second phase was that the average rate of unemployment could be lowered by the proper use of monetary and fiscal policies in much the same way in which these policies were used to reduce purely cyclical unemployment, except that as a consequence of aiming at a lower average rate of unemployment it would be necessary for society to accept a certain degree of price inflation. Empirical judgments were made that the welfare gains from some lowering of the unemployment rate in the United States, from 5.5 to 3.5 percent, exceeded the social costs of the inflation, believed to be a steady 2 percent per year.

Monetarist critique of Keynesian analysis also can usefully be separated into two different sets. The first, which we call the extreme monetarist critique of Keynesian models, is aimed at the use of monetary and fiscal policies for business cycle stabilization. The second set of critiques, undertaken by what we shall call moderate monetarists, is aimed at the idea that monetary and fiscal policies can be used to lower the average rate of unemployment.

Extreme Monetarist Critique of Keynesian Stabilization Policies

The monetarist view of the problem of business cycle instabilities is that they have been caused and reinforced in the past dominantly by disturbances emanating from financial sectors. It is maintained that the real sector of an economy is inherently very stable, and the frequency and amplitude of business cycles could be minimized by a government policy aimed at letting the money supply grow at a constant rate equal to the long-run trend of growth of real output. This policy recommendation is backed by a number of other empirical judgments, such as that the demands for money and money supply functions are stable and that the income elasticity of the demand for money is 1. Monetarists envision that a steady rate of increase in the money supply will limit booms, because excessively optimistic expectations about the profitability of investment and resultant large demand for loans lead to higher interest rates, which reduce the boom level of investment. An analogous process of falling interest rates during a recession limits the downturn of business activity. During extremely large swings in cyclical expectations, the stabilizing influence of the interest rate changes accompanying steady money supply growth is reinforced by the effects price level changes have on the real value of money. This is the so-called wealth effect made famous by A. C. Pigou and Don Patinkin. Boom-caused inflation lowers the real value of money held by the public and reduces the desire and ability to spend and invest, thus cutting into the boom, and vice versa for depressions and falling prices.

Monetarists argue that the alleged countercyclical variations in the money supply brought about by deliberate policies of central banks in the past often have increased rather than decreased the amplitude and frequency of business cycles, for three reasons. First, monetary policy based on orthodox Keynesian views of the problem considered its primary objective to be to stabilize the interest rate and through it the level of income and employment. As is well known from the *LM–IS* model of the Keynesian system, full employment is associated with one unique interest rate, though in complex *LM–IS* models the rate may vary over the business cycle. The basic rule guiding monetary policy therefore has been to attempt stabilization of that interest rate by a strategy known as "leaning against the wind," increasing the money supply when the interest rate rises and reducing the money supply when it falls. Such a policy rule is alleged to add to instability because it raises the money supply when boom expectations lead to excess demand for credit and real goods and services, both of which therefore tend to be realized to a greater degree than when the money supply was not increased. An analogous process leads to deepened recessions.

Second, the Keynesian framework of analysis neglects the role of prices and expectations about the rate of inflation in the determination of the demand for credit, the interest rate, and the real quantity of money supplied. As a result, on occasion the monetary authorities have interpreted a rise in the interest rate as a sign of tightening credit, which they ordered to be mitigated by an increase in the money supply, while in reality the rise in the interest rate was due to the expectation of a higher rate of inflation and not monetary tightness. Under these conditions the increase in the money supply further eased credit and fueled the boom and inflation.

Third, changes in the money supply and interest rates caused by monetary authorities affect spending on real goods and services, not immediately but with lags of varying and unknown length. According to the extreme monetarist critics of discretionary monetary policy, easing of credit, even if timed properly for current conditions of recession, may not induce higher levels of aggregate spending until the time when independently developing business cycle forces have already caused the appearance of excess demand.

Extreme monetarists argue that fiscal policy, defined as government deficit and surplus spending financed through the sale and retirement of bonds, also is unable to stabilize aggregate demand over the business cycle, because of political difficulties in getting taxation and expenditure decisions through democratic legislatures quickly and in the right magnitudes. Furthermore, fiscal policies tend to have effects on real expenditures only with unknown lags, so that they may be destabilizing as well as stabilizing. Most fundamentally, however, monetarists argue that government budget deficits do not increase aggregate expenditures, for a number of reasons. At the highest level of theoretical abstraction, taxpayers, who have to service and repay the government bonds issued to finance the deficit spending, should rationally reduce their own real expenditures in anticipation of the future tax payments, thus offsetting the increase in aggregate demand created by the government deficit spending. Still at a high level of abstraction is the argument that government expenditures on investment not justified on efficiency grounds must compete with and therefore lead to a reduction in private investment which offsets the stimulative effects of the public investment. If the government incurs its deficit by spending on consumption, total social investment declines, and in order to maintain the capital stock at its efficient level private savings have to rise, offsetting the aggregate expenditure increase caused by the government's deficit spending. At a more practical level of analysis, extreme monetarists point to the money market effects of government deficit financing, which leads to higher interest rates and the crowding out of private borrowers whose investment projects, especially residential housing, are sensitive to the cost of credit. As a result, the reduced private investment expenditures offset the stimulation of aggregate demand created by the initial government deficit spending. For all of these reasons, extreme monetarists recommend that discretionary fiscal policy aimed at the stabilization of aggregate demand be stopped, and that governments be required to maintain balanced budgets over the full cycle of recession and boom.

Moderate Monetarist Critique of the Phillips Curve Tradeoff

There are many economists who believe that while governments can use discretionary monetary and fiscal policies to reduce successfully the magnitude and frequency of business cycles, they cannot use these policies to reduce the average rate of unemployment over the full business cycle, as is implied by the Phillips curve analysis. According to this view the average rate of unemployment over the business cycle with stable prices or a constant rate of inflation is known as the "natural rate of unemployment," and is determined by structural characteristics of the economy and workers' preferences for work and leisure. More specifically, the rates of technical change, output, and labor force growth; the levels of unionization; legal minimum wage levels; real wages; the level of competition in factor and goods markets; unemployment insurance and welfare payments, and many other factors determine the natural rate of unemployment. Therefore, it can be lowered only by appropriate changes in these structural characteristics, not by aggregate-demand management.

Moderate monetarists believe that the Phillips curve argument about the existence of an unemployment-inflation tradeoff is based on an incomplete specification of the mechanism determining the division of increased aggregate demand into its components of increased real output and inflation. The missing element in the specification of the mechanism is expectations of workers about the future rate of inflation. A monetarist explanation of the Phillips curve phenomenon, incorporating expectations in the proper way, is as follows.

Consider that initially price stability has prevailed for a long period of time and is expected to do so in the future. The labor market is in equilibrium in the sense that all unemployed persons are between jobs or voluntarily out of the labor force. Now if the government is dissatisfied with this level of unemployment and labor force participation and wishes to lower it, the Phillips curve analysis suggests the need to increase aggregate demand through a permanently greater rate of increase in the money supply or by running a permanent government budget deficit. The initial results of these policies are that business inventories are lowered, and generally favorable sales conditions cause firms to want to hire more workers. However, in order to do so they have to offer higher wages, since in the initial conditions the only people who did not work were those who, at the going wage rate, preferred leisure over work. The additional employment lowers the recorded rate of unemployment and raises labor force participation and the rate of real output growth, and the policy of aggregate-demand expansion apparently has worked as predicted.

But now comes the cost of the policy. Increased wage payments are reflected in higher prices of output after some time lag, and the resultant inflation reduces real wages. The workers who were lured into employment by the higher wages find that inflation has lowered them again, and since their basic work-leisure preferences are unchanged, they again leave employment. The nature of the unemployment insurance laws induces and permits workers and employers to hide the true motives for dropping out of the work force so that unemployment benefits can be obtained. As a result the recorded rate of unemployment temporarily is raised above the natural rate, but as statutory limits in the length of unemployment insurance payments are reached, the economy drifts back toward its natural rate of unemployment. But now, because of the permanently greater rate of expansion of aggregate demand, the rate of inflation is positive. For example, with a balanced government budget, and a rate of increase in the money supply of 2 percent above long-run average growth in real output, the inflation rate will be 2 percent per year.

If the government wishes to maintain the low unemployment level achieved by the initial increase in aggregate expenditure, it has to keep on increasing its rate of monetary and fiscal stimulation in order to maintain the excess demand for goods which is translated into demand for labor and continuously higher wages, with inflation lagging behind. By pursuing these policies the government can maintain a rate of unemployment below the natural, but only at the cost of accelerating inflation, not at the cost of a steady rate, as the simple Phillips curve analysis implies. In the longer run the accelerating inflation becomes so large that its social cost exceeds the gains from greater employment, and the government has to abandon its policies and return to a lower rate of increase in aggregate demand. However, this adjustment process in the downward direction occurs at great cost. The expectations about the rate of inflation are rooted in the minds of the workers, and as wage rates fail to rise at the recently experienced pace, real income falls below normal and many workers prefer leisure at this real rate of pay. As a result, the recorded unemployment rate rises above the natural, and the rate of growth in real output falls below the long-run average. The economy loses on the downturn what it gained on the upturn. In the presence of strong labor unions the turnaround in government policies designed to lower the inflation rate is accompanied by disruptive strikes as the workers attempt to protect their real incomes.

Business which faces falling demand for its output resists the payment of higher wages. To the extent that business is forced into paying higher wages the prices of products continue to rise, and the economy goes through a period of inflation combined with high unemployment and slow growth, the so-called cost-push inflation and stagflation.

After an economy has gone through a number of cycles of this sort, the public learns to expect inflation, unionization and escalator clauses in wage contracts spread more widely, and the employment benefits from an acceleration of aggregate demand are smaller and smaller. Government attempts to reduce the strength and duration and welfare costs of the cost-push inflation phase, through the initiation of wage and price controls, higher unemployment and welfare benefits, and other nonmarket measures, lead to further changes in the structure of the economy and raise the natural rate of unemployment. Consequently, attempts to lower permanently the rate of unemployment through aggregate monetary and fiscal policies cannot succeed in the longer run and may actually raise unemployment.

The preceding analysis leads moderate monetarists to the policy recommendation that aggregate-demand management policies be aimed at the maintenance of price stability over the full business cycle, letting the average rate of unemployment go to its natural level. If the natural rate of unemployment is considered to be too high, policies should be aimed at increasing competition in factor and product markets, the provision of more labor-market information, the elimination of minimum wage laws, and other such structural changes.

The preceding monetarist critique of Keynesian policy principles with respect to both short-run stabilization and the Phillips curve tradeoff, is highly controversial, which is probably why so many economists and politicians consider economics to be in a crisis during the 1970s. The following analysis of the monetarist principles applied to the international economy is even more controversial and less well understood.

II. INTERNATIONAL MONETARIST VIEWS

The division of Keynesian policies into those dealing with business cycles and those aimed at lowering the unemployment rate permanently can be applied also to the analysis of the most basic international monetarist proposition: All persistent balance-of-payments imbalances are due to increases in the money supply at a rate above that at which real economic output is growing.

Balance-of-Payments Effects of Stabilization Policies

As a norm by which to judge the effects of government policies, we should consider a world in which all countries adhere to extreme monetarist principles for domestic demand management, letting the money supply grow at a steady rate equal to the average growth rate of real output and maintaining a balanced government budget over the full business cycle. In such a world the price levels in every country and in the world as a whole are stable. In the long run countries' exchange rates are constant, except for changes in the determinants of the real terms of trade known from the pure theory of international trade. Here we assume that such terms of trade effects are so small over the time period under consideration that they can be ignored for our purposes of analysis. As a result of business cycles and other disturbances, countries tend to experience temporary disequilibria in the foreign exchange markets. These manifest themselves as changes in reserves under fixed exchange rate systems, as exchange rate fluctuations when rates are free to adjust, and as a combination of exchange rate and reserve changes under systems of managed float. But because of the fundamental price stability, reserve changes and exchange rate fluctuations net to zero.

Now let us assume that governments attempt to use monetary and fiscal policy to reduce the amplitude and frequency of business cycles, while continuing to aim at price stability in the long run. Whether these government policies are successful in stabilizing economies or they add to instability, as the monetarists claim, the long-run average price stability assures that reserve and exchange rate changes net to zero. We reach the important conclusion, therefore, that any balance of payments disequilibria persisting over a long period must be due to attempts of governments to reduce permanently the rate of unemployment through monetary growth rates in excess of real output growth rates. We now turn to a more detailed analysis of this proposition.

Fiscal Policy and Temporary Payments Imbalances

Let us assume that all of the world's countries adhere to the principles of maintaining price stability over full business cycles, except for the small country A, which attempts to lower its unemployment rate by running a perpetual government budget deficit while keeping the money supply growing at a constant rate equal to its growth rate of real output. The country has a managed exchange rate and there are no short- and long-term capital flows.

In the section above dealing with the monetarist critique of the use of fiscal policy in an attempt to lower unemployment permanently in a closed economy, we gave a number of reasons why such a policy must fail in the long run: Taxpayers reduce expenditures in order to finance debt service and retirement in the future, the private sector adjusts its capital formation to assure maintenance of the desired total social capital stock, and government financing crowds out private investment financing. These processes can be expected to take place in an open as well as a closed economy. In the long run, a permanent fiscal deficit cannot be expected to lead to a permanent increase in aggregate demand and therefore to a continuous balance-of-payments deficit, depreciating exchange rate, or both. In the short run we can expect the operation of some lags in the adjustment of public spending to the budget deficit, and as a result a balance-of-payments deficit will develop. However, after the full adjust ment of the private sector, the deficit may turn into a temporary surplus, or the country may end up with a permanently lower stock of reserves or higher price of foreign exchange. For our present purposes of analysis the main point is that in the longer run the permanent budget deficit will only affect the mix of national output and cannot lead to a permanent imbalance in the foreign trade sector.

Monetary Policy and Permanent Payments Imbalances

Let us now assume that country A attempts to achieve a lower unemployment rate by increasing its money supply at a rate of n percent above the long-run growth rate of real output, keeping its government budget balanced over the full business cycle. Under these conditions, in the closed-economy case and according to the monetarists, in the long run inflation is at the rate of n percent per year, the nominal interest rate is n percentage points above the real rate of interest and productivity of capital, but the level of unemployment is at its natural rate. In essence, the change in the money supply has no significant long-run effects on the capital stock, society's rate of time preference, real wages, and labor's preference for leisure. In an open economy, in the long run and under freely floating exchange rates, the domestic inflation must lead to a constant and continuing excess demand for foreign exchange. This demand is eliminated by the constant, continuing depreciation of the exchange rate at n percent per time period, because the money supply increases affect only the price level, and neither comparative advantage nor absorption expenditures in the long run. In our analysis of the monetarist views above we noted that if in the closed-economy case a country uses monetary policy to maintain a certain unemployment rate below the natural, then it must increase continuously the rate at which it increases the money supply. Under these circumstances the inflation rate must accelerate, and with it the rate of depreciation of the exchange rate. Ultimately, as in the closed-economy case, the inefficiencies and social problems associated with very high rates of inflation tend to force the abandonment of the policy goal of an unemployment rate below the natural rate, and therefore to bring an end to the acceleration in the rate of increase of the money supply.

In the case where a country manages its exchange rate rather than letting it float freely, the preceding analysis needs to be amended only slightly and in ways obvious from the study of the simpler cases. The excess demand for foreign exchange accompanying the increase in the money supply and price rises is to some extent financed by running down international reserve holdings. In the longer run this financing causes the reserve holdings to be below their desired normal level, and exchange rate devaluations are induced. In the long run the results are the same as those under a freely floating exchange rate regime: persistent exchange rate depreciation, which is attributable to an excessively rapid growth in the money supply.

Reserve Currency Country under Managed Exchange Rates

We now turn to the analysis of the monetarist view of international adjustment in a world of pegged but adjustable exchange rates, in which one large reserve currency country increases its money supply at a constant rate. This case is of particular historical interest since it describes the situation of the United States and the world in the 1960s and is believed to explain the worldwide inflation of the 1970s. As is well known from the discussion of postwar international monetary problems, the very large size of the U.S. economy and some historically determined factors have made the U.S. dollar the primary form in which the countries in the rest of the world have held their international reserves. As a result, during the 1950s and 1960s U.S. balance-of-payments deficits led to automatic increases in the aggregate supply of international reserves.

Given these characteristics of the international monetary system, let us consider that after a period of price stability and balance-of-payments equilibrium among all countries in the world, the United States alone changed its basic policy and increased the money supply at a constant rate n percent above the growth rate of real output, in order to move towards a lower rate of unemployment. The continuous increase in the money supply generated inflationary pressures and, with managed exchange rates, a balance-of-payments deficit. The role of the dollar as reserves implied that the United States could finance its deficits without using international reserves, and deficits did not force the United States to an exchange rate change, as they would an ordinary small country. Consequently, the domestic price increases which accompanied the increases in the money supply were not adjusted for by a corresponding continuous decrease in the exchange rate, and U.S. balance-of-payments deficits during the period were continuous.

As a result of these developments, countries in the rest of the world suffered from excess demand through the U.S. payments deficits, experienced balance-of-payments surpluses, and accumulated international reserves. In theory the other countries could have reacted to these events by letting their exchange rates appreciate continuously relative to the U.S. dollar and by keeping their domestic money supplies constant. That this would have been a technically feasible policy is seen most readily by assuming the existence of freely floating exchange rates. Under these conditions the excess supply of dollars would have been eliminated continuously and smoothly through exchange rate adjustments, and the inflation caused by the U.S. increases in the money supply would have been confined to the United States.

In fact, however, countries in the rest of the world did not behave in the manner postulated in the preceding paragraph. Swept by the same notion as the United States, that unemployment could be lowered by continuous increases in the money supply, these countries welcomed the trade surplus with the United States as a stimulus to demand and welcomed the growth in their reserves in the form of dollars. As a result, the U.S. deficits went on for longer than seems wise in retrospect, and the world in the beginning of the 1970s was holding vast quantities of reserves in the form of U.S. dollars. These reserves are equivalent analytically for the world as a whole to quantities of money in a closed economy. If these reserves were excessively large, as some analysts claim, they induced countries to run payments deficits to get rid of them. But as all countries attempted to attain the same objective, the only result was worldwide excess demand and inflation. The process comes to an end only once the inflation has reduced the real value of the reserves to the desired amount relative to individual countries' incomes and payments instabilities, assuming there are no further continuous increases in reserves.

It follows from the preceding paragraph that economists and, especially, politicians who believe that it was time during the 1960s for the United States to behave like any other country and revalue its currency in response to payments imbalances blame the U.S. government for the world inflation of the 1970s. The monetarist analysis attributes the U.S. inflation to excess money creation, but there is no reason that it should necessarily have caused worldwide inflation. However, once the rest of the world did permit international reserves to grow, for whatever reason, then worldwide inflation is perfectly consistent with the monetarist view, since in a world of managed exchange rates, reserves play the same role as money, and the world as a whole is a closed economy.

Some Casual Empirical Support of the Monetarist Views

The condition of some countries in Western Europe during the 1960s and 1970s is at least consistent with the international monetarist views of adjustment. During the 1960s Britain was publicly committed to a lowering of the unemployment rate and an acceptance of some necessary inflation, through the alleged Phillips curve tradeoff. Above-normal increases in the money supply succeeded initially in raising employment because of workers' failure to anticipate inflation and the existence of some nontraded goods. However, after some time, workers anticipated inflation, and unions resisted erosion of real incomes by militant demands for rapidly rising wage rates. Large deficits began to develop and devaluation of the pound sterling became necessary. However, it is nearly impossible to prevent reduced absorption altogether, if only as a result of imperfections in capital markets and lags between price increases and adjustments of factor payments. For example, high nominal interest rates accompanying inflationary expectations reduced the flow of resources to the housing industry and adversely affected other industries with heavy borrowing requirements and long investment gestation periods, such as high-technology industries. To prevent inefficiencies and inequities caused by these capital market imperfections, the British government provided direct subsidies and increased the money supply at increasing nominal rates, in order to prevent further rises in the interest rate. The monetarist model implies that this vicious circle has been caused by, and can be broken only by abandonment of, efforts to use monetary policy to achieve a permanent increase of employment from the natural rate of unemployment. Britain's experience was matched to some degree by that of Italy and France and, as we argued earlier, of the United States.

There were two countries in the world which did not adopt the policy of attempting to reduce permanently the rate of unemployment. These two countries were Germany and Japan, where the public was more concerned with the maintenance of price stability than lowering the unemployment rate. The experience of these countries also is consistent with the monetarist model, since it involved rates of increase in the money supply below those in the rest of the world, consequent lower rates of price increases, upward valuations of currencies, and perpetual payments surpluses, all in a beneficial cycle.

It should be noted that our very cursory analysis of the experience of some countries in the 1960s and 1970s is only *consistent* with the monetarist view of the world. According to many economists the experience is also consistent with many other explanations, such as failure of the United States to finance the Vietnam War through appropriate tax increases, the militancy of unions growing for reasons other than inflation, the growth of the welfare state more generally, conflict between the working and capitalist classes, and increasing costs of production, generally because of diminishing stocks of the world's resources relative to the growth in demand. We cannot evaluate the merit of these explanations here. Monetarists would argue that such influences have existed throughout history and have been accompanied by either price stability or inflation, depending on monetary policy. Readers have to judge for themselves the merit of these arguments.

III. OTHER MONETARIST ANALYTICAL APPROACHES

In recent years the traditional models of international adjustment based largely on Keynesian concepts have been criticized on a number of grounds which have nothing to do with the fundamental views of the monetarists presented in the preceding parts of this chapter. In other words, these criticisms of traditional models are valid and should be acceptable to all economists, whether or not they believe in the existence of a Phillips curve tradeoff and the causal effects of excess money creation on inflation. However, because these criticisms have been advanced most prominently by economists who also have advanced the monetarist views of the balance of payments, often in the same papers, these criticisms are now considered to be part of the monetarist challenge to orthodox balance-of-payments theory. In the remainder of this chapter we present a brief outline of these criticisms. First we discuss the implications of the traditional assumptions that goods markets are imperfect and that there are many nontraded goods. Second, we analyze the effects of the assumption of imperfect capital markets. The section closes with a consideration of the problems raised by the fact that balance-of-payments imbalances involve flows which are financed from stocks of reserves and which are determined by or influence domestic stocks of money.

Perfect Competition in Goods Markets

Orthodox international adjustment theory, going back to David Hume, suggests that an excess creation of money leads to the following sequence of events through time in a country with a fixed exchange rate regime. First, there are increases in employment and domestic prices, which are then followed by purchasing adjustments of traders to changed relative prices, which lead in turn to a trade deficit. Given such a sequence of events, it is possible for the government to correct the payments imbalance by a devaluation which eliminates the relative price advantage of foreign goods. However, there has now developed a challenge to the validity of this analysis and of the important policy implication that devaluation can be used to correct differential domestic and rest-of-the-world price level increases. This challenge is based on the view that goods markets are so perfect that through cheap and efficient arbitrage the prices of traded goods in all countries remain the same at the given exchange rates.

This fact, for which more and more empirical support is found, leads to the revised view of the sequence of events following an excess creation of money in a small country with a fixed exchange rate regime. Assuming that in the small country all goods are traded, the increased aggregate demand following the excess creation of money leads immediately to a balance-of-trade deficit, while domestic prices and employment remain unchanged. Because the trade deficit has to be financed by government sales of foreign exchange at the pegged exchange rate, in effect the excess money created is equal to the loss of reserves.

The preceding analysis has been amended to take account of the fact that most countries have some nontraded goods and services whose prices can be raised by the excess creation of money, so that there can be divergence of national price levels, and some employment effects can take place. However, the extent to which a country can rely on the operation of these traditional adjustment processes depends on the size of the nontraded goods sector and the elasticity of substitution between traded and nontraded goods. Since the size of nontraded goods sectors of countries is an increasing function of the size of countries and has declined steadily in recent years with the revolution in transportation technology, many countries of the world, but especially of Western Europe, have had in fact little opportunity to influence domestic demand while maintaining fixed exchange rates. We conclude, therefore, that the traditional theory of international adjustment, which assumed implicitly that international goods markets are imperfect, nontraded goods sectors are large, or both, should be amended to reflect the existence of highly perfect goods markets. This adjustment of the theory leads to the important policy conclusions that in a small country with a fixed exchange rate and a small traded goods sector, monetary expansion cannot lead to increased employment, and domestic inflation is determined completely abroad.

In the light of the analysis presented in the first two sections of this chapter, it is easy to understand the further ramifications of this conclusion for the use of monetary policy to affect employment and the choice of an exchange rate regime. The spillover of excess money creation into trade deficits can be avoided by the adoption of a freely floating exchange rate regime. But if the initial unemployment is at the natural rate, then the attempts to increase employment through monetary policy lead to domestic inflation and currency depreciation at rates equal to the rate at which the money supply increase exceeds the growth in real output. This important conclusion about the inability to lower unemployment through monetary policy is the same as that reached above through the use of the strict monetarist approach. But the current model has as an additional analytical innovation not found in either the pure monetarist or the traditional Keynesian models: the empirically verifiable propositions about the perfection of goods markets and the size of nontraded goods sectors.

Perfect International Short-Term Capital Markets

Some versions of the traditional models of the international adjustment mechanism emphasize that an increase in the money supply causes a lowering of the interest rate and the subsequent increase in aggregate demand through higher investment. It has always been known that in an open economy the fall in the interest rate and therefore the effect of a given amount of monetary expansion on aggregate demand depends on the interest elasticity of international short-term capital flows. Long before a monetarist approach to the balance of payments had been identified, Mundell analyzed the implications of assuming that the interest elasticity of international short term capital flows is infinity.

The results of his analysis are well known: When the exchange rate is fixed, the money supply increase exerts downward pressures on the interest rate and induces short-term capital outflows exactly equal to the excess money creation, without any effects on employment or prices. When the exchange rate is freely floating, then the money supply increase induces downward pressures on the interest rate, but the resultant capital outflows cause a depreciation of the exchange rate, which in turn results in the development of a trade surplus and an increase in aggregate demand and employment.

This body of analysis has become increasingly more relevant in recent years as international short-term capital markets have become integrated through institutional and technological developments such as multinational corporations, Eurocurrency markets, jet airplanes, computers, and communications satellites. More important for our purposes of analysis, however, the model readily can be extended to incorporate the concept of the natural rate of unemployment and the absence of a Phillips curve tradeoff. Our preceding discussions concerned with these points make it unnecessary to repeat the analysis in detail, and we can state the conclusion that the increase in the money supply will not lead to a lower unemployment rate, even if the country has freely floating exchange rates, if initially the economy was at its natural rate of unemployment. The excess demand created by the trade surplus leads to domestic price increases, which offset the relative price advantage caused by the exchange rate depreciation in the wake of the capital outflows. In long-run equilibrium, the domestic inflation and exchange rate depreciation offset each other and eliminate the trade surplus. The price level rises and the exchange rate falls at the rate by which the money supply increase exceeds the growth in real output.

Stock-Flow Relationships

The traditional Keynesian model of the international adjustment mechanism has as one of its crowning achievements the proposition that a monetary and fiscal policy mix can be achieved in such a way that even in the presence of international short-term capital flows it is possible to achieve both internal and external balance. This model can be attacked on many grounds centering on the *LM–IS* curve analysis, which is central to the monetary-fiscal policy arguments.

However, the monetary-fiscal policy mix model can also be attacked on the fundamentally different ground that payments imbalances represent a flow, while their financing affects stocks. Thus, if a country finances a trade deficit by a corresponding inflow of capital, its stock of indebtedness toward the rest of the world rises in every period. Analogously, a country's lending to the rest of the world increases with the financing of a trade surplus in every period. As these stocks of foreign indebtedness or credit grow and, in principle, could approach infinity, there must come points where further credits are not granted because of the risk of default or because the foreign lending or borrowing places excessively large real burdens on future generations. The traditional Keynesian monetary and fiscal policy mix models therefore need to be adjusted for changes in elasticities of short-term capital flows induced by the growth in foreign indebtedness. In the long run the possibility of using the mix policies disappears completely as stocks of foreign indebtedness approach infinity and the elasticities become zero.

An important corollary to this analysis is the problem that servicing this growing stock of foreign indebtedness requires growing interest payments, which in turn have to be financed by short-term capital inflows. As a result, even in a static world, interest rate differentials have to be widened continuously to attract more funds. If there are institutional barriers to the levels domestic interest rates can reach, then the use of the monetary-fiscal policy mix for balance-of-payments purposes is constrained for reasons not previously recognized.

More generally, there have been criticisms of traditional international adjustment models for failing to distinguish between what has been called quasi or flow equilibrium on the one hand and true or stock equilibrium on the other. The preceding example of the problem of total short-term capital indebtedness is the best known application of the principle, but it has also been used in connection with the demand for money and long-term assets.

These criticisms of traditional models are valid logically and empirically in the long run. However, in the short run, for which most policies are designed, their empirical relevance is open to some question. The monetary-fiscal policy mix models imply that under fixed exchange rates internal and external balance can be achieved as a matter of long-run policy choice, but in the real world, for all countries, the balance of payments is subjected continuously to random shocks of nature and from government policies, originating domestically and abroad. Thus few policy makers ever considered the prescriptions flowing from the mix model as anything but providing short-run solutions to short-run problems. Yet, under some circumstances, successions of short-run solutions can have empirically important stock effects, and the usefulness of the traditional international adjustment models for policy making undoubtedly has been increased by the consideration of flow and stock effects.

IV. SUMMARY AND CONCLUSIONS

The monetarist challenge to the conventional Keynesian view of international adjustment emerges clearly and directly from the view of the monetarist school on domestic macroeconomic stabilization policies. According to this school, monetary and fiscal policies cannot affect real variables in the economy. The rates of economic growth and unemployment in the long run are determined by market forces, and fiscal policy can affect only the ownership of the capital stock, while monetary policy changes the price level. The cyclical instability of capitalist economies is due primarily to psychologically caused changes in demand for investment, while the demand for money is stable. Cyclical instability is dealt with through assurance of an orderly, steady growth in the money supply, since countercyclical monetary and fiscal policies affect aggregate spending only through lags of uncertain length and often are destabilizing rather than stabilizing. Efforts to move to lower average unemployment through planned acceptance of inflation must lead to accelerating inflation and ultimate failure.

This view of the world has its counterpart in the international sphere. Under freely floating exchange rates, the trade balances of countries would always be determined by real forces underlying productivity and comparative advantage. In such a world inflation in any one country and continuous exchange rate depreciations are caused only by excessively expansive monetary policy, though observed relationships may be complicated by lags in adjustment and changes in wealth and reserve holdings. Under managed exchange rates, these propositions about the causes of inflation and exchange rate changes are influenced by lags introduced through government behavior, but they are not changed basically. Inflation and payments imbalances of one country and worldwide inflation are caused by too rapid expansion of the money supply.

Do these arguments mean that we have to abandon our Keynesian tools of analysis? Most economists will probably answer this question in the negative. After all, traditional Keynesian international adjustment models stress the importance of adjusting absorption to restore payments equilibrium, and maintain that failure to do so leads to continuous devaluations. The Keynesian model implies that absorption can be reduced by lowering the money supply, which is perfectly consistent with the message of the monetarists.

However, the monetarist challenge should encourage Keynesian economists to expand the $LM–IS–FE$ analysis to reflect properly the difference between nominal and real interest rates and in the process pay more attention to expectations about inflation and the real quantity of money. Most importantly, the monetarist challenge should lead to a fundamental reexamination of the proposition that the natural rate of unemployment can be reduced through monetary and fiscal policy and the acceptance of some positive rate of inflation in anything but the shortest run. As Johnson put it, Keynes's dictum that we are all dead in the long run is valid, but this does not permit us to pretend that therefore we can forever be making economic policies which consider only short-run effects. At some point successions of short-run policies must have effects on long-run relationships. Acceptance of the monetarist argument that the Phillips curve tradeoff is not possible does not imply the necessary acceptance of the other monetarist prescriptions about the steady growth in the money supply, the disuse of discretionary fiscal policy, and the need for freely floating exchange rates for stabilization purposes.

As a general methodological proposition about the merit of the traditional Keynesian model against the monetarist models of the international adjustment mechanism, it is almost trivial to observe that if we had genuine general equilibrium models and knew all of the adjustment parameters empirically, either approach would be equally valid. Of course, we do not have such theoretical and empirical models, and from this fact arises precisely the need to simplify and theorize. Under these conditions the value of one theory over another is determined by their relative abilities to explain real-world phenomena and to predict the consequences of certain government policies. Judged from this point of view, the Keynesian traditional models, in the opinion of many economists, have failed badly in recent years. This phenomenon explains in part the widespread interest in monetarist models. But it is too early to reach a verdict on the ability of the monetarist models to explain and predict consistently better than did the Keynesian models. There simply is not enough empirical work to reach a verdict on this question.

Perhaps the safest prediction about the future of the monetarist models of the international adjustment is that, like many other apparently revolutionary analytical tools and approaches, they will be added to economists' kits and increase the stock of knowledge in economics, but they will not lead to a fundamental revision of its basic core.

BIBLIOGRAPHICAL NOTES

The monetarist approach to the balance of payments pervades much of Mundell's writing in his two books (1968, 1971). Johnson (1972) provides a comprehensive statement of the theory. A number of contributions have been collected in Frenkel and Johnson (1975). Dornbusch (1973a, 1973b) and Mussa (1974) present extensions and modifications of Mundell's models. One of the earliest empirical studies of the monetarist approach, though conceived independently of the recent theoretical discussions, is Triffin and Grubel (1962). The domestic monetarist principles are developed in Friedman (1968) and Friedman and Schwartz (1963). Masera (1974) presents an attempt to integrate the monetarist and Keynesian models.

CONCEPTS FOR REVIEW

Natural rate of unemployment
Business cycle instability
Wealth effect
"Leaning against the wind"
Price expectations and shifts in the
 Phillips curve

Wage-push inflation
Stagflation
Money illusion
Nontraded goods and inflation
Perfect goods market arbitrage

POINTS FOR FURTHER STUDY AND DISCUSSION

1. Calculate the proportionate increases in the money supply and consumer prices of the United States, Britain, and Germany by five-year periods, from 1950 until 1975. Are the results consistent with the quantity theory of money and the monetarist approach to the balance of payments?

2. Summarize the estimates about the Phillips curve tradeoff which had been made during the 1960s for the United States, Canada, and other countries and compare them with the actual experiences of the 1970s.

3. Review the literature of the early 1970s concerning the role of the United States in the worldwide inflation of the late 1960s and early 1970s.

4. Describe the determinants of the natural rate of unemployment and discuss policies suitable for lowering this rate.

5. Analyze the proposition that during price stability and over the full business cycle, on the average, nonworking people are either between jobs or voluntarily idle.

20 An Integrated View of the Adjustment Mechanism

AFTER STUDYING the highly abstract models of the international adjustment mechanism presented in the six preceding chapters, students may be tempted to ask how, in practice, countries deal with payments imbalances under a wide variety of real-world conditions. More specifically, they may wish to know under what circumstances countries use financing, income adjustments, direct controls, and exchange rate changes. What criteria of choice are various countries using in their selection of particular adjustment policies.

In this chapter we attempt to provide a practical, integrated approach to the determination of balance-of-payments adjustment policies by considering first the characteristics of the disturbances giving rise to them and the implications these characteristics have for the use of the adjustment policies. We conclude that disturbances are best seen as being the outcome of a random process which tends to equalize positive and negative influences on the balance of payments for most of the countries most of the time. Because of certain social costs which result from exchange rate instabilities, countries reduce the real cost these disturbances would have on their economies by financing the imbalances and maintaining the exchange rate fixed as long as possible. Currency revaluations tend to be necessary in relatively few cases, when countries suffer from long runs of successive surpluses or deficits which are shown to be the outcome of the assumed random process which determines the imbalances.

In the second part of this chapter we consider a country which is subject to balance-of-payments deficits and surpluses in the random pattern analyzed in the preceding section. Such a country will be seen to use rationally all available adjustment policies as it deals with short and long runs of payments imbalances in the same direction. An efficient policy mix requires the use of all policies, up to the point where at the margin the social cost of using each one is equalized.

The material to be presented in this chapter, especially the arguments about the efficiency of financing and the use of controls, is rather controversial and is not based on any existing literature. Nevertheless, the very nature of the different adjustment models presented in the preceding chapters seems to ask for some integration and overview. It is hoped that the attempted integration will be of help to students and will be found to be correct.

I. THE NATURE OF BALANCE-OF-PAYMENT DISEQUILIBRIA

In the real world countries faced with payments imbalances need to decide which of the available methods of adjustment discussed in Chapters 14–18 should be used to deal with them. The problem of choice arises from two basic problems. First, the use of each of the adjustment methods is associated with some welfare cost, and second, it is never known whether a certain imbalance is due to some long-lasting cause or it is likely to be self-reversing or to be offset by a disturbance affecting the payments imbalance in the opposite direction. The countries which, after World War II, created the International Monetary Fund agreed to use methods for dealing with payments imbalances according to a code of behavior which specifies that all payments imbalances are to be financed, or eliminated, through income and domestic price adjustments, except when the imbalances are due to a "fundamental disequilibrium" and exchange rate adjustments are required.

This code of behavior is deceptively simple and unambiguous. Its rationale is that exchange rate adjustments to all imbalances lead to social costs. The precise nature of these costs will be discussed in Chapter 22, which deals with the arguments for and against freely floating exchange rates. They can be summarized as follows. Exchange rate changes give signals to producers and consumers about changes in relative prices and scarcities, to which they adjust through changing their mix in output and consumption. These changes in production and consumption patterns give rise to adjustment costs. Furthermore, the changes in the exchange rate through the prices of traded goods influence the stability of the domestic prive level, which in turn leads to welfare losses because of external effects on the usefulness of money in the economy. If payments imbalances are due to random disturbances (such as bad harvests or business cycles) which over time average to zero, government stabilization of the exchange rate minimizes these social costs of fluctuations. Reserves lost in one period are regained in another, leaving the country on the average, through time, with a constant stock of international reserves. However, if the payments imbalances are due not to random disturbances but to some fundamental force, such as differential rates of inflation or of population or productivity growth, then the payments imbalances are symptomatic of what is known as a fundamental disequilibrium. Under these conditions, government stabilization of the exchange rate leads to cumulatively very large reserve losses or gains, which ultimately have to be terminated through an appropriate exchange rate change. The undesirable large changes in reserves should be avoided through an exchange rate change immediately when a fundamental disequilibrium affects a country's balance of payments.

The problem with this code of behavior is that in practice it is impossible to know whether or not a payments imbalance is due to a fundamental disequilibrium or a random disturbance. During the 1950s many articles were written on this subject, reaching the conclusion that while it is easy enough to define or describe the nature of random disturbances and fundamental influences on the balance of payments, there is no method for ascertaining in the real world whether a given imbalance is due to one cause or the other. In order to appreciate this point let us consider briefly the nature of disturbances according to six broad categories of origin.

First, there are the types of disturbances which used to be emphasized by classical economists: variations in the quality and quantity of harvests and other natural influences on economic activity, wars, and politically and economically motivated civil unrest. Second, there are disturbances originating from the operation of market economies in which investment and savings decisions are made by independent groups in the economy, on the basis of uncertain views about the future. As is well known from Keynesian economics and business cycle theories, differences between desired savings and investment lead to economic processes (some of them self-reinforcing) which affect employment, prices, and the balance of payments. Third, there are disturbances emanating from the action of government attempting to deal with externalities, provide public goods, or change the income redistribution. While the adoption of these policies tends to be designed such that the impact on stability is minimized, some instability normally does result. This is considered to be a necessary cost of achieving otherwise socially desirable objectives. Fourth, these domestic government policies have their counterpart in the international sphere. Here they involve the formation of customs unions, reform of the international monetary system, and other efforts to reorganize the international order or redistribute income among countries. These efforts to change the international economic order tend to produce some economic instability, but this is considered to be a normal cost of achieving the otherwise worthwhile social objectives. Fifth, there are disturbances caused by the efforts of individual countries to enrich themselves at the expense of others, through the use of tariffs or quota restrictions on exports or in many other ways. Sixth, there are disturbances resulting from efforts of countries to deal with the instabilities stemming from the five causes just discussed. Government policies designed to stabilize the economy sometimes have the opposite effect because they are made with incomplete knowledge about changing interdependencies and magnitudes in the economy.

The first two categories of disturbances can be assumed to be random and can be expected to be reversed or offset by analogous developments which have the opposite effects on the balance of payments. For example, by definition, below-average harvests must be followed by above-average harvests, booms by recessions, and so on. Irreversible events and trends affecting the balance of payments may be expected to result from government actions in Categories 3–6. For example, efforts to move to a permanently lower rate of unemployment by taking advantage of the Phillips curve tradeoff result in a permanently higher rate of inflation or price level which, in the presence of downward price and wage rigidities, leads to fundamental payments disequilibria best dealt with by exchange rate changes. Similarly, customs unions may increase producers' competitiveness, tariffs may permanently lower import demand at a given exchange rate.

Yet while all events in Categories 3–6, taken individually, have these clear-cut, nonreversible effects on a country's balance of payments, taken together they often tend to cancel each other. A country may suffer from inflation as a result of attempts to lower unemployment permanently, but the balance-of-payments effect of the inflation may be reversed in the next period by inflation abroad, which may have been caused by similar policies for dealing with unemployment, or genuine classical random shock such as a bad harvest, or the initiation of a costly program of environmental pollution control. In practice, the balance of payments of each country is perpetually influenced by large numbers of such events, some of which are canceling each other even before they can affect the balance of payments. The overwhelming proportion of these influences cannot be predicted with respect to either their timing or the magnitude of their effects on the balance of payments. In such a world deliberate policies aimed at the elimination of payments imbalances, such as income adjustments and direct controls, ceteris paribus can work in the manner and direction analyzed in Chapters 14–18, but because of unpredictable changes in the ceteris paribus conditions often they are swamped and fail to produce the expected improvements in the balance of payments. For this reason it is useful to consider deliberate balance-of-payments policies as being part of the many basic influences determining actual and unpredictable balance-of-payments changes.

A Random-Walk Model of Payments Imbalances

The preceding considerations about the nature of balance-of-payments disturbances have led some economists to conclude that it is best to abandon the distinction between fundamental and nonfundamental payments disequilibria and instead treat all imbalances as if they were part of a "random-walk" process. The nature of such a process is best understood by assuming that under fixed exchange rates, in each period a country's payments imbalance is decided by the toss of a true coin, and the rule is that the head of the coin represents a $1 billion surplus and the tail a $1 billion deficit. On average and in the long run, our best guess is that under these assumptions the plus and minus events will net to zero, since heads and tails of the coin show up an equal number of times. But for any particular time in the future we can calculate the probability of cumulative losses of different sizes or the number of times heads or tails will show up in sequence.

In Figure 20–1, which shows a so-called probability tree, we start from balance at Period 0. At this point the probability is .5 that the cumulative imbalance is −1 or +1 at the end of Period 1. By looking at Period 2 we

FIGURE 20–1
A Random-Walk Process

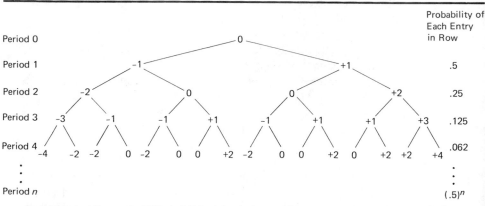

In any period the probability is 0.5 that the balance of payments shows either a surplus of 1 or a deficit of 1. At the end of Period 1, therefore, the cumulative payments imbalance is either −1 or +1, as shown in Row 2. At the end of the second period, the postulated balance-of-payments behavior results in a cumulative effect of either −2, 0, 0, or +2, as is shown in Row 3. At the end of the third period, the possible cumulative effects are shown in Row 4, and so on for all other periods.

At period zero, it is impossible to predict what will be the cumulative balance-of-payments imbalances at any point in the future. However, it is possible to predict that at the end of the Period 4, they will be −4 and +4, with a probability of .062 each, −2 or +2 with a probability of .25 each, and zero with a probability of .375. What size of cumulative payments imbalances can be financed and which require exchange rate adjustment are determined by the availability of international reserves.

can see that if the imbalance has been -1 in Period 1, in Period 2 it is -2 or 0, with a probability of .25 each; if it has been $+1$ in Period 1, then it is $+2$ or 0, with a probability of .25 each, in Period 2. And so on for all later periods. The main point is that for any given period there is the nonzero probability of very large cumulative gains or losses, even though the average of all payments imbalances nets to zero. In Period 4, for example, the probability of a -4 cumulative deficit is .062, and it can readily be seen from Figure 20–1 that the extreme right- and left-hand branches of the tree involve cumulative increases and decreases, respectively, of one unit per time period. Yet adding up all sums of Period 4 results in a total equal to zero.

Countries on the interior and extreme outside branches of the probability tree, however, alike enjoy welfare gains through the many periods of stability of the exchange rate. On balance, if the costs of welfare, due to the use of income adjustments, direct controls, the necessary exchange rate adjustments, and the cost of holding reserves are less than the welfare gains derived from the fixed exchange rates, then the system leads to an overall lower cost of dealing with economic instability than that which would be incurred if exchange rate changes were the only method for dealing with payments imbalances. We return to the problem of the welfare implications of international monetary systems in Part Five, especially Chapter 25.

The preceding description of the cost-minimizing behavior of countries faced by payments imbalances following a random-walk process agrees roughly with behavior observed during the postwar years. Most countries, during most periods, maintained fixed exchange rates, averaged reserve losses and gains, and used income adjustments and controls only rarely. The newspaper headlines and scholarly commentaries paid greatest attention to the episodes during which countries lost or gained large quantities of reserves, were forced into costly income adjustments and controls, and finally had to devalue. But seen as part of the total picture, these episodes were relatively rare, as is implied by the low probabilities attached to the branches on either end of the probability tree.

Before we turn to an overview of balance-of-payments adjustment behavior in terms of the analytical tools developed in the preceding chapters, it is necessary to discuss briefly the formal conditions of an efficient mix of the alternative adjustment policies, income changes, direct controls, and exchange rate changes. For this purpose we can consider that a country engages in balance-of-payments stabilization policy to produce a good which is the welfare of society, that the adjustment policies are factor inputs in the production process, and that the original disturbances, costs of controls, income, and exchange rate changes determine the production function. Now, if we compare the country's behavior with that of the firm we can draw on the well-known condition of efficiency of production: At the margin the cost of each factor input is equal. Applied to the theory of the balance-of-payments policy mix, it implies that the use of each of the policies should be pushed to the point where at the margin the costs are equalized. This formal statement of efficiency is of little practical use to policy makers in the real world, as we shall see in the next section, but it is useful in explaining and rationalizing the behavior of countries actually observed. Of course, the theoretical optimality of the simultaneous use of all policies does not imply that countries necessarily always employ them in optimal relative intensity.

II. AN OVERVIEW OF THE MODERN THEORY OF THE ADJUSTMENT MECHANISM

In Figure 20–2 we present schematically what policies a small country, A, initially holding an equilibrium stock of international reserves and at full employment, undertakes as it is faced with payments imbalances of a nature discussed in Section I of this chapter. We begin the analysis by assuming that in the initial period a deficit develops as a result of, say, a bad harvest. Starting in the upper left corner of the diagram, it can be seen that the first policy response is financing of the deficit through the use of international reserves. If in the subsequent period the imbalance is reversed or offset, the "problem" of the imbalance has been "solved," as is indicated by arrow a from Box I, Financing. We can note immediately the economic advantage of financing under these conditions. No relative price changes between tradables and nontradables take place, and the accompanying adjustment costs are saved. In effect, the country overcomes its temporary excess demand for foreign goods and assets by drawing down wealth held in the form of international reserves. This method of dealing with a payments imbalance is especially suitable if disturbances are random. In the particular model of random shocks presented in Figure 20–1, in Period 2 the probability is 0.5 that the deficit is eliminated by reversal or offsetting of the basic disturbance.

Let us go on to consider the case where deficits recur for a number of periods, as well they may under the random-walk hypothesis. In this case financing continues initially, as arrows b and c from Box I to Box II, Expenditure Changing, indicate. As we have seen in Chapter 16, the financing does not prevent the automatic operation of adjustment through changes in income and the money supply, operating through processes of changed domestic absorption of goods and services well known from Keynesian and monetary economics. If these induced absorption changes (see arrow d) are consistent with full-employment targets, and if at full employment, with the given exchange rate, payments are balanced, then the basic problem of the payments deficits is solved. Such an outcome is

Payments Imbalances Are
Deal- by:

I FINANCING —b→ If imbalances are not reversed or offset —c→ **II EXPENDITURE CHANGING** —d→ If absorption changes are consistent with full-employment target and if, at that full employment, productive capacity equals demand for output

a

If imbalances are reversed or offset

(Problem is solved)

(Problem is solved)

II EXPENDITURE CHANGING

Changes Absorption through automatic
1. Direct income changes
2. Income multiplier
3. Money supply changes

—e→ If conditions under (*d*) are not met and
1. Automatic income changes are suppressed
2. Reserves run low
3. Imbalances continue

III EXPENDITURE SWITCHING

f *j*

A DIRECT CONTROLS OR SUBSIDIES   B EXCHANGE RATE CHANGES

g *k* *i*

h

If controls are temporary and markets do not overcome them and if
1. Imbalances are reversed or offset
2. Expenditure changing works
3. Exchange rate changes work

(Problem is solved)

If controls are in operation too long, markets overcome them, imbalances reappear

m

Back to I, II, and III and continued exchange rate changes until absorption is changed

Result in
1. Implicit relative price level changes
2. Changed absorption through
   a) Money illusion
   b) Income redistribution
   c) Wealth effects

r

If absorption is not changed because of union action, escalator clauses, monetary policy, or other policies to maintain absorption and wealth positions

p

If allowed to work

(Problem is solved)

n

A country suffering from payments imbalance typically attempts to finance it in expectation that the disturbance is reversed or offset in the next period, as is indicated by Box I, Financing, in the upper left corner of Figure 20–2. Arrow *a* and the oval entry shows solution of the problem. Arrows *b* and *c* point to Box II, Expenditure Changing, which is needed if imbalances continue. If this policy is successful, the problem is solved (arrow *d*); if it is not, the imbalances continue, arrows *e* and *f* point to the need for Box III, Expenditure Switching, policies, through either A, Direct Controls or Subsidies, or B, Exchange Rate Changes. As in the case of other adjustment policies, if expenditure switching is successful and eliminates imbalances, or if they are reversed or offset automatically, the problem is solved (arrows *h* and *p*). If imbalances continue for a variety of reasons (arrows *k* and *r*), financing and expenditure changing and switching have to be repeated (arrows *m* and *n*).

especially likely if the initial deficits are caused by a cyclical boom or excessively expansionary monetary and fiscal policies.

On the other hand, if the preceding requirements with respect to employment targets are not met, and the government suppresses the automatic income adjustments through appropriate monetary and fiscal policies, the deficit may be permitted to continue for a number of periods, always in the hope that it reverses itself or is offset automatically. If this happens, again the problem is solved, and financing has permitted maintenance of income and the avoidance of resource shifts.

However, let us now consider the case indicated by arrow *e* and assume that deficits continue, automatic income and absorption adjustments have been suppressed, and as a result of financing for a number of consecutive periods, reserves have become very low. Under these conditions, the country has to consider the policies included under Box III, Expenditure Switching. These consist of A, Direct Controls or Subsidies, and B, Exchange Rate Changes. The direct controls and subsidies for trade, capital flows, and exchange rates embrace policies which in the analytical framework of Chapter 11 cause shifts in the demand and supply curves for foreign exchange. Thus they eliminate the deficit and the need for the continued use of reserves, which we had assumed were running low. As arrow *h* indicates, if the controls are in effect for only a short period and random events improve the balance of payments, income changes or exchange rate changes eliminate excess demand for foreign exchange, and the problem is solved. But if the controls and subsidies are maintained for a long time or are instituted frequently, markets develop methods for circumventing them and make them ineffective. Under these conditions they produce inefficiencies and fail to assist the country in reaching payments equilibrium. The consequences of such prolonged maintenance of direct controls and subsidies are shown by arrows *k* and *m*; further financing is required.

We now turn to the alternative of achieving expenditure switching through exchange rate changes. A depreciation has the main effect of changing the relative costs of foreign and domestic goods and thus inducing the public to buy less abroad and more home-produced goods. This effect reflects classical thinking about the international adjustment mechanism, and under normal conditions devaluation of a country's currency eliminates payments deficits, ceteris paribus. However, Keynesian economics and the new monetarist approach to balance-of-payments theory suggests that exchange rate changes also have a number of important other effects which have to come into play if the elimination of the payments deficit is to become effective. First, there is the interaction of the exchange rate change with the marginal propensity to import out of income, which affects the choice of optimum expenditure policy. We discussed this relationship between policies of expenditure switching and expenditure changing and their impact on internal and external balance in Chapters 16, 17, and 18, using the analytical models developed by Trevor Swan and Robert Mundell. Second, we showed in these chapters that exchange rate changes have an automatic effect on domestic prices which in turn leads to money illusion, income redistribution, and a reduction in the value of money held by the public. With arrow p we indicate that if exchange rate changes are permitted to work their relative price effect and to induce reduced absorption through money illusion, income redistribution, or the wealth effect, then the balance-of-payments problem is solved, even though the basic disturbance is not reversed or offset and international monetary and fiscal policies do not change absorption.

On the other hand, with arrow r we show the possibility that the changes in absorption induced by the exchange rate changes are eliminated because workers have no more money illusion, income redistribution effects are eliminated by social policies of the government, and the government restores real money balances through appropriate policy, then the exchange rate change does not correct the payments imbalance. Arrow n indicates that under these conditions there are again payments imbalances, which must be financed until they are either reversed or offset automatically or eliminated through expenditure-changing or expenditure-switching effects. As long as monetary and fiscal policies are maintained to keep absorption at disequilibrium levels, this process continues. As we noted above, the process involves domestic price increases. When these price rises are considered to produce a greater social cost than reduction in absorption through restrictive monetary and fiscal policies, the country will introduce them, and thus it will finally deal effectively with the disturbances which caused the balance of payments deficits.

The preceding analysis can readily be applied by strict analogy to the case where a country experiences random shocks to stability leading to payments surpluses. There are a number of asymmetries, however. The most important is that pressures on countries to engage in policies under Box III, Expenditure Switching, are less if the imbalance leads them to accumulate reserves, which presumably can be done almost without effective limit, than if they are faced with a loss of reserves, which must cease when reserves have reached a level of zero. Furthermore, if countries in payments surplus do appreciate their currencies, it is politically more acceptable to permit the automatic operation of income and absorption effects to raise employment than it is to permit the operation of these forces in the downward direction. For these reasons, balance of payments "crises" mostly involve countries in deficit, rarely countries in surplus.

We should note finally that the arguments of this chapter would be modified only slightly if it were assumed that exchange rates could be changed gradually, as under a system of managed float, than if they had to be changed in discrete and officially announced steps, as under the parity system. Under the managed float and parity systems countries have to enter the same calculus about the welfare effects of exchange rate instability, the randomness of disturbances, and the costs of financing, income changes, and direct controls. The important difference between the parity and managed float systems is that, under the latter, runs of payments imbalances in the same direction can trigger smooth and gradual exchange rate adjustments, and countries tend to be tempted less to defend a fixed rate for a long period of time in the hope that the run of imbalances will cease. As a result, it is likely that under the managed float, countries can avoid the traumatic economic and political difficulties which are associated with the decision to revalue a currency by a discrete amount after reserves have run low and other adjustment policies have become too costly, as was the case under the parity system. Yet, in principle, the same criteria should be used in arriving at the decision to change the value of a currency through a gradual float or through a discrete, officially announced revaluation. For this reason, the models presented in this chapter are useful for understanding balance-of-payments policies under both systems, parity exchange rates and managed floats.

BIBLIOGRAPHICAL NOTES

Since this chapter is intended to serve only as a general outline of the field covered in Part Four, no references covering specific points are given here. They have been supplied at the end of the chapters in which the points are made in greater detail. References to general treatises of the international adjustment mechanism and monetary system are the scholarly, synthesizing work by Stern (1973a), which contains also a very up-to-date bibliography, and the treatises with strong viewpoints and some dashes of original contributions by Sohmen (1969) and Yeager (1966). Some of the most influential writings in the field during the past 15 years are in Mundell (1971) and Johnson (1962). Heller (1966) introduced the random-walk model into the literature on financing and the demand for reserves.

CONCEPTS FOR REVIEW

Random walk
Probability tree
Fundamental disequilibrium

Branch of probability tree
Efficient mix of adjustment policies

POINTS FOR FURTHER STUDY AND DISCUSSION

1. Survey a number of other textbooks and treatises in international economics and compare:
    a. What they assume about the nature of disturbances giving rise to the need for an international adjustment mechanism and monetary system.
    b. The methods of presenting the modern theory of the adjustment mechanism.

2. Work out the formula and present schematically a random-walk process based on a biased coin.

3. Read some of the large literature on the evidence that stockmarket prices are following a random walk. Find out what a random walk for stock market prices implies for the profitability of speculation. Analyze a lengthy period of daily exchange rates to find out whether or not they follow a random-walk pattern. Explain your findings in the light of what you already know about the theory of exchange rate determination.

part five

THE INTERNATIONAL MONETARY SYSTEM

21 The Gold Standard

FOUR DIFFERENT TYPES of the international monetary system which have existed in history or which have been suggested for adoption by economists are discussed in Part Five. These four systems are the gold standard, freely floating exchange rates, the gold exchange standard, and managed exchange rates with centrally created reserves. These systems are discussed separately in each of the four chapters of this part. The concluding chapter of Part Five not only describes the current IMF system and discusses practical problems of choice in various areas facing it, it also contains a model of an optimum international monetary system based on centrally created reserves.

The principle of exposition adopted for each chapter is the presentation of a basic model of how the system is supposed to work ideally. In other sections we summarize the historic development and performance of this basic model, identify the policies which would be necessary to make the ideal system work under current conditions, and specify what the welfare costs of these policies would be.

I. THE BASIC MODEL

The theoretical blueprint of the basic classical gold standard is based on assumptions about the real world that are normally made in the teaching of classical economic theory and general equilibrium analysis: the economy operates under conditions of perfect competition, prices and wages are perfectly flexible, there is always full employment of resources, money is held only for transaction purposes, and the institutional arrangements determining this transaction demand change only slowly. In addition, it is convenient to assume that the money supply consists entirely of gold, which is also acceptable in the settlement of debts between nations. For heuristic reasons the following discussion proceeds in terms of a two-country world, where there are neither technical change nor economic growth and where there are no autonomous capital movements between the two countries.

In an economy where these basic conditions are met, the quantity theory of money holds. This theory can best be explained by presentation of the basic and well-known identity: $M \times V \equiv P \times Q$, where M is the quantity of money, V is the transactions velocity of money (i.e., how often a unit of money is spent over a given time period, a fact determined by the economy's institutions regarding patterns of payments and receipts), P is an index of all prices in the economy (i.e., the price level) and Q is an index of the volume of physical transactions resulting from a given full-employment level of national output. Alternative specifications of this identity consider Q to be the physical volume of goods and services produced over a given time period. With this specification of Q, V is defined as the income velocity of money. Either definition of Q and V is legitimate, and no substantive changes in the conclusions of the basic analysis follow from the adoption of one or the other definition. Under both systems, given the indexes of Q and P and the nominal value of M, V is derived by simple division, i.e., $V \equiv PQ/M$.

The basic identity of the equation $MV \equiv PQ$ can be made into an analytically useful theory by the assumption that V is unalterably fixed in the short run and that P adjusts passively to exogenous changes in M or Q. According to this theory, it follows that if a government tries to increase the quantity of gold circulating in its country through the imposition of appropriate laws and regulations, then the result of such efforts will be an increase in P proportional to the increase in M, since Q is given at its full-employment level and V is constant. Alternatively, with M unchanged, the autonomous decrease of Q resulting from a poor harvest, flood, or war devastation also results in an increase in P proportional to the decrease in Q.

The preceding example of a government-induced increase in M is of great historical interest, since it describes the activities of the mercantilist governments of the 17th and 18th centuries, and it stimulated David Hume to present a well-articulated version of the quantity theory of money, which he then applied to the demonstration of the absurdity of these mercantilist policies. As the increase in circulating money raised the price level, the country's balance of trade would turn to a deficit requiring settlement in gold and continuing until the domestic money supply had returned to its previous level, thus eliminating all of the gold gains the mercantilist policies had achieved through the imposition of unpopular and socially costly restrictions on international economic relations.

The same quantity theory model of the economy was later used to analyze more formally the process of international adjustments under the gold standard. Under classical assumptions about the real world, the most prominent sources of disturbance to international equilibrium were natural or man-made catastrophes which reduced the physical quantity of a nation's output during a given period of time. The result of such catastrophes is an increase in the domestic price level, which induces foreigners to reduce their purchases and domestic residents to increase their purchases abroad, leading to a payments deficit and an outflow of gold. As a result of the reduced stock of money in the economy, the price level falls and the size of the deficit in the following period is reduced. With the national output remaining at its catastrophe-reduced level, the deficit, gold losses, and price reductions continue in subsequent periods until prices reach a level where the payments imbalance is zero. The attainment of this equilibrium is aided if the gold transfers cause an increased money supply and a rise in the price level in the rest of the world, thus helping to offset some of the initial price disadvantage of the country with the basic difficulties. The adjustment mechanism ultimately produces the condition where at the temporarily lowered level of Q, the quantity of M is just sufficient to keep the economy at the price level P which, given V and the price level in the rest of the world, results in balanced external payments.

After the country with the original disequilibrium restores its national output to the normal level, its existing price level falls further still, as it must if the basic identity $MV \equiv PQ$ is to hold and M and V are given. The lower price level causes the appearance of a trade surplus, an increase in M and a rise in prices. This process of gaining gold and raising the price level continues until the old, precatastrophe levels of the money supply and prices are reached in both the original deficit country and the rest of the world, and international payments are balanced.

This basic model is applicable in modified form to the explanation of adjustments to causes of payments disequilibrium other than natural catastrophes, such as changes in taste and technology, shifts of capital, domestic inflation due to excess spending, and others. In all of these cases resultant deficits are cured by domestic price reductions, which the gold losses bring about automatically in the manner described. However, as for the ultimate adjustments, the present cases differ from those of natural catastrophes in that the original national incomes, prices, and gold stocks may not be reestablished in the new equilibrium. For example, as a result of a change in tastes, a country may find its output valued lower by the rest of the world, the terms of trade moved adversely, and the value of national income lowered, thus requiring less gold for normal transactions.

In general, the basic mechanism for the international adjustment of national payments imbalances under the gold standard has several outstanding advantages. First, there is the expectation of stable, long-run prices between all countries. Price levels between countries may diverge occasionally and temporarily, but such episodes are likely to be no more intense or lengthy than price divergences between the regions of a major country, each of which is also subject to natural catastrophes. As was argued before, such stability of prices and values between nations encourages the development of international trade and the free flow of capital. From this point of view the whole world becomes one "country," with the only essential difference that there are national governments, with the right to tax and wage wars and restrict the free movement of people. Otherwise, the allocation of resources in the world as a whole tends to be efficient as it is within a single country.

Second, implicit in the analysis of the gold standard's financial mechanism is a beneficial flow of real resources. When a country finds its output temporarily reduced by one event or another, its population, *ceteris paribus,* would have to reduce its standard of living drastically, and by the full amount of the lost output during the period when the harvest failed or productive resources have been destroyed, if it did not have the option to use some of its circulating gold to purchase goods from foreigners and thus decrease the severity of the imposed income reduction for the moment. Ultimately the country's population has to absorb the consequences of the original calamity through a reduced standard of living, but under the gold standard it can do so over a longer period of time and with smaller sacrifices per time period than it would have to without the gold standard. Since this benefit is available to all nations on the gold standard, this organization of the international payments system amounts to an efficient and equitable system of insurance against natural catastrophes and mutual assistance for the world as a whole.

Third, the gold standard as described in the basic model functions without any government intervention. This is a great advantage in the eyes of people who believe that the efficient allocation of resources is such a complex problem that no human being can ever have all of the relevant information and necessary foresight to devise policies that can assure that the economy operates efficiently. In addition, such government intervention in the economic sphere represents a reduction in economic liberty, and in the long run, personal freedom in a pluralistic society cannot exist without liberty in the sphere of economics. From this point of view it is a great advantage that the gold standard operates without economic policies made by the governments, and thus it permits the restriction of government activity to provisions for national defense, other genuinely public goods, and the maintenance of domestic law and order.

II. THE MODEL AND THE REAL WORLD

An important set of theoretical modifications of the gold standard model was undertaken in response to empirical findings. Professor Frank Taussig at Harvard and some of his students had examined statistics of price and gold movements during periods when the gold standard was in actual operation. They discovered that even some of the severest disruptions of balance-of-payments equilibria were accompanied by actual gold movements of such minor size that they had to be considered incapable of explaining the process of adjustment predicted by the basic classical model.

The theoretical modifications of the basic gold standard model that developed in response to these findings fall into three distinct groups. First, the model was adapted to account explicitly for private short-term capital movements. Thus, if, as in the framework of the previous analysis, the cause of the international disturbance is assumed to be the failure of a harvest, the deficit causes prices to rise and gold to be exported in the manner described before. The additional element of the analysis is, however, that farmers try to borrow funds to tide them over the period of calamity. Since this demand represents a net addition to the equilibrium quantity of loans demanded and supplied at the existing interest rate, the market rate of interest goes up. In real terms, because of the destruction of resources in the deficit country, the marginal productivity of capital is temporarily raised.

As a result of this rise in the interest rate, private short-term capital is attracted into the deficit country. These capital imports are equivalent to the export of goods and services, in fact they *are* the export of claims on assets, enabling the deficit country to increase its imports of food products above the levels permitted by its own current exports of goods and services alone. The resultant increase in food supplies keeps down the rise in prices and the loss of gold. The extent to which this process is effective depends on the institutionally determined interest elasticity of private short-term funds. If the elasticity is very great, a very small rise in the interest rate causes sufficient capital inflows to prevent any further price increases and gold losses. At lower elasticities the benefits are correspondingly smaller.

In real terms these capital imports amount to the mortgaging of national assets other than gold, in return for the temporary loan of resources needed to overcome the effects of the bad harvest. Mortgaging of these assets other than money has the advantage of limiting the extent to which the price level has to rise initially and fall in the subsequent period of adjustment.

In the model with short-term capital flows the assets are repurchased from foreigners when, upon the restoration of the crop to its normal level, the farmers begin to repay their loans and interest rates fall. Consequently, foreigners divest themselves of their holdings, acquire gold, and repatriate it. As a result of this, gold transfer prices fall in the country that had the poor harvest and rise in the other one, causing the appearance of a trade surplus for the former and the transfer of the real resources borrowed originally.

In the real world during the gold standard, private short-term capital was rather interest elastic because of the confidence investors had in the stability of exchange rates and national price levels. However, as will be discussed below, the private short-term capital movements under the gold standard were dominated by events in London and worked primarily to the benefit of the United Kingdom rather than of all countries, as the theoretical model suggests.

The second modification of the basic classical model represents an explanation of the small actual gold movements discovered by Taussig, which is essentially a logical rival to the explanation involving capital movements. This modification received a complete and thorough explanation through the systematic development of Keynesian economics. In this system of analysis the classical model of the economy is made more realistic by the explicit recognition of the downward rigidity of real wages and prices.

In the Keynesian model exogenously caused decreases in aggregate demand, such as those following a poor harvest, have further repercussions. Suppliers of farmers find their sales decreased, since the farmers do not have the purchasing power to buy the normal quantity of farm inputs and consumer products. Other businessmen and workers find their stocks of merchandise increased beyond desired levels, both directly through the suppliers' reduced sales and indirectly through the suppliers' own reduced demand for stocks, investment, and consumption goods. The reaction of business throughout the economy to these developments is the laying off of workers, which in turn causes the disappearance of additional purchasing power, resulting in a vicious circle, until renewed bumper crops and increased sales start the economy on a beneficial cycle.

Temporary or permanent reductions in aggregate demand affect the international trade balance in this fashion because of a phenomenon that is known as the marginal propensity to import. It has been observed that at constant relative price levels between countries, a given country's imports tend to vary roughly proportionately with its income. Thus, a country whose imports fall by $15 million when its income level is lowered by $100 million is known to have a marginal propensity to import equal to $0 \cdot 15$, which is normally constant over a wide range of income changes.

An application of these ideas to the problem of adjustments under the gold standard leads to the following simplified pattern of events. The assumed failure of the harvest immediately and directly reduces national income. Along with this income reduction occurs a fall in imports, representing initially only those foreign products the farmers otherwise would have purchased. Soon, however, other business activities are curtailed, national income falls, and imports are reduced further. If the unemployment following the initial disturbance and the import propensity are great enough, the resultant lowering of imports can eliminate all deficits that would have appeared otherwise and thus reduce the need for actual international movements of gold.

During the periods when the gold standard was actually working in the world, price flexibility decreased progressively and the Keynesian income fluctuations increased, both along with the rise in general industrialization and unionization. Empirically, therefore, income adjustments tended to be more important during the last decade of the 19th and early 20th centuries than they were before.

A third explanation of the Taussig findings complements the other and does not change the basic classical model in a significant manner. It is recalled that the preceding analysis assumed that gold was the only money in the economy, and that there was a one-to-one correspondence between gold lost in balance-of-payments deficits and reductions in domestic money supplies. This system is also known as the "gold specie" standard.

In the real world, these conditions never prevailed strictly. Even when gold coins made up the bulk of the hand-to-hand money, fractional coins often consisted of some other metal or substitute, and major transactions were frequently carried out through the shipment of drafts and cheques substituting for the actual gold. The existence and the proliferation of these gold substitutes serving as money eventually loosened the one-to-one link between changes in a nation's gold stock and money supply. However, the essential feature of the system was retained, in the sense that all forms of monetary assets could readily be exchanged into gold. The resultant system is known as the "gold bullion" standard.

Quantitatively the most important source of gold substitutes was the banking system and the demand deposits it created. However, because gold tended to serve as the liquidity reserve of the banking system, any changes in a country's stock of monetary gold influenced these reserves and the quantity of demand deposits outstanding. In fact, because of the multiple expansion of deposits on the gold base, a given change in the gold stock normally had a multiple effect on the total money supply, and, for this analytically highly important reason, relatively small flows of monetary gold between countries were capable of producing the kind of reductions in the money supply and price levels under the gold bullion standard which the basic classical model of the gold specie standard envisaged.

The theoretical models explaining international payments and adjustments under the gold standard just presented are analytical prototypes. In the real world there existed a blend of all four: internal disturbances would tend to cause domestic price changes and flows of gold between countries. But there would also be amplified effects on national supplies of credit money. Short-term capital flows would reduce the need for price changes and gold flows. Income effects would tend to influence balance of payments through changes in the demand for imports. However, logically and for the sake of easy exposition, it is useful to distinguish these four elements of the adjustment process. One of the main features of this adjustment process, it is worth pointing out, is its automaticity and the absence of any governmental activity.

In recent empirical studies of the gold standard two additional important elements of this theoretical construct have been considered. The first of these elements concerns the role of government discretionary policies in the operation of the system. The government policies relevant in this context are those of exchange rate revaluation, in the form of redefining the gold value of domestic currency, and monetary policy, in the form of changing the quantity of money or the cost of credit. Arthur Bloomfield (1959), in an important study of actual government policies during the period 1880–1914, which he considers to be the time when the gold standard was most firmly established in the world, discovered that governments did in fact occasionally vary the price at which they purchased or sold gold bullion, in rather subtle and discrete ways. For example, countries would sometimes open offices for the purchase of bullion in border cities, lowering the cost of gold shipment and thus encouraging the importation of gold from neighboring countries at the outwardly fixed and unchanged unit price. In general, however, such interferences were rare and quantitatively insignificant.

In the realm of monetary policy, governments had more range for important actions because gold flows, through their effect on bank reserves, had a direct connection with countries' supplies of credit money. To prevent severe credit contractions, financial crises, and unemployment, central banks, through discretionary open-market operations, could offset gold losses and, by maintaining the base on which the credit money was built, prevent the contraction and other disruptions of the economy from taking place. Bloomfield's study revealed that in fact central banks seemed to engage in such offsetting policies quite frequently. However, it is clear that as long as these policies did not neutralize completely the effects of the gold losses, and instead only lessened their influence, the basic working of the system is not destroyed but only slowed down. Changes in discount rates were similarly used by governments to reduce the domestic impact of gold flows by reinforcing the interest rate mechanism and directing private capital flows in the manner suggested in the basic model. Natural catastrophes and gold losses, for example, under the model discussed above, would lead to interest rate increases and private capital inflows which governments could speed up or reinforce through the appropriate increase in its discount rate. Ultimately, the most important question about the role of these government policies is whether in fact they prevented basic adjustments and caused periods of disequilibrium with all their manifestations, such as unemployment, revaluations, the imposition of tariffs, and other restrictions on trade. The evidence suggests clearly that government policies did not cause these effects and that, while they may have modified the working of the gold standard system, they did not alter it basically from the way the theoretical blueprints suggest.

The second important element of the real world concerned the central role of Britain, which at the time dominated world trade and finance as no other country has since. Because of this position of dominance, Britain enjoyed an exceedingly high interest elasticity of private capital flows, so that a slight change in the discount rate was sufficient to alter the balance of payments by significant amounts. In the framework of the basic models introduced above, such management of private capital flows merely serves to minimize the flow of gold, and while it slowed down the fundamental adjustment process, it did not prevent it from working altogether. If a deficit in the balance of payments is reduced by an increase in the discount rate, the increased level of interest rates at the same time restricts domestic demand, lowers prices, and thus restores equilibrium in foreign trade, and vice versa for reductions in the discount rate. For small rises in the discount rate the resultant adjustments were small also, and a given required basic adjustment took longer to be completed.

Robert Triffin (1968) suggested in a study that the adjustment process, in the case of British deficits, may have worked not by restricting domestic demand but by improving Britain's terms of trade in the following way. The cost of credit was an important factor in determining the size of physical stocks of raw materials held in Britain. As the discount rate was raised, new purchases of raw materials fell off, and the resultant glut of products abroad caused a lowering of their prices, thus improving Britain's terms of trade and balance of payments. The burden of adjustment in real terms to a British disequilibrium thus fell primarily on the rest of the world rather than on Britain and the rest of the world in more equal measure, as the basic model suggests. Triffin may be correct in his analysis of the 19th-century gold standard experience, though more work needs to be done on the historic development of prices and interest rates to clinch the case. However, this finding does not invalidate the theoretical analysis of the gold standard mechanism in a world of roughly equal sized countries which was presented above and which is relevant for the current discussion of the alternative forms of monetary organization.

III. HISTORY OF THE GOLD STANDARD

Implicit in the analytical models of the gold standard just presented is the dual role of gold as, first, a means of settling payments imbalances between nations and, second, the standard of value to which all national currencies are linked. The institutional arrangements under which gold can play these roles exist when national governments purchase and sell gold bullion and mint gold coin in unlimited quantities at fixed prices, and when there are no legal obstacles on the melting of coin or export of the bullion.

Historically, gold coins have circulated since antiquity, but these formal institutional requirements of the gold standard were not met until the development of strong national governments in Western Europe during the 18th and 19th centuries. One of the most serious obstacles in the development of the gold standard was the fact that gold and silver coins had circulated side by side for many centuries, so that when governments began to assert their monetary sovereignty they were forced to establish ratios of exchange for gold and silver bullion. Depending on the ratio chosen and technological developments in the production and industrial use of the two metals at various times, one or the other tended to be overvalued and to drive the other metal from circulation, as a result of the working of Gresham's famous law.

Great Britain was the first major country to meet the formal conditions of being on the gold standard when, in 1821, the Bank of England was legally required to redeem its notes in gold bars or coin, and when all prohibition on the melting of coin and export of gold were repealed. Around 1850 the world price of gold fell relative to silver when supplies from the newly discovered fields in California and Australia came on the market. As a further result, in the United States and France, Gresham's law caused the disappearance of silver coins, and the two countries moved from the bimetallic standard to the de facto gold standard. Belgium, Switzerland, and Italy had standard monetary units equal to those of France and also went on the gold standard at the same time. However, by 1870 some countries, such as Germany, were still on the silver standard, and wars and revolutions had forced other countries into issuing inconvertible currencies. Among the latter group of countries were Russia, Austria-Hungary, Italy, and the United States. After the Franco-Prussian war of 1870, however, Germany obtained sufficient gold payments from France as reparations to enable her to adopt a genuine gold standard, and during the following decade a sufficiently large number of the remaining major countries of the world had passed the necessary legislation. Many observers therefore consider the year 1880 as the beginning of the "universal" gold standard era. Strictly speaking, however, Russia, Austria-Hungary, India, and Japan met the gold standard requirements only after 1895, and for this reason some observers put the beginning of the gold standard era as late as 1900.

The exact beginning of the gold standard era is not really very important because its effective life, ending with the outbreak of World War I hostilities in 1914, was perhaps 15 or 35 years, and thus it represents even at maximum a very short span in the history of the world or even of the industrialized West. Yet, the period is remembered with nostalgia by many people, and some influential economists and politicians have urged that it be reinstituted in the 1960s. Why, then, is this period of the gold standard held in such high esteem?

The answer to this question is to be found in the standard's alleged record of performance in contributing to an increase in the welfare of mankind. Human welfare has many dimensions, but two of the most important are the level and stability of real income and the degree to which individuals are free to shape their own destiny. With respect to the first, the last half of the 19th century saw a remarkable growth in per capita real income which was made possible through the techniques of mass production, the falling of food prices caused by the opening of the North American prairies for cultivation, and the availability of low-cost steamship and railroad transportation. Economic stability was reasonably great, interrupted only by occasional depressions and financial crises. Even during the long period of falling world prices in the 1880s and 1890s, per capita incomes continued to rise. In the decade following the California gold discoveries in 1849 and after the Alaska discoveries and the development of the cyanide process for refining South African gold about 1895, gold production increased rapidly and caused world prices to rise. These inflations created a sense of well-being in business and the general public throughout the world. The gold standard *contributed* to these developments by encouraging an efficient allocation of resources and pattern of development. During the gold standard era goods were exchanged freely in international trade, so that production tended to locate in technically optimum places; capital flowed to wherever productivity was highest without restrictions and in the confidence that world prices would be stable.

In the second important area of human welfare, the last half of the 19th century saw a movement toward greater personal and political freedom. Governments by and large pursued policies of enlightened nationalism, channeling people's energies into economic development and industrialization and permitting individuals a maximum of freedom to move geographically, to choose occupations, and to advance themselves socially. As compared with the level of government activities in the economy prevailing during the preceding period of mercantilism and the following period of neomercantilism and nationalism of the 1930s, government activity during the gold standard era was at a minimum. Most important, governments acted as if they were part of a world community, obeying rules of behavior that served the purposes of a smoothly functioning international economy. In cases of conflict between the interests of the world community and domestic welfare, the latter was subordinated to the former. Such internationalist policies did not have the same serious consequences for domestic welfare at that time as they would at present, because the degree of industrialization was lower, and consequently any slowdown in business activity would typically affect the living standards of smaller proportions of the population. For all of these reasons the gold standard period is considered by many as having been a desirable one in which to live, and one worth recreating for the present world.

This favorable interpretation of the gold standard's history has been challenged, and it is not clear to what extent the international monetary organization of the time was responsible for the growth in world welfare, and to what extent the preceding description of the "good old times" of the late 19th century made the mistake of confusing causes and effects. It can easily be argued that the real causes of the observed increases in overall well-being were the movement of Western societies toward democracy and the acceleration of industrial development which was taking place for other reasons. The gold standard, from this point of view, merely was a passive agent, facilitating but not influencing in any meaningful way this development. Subsequent growth in many of the world's economies, especially the rapid gains in real income in the United States, Western Europe, and the Soviet Union since the end of World War II, suggest strongly that the gold standard is not a necessary condition for real economic development.

But what about personal liberty and freedom from government intervention which characterized economic growth under the gold standard and which was restricted to varying degrees in the rapid-growth situations after World War II? Would a gold standard in this period have enabled the world to make the same gains in income without this loss of personal liberty and this growth of government activism in the economy? It is doubtful that it would have done so. Government involvement in capitalistic economies had become necessary because of the nature and complexity of the 20-century industrial structure, which requires the provision of public goods in quantities not technically feasible or necessary in the 19th century. The taxation and expenditures caused by these public goods makes government activism unavoidable. Moreover, the modern industrial economies are subject to at least the same instabilities as were the economies of the 19th century, but because of their populations' greater size and dependence on industrial employment, they create much greater human misery than did the same fluctuations in the 19th century. As the analysis of this chapter has shown, the working of the gold standard involves surrender by national governments of the right to engage in domestic stabilizing policies that are in conflict with the economic forces set in motion by the payments deficits and gold flows. Governments are not, and because of the severity of welfare losses should not be, willing to give up the rights to engage in these policies. Standards of government activity and optimum personal and economic liberty determined under the technical conditions prevailing in the 19th century are not applicable in the 20th century. And neither is the gold standard with which they are associated.

BIBLIOGRAPHICAL NOTES

The classic on the gold standard mechanism in Hume (1752). A two-volume definitive history of the gold standard was written by Brown (1934). Bloomfield's (1959) short pamphlet has much solid analysis and empirical evidence on the working of the gold standard. Taussig's findings are reported in his textbook (1927), pp. 239, 261. Triffin (1968) critically analyzes the gold standard model and its actual performance. References to contemporary proponents of the gold standard are Rueff (1961) and Heilperin (1962).

CONCEPTS FOR REVIEW

Quantity theory of money
Transactions velocity of money
Gold specie standard

Gold bullion standard
Gresham's law

POINTS FOR FURTHER STUDY AND DISCUSSION

1. Write a report on the history of the gold standard, paying special attention to a precise definition of its operation, the countries fully subscribing to it, and evidence on whether or not these countries behaved as the simple model suggests they would.

2. Survey the writings of traditional conservative economists such as Friedrich Hayek, Jacques Rueff, Ludwig von Mieses, Milton Friedman, Gottfried Haberler, Henry Simons and of recent monetarists such as Karl Brunner, Alan Meltzer, David Laidler, Harry G. Johnson and Michael Parkin to find out their views on the merits of the gold standard v. freely floating exchange rates.

3. Find estimates of gold production in recent years and discover what proportions of this output went into international monetary reserves and into industrial uses and private hoarding. How great has been the increase in the value of the world's gold stock as a result of recent price increases? As a result of these developments, what has happened to the ratio of gold to international reserves? How adequate therefore would be the stock of gold in the world if it were to serve as a base for a gold standard system?

4. Collect statistics on the price of gold in terms of sterling or dollars over the past 50 or 100 years. Has the price always gone up? What would have been the rate of return from holding gold for speculation over the entire period or some subperiods?

22 Freely Floating Exchange Rates

THE SYSTEM OF freely floating exchange rates has many articulate advocates among economists, most notably the University of Chicago's Milton Friedman, Egon Sohmen of the University of Heidelberg, and Leland Yeager of the University of Virginia, who have produced persuasive scholarly treatises to back their recommendations. However, freely floating exchange rates have never been popular with businessmen or politicians, and in recent years academic economists have developed some sophisticated arguments against freely floating rates which represent an effective challenge to the traditional views on the subject.

In this chapter we attempt to sort out the arguments and evidence underlying the case for and against freely floating rates. Because of the existing lack of agreement among scholars, however, students are warned to treat the material presented and the conclusions reached with skepticism. We oppose the use of freely floating rates on the basis of arguments on which the final judgment has not been reached.

The organization of the analysis in this chapter is as follows. First, the case for freely floating exchange rates is made in its most forceful form. We then present arguments against this case which are based on political judgments and the existence of market imperfections. The validity of the arguments in these two classes of objections will be seen to be questionable on theoretical and empirical grounds. The real case against freely floating exchange rates is presented in the final parts of this chapter, where we analyze the recently developed theories of optimum currency areas and optimum exchange rate stability. These theories argue that freely floating rates involve welfare costs, due to externalities from economic instabilities, which can be reduced through exchange market intervention.

438

In the presentation of the arguments involving political judgments and market imperfections, we proceed by stating the case against freely floating rates as forcefully as possible and then give a reply in the form of an examination of the theoretical and empirical validity of that argument. This expositional approach reflects real-world conditions, under which proponents of freely floating rates present a rather straightforward and simple case against their opponents, who make their case by drawing on the lessons from a long history of intervention and the practical experience and knowledge of traders, bankers, and government officials.

Before we turn to the main parts of this chapter it is necessary to reiterate an important point made earlier in this book: The system of freely floating exchange rates to be discussed first in this chapter is characterized by the total absence of any government intervention in the foreign exchange markets. If there is any foreign exchange market intervention at all, even just intervention designed to level exchange rate fluctuations or to smooth trends during a day or a week, the system of international monetary organization is then one of managed float. The arguments for and against the managed float system are presented in section five of the present chapter and in section four of Chapter 24.

I. THE BASIC MODEL

According to the advocates of freely floating exchange rates, their universal use would provide the world with benefits falling into three classes. First, there would be the benefits arising from increased efficiency in the allocation of resources. This is so because, according to the argument of its proponents, the exchange rate is nothing but a price, and theory suggests that prices determined in free markets lead to the efficient allocation of resources. Furthermore, there are benefits from the savings of real resources used up in the management of exchange rates. Second, free societies benefit from the absence of government control over an important price which can be manipulated to achieve certain political objectives and constrain the freedom of individuals. Exchange rates are particularly objectionable instruments for the attainment of income redistribution and other social objectives, since their control often is out of the hands of elected parliaments and instead in the hands of bureaucrats who may try to impose their views on the public. Third, in a world in which governments use discretionary monetary and fiscal policies to combat business cycles and try to trade off higher employment for inflation, benefits accrue from freely floating exchange rates because they permit the optimal pursuit of these stabilization and employment policies, free from all balance-of-payments constraints.

These basic arguments in favor of freely floating exchange rates are buttressed by a wide range of considerations familiar to students of price theory and those who are acquainted with models of how the market and governments should deal with market imperfections and externalities. Thus, if there are market imperfections which prevent the attainment of efficiency, such as oligopolies or monopsonies, then these imperfections should be dealt with directly, not through the introduction of an added social cost in the form of a nonmarket price for foreign exchange. In this context the analysis of second-best policies and tariffs presented in Chapter 8 is relevant. If society desires public goods, such as higher income of workers in import-competing industries or the maintenance of an industry important for defense which would be eliminated by imports, then a democratic parliamentary system should provide them directly and according to the wishes of the electorate, not indirectly through the pegging of exchange rates, which is out of the control of the legislature. Externalities arising from pollution and similar nonmarket effects on welfare, according to some recent theorizing, should induce the creation of new voluntary social organizations which internalize the externalities. For example, residents around a polluted lake have the incentive to form an association to reduce pollution through collective action limited to the affected people. Central government action to force the residents around the lake into adopting a pollution-control program is neither necessary nor likely to lead to an efficient solution.

It is quite obvious, therefore, that freely floating exchange rates tend to be favored by individuals who attach great weight to the social benefits of personal freedom and deliberate collective action at the most decentralized level possible. It is therefore no coincidence that the most articulate spokesmen for freely floating rates, Friedman, Sohmen and Yeager, in their other writings also tend to favor market over government solutions to economic and social problems. However, these attributes of the proponents for freely floating rates should not prevent a careful and objective analysis of the theoretical arguments and empirical evidence they use in making their case.

II. POLITICAL ARGUMENTS AGAINST FREELY FLOATING RATES EVALUATED

A. The Anchor Argument

Contention. In democracies, elected officials face the temptation to use economic policies to assure reelection. Low levels of unemployment and the temporary euphoria accompanying periods of inflation are particularly useful methods of achieving these ends. Yet inflation in the long run is bad for the economy and the moral and ethical values of society. For this reason, many Western governments have independent monetary authorities and other institutional arrangements which serve to isolate economic policy making from short-run political manipulation. Fixed exchange rates have traditionally helped national monetary authorities in their fight for price stability, because inflation tends to cause payments deficits and reserve losses, which the guardians of price stability then have used as a justification for the imposition of monetary and fiscal stringency and a slowdown in the rate of inflation. Under flexible exchange rates, international payments deficits would never occur, and monetary authorities would lose their anchor for restraining monetary expansion.

Answer. This argument about the disadvantages of flexibile exchange rates is based on a rather cynical view of democratic processes, namely the idea that central bankers or other economic technicians know better what rate of inflation is in the long-run interest of a nation than the public does. Price stability is not a constitutional right. Politicians and the government's executive should be sensitive to the public's desired relative quantities of inflation and unemployment. If the public wants to trade some unemployment for a somewhat higher rate of inflation, and it makes this preference known by electing candidates who stand for such a policy, it ought to be able to do so without being encumbered by monetary (or any other) anchors thrown out by conservative elements in society. From this point of view the loss of the monetary anchor implied by the institution of flexible exchange rates is a blessing rather than a disadvantage.

B. The Internationalist Argument

Contention. It is no coincidence that internationalism was strongest during the period of the gold standard in the 19th century. The level of international financial integration was high, and successful operation of the system of fixed exchange rates requires substantial intergovernmental consultation and cooperation. This internationalism helped to raise world welfare by permitting people and capital to move between countries with relative ease. Flexible exchange rates, on the other hand, would encourage nationalism by making it easier for governments to pursue policies without regard for the consequences to other countries. In such a world governments would tend to compete with each other in many ways, and in the process they would erect barriers to the free circulation of people and capital.

Answer. As it was argued in the discussion of the gold standard, countries began to renounce this system because industrialization and downward rigidity of wages made internationalism socially too costly. The gold standard worked because other necessary conditions for internationalism were right and not because there was a gold standard. It is, therefore, an illusion to believe that rigid exchange rates or the gold standard would bring an end to the current wave of nationalism. In the same way, flexible exchange rates would probably do little to increase nationalism.

However, fixed exchange rates have caused the erection of many controls on trade and capital movements which appear to be manifestations of nationalism, but in reality have been motivated by balance-of-payments problems. Many of these barriers to trade and capital flows may be eliminated once flexible exchange rates bring to an end all balance-of-payments problems. It may well be that such economic liberalization would be an important aid to greater international economic integration and cooperation than exists under the system of the adjustable peg.

III. MARKET IMPERFECTIONS AS ARGUMENTS AGAINST FREELY FLOATING RATES EVALUATED

A. Elasticity Pessimism

Contention. The price elasticities of import demand for internationally traded goods are low. If they are so low that the Marshall-Lerner condition is not fulfilled, and the elasticity of demand for a country's imports and the elasticity of the world's demand for its exports sum to less than 1, then a country's trade balance fails to improve if its exchange rate depreciates, and depreciation alone does not restore balance. Even if the sum of import elasticities is greater than 1, generally low elasticities imply that the attainment of any proportionate balance-of-trade improvements require large proportionate changes in exchange rates. Such wide fluctuations are an impediment to international trade and capital flows.

Answer. There is very little empirical evidence to suggest that the import elasticities facing one country are very low. At times in the past when countries did not experience improvements in their balance of payments after devaluation, they normally had failed to engage in the necessary policies for domestic expenditure reduction. As a result, aggregate demand continued to exceed aggregate supply. The basic cause of the deficit was not removed, and it wiped out the otherwise beneficial effects of the devaluation.

As we have seen (in Chapter 14), the belief in the existence of high elasticities is based on both theoretical and empirical evidence. While it is true that the elasticity of world demand for any one product may not be high, the demand elasticity for any one country's output of that product is high. Thus, for example, the world consumption of tea probably would increase by less than 10 percent if tea prices would fall by 10 percent. However, if *one* country would lower the price at which it is willing to sell tea by 10 percent below the prevailing world price for the identical quality product, it could sell all it can produce domestically. As to empirical evidence, econometric measurement of demand elasticities in recent years have found elasticities to be quite high.

In general it is true that demand elasticities are a function of time. A day after reduction in the price of tea by one supplier, his sales can be expected to increase only little because the price change may not be known or because buyers have stocks of tea or are contractually bound to deliveries from other higher priced sources. But after some time the price reduction will be known widely in the market, consumers' stocks need to be replenished, existing contracts between buyers and sellers come up for renewal, and buyers will take advantage of the lower price in increasing quantity. Because of this fact a given disequilibrium in foreign demand would tend to cause initially wide price movements, which eventually tend to be narrowed as the forces responsible for high trade elasticities in the long run come into effect. How big might these initial fluctuations be?

First, it must be remembered that very rarely are there events which suddenly affect a country's balance of trade. Bad harvests, technical change, or domestic inflations show their disequilibrating effects slowly. As a result, the factors causing trade elasticities to be high have sufficient time to operate. Second, even if payments disturbances are not gradual, the resultant persistent patterns of prices, such as are suggested by the analysis of elasticities through time, tend to be exploited by speculators. Knowing that the exchange rate will fall after its initial rise, they sell it at the high price and repurchase it at the low price. In so doing, of course, speculators prevent the rise in price from becoming as high as it would have been otherwise and thus stabilize the exchange rate.

B. Destabilizing Speculation

Contention. Foreign exchange speculation makes a system of freely fluctuating exchange rates unstable. Once an exchange rate begins to depreciate, speculators will have the tendency to expect further depreciation. Acting upon these expectations, asset holders sell the currency, exporters slow down sales and payments, and importers speed up purchases and payments. This speculative activity brings further currency depreciation, causes speculators' expectations to be realized, and feeds further speculation, in a cumulative, vicious cycle in which speculators make their own expectations come true. Even if the process is not infinitely cumulative, speculators are bound to cause large swings in exchange rates which are an impediment to international trade and capital flows.

Answer. The arguments about the cumulative process of self-fulfilling speculation are not well founded. Consider a situation where asset holders, exporters, and importers have engaged in their activities for one week, and they have in fact forced a decrease in the exchange rate. In the following week asset holders have fewer assets to draw upon, interest rates at which speculative funds can be borrowed have risen, and exporters and importers face lowered domestic and higher foreign prices and also higher domestic interest rates at which to finance their payments leads and lags. All of these "real forces" ultimately set a limit to the ability of asset holders and traders to carry on their speculative activities. Only if a government, through inflationary policies, keeps interest rates low and domestic goods prices high and thus prevents these real forces from developing can there be a cumulative depreciation of the currency. Under these circumstances the blame for the domestic inflation and exchange rate depreciation should be put on the government's inflationary policies, not on the speculators.

If real forces work without impediment, and speculators through faulty judgements sell at lower prices than those warranted by existing worldwide conditions of prices, demand, and supply, then the speculators lose money on their activities. In the long run speculators who have a tendency to misjudge real forces drop out of the market, and only those who are capable of forecasting "normal" prices remain active. This group of speculators serves a socially useful function of evening out temporary fluctuations. For example, if a country's harvest fails and the exchange rate falls, speculators anticipating that the future exchange rate will return to its "normal" level after the next harvest buy currency at the price below normal, in expectation of profits from future sales. As a result the price falls less than it would have in the absence of the speculators' purchases, who, from a social point of view, are "lending" resources to the country to overcome the temporary effects of a bad harvest.

It has been argued that the elimination of destabilizing unsuccessful speculators, as predicted by the theory, does not take place effectively, since dropouts always tend to be replaced by new entrants willing to risk their capital, so that at all times there exists a "floating" population of destabilizing speculators. Such a phenomenon is theoretically possible. It has also been shown that some speculators can profit consistently even though their purchases and sales add to price instability. To derive these results, very strong assumptions about the speculators' behavior and price-forecasting abilities have to be made, though the logical possibility represents an important qualification of the basic arguments about profitability of speculation and stability. However, the entire controversy over the effects of speculation on foreign currencies can ultimately be settled only through experience. Unfortunately, the evidence drawn from past experience is mixed. The Canadian exchange rate did not suffer greatly from speculative instabilities, but it is not clear to what extent this has been due to limited government intervention. Other historic experiments with the use of freely flexible exchange rates have nearly always been accompanied by unsettling speculation. However, these experiments are not really a fair test, since they were always introduced after major economic crises and after conventional pegging operations proved totally inadequate to deal with the problems. The best known experiments in this category are when the United States did not maintain stable exchange rates with gold standard countries from the Civil War until 1879, and when several European countries let their currencies float after World War I, until restoration of a quasi gold standard in the twenties.

In general, the uncertainty of the effects speculators are likely to have on freely floating exchange rates is undoubtedly one of the most important obstacles standing in the way of the widespread adoption of floating rates. In other markets, such as for corporate securities or commodities, speculators frequently do engage in unsettling activities. However, it should be noted that such speculation for the most part takes place in relatively thin markets where speculators' limited resources have the greatest leverage. This fact has an important implication for flexible exchange rates also in that it suggests stability might be greater the deeper a market and the larger the geographic area within which rates are fixed and whose external rate is free to fluctuate. These considerations will be taken up in the next section, on optimum currency areas.

C. Costs of Transition Period

Contention. The switchover from pegged rates to flexible rates is bound to be accompanied by chaos in the exchange markets, upsetting international patterns of trade and capital flows and causing in turn upheavals in many domestic markets. Empirical evidence suggesting the likelihood of these events is very strong. Their real social cost tends to be very large, and it might take a long time of superior performance by the flexible exchange rate system to amortize this cost of transition.

Answer. The chaos resulting from the transition is a once-and-for-all cost, while the benefits can be expected to last for as long as the system is maintained, so that even if initial costs are high there may be a substantial positive return to the introduction of flexible rates. Furthermore, the cost should be compared with the sum of the costs incurred by the chaos accompanying the revaluation of major currencies under the pegged system. It is not legitimate to set up a smoothly functioning system of pegged rates as a standard of comparison. Instead the proper base of comparison should be the historical performance record of the system the flexible rates are to replace. Moreover, the chaos expected to follow from a sudden freeing of all exchange rates could be reduced considerably by the use of policies specifically designed to cope with transitional problems. For example, countries could introduce universal flexibility by the gradual widening of intervention margins and by progressive limitations on the frequency and intensity of pegging operations.

The available historical evidence suggests that frequently the introduction of flexible exchange rates has been accompanied by chaos in internal and external economic conditions. However, it is highly misleading to infer from this simultaneity of events the causal relationship running from the introduction of the rates to the chaotic conditions. Historically, domestic inflation and the mismanagement of external accounts, often caused by wars and their aftermath, has tended to lead to such difficulties for governments that flexible exchange rates were the only solution. Without their use the chaos might have been greater still.

IV. MARKET FAILURES: THE OPTIMUM CURRENCY AREA ARGUMENTS

During the 1960s Robert Mundell of Columbia University and Ronald McKinnon of Stanford University introduced a new element into the discussion over the merit of freely floating exchange rates. This new element can be appreciated most readily by consideration of the following question. If freely floating exchange rates provide monetary authorities with the freedom to pursue stabilization policies, then why would it not be optimal to make every small region of the world into a "currency area" by endowing it with its own money, monetary authority, and a freely floating exchange rate with the rest of the world? According to the theory, such a system would permit regions notorious for their unemployment, such as southern Italy, Appalachia in the United States, and the Maritime provinces of Canada, to move to full employment. Anyone who considers it appropriate that such regional currency areas be created has to face the question which logically follows: Why is it not even better if still smaller currency areas were selected encompassing counties, villages, or even individual firms and workers? Anyone who feels that such regional currency areas are not optimal must consider whether the current nation-states are optimum currency areas or if it would not be better to combine some of them into larger entities with fixed exchange rates among them but freely floating rates towards the rest of the world.

Anyone who admits that these questions are legitimate (and every economist on record does so) implicitly also admits that the arguments for and against freely floating exchange rates discussed above are omitting some important elements of costs and benefits which should enter the social calculus over whether or not countries would maximize their welfare by adopting freely floating exchange rates toward the rest of the world. Let us now make explicit the costs and benefits resulting from currency area formations as they have emerged during the 1960s. We will use the analytical simplification of considering only the enlargement of a currency area, though, of course, the analysis could also be carried out for the case of dividing an existing country into a number of separate currency areas.

Consider that the world consists of three independent countries which have freely floating exchange rates among themselves initially. We make the important assumption that all markets and economic processes work perfectly, as is assumed by the proponents of freely floating rates. We assume that we can measure world welfare under these conditions and take the initial level of world welfare as the standard by which we evaluate the merit of the following institutional innovation. Two of the countries link their currencies permanently and create one monetary authority. The new currency area's exchange rate floats freely. The two countries are assumed to retain all other forms of national economic sovereignty, specifically the right to regulate foreign trade, make fiscal policy, tax, and provide public goods according to each nation's tastes. We consider here only the welfare levels in the two countries forming the currency area. If it improves, they are assumed to be an "optimum currency area." In a social welfare calculus for the world as a whole, one needs to analyze also the welfare effects of the currency area formation on the third country. Consideration of all possible currency area combinations and world welfare effects would result in the choice of a global network of currency areas representing optimum optimorum. Here we are interested only in developing the criteria for deciding how one currency area enlargement affects welfare. The same criteria can be used to analyze the effects of all other combinations of countries and regions into particular networks of currency areas.

The welfare of the population in the new currency area is assumed to be an increasing function of three elements: real income, the stability of real income, and independence in choice of target unemployment levels and rates of economic growth. The formation of the currency area affects these three elements of welfare through the following processes.

Real Income

After formation of a currency area the stock of labor, capital, and technology in the area are unchanged, and therefore they do not affect income levels directly. However, the fixed exchange rate between the two countries eliminates instabilities and uncertainty, which exist even when markets work perfectly and speculation stabilizes markets, as we argued above. As a result of this reduced instability producers are encouraged to consider the entire currency area rather than just their own country as their marketing territory, and they establish plants of optimum size in cases where the smaller national currency areas previously did not support such plants. For the same reason of reduced instability, capital is allocated more efficiently throughout the new currency area. The consequences of these changes in the pattern of production and capital flows are greater productive efficiency and therefore higher income in the currency area.

According to Mundell and McKinnon, one of the most important effects of the currency area formation is that the price level is stabilized. This follows from three facts. First, in the larger area random shocks to stability are likely to be offsetting; when one of the countries has a bad harvest, for example, the other is likely to have a bumper crop. Generally this benefit is an increasing function of the territorial size and geographic and industrial diversity of a currency area. Second, it is well known that the consumer price index in every country is calculated by weighting individual items relative to the quantities in which they are purchased by the average consumer. Third, we know from our analysis of Chapter 11 that the domestic prices of tradable goods are determined by rest-of-the-world prices times the exchange rate. As a result of the latter two facts, changes in the exchange rate influence the domestic prices of tradable goods, and for any given changes in the prices of these tradables the consumer price index fluctuates more the greater is the share of these goods in the consumer's market basket. In the new currency area, tradables carry a smaller weight in the market basket than they do in each of the original countries. A combination of all three facts leads to the conclusion that a given set of disturbances facing the two countries in the currency area causes less price instability because disturbances are likely to be offsetting internally and to result in smaller exchange rate fluctuations. Furthermore, the remaining exchange rate fluctuations have a smaller impact on the price indexes because tradables are a smaller proportion of all goods used in the calculation of the index.

The most important effect of the increased price stability is on the usefulness of money as a medium of exchange, unit of account, and store of value. It is a well-known proposition from monetary theory that people are inclined to hold more money the more certain is its purchasing power in the future. This argument is not to be confused with the one concerning the rate of inflation. Money holdings are a decreasing function of the expected rate of inflation, because the latter represents a tax. But whatever the expected rate of inflation and the associated demand for money, people are willing to hold more money the more certain is this expected rate of inflation.

To see that this is so, consider that in a certain country the average inflation rate is zero, but this average is composed of random increases and decreases of 10 percent each in equal numbers of time periods over a long time horizon. We make the normal assumption that individuals typically hold money because they cannot predict exactly when they need to make an expenditure, and it costs real resources to convert other assets into cash on quick notice. Let us assume furthermore that wealth holders can hold their net worth either in the form of money or as real assets whose value in exchange for other assets and consumption goods fluctuates together with the price index. Under these conditions, a person who holds all of his wealth in real assets enjoys perfect stability of value of his wealth in exchange for assets or consumption goods, even though the price index measured in currency units fluctuates randomly, as postulated. On the other hand, if he holds all of his wealth in money, his net worth in terms of consumption goods and real assets fluctuates. Since all people, ceteris paribus, prefer a certain and predictable level of wealth through time over levels which are uncertain and unstable, holding wealth in the form of real assets is preferable to holding money, under the assumed conditions of price instability.

What proportion of the wealth is actually held in the form of money under the conditions described here depends on the random patterns of expenditure and receipts, as well as on the cost of exchanging real assets for money and the losses incurred when cash is not on hand to make emergency expenditures. As long as these costs and losses are nonzero, there will be some cash holdings, in spite of the greater value certainty of real asset holdings. However, for our purposes of analysis, we reach the important conclusion from the preceding considerations that, ceteris paribus, in a country the public's money holdings are an increasing function of price stability.

We know that in the absence of money, economic activity would be reduced to barter and valuable resources would be used up to match specific needs of consumers and availabilities of producers. In fact, modern industrial economies simply could not function. Money therefore has a social productivity which permits the saving of the resources otherwise used up in barter, and it encourages the development of specialization in production, which is the source of much of the productivity of modern industrial economies. It is important to note that most of these benefits accrue to society in the form of externalities. From these facts about the social productivity of money it follows that the more stable the price level is, the more money the public is willing to hold, and the further the economy moves along the spectrum from the costly system of barter to the optimally efficient monetary economy. Because the currency area enlargement considered here tends to increase price stability, it produces the kinds of positive externalities associated with the increased use of money, and it raises the welfare of the population in the two countries above the levels they enjoyed before the union.

The final effect on real income resulting from currency area enlargement is due to savings made possible by the elimination of speculators and forward exchange brokers, who previously served trade and capital flows between the two countries which are now joined in the currency area. Furthermore, private individuals can forego the often tedious labor of changing money when traveling into the other country or converting foreign into domestic currency prices when planning budgets and managing portfolios encompassing goods and assets from the other country in the currency area. All of the resources saved by the reduced need for speculators, foreign exchange brokers, money changing, and price conversion can be used to increase the real income and welfare of the people living in the two countries joined in a currency area.

Stability of Income

The main cost of currency area formation is that it reduces the ability to pursue monetary policy for stabilization of income without constraints in each of the two previously independent countries. Thus it is possible that random disturbances will cause unemployment in one of the two countries and inflationary pressures in the other. Whereas, before the currency area formation, the monetary authorities in each country could apply the policies most appropriate for the remedy of its own problem, the single authority serving both countries in the enlarged currency area must compromise and adopt a policy of monetary neutrality which imposes real costs on both countries. Mitigating this difficulty somewhat is the fact that within the larger currency area disturbances of opposite effects on income and employment tend to be arbitraged more readily by private entrepreneurs and capital flows. As the examples of regional unemployment pockets in Italy, Canada, and the United States mentioned above indicate, however, this arbitrage would tend not to be perfect, and it must be concluded that reduced average income and employment stability caused by constraints is one of the costs of currency area enlargement.

McKinnon, in his article on optimum currency areas (1963), stresses the fact that exchange rate devaluations involve decreases in workers' real income. Because of money illusion, they are more willing to tolerate these decreases than equal adjustments made through money wage cuts, monetary policy, or taxation. For example, if a country in balance-of-payments deficit because of cyclical excess demand devalues its currency by 10 percent, and if tradables represent 20 percent in the workers' market basket, then the price index based on this basket must increase in terms of domestic currency units by 2 percent, for reasons discussed above. Now if under such conditions workers do not ask immediately for a 2 percent increase in money wages because they have not realized the implications of the devaluation and resultant inflation for their real incomes, they are said to be suffering from money illusion. When there is such money illusion workers are induced by currency devaluation to accept lower real incomes, thus setting free resources which can be used to increase exports or reduce imports, which is, as we have seen in Part Four, a necessary condition for attaining balance-of-payments equilibrium.

In the context of optimum currency areas, McKinnon's argument is that workers are more likely to suffer from money illusion the larger is the currency area and therefore the smaller are the share of tradables in the price index and the price rise accompanying a given-sized devaluation. For example, in Appalachia, whose dominant industry is coal mining, nearly all goods are tradable. If Appalachia had its own currency and suffered from a payments deficit, depreciation of its exchange rate by 10 percent would raise prices by nearly 10 percent. While workers may accept the consequences of a 10 percent devaluation in a country with a small proportion of tradables, they are less likely to do so in one where tradables are as important as they are in Appalachia. From this argument it follows that any given random shock resulting in excess demand and leading to a depreciation of the currency is more likely to be eliminated in a larger than in a smaller currency area. On the basis of this argument, then, the larger currency area can be expected to be able to achieve payments equilibria more easily, by being able to reduce excess demand through the use of both restrictive monetary policy and a downward floating of its currency, than could either of the two countries in isolation. The welfare in the newly formed currency area therefore is likely to be increased. We can note, however, that the validity of this argument depends decisively on the assumed strength of money illusion in the large and small currency areas. In periods of general economic instability and rapid inflation, workers tend to become very sensitive to all price changes, and money illusion tends to disappear. In the extreme, when workers and other factors of production receive incomes indexed according to inflation, the postulated advantage of currency area enlargement disappears completely.

Independent Targets

As we have shown in Chapters 16, 17, and 18, Keynesian economics, as it developed in the period after World War II, suggests that countries have two important macroeconomic policy choices. We can summarize these again, as follows.

First, evidence suggests that countries have a choice of achieving any desired level of unemployment through appropriate aggregate-demand management, as long as they are willing to accept the inflation which, according to the so-called Phillips curve tradeoff, accompanies the particular unemployment. Countries are considered to have not only different rates of employment-inflation tradeoff, but they are also different with respect to their preferred points on the spectrum of choices confronting them. Thus, after public discussion of the issues, the United States and Canada decided to aim for a target of 3 to 3.5 percent unemployment, in expectation that it would be accompanied by an annual inflation rate of about 2 percent. Germany, on the other hand, aimed for zero inflation, with only 1.5 to 2 percent unemployment. From our analysis of the foreign exchange market, it follows that such different rates of inflation cause changes in the exchange rates of one country with the rest of the world. If two countries had pursued different optimal rates of inflation without balance-of-payments constraints because of freely floating rates, they could not continue to do so after they adopted one common currency. As a result, one or both countries have to adjust their rates of inflation to a level acceptable to the entire area. In so doing, both countries suffer a loss in welfare, since they have moved from their prior optimum position.

Second, Keynesian economic analysis suggests that equal levels of aggregate demand can be achieved by fiscal restraint and monetary ease and by fiscal ease and monetary tightness. The two policy mixes have important effects on economic growth. When fiscal policy is tight, interest rates are low and investment is encouraged; when fiscal policy is easy, monetary restraint leads to high interest rates and capital formation, and growth is discouraged. Depending on the structure of their economies and tastes for present as against future consumption, countries tend to adopt preferred mixes of fiscal and monetary policies. If they do, freely floating exchange rates eliminate all balance-of-payments problems, but under a common currency, one or both have to adjust their policy mix to one that is acceptable to the residents of both countries. If the previous policies were optimal, any move away from them must cause a reduction in welfare.

Sacrifices of optimal full employment or inflation and growth policies are likely to be required as a consequence of currency area formation, and they may well be considered to involve the greatest welfare losses from the point of view of politicians and the public. However, during the past decade economists have begun to question the validity of the Keynesian economic analysis which has led to the view that there exists a tradeoff between inflation and unemployment and a choice of growth rates, as we discussed in Chapter 19. The model of monetary and fiscal policy mixes to achieve different growth rates has been shown to involve questionable assumptions about real and nominal rates of interest, about the substitution of government for private securities in the wealth portfolios of the public, and about the effects of balance-of-payments flows on stocks of reserves. We cannot evaluate the merits of these challenges here. For our purposes of analysis, it may be best to conclude that currency area enlargement involves some social cost in the form of reduced choice of inflation-unemployment and growth mixes, but this cost may be considerably smaller than economists believed during the 1950s and 1960s.

Summary and Conclusions

Let us now put together the different sources of welfare effects arising from the formation of a currency area by two countries which previously had their own currencies and freely floating exchange rates. The welfare of the residents in the area is likely to rise because of higher income due to greater efficiency in production and capital allocation, to the greater usefulness of money, and to savings in transactions costs. The effect of currency area formation on economic stability may well be negative, because of the constraints the common currency puts on the use of monetary policy to combat regional unemployment problems. To mitigate these constraints it is likely that disturbances within the area will be offset, and private market arbitrage and speculation will work more perfectly. As a result, the welfare of the public in the currency area may be reduced by increased economic instability. Another effect of currency area formation on welfare is due to the fact that the individual countries cannot continue to pursue independent targets of unemployment or inflation and the monetary-fiscal policy mix for growth. Welfare losses from these constraints are probably smaller than had been believed during the 1950s and 1960s, when the development of Keynesian economic analysis gave rise to the theoretical concepts.

In the real world none of these effects on welfare can be estimated with precision, and therefore the net effect of any contemplated currency area formation on the well-being of the public cannot be established. However, these considerations do give some important insights into the direction of the welfare effects. They also increase understanding of why most experts are reluctant to recommend splitting individual countries into small currency areas to solve regional problems of unemployment and economic instability more generally and why, on the other hand, European countries are moving toward the establishment of a European Currency Area. We can presume that the public debate and political processes accompanying moves toward currency area formation represent a sorting out and informal estimation of the welfare costs and benefits we have discussed theoretically.

Analytically, the optimum currency area arguments about the consequences of freely floating exchange rates are of extreme importance, because they point to the existence of externalities that competition in factor and goods markets will not eliminate. As such, they are in a completely different category from the arguments against freely floating rates made in the preceding two sections of this chapter. Imperfectly working political processes and markets call for policies which would eliminate them directly rather than through the pegging of exchange rates. The welfare effects discussed in this section, on the other hand, would exist even if markets were perfect. Their elimination involves changes in institutions, such as combining groups of nation-states into currency areas, which internalize the externalities.

In the next section we use the tools of analysis developed in the optimum currency area arguments above to show that by increasing the stability of exchange rates through time, countries can internalize the same externalities that they can by geographic extensions of the area of stability through optimum currency area formation. Out of this reasoning we develop the concept of optimum exchange rate stability, which involves less than freely floating exchange rates, even in the presence of otherwise perfect markets and political institutions.

V. THE CASE FOR OPTIMUM EXCHANGE RATE STABILITY

The argument against freely floating exchange rates to be presented in this section involves a dynamic framework of analysis and the efficiency of market allocation mechanisms under uncertainty and over time. This dynamic framework of analysis is not developed very well, and much of the thinking of economists in this area is based on the generalization of results from comparative static analysis. However, one important, explicit, and well-developed analytical link between time periods under uncertainty is the speculator. The role of speculators in the efficient allocation of resources through time can usefully be summarized as follows.

Consider that at the present time all agricultural product prices are in equilibrium, in expectation of an average-sized harvest. Suddenly a natural catastrophe lowers expected yields. Speculators, specializing in the analysis of the effect of the particular event on the availability of agricultural products in the future, decide that there will be a shortage next year. They act on their expectations and purchase stocks currently available. These purchases raise present prices and reduce current consumption. If there is a bad harvest in the next period, as the speculators expected, prices stay high and consumption remains low. This is necessary, since a less than normal quantity of output is available. Under these conditions speculators make a profit, but they also have done society a service by signaling to the market earlier than would have been the case otherwise that a shortage was imminent and that it was necessary to consume less in one period of relative plenty to avoid a very drastic reduction in consumption in the following period. If, on the other hand, the shortage anticipated by speculators does not take place, then prices after the harvest fall, and speculators lose on the sale of the stocks they have accumulated. It is reasonable to assume that speculators who habitually forecast badly lose their means for speculation, so that on balance those who remain tend to forecast correctly on average. Therefore they provide a beneficial service to society through their specialized study of likely future events.

It is worth noting here that perfectly working speculative markets cannot and should not eliminate all price instability. This is an important point, since it is not a legitimate criticism of the free market mechanism that it does not achieve perfect stability. This proposition follows from the fact that a necessary condition for efficient resource allocation is that any activity should be pushed to the point where marginal cost equals marginal benefit. The marginal benefit from price stability is a decreasing function of stability and reaches zero when fluctuations are zero. Since the marginal cost of keeping stocks of goods necessary for price stabilization is always positive, optimality must be reached before prices are kept perfectly stable. In other words, the profit motive guiding the behavior of rational spectators will not lead to perfect stability of prices through time. This argument in general form is applicable to commodity prices as well as to exchange rates, spot and forward.

Let us now assume that in fact a country, which may or may not be an optimum currency area in the sense discussed above, lets its exchange rate float freely, and speculators are stabilizing it in both the spot and forward markets. The problem of the optimality of freely floating exchange rates can now be put as follows: If this country acquired international reserves and undertook to reduce the variance of exchange rates through time from the level they achieved under the specified free market conditions, would welfare in this country be raised? In our discussion of the optimum currency area arguments, we have already provided the ingredients of our answer to this question. Welfare would be increased through three different processes. First, the instability of prices of foreign goods and assets is reduced even further than was permitted by the speculative markets and forward contracts. As a result, trade and international specialization are increased, leading to the welfare gains discussed in Part One of this book. Furthermore, capital is allocated more efficiently throughout the world, raising output and welfare. Second, because of the link between exchange rates and the prices of tradable goods, the domestic price level in the country shows a smaller variance, with the implications for the usefulness of money, efficiency, and specialization discussed above. Third, individuals save resources by the reduced need to pay attention to the prices of foreign goods and assets. They also are induced to hold foreign currencies and thus save the costs of money changing.

The argument about the beneficial effects of exchange rate stability on trade and capital flows is the one made most strongly by businessmen and bankers and underlies the case for the gold standard discussed in the preceding chapter. However, the stress of these arguments is on the reduction of uncertainty brought about by the pegging of exchange rates. This stress leaves open the argument to criticism by the proponents of freely floating rates that forward exchange markets can be used to eliminate the uncertainty. In our analysis the emphasis is on the instability of foreign prices and assets, which exists even if forward markets are well developed and permit the elimination of all uncertainty.

If welfare is raised by the stabilization of exchange rates, the important conclusion emerges that international reserves needed for the foreign exchange market intervention and stabilization by the government have a positive social productivity. It should be noted that such productivity is logically inconsistent with the assumption that freely floating exchange rates lead to greatest efficiency. In the analytical framework we have developed here, therefore, international reserves closely resemble money in domestic economies, which also is known to have a social productivity, because without it economies would have to operate under the inefficient system of barter.

We have established the crucially important points that international reserves have a positive social productivity, even in a country where there are no market imperfections, because they allow governments to reduce exchange rate fluctuations and internalize the externalities associated with them. We can now turn to the development of the concept of optimal reserves and tie this up with optimal exchange rate stability.

Optimal Reserves and Flexibility

From our analysis of the benefits from exchange rate stabilization follows this question: Why don't governments act to eliminate all exchange rate fluctuations and therefore maximize social welfare? The answer is that it costs something to stabilize exchange rates, and the social benefits from stabilization in the form of externalities are decreasing at the margin. The costs of exchange market intervention consist of the opportunity cost of holding reserves, say gold or dollars, rather than real assets with a social productivity, such as real capital. Furthermore, governments incur the costs of information gathering and decision making about the proper level of intervention. Efficiency therefore demands that exchange rate stabilization be pushed only to the point where marginal social costs equal marginal social benefits.

The condition of optimality can be illustrated with the help of Figure 22–1, in which we measure the marginal productivity of resources and reserves on the vertical axis and the quantity of reserves held by the individual country along the horizontal axis. The distance OR represents the marginal productivity of resources in the country, which is also equal to the opportunity cost of reserves yielding no interest, such as gold. The schedule $MPMP'$ represents the marginal productivity of reserves, which is positive, according to the analysis just presented, and a decreasing function the quantity of reserves. The latter property arises from the facts

FIGURE 22–1
Productivity of Reserves

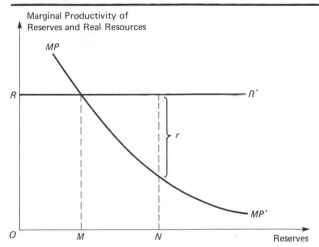

The marginal productivity of international reserves is shown as a decreasing function of the quantity of reserves held ($MPMP'$). The marginal productivity of real resources is OR in country A. This country's equilibrium level of reserve holdings is OM if reserves yield no interest and ON if they yield an interest rate r, because for efficiency all asset holdings should be pushed to the point at which their real plus monetary yields are equal.

that the ability to stabilize rates is greater the larger is the country's stock of reserves, and the social benefits from stabilizations are decreasing at the margin. Optimal reserve holdings in the form of gold are OM where marginal costs and benefits are equal, abstracting from costs of information and decision making. The optimal exchange rate stability is that which can be achieved by maintaining the average target level of reserves, OM, when dealing with the country's periodic excess demand and supply conditions in the foreign exchange market, in the manner analyzed in Chapter 20.

We can note briefly that if the country could hold its reserve in the form of an asset yielding interest rate r, the optimum reserve holdings would be ON; the marginal productivity of average reserve holdings would be lowered; and the optimum stability of exchange rates would be increased, as compared with the situation encountered when reserves yield no interest. This conclusion follows directly from the efficiency condition, which implies that in equilibrium the marginal productivity of average reserve holdings must be equal to the opportunity cost of holding the reserves, which is equal to the marginal productivity of domestic real resources minus the interest yield on the reserves. An individual country cannot alter the productivity of domestic real resources or the interest yield on reserves, so its optimum reserve holdings and exchange rate stability are uniquely determined. However, as we shall see in Chapters 23 and 24 on the IMF system, the world as a whole can alter the interest yield on reserves and therefore the average reserves held by each country, the average stability of exchange rates, and consequently the overall efficiency of the international monetary system.

Assumed Government Wisdom

The case for managed exchange rates made in this section rests importantly on an empirical judgment, the validity of which is not undisputed. This judgment is that governments charged with the welfare-increasing management of exchange rates on average stabilize rather than destabilize the rates. The latter outcome may arise either in short-sighted attempts to exploit the international community or through ignorance and incompetence. If this is the case, then it is possible that freely floating exchange rates are welfare maximizing, even though it is correct that further exchange rate stabilization of markets without imperfections would increase welfare.

A number of economists believe that there is much evidence in economic history of economic mismanagement by governments, which arose for a number of reasons. For example Friedman argues that the Great Depression of the 1930s was caused by the lack of understanding of the nature of monetary policy and the incompetence of monetary authorities in the United States and other countries. There is convincing evidence that countries sometimes attempt to enrich themselves at the expense of the rest of the world and succeed in doing so for periods of time. On the other hand, many economists hold the view that economic management, through the use of monetary and fiscal policies combined with a system of managed exchange rates since the end of World War II, has produced a long period of real economic growth and stability which is unprecedented in economic history. There is also evidence that governments are improving their ability to deal with instability and to manage exchange rates in a stabilizing fashion. There appears to be increasing recognition of the benefits of international cooperation and willingness to work together in international economic agencies. The optimum management of economic instabilities and exchange rates may be an elusive goal, and setbacks are inevitable, but many economists believe that improvements will continue to be made in the longer run.

We have no way of establishing with scientific rigor the validity of either of the two views about governments' ability to increase economic stability through monetary and fiscal policy and management of the exchange rates. There is simply no way of finding out whether some disturbances would not have occurred under laissez-faire and how the economy would have handled them without government policies. The debate over these issues will continue for long into the future, and students have to choose sides on their own. Whatever the outcome of these deliberations may be, the arguments about the superiority of managed exchange rates over laissez-faire solutions of the gold standard or freely floating exchange rates follow logically from the assumption that governments, on average, are able to reduce economic instability resulting from exogenous shocks of nature, their own activities of income redistribution and public goods provision, international economic conflicts, and their mistakes in carrying out the stabilization policies.

The Coase Theorem

We conclude this chapter by dealing briefly with the objections to government interference, even in the presence of externalities, developed in recent years at the University of Chicago Law School, most notably by Ronald Coase. According to this view, society tends to create new institutions to internalize externalities. For example, as we have noted, homeowners around a lake create externalities through dumping waste into the lake, and each suffers from the unpleasantness of the pollution and the reduced value of his property. Individual homeowners cannot prevent the pollution because they know that their own reduced dumping of wastes is insufficient to achieve the required cleaning effect. Only collective action will do to solve the problem. Knowledge of these facts creates incentives for the homeowners around the lake to create an association and to agree collectively on the building of sewers and other measures to reduce pollution, to the point where the marginal costs equal the marginal benefits in the form of reduced negative externalities. If no such association is formed, homeowners reveal by their inactivity that the cost is not worth the benefit of the elimination of the pollution. Any standards of pollution control imposed by a government body other than the association of homebuilders would tend to be nonoptimal.

This argument against government interference can and has been refined to take account of transactions costs, problems of information and organization, and others, all of which may prevent the socially optimal degree of internalizing externalities. In spite of these objections, the argument remains most persuasive. However, it may be considered to provide the rationale for rather than against control of the money supply and managed exchange rates by governments. In the case of the lake, externalities affect people in a clearly defined geographical area. The optimum organization for the internalization of externalities is this region. The externalities arising from financial instability and foreign trade, on the other hand, involve nations and, according to the optimum currency area arguments, perhaps even regions comprising more than one country. For these types of externalities, the optimal size of organization for their internalization, therefore, may well be entire countries or optimum currency areas. From this point of view, central banks controlling the money supply and managing the exchange rate are institutions designed to internalize the externalities from economic instabilities within the appropriate territory, and exchange rate stabilization is consistent with efficiency.

BIBLIOGRAPHICAL NOTES

The classic on flexible exchange rates is Friedman (1953). A more complete discussion is in Sohmen (1969). At a more popular level and introducing broader political considerations is Brittan (1970). Detailed discussion of the literature on the effects of speculation on flexible exchange rates and on the experience of different countries during actually floating rates are discussed in Stern (1973a), ch. 3. The classics on optimum currency areas are Mundell (1961) and McKinnon (1963). Grubel (1970), Ishiyama (1975), and Willett and Tower (1970) attempt to synthesize the original arguments. Johnson and Swoboda (1973) contains the papers delivered at a conference on optimum currency areas. The paper on which the last part of the chapter is based is Grubel (1973). The interpretation of the causes of the Great Depression is in Friedman and Schwartz (1963). The reference to Coase is (1966).

CONCEPTS FOR REVIEW

Anchor argument
Internationalist argument
Destabilizing speculation
Market failure versus market imperfection
Optimum currency area
Productivity of money

Productivity of international reserves
Money illusion
Nontraded goods
Optimum exchange rate stability
Coase theorem

POINTS FOR FURTHER STUDY AND DISCUSSION

1. Survey the literature and write a report on Canada's experience with floating exchange rates during the 1950s and 1960s.

2. Survey the literature and write a report on the studies designed to establish whether speculators tend to stabilize or destabilize the exchange rate.

3. According to regional economists, there are regional transportation territories, regional pollution control territories, regional administrative territories. Can you think of anything that these optimal regional territories and optimum currency areas have in common?

4. Survey the literature on the demand for international reserves and write a report on the evidence concerning the relationship between nations' reserve

holdings and economic instability. Can you think of any reasons why the causal relationship between observed instability and reserve holdings may run in both directions?

5. Consider the special characteristics of an economically depressed region within your country, state, or province and analyze the benefits and costs of giving this region an independent monetary authority.

23 The Gold Exchange Standard

THE HISTORY OF postwar international economic problems cannot be understood without an appreciation of the factors which led to the growth and decline of the dollar-gold exchange standard. This form of international monetary organization evolved after World War II, not with deliberate planning but as the natural outcome of U.S. economic, military, and political world dominance at the time. The resultant system had several built-in shortcomings of a technical nature, but its most fatal flaw became evident when the relative U.S. strength declined and suffered heavily under the strain of the Vietnam War. At this point, the countries of Western Europe, Japan, the Arab countries, and the developing countries demanded a greater share of world economic power and prestige. As they conceived it, the only way to attain this objective was to reduce the power and prestige of the United States. This meant a dismantling of the dollar-gold exchange standard and the removal of the U.S. dollar from its central position in this postwar international monetary system. The United States acceded to this desire of the rest of the world, and after 1971 it actively encouraged negotiations for an international monetary system in which the dollar would play a less essential role and the United States, in principle, would be equal to all other countries.

We tell the story of the rise and the fall of the dollar-gold exchange standard by presenting first a theoretical blueprint of its operation, second a history of the system, and third, an analysis of the shortcomings of the system which is suggested by the history. In Section IV we discuss various proposals for reform of the gold exchange standard, some of which were presented during the 1950s and 1960s and some of which are still being recommended by some economists during the 1970s. The chapter closes with an analysis of the proposition that the U.S. dollar's removal from its central role as an international reserve currency will not necessarily end its use in private markets.

I. THE THEORETICAL BLUEPRINT

The gold exchange standard evolved from the gold standard but differs from it most basically in that under its operation international reserves consist of both gold and convertible national currencies. Consequently, the world's payment mechanism can function properly with a smaller quantity of gold than under the gold standard, thus economizing on the use of the precious metal. The gold exchange standard's most important features can best be demonstrated by the use of a simple model.

Consider a world consisting of many countries, one of which is called "Banker" and the rest of which are known as "Other." All countries are assumed to have fixed exchange rates and independent monetary and fiscal systems, and thus they have the need to hold international reserves for the settlement of payments imbalances. Initially, this world is assumed to be on a gold standard, using only gold to settle intercountry debts. Then the decision is made to institute the gold exchange standard, which requires the universal adoption of the following rules.

First, all gold held by Other is turned over to a Banker. Second, Banker issues to Other its own currency obligations, CO for short, in return for the gold, and commits itself to hold only gold as reserves. The Banker obligations are convertible into gold on demand and pay a low interest rate to bearer. Third, the national governments in Other agree to accept these Banker obligations as a means of payment, as they had previously accepted gold. Fourth, it is agreed that Banker can issue national obligations in excess of its gold stock as long as it maintains a minimum ratio of obligations to gold. Fifth, all newly mined gold not needed for industrial purposes is turned over to Banker at a predetermined, fixed price.

It is easy to see how such a system economizes on the use of gold. If Banker maintains a ratio of 25 percent gold behind the obligations held by Other, then $100 of gold permits the existence of $400 of COs and a total stock of reserves of $500. The degree of economizing is greater the smaller is the ratio of gold to COs. In Figure 23–1, at time t_0 the initial stock of gold, OG_0, is shown to support a stock of currency obligations of $G_0 P_0$, at an assumed ratio of OG/OP equal to 0.25.

The growth in the potential supply of COs depends upon two factors. First, with constant OG/OP ratio, the rate of growth of the gold stock determines the rate of growth of the stock of COs. In Figure 23–1, this dependence is shown by the fact that the two lines labeled gold and currency obligation potential, OG/OP = constant, are parallel on the semilog graph. Between time t_0 and t_1, both stocks are assumed to grow at the rate

FIGURE 23–1

A Model of the Gold Exchange Standard

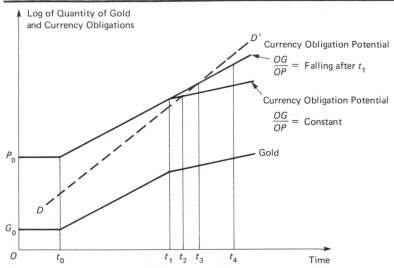

Under the gold exchange standard, the World Banker holds gold reserves growing from time t_0 to t_1 at a certain rate and after t_2 at a slower rate, as shown. Under the assumption that gold must represent a certain fraction of Banker's total obligations, the obligation potential grows like the line labeled currency obligation potential, OG/OP = constant to OG/OP = falling after t_2. The line DD' shows the actual growth of Bankers' currency obligations. They would have exceeded the potential at time t_2 had it not been for an international agreement to lower the gold-backing ratio required for Banker's obligations. The new currency obligation potential is shown as the top solid line after t_1. At t_3, currency obligations of Banker exceeded those permitted even under the more liberal gold-backing requirements. Time t_3 signaled the end of the gold exchange standard, circa 1971.

r_0 (equal to the slope of the lines); between t_1 and t_4, they are assumed to grow at r_1, where $r_0 > r_1$.

Second, for any given growth rate in the stock of gold, the rate of growth of the currency obligation potential depends on the ratio OG/OP. Thus in Figure 23–1, the uppermost solid line segment between point t_1 and t_4 shows that the currency obligations potential continues growing at r_0, even though the gold stock grows only at r_1. This is achieved by a constant fall in the OG/OP ratio, which in the graph is shown to be from 0.25 at t_1 to 0.20 at t_4. (The line DD' will be explained below.)

The currency obligations are held by Other countries, since they are readily exchangeable into gold, are acceptable by others as money, and bear interest. They are thus, in every essential respect, as good as gold and are superior to it in the sense that they yield a return and there is no need to guard a physical stock, since the CO certificates are useless to private individuals.

The preceding theoretical model permitted the analysis to be focused on some important relationships. However, to keep it simple, it was assumed that Other held only Banker's currency obligations. It is easy to modify the model by considering the possibility that Other countries wish to maintain a certain fraction of their international assets in the form of gold. If this is so, two major consequences follow. First, the degree of gold economizing inherent in the gold exchange standard is smaller than it is otherwise, and with a given ratio of gold to currency obligations maintained by Banker. Second, unless Other countries agree firmly to maintain a fixed ratio of gold to COs, the system can become unstable whenever Banker's solvency becomes suspect. Countries then begin to convert COs into gold and produce what is equivalent to a "run on the bank." This possibility and its relationship to some other features of the system will be discussed below.

II. HISTORY OF THE SYSTEM

The theoretical model just presented is an idealization of the basic idea of how the world could economize on the existing stock of gold. However, between this theoretical ideal and the real world there have been, and continue to be, great differences which can best be discussed in the context of actual past events.

The gold exchange standard has never been based on an explicit agreement among nations but, as has been mentioned before, represents the outcome of historic evolution. Thus, even during the heyday of the gold standard before 1914, some central banks held national currencies as international reserves. In 1885 the central banks of Denmark, Norway, and Sweden were authorized to hold balances with each other and to count these balances as reserves on which the issue of notes was based. In 1894, Russia began to hold some of its reserves in Berlin and other places. According to Nurkse (1944), in 1913 15 European central banks together held about 12 percent of their total reserves in the form of foreign exchange.

In 1922, the Genoa Conference met to consider problems of reconstructing a viable international financial system after the turmoil created by World War I. One of the problems confronting the Conference was that as a result of the general rise in prices and the retention of the old price of gold, the metal's production had declined by one third, and the value of the existing stock had become a smaller fraction of world output and trade than it had been before the war. For this reason, the Conference recommended the adoption of a gold exchange standard to economize on the use of existing stock and future output of gold.

While official agreement on the implementation of the recommendations was never achieved, the basic ideas nevertheless had considerable influence. Most major countries in the world subsequently adopted the legislation permitting their central banks to hold gold and foreign assets exchangeable into gold, some without and some with limitations on the fractions of reserves that had to consist of gold. After advantage had been taken of these laws, foreign exchange in 1927 and 1928 represented as much as 42 percent of 25 major countries' total reserves, and it ranged around 19 to 27 percent during the periods 1924–26 and 1929–31. From the point of view of economizing on gold, the system, therefore, was quite successful for a number of years.

However, by 1932 foreign exchange in the international portfolio assets of the 24 countries had fallen to 8 percent, and thereafter it fell even further. The events leading up to this demise of the standard show quite clearly the importance that must be attached to the absence of a formal agreement on its operation. Thus, in 1926 France initiated strict domestic measures to restore confidence in the French franc. The external value of the franc was stabilized at a level which represented a significant undervaluation. As a consequence, France began to run balance-of-payments surpluses and to accumulate a very large stock of reserve assets, at first almost completely in the form of foreign exchange. However, a law passed in June 1928 prohibited the French central bank from acquiring any more foreign exchange. In 1931 France began to convert the previously acquired foreign exchange holdings into gold. By that time the worldwide depression had caused Great Britain to be in serious balance-of-payments difficulties. The French conversion of sterling holdings into gold added significantly to the pressures and probably was a major contributory cause to Britain's suspension of convertibility of the pound into gold. Since most central banks were required to hold foreign exchange convertible into gold, sterling's inconvertibility forced them to dispose of their holdings of that currency, further aggravating the crisis. During the same period large quantities of dollar holdings also were exchanged into gold. These events caused the extinction of large sums of international reserves, since the pound and the dollar had been the most important reserve currencies.

The main reasons for this observed desire to convert foreign exchange assets into gold were twofold. First, countries believed that their national prestige was enhanced if their currencies served as reserves for other nations, and they were thus members of the glamorous group of countries serving as World Bankers. In order to qualify for this role, currencies had to be freely convertible into gold, which in turn necessitated maintenance of a substantial share of total reserves in the form of gold. Consequently, those countries that wanted to have their currencies qualify as international reserves began converting some of their own assets into gold, and in the process they reduced the entire system's effective economizing on the metal and created an unhealthy competition for the existing stock.

Second, according to the theoretical model of the gold exchange standard presented above, the real economic incentive for holding foreign currencies rather than gold is that the former has a positive yield, as compared with the zero yield on the latter. During the depression of the thirties, competitive devaluations of national currencies in relation to gold had the effect of endowing gold with capital value gains and a resultant positive rate of return which tended to exceed that available in foreign currencies. Moreover, the frequent devaluations made the value of foreign currencies uncertain and reduced their usefulness as international reserves. Because of this capital value uncertainty, and the changes in the relative rates of return on gold and currency holdings, many countries switched their reserves from currencies into gold.

Analytically, these events, and the causes leading up to them, were due to the absence of any formal agreement among the countries of the world as to, first, which ones would serve as Bankers; second, that Others would keep down their gold holdings; and third, that Bankers' exchange rates in terms of gold must never be changed. If agreement on these matters had existed, the gold exchange standard might well have worked.

The developments after World War II led again to the establishment of a gold exchange standard, and its history reemphasizes that this form of international monetary order requires as a necessary, though by no means a sufficient, condition sound international cooperation.

The composition of international reserves held by all countries in the world outside of the Communist bloc is shown in Table 23–1. As can be seen, the share of gold in the total fell steadily from a high of 70.2 percent in 1950 to a low of 20 percent in 1974. On the other hand, international reserves in the form of foreign exchange, mainly U.S. dollars and U.K. sterling, represented 26.4 percent in 1950 and rose to 70 percent in 1974. International reserves provided by the International Monetary Fund have remained a relatively insignificant part of the total, in spite of the fact that between 1954 and 1974 they increased from 3.2 percent to 10 percent of all international reserves.

Like so many human institutions, the International Monetary Fund (IMF), set up at Bretton Woods on the eve of World War II, was essentially designed to deal with the problems of the past. The rules guiding the relations among member states were set up to prevent the repetition of conditions which had haunted international economic relations during the thirties: competitive devaluations, discrimination in foreign exchange dealings and tariffs, lack of convertibility, and disorderly capital flows. The IMF was quite successful in achieving these objectives. However, the organization's provision of international reserves was totally inadequate. While the national ownership of freely spendable assets provided by the IMF under a quota system was raised twice in 25 years, it

TABLE 23-1
International Reserves

A. In Billions of U.S. Dollars

End of Year	Gold	Foreign Ex- change	IMF Posi- tion	SDRs	Total	Annual Growth Rate
1948.....	$34.5	$ 13.4	$ 1.6	—	$ 49.5	
1950.....	35.3	13.3	1.7	—	50.3	1.0%
1952.....	35.8	14.2	1.8	—	51.8	1.4
1954.....	36.9	16.7	1.8	—	55.4	3.5
1956.....	38.1	17.8	2.3	—	58.2	2.4
1958.....	38.0	17.0	2.6	—	57.6	−0.5
1960.....	38.0	18.6	3.6	—	60.2	2.3
1962.....	39.3	19.9	3.9	—	63.1	2.4
1964.....	40.8	23.7	5.4	—	69.9	5.1
1966.....	40.9	24.6	6.2	—	71.7	1.3
1968.....	38.9	32.0	6.5	—	77.4	4.0
1969.....	39.1	32.4	6.7	—	78.2	1.0
1970.....	37.2	44.8	7.7	$ 3.1	92.8	18.7
1971.....	39.2	78.2	6.9	6.4	130.7	40.8
1972.....	38.8	103.6	6.9	9.4	158.7	21.4
1973.....	43.1	123.1	7.4	10.6	184.2	16.1
1974.....	43.8	153.5	10.8	10.8	218.9	18.8

B. In Percentages

Year	Gold	Foreign Exchange	IMF Position	SDRs	Total
1948.....	69.7%	27.1%	3.2%	—	100%
1950.....	70.2	26.4	3.4	—	100
1952.....	69.1	27.4	3.5	—	100
1954.....	66.7	30.1	3.2	—	100
1956.....	65.5	30.6	4.0	—	100
1958.....	66.0	29.5	4.5	—	100
1960.....	63.1	30.9	6.0	—	100
1962.....	62.3	31.5	6.2	—	100
1964.....	58.3	33.9	7.7	—	100
1966.....	57.0	34.3	8.6	—	100
1968.....	50.3	41.4	8.4	—	100
1969.....	50.0	41.5	8.6	—	100
1970.....	40.1	48.3	8.3	3.3%	100
1971.....	30.0	59.9	5.3	4.9	100
1972.....	24.5	65.3	4.3	5.9	100
1973.....	23.4	66.8	4.1	5.8	100
1974.....	20.0	70.0	5.0	5.0	100

Source: International Financial Statistics.

remained only a small part of total international reserves, as can be seen from Table 23-1. Credits extended by the IMF to members in balance-of-payments difficulties served in some measure as substitutes for owned reserves, but they never became a significant share of total instruments available to countries for the settlement of debts.

In the absence of an orderly provision of reserves by international agreements, the world developed a temporarily very successful gold exchange standard almost by accident. The United States emerged from World War II with an overwhelmingly dominant economy in terms of productive capacity and national wealth, including reserves of monetary gold. In the eyes of the rest of the world dollar holdings were more desirable than gold, since they were readily exchangeable into the metal and brought interest to their holders. During the 1950s U.S. balance-of-payments deficits were welcomed as a source from which the reconstructed nations of Western Europe could replenish their depleted stocks of international reserves. They did so, holding mostly dollars but also exchanging some of them for gold, thus reducing the U.S. gold stock. It has been argued, and it is probably correct, that these deficits made possible the widespread return to convertibility in 1958 and that they made a significant contribution to world prosperity after 1950. The United States had thus, without formal international agreement, taken on the role of a World Banker and helped sustain an efficient monetary system.

The United Kingdom emerged from World War II reduced in relative economic and military power, but still at the heart of a Commonwealth and with the tradition and know-how of a World Banker. Because of sterling assets held by Commonwealth members and the facilities provided by London's private financial intermediaries, the United Kingdom's national obligations served as international reserves to some extent, though they never were very significant and tended to become less so as Commonwealth ties were loosened during the fifties and sixties.

In 1960 Robert Triffin published a now famous book in which he analyzed the characteristics of a world monetary system based on reserves in the form of gold and national obligations. Showing that the U.S. stock of monetary gold grew at a slower rate than its stock of dollar obligations (it actually fell), he predicted a crisis of confidence in Banker's liquidity. This crisis promptly occurred later in 1960, when, for the first time since the thirties, the value of U.S. short-term obligations exceeded the value of U.S. gold holdings. It manifested itself through speculative private sales of dollars and some official demand for gold for dollars, in expectation of a devaluation.

The historic development of the liquidity positions of the United States and the United Kingdom is shown in Table 23–2. The United States experienced a steady decrease in her holdings of international reserves and an equally steady increase in external liquid liabilities, nearly all of which were to foreign official monetary authorities. The simultaneous rise in liabilities and decrease in assets resulted in a sharp fall of the ratio of reserves over liabilities, from 2.73 in 1950 to 0.14 in 1974. The ratio fell below 1 for the first time in 1960, the year of the first dollar crisis.

TABLE 23–2
External Assets and Liabilities of the United States and United Kingdom
(billions of U.S. dollars)

	United States			United Kingdom		
End of Year	(1) International Reserves	(2) External Liquid Liabilities	(3) $\frac{(1)}{(2)} \times 100$	(1) International Reserves	(2) External Liquid Liabilities	(3) $\frac{(1)}{(2)} \times 100$
1975	15.9	125.5	0.13	—	—	—
1974	16.1	119.0	0.14	6.9	117.9	0.06
1973	14.4	92.4	0.16	6.5	95.8	0.07
1972	13.2	82.9	0.16	5.6	72.3	0.08
1971	13.2	67.8	0.19	6.6	52.1	0.13
1970	14.5	47.0	0.31	2.8	40.4	0.07
1969	17.0	45.9	0.37	2.5	32.2	0.08
1968	15.7	38.5	0.41	2.4	20.6	0.12
1967	14.8	33.2	0.45	2.7	11.8	0.23
1966	14.9	29.8	0.50	3.1	12.5	0.25
1965	15.5	29.1	0.53	3.0	11.9	0.25
1964	16.7	29.0	0.58	2.3	11.8	0.20
1963	16.8	26.3	0.64	3.1	11.4	0.27
1962	17.2	24.1	0.71	3.3	10.7	0.31
1961	18.8	22.9	0.82	3.3	9.9	0.33
1960	19.4	21.0	0.92	3.7	10.9	0.34
1959	21.5	19.4	1.11	2.8	9.8	0.29
1958	22.5	16.8	1.34	3.1	9.4	0.33
1957	24.8	15.8	1.57	2.4	9.2	0.26
1956	23.7	14.9	1.59	2.3	9.6	0.24
1955	22.8	13.5	1.69	2.4	10.0	0.24
1954	23.0	12.5	1.84	3.0	10.4	0.29
1953	23.5	11.4	2.06	2.7	9.8	0.28
1952	24.7	10.4	2.38	2.0	9.0	0.22
1951	24.3	8.9	2.73	2.4	10.0	0.24
1950	24.3	8.9	2.73	3.4	9.8	0.35

Source: *IMF Statistics:* U.S., lines 1d, 4d; U.K., lines 1d, 4b, 4c.

While the U.S. time series is characterized by steady and pronounced trends, the British series exhibits very few trends but substantial and persistent fluctuations between 1950 and 1967. Also remarkable is the fact that the U.K. reserves has been much lower than the U.S. ratio throughout the period, averaging about one half of the lowest ratio attained by the United States in 1967. Because of the low initial ratio very little growth in external liabilities, i.e. international reserves in the form of pound sterling, took place during the period up to 1967. Threafter external liabilities rose sharply and caused a dramatic fall in the U.K. reserves/liabilities ratios.

Figure 23–1 above lends itself well to a somewhat abstract but nevertheless useful explanation of the events during the fifties. The line labeled *DD'* shows the world demand for dollars, which is equal to the supply actually made available by U.S. deficits. It is shown to grow at a faster rate than the currency obligation potential, which in the theoretical world of the gold exchange standard (presented in the first part of this chapter) is determined by the rate of growth in the gold stock and the ratio of gold to obligations considered necessary by the "depositors." Between period t_0 and t_2 no problem arose, since U.S. gold reserves exceeded U.S. obligations by a margin considered safe by the holders of the dollars. However, at period t_2 (1960?) depositors became alarmed and started the "run" on the Bank, because the ratio of Banker's obligations to gold had begun to exceed the "safe" level.

At that time the leaders of the Western world realized that the gold exchange standard needed to be improved by official agreements, and that it was necessary to accept a decrease in Banker's ratio of gold to demand obligations. An assumed acceptable rate of decrease in this ratio is shown in Figure 23–1 by the relationship between the uppermost solid line, currency obligation potential, OG/OP = falling after t_1, and the line labeled gold. At the same time, however, diplomatic pressure was brought to bear in the United States to decrease the rate at which the actual supply of its obligations grew in the future. For a number of reasons, the United States was unable to reduce the balance-of-payments deficit, and after time t_3, dollar obligations relative to gold again began to exceed those considered prudent for a Banker. In 1967 private speculation against the dollar once more became rampant.

More generally, during the 1960s and early 1970s two developments took place which destroyed some of the necessary conditions for the operation of the gold exchange standard based on the dollar. First, the U.S. economy grew more slowly than that of the major European countries, which had formed the European Economic Community (EEC). As a result, the economic dominance of the United States in world trade was diminished, and that of the EEC countries grew correspondingly. These facts can readily be discerned from an inspection of the tables on world trade in Chapter 6. Simultaneously with the relative economic growth of Europe came the desire of some of its leaders, especially Charles de Gaulle, to attain political and military power and prestige commensurate with Europe's newly found economic status. Second, the United States lost its reputation as a country in which assets were safe. The Vietnam War revealed certain weaknesses in U.S. military power and the country's willingness to use it fully in the preservation of the existing world order, in the manner of the past. Domestic race riots, university campus unrest, and political scandals brought into question the internal political stability of the nation. Most important, the United States went through a period of inflation, and at the close of the 1960s it was suffering rapidly worsening balance-of-trade deficits and capital account imbalances. The resultant overall U.S. payments deficits in 1970 ($10 billion) and in 1971

($30 billion) resulted in such an increase in international liquidity and U.S. obligations toward the rest of the world that the continued U.S. role as World Banker came into question, both within the United States and in the rest of the world.

The main surplus countries receiving the dollars from the U.S. deficits were the members of the EEC and Japan. It is important to note that these countries would have been capable technically of saving the dollar-gold exchange standard if they had had the desire to do so. All they would have had to do, in the presence of large U.S. deficits, was to revalue upward their own currencies relative to the dollar. These revaluations did not take place, and instead diplomatic pressures were brought to bear on the United States to solve the problem through policies of its own. On August 15, 1971, President Richard Nixon announced unilaterally the legal suspension of gold convertibility, a 10 percent surcharge on all imports, and a host of domestic policy measures. This date signals formally the end of the gold exchange standard. It was forced upon the world by a basic desire of the EEC countries to diminish the power and prestige of the United States through ending the role of the dollar as the most important international reserve asset. In the United States, many economists and political leaders had begun to question the value to the United States of continuing to play the role of World Banker as part of a general reappraisal of the country's role in world affairs after the Vietnam War fiasco. As we will show below, the economic benefits accruing to the World Banker in the form of seigniorage (to be explained below), or more simply the profits from banking, were minor, and the U.S. public became disenchanted with the alleged prestige accruing to it through the banking role, in line with its dislike of the U.S. position as policeman of the world. As a result of this public attitude, U.S. policy makers would not and could not use the remaining U.S. military power and economic influence to push through a solution to the U.S. deficits in 1970–71 which would have preserved the dollar-gold exchange standard.

III. THE SHORTCOMINGS OF THE GOLD EXCHANGE STANDARD

The preceding description of the history of the gold exchange standard and of the U.S. experience as the World Banker brings out the basic dilemma inherent in the gold exchange standard: Since gold is the ultimate standard of value, its value relative to the Banker's currency must never be changed. With the price of gold thus fixed, only by coincidence does its supply grow at the same rate as the welfare-maximizing demand for reserves. Consequently, countries holding Banker's obligations must be willing to accept changes (and historically they have been mostly decreases) in the Banker's liquidity position.

International agreements formalizing this willingness have been difficult to reach in practice, since there always appears to be at least one maverick noncooperating nation which finds such agreements contrary to its own national interests and sabotages them through hoarding of gold and other means.

However, even if such agreements on the Banker's liquidity position could be reached among the governments of the world, the gold exchange standard has several other glaring weaknesses. First, private holders of national currency obligations may not be convinced that Banker has a sound liquidity position, even if their governments are. With the price of gold fixed in the downward direction through the basic setup of the system, switches from national currency obligations into gold are safe and relatively cheap. Periodic private speculation against the dollar and sterling has taken place in the past, in spite of strong cooperation among central banks, and it can be expected to take place in future. Such speculation causes shifts of private capital, delays or speedups in commercial purchases and deliveries, and changes in exchange rates and in general it has unsettling and harmful effects on world trade, capital flows, and welfare.

Second, the growth in total international reserves depends on Banker's balance-of-payments deficits. At present and for the foreseeable future, governments do not seem to be able to set the size of their balance-of-payments deficits with precision. Consequently, the actual growth in reserves is likely to be erratic, unpredictable, and unrelated to need, probably adding to world instability, because Banker and Other countries are unable to regulate their balance of payments in the necessary optimum fashions.

Third, the Banker nation surrenders the right to use devaluation as a policy instrument in the quest for domestic stability, full employment, growth, and balance-of-payments deficits of the required size. Since at least 1960, U.S. economic policy making has been severely constrained by an allegedly excessive balance-of-payments deficit that could not be rectified by devaluation. As a result, the United States had to impose measures to reduce imports and capital outflows and to set high interest rates which conflicted with the objective of increased domestic economic growth.

However, a cooperation among countries of a kind somewhat different from those discussed above can eliminate this constraint on the Banker's policies. It is known that if there are two countries, one's surplus is the other's deficit, and vice versa. Consequently, if one country's international payments are balanced, so are those of the other. Similarly, the sum of all imbalances of $n - 1$ countries is equal to the imbalance of the nth country. From this relationship arises the possibility that the size of Banker's external deficit can be determined by the appropriate exchange rate and interest rate adjustments by all the other countries. In practice, the United States has been unable to make other industrial countries take appropriate actions to free it for the need for balance-of-payments adjustments.

Moreover, the question might be raised whether the costs of such cooperation do not exceed the benefits derived from it. It requires that Other countries agree, through political bargaining, on which should do the adjusting, by how much and how frequently. It is not clear that the resultant frequency and size of exchange rate adjustments are optimum, from the point of view of maximizing world trade and capital flows.

A fourth weakness of the gold exchange standard, related to the two preceding points, is the difficulty that, under the system, some human beings have to determine what the desired rate of increase in the supply of reserves should be in the future. Such judgments are not only technically very difficult to make, because of the uncertainties surrounding the timing and magnitude of business cycles, rates of growth, and so on, but they also involve intercountry comparisons of utility, since the rate of reserve growth has effects on worldwide rates of inflation, and price increases are disliked by countries in differing degrees. The resultant need for political bargaining and possible delays in decisions have been discussed above.

A fifth shortcoming is that under the gold exchange standard the world's richest economy is the most likely candidate for the role of the World Banker. Successful operation of the scheme assures that Banker receives a regular flow of resources called "seigniorage," by analogy to the resources which used to accure to sovereign rulers of the past who had the right to mint coin with a face value larger than the intrinsic metal value in the coin and the cost of manufacturing, and so on. This seigniorage accrues to Banker because the only way the rest of the world can acquire Banker's national obligations is by running a balance-of-payments surplus, thus transferring real resources or claims on assets to Banker. However, as in the case of gold coins, the value of the seigniorage is not equal to the face value of the coins, so the nominal value of the resources accruing to Banker has to be adjusted for various "costs" to arrive at an estimate of the value of the seigniorage.

The present value of the seigniorage acquired in one year can be determined as follows. Assume that there are interest payments on Banker's obligations at the annual rate r, that costs of running the business are equal to c percent per annum on deposits, and that Banker can place the acquired resources in the open market at an annual rate of R, which is equal to the marginal productivity of capital. Discounting the future annual payments at the social discount rate of d, the present value of seigniorage (S) due to one year's deficit (D) is

$$S = \left[\frac{R - r - c}{(1 + d)} + \frac{R - r - c}{(1 + d)^2} + \frac{R - r - c}{(1 + d)^3} + \cdots + \frac{R - r - c}{(1 + d)^n} \right] \times D$$

where n is the year at which the Banker's currency obligation is traded in by running a balance-of-payments surplus with the rest of the world. If n approaches infinity, present value becomes $[(R - r - c)/d] \times D$. As can be seen from this formula, assuming $r = 0$, $c = 0$, and $R = d$ makes the value of seigniorage equal to the deficit, D.

A calculation of the benefits to the United States or the United Kingdom of being the World Banker in practice is quite complicated, since it is difficult to determine the costs associated with the role, especially how big gold reserves would have been if the country had not served as the Banker, when the resources have to be repaid, and what rate of interest is paid on outstanding obligations. However, it may be worth noting that the total obligations of the United States held by foreign official institutions were valued at $16 billion in the fall of 1967, while those of the United Kingdom were £2 billion before the November 1967 devaluation. Under the assumption that $R = 10$ percent and $r + c = 5$ percent, then these obligations resulted in a flow of resources valued at $800 million to the United States and £100 million to the United Kingdom during the year 1967. Moreover, since Banker's currency is widely used as a means of payment in private transactions of international trade and finance, private foreigners tend to keep quantities of this country's currency as transactions balances, which in turn are a source of seigniorage in the same way as the officially held balances. Moreover, the World Banker also sells other banking and kindred services, such as insurance and brokerage, to international business clients, and these are a source of comparative advantage and a gainful use of resources.

However, this last group of added advantages should not be attributed to the position of being the World Banker, since causation probably runs the other way: A country dominating world trade and finance through its relative size and financial and industrial development logically grows into the role of issuing currency obligations acceptable to governments as official reserves. Certainly, the United States and Great Britain were the dominant trading nations long before they became World Bankers.

The phenomenon of seigniorage thus is the main source of a transfer of real resources from the poorer to the richest nations of the world. Such a redistribution of income is neither efficient nor equitable and must be considered as being an undesirable by-product of the gold exchange standard.

A sixth weakness of the gold exchange standard is that gold retains a central role in the operation of the system. Banker continues to purchase all gold offered in the free market at a fixed price. From a social point of view, the process involved is that resources of labor and capital are used in some areas of the world to mine and refine gold. More resources are used to rebury and guard it at the Banker's central depositories, such as the New York Federal Reserve Bank and Fort Knox in the United States. Such a process tends to be socially wasteful, as has been recognized by most national governments, which over the past few decades have severed previously existing ties between their fiat money supplies and gold. Logically, such a severance would also be possible for the gold exchange standard, because if agreement on the working of the system were perfect and reliable, Banker would never have to exchange his national currency obligations into gold. However, if such a break with gold were to be made, the essence of the gold exchange standard would be destroyed, and the emergent systems would fall into the analytical category of schemes known as centrally created reserves, which will be discussed in Chapter 24.

A final shortcoming is that the gold exchange standard contains no effective and equitable method for assuring adjustment to balance-of-payments disequilibria. Under the gold standard, adjustment is automatic through the effects gold movements have on money supplies. Freely fluctuating exchange rates carry directly all burden of adjustment to disequilibrating disturbances. Under the gold exchange standard, when Other countries incur deficits, they sooner or later feel the discipline of running out of reserves, so that real adjustments are forced upon them. But when the Banker runs deficits excessive in the light of the world's demand for its obligations as reserves, adjustment pressures of the normal kind are lacking. Yet, these Banker deficits are excessive by definition and force hardships upon the countries at whose expense they occur. Efficiency and equity might demand that at least part of the necessary adjustment to the imbalances be undertaken by the Banker. Moreover, also among Other countries, there is no effective adjustment mechanism working on the surplus countries. During the 1950s, for example, Germany and the Netherlands ran substantial and consistent balance-of-payments surpluses, the elimination of which would have required exceedingly severe deflation by the other major industrial countries of the West. Only after many years of surpluses did the diplomatic pressures of the deficit countries force Germany and the Netherlands into an upward revaluation of their currencies.

In spite of the success of diplomatic pressures in this episode and the general development of unwritten "rules of the game" allegedly guiding the behavior of countries with imbalances in their external accounts, the absence of any compelling method by which the burden of adjustment is put on Banker and Other surplus, as well as deficit, countries has turned out to have been the most serious shortcoming of the gold exchange standard. The domestic economic and political difficulties besetting the United States during the late 1960s and early 1970s were aggravated by large trade deficits and staggering increases in external liabilities. As the World Banker the United States could not alleviate these external economic problems unilaterally without upsetting the system. Other countries were unwilling to come to the rescue of the United States, for the political and economic reasons given in the summary of events in the preceding part of this chapter. The resultant impasse, caused by the absence of genuine international agreement on the existence and operation of the gold exchange standard, brought the August 15, 1971, legal suspension of U.S. dollar convertibility into gold. With it came the end of the system whose very essence had been the convertibility of Banker's obligations into gold.

IV. PROPOSALS FOR REFORM OF THE GOLD EXCHANGE STANDARD

Following the 1960 dollar crisis and Triffin's diagnosis of the world monetary system's ills, scholars, central bankers, and bankers such as Edward Bernstein, Per Jacobson, Friedrich Lutz, S. Posthuma, Robert Roosa, Henry Wallich, and Xenophon Zolotas published treatises containing their own diagnosis of the problem and prescriptions towards its solution.

Most of these writers saw the short-run solution of the issues of the times to be increased international cooperation, as is well exemplified by the title of Wallich's paper, "Co-operation to Solve the Gold Problem" (1961). The many areas in which strong cooperation is needed to make the gold exchange standard work have been discussed above. They include consultation on the consistency of national economic policies, the sharing of the adjustment burden, and the granting of mutual credits, especially to the United States as the World Banker. The latter step can be interpreted as an agreement to accept a lower Banker's liquidity ratio. However, some of these analysts considered such cooperation agreements as being insufficient, and they demanded that the United States strengthen the existing system by granting gold guarantees on the dollar balances held by foreign governments. It is interesting to note that this proposal was not supported by American experts. However, Roosa, who at the time was Under Secretary of the U.S. Treasury for International Monetary Affairs, argued for, and was able to introduce, the practice whereby the United States sold to foreign governments bonds denominated in their own currencies. These bonds, known as Roosa bonds, provided the equivalent of a gold guarantee to countries that chose not to devalue their currencies in case the United States did so, but they provided only a guarantee of fixed value in national currency for those that kept their exchange rates pegged to the dollar. These bonds never became a large share of U.S. obligations. In general, the system was well able to deal with the short-run problems after many of the experts' recommendations for cooperation had been put into effect.

While there was rather broad agreement on the short-run solution to the crisis of confidence, two broad proposals were made to solve the problem of supplying world liquidity in the long run. These proposals were made in recognition of the fact that the supply of liquidity for nearly a decade had depended on U.S. deficits, and it threatened to dry up once the U.S. balance-of-payments deficit was eliminated. The characteristic common to the proposals discussed here is that they all sought the solution within the framework of the existing institutional set-up.

The first set of proposals concerned the systematic use of more national currencies as international reserves. Thus, if and when the United States began to run a balance-of-payments surplus, the stock of outstanding dollar obligations should not be reduced, but instead the United States should begin to hold other foreign currencies. This practice would assure a growth in total world reserves and facilitate the adjustment problems of deficit countries. The main difficulties with this solution are the same as those with the gold exchange standard with one or two Bankers. The rate of growth of world reserves depends on national balance-of-payments deficits. A country running large payments deficits makes available large supplies of its currency, but it also reduces the attractiveness of its obligations as reserves. Furthermore, there exists the danger of frequent and unsettling shifts of previously accumulated reserves, away from weakening to strengthening currencies.

Most of the preceding shortcomings of the multiple currency reserve approach can be remedied by appropriate agreements, and some of these were proposed. For example, gold guarantees on all currencies would make it unnecessary to be afraid of devaluations, and the speculative shifts could be prevented. To even out short-run fluctuations in balance of payments and assure constant demand for all eligible currencies, it had been proposed that all countries hold currencies and gold in specified proportions.

The preceding set of proposals for a multiple currency reserve system never were implemented. One reason for official coolness toward the plans may have been the recognition that they require such a large degree of international cooperation and agreement that they would be exceedingly difficult to negotiate. Moreover, if such agreement were attainable, it might better be used to put into effect a more fundamental reform of the system, along the lines discussed in the next chapter.

The second broad approach to the long-run liquidity problem emphasized the potential role of the International Monetary Fund. It suggested the creation of more owned reserves, especially the expansion of the quotas, and more credit facilities, and urged generally a greater willingness of countries to use the IMF facilities. The main trouble with these proposals was that they fell short of granting the IMF the right to create internationally acceptable means of payment by fiat, since the unconditional drawing rights and conditional added credits would have to be repaid by the countries to which they were granted initially. Moreover, to attain some of the drawing rights, countries would have to surrender gold to the fund.

Some of the proposals for modification of the IMF made after 1960 were in fact implemented, such as an increase in quotas and the development of added credit facilities, the most important of which became known as the General Agreement to Borrow (see Chapter 17). These changes have strengthened the existing gold exchange standard, but public and official thinking about the future of the IMF slowly moved toward acceptance of the notion that the world needs an authority which can create owned and nonextinguishable means of payment which are acceptable for the settlement of debts among nations. It is difficult to pinpoint the precise time of the idea's intellectual victory. However, it is a historic fact that at the September 1967 meetings of the International Monetary Fund in Rio de Janeiro, the Board of Governors approved the outline of a scheme for the creation of fiat reserves, known as SDRs (special drawing rights). These are discussed more fully in Chapter 24.

In 1966, when U.S. payments deficits were large and growing and gold speculation was rampant, three U.S. economists, Emile Despres, Charles Kindleberger, and Walter Salant argued in a famous article (1966) that the crisis was due to the role of gold in the system, and attempts to end the role of the dollar in private and official use in the world would not only be harmful for world welfare but would also prove to be very difficult. According to this view, the simplest solution to the problem would be to end the convertibility of dollars into gold and let market forces regulate the quantity of short-term dollar obligations the world needed for private and official uses. Under the resultant dollar standard, the United States would pursue monetary and fiscal policies for maximum domestic stability and growth, without regard for its balance of payments. Other countries, through their balance-of-payments policies, would regulate the U.S. payments imbalances such as to obtain just the desired quantities of dollars in their private and official portfolios.

This policy was decried in some foreign circles as a form of dollar imperialism. In later years Ronald McKinnon (1969), Lawrence Krause (1970), and Gottfried Haberler and Thomas Willett (1971) further pushed the arguments in favor of a world dollar standard. The policy prescriptions to the United States following from this view were that the country should follow a policy of "benign neglect" of her balance-of-payments problems, which means not taking any policy actions at all to alleviate imbalances. In analogy with the Despres-Kindleberger-Salant argument, any country that wished to reduce or slow down the growth in its dollar holdings should be expected to appreciate its exchange rate against the dollar. Accordingly, any actual accumulation of U.S. dollars by foreigners was entirely a revelation of a preference of dollars over other forms of wealth holding.

The U.S. government did not follow these policy prescriptions. Instead, on August 15, 1971, as noted above, it suspended the convertibility of dollars into gold and, importantly, imposed a 10 percent surcharge on all imports, which was to be removed after agreement had been reached on the realignment of exchange rates. In December 1971 the Smithsonian Agreement was reached among the ten largest industrial nations of the Western world (the Group of Ten, consisting of Belgium, Canada, France, Germany, Italy, Japan, the Netherlands, Sweden, the United Kingdom, and the United States), to devalue the dollar in terms of gold to $38 from $35 per ounce and to increase the value of most currencies in terms of dollars. In February 1973 there was another devaluation of the dollar by 10 percent in terms of gold, after an intensive effort of the U.S. Under Secretary of the Treasury for International Monetary Affairs, Paul Volker, to persuade countries in payments surplus to permit an appreciation of their currencies in terms of the dollar, in order to permit an elimination of the U.S. payments deficits.

The important fact emerging from these events for our purposes of analysis is that the United States did not follow a policy of dollar imperialism or benign neglect. Instead, the U.S. government initiated and participated in international agreements in which efforts were made to dismantle the dollar-gold exchange standard of the postwar years in a manner acceptable to all countries of the Western economic community.

While it has been fairly easy to reach international agreement on exchange rate changes, by the end of 1975 it had not been possible to reach agreement on the shape of a new international monetary order, except in the most general terms that the dollar-gold exchange standard be replaced by a system in which international reserves are created centrally. We will discuss in the next chapter problems surrounding the creation of an international monetary system based on centrally created reserves.

V. THE FUTURE ROLE OF THE DOLLAR

The likely end of the U.S. dollar an official reserve asset, which has been demanded by the rest of the world through such means as forcing the 1971 dollar devaluation and which is being accepted, if not pushed, by the U.S. government, leaves open the question of the future role of the U.S. dollar in the private sector. In the remaining part of this chapter we present the reasons why the U.S. dollar is likely to continue to be the dominant private international unit of account, medium of exchange, and store of wealth, even though it may be replaced by centrally created reserves in some other functions it had served under the gold exchange standard.

All economic exchanges in modern market economies involve a price and money. When currency units are used to express prices of goods, services, and assets, money is paid to serve as the numeraire, or unit of account. When money changes ownership in the purchase or sale of goods, services, and assets, it is said to serve as a medium of exchange.

Because of its ready acceptability in exchange, money often also serves as a temporary store of value. The economic benefits accruing to society from having money in these uses are well known and are discussed in every elementary textbook on money and banking. All textbooks, however, restrict their discussion to the domestic economy. Yet, after a little thought it is obvious that similar benefits accrue to the world economy from having an "international money" which serves as a convenient unit of account, medium of exchange, and temporary store of value in transactions involving internationally traded goods and assets.

International Unit of Account. Consider, for example, the savings resulting from the fact that the prices of coffee, tin, rubber, and wheat are quoted in U.S. dollars in each producing country and at major commodity trading centres instead of in Brazilian cruzeiros, Columbian pesos, Ugandian shillings, Guatemalan quetzales, and Ethiopian dollars, to name just a few currencies of the main coffee-producing countries of the world. If quotations were not in dollars, Canadian, German, French, or U.S. importers who wanted to compare the current and expected future prices of coffee from the various sources would have to gather and evaluate information about the current and expected future exchange rates of each of these currencies, in terms of their own. Similarly, the exporters and producers of these goods would have to engage in this kind of research activity to make correct pricing decisions.

Because prices of most internationally traded goods, services, and assets are quoted in dollars, exporters and importers everywhere can readily compare prices from all sources and convert them into domestic currency values by knowing only the exchange rate of their own currency with the dollar. Information about future exchange rates needed for most business decisions can also simply be expressed in terms of likely changes in the domestic currency price of the dollar. Since in every country there are many users of the information about present and future dollar exchange rates, it is well researched, publicized widely, and available cheaply to individual decision makers.

Medium of Exchange and Store of Wealth. The use of dollars also lowers resource expenditures connected with the task of bringing together buyers and sellers of national currencies used in the exchange of internationally traded goods and assets. Because the U.S. dollar is so readily acceptable as a means of payment, many firms save brokerage expenses by receiving and paying out U.S. dollars, often involving business partners who are not U.S. residents. These uses of dollars have received a great boost by the growth of the multinational corporations, which engage in much simultaneous importing and exporting. However, the savings have become available also to smaller national firms, as a result of the development of an efficient international money market. In this market dollar balances can be lent or borrowed at competitive interest rates to bridge gaps between the times payments in dollars are received and have to be made. These investment facilities thus have enhanced the dollar's usefulness as a means of payment. They also make it more attractive as a store of wealth. Many of these benefits from having an international money have been experienced by international travelers whose U.S. dollars were acceptable directly in the payment for goods and services and which could be exchanged easily and at low cost into other currencies. Many shops at airports and other places frequented by tourists quote prices in dollars for the convenience of not only U.S. but all foreign tourists.

Economies versus Government Policy

It is important to note that savings resulting from the use of an international money in the functions just discussed accrue to the transactors directly. Consequently, the forces of the market, without any incentives from governments, tend to choose such a currency. Once a currency is beginning to be employed in this manner, all users benefit simultaneously, as more and more transactions are denominated in it, its acceptability spreads and opportunities for trading and borrowing are developed. In terms of technical economics, the use of a currency for these purposes initially is stimulated by the expectation of private gains, but the social gains exceed the sum of the private gains because of the appearance of external scale economies which lower the overall cost of economic transactions.

What remains to be explained is why the market in recent years has chosen the dollar rather than any other currency as the international money. The answer to this question is rather simple and follows directly from the statistics presented in Chapter 6. Because of the relatively large size of the U.S. economy and trade, prices of goods traded by the United States and quoted in dollars represented a large fraction of all goods in world trade, dollars were relatively most frequently needed in international payment, and the dollar exchange rate was researched and publicized most widely of all currencies. Consequently, the costs of using dollars as the international money automatically were lower than those of using any other currency.

Likely Future Rival Currencies

The preceding analysis suggests an answer to the question whether the dollar is likely to continue in its role as unit of account, medium of exchange, and store of value in private international transactions after the devaluation and suspension of gold convertibility in 1971. The dollar is likely to continue in this role until its comparative advantage is lost through the development of a national currency of greater relative importance in international trade. Such an event is not likely to take place, within the foreseeable future, through differential rates of growth in any of the existing national economies. A serious rival to the dollar's role is much more likely to develop through economic and monetary integration in Western Europe. However, it is extremely hazardous to make predictions as to the date of such a monetary union. Some sceptics maintain that it may never come.

A further consideration supports the prediction for a long use of the dollar in its role of international private money. Familiarity, institutions, and custom acquired through time will have given the dollar an advantage which can be overcome only if the European currency area is substantially larger than that of the United States. The continued use of the British pound sterling in some countries as international money many years after Britain's size advantage had been lost is an example of strength of institutions and customs in the market's choice of a particular national currency.

Effects on U.S. Welfare

The use of U.S. dollars by private foreigners affects U.S. public welfare only indirectly and marginally. One of the main sources of benefit arises from the export of banking and related services. These are believed to be subject to internal and external economies of scale in production. The most important cost can appear when internationally mobile dollar balances move around the world in search of higher interest or speculative gains, destabilizing the U.S. balance of payments and complicating the operation of U.S. domestic monetary policy. How serious the consequences of these capital flows are on the U.S. economic well-being depends on the quantity of U.S. international cooperation in preventing these flows, and the ability of domestic monetary policy makers to use the appropriate instruments. In general, these problems do not seem to be too serious, or at least not too difficult to solve by future institutional innovations. But even if some analysts concluded that the social benefits are smaller than the costs, it may turn out to be beyond the capability of U.S. policy makers to stop the private use of dollars abroad as the unit of account, transactions currency, and store of wealth. The only way they could do so would be through taxation and controls, which in turn impose what probably would be considered to be excessively high political and economic costs on the U.S. economy.

BIBLIOGRAPHICAL NOTES

A perceptive analysis of postwar monetary problems is given in Triffin (1960) and Hirsch (1967). Surveys of the literature on international monetary problems include Cohen (1975), Williamson (1973), and Grubel (1971a). The theoretical issues are dealt with explicitly by Johnson (1967c). Books of readings of the most important articles in the field are Meier (1974), Officer and Willett (1969), and Grubel (1963), which contains most of the early proposals for reform of the gold exchange standard. On the merit of being the World's Banker, see Triffin (1960), Kenen (1960), Boyer de la Giroday (1974), and Officer and Willett (1969). Despres et al. (1966), McKinnon (1969), Haberler and Willett (1971) and Krause (1970) make the case for a world dollar standard and benign neglect.

CONCEPTS FOR REVIEW

U.S. dollar role as unit of account, store of wealth, and medium of exchange
Official intervention currency
Gold exchange standard
World Banker
Other countries

Seigniorage
Multiple currency approach
Roosa bonds
Dollar standard
Benign neglect
Dollar imperialism
Currency obligation potential

POINTS FOR FURTHER STUDY AND DISCUSSION

1. Compare the causes of the decline of the gold exchange standard based on the British pound sterling and the U.S. dollar.

2. Update calculations about the benefits from being the World Banker found in the literature, taking special account of nominal against real yields on U.S. dollar assets held by the rest of the world.

3. Analyze advantages and disadvantages encountered by firms attempting to write private contracts in terms of SDRs. Investigate reports that some New York banks are accepting deposits and are making loans denominated in SDRs. What does this development mean for the future of the U.S. dollar in private business?

4. What is the value of seigniorage accruing to the issuer of a monetary asset worth $1 million bearing an interest rate of 3 percent for 20 years? Assume that it costs nothing to issue the asset and that the proceeds are invested at 5 percent.

5. Study the latest statistics available on the composition of international reserves. Does the evidence suggest that the dollar gold exchange standard has come to an end? Try to explain the existing facts.

24 An International Monetary System Based on Centrally Created Reserves

HISTORICALLY, the monetary sectors in the industrialized economies of the West have evolved from decentralization and laissez-faire to centralization and strict control. This evolution was accompanied and caused by the growing recognition that the money supply is too important an element in economic growth and stability of nations to be left uncontrolled by man. If this historic evolution in national economies is a reliable guide to coming developments in the international monetary sector, then the ultimate form of international monetary organization will be one resembling the U.S. Federal Reserve System, the Bank of England, or any other national central banking system, with the world supply of reserves firmly in the conscious control of man. Accordingly, the function of such a world agency will be nearly identical to that of the national central banks in that it is to provide the community of nations with liquidity sufficient to enable the system's operation at maximum efficiency.

The most important difference between national monetary authorities as they are known today and an international central bank now being envisioned is that the former is part of a complete government executive department, with the power to tax and enforce its legislation, while the latter essentially is a voluntary association of nation-states, with practically no effective power to oversee execution of its orders. The existence of this difference will be seen to be at the heart of many of the difficulties encountered in the negotiations for the establishment of a world monetary order based on a system of centrally created reserves.

More specifically, the basic institutional environment to which the international monetary system has to be fitted is the continued existence of independent nation-states. One of the most important rights of these sovereign nations is the making of economic policy through regulation of the money supply, exchange rates, and fiscal policy. The existence of this right must be recognized explicitly in all reform plans based on a central reserve creating agency, and it imposes two important limitations on a world monetary authority.

First, the "money" issued will not be circulating publicly. Day-to-day private transactions of international trade and finance will continue to be executed in national currencies. The centrally created international money will be used only by national governments in the settlement of debts arising among themselves as a result of official intervention in the foreign exchange markets.

Second, whereas national central banks can regulate the quantity of money in the economies over which they have jurisdiction, by influencing the quantity of the banking system's reserve assets, the discount rate, and the fractional reserve requirements, the international agency has no such powers to regulate total liquidity in the world. This is primarily because national governments continue to be free to set the levels of their money supplies for purposes of domestic stability and with only little regard to their level of international reserves. Therefore, the total quantity of money *privately* used in the world, through its effects on monetary rates of interest, has an important influence on national and average worldwide employment and prices and is not under the control of the international agency.

None of the plans for international monetary order to be analyzed below envision the extinction, or even the significant reduction, of national monetary sovereignty. However, the establishment and operation of a central international monetary agency, even on the limited basis just suggested, implies the surrender of some economic sovereignty and close cooperation among nations. Moreover, it is likely that the experience of working together, bargaining, and communicating provided by such an international organization will make its own contribution toward greater understanding and trust, thus paving the way for future increased cooperation and surrender of sovereignty. However, such developments are speculative, and all plans for a new international monetary order proceed from the assumption that it will serve a voluntary association of independent nation-states.

In the present chapter we present a history of the IMF which permits us to put into perspective the need for reform now confronting the world. Section II discusses the nature of special drawing rights (SDRs), which since 1968 have put the IMF into a position to create genuine owned reserves and which represent an important step in the evolution of a world central bank. Section III considers what to do with the social savings which centrally created reserves can create. In Section IV we apply concepts derived from the optimum-quantity-of-money argument to the case of the international monetary system and find criteria for an optimal interest rate on SDRs and an optimal quantity to be created. In the concluding section of this chapter we discuss some other important issues confronting reformers of the international monetary system in the 1970s and beyond. These problems are what to do with gold in the system, what form to choose for an international adjustment mechanism and finally, how to meet the need for an intervention currency.

I. A HISTORY OF THE EARLY IMF

The International Monetary Fund (IMF) was created by international agreement at Bretton Woods, New Hampshire, in July 1944 and opened for currency operations on March 1, 1947, claiming a membership of 30 nations. Its headquarters are now in Washington D.C. The charter and declared objectives the IMF adopted were those originally proposed by the United States and its key negotiator, Harry Dexter White, rejecting the more visionary proposals made by Britain and its chief representative, John Maynard Keynes. While Keynes had wanted the IMF to become a genuine world central bank, with the power to issue its own currency obligations and limited power to encroach on the economic sovereignty of member states, the U.S. proposals were pragmatic and were aimed at enabling the IMF to prevent the major abuses and shortcomings of the international monetary system during the 1930s: competitive devaluations, exchange and trade restrictions, and a lack of international reserves.

The problem of competitive devaluations was tackled by agreement that countries generally should adhere to the maintenance of parity exchange rates. These rates were declared and registered legally with the IMF, and every country committed itself to maintain them within a margin of maximum plus or minus 1 percent unless "fundamental" payments disequilibrium required a change of the parity rate. Changes in parity greater than 10 percent could be undertaken only with agreement from the IMF, while changes smaller than 10 percent required no such permission. On the question of freeing international trade and payments from restrictions, the main policy tool of the IMF was to set out guidelines for the use of such restrictions.

In the pursuit of the declared objectives of exchange rate stability and removal of controls on trade and payments, the IMF was severely handicapped by the absence of any real power of enforcement. Its main role was that of a forum for the meeting of the representatives of various countries to exchange information and set and maintain of standards of behavior through the evaluation of policies and public pronouncements. However, even in these activities the IMF was constrained by the ability of individual countries to censure any official publications they deem to be against the national interests. It is difficult to know what role the IMF played behind the scenes in nonpublic consultations, as a neutral forum for the exchange of information, as a place where other nations collectively could confront the United States, and as a guardian of public morality during the postwar years, when exchange rates were relatively stable, restrictions on trade and payments were removed progressively, and ultimately (in 1958), all currency restrictions were removed by the major European countries. A history of the IMF from this point of view still needs to be written.

In the third area of responsibility, the provision of international reserves, the IMF also has failed to play a major role, though the unplanned development of the dollar gold exchange standard discussed above prevented the appearance of a serious liquidity shortage in the postwar years. The provision of international reserves through the IMF originally was based on the creation of a pool of gold and national currencies, $8.8 billion in 1944, which were contributed by member countries and could be drawn upon by members according to a system of quotas and a set of rules. The quotas were designed to reflect the economic size and importance of each country's national economy and international trade. The quotas originally set in 1944 have been revised several times in the past as other countries have joined the IMF (there were 125 member countries in 1973) and some grew in relative economic size and importance, such as Germany and Japan. The total size of quotas in 1974 was $29.2 billion.

The IMF pool of reserves was set up by requiring that each country make a payment to the fund equal to its quota, 25 percent in the form of gold and 75 percent in its own national currency. If a country is in short-run balance of payments disequilibrium it may draw from this IMF–held pool, subject to differing degrees of restrictions and costs, depending on its total borrowing. The actual process of drawing involves a deposit of the amount to be borrowed in the form of domestic currency of the borrowing country with the IMF. In return the IMF makes available to the borrowing country a currency useful for intervention in foreign exchange markets, usually, in the past, dollars. A country can thus obtain amounts of reserves equal to 25 percent of its quota, the so-called gold tranche, automatically and without restriction. Further borrowings, up to a maximum of 200 percent of its quota, may be made, but these are accompanied by increasingly more stringent conditions as to repayment, cost, and the pursuit of domestic policies specified by the IMF. Repayment of the borrowed funds has to be undertaken within three to five years, in the form of gold or convertible currencies. There are limitations on the currencies that can be used for repayment, and a number of other regulations guide the rate of borrowing and repayment.

It is not important for us to spell out in detail these rules and regulations guiding borrowing. Instead, we should note the important fact that the IMF system did not result in a net increase in unconditionally owned world reserves. The unconditional gold tranche is simply equal to the amount of gold each country had to pay into the pool, and every country's reserves therefore are the same as they would have been in the absence of the IMF. The other uses of the IMF borrowing facilities under the quota system involve conditional credit, which has the undesirable property that it is not necessarily available when needed in an emergency and in the quantities needed. Furthermore, since credit is repayable, any increase in liquidity resulting from the extension of a loan ultimately is extinguished. Because of these properties of conditional quota credits, they are not counted as part of international reserves. Instead, the entry in Table 23–1 (Chapter 23) labeled "IMF Position," which is counted as part of international reserves, essentially reflects only the sum of gold tranches. These grew slowly in absolute value, from $1.6 billion in 1948 to $7.4 billion in 1973, and represented a maximum of 8.6 percent of global reserves in 1966 and 1969.

In 1961 the initial credit facilities in the framework of the quota system were supplemented by the General Agreement to Borrow. As we noted in connection with short-term capital problems in Chapter 17, this agreement enabled the IMF to borrow up to $6 billion from any members of the Group of Ten countries and to lend these funds to countries suffering from temporary payments disequilibriums caused by short-term capital flows.

In sum, the early history of the IMF, from its inception at the end of World War II, was one in which the institution kept a relatively low profile, while the dollar gold exchange standard and parity exchange rates provided a relatively smoothly functioning international monetary system. The IMF served as a useful forum for the exchange of ideas and the codification of international norms of behavior. In addition, the IMF created some additional facilities for conditional borrowing of reserves. However, in the two decades following its creation, the IMF failed to evolve into an institution which created genuinely owned reserves in the manner envisioned by Keynes and others who saw the IMF as a future world central bank.

After the first dollar crisis of 1960 (described in the preceding chapter), Robert Triffin of Yale University analyzed the difficulties inherent in the dollar gold exchange standard and developed the theoretical case for enabling the IMF to create genuinely owned international reserves. Triffin's visionary plan received much public attention and support from intellectuals, but it took almost seven years to persuade the governments of the United States and other leading countries to agree to such a revolutionary change in the institutional characteristic of the IMF. To the surprise of many observers, at the 1967 annual meeting of the IMF in Rio de Janeiro, partly through the personal efforts of Henry Fowler, who was head of the U.S. delegation and the U.S. Under Secretary for International Monetary Affairs, agreement was reached for the creation of genuine net addition to international reserves, the so-called special drawing rights, or SDRs. In 1970 the first SDRs were distributed and, as can be seen by referring to Table 23–1, in 1973 the amount of SDRs created came to $10.6 billion, or 5.8 percent of total reserves.

II. THE NATURE OF SPECIAL DRAWING RIGHTS

The mechanism of creation, distribution, and use of SDRs can be summarized as follows. After general agreement has been reached among members of the IMF about the total number of SDRs to be created in a given time period, each country is then credited in its account with a certain number of SDR units, determined by the relative size of its quota. For example, if in a given year 1 billion SDRs are to be created, country A, whose quota represents 10 percent of all quotas, receives a credit of 100 million SDRs. Now if this country needs foreign exchange to intervene in the market in support of its currency, it notifies the IMF of its intention to use its SDRs for this purpose. The IMF then informs country A which national currencies are eligible for such withdrawal, and country A then specifies the currencies of which country or countries it wishes to acquire. For example, country A may decide to obtain 50 million SDRs worth of DM at the current exchange rate. Under these conditions country A's SDR account is debited and Germany's is credited with 50 million SDRs. In a later period, when country A has a payments surplus and accumulates foreign exchange, it can reacquire SDRs by selling to the IMF eligible foreign currencies.

Country A does not have to repay the SDRs used in this manner, though it must maintain an average of 30 percent of its past cumulative allotments over any five-year moving period. Countries whose currencies are acquired for intervention in private markets are not obligated to hold more than three times their original allotments. Once a country has reached such a point, the IMF declares its currency ineligible for further withdrawals.

Once every year the IMF charges every country interest on all cumulative past allotments, and credits every country with interest on the average actual holdings of SDRs during the past year. As a result, a country which exactly holds its past allotments receives an equal credit and debit of interest. A country which has used SDRs to acquire currencies owes a net debit, and a country whose currency was withdrawn receives a net credit for interest. The interest rate on SDRs originally was set at 1.5 percent per year and raised to 5.0 percent in 1975.

SDRs cannot be converted into gold or any other lasting, ultimate standard of value. Their value derives, simply and importantly, like that of domestically circulating money, from the fact that they are acceptable without conditions in the settlement of debts among nations, though the process of use for this purpose is obscured by the kind of institutional arrangement, exchange into currencies acceptable in private markets, we have just discussed. The determination of the value of an SDR in exchange for national currencies, however, is a fairly complicated matter.

The Value of SDRs

Originally the value of an SDR was set at one U.S. dollar, both having the same weight in gold in 1970. The exchange value of the SDR against other currencies was simply equal to their market rate against the dollar. For example, if a DM was worth $0.25, then the SDR value of one DM was also 0.25. However, with the cessation of U.S. gold convertibility, changes of the dollar exchange rate against gold and many other currencies, and the general moves to end the key role of the U.S. dollar in the international monetary system, after July 1, 1974, the value of SDRs was determined in terms of "basket" of 16 main currencies. The currencies in the basket are those of countries which during the period 1968–72 had world trade equal to at least 1 percent of the world's total. The method for calculating the SDR value under this method can best be explained with the help of Table 24–1.

In Column (1) we show the names and in Column (2) the weights each currency has in the SDR basket. According to the *IMF Survey*, July 8, 1974, "Relative weights for each currency are broadly proportionate to the country's exports, but are modified to recognize that the share in trade does not necessarily give an adequate measure of a currency's weight in the world economy" (p. 213). As a result of past SDR valuation methods in terms of gold and dollars, the U.S. gold devaluation had resulted in an SDR value of $1.20635 on July 1, 1974. In order to maintain continuity with this value, it was necessary to derive an index called "Units of Currency in One SDR," shown in Column (3) of Table 24–1, which reflects not only the currency's weight in the basket but also its market value in terms of dollars. Thus, with the U.S. dollar weight at 33 percent and the unit currency value of 1.0, .33 × 1.0 × 1.20635 = 0.3980955, or roughly 0.4. For other currencies the units shown in Column (3) were chosen in a similar manner, though, as can be seen, the numbers are rounded for ease of calculation and because excessive precision would be misplaced, since the weights were determined somewhat arbitrarily.

The value of an SDR is calculated daily by the IMF, using as the fundamental input the index units of currency in one SDR shown in Column (3) and the daily market exchange rates of individual countries in terms of dollars. In Column (4) we show the individual rates on July 2, 1974. Column (5) represents the result of dividing Column (3) by (4), which establishes the dollar value of one SDR for the day. As can be seen, it was 1.206375 on that date, slightly more than the 1.20635 on July 1,

TABLE 24-1
The Valuation of SDRs by the Currency Basket Method

(1)	(2)	(3)	(4)	(5)	(6)
			Exchange Rates,		
		Units	July 2,	U.S.	Currency
		of Cur-	1974,	Dollar	Units
	Weights	rency	Units	Equiva-	per SDR,
	(per-	in One	per	lent of	July 2,
Currencies	cent)	SDR	Dollar	SDR	1974
U.S. dollar	33 %	0.400	1.0000	0.400000	1.206375
Deutsche mark	12.5	0.3800	2.55750	0.148583	3.085304
Pound sterling	9	0.0450	1/2.38800	0.107460	0.505182
French franc	7.5	0.4400	4.81350	0.091410	5.806886
Japanese yen	7.5	26.0000	285.90000	0.091410	344.9026
Canadian dollar	6	0.0710	1.02850	0.073024	1.240757
Italian lira	6	47.0000	646.50000	0.072699	779.9214
Netherlands guilder	4.5	0.1400	2.66350	0.052562	3.213180
Belgian franc	3.5	1.6000	38.1000	0.041995	45.962888
Swedish krona	2.5	0.1300	4.37500	0.029714	5.277891
Australian dollar	1.5	0.0120	0.67227	0.017850	0.811010
Danish krone	1.5	0.0990	5.44350	0.018392	7.215329
Norwegian krone	1.5	0.0990	5.44350	0.018187	6.566902
Spanish peseta	1.5	1.1000	57.2700	0.019207	69.089096
Austrian schilling	1	0.2200	18.25500	0.012051	22.022376
South African rand	1	0.0082	0.66669	0.012300	0.804278
	100.0%			1.206375	

One SDR = $1.206375
One dollar = SDR 0.828930

Examples for other currencies:					
Ecuadoran sucre			25.000103		30.1595
Irish pound			2.3880		0.505184
Kuwaiti dinar			.291900		0.352142
U.A.E. dirham			3.954881		4.77107

Source: *IMF Survey*, July 8, 1974, pp. 209–13. Column (6) was found by multiplying Column (4) with 1.206375.

1974, the day on which the past and the new systems of calculation were linked. In Column (6) we show the number of currency units of individual countries required to purchase an SDR. The figures in Column (6) are simply the product of Column (4), the current exchange rate, and the current, calculated value of the SDR currency basket, 1.206375. The last four currencies shown in Table 24–1 are not used in the calculation of the SDR value. The value of these currencies in terms of SDRs is shown in Column (6) and is found by multiplying the dollar price shown in Column (4) by 1.206375.

In announcing the new method for the valuation of SDRs in July 1974, the IMF was careful to explain that the use of the dollar exchange rates of all currencies in the basket was a matter of computational convenience and ease of obtaining data; it was not meant to confer or imply any special status for the dollar in the international monetary system. This statement and the very institution of the new SDR valuation procedure are symptomatic of the desire of the world, acting through the IMF and with the consensus of the United States, to remove the dollar and gold from their past positions of dominance in the official international monetary system. This fact is obvious once we realize that except for minor inaccuracies due to weighting, the relative values of currencies shown in Column (6) could be found, as they had been before July 1, 1974, by defining the values of SDRs and dollars in terms of gold, thus maintaining a fixed relationship between SDRs and dollars and deriving the SDR value of other currencies on the basis of market exchange rates in terms of dollars. This procedure used to produce a fixity of the SDR value of the dollar which was changed only when the official dollar price of gold was changed, while all the other currencies' values changed with market prices. Under the new system the value of a dollar in terms of SDRs fluctuates daily, just as does the value of all other currencies. Symbolically, the dollar has been made equal to all other currencies. Also, the official dollar price of gold no more determines the dollar value of SDRs directly, though how precisely the units of currency per SDR index of Column (3) would be affected by an official change in the dollar price of monetary gold is not clear and may not yet have been determined by the IMF.

Despite this symbolic demotion of the dollar, however, it is obvious that the reality of the dominance of the dollar in world trade and finance cannot be denied. There is no national currency other than the dollar for which in all market economies of the world it is possible to obtain meaningful daily exchange rates. For this reason the IMF chose to calculate the basket value of the SDRs using dollar exchange rates. We have discussed already above in other contexts the fact that the dollar's use in private transactions and as a measure and store of value brings many externalities. We have just seen that they exist also in some official uses for the dollar. These externalities are likely to persist, as is the dollar's dominance in private and some official uses, in spite of concerted efforts to treat the dollar as equal to other currencies in official international affairs.

In sum, the most important characteristics of SDRs are that they can be used unconditionally, with the minor proviso that the currencies obtained with them cannot be turned into gold at a central bank, that they are not extinguished through use or repayment, and that they cannot be converted into gold or any other ultimate standard of value. SDRs therefore have all the characteristics of genuine money, and they represent a net addition to international liquidity as useful as gold or dollars. Since it costs practically nothing to create SDRs through bookkeeping entries at the IMF, their use in place of gold gives rise to social savings for the world equal to the resources saved by not having to mine, refine, and guard gold. The SDRs can be created at a rate to assure an orderly and adequate growth of international reserves. Once SDRs have replaced dollars as reserves in the portfolios of central banks, the United States will be relieved of the burden of being the World Banker, and the international monetary system bestows no special prestige or privileges on any one nation. Most generally, the SDR system makes the IMF into an international central bank for national central banks, which parallels to an important degree the development of central banks within individual countries. As such the IMF with SDRs represents a major and significant act of international cooperation for the benefit of the world as a whole.

In the remaining parts of this chapter we analyze the functioning of the SDR system from several different points of view. First we consider the mechanisms by which the system presently distributes, and is being challenged to distribute in the future, the social savings accruing to the world from the substitution of the SDRs for gold. Next we consider theoretical guidelines which should determine the growth of SDRs through time and the rate of interest charged and paid on their use. Finally we discuss a number of other issues related to the proper functioning of an SDR system.

III. WHAT TO DO WITH SOCIAL SAVINGS FROM CENTRALLY CREATED RESERVES

In the long run one of the most important benefits of having an international monetary system based on centrally created reserves is that the use of these inexpensively producable reserves in place of gold results in large resource savings for the world as a whole. For example, in 1970 the world's central banks held in their portfolios approximately $93 billion of reserves. If the demand for such reserves grows at a real rate of 5 percent a year, then if only gold had been used, it would have been necessary that year to produce about $5 billion of gold. In future years this resource use would become larger, growing at the rate of 5 percent a year, that is, doubling about every 16 years. Further resources would be required to store and guard this gold hoard. There are some economists and politicians who believe that for the world as a whole the value of these resources is negligibly small. They have argued for the retention of gold, revalued periodically in terms of national currencies, as the only source of international reserves. However, the development of the SDRs discussed above means that the world may be able to look forward to substantial real resource savings in the future, when SDRs replace gold in central bank reserve portfolios.

Out of this fact arises the question of how these resource savings, which in technical language have become known as seigniorage, should be distributed. As noted in Chapter 23, the term "seigniorage" has in the past been used to describe the revenue of sovereigns who before the development of democratically controlled governments had the monopoly right to issue coins with a face value greater than their true metal content. The difference between the face and metal content value of coins minus the cost of minting is known as seigniorage. Historically it represented an important source of revenue to sovereigns.

More precisely, the present value of social seigniorage (SS) arising from the issue of D units of paper money over a given time period is equal to

$$SS = \left[\frac{R - c}{1 + d} + \frac{R - c}{(1 + d)^2} + \frac{R - c}{(1 + d)^3} + \cdots + \frac{R - c}{(1 + d)^n} \right] \times D \quad (24\text{--}1)$$

where n is the period at which the paper money has to be "cashed in" or is replaced by a commodity substitute; R is the marginal social productivity of the resources, D, which would have been required to produce commodity money of equal value; c is the social unit cost of servicing the fiat money, such as printing and replacing worn-out paper money, policing against counterfeiting, and providing check clearing services; and d is the social rate of discount. Assuming constancy of R, c, and d throughout the life of the fiat money, and assuming that life to approach infinity, the present value of social seigniorage from the issuance of D units of paper money is

$$SS = \left[\frac{R - c}{d} \right] \times D \quad (24\text{--}2)$$

Thus, if c is zero and $R = d$, the value of the social seigniorage is equal to the face value of the money issued.

It should be noted that the present value of seigniorage accruing to the issuer of money was found to be

$$S = \left[\frac{R - r - c}{d} \right] \times D \quad (24\text{--}3)$$

under the assumption of an infinite life of the money and where r is the interest rate paid to the holders of the money. Thus, it is seen that the essential difference between the two concepts is found in the term r. As will be shown below, the payment of interest to money holders is one of the methods for the distribution of social seigniorage away from the issuer of the money and to those who hold it.

Logically, there exist three basic methods for the distribution of social seigniorage, each of which has been embodied in a class of reform proposals made in recent years. The three methods of distribution for convenience will be called the central government, the free market, and the transactions demand methods. These will be discussed with the reform proposals based on them.

Central Government Method

National monetary authorities never face any "problem" in connection with the distribution of social seigniorage, even though it is substantial, as growing economies are supplied with large quantities of needed paper money. In the United States, for example, the cumulative total value of seigniorage from the issuance of paper money alone was $40 billion at the end of 1967, assuming that the cost of the money's production and maintenance has been zero in the past and will continue to be so in the future. In recent years the seigniorage has been about $4 billion per annum.

The seigniorage accruing to national monetary authorities rarely gives rise to any discussion because the creation of money is part of the central government activity, and, as such, the excess of the face value of the paper money over its cost of production and administration goes directly into the general revenue of the treasury. In the United States, for example, the mints responsible for producing currency are an administrative division of the Treasury, and "profits" from their operation enter government revenue directly. From there this seigniorage is distributed to society as a whole by the purchase of public goods or through the redistribution of income. The process of distribution can best be understood by realizing that in theory government expenditures for public goods and income redistribution are determined by society's needs and available alternative resource uses, while taxation rates are set to raise revenue sufficient to meet the cost of these expenditures. The existence of seigniorage permits these tax rates to be lower than they otherwise would have to be.

Another way of looking at the process of seigniorage distribution by national governments is to consider that the newly issued money each year permits the government to purchase certain quantities of goods and services with "cash" which it did not obtain through taxation and which does not add to the rate of price increase existing otherwise, since the public needs this cash to carry on business activity at the new level reached during the year.

The purchase of world public goods, or the redistribution of world income with the seigniorage from the issue of international reserve assets, was proposed by Sir Maxwell Stamp in 1962. In his plan he proposed that the seigniorage from world liquidity creation be channeled to the less developed countries. Such an objective can easily be attained by issuance of the agreed-upon quantity of reserve assets to the less developed countries, which would then spend them on real resources in the developed countries. By agreement the latter countries would accept these assets and treat them as reserves. The resultant flow of resources from developed to less developed countries would not have to be reversed, as long as the developed countries continued to abide by the agreements setting up the monetary order, and economic conditions did not call for a decrease in average holdings of reserves.

Pursuing the logic of Stamp's basic idea, it follows that, after the disappearance of the less developed countries' need for capital, seigniorage could be used to support other worldwide programs of income redistribution as appear desirable at the time. Or, alternatively, seigniorage could be spent directly on world public goods and services, as, for example, a supranational peace-keeping force, international courts of law, the maintenance of agencies to regulate and maintain international air, land, and sea ways, or the collection and interpretation statistics in economics, demography, and meteorology.

Since about 1970 the distribution of newly issued SDRs directly to developing countries has received much attention from politicians and economists. The proposal known as LINK has come to be an item for negotiation in the official talks about reform of the international monetary system, which have been continuing since the Smithsonian Agreement was reached in December of 1971. The LINK proposal derives its name from the fact that it calls for a link between the creation of international liquidity and the provision of development assistance.

The arguments in favor of LINK are essentially moralistic, though in some versions they are obscured by technicalities and failure to understand monetary theory. The arguments are that the developed countries owe the developing countries assistance as a matter of human decency, and, since legislatures in the developed countries are not willing to vote sufficient quantities of such assistance, the need arises to find ways to overcome this resistance by the legislatures. One way of doing so is to use the LINK scheme, which would put the resource transfers outside the legislative process, since the acquisition of SDRs would be part of an automatic process under which national central banks allocate national wealth efficiently. Defenders of the scheme in developed countries seem to be taking the view that legislators basically would like to provide foreign assistance, as humanitarian and broad-minded leaders of their societies, but the democratic process, which gives votes to large numbers of narrow-minded and selfish people, prevents them from doing so. Since the LINK proposal involves highly technical matters of international finance it cannot become a political issue, and legislators have an opportunity to discharge their humanitarian obligations without facing the penalties the democratic process would impose upon them otherwise.

The arguments against LINK are that it would, in a most cynical fashion, bypass the democratic process in the expenditure of resources which is the cornerstone of Western societies. Furthermore, the scheme would create conflicts within the IMF which would endanger the functioning of the SDR system itself. Developing countries would have great incentives to vote for large annual allocations of SDRs, erring, where judgment is a requirement, on the side of creating too many reserves. Developed countries, on the other hand, would have incentives to vote for smaller increases in reserves. If ever the developing countries should obtain a voting majority on these decisions, the developed countries might be forced into withdrawal from the entire SDR scheme. The very fact that the LINK proposal has become an agreed-upon major item of overall reform of the IMF in the 1970s is indicative of the voting power of the developing countries in this organization.

There is also the technical but important matter, to be developed further in the next section of this chapter, that the efficiency of the international monetary system using SDRs and managed exchange rates demands a higher interest rate on the SDRs than is paid at present. Under the LINK scheme, the real resource transfer from a given number of SDRs is smaller the higher is the interest rate on the SDRs. In the extreme, if SDRs carried an interest rate equal to the marginal productivity of real resources, then the developed countries under the scheme would receive resources the marginal product of which would have to be paid to the developing countries, and their net gain would be zero or limited to gains of consumer surplus. The LINK scheme therefore might prevent attainment of agreement on a socially optimal interest rate on SDRs.

Free Market Method

Free market economies have developed substitutes for commodity money, the best known of which are the various forms of negotiable instruments, above all checks and demand deposits. In the process, the free market has solved automatically the problem of distributing social seigniorage through the payment of interest.

The role of interest in the distribution of social seigniorage can be explained most easily by the following schematic sketch of the historic evolution of the banking business. Goldsmiths are alleged to have taken on the job of storing bullion for their customers, at first simply as a sideline to their regular business. They issued certificates of deposit to the owners of the gold, which began to circulate freely in place of the gold itself, since every new owner was confident that he could obtain the metal whenever he needed it. Only rarely did special circumstances give rise to the actual conversion of certificates into the metal. The smarter goldsmiths eventually realized that it was quite safe to keep only a fraction of their deposits backed by gold, and they began to convert a fraction of their gold deposits into income-yielding investments such as securities, loans, houses, land, merchandise inventories, and machines.

The gold put back into circulation in this manner was redeposited with other goldsmiths and in turn was used to make more investments after an appropriate fraction had been retained for liquidity purposes. Ultimately the circulation of certificates exceeded the existing stock of gold by a multiple, the exact size of which was determined by the fraction of gold deposits retained as a liquidity reserve. How large a fraction of deposits needed to be retained depended on the stability of the demand deposits and the cost and availability of liquid secondary reserves, as is well known from the theory of banking.

The first goldsmiths who made these productive investments with their customers' deposits earned extraordinarily high profits. However, in a free market such high profits attract new entries into the business, and soon competition for these profitable deposits began to develop. The main forms in which this competition expressed itself were the provision of more services to depositors, as for example check-writing privileges, and the payment of interest. The costs of doing business and the interest payments tended to rise through competitive responses, until in the end profits from the banking business were reduced to normal.

In terms of the preceding discussion of seigniorage, the formal condition for competitive equilibrium is:

$$S = \left(\frac{R - r - c}{d} \right) \times D = 0 \qquad (24\text{--}4)$$

where S is the present value of seigniorage accruing to the issuer of D units of paper money; R is the yield on the investments made by the money issuer; c is the cost of administering the business per unit of deposit, including a normal profit to the entrepreneur and his capital; and d is the social rate of discount. From this equation it follows that the interest rate on deposits with the goldsmiths (r) is $r = R - c$. Since the marginal productivity of investments and the cost of carrying on the banking business are determined by technological conditions in the economy as a whole, the yield on deposits of money is seen to be determined by the same factors.

In this situation of competitive equilibrium, society still reaps benefits from social seigniorage due to the use of paper money in place of the gold. However, these benefits accrue to the holders of the money in the form of interest and services on their deposits and, consequently, in proportion to the extent to which they contributed to the demand for paper money and the generation of the social savings.

Of the major proposals for reform of the international monetary system made in recent years, only that by Triffin places emphasis on the role of interest. He argues that the payment of interest to the holders of centrally created reserves makes these assets more desirable than gold. According to his plan, the central authority would receive deposits of gold and national currencies, in return for which it would issue the international fiat money. The national currencies thus received would be invested in the securities markets of member nations, yielding an interest income to the Bank at the rate R per unit of outstanding fiat money. Though Triffin does not discuss these issues explicitly, his bank would presumably pay interest to the holders of the money at a rate high enough so that the profits from these investments are zero after payment of operating costs (c). In terms of the preceding analytical framework, these conditions are equivalent to the condition $S = R - r - c = 0$.

The method of distributing the seigniorage through payment of interest to the money holders has the disadvantage of requiring the central authority to manage a very large asset portfolio, with all of the difficulties of judging credit worthiness of debtors, maintaining maturity structure of the portfolio, collecting and disbursing interest and dividends, and so on. The investment decisions by a group of directors could mean doom or success to private entrepreneurs and governments, especially since the investments represent demand for a country's debt instruments and influence the level of national exchange rates. For these reasons, political pressures on these directors would tend to be strong and, in general, their positions would represent an undesirable concentration of economic power. It would most likely be possible to routinize the portfolio management of the authority and leave little discretion and power to directors. However, such a system might prove to be quite inflexible and incapable of adjusting to changing conditions, thus aggravating cyclical instabilities and hindering secular adjustments in international trade and finance. Consequently, management by rule may be as undesirable as leaving too much discretionary power in the hands of the directors.

In spite of these objections, the free market method of distributing social seigniorage carries considerable intellectual appeal, since it approximates the solution perfect competition would attain. However, chances for its adoption are not good, primarily because of the availability of a superior method of distributing seigniorage called the transactions demand method.

Transactions Demand Method

The distribution of social seigniorage under the central government method and the Stamp plan discussed above results in the ultimate transfer of resources between countries when the initial recipients of the newly created money spend it. Thus, if the initial recipients could be required to hold on to it, no other countries in the world would be required to give up resources as a result of fiat money creation and distribution. But while "money" that can never be spent is not really money, and the preceding analysis is unrealistic, it dramatizes the point that it is the expenditure of paper money received free initially which gives rise to resource transfers and the problem of social seigniorage distribution.

Analytically, the permanent hoarding of the newly issued reserves is equal to the maintenance of an average balance of cash equal to the sum received. Thus, if countries are required to aim for a holding of average reserve balances just equal to the sum they were given from the fiat money-creating agency, the reserves would be available for purposes of meeting temporary balance-of-payments deficits. In this way they would serve the purposes for which they were created, without causing inter-country resource transfers attributable to their creation and distribution. Periods of temporary shortage below the sum of fiat money received have to be met by periods of excess holdings above that sum, and accounting of a country's position in this sense requires keeping a running total of reserve unit days in surplus and deficit.

If newly created reserves are distributed among nations so that each country receives only such quantities as it tends to hold on the average, the *creation* and *distribution* of reserves in this manner involves no inter-country transfer of resources and retains a theoretical neutrality of money in the allocation of resources. This is strictly true only if interest adjustments are incorporated into the calculation of average reserve balance shortages and surpluses in order to reflect the fact that real resources acquired today in exchange for fiat money are worth more than these resources repayable in the future.

The concept of social seigniorage distribution according to these general principles was incorporated in both the White and Keynes plans which served, respectively, as the U.S.– and U.K.–backed blueprints for the establishment of the International Monetary Fund. Under the IMF charter the concept is reflected in the quotas, which determine the quantity of internationally acceptable assets, such as dollars, sterling, or gold, a country may obtain in return for its own currency. These same quotas serve as a basis for the distribution of special drawing rights.

To the extent, therefore, that quotas do in fact reflect long-run average demand for reserves of individual countries, the distribution of SDRs on this basis does not lead to an intercountry transfer of income or wealth. Unfortunately, there are no universally accepted methods for establishing whether or not current quotas reflect long-run average demand. Historically, quotas were determined on the basis of both economic and political criteria.

Thus, White's proposed formula for the computation of national quotas under the IMF favored the United States, since it based the calculation of quotas on the level of gold holdings, national incomes, and fluctuations and scale of international payments at the time when the U.S. position in these respects was extraordinarily strong. Keynes's formula, on the other hand, provided that the level of each country's exports and imports for the three years immediately before the war be used as a base. This formula would have been relatively favorable for the United Kingdom, because of the country's relatively strong position in the period just before the war. Ultimately, the IMF agreements provided for quotas based on the White plan, though the formula was not made part of the official document, and political considerations appear to have modified somewhat the distribution resulting from the mechanical application of the formula alone.

However, since the original determination of quotas, dominance of the IMF and world economic and financial scene by the United States and United Kingdom has diminished, and the growing power and influence of Western European countries and of the developing countries led to the revision of quotas in 1959 and 1974. It may not be unreasonable to expect further revisions of quotas in the future, so that they reflect with increasing accuracy the long-run average demand for reserves by the individual countries of the IMF.

However, we should note here briefly that even if quotas lead to the allocation of SDRs to individual countries in quantities different from their long-run average demand, the implicit intercountry transfer of income and wealth may be negligibly small if the interest rate on SDRs is close to the productivity of real resources. This is required for efficiency, according to some criteria to be developed in the next section. For example, if a country perpetually holds 100 million SDRs less than have been allocated to it because it has run a trade deficit of that size, it enjoys the benefits of having perpetually 100 million SDRs worth of real resources obtained from the rest of the world. But now if that country has to pay, every year, interest on these SDRs equal to the marginal productivity of the real resources acquired, then the present values of the marginal yield of the resources and of the interest payments are equal, the net benefits are zero, and the net cost to the rest of the world is nil. More generally, the intercountry transfer of real resources due to perpetual differences between holdings and allocations of SDRs is a decreasing function of the marginal productivity of real resources and the real interest rate on the SDRs.

IV. THE OPTIMUM QUANTITY AND COST OF INTERNATIONAL RESERVES

Two important problems confronting the IMF are the choices of how many SDRs to create and what interest rate should be attached to their use. We now turn to a discussion of these subjects, using the concept of the optimum quantity of domestic money which was first published by Milton Friedman in 1969.

It is easiest to explain the international monetary case by first presenting a brief summary of Friedman's argument about the optimum quantity and cost of money in the domestic economy. The first step in Friedman's argument is to recall the familiar price-theoretic theorem that a necessary condition for the efficient operation of an economy is that the price of any good or service be equal to the marginal social cost of producing it. We then need to realize that currency and money, more generally, provide the services of liquidity and that efficiency therefore demands that the cost of liquidity services be equal to the social cost of producing them. The price of money is equal to the opportunity cost of the foregone earnings resulting from the holding of money rather than an interest-earning asset, say bonds, which, for the sake of this theoretical argument, we can consider to have a yield equal to the marginal productivity of real resources or the rate of interest. Therefore it follows that under present institutional arrangements, the cost of money services is equal to the rate of interest in the market. However, the social marginal cost of producing money is very close to zero, given that it costs very few real resources to print currency and protect it against counterfeiting. The efficient price of money therefore also would be close to zero. Such a condition would be attained by paying interest on money at a rate very close to the interest rate on bonds. If such interest were paid, the public would be induced to increase its holding of money and to consume more of its liquidity services. Since it costs society near to nothing to produce this money, the benefits derived from the public's increased consumption of money's liquidity services are a clear social gain, due ultimately to an increase in the efficiency with which the economy operates.

One serious problem standing in the way of the realization of this efficiency gain is the fact that the very nature of money makes it technically very expensive to pay interest to its holders in a manner similar to that with which the holders of bonds or savings deposits are paid. It is not inconceivable that any technically feasible method for the payment of interest on money in this manner would absorb real resources sufficiently large to wipe out the efficiency gains. However, Friedman proposed one indirect method for making money holders receive a return. Under this method, the government would create money at such a rate that the price level falls at an annual rate nearly equal to the interest rate. Under this condition, the nominal interest rate on bonds would fall to nearly zero, because bond holders would receive an annual capital gain nearly equal to the interest rate. The efficiency condition that the productivity of real resources and the real interest rate on bonds be equal would be retained, but the opportunity cost of holding money would be almost zero, because money holders would make an annual capital gain nearly equal to the rate of interest. It is not too difficult to understand, after our discussion of the Phillips curve controversy and the monetarist approach to balance-of-payments adjustment in preceding chapters that such an institutional arrangement for paying interest on money through the generation of a falling price level is primarily of theoretical rather than practical interest.

Let us now turn to the application of the argument for an optimum quantity of money to the case of international reserves. For this purpose we redraw here Figure 22–1 (Chapter 22) as Figure 24–1 and recall the arguments about the existence of a demand curve for reserves by an individual country made in Chapter 22. In Figure 24–1 we measure along the horizontal axis the quantity of reserves and along the vertical axis rates

FIGURE 24-1
The Optimum Quantity of International Reserves

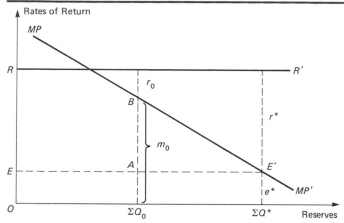

The line MP–MP' shows the marginal productivity of aggregate world reserve holdings as a decreasing function of quantity. The marginal productivity of real resources is OR. According to the principles of efficiency, the returns from wealth-holdings are maximized if marginal returns on all forms of assets are equal. Therefore, if the monetary returns on reserves are r_0, efficient holdings are $O\sum Q_0$; if monetary returns are r^*, efficient holdings are $O\sum Q^*$. Under the assumption that e^* is the marginal cost of producing reserves, $O\sum Q^*$ is the optimum quantity. By setting the interest rate on reserves at r^* rather than r_0 and inducing increased holdings, the world gains $AE'B$ additional output at zero cost of production.

of return. These are the marginal productivity of real resources (OR), the interest rate on reserves (r), and the marginal social productivity of reserves giving rise to the demand curve for reserves. In contrast with Figure 22–1, however, the quantities, interest rate, and functional relationships are those for the world as a whole rather than just one country. They are derived by adding up the demand for reserves schedule by individual countries. In Figure 24–1, OR is the marginal productivity of real resources, which is assumed to be the same in all countries of the world, and $MPMP'$ is the sum of all individual countries' demands for reserves schedules.

Recall that according to our analysis of Chapter 22, the individual country aims for an average level of reserve holdings where the marginal productivity of these reserves, M_0 plus the interest yield, r_0, on them, is just equal to the marginal productivity of real resources, OR. This condition is met for the aggregate world demand schedule for every country when reserves are at $\sum Q_0$. While this supply of reserves represents an equilibrium, given the interest rate set at r_0, the optimum-quantity-of-money argument implies that for efficiency the interest rate must be such as to make the price of liquidity services from money equal to the marginal social cost of producing them. Let us assume that the long- and short-run marginal costs of producing reserves are constant at OE. It follows that the IMF should set the rate of interest on them at r^* and that the new, efficient, equilibrium supply of reserves would be $\sum Q^*$. All countries would be induced to increase their holdings of reserves, in the aggregate, from $\sum Q_0$ to $\sum Q^*$ and to derive gains in real income through the ability to capture externalities from greater exchange rate stability. The total gains in income are equal to the triangle $AE'B$.

The preceding theoretical arguments represent a fairly simple modification and graphic exposition of Friedman's basic analysis. We now need to discuss some institutional factors and real-world facts, to make it applicable to the IMF and SDR system. We have noted that the interest rate on SDRs set during the negotiations in Rio de Janeiro was 1.5 percent and was raised in 1974 to 5 percent per year. The average cost of running the IMF in 1971 came to about 1 percent of the value of outstanding SDRs, and it may not be unreasonable to assume that this figure reflects also long-run marginal costs. Therefore, the 5 percent interest rate would be optimum if the marginal productivity in the world is 4 percent. According to the judgments of some economists, this rate may be about equal to the long-run yield of investment in developed countries. However, we should note that the concept of the marginal productivity of capital involves a real rate, while the interest rate on SDRs is nominal. As a result, any world inflation reduces the real yield on SDRs below that on real resources and thus creates nonefficient incentives for surplus countries to reduce lending and for deficit countries to increase borrowing through SDR financing. The optimum-quantity-of-money argument applied to the international sphere thus implies that the interest rate on SDRs should be indexed to world inflation. Such a reform would bring the cost and return features of the SDR system very close to the theoretical optimum.

Knowledge of the proper interest rate on SDRs, however, does not imply knowledge about the optimum quantity of reserves created. In other words, in Figure 24–1 we know approximately the empirically correct level of r^* and e^*, but we do not know the elasticity of the $MPMP'$ schedule and the implicit optimum quantity of reserves $O \sum Q^*$. Much the same absence of knowledge characterizes the domestic demand for money schedule. Historically, there are available no periods with different, substantial positive rates of return to money holdings which could permit empirical estimates to be made. However, domestic monetary theory suggests that this difficulty created by the lack of knowledge about the demand function can be overcome by the simple, practical expedient of letting the supply of SDRs grow at a steady rate. This rate may be fixed for a number of years at, say, the rate at which international trade has grown over the past decade. After such a number of years has elapsed, the performance of the world economy should be evaluated in much the same way in which domestic monetary policy is evaluated. Thus, for example if during a given period world trade growth had slowed down, the incidence of restrictions on trade and payments had grown, and the instability of exchange rates had increased, we might conclude that the growth in reserves was too small. Sophisticated performance criteria might be developed and monitored by the IMF, though we can expect the elapse of a considerable length of time before the IMF will be in the position of national central banks and able to engage in genuinely countercyclical creation of international reserves.

We can close our analysis of the optimum quantity of price of SDRs by considering that, according to our model of the determinants of the demand for reserves, the existence of an optimum quantity and price of SDRs also implies that countries would maintain an optimum exchange rate stability through time. This important conclusion follows directly from the foreign exchange model developed in Chapter 11 and the arguments about the nature of payments disturbances and the methods of adjustment presented in Chapters 14–20. According to these models, countries faced with given sets of balance-of-payments disturbances try to finance them until they run low on reserves. At this point they use all methods of real adjustment, including exchange rate changes. The need to adjust exchange rates is thus determined by the stock of reserves normally held by each country, and it follows that if the stock is socially optimal, the changes in exchange rate countries are forced to make will be optimal also.

V. MISCELLANEOUS PROBLEMS OF INTERNATIONAL MONETARY ORGANIZATION

In the remaining section of this chapter we turn to the analysis of a number of miscellaneous issues confronting the reformers of the international monetary system. While these issues, in some respects, are as important as those concerning the distributions of seigniorage and the quantity and cost of international reserves to be created, we will treat them here more briefly and with less analytical rigor. This is partly because there exist no theoretical concepts equivalent to those of seigniorage and optimum quantity of money and partly because of a lack of space. Students interested in pursuing further some of the issues raised here are referred to the readings suggested at the end of the chapter.

The Role of Monetary Gold

Monetary theorists used to insist, until the 1930s, that the ultimate value of money was guaranteed only through its convertibility into gold. In a somewhat more sophisticated version of the theory, they also maintained that if such convertibility was maintained legally, it put an effective constraint on the ability of governments to increase the money supply by

inflationary quantities. At the beginning of control by modern governments over the issue of currency, in fact, bank notes and coins were
convertible into gold. However, during the economic difficulties of the
1930s and World War II, all of the major Western countries abandoned
this convertibility feature of domestic currencies. Accordingly, monetary
theory began to explain that the value of a currency was determined not
by its convertibility into some ultimate standard of value but by its acceptability as a means of payment. Such acceptability depends on the government's willingness and ability to keep money scarce and maintain its
aggregate supply in a relationship to need such that prices remain stable.
Since the end of World War II the governments of all Western, developed
countries have controlled their money supply rather well, according to
these principles, and the major currencies have remained acceptable and
relatively stable in value.

In the international monetary sphere gold has historically played a role
analogous to that in national monetary systems. As we have noted already, during the pure gold standard gold was the only form of domestic
and international money. During the development of the gold exchange
standard, the metal continued to serve as the ultimate standard of value
and the safest and most liquid reserve asset a country could hold. However, as countries showed a great willingness to hold the national obligations of the World Banker countries, Britain and the United States, and
rarely, if ever, demanded gold, the parallel with domestic money convertibility became obvious. Convertibility into gold of dollars held as international reserves theoretically served to put a constraint on the ability of
Britain and the United States to increase their obligations at will, if they
were following sound banking practices, and maintained a backing of gold
for these obligations at a certain fraction of the total. Gold and convertibility thus in theory protected the world from inflationary increases in international reserves in the form of dollars and sterling.

During the 1960s, however, it became obvious to many observers that
this simple model of the gold exchange standard had a major shortcoming.
In theory the production of gold and additions to the stock of monetary
gold held by the banker countries should grow with world economic
development generally and the demand for reserves specifically. However, since the 1930s the official price of gold had been fixed at $35 an
ounce by the U.S. Treasury, and that agency's vast holdings of gold (as
mentioned above) assured that the private market price was at the same
level. At this price world production of gold stagnated, and in the face of
increasing industrial demand for the metal, world monetary gold holdings
ceased to grow. As a result, gold backing for the U.S. dollar obligations to
the rest of the world fell throughout the 1950s and 1960s, and (as we noted
in connection with the history of the gold exchange standard) in the early
1960s an international understanding was reached among the major West-

ern countries that they would refrain from converting dollars into gold and that they would accept a lower ratio of U.S. gold holdings to foreign short-term dollar obligations.

However, these understandings did not solve the problems of excess demand for gold in industrial uses at $35 an ounce and the development of strong private speculation that at some point in the future the official price of gold would have to be raised to preserve the gold exchange standard. In response to these developments, in 1968 at Washington, D.C., the pathbreaking international agreement was reached to establish a two-tier gold market, one at $35 an ounce for official gold and one free market in which the price would be determined by private demand and supply. The major governments participating in this agreement committed themselves not to use monetary gold already in their portfolios or obtained through conversion with other governments for sale in the private markets. In effect, the agreement had locked monetary gold into the vaults of central banks. Very significantly, the theoretical constraint on the U.S. issue of dollars as reserves had been removed effectively, because the convertibility of the dollar into gold, while still operative legally, had ceased for all practical purposes. Furthermore, there was virtually no chance that there would ever be any new additions to the world's monetary gold at $35 an ounce and therefore a renewed functioning of the gold exchange standard along the traditional model. While after 1968 most major countries did not embarrass the United States by continued conversion of dollars into gold, France, under the leadership of Charles de Gaulle, deliberately acted as a maverick in order to force an end to the dollar gold exchange standard and an official revaluation of the price of gold, all as part of the general's design for a more important role for France and Europe in world affairs. The resultant U.S. gold losses and the severely deteriorating U.S. balance-of-payments deficits in 1970 and 1971 finally forced the United States into a legal suspension of gold convertibility on August 15, 1971. This convertibility has since not been restored, and the role of gold in the international monetary system remains in doubt.

In the United States there are strong intellectual and political forces at work which want to see the world monetary system reformed rationally, ending the roles of both gold and the dollar as international reserves. The intellectual forces see gold as a barbaric relic of the past, the supply of which historically has fluctuated with new discoveries of gold fields and the development of new mining technologies. Furthermore, while not of overwhelming importance, given the productive capacity of modern economies, the resources used up in the production of gold have many more socially productive application in industry. It seems to many observers to be a deplorable symbol of irrationality to produce gold at great expense from the bowels of the earth, only to rebury it in the vaults of central banks. Importantly, the development of monetary theory and the experiences of national governments suggest that the usefulness of any money, including international reserves, depends not on its convertibility but on limitations on its supply. Such limitations could be achieved through central control over the supply, as by the IMF and the creation of SDRs under its auspices. The political and intellectual forces agree on the undesirability of having the United States return to gold convertibility because it would tend to reintroduce the use of dollars as international reserves and establish the responsibility of the United States for the adequate and orderly growth of these reserves.

However, it is not certain whether or when the complete demonetization of gold can be achieved. Efforts to do so have been marked by a number of setbacks and successes since August 15, 1971. In December 1971, as a concession to countries wanting to retain the traditional role of gold, the official U.S. price of gold was raised to $38 an ounce under the Smithsonian Agreement for the revaluation of major currencies. In February 1973, another dollar devaluation raised the official U.S. gold price to $42.20 an ounce. In December 1974, private gold speculators drove the price of gold in the London bullion market to a peak of $200 an ounce, and during 1975 and 1976 it stayed at a price between $100 and $150. This high private market price of gold is indicative of the fact that a large number of speculators throughout the world do not believe that the United States and a few of the other important Western countries are either genuinely willing or able to remove gold from its traditional role in the international monetary system. The U.S. government, within the limits of its own ability, has taken two important steps to signal to the world its determination to move in this direction, first, by permitting U.S. residents to hold gold legally and second, by auctioning off 2 million ounces of monetary gold to private markets in January 1975. Furthermore, international agreements reached in 1975 required that the IMF sell one sixth of its gold holdings in the open market and distribute the proceeds as grants to developing countries. These partly symbolic actions of the U.S. government and the IMF caused a dramatic fall in the free market price of gold during 1975 and 1976.

Only time will tell whether the world has rid itself of the cross of monetary gold. The stocks of gold in the possession of central banks, at prices of around $100 per ounce, are equal to several decades' worth of industrial use, net, of newly mined gold. The decision by all central banks of the world to sell their holdings of monetary gold, therefore, would depress the price of gold severely and would have serious income and wealth effects on the world's gold-mining industry and the industrial users and hoarders of the metal. Relatively short-run effects of this sort must be given due consideration and are likely to complicate reaching any international agreements in the future, regardless of how good is the intellectual case for the demonetization of gold in the long run.

Control over the Adjustment Mechanism

In preceding chapters we have made the point that under any conceivable form of international monetary organization, long runs of adverse random shocks on occasion have made it necessary for certain countries to subject their economies to real income or exchange rate adjustments in order to maintain its balance of international payments in the long run. Such adjustments as the gold standard and the system of freely floating exchange rates have the advantage that they take place automatically and continuously. Under the system of managed exchange rates, on the other hand, the adjustments require deliberate policy decisions.

One of the serious problems afflicting an international monetary system in which adjustment requires deliberate policy action is that governments, in their efforts to stabilize the domestic economy, may be tempted to abuse the existing institutions of international cooperation for short-run gains. Thus, they may undervalue their country's currency in order to stimulate net exports and domestic employment, as was common practice during the 1930s. Alternatively, they may run large and continuous balance-of-payments deficits in order to borrow real resources from the rest of the world in some perceived or real emergency. As an example of such behavior we can cite the U.S. deficits in the late 1960s and early 1970s, which allegedly permitted conduct of the war in Vietnam without the otherwise required decreases in real domestic U.S. income. While such abuses of the system are a continuous and real threat, most countries realize that they benefit greatly from international cooperation and that it is in their own interest not to abuse the system and cause its breakdown. Moreover, the IMF system has had two institutional measures to safeguard against abuses by maverick and short-sighted governments.

First, there is the scarce-currency clause, which in principle can be invoked if a country is in perpetual large balance-of-payments surplus. Once a surplus country's currency has been pronounced officially as being "scarce," the rest of the world is entitled to impose tariffs and quantitative restrictions on imports from this country. The scarce-currency clause was made part of the original Articles of Agreement setting up the IMF in regard for the problems of the 1930s, especially the large U.S. surpluses resulting from an undervaluation of the dollar. The clause has never been invoked during the postwar years, because immediately after the war the U.S. surpluses were to a considerable degree dispersed through Marshall Plan aid. Thereafter, the United States ran persistent deficits, and no other large country's surpluses created any real difficulties for the rest of the world. However, the provision is still on the books and could be used as a safeguard measure against abuse of the system in the future.

Second, under the IMF rules until 1973, member countries were required to declare parity exchange rates, which they were committed to maintain within a margin of plus or minus 1 percent through foreign exchange market intervention. As noted above in this chapter, changes in parity of less than 10 percent could be undertaken without consultation with the IMF, while greater changes required IMF consent. As a very important part of the required mechanism for the functioning of this system, the IMF consulted regularly with national governments about their domestic and balance-of-payments conditions, and as a result it was able to represent the world's collective interests as an input into national policy formation. The IMF influence through these channels is not widely known and was not backed by any real power, except the power to withhold credit from smaller nations. However, it seems to be widely believed that the parity system was very successful in maintaining exchange rate stability during the postwar years and preventing abuse of the system. There were no major countries running excessively large and persistent surpluses or deficits to cause problems for the rest of the world, except for the case of the United States which, as the World Banker, was in a special position. Because of these judgments about the success of the parity system in the postwar years, the governments of most countries in the IMF have demanded that parity exchange rates be retained as a permanent feature of the reformed IMF in the future, though with intervention bands remaining at the 2.25 percent on either side of parity, agreed upon at the Smithonian Agreement in December 1971. The widening of the band is considered to be a weapon in the fight against currency speculation rather than an aid to international adjustment.

However, there is widespread agreement among academic economists and support from some governments for the view that the parity exchange rate system is clumsy and provides excessive exchange rate stability, thus preventing real adjustment. The reasons for this view are that under the parity system a change in a country's exchange rate involves a major political decision which entails fights among parties gaining and losing from currency revaluations within governments and legislatures. Furthermore, while such public debates proceed, speculators tend to take positions, upset foreign exchange markets, disturb normal trade and capital flows, and often influence the outcome of the deliberations about exchange rate changes.

There are two fundamental alternative approaches to parity exchange rates for safeguarding the international monetary system against abuse by maverick or short-sighted member nations, while simultaneously promoting greater exchange rate flexibility. First there is the formal automatic system, which is based on some indexes designed to reflect countries' balance-of-payments conditions objectively. These indexes are to be used to trigger automatic changes in the official exchange rate of a country and force its government to maintain this rate within specified margins through appropriate intervention in the foreign exchange market. One simple variant of a family of proposals in this category has been advanced by John H. Williamson of Warwick University. It involves the "crawling peg," operating as follows. At any given moment a country is committed to maintain its pegged exchange rate within a margin of X percent at a level equal to the moving average of the market exchange rate over a preceding period of Y weeks, where both X and Y are subject to negotiations. Under this scheme, a country experiencing a persistent balance-of-payments deficit can let its exchange rate drift lower within the margin, and as it does so the pegged rate, together with its intervention margin, also drifts lower through time. Under this system, over a long enough period substantial readjustment of exchange rates can take place smoothly and without the traumatic political problems and large adjustments necessary under the parity system. The principle of automatic adjustment according to rules and changes in objectively observable indexes permits many variations. Indexes can be designed to include not only historic market exchange rates but also countries' reserve holdings, inflation rates, employment levels, consideration of trade and capital flow balances, and many more. The essence of all proposals in this family is the automatic adjustment of a pegged rate according to some formula.

The second method for safeguarding against abuse of the system is informal, requiring neither the construction of performance indexes nor automatic rules for the determination of the exchange rate. Under it the IMF bureaucracy would take aggressive actions in evaluating and applying pressures on countries whose exchange rates are in disequilibrium, according to broad and widely accepted economic criteria administered flexibly and most suitably for the time and circumstances of the case. This system might involve either pegged exchange rates registered with the IMF or simply floating but managed rates, without any official commitments to a peg or parity. The latter arrangement seems preferable to the former, since pressures for adjustment can be brought continuously, and potentially heated arguments over changes of a particular rate between the IMF and national governments could be avoided. The IMF pressures on governments could be applied at different levels of intensity according to circumstances, starting with secret consultations among officials and escalating into publicity, the withholding of IMF privileges, penalties such as the charging of interest rate fines on excessive SDR imbalances, and ultimately the imposition of collective sanctions as envisaged under the scarce-currency clause.

The choice of methods for assuring exchange rate adjustment involves important judgments which have to be made without much relevant prior experience. However, it does seem that the very plethora of possible criteria for automatic adjustment will make it difficult to reach agreement on one set. During negotiations every country will want to safeguard or maximize its own interest by advocating indexes and rules most favorable to its own conditions. Economics and statistics are useless in providing criteria for the choice of an objectively best set of rules. Once a set of rules has been agreed upon, the problem arises that it is likely to be unsuitable for economic, political, and military power conditions in the future. These kinds of considerations tilt the scale in favor of cooperative surveillance of international exchange rates under a set of broad and widely accepted economic criteria. The disadvantage of this approach is that significant power is given to an international bureaucracy, which may at times be technically incompetent or dominated by political alliances attempting to use the system to achieve certain narrow economic or political objectives. However, the constitutions of most democratic countries have devised methods for checks and balances between legislatures, the government, and bureaucracies, and it should be possible in principle to develop such institutions within the IMF. Only the future can tell whether countries will be more willing to surrender national sovereignty to objective but essentially arbitrary rules or to a system of principles administered by an international agency staffed by fallible civil servants and guided by always less than perfect but democratic voting processes. In 1975 the official U.S. government position on these issues switched from previous strong support of pegs and automatic rules to support of very general rules for the guidance of adjustment behavior, to be written into the charter of a reformed IMF.

The Problem of an Intervention Currency and the Future Role of the Dollar

One of the essential features of the IMF–SDR system which distinguishes it from a conventional central bank system for money creation is that SDRs do not circulate in private markets as do the obligations of national central banks. Instead, SDRs circulate only among central banks which are members of the IMF. Recall from our discussion of the SDR system above that because of this feature, central banks wishing to use SDRs for intervention in public foreign exchange markets have to obtain an eligible national currency from the IMF, which credits the country whose currency is thus used with a corresponding amount of SDRs. In practice nearly all countries have found that foreign exchange market intervention is carried out most smoothly and efficiently with U.S. dollars, because of the dominance of this currency as a standard of value, means of payments, and store of short-term purchasing power in private markets.

The use of the dollar as an intervention currency has the further advantage of permitting the world to deal with what is known technically as the $n - 1$ problem. It arises from the fact that if there are n currencies, only $n - 1$ are independently determined. The nth currency is implicit. For example, if there are only two currencies, the dollar and the pound, the only independently determined rate is either the price of pounds in terms of dollars or the price of dollars in terms of pounds. Once we know one of these two prices, the other is implicit as the inverse of the first. The example could be expanded to include more than two currencies, but the most salient fact is obvious. If the values of all currencies in the world are expressed in terms of dollars, then it is unnecessary to have an added list of values of foreign currencies in terms of dollars. This fact has an important implication for the operation of foreign exchange market intervention programs: If every country other than the United States pegs its currency at a certain level to the dollar, the United States cannot intervene simultaneously. That this is so can be seen most readily in the two-country dollar-sterling case. If Britain intervenes to peg the price of the pound at 2.4 dollars, the United States cannot intervene at any other price without setting in motion large-scale private arbitrage which would be profitable for the arbitragers but costly for the U.S. or U.K. authorities. For this reason, the world benefits from having one country which refrains from all foreign exchange market intervention. This role has been and continues to be played by the United States and the dollar.

From this widespread use of the dollar as an intervention currency arises the question whether it is possible to reform the international monetary system in the future so that this particular role of the dollar is ended, just as the creation of SDRs and the end of convertibility in principle can and probably will put an end to the gold exchange standard and to the use of dollars as official reserves. The IMF already makes it possible for countries to use currencies other than dollars for intervention, but this facility is of little practical importance and should be interpreted as part of the concerted political effort to remove the dollar from its past position of eminence in official international agencies. If and when the European Economic Community achieves complete monetary union and one common currency, it may replace dollars as the optimum intervention currency. The other replacement for dollars in this role would be SDRs themselves. However, such an institutional arrangement involves more than just a simple bureaucratic change. Instead, it represents a really major surrender of national monetary sovereignty to an international organization, going far beyond that required under the system where SDRs are acceptable only for payment among central banks. For SDRs to be useful as an intervention currency in private markets they must be acceptable as means of payment in both domestic and private transactions, for otherwise no other private wealth holders would acquire them in voluntary exchange with central banks. However, if this were done, the SDRs would add to or reduce the money supply of individual countries and force them to forego the seigniorage from domestic money issues. Since control over the money supply is an important tool of economic stabilization policy, and seigniorage from currency issue is an important source of implicit taxation for some countries, most countries are likely to resist the use of SDRs as intervention currency for the foreseeable future, though their ultimate use for this purpose seems to be probable in the long run.

The use of dollars as intervention currency inevitably causes national governments to hold inventories of dollars, since it is not possible to draw them from or return them to the IMF only just as needed or as they are accumulating during the process of intervention. As a result, there is a danger that countries, in order to save transactions costs, may return to holding dollars as international reserves, in spite of international agreement to end the dollar gold exchange standard and the desire of the U.S. government that other countries do not use dollars for this purpose. There are two ways in which this problem could be solved. First, if interest rates on SDRs are substantially above U.S. treasury bill rates, individual countries have incentives to minimize their holdings of dollars and could be expected to limit them strictly to transactions balances. Second, international agreement could be reached according to which countries obligated themselves to hold dollars only up to a certain maximum, which could be defined as a fraction of every country's IMF quota or some other index of need. Such an agreement should not be too difficult to reach or enforce, since the benefits from holding dollars as reserves accruing in the form of lower transaction costs are relatively trivial and few governments would find it worthwhile to circumvent the agreements.

The passive role of U.S. authorities in foreign exchange markets necessary when the dollar is used as the convenient $n - 1$ currency and as the vehicle for intervention in a sense leaves the United States unable to influence the dollar exchange rate and therefore its balance of payments. The U.S. government has bad memories of the dollar–gold exchange era when this U.S. passiveness led to large payments deficits, and the role of the dollar as international reserves prevented it from taking any unilateral action, for fear of a collapse of the entire international monetary system. The Nixon program of August 15, 1971, represents such a unilateral step and was taken only after conditions had become intolerable. The ultimate consequences of the step for world trade and welfare still have to be evaluated. Because of this history of U.S. impotence to deal with balance-of-payments problems, the U.S. government is eager to assure that in any reformed international monetary system the United States has effective control over its exchange rate and balance of payments. Our analysis of this section suggests that at present the world needs the dollar as an intervention currency and that the United States should not and perhaps even cannot prevent the use of the dollar for this purpose. It is unrealistic to believe that the dollar can be made to be like any other currency through some institutional tricks. However, the United States does have the right to demand safeguards against the repetition of the dollar–gold exchange problem of the pre–1971 period. Agreements to keep national official dollar holdings to a maximum size for transactions purposes, as described above, is one part of such a safeguard. However, there remains the problem that even if dollar holdings are kept small, countries run large surpluses with the United States and accumulate large quantities of SDRs. At present U.S. authorities are known to consult with the authorities of major Western European countries about exchange market intervention whenever the value of the dollar is at an undesirable level and to ask for intervention by these authorities to rectify the situation. These informal working arrangements should be capable of dealing with the problem, especially since the United States always has the option of announcing to any foreign government that it would engage in unilateral sales or purchases of its currency if it is believed to be out of line. Further safeguards have to be built into the system through multilateral surveillance of the balance of payments and reserve positions of individual countries through the IMF, as we discussed above.

BIBLIOGRAPHICAL NOTES

References to the literature applicable to this chapter overlap to a considerable degree with those provided for Chapter 12, and students are referred to them for further readings. The optimum quantity of money argument is made by Friedman (1969). Machlup (1968) provides a good explanation of the functioning of the IMF after the 1968 Rio de Janeiro Agreements to create SDRs. On the proposal to link SDR creation to aid, see Grubel (1972), which contains references to other articles. Oppenheimer (1969) makes the case for keeping gold in the center of the international monetary system.

CONCEPTS FOR REVIEW

Parity exchange rates
IMF quotas
Special drawing rights
Gold tranche
General Agreement to Borrow
Social seigniorage
Currency basket method for SDR valuation
Market, demand, and central government distribution methods for social seigniorage

LINK proposal
Optimum quantity of reserves
Smithsonian Agreement
Scarce-currency clause
Crawling peg
The $n - 1$ problem

POINTS FOR FURTHER STUDY AND DISCUSSION

1. Study the historic record on the determination of the IMF quotas and try to determine whether they reflect fairly the "importance" of countries' economies in the world.

2. Consider the rates of return in terms of DM earned from holding international reserves as gold, in U.S. short-term treasury bills, and as SDRs, from the point of view of Germany between 1960 and 1975. Include in your rate-of-return calculation capital value changes due to changes in the prices of the assets, general inflation, exchange rate changes, and interest earnings.

3. Argue precisely why the benefits accruing to developing countries from the operation of the LINK program are a decreasing function of the interest rate on SDRs. Could there still be benefits to developing countries from the LINK even if the SDR interest rate were equal to the marginal productivity of capital in developed countries?

4. Consider advantages and disadvantages of different variants of proposals for the operation of crawling pegs or other objective determinants of exchange rates. Can you think of any objective criteria for choosing one variant over the other?

5. Compare the size of the United Nations budget during the period 1965–70 with the growth in international reserve holdings during the same period. Would the distribution of SDRs under the central government method to the UN have resulted in a sufficiently large resource transfer? Argue the case for and against using SDRs for this purpose.

6. Analyze what institutional innovations would be required to make it possible to use SDRs as an official intervention currency with and without bringing about a loss of national monetary sovereignty.

part six

INTERNATIONAL FACTOR MOVEMENTS AND THE ECONOMICS OF INTEGRATION

25 International Factor Movements: Motives and Welfare Effects

THE CAUSES and welfare and balance-of-payments effects of international factor movements, especially of capital, are discussed in this and the following chapter. As topics of special interest we discuss the problems raised by the existence of multinational enterprises and the brain drain, which since the 1960s have caused great public concern in many countries of the world.

In parts of this book dealing with the pure theory of international trade, we made the assumption that factor movements were zero. Relaxation of this assumption has no effect on the key theorems of the pure theory in comparative static analysis concerning the gains from trade, the effects of trade on factor prices, and so on. This is because even if there are factor movements, it is possible in principle to consider factor endowments of countries at any given moment in time and derive from them patterns of comparative advantage, gains from trade, and so on. However, analysis of trade patterns through time would be influenced by the effects international factor movements have on factor endowments. There is no need for the development of a new body of analytical tools, since if we know changes in factor endowments through time we can simply use the existing models of growth and international trade presented in Chapter 5 and analyze their effects on comparative advantage, factor prices, and the gains from trade. Under the assumption that capital and labor flow into countries that are relatively poorly endowed with these factors, we reach the fairly obvious conclusion that factor movements through time narrow differences in relative factor prices and diminish the quantity of international trade.

In this context it is possible to produce formally, as Robert Mundell

(1957) has done, the interesting result that factor movements which tend to equalize stocks in all countries are a substitute for trade in maximizing efficiency of the world economy and equalizing goods and factor prices. To make this point simply, consider the traditional Heckscher-Ohlin model of the world as consisting of two countries with given quantities of labor and capital producing two goods, given tastes, and so on, in equilibrium initially under complete autarchy. Then consider that the economic isolation of the two countries is ended, not by permitting trade but by allowing only the free flow of capital and labor. Under these assumptions, factors move until their prices in the two countries are equalized absolutely and relatively. Once this condition is attained, world output is maximized, since every factor of production has the same marginal productivity in all countries. Also under this condition, the removal of barriers to trade would not result in trade, since maximum world output has already been attained and further gains from trade are not possible. Therefore it follows that the perfect mobility of capital and labor is a substitute for international trade in its effects on the efficiency of world output and on factor prices. If we introduce into this analysis the element of realism that transportation costs for goods have to be paid time after time, while factors move only once, we reach the conclusion that factor price equalization and the attainment of maximum world production through free international labor and capital flows and no trade leads to a greater value of real world output than does free trade without factor movements. Our extension and critical analysis of the simple Heckscher-Ohlin model in Chapter 4 has suggested the need to be careful about drawing too many real-world implications from the preceding analysis. For example, the existence of natural resources as factor inputs in addition to capital and labor, of product differentiation, and of economies of scale would, for obvious reasons, cause us to modify the results of the preceding simple analysis. Space constraints prevent us from undertaking such modifications here.

Instead, we now turn to the main task of this chapter. Section I presents some facts about the size and nature of past international capital flows, which are summarized most conveniently by a table giving the international investment position of the United States in some recent years. In Section II we analyze the motives for international capital movements, which are higher rates of return and greater stability of earnings through time. In this part we present the modern theory of direct investment, which is needed because the classical theory of the determinants of capital flows cannot explain the phenomena of direct investment. In Section III we discuss the welfare effects of international capital flows, supplementing the classical model by the consideration of the effects of direct investment and of knowledge capital flows.

The next chapter deals with some special problems raised by international factor movements: the growth of multinational enterprises, the balance-of-payments effects of capital flows, and the transfer problem. The chapter includes a review of some central issues surrounding human migration generally and the migration of highly skilled persons specifically. This has given rise to the phenomenon widely known as the brain drain, which has the analytically interesting feature of involving the international flow of human capital.

I. SOME FACTS ON CAPITAL FLOWS

With the help of Table 13–1 in Chapter 13, which gives the U.S. balance of payments for 1973, we are able to get an indication of the magnitude of capital flows relative to other international transactions of the United States. In that year the sum of current account credits and debits was $205.2 billion, while the sum of capital outflows and inflows was $35.3 billion, which made capital transactions equal to 17.2 percent of current account transactions. While these balance-of-payments statistics are of great importance for the management of the exchange rate, from the point of view of welfare effects the more relevant statistics are estimates of countries' total assets held abroad and of domestic assets held by foreigners, since they reflect the cumulative effects of not only past capital flows but also of reinvested earnings, which do not appear in balance of payments statistics.

In Table 25–1 we present the international investment position of the United States at the end of the years 1960 and 1973. In analyzing the U.S. position we refer only to the 1973 statistics and return to the 1960 data only for some comparisons between the two years. The upper half of Table 25–1 shows foreign assets held by Americans, separated into categories of private-owned and U.S. government–owned assets, where the former are $172.9, or 76.5 percent of the total, and the latter are $53.2 billion, or 23.5 percent. Private assets consist of short-term holdings with a maturity of less than one year ($29.5 billion); long-term holdings in the form of securities, which are bonds and equities representing less than 10 percent of the foreign firm's outstanding common stocks ($25.1 billion); direct investment, which involves the outright ownership of enterprises or holding of more than 10 percent of outstanding common stocks ($107.3 billion); and "other" ($11.0 billion). U.S. government assets are made up of nonliquid short-term obligations ($2.6 billion); reserve assets of gold, foreign exchange, and IMF positions ($14.4 billion); and long-term obligations obtained primarily by the granting of loans in the framework of foreign assistance programs to developing countries ($36.2 billion). On the liabilities side of the U.S. international investment we find similar

TABLE 25–1

The International Investment Position of the United States (end of years, book value)

	1960		1973		
	Bil-lions of U.S. Dol-lars	Per-cent	Bil-lions of U.S. Dol-lars	Per-cent	1960–73 Growth Percent
Assets abroad					
I. Private					
1. Short term	$ 4.8	5.6%	$ 29.5	13.0%	615
2. Long term					
a. Securities	9.5	11.1	25.1	11.1	264
b. Direct investment	31.9	37.3	107.3	47.5	336
c. Other	3.0	3.5	11.0	4.9	367
Total private	$49.2	(57.5)%	$172.9	(76.5)%	351
II. U.S. government					
1. Short term nonliquid	$ 2.9	3.4%	$ 2.6	1.1%	−10
2. Reserve assets	19.4	22.7	14.4	6.4	−26
3. Long term	14.0	16.4	36.2	16.0	259
Total government	$36.3	(42.5)%	$ 53.2	(23.5)%	147
III. Sum of private and government	$85.5	100.0%	$226.1	100.0%	264
Liabilities to foreigners					
I. Private					
1. Liquid to private foreigners	$ 9.1	22.3%	$ 25.8	15.8%	174
2. Long term					
a. Securities	9.9	24.3	36.8	22.5	372
b. Direct Inv. in USA	6.9	16.9	17.7	10.9	257
c. Other	2.9	7.1	15.9	9.7	548
II. To foreign official agencies					
1. Liquid	12.0	29.4	63.6	39.1	530
2. Other	0.0		3.2	2.0	
III. Sum of private and official	$40.8	100.0%	$163.0	100.0%	400
Net International Investment Position: Assets minus Liabilities	44.7		63.1		141

Source: *U.S. Survey of Current Business*, vol. 54, no. 8 (August 1974), Part II, p. 5. See source for definitions and coverage.

categories of wealth obligations as on the assets side. While total U.S. assets were worth $226.1 billion in 1973, the liabilities came to only $163.0 billion, leaving a net U.S. asset position of $63.1 billion.

This figure of net U.S. asset holdings abroad should be put in relation to the overall stock of U.S. physical capital, in order to permit a perspective on the importance of foreign asset holdings for the U.S. economy as a whole. Unfortunately, national capital stock estimates are difficult to obtain for recent years because of innumerable problems associated with calculating stock figures to reflect properly the amount of depreciation and capital gains. However, the official U.S. Department of Commerce publication *Historical Statistics of the United States* gives the 1956 value of U.S. wealth in the form of houses, machines, factories, and so on as $1,448 billion (p. 151). In the same year the net foreign asset position was $17.8 billion, or 1.2 percent of the total. Since 1956 the net U.S. foreign asset position has grown 3.54 times. During the same period the value of the U.S. gross national product has risen 3.07 times. Under the reasonable assumption that U.S. reproducible wealth grew at about the same rate as output and reached about $4.4 thousand billion in 1973, we conclude that in this year the net U.S. foreign asset position represents only about 1.4 percent of total U.S. wealth, while the gross foreign asset position of $226.1 billion represents only 5.1 percent of the total.

We can note the following interesting facts about the changes in the U.S. international investment position between the years 1960 and 1973. First, while total U.S. assets abroad grew 2.64 times, foreign ownership of U.S. assets grew 4.00 times, causing the U.S. net position to rise only 1.41 times. Second, private U.S. holdings of foreign short-term assets grew dramatically 6.15 times, reflecting speculation against the dollar in expectation of further devaluation, which probably was undertaken primarily by large multinational enterprises. Third, direct investment holdings by U.S. firms abroad grew 3.36 times during the period and moved from a share of 37.3 percent in 1960 to 47.5 percent of total assets in 1973. This fact also calls attention to the importance of developing a good understanding of the causes and effects of direct investment and multinational enterprises. Fourth, U.S. holdings of foreign securities rose 2.64 times during the period but were at 11.1 percent of total U.S. foreign asset holdings in both 1960 and 1973. The U.S. holding of foreign securities and foreign holding of U.S. securities are due to benefits from diversification of risks, which are explained in a recent extension of foreign investment theory presented in the next section of this chapter. Fifth, the foreign ownership of U.S. assets was dominated in both years by liquid obligations toward foreign official agencies which represent the dollars held as international reserves. In the preceding chapter we discussed the causes of the 5.30 times growth of these U.S. liabilities. Sixth, foreign private investors show a relative preference for holding U.S. securities rather than direct investment assets, and this preference has grown over the period under discussion when security holdings rose 3.72 times, while direct investment rose only 2.57 times.

In the theoretical parts of this chapter we will focus exclusively on private foreign capital holdings in the form of securities and direct investment. Table 25–1 shows that these forms of asset holdings are quantitatively the most important of all items in the balance sheet. Other large entries in the U.S. foreign balance sheet have been discussed already, such as liquid private balances, in the chapter on international adjustment with short-term capital flows (Chapter 17), and liquid balances held by official agencies, in Chapter 23 on the gold exchange standard. U.S. government long-term assets of $36.2 billion in 1973 consist mostly of foreign assistance loans at very low interest rates. These have been motivated largely by noneconomic criteria; their effects were touched upon in Chapter 5 on international trade and economic development.

In further preparation of our theoretical analysis we present, in Tables 25–2 and 25–3, some salient facts about the regional and industrial compo-

TABLE 25–2

Direct Investments by Area and Countries (year end 1973, book value, billions of U.S. dollars)

(1)	(2) U.S. Investment Abroad		(3) Foreign Investment in U.S.		(4)
Area or Country	(dollars)	(percent)	(dollars)	(percent)	(2) ÷ (3)
Canada	$ 28.1	26.2%	$ 4.0	22.6%	7.0
Europe	(37.2)	(34.7)	(12.1)	(68.4)	3.1
United Kingdom	11.1	10.4	5.4	30.5	3.0
European Economic					
Community	19.3	18.0	4.5	25.4	4.3
Other Western Europe ..	6.8	6.3	2.2	12.3	3.1
Japan	2.7	2.5	0.3	1.7	9.0
Latin America	18.5	17.2	0.4	2.3	46.3
Australia, New Zealand,					
South Africa	6.1	5.7	0.9	5.1	23.1
Other	14.7	13.7			
Total	$107.3	100.0%	$ 17.7	100.0%	6.1

Source: *U.S. Survey of Current Business*, vol. 54, no. 8 (August 1974), Part II, pp. 7 and 16.

sition of direct investment. Table 25–2 shows that 26.2 percent of U.S. direct investment in 1973 was in Canada, 34.7 percent in Europe, 17.2 percent in Latin America, and the rest in the remainder of the world. Developing countries of Asia and Africa, therefore, have received only about 13.7 percent of the total U.S. direct investment in the past. We can

TABLE 25-3

Direct Investment by Industries (year end 1973, book value, billions of U.S. dollars)

		Dollars	Percent
I.	U.S. investment abroad		
	1. Mining and smelting	$ 7.4	6.9%
	2. Petroleum	29.6	27.6
	3. Manufacturing	45.8	42.7
	4. Other	24.4	22.8
	Total	$107.2	100.0%
II.	Foreign investment in U.S.		
	1. Petroleum	$ 4.4	24.9%
	2. Manufacturing	8.4	47.5
	3. Trade	1.0	5.6
	4. Insurance	2.7	15.3
	5. Other	1.2	6.8
	Total	$ 17.7	100.0%

Source: *U.S. Survey of Current Business*, vol. 54, no. 8 (August 1974).

also note from Column (4) of Table 25–2 that U.S. direct investment abroad in 1973 was 6.1 times larger than foreign direct investment in the United States. However, this ratio is only 3.1 for Europe and 46.3 for Latin America. The fact that simultaneously the U.S. has direct investments abroad, and the rest of the world, but especially Canadian and European firms, has direct investments in the United States, is a puzzle if one assumes that capital flows only into the countries with the highest productivity of capital. The modern theory of direct investment is designed to resolve this puzzle.

Table 25–3 contains data on the industries in which direct investments have been made. Manufacturing is the preferred form for direct foreign investment by Americans abroad and foreigners in the United States, representing over 40 percent of the total in both cases. About one quarter of direct investment by Americans and by foreigners is in the petroleum industry, while U.S. direct investment in mining and smelting abroad represents only 6.9 percent of total U.S. foreign direct investment holdings. Foreign direct investment in the U.S. insurance industry represents a significant 15.3 percent of the total. The explanation of this phenomenon can readily be found in the general theory of foreign investment to be presented below.

II. MOTIVES FOR CAPITAL MOVEMENTS

In conventional price theory it is assumed that wealth holders try to maximize only the rate of return from their assets. This assumption has been a most useful simplification of the real world and has led to the explanation of wide ranges of observed phenomena. All of the important price-theoretic theorems about efficiency, Pareto optimality, and the international trade theorems derived from the Heckscher-Ohlin model are based on this assumption. We will adhere to it in the first half of our discussion of motives for international capital flows. However, in the second half we introduce the analytical refinement that because of uncertainty about rates of return on assets in the future, investors purchase assets which give them not only a high rate of return but which also promise relatively stable earnings through time. The models of portfolio management based on this principle permit us to explain a range of empirical phenomena which the simpler return-only maximization models cannot.

Rates of Return

Under the assumption that investors are concerned about maximizing only the rate of return of their wealth, the motive for foreign capital flows is simple and straightforward: Country A residents buy foreign country B assets because they yield a higher rate of return than domestic country A assets. In the traditional theory of international capital flows, specified at the same level of abstraction as the Heckscher-Ohlin model, the causes of these differences in rates of return are considered to be due to differences in relative factor proportions and factor prices which are maintained through time, because of obstacles to free trade or because of differential rates of domestic growth in the stocks of capital and labor in the two countries. Under the further assumption that the marginal productivity of capital in both countries under perfect competition in capital markets is equal to the interest rate on bonds, the traditional theory of the motives for international capital flows thus explains why wealth holders in the relatively capital-rich country A purchase country B bonds which, through the process of international adjustment discussed in preceding chapters, results in a flow of real capital from country A to B. This theoretical model explains well the behavior of British investors in the 19th century. They purchased large quantities of foreign bonds issued to finance the building of railroads and other industries in India and North America. At the time Britain was indeed the country of the world most richly endowed with capital, and foreign investment involving direct ownership of productive facilities was virtually unknown.

However, as can be remembered from our analysis of the U.S. international investment position in 1973, holdings of non-control-conferring foreign securities represent only a small proportion of foreign asset holdings in recent times, and the bulk consists of direct investment. Furthermore, while in the 19th century the rest of the world owned practically no

British long-term assets, our data revealed that in recent times U.S. capital outflows were to some degree matched by capital flows into the United States. These two facts are not consistent with the traditional model, for the following two reasons. First, if rates of return in country B are higher than in country A, entrepreneurs resident in B should sell bonds in A and build manufacturing facilities in B, under their own control, with the funds thus obtained. As residents and citizens in the country of the direct investment, they should be much more familiar with local conditions than foreign entrepreneurs, and therefore they should be able to earn a higher rate of return from direct investment than foreigners. Second, if the productivity of capital is higher in country B than in A, there should be no capital flows at all from B to A.

The explanation of these two phenomena is found not within the rate-of-return maximization assumption but by relaxation of the assumption of perfect competition and markets, which underlies the traditional capital flow model derived from the Heckscher-Ohlin framework. In this sense the modern theory of foreign investment represents an extension of the traditional model, much as does the theory of intraindustry trade for the pure theory of trade. Before we turn to a detailed analysis of the imperfections underlying the modern theory of foreign investment, we need to consider briefly three preliminary matters. First, in the 19th century markets also were not perfect, and the question arises why direct investment has become so important only in recent decades. The answer to this question has been provided by Charles P. Kindleberger of the Massachusetts Institute of Technology, who attributes the recent growth in direct foreign investment to the development of technologies in transportation and communication. These have made it possible to maintain effective control over foreign business at reasonable cost, primarily through the availability of fast, reliable, jet air transportation, the telephone, and electronic data processing. A similar lowering of the cost and speed of transport and communication in the last third of the 19th century, through the development of railroads and the telegraph, caused an analogous spread of centrally owned manufacturing and trading enterprises in the United States which resulted in the famous Sherman and other antitrust legislation. Kindleberger's explanation of the relatively recent rapid growth of direct foreign investment and its main vehicle, the multinational enterprise, provides a useful perspective on the nature of the problems these enterprises have caused and on how they might best be dealt with.

The second matter regarding the theory of foreign investment to be considered is that it is difficult to obtain reliable estimates on the comparative profitability of investment in the United States and abroad, and it is even more difficult to do so for investments of other countries in the United States and third countries. However, in Table 25-4 we present a time series on after-income tax rates of return on U.S. direct investment

TABLE 25–4

Rates of Return on Investment in Manufacturing (in percent, after income taxes)

Year	Foreign	Domestic	Year	Foreign	Domestic
1960	10.1%	9.2%	1967	9.1%	11.7%
1961	10.3	8.9	1968	9.9	12.1
1962	10.3	9.8	1969	11.9	11.5
1963	10.6	10.3	1970	11.0	9.3
1964	11.9	11.6	1971	11.2	9.7
1965	11.0	13.0	1972	13.8	10.6
1966	10.1	13.4			

Note: Foreign rates of return were computed by dividing earnings by mean of current and preceding year-end book value of investment.

Source: *Survey of Current Business*, August 1974, p. 16, and October 1968, p. 26, for foreign returns; *Economic Report of the President*, February 1974, p. 337, for domestic returns.

in manufacturing abroad and on U.S. corporations engaged in manufacturing, including their foreign operations. These data suffer from some lack of comparability in the valuation of the investment and of income tax–distorted earnings too complicated to discuss here, but they may be taken as being roughly comparable. They reveal that the rates of return from foreign investment averaged the same as for domestic investment at 10.9 percent during the period 1960–72, with slightly larger fluctuations in the domestic than in the foreign rates of return. The relationships of the data for rates of return on foreign and domestic investment in manufacturing are shown graphically in Figure 25–1.

Given the data imperfections underlying these statistics, we can conclude that the phenomenon of direct U.S. foreign investment in manufacturing is at least consistent with the rate-of-return maximization assumption. In the next section, on the risk diversification motive, we present some data on returns from foreign equity investment which lead to the same conclusion about the maximization of returns. But the need remains to explain why capital flows to the higher yield country through direct investment rather than through lending through bonds, and how it is possible that direct investment is induced to move both into and out of the high-yield countries.

The third matter to be considered is that it might be argued logically that the reason why direct investment has taken the place of lending through bonds is that the capital-receiving countries suffer from an absence of local entrepreneurs. This explanation does not stand up very well to the facts of the real world, though it may contain an element of truth in some instances. As we have noted already, most of the U.S. direct investment is in the industrialized countries of Western Europe and Canada. These countries could hardly be considered as having a scarcity of entrepreneurs. On the other hand, visitors to developing countries are always

FIGURE 25–1
Rates of Return on Investment in Manufacturing

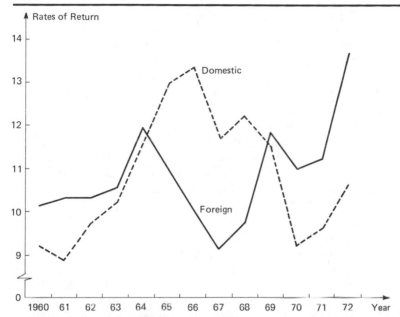

The rates of return on investment in manufacturing plotted show that during the period between 1960 and 1972 domestic (U.S.) and foreign rates were synchronized imperfectly, though averages were about the same. These data show that companies having manufacturing investments in both the United States and abroad tend to have more stable earnings than companies without such internationally diversified operations.

struck by the ubiquitous entrepreneurs trying to make a living from trade or the sale of services. These countries seem not to lack entrepreneurs either, and we must reject differences in the supply of entrepreneurial talents as an explanation of direct foreign investment.

Factors Inducing Direct Foreign Investment. We now turn to the task of providing logical and empirically valid explanations of direct investment and two-way capital flows by considering ways in which imperfect markets induce foreign ownership of the means of production. In so doing we draw on fundamental contributions by Kindleberger and Richard Caves of Harvard University.

Technical Externalities. The operation of enterprises for the mining and processing of raw materials, such as copper and aluminum, have certain characteristics which encourage vertically integrated, worldwide ownership. The capital investment in mines, smelters, and their supplies of energy is very high, and the size of output at which cost per unit of output is minimized is very large, so that the failure to operate these plants continuously at optimum output levels tends to raise substantially costs of output per unit of input. The mines, smelters, and further processing plants usually are located according to the availability of ores, energy, water, labor, transportation facilities, and so on, often in different countries. Transportation costs between these facilities tend to be high and can be minimized by the proper design of integrated loading and shipping facilities. Given these technical characteristics of the business of mining, processing, and transportation of raw materials, firms that can integrate all operations, build all component parts of the system to fit optimally, and develop and invest in new technologies with minimum disruptions to the system are able to sell the final product at a lower average cost than competitors that are not so integrated. In price-theoretic terms, the cost savings available from such worldwide integration of the operation of different production stages are considered to be externalities outside the control of component firms. Vertical integration of firms permits internalization of these externalities and results in the flow of capital from one country to many others in the world. For example, the Canadian aluminum company Alcan owns bauxite mines in Australia and Jamaica, smelters in Canada, and production facilities in the United States and Europe. The latter operations are usually located near centers of consumption, in order to minimize relatively high transport costs for finished products and to maintain ready contact with changing demand by consumers. The main point of this example is that it provides explanations for direct investment giving control over the size of foreign operations and the technology used by them and for the flow of capital from the relatively capital-poor Canada to the capital-rich United States.

Factor Market Imperfections. Consider that there are two entrepreneurs, one a native and resident of Singapore, the other a citizen of the United States, who could in principle produce profitably a given product in Singapore. As mentioned above, the Singapore entrepreneur is likely to be able to produce the product at a lower cost, since he is very familiar with local customs, factor and products markets, government regulations, and so on. Yet, very often the U.S. rather than the Singapore entrepreneur will establish the production facility, because only the former can obtain the necessary funds in the U.S. capital market. Such a condition may be considered to be due to a capital market imperfection in the form of oligopolistic collusion between U.S. lenders and borrowers, or to the large size of the U.S. borrowers relative to that of the Singapore borrowers. However, it may also be considered to be the outcome of efficient market processes, in which the cost of obtaining information about the Singapore rather than the U.S. entrepreneurs is so much greater as to outweigh the Singapore entrepreneur's higher return on the investment. As a consequence, the U.S. wealth holders lending the funds for the Singapore investment obtain a higher yield by lending to the U.S. entrepreneur, who needs little credit investigation, rather than to the Singapore entrepreneur, who has to be investigated at great cost. Whether we consider the market imperfection or information-cost explanations to be relevant, in either case we have established reasons for direct investment rather than the international lending of funds through bonds.

A second category of factor market imperfections arises in connection with markets for knowledge about techniques of production and management. Thus, a local entrepreneur in Singapore could have a more profitable investment project than the U.S. entrepreneur, if only he had the technical and managerial know-how available to the U.S. entrepreneur as a result of research and past experience. The U.S. entrepreneur can use this know-how in foreign investment projects at an effectively zero marginal cost, since the investment in its production has already been made for domestic uses. Some types of technical knowledge tend to be available to the foreign entrepreneur through licensing from its developer. Under these conditions, a local entrepreneur may be able to pay licensing fees to the U.S. entrepreneur large enough to result in higher U.S. profits from the sale of the know-how than from the use of the know-how through direct investment. We do in fact observe a large and growing international market for technical knowledge.

However, there also exist types of know-how which cannot be marketed. Such knowledge is due to learning by doing, and since it is embodied in the managers and labor of a firm it cannot be sold separately. Other nonmarketable knowledge tends to exist in industries in which technology is developing rapidly, as in computers, pharmaceutical, chemical, and aerospace products. In these industries evolution of technology is continuous, and licensing of a process today tends to lead to obsolete production facilities tomorrow. In such dynamic, high-technology industries, local entrepreneurs simply cannot purchase the knowledge, and foreign direct ownership of the means of production is typical.

Product Market Imperfections.   The explanation of foreign direct investment in this category is dependent on the existence of product differentiation and oligopolistic market structures, as, for example, in the automobile and razor blade industries. In these consumer-good industries we find typically heavy investment by firms in the development, design, and advertising of products differentiated by some minor functional characteristic, quality, or style, as we discussed in Chapter 4 in connection with the explanations of intraindustry trade. A local entrepreneur, because of his familiarity with his country's customs, labor market, government, and so on, may be able to produce Volkswagens or Gillette razor blades more cheaply than foreign entrepreneurs can. But there is no market for the designs or formulas required for the production of such goods or, where there are no commercial secrets, the designs may be protected by patent or copyright laws.

The owners of these inputs required by local entrepreneurs are unwilling to sell them because of the need to maintain strict quality control and to assure continuity in the evolution of product lines. It would be most harmful for the reputation and sales of Gillette razor blades worldwide if an independent producer in one country acquired the right to manufacture Gillette-designed blades under that brand name but produced and marketed a substandard product. Similarly, it would create chaos for VW marketing if an independent producer in one country continued to sell previous models in competition with current models. One characteristic of industries producing differentiated products of this type is that their advertising has considerable spillover effects in all countries of the world, and there are large economies of scale in the design and launching of worldwide advertising campaigns. These facts would create benefits to foreign entrepreneurs owning production rights to the differentiated products being advertised, for which the originators of the advertising would not receive compensation. At the same time, these facts make it very costly and therefore noneconomic for local entrepreneurs to compete with the foreign enterprises in this field through attempts to create and advertise local substitute products. For all of these reasons, we find a predominance of direct foreign investment in industries producing differentiated consumer goods with heavy development and advertising costs.

The preceding analysis can be amplified by considering the following stylized account of events which might have caused the establishment of Ford and General Motors automobile production facilities in Australia. It is a technological fact that dies used in shaping car body parts can be used in presses longer than they are required in the regular cycle of model changes. Now let us assume that initially there was peace in the domestic oligopolistic market for U.S. cars, each firm's share of the market being determined by costs of production, history, and so on, as we might find explained in studies of oligopolistic behavior. Suddenly, in one year Ford Motor Company decides that it would not scrap its technologically sound but stylistically obsolete dies but instead would establish an Australian subsidiary and have it use these dies in the production of a new model. Through time the Australian subsidiary would then always use the most recently obsolete U.S. dies in launching its "new" models for the local market. This actual Ford company practice gave it a competitive advantage over any actual or potential local producers who had to design and develop dies for Australian use only. It also lowered costs of production in U.S. Ford plants, since the investment in dies could be amortized over a larger number of automobiles. This lowered cost of domestic production permitted Ford to reap higher profits, advertise more heavily, invest more in product design, and generally disturb the peace in the oligopolistic industry and gain a greater market share at the expense of General Motors. The resultant competitive response of General Motors was that it also would make a direct investment in Australia and use its obsolete dies.

This highly stylized account of the events leading to direct investment by U.S. automobile companies in Australia does not agree completely with the facts and leaves out many institutional details and complications. Yet, it captures the essence of the motives for direct foreign investment in the automobile industry and similar industries: the existence of oligopolistic market structures, product differentiation, heavy fixed investment in the design and advertising of new products which can be used abroad at very low marginal cost, and the inability of local entrepreneurs to compete unless they too are large enough to engage in worldwide operations and finance product differentiation and development. In Europe, as in contrast with Australia, the direct investment of U.S. car firms with the competitive advantages mentioned above caused many smaller firms to go out of business or to merge and reach a size sufficient to compete throughout the world, using the same strategies as the U.S. firms.

Government Subsidies. A special kind of market imperfection, if we may call it by this name, is caused by the policies of governments. To bring out clearly the case where such government policies lead to direct foreign investment, let us assume that all of the motives for foreign investment just analyzed were of insufficient strength to induce a U.S. manufacturer to open a plant in Peru, even though there was a sufficiently large market for its output within Peru and neighboring countries. The Peruvian government, in its efforts to industrialize the country, considers it desirable to have such a plant, which would increase employment and save scarce foreign exchange. Borrowing abroad, even by the Peruvian government, and lending to a local entrepreneur would be successful in getting the plant only at an extremely high cost, because the local entrepreneur would need to produce the very expensive knowledge capital to launch the differentiated product. Under these conditions, it is rational for the government of Peru to subsidize the U.S. manufacturer's operation in Peru through any of a host of possible methods, such as the free provision of a factory building or the granting of a tax holiday. As a result of such a subsidy we would find direct investment which otherwise would not have been undertaken.

Direct foreign investment is also often induced by the imposition of import tariffs as part of a more general government program of development through import substitution. Under these conditions the government does not necessarily desire foreign capital inflows and resultant foreign ownership of the protected industries. However, our considerations above about the characteristics of many goods suggest that local development of import substitutes would tend to be very expensive, and multinational enterprises therefore often are induced by tariffs to establish means of production which otherwise would not have been profitable. Case studies of foreign investment in Australia, Canada, and developing countries have revealed that direct foreign investment is motivated to a very important degree in the protective structures of these countries. Yet, tariffs only raise the profitability of investing in protected industries. We need the modern theory of direct foreign investment to explain why this profitability does not simply lead to capital inflows through bonds.

In sum, profit-maximizing entrepreneurs are induced to make direct foreign investments because of the opportunity to internalize external benefits from the global integration of production, to take advantage of the low marginal cost of using nonmarketable knowledge capital in production techniques and the design and marketing of differentiated products, to exploit advantages conferred by the existence of imperfect knowledge and financial capital markets, and to enjoy the benefits of government subsidies. These factors explain not only direct investment generally, in contrast with lending through bonds, they also explain two-way investment, since the particular imperfections and benefits can accrue to entrepreneurs in all countries, not just the one with the greatest relative capital endowment. Of all of the theoretically relevant factors, empirically the most important undoubtedly is the one relating to the low marginal cost of knowledge capital in the design and marketing of differentiated products. This category of motives to a large extent underlies the direct foreign investment by such well-known giant multinational enterprises as General Motors, Ford, IBM, Procter and Gamble, Du Pont, Gillette, Nestle, Unilever, General Foods, Volkswagen, Fiat, General Electric, and Bayer, to name just a few.

Risk Diversification

Risk diversification is a potential motive for foreign investment which apparently has always been important for businessmen but which has entered formally into the literature on the determinants of foreign investment only recently. There has been a considerable lag in its introduction after the development of so-called portfolio models for the choice of domestic assets in a world of uncertainty. In order to develop the argument that international diversification gives rise to a motive for foreign investment, we discuss the nature of investment risks and how the portfolio model handles them analytically. We then introduce foreign assets into the set from which investors select their portfolios, consider how foreign and domestic assets differ, and finally present some empirical evidence on the benefits from international diversification of assets.

Wealth holders face many types of risk in connection with their investments. The profitability of firms may decline because of cyclical economic influences, poor management, changes in tastes of consumers, technological innovations, government regulations, and so on. Such changes in profitability are reflected in the capital value and dividend or interest yields of securities of these firms. Every investor faces the risk that an investment may become worth nothing, as a result of bankruptcy or government expropriation. In the case of foreign investments, many of these risks are magnified because of poorly developed markets, heavy government involvement in the economy, unstable governments, and fluctuations in exchange rates.

Risks of asset holdings due to all of these sources, along with the rate of return of assets, are the two most important determinants of the composition of portfolios of investors who like higher rates of return but can reasonably be assumed to dislike greater risk. In capital markets, investors find assets with many different combinations of risk and return. The modern theory of portfolio choice formalized by Harry Markowitz and James Tobin of Yale University during the 1950s assumes that, in principle, investors form probability distributions about the rates of return expected to be realized from every asset at the end of a certain period, taking into account all of the risks mentioned above. For example, an investor's research may have convinced him that a share in firm A held five years will yield 10 percent with a probability of .5 and 9 and 11 percent with a probability of .25 each. We have already developed such a probability distribution (represented graphically in Chapter 11, Figure 11–4, Panel A) in connection with our analysis of speculation in the foreign exchange market. This same figure can be considered to reflect the probability distribution of expected returns from firm A assets if we measure annual rates of return instead of exchange rates along the horizontal axis and consider the values .9, 1.0 and 1.1 to be rates of return of 9, 10 and 11 percent, respectively. Figure 11–4, Panel B, shows by analogy the probability distribution of returns from holding asset B, which has 10 percent as the most likely rate of return, just like asset A. However, as can be seen from Panel B, there is a wider range of possible outcomes for asset B than for asset A. Of necessity, the probabilities of attaining each outcome differ between assets A and B, since in both cases they have to sum to 1.0. The range of possible outcomes can be measured statistically as the variance of the distribution, and it is assumed to measure the riskiness of an asset. According to this terminology, asset B is riskier than asset A.

The traditional theory of investment presented in the preceding section on rates of return is concerned only with the rate of return of assets as the determinant of investors' choices. Within this analytical framework, investors would find assets A and B described above equally attractive. The modern portfolio theory of investment implies that asset A is superior to asset B because the former is less risky than the latter, assuming that investors dislike risk. Portfolio theory, however, is concerned not just with the choice between two assets but rather with the optimal composition of asset portfolios. For this purpose investors are assumed to consider not only the variance of each asset about its mean rate of return but also the expected correlation in the fluctuations of returns among assets. For example, by holding two assets whose rate-of-return fluctuations are perfectly negatively correlated, an investor can eliminate all risk in his portfolio. This is so because a perfect negative correlation means that when the rate of return on asset A is above its average, the rate of return on asset B is below average by the same proportional amount, and vice versa. Fluctuations just cancel one another.

The benefits from the diversification of portfolios are available to a smaller degree whenever the correlation of changes in returns between assets is less than perfect. It may be useful to demonstrate this proposition with the help of a simple example. Consider two assets, A and B, with given equal expected rates of return $R_A = R_B = 5$ percent; expected equal variances of $V(R_A) = V(R_B) = \sigma_A{}^2 = \sigma_B{}^2 = 10$ but a covariance between the rates of return $\sigma_{A,B} = 0.3$. It is clear that a portfolio consisting only of either asset A or B alone would have an expected rate of return of 5 percent and a variance of 10. But let us consider a portfolio consisting of one half of asset A and one half of asset B, i.e. $P_A = P_B = 0.5$, where P_A and P_B represent the proportions of the total portfolio held in assets A and B, respectively. It is intuitively obvious that the expected rate of return on this portfolio is also 5 percent, as may be verified by substitution of the appropriate values in equation 25–1, which is a formula for the expected rate of return for any two-asset portfolio:

$$E(R_{A,B}) = P_A R_A + P_B R_B \qquad (25\text{–}1)$$

The analogous formula for the variance of a two-asset portfolio is:

$$V(R_{A,B}) = P_A{}^2\sigma_A{}^2 + 2P_A P_B \sigma_{A,B} + P_B{}^2\sigma_B{}^2 \qquad (25\text{–}2)$$

The derivation of both equations cannot be undertaken here, but it can be found in the literature cited at the end of the chapter. Inserting the appropriate values in Equation (25–2) gives the result that the variance of the portfolio is only 6.5, less than the 10 of each asset alone. It can readily be seen that if the covariance were -1, the value of the portfolio's variance would be zero.

In the real world investors face a large menu of assets with different expected rates of return, variances, and covariances. The theory of portfolio choice analyses how investors choose from these assets a particular set which provides their portfolios with just the combination of risk and return appropriate for their preferences and needs. Portfolio choice of this sort can be stylized with the help of Figure 25–2, where expected rates of return are measured along the horizontal axis and the standard deviation of returns along the vertical axis. We show the available individual assets A–E as points in this space. The investor can combine these five assets in his portfolio in any conceivable proportions, deriving for each set a different standard deviation and expected rate of return. The precise rates of return and standard deviation of each portfolio are determined by the

FIGURE 25–2
Model of Portfolio Choice

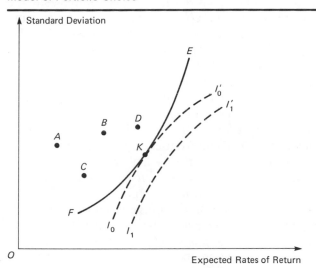

Individual assets A–D have the expected rate of return and standard deviation characteristics as shown. However, as a result of expected covariances of returns among
these assets, their efficient combination in a portfolio permits attainment of the mixture
of standard deviation and rate of return indicated by the frontier FE. Indifference curves
reflecting the tastes of risk avoiders are representative of investors' risk-return preferences and determine the choice of a welfare-maximizing portfolio, such as K.

variances, covariances, expected rates of return, and proportion of each
asset in the portfolio, according to principles developed above in our
example of the two-asset portfolio. However, not all portfolios are of
equal interest to the investor. There exists a set, known as the efficient set
(shown as the line FE in Figure 25–2), which has the characteristic of
giving for every feasible rate of return the smallest standard deviation
attainable from all possible combinations of assets. A mathematical
method known as quadratic programming is available to compute such
frontiers as FE from given information on expected rates of return, variances, and covariances of assets. The taste of investors with respect to
return and risk are reflected in an indifference map, of which two representative curves, $I_0 I_0$ and $I_1 I_1$, are shown in Figure 25–2. The investor's welfare is greater at indifference curve $I_1 I_1$ than at $I_0 I_0$. The greatest level of
welfare attainable from the menu of assets available to the investor is
reached at point K, which is the point of tangency between the efficient
portfolio set and the indifference map. Point K represents a unique combination of assets and, as can readily be seen from Figure 25–2, it provides a
higher level of welfare than is attainable by the holding of a portfolio
consisting of only one of the available assets alone.

The portfolio model of investment can now readily be applied to an explanation of foreign investment by considering the fact that typically the rates of return on all assets within one country are subject to the same influences, such as the business cycle and government policies. For this reason there exists a higher degree of correlation of returns among assets from one country than among the assets from two countries. As a result, an efficient portfolio frontier of assets including foreign assets is likely to permit the attainment of a higher level of welfare than does the efficient frontier of domestic assets only. In terms of Figure 25–2, if assets A–E are all domestic ones, then the inclusion of foreign assets in the menu of choice would be likely to produce a new efficient frontier outward and to the right of the *FE* line shown. In order to attain this higher level of welfare, investors have to include foreign assets in their portfolios, and consequently they cause international capital movements.

The usefulness of this model of international diversification can be appreciated by considering the fact that the preceding argument can be made for any individual country, so that it is possible for capital to flow in both directions, which is an empirical phenomenon we noted above. Thus the portfolio model can explain two-way capital flows involving financial instruments such as bonds and equities, which could not be explained by the factor and product market imperfections relevant to direct investment. According to the model, capital could flow between countries even if the rates of return are the same in both, as long as diversification reduces the risks of total portfolios. The same principles can explain the otherwise puzzling phenomenon that wealth holders in one country purchase assets of another country with lower expected rates of return than domestic assets.

Empirical evidence lends considerable support to the hypothesis that risk diversification is an important motive for foreign investment. For example, Table 25–4 and Figure 25–1 above indicate that realized rates of return from domestic and foreign direct U.S. investment in manufacturing were the same. Under the reasonable assumption that over the period realized earnings averaged anticipated earnings, the U.S. investors could have been motivated by the desire to stabilize overall earnings. The divergent pattern of rates of return evident from Figure 25–1 suggests that foreign diversification would have achieved this goal. In a study of the stability of earnings of large U.S. corporations (1974), Alan Rugman of the University of Winnipeg found that this stability is an incrasing function of firms' foreign investment as a proportion of the total. Such greater stability of earnings of U.S. firms with high proportions of their production facilities abroad is due not only to different phasing of cyclical demand variations, which could be taken advantage of by exports from the United States, but also to different cyclical variations in costs of labor and capital. Furthermore, internationally diversified production facilities of high-technology industries discourage government expropriation and militant union policies, since a factory producing a part of a computer assembled elsewhere and being redesigned continuously would soon be worthless if expropriated and cut off from multinational headquarters. Vertically integrated firms manufacturing primary products which have plants engaged in the same operation in different countries have a certain range of flexibility in scheduling production to avoid disruptions due to government and union actions. This tends to stabilize their earnings relative to those of firms with production facilities in only one country.

Benefits from international diversification accrue not only to multinational firms making direct investment but also to holders of financial assets. We have estimated the rates of return investors could have earned by the ownership of equities in 11 major countries during the period 1959–66, assuming the purchase of a "basket" of securities in the share-price index of the country and considering income from dividends, capital gains, and exchange rate changes. Using monthly data, the standard deviation of each country's rate of return and the correlation in the fluctuations of the returns among all countries were computed. The results of these calculations are shown in Table 25–5, where both the widely differing rates of

TABLE 25–5
Risk and Return from Investing in Foreign Stock Market Averages, 1959–66

Country	Rate of Return: Percent per Annum	Risks: Standard Deviation	Correlation (R) with U.S.
U.S.	7.5%	43.7	100
Canada	6.0	41.2	0.70
United Kingdom	9.6	65.3	0.24
West Germany	7.3	94.7	0.30
France	4.3	49.6	0.19
Italy	8.1	103.3	0.15
Belgium	1.1	37.6	0.11
Netherlands	5.1	86.3	0.21
Japan	16.5	92.5	0.11
Australia	9.4	34.9	0.06
South Africa	8.5	61.9	−0.16

Source: Herbert Grubel, "Internationally Diversified Portfolios," *American Economic Review*, December 1968.

return from holding these countries' shares and the wide range of correlation between the returns of the United States and other countries can be noted. The high correlation between the U.S. and Canadian returns is indicative of the similarity of the influences determining economic conditions in these two close neighbors, while the very low correlation of Australian with U.S. returns and the negative correlation of South African with U.S. returns is also consistent with the theoretical expectations about the determinants of these values. These explanations are dominately the relative economic isolation of Australia and the countercyclical profitability of South African gold mining shares.

On the basis of the information contained in Table 25–5, an electronic computer program selected eight efficient portfolios which were plotted as the efficient frontier shown in Figure 25–3. For reference

FIGURE 25–3
Benefits from International Portfolio Diversification

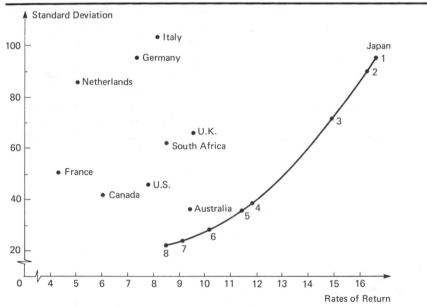

Source: Herbert Grubel, "Internationally Diversified Portfolios," *American Economic Review*, December 1968.

Each point in the space which shows standard deviations and expected rates of return represents actual observations of an individual country's stock market averages (see Table 25–5 for details). The frontier labeled 1–8 has been computed from actual returns and variance and covariance information. It shows different portfolios of maximum returns and minimum variance which could have been reached by the holding of individual-country stock market averages, in proportions calculated by computers.

we show the risk and rate-of-return combinations presented by investment in only one country's stock market average. As can be seen, an investor in the U.S. average who diversifies optimally could have maintained the same level of risk as he experienced from his U.S. holdings, but he would have increased his rate of return from 7.5 to about 13 percent. Alternatively, he could have retained his U.S. rate of return but reduced the standard deviation from 47 to 23. Analogous gains would have been available to investors in other countries' averages. The precise choice of a spot on the frontier depends on the tastes of the investors. However, it is interesting to consider what countries' assets would have had to be held to reach point K, the welfare-maximizing position of Figure 25–2. According to the computations, portfolio 6 consists of assets from the following countries: United States (12.3 percent) United Kingdom (10.7 percent), Italy (1.7 percent), Japan (17.0 percent), Australia (42.6 percent) and South Africa (15.7 percent). The highest risk-return portfolio would have consisted entirely of Japanese assets.

We should note that the evidence on the gains from the international diversification of assets presented here is based on actual events. In the real world investors have to form expectations about the future, and we cannot infer from the data available to us that investors had anticipated the actual return patterns on which the calculations are based or that any investors did reap such gains from international diversification. However, these facts do not invalidate the conclusions of the study: there existed large potential gains from international diversification during the period. Furthermore, to the extent that we are prepared to consider the past as helpful in predicting the future, the study implies that international diversification of portfolios will lead to gains in welfare and to some international capital flows which could not be explained otherwise. At a different level of analysis, the evidence is consistent with the observed growth during the past 15 years of internationally diversified mutual funds.

In sum, we have shown that in a world of uncertainty the holding of any assets is associated with risks, which investors dislike. They can reduce the overall riskiness of their wealth portfolios by proper diversification of assets. Foreign assets increase the opportunity to reduce risk because the correlation of changes in returns among domestic and foreign assets tends to be smaller than that among domestic assets alone. This lower correlation exists because business cycles are not synchronized perfectly in all countries and because governments have different abilities to deal with economic instability. Empirical evidence concerning the characteristics of rate-of-return patterns from stock market investments implies the availability of substantial benefits from international diversification of financial assets. Other evidence on the stability of earnings of multinational enterprises suggests that it is an increasing function of the proportion of total investment abroad. International diversification thus, in principle, is capable of explaining capital flows between countries which could not be explained by or which are contradictory to the rate-of-return maximization motive for foreign investment.

III. WELFARE EFFECTS OF CAPITAL FLOWS

The traditional analysis of the welfare effects of international capital flows makes a number of assumptions: (1) all countries are at full employ-

ment, (2) there are no government taxes or expenditures, (3) capital flows
have no terms-of-trade effects, (4) factor and product markets are perfect,
(5) the only form of investment is through bonds, (6) there are no externalities associated with investment, and (7) real resources are transferred
between countries fully and without adjustment problems. In such a world
capital moves from country A, with the higher capital/labor ratio and the
lower marginal productivity of capital, to country B, with the lower
capital/labor ratio and the higher marginal productivity of capital. If the
capital flows are marginal in size relative to the existing stocks in either
country, the capital flows produce a net gain in world output equal to the
difference between the marginal productivity of the capital in the two
countries, which in turn is a proxy for the world welfare gain. In the
simplest possible terms, international capital flows improve the efficiency
of resource allocation in the world and thereby raise world output and
welfare.

However, if capital flows are not marginal, the gains in world output
are accompanied by a number of problems, the nature of which can best
be developed with the help of Figure 25–4. Along the vertical axis we
measure the marginal productivity of capital assumed to be equal to the
interest rate, and along the horizontal axis, between the two vertical lines
O_AO_B, we measure the total quantity of capital in the world, which is
assumed to consist of countries A and B. The marginal productivity

FIGURE 25–4
Output and Welfare Effects of Capital Flows

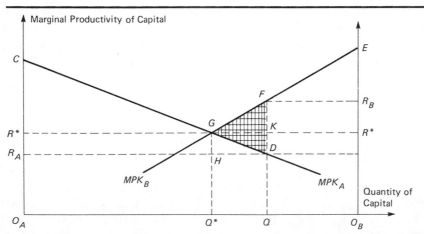

The distance O_AO_B represents the total stock of world capital. Before trade, country A
holds O_AQ of capital and its total output is O_AQDC; country B's output is QO_BEF. The
shift of Q^*Q capital from country A to country B equalizes returns in both at R^* and
increases world output by GDF, of which GDK accrues to country A and GKF to
country B. The area Q^*QKG is the rent paid by country B to country A, but the total
increased output of country B is Q^*QFG, leaving it the gain of GKF.

schedules of capital in the two countries are shown as MPK_A and MPK_B, with the vertical line at O_A treated as the zero axis for country A and the quantity of capital measured by moving to the right from O_A. For country B the vertical line at O_B is the zero origin, and the quantity of capital is increased by moving to the left.

Let us now consider that the initial position, before trade and capital flows between the two countries are possible, has country A with a stock of capital equal to $O_A Q$ and country B with the stock $O_B Q$. Under these conditions the marginal productivities of capital and the interest rates in the two countries are $O_A R_A$ and $O_B R_B$. Total output is $O_A QDC$ and $QO_B EF$ in countries A and B, respectively, on the grounds that the sum of marginal products under the MPK schedules is equal to total output. The share of this output going to labor is $R_A DC$ and $FR_B E$ in countries A and B, respectively. The difference between total output and labor's share in country A is equal to the rectangle $O_A QDR_A$, which represents the quantity of capital, $O_A Q$, times the interest rate $O_A R_A$. By analogy $QO_B R_B F$ is the capital's share of output in country B.

Now let us assume that restrictions on capital flows are removed between the two countries. Investors in country A will buy high-yield bonds in country B and real capital is transferred from A to B until equilibrium is reached when interest rates in both countries are equal to R^*. The amount of capital is $O_A Q^*$ and $O_B Q^*$ in countries A and B, respectively. Country A's output has fallen by the area $Q^* QDG$, while output in B has risen by $Q^* QFG$, leaving a net gain in output equal to the shaded triangle GDF.

However, this gain in world output is accompanied by some important income distribution effects. Thus, country A's earnings on the capital lent to country B are equal to the rectangle $Q^* QKG$, that is, the quantity of capital times the rate of interest. Since initially output attributable to the $Q^* Q$ capital in country A was equal to $Q^* QDG$, country A's net gain is about one half of the world gain or GDK. Under our assumption of linear schedules of the marginal productivity of capital, the world gains in output due to the capital flows are distributed about evenly between the two countries. The distribution would be exactly even if the elasticities of the MPK_A and MPK_B schedules were the same in the range $Q^* – Q$.

Let us now consider the income redistribution effects of the capital outflow from country A on the income of labor and capital in that country. We can note first that the rate of interest is raised from $O_A R_A$ to $O_A R^*$, while the wage rate must be lower because of the lower capital/labor ratio. From Figure 25–4 we can see that labor's income has fallen from $R_A DC$ to $R^* GC$, with all of the loss accruing to the owners of capital in Country A. There is an analogous increase in income of labor in country B, which the reader can readily work out by himself. These internal income redistribution effects due to capital flows explain why organized labor in a heavy capital-exporting country, such as the United States, tend to lobby with the U.S. legislature for restrictions on capital exports. Knowledge of their existence also makes economists concerned about the low income of labor in developing countries suggest that it is not in the interest of poorer nations to restrict capital inflows. We return to this point below in our discussion of the problems raised by the existence of large multinational enterprises.

In our analysis of the gains from trade we have discussed the problems raised for economic policy advisers by the existence of simultaneous efficiency gains and income redistribution effects of a given policy. In using the principles already developed we can conclude that the free movement of capital between countries raises world output and therefore is desirable. The problem of income redistribution effects raised by this free flow of capital should be treated as a separate issue, to be solved by the political process used in most countries to modify the income distribution created otherwise by the free operation of market forces.

Relaxing Some Assumptions

We now increase the realism of our analysis of the welfare effects by relaxing some of the assumptions which were made above, in order to permit us to focus on the classical case of increased efficiency in the world economy.

Terms of Trade. Foreign investment can affect the terms of trade of capital-exporting and capital-importing countries and thus change welfare in a manner familiar from our analysis of the gains from trade. For example, the oil and natural-resource exploration activities of firms from industrial countries are likely to have caused the world prices of oil and raw material to be lower than they would have been otherwise. Consequently the terms of trade of countries exporting these products (often developing countries) are worse than they would have been. On the other hand, investment in manufacturing facilities in developing countries tends to lower the world price of manufactures, favoring developing countries. It is impossible to estimate the net effects of these investments on the terms of trade between developing and industrial nations. The set of effects just presented are only the most obvious resulting from foreign investment; a complete analysis would have to take account of many more, such as the income and resultant demand for imports, the rates of discovery of natural resources, and capital formation, which otherwise would have taken place in the two regions. Information on such matters simply is not available for either regional groupings of nations or individual countries. Economists who have tried to deal with the problem of terms-of-trade effects empirically have reached the conclusion that in all likelihood they are offsetting for most countries and are negligibly small relative to the efficiency gains and some other effects of capital flows to be discussed next.

Employment. Capital flows may interfere with macroeconomic stabilization policies of the type discussed in Part Four of this book. Thus, capital outflows can make it more difficult to generate aggregate expenditures necessary to lower unemployment, while inflows may aggravate already existing excess demand, especially because direct foreign investment is often accompanied by demand for labor, construction, and materials. On the other hand, foreign investment may also be timed to assist cyclical stabilization policies. In general, the employment effects of foreign investment are probably procyclical because foreign, like domestic, investors are attracted by good domestic business conditions and repelled by bad conditions. Overall, however, in most countries the employment effects of foreign investment are dominated by domestic sources of instability. We can conclude that the influence on welfare by these effects is negligibly small.

Developing countries tend to suffer from structural rather than cyclical unemployment. In these countries, foreign investment can lead to the employment of labor which otherwise would have had a zero or extremely low productivity in traditional agricultural work or service industries in cities. Under these conditions the welfare effects of foreign investment in the receiving country and for the world as a whole are much larger than those envisaged in the traditional model presented above. Underemployment and unemployment characterizing developing nations does not fit into the traditional capitalist micro and macro models, according to which it represents only temporary disequilibrium in labor markets. For this reason it is difficult to give greater precision to the nature and quantity of the welfare gains due to the employment effects of foreign investment, beyond the general ones we have just discussed.

Knowledge Capital. At several points in this book we have noted the fact that physical, human, and knowledge capital are complements in the production process and are increased in the same manner by the sacrifice of current consumption. Some forms of knowledge capital can be purchased in international markets through licensing arrangements. However, some of the most important forms of knowledge capital are inseparable from the operation of business and cannot be purchased separately. As we have argued above, this knowledge, embodied in managerial know-how, product differentiation, marketing experience, and the evolutionary process of high-technology and research-intensive products, represents the most important motive for direct foreign investment. A country receiving such direct investment tends to pay for the knowledge capital through the fact that the sum of factor prices of the machines alone is smaller than the price of the total package of investment. The capital-exporting country in the short run may be able to make windfall profits from the export of real machines marked up in price to reflect the value of the knowledge they embody in the package as a whole, since the marginal cost of using the already existing knowledge capital is zero. Recall the example given above of the increased profits of the automobile industry from the export of body dies which are obsolete for domestic marketing purposes but sound technically. However, we can note that one effect of these exports of knowledge capital is to raise the relative rate of return from knowledge over real capital formation, which induces firms to engage in more model changes and more advertising, though domestic real investment may be increased also. Such added expenditures cease only once the marginal rate of return on both forms of capital formation are equalized. At this point the markup over cost on the export of the bundle of real machines reflects truly the long-run marginal cost of producing the knowledge capital. The exporting country still enjoys gains from the more efficient allocation of savings in the two forms of capital formation, but it would be wrong to consider the markup on the factor cost of the exported bundle of machines as being equal to these gains in the longer run.

The capital-receiving country may gain from the receipt of knowledge capital of the sort just discussed if it leads to certain spillover effects. For example locally employed workers can learn production management, financial, and marketing skills which are portable and can be used in other industries or to set up domestic competition. The machines themselves tend to become obsolete and are sold for secondhand use. local entrepreneurs may be able to adapt the machines for employment in industries supplying local markets that are of no interest to the foreign company. In so doing local entrepreneurs may be able to acquire knowledge about manufacturing techniques not otherwise available. In terms of the analytical framework of Figure 25–4 the spillover effects of the knowledge capital flows embodied in foreign direct investment tend to shift upward the marginal productivity of capital schedule (MPK_B) of the importing country, which has obvious effects on the distribution of capital and incomes and output gains in the new equilibrium.

Competition. Competition in many countries of the world is restricted by collusion among producers and labor. As a result, some owners of capital and some workers earn a rent, and the efficiency of the economy is reduced. Often such conditions are caused or condoned by government policies, the most frequent of which involves tariffs on imports. Under these conditions foreign direct investment can increase competition, since the foreign owners are not part of the collusive agreement, and in order to sell their output they need to compete with established producers through the lowering of product prices or the marketing of superior qualities and styles at the same price as competitors. Such competition increases the overall allocative efficiency of the economy and eliminates rents to factors of production.

The banking industries in many countries have had a tradition of protection from competition through legislation designed originally to create greater stability in the supply of money and the financial sector generally. Foreign direct investment in the form of banking has grown rapidly in recent years, motivated by the profit opportunities created by the high prices and limited services offered to the public in many countries in which strong banking oligopolies have existed for a long time. The development of Eurodollar markets, personal loan and checking services, and bank credit cards in many countries have been initiated or stimulated by foreign branch banks. The effect on competition undoubtedly would have been even greater if legislation had not interfered with the operation of foreign banks in many countries.

Government. One of the most important influences on the estimation of welfare effects from foreign investment not captured by the traditional analysis arises from government taxation of investment income and the distribution of earnings. The basic problem arises from the fact that both capital-exporting and capital-importing countries tax income from investments, and if investors were taxed twice, motives for the efficient allocation of resources in the world would be distorted. For this reason most governments have signed double-taxation agreements to avoid this inefficiency. It is easiest to explain these issues with the help of a brief example.

Consider a U.S. investor who has found out that he could build a plant either in the United States, earning $100, or abroad, earning $102. If taxes were 40 percent of his earnings in the United States and abroad and his income was taxed twice he would have an after-tax income of $60 from investing in the United States and $20.40 from the foreign investment. The latter figure is derived by assuming payment of $40.80 taxes to the foreign government and $40.80 taxes to the U.S. Treasury. Clearly, under these conditions the U.S. investor would build the U.S. rather than the foreign plant and maximize his after-tax income. However worldwide allocative efficiency would be harmed because the building of the foreign plant would have increased world output by $2. To avoid this distortion of investment motives, double-taxation agreements permit the U.S. investor to claim the $40.80 foreign tax payment as a credit in calculating his tax obligations to the U.S. government. In the case of equality of tax rates, the U.S. investor owes nothing to the U.S. Treasury. If the foreign rate is less than the U.S. rate, he pays the U.S. Treasury the difference. Foreign tax payments in excess of U.S. obligations are not rebatable, though investors can consolidate incomes and taxes from different countries in calculating their U.S. tax obligations. By doing so they are able to offset payments at a rate above the U.S. rate in some countries with those below the U.S. rate in others. Under these double-taxation agreements the investor considered above has an after-tax income from the foreign investment of $61.20—$102 gross income minus $40.80 foreign and no U.S. taxes— as against a return of only $60 from the U.S. investment. The investor is thus motivated to move capital to the socially most productive location abroad.

Let us now turn to an examination of the welfare effects of the double-taxation agreements from the point of view of the United States and the rest of the world. If the investment had been in the United States, the U.S. Treasury would have received $40 to spend on public goods or use in place of other tax receipts. But with the investment abroad, the U.S. Treasury and the public forego the income of $40. The foreign country's treasury, on the other hand, receives $40.80 tax revenue and can spend it on public goods or reduce other taxes by an equivalent amount. We conclude, therefore, that in this case the United States population as a whole lost $40 and the private investor had a net gain of $1.20 by making a foreign rather than a domestic investment.

The preceding example can be generalized to take account of larger differences in before-tax incomes at home and abroad, different domestic and foreign tax rates, the effects of government expenditures on goods and services consumed by the investment, and the size of foreign investment in the United States. Furthermore, the model has to account for the existence of foreign withholding taxes on dividends, which further reduce the social returns from U.S. investment abroad. An empirical study of the private rates of return from U.S. asset holdings abroad during the period 1960–69 found that the social after-tax rates of return on direct investment averaged minus 5.9 percent per annum, under the assumption that if this investment had been made domestically rates of return would not have fallen and spending by the U.S. government out of general revenue would not have increased. While these results are to be treated with some caution, they are indicative of the existence of potentially large welfare effects of international capital flows which the traditional model fails to take into account. For countries which are large net importers and exporters of capital, it may well be that the taxation effects dominate all others in their influence on welfare.

Uncertainty. In the model presented above we analyzed how in a world of uncertainty the international diversification of portfolios can increase the stability of earnings through time. While we used this model to indicate that diversification represents a motive for international capital flows which is basically different from the traditional one of higher returns, it is easy to use this same model to show the welfare gains from international diversification. The indifference curves in Figure 25–2 represent the combinations of rates of return and stability of earnings through time which leave an investor equally well off, in strict analogy with indifference curves representing equal utility derived from the consumption of different combinations of apples and oranges familiar from elementary consumer-demand theory. As we have shown above in connection with Figure 25–3, portfolios diversified internationally permit investors to reach a higher indifference curve and thus enjoy a gain in welfare.

Externalities.   Foreign investment, especially in the form of direct investment, may be accompanied by positive or negative externalities in both exporting and receiving countries. In a sense the terms of trade, employment, competition, and technological spillover effects just discussed are externalities because they change public welfare in ways for which the private entrepreneurs are neither charged nor compensated. However, there exists a separate group of externalities which are mostly noneconomic and have been raised most often in connection with the debate over the merits of multinational enterprises. They involve such arguments as the loss of national identity and sovereignty, distortion of social values, and technological dependence. This debate has become very heated and has generated a great deal of public interest in recent years. For this reason we will discuss this particular class of externalities in Chapter 26 under the heading "The Problems Caused by Multinational Enterprises."

Optimum Tariff on Capital Exports.   A country exporting capital which is large enough to affect the rate of return to capital in the rest of the world can be considered as facing a less than perfectly elastic demand curve for its capital. As a result, such a country is able in principle to improve its welfare by restricting free capital outflows through the imposition of an export tax on capital. The argument leading to this conclusion is essentially the same as the one which led to the optimum tariff on imports discussed above and the restriction of output by producers in imperfect competition. It can be summarized as follows.

The marginal foreign investment is motivated by the higher rate of return accruing to its private owner. However, since under the conditions considered here the marginal investment lowers the rate of return on all previous foreign investment, the social rate of return is equal to the gain on the marginal unit minus the losses on the inframarginal units. It is clear that because the demand curve is downward sloping, the marginal rate of return must always be lower than the average rate of return. As in the case of the firm in imperfect competition, the capital-exporting country maximizes its welfare by permitting exports only up to the point where the marginal rate of return is equal to the opportunity cost of the capital in domestic use. But since the marginal is below the average rate of return, the capital-exporting country exploits its monopoly optimally by preventing exports before the rate of return abroad is equal to the domestic rate of return on capital. Private wealth holders can be induced to restrict capital exports to just this optimal level by the imposition of an export tax just equal to the difference between the domestic and foreign rates of return in equilibrium. While the capital-exporting country can thus improve its welfare, the world as a whole loses because the export tax prevents the equalization of the marginal productivity of capital in all countries.

The real-world importance of the argument for optimum export tariffs on capital is probably very small, since the ability of any country to influence the rate of return on capital through its exports is rather limited. Domestically feasible capital exports, even by the United States, represent a very small addition to the capital stock of the rest of the world, and decreases in the marginal productivity of capital in this range of change are negligibly small. Furthermore, in a time when countries have been negotiating successfully for mutual reduction in tariffs to maximize world gains from trade, it would be very inconsistent to apply restrictions on capital flows.

BIBLIOGRAPHICAL NOTES

The subject of long-term foreign investment has received attention from economists only relatively recently, and there is no traditional literature linking up directly with the writings beginning in the 1960s. Mundell (1957) develops the argument that capital flows and trade are substitutes. Most of the best articles on the modern theory of foreign investment are reprinted conveniently in Dunning (1972).

On the motives for direct foreign investment, the classics are Kindleberger (1969) and Caves (1971). The diversification argument has been made in Grubel (1968) for portfolio investment and Rugman (1976) for direct investment. Richardson (1971) analyzes the initial foreign investment decision.

The classics on the welfare effects of foreign investment are MacDougall (1960), generally, and Johnson (1970b), specifically in the context of the multinational enterprises. Grubel (1974) makes the theoretical and empirical case about welfare effects due to double-taxation agreements. Krause and Dam (1964) discuss the laws underlying foreign taxation of income and the effects they have on efficiency and welfare.

CONCEPTS FOR REVIEW

International investment position
Direct investment
Portfolio investment
Risk diversification

International diversification of
  portfolios
Multinational enterprise
Optimum tariff on capital exports

POINTS FOR FURTHER STUDY AND DISCUSSION

1. Assume that free factor movements have equalized the marginal productivity of capital and labor in all countries and describe conditions under which trade would still take place.

2. There has been a lengthy discussion in Britain about the social profitability of foreign investment in the 19th and early part of the 20th centuries. Study this

literature and apply the principles for the evaluation of gains and losses to U.S. investments in the postwar years.

3.   There have been surveys of businessmen as to their motives for foreign investment, undertaken mostly in the framework of business school research projects. Study the literature on this subject and discuss whether or not it is consistent with the economic analysis of investment motives.

4.   Using publications about the performance of U.S. and foreign-based mutual funds, try to establish whether or not internationally diversified mutual funds have increased in number tween 1960 and 1975. Does the European mutual fund industry show a greater preference for international diversification than the U.S. industry? Do the facts agree with your expectations? Selecting a few mutual funds at random, compare the performance in terms of rates of return and variance in the rates of return of those funds that were and were not internationally diversified.

5.   Find out from a local bank that has branches abroad or from a local branch of a foreign bank what services it can provide. From these facts try to establish the sources of comparative advantage of foreign branch banks which permit them to compete with local banks. Are your findings consistent with the modern theory of foreign investment?

26

Some Special Problems Raised by International Factor Movements

A NUMBER OF special problems related to the effects of factor movements on welfare in receiving and sending countries are analyzed in this chapter, with emphasis on externalities not captured by the price-theoretic analysis of the preceding chapter. These externalities, which are immeasurable but very important in the welfare calculus of some people, arise in connection with (and are responsible for) the heated public debates about the noneconomic welfare implications of the large multinational enterprises and of the brain drain. We discuss these topics in Sections I and IV. In Section II we analyze the balance-of-payments effects of foreign investment which gave rise to some public debate during the 1960s and led to some onerous restrictions on U.S. capital exports. The topic of the transfer mechanism presented in Section III fits into this chapter because it tends to arise in connection with large capital flows, though its origin historically is found in the problems encountered when Germany, after World War I, was obliged to make extremely large reparations payments to the victorious allies. The analysis is directly relevant to the problem of how the rest of the world can amortize its large obligations to the oil-producing nations as a result of the sharp oil price increases in 1974.

I. THE PROBLEMS CAUSED BY MULTINATIONAL ENTERPRISES

During the 1960s direct foreign investment by firms with completely owned subsidiaries or branches in many countries, the so-called multinational enterprises (most of them with a U.S. base but many also with European headquarters) rapidly increased the value of their foreign holdings and the number of countries in which they operated. The size of these firms, combined with projection of past growth rates into the future, conjured visions of world domination by powerful organizations. Some statistics about the multinational enterprises (MNEs) indeed are staggering. It has been estimated that in 1969 sales by foreign-owned direct investment were $1,350 billion, while the free-world total output was worth $2,000 billion. We should note, however, that the sales figures are not strictly comparable with GNP estimates, since the latter represent total value added, while the former include much double counting. Thus, the value of all sales of business in the free world would be a multiple of free-world GNP. More meaningful is the statistic that the profits of the largest MNE, General Motors, exceed the government expenditures of some smaller industrial nations like Belgium or the Netherlands. The growth of direct foreign investment in recent years has been extremely rapid. In Australia in 1955–59 the addition to the number of foreign-owned firms was twice as large as that during 1950–54. Statistics on foreign ownership of capital in Canada indicate the extent to which a small country's economy can be owned abroad. In 1961 the percentages of industries owned by foreigners were as follows: automobiles, 90; rubber, 81; electrical apparatus, 64; chemicals, 44; pulp and paper, 43; beverages, 23; iron and steel, 19; and textiles, 15. In 1966 Canadian exports of manufactures were valued at $5.3 billion, of which $2.5 billion, or 48 percent, were produced by foreign-owned companies in Canada. Analogous figures for Britain were 17 percent, in the Benelux countries, France, and Germany the figure was about 7 percent in each.

Facts such as these have been dramatized and presented to the public in some best-selling books, such as *The Silent Surrender* (1970) by Kari Levitt of the University of Toronto, documenting the Canadian problem, and *The American Challenge,* (1969) by J. J. Servan-Schreiber, the editor of France's influential weekly magazine *l'Express,* concerning the European interests in this issue. Governmental inquiries into the problems caused by MNEs and possible methods for dealing with them have been held in Canada, Australia, France, and many developing countries. The United Nations appointed a "Committee of Wise Men" to write a report on MNEs in 1973–74 and the role of the United Nations in regulating them. After the steep rise of oil prices in 1974, the Arab countries accumulated large quantities of financial assets, some of which they sought to invest in common stocks of major U.S. and European (especially German) corporations. In response to this possibility the U.S. and German governments prepared legislation to restrict ownership by Arab financial interests of important corporations under their national jurisdiction.

However, all governments and international agencies which are confronted with demands for control of the activities and growth of MNEs are faced with two very important problems. First, since MNEs bring many benefits to host countries in the form of employment, growth, immediate foreign exchange income, tax revenue, and technological know-how, any control measures which reduce these benefits are costly. Of course, it may still be socially beneficial to control the MNEs if the marginal costs are smaller than the marginal benefits from doing so. Second, while it is easy to state this principle for dealing efficiently with MNEs, in practice it is extremely difficult to obtain even reasonably accurate estimates of marginal social costs and benefits and of how they are affected by particular forms of control. This is due partly to the nature of the costs and benefits, which take the form of externalities and therefore cannot be measured directly, and partly because the task of measurement is complicated by the natural tendency of individuals or firms within a country to organize political resistance and mobilize public opinion when they are injured by the MNEs, even if the injuries are simply a part of the adjustment necessary to increase the efficiency of the economy.

The welfare benefits of capital flows were dealt with in the preceding chapter, so we turn to a discussion of the alleged harmful effects of MNEs. We can distinguish three classes of effects brought about by the MNEs: losses of national sovereignty, externalities due to market failures, and income distribution. We describe first the welfare costs as they are seen by proponents of control over the MNEs and then present theoretical arguments or empirical evidence about the existence of the welfare costs and how best to deal with them.

Losses of National Sovereignty

The costs and benefits of MNEs have been discussed very widely in Canada because a significant proportion of that country's industry is owned by MNEs, most of which have their headquarters in the United States. For this reason we can draw readily on examples from the Canadian experience to illustrate how MNE activities lead to a loss of national sovereignty, though the examples are applicable to most countries.

MNEs in Canada cause losses of national sovereignty through the following processes. First, managers of MNEs have to adjust their activities to be consistent with global profit objectives. As a result, if a Canadian subsidiary of a U.S. firm wishes to export goods to a Communist country, and U.S. foreign policy prohibits such exports, the Canadian firm may be asked by its U.S. headquarters to comply with U.S. regulations to assure the maintenance of good relations between the MNE and the U.S. government, which is important for future global profitability. Second, the MNE managers are also likely to have access to foreign capital markets more readily than those of purely Canadian-owned firms. Therefore they are able to avoid more readily the effects of Canadian monetary policy, shifting funds abroad when credit is easy, borrowing abroad when it is tight. This behavior makes the pursuit of macroeconomic stabilization policy in Canada more difficult. It also results in allocative inefficiencies, as some Canadian firms without such foreign contacts have their activities constrained relatively more heavily, and causes added instabilities of demand for foreign exchange.

Third, foreign-owned enterprises can resist the efforts of countries to reform their social order. Special tax levies on capital and profits aimed at income redistribution can be avoided by the use of interfirm accounting prices which shift reported profits abroad. Through the financial support of political candidates or through bribery in some countries, foreign firms can influence the shaping of economic policies involving pricing, taxes, and public ownership. U.S. blockades, economic sanctions, and military and diplomatic pressures are remembered from the cases of Cuba and Chile. For these reasons political parties whose aim it is to replace capitalism with socialism or communism often offer the most vocal opposition to MNEs, which they accuse of constraining national sovereignty in the pursuit of revolution or fundamental social and economic reform. This interpretation of the motive of opposition of MNEs by some political parties can be discovered by reading the book *Silent Surrender,* by Kari Levitt, which argues the case for restrictions on foreign direct investment in Canada.

Fourth we noted above that one of the important motives for the growth of MNEs has been the effort to spread the use of knowledge capital over larger units of output. Research and development therefore are known to be undertaken on a large scale by MNEs in the particular industries in which they operate. The production of knowledge capital requires factor inputs and learning by doing and is subject to scale economies. This causes MNEs to locate this activity only in certain countries, primarily the United States, Britain, and West Germany, where conditions permit low costs of production. As a result, other countries have smaller research establishments than they would have if knowledge capital production were not planned centrally and with the view of worldwide cost minimization. As a result, the research and development expenditure patterns of MNEs deprive certain countries of stocks of highly skilled people, whose presence confers great benefits to society in the form of a more interesting intellectual life and spillover of knowledge into the solution of strictly local problems. It also limits their ability to engage in crash scientific and development programs should the sudden need for them arise, as it has in recent years with the energy and food crises.

Fifth, the influence of MNEs on consumption patterns throughout the world has been very great, through advertising and the sale of cheap substitutes for local products. The most widely quoted example in this context is Coca-Cola, which has replaced many local drinks, but analogous examples abound in many other consumer goods industries. Foreign-owned magazines, book publishers, and record distributors compete with local talent and content. Intellectuals in many countries deplore the changes in national tastes in consumption and losses of the intellectual and cultural sovereignty which have resulted from these trends and which have been aggravated by the growth of MNEs.

Sixth, a source of concern over the loss of national sovereignty which is not discussed in Canada as much as it is in the United States is that the rapid increases in financial asset holdings of the Arab countries after rises in oil prices in 1974 could be used to purchase control over major Western corporations. In the United States a newspaper reporter dramatized the resultant problem by stating that it was conceivable that Arab directors sitting on the boards of IBM, Boeing, and General Electric could have enough voting power to delay or sidetrack the development of new computers, aircraft, and weapons needed for national security. Alternatively, they might engage in espionage for foreign commercial competition and hostile governments.

There are many economists who believe that the loss of national sovereignty through these mechanisms simply is a necessary cost of living in a world of nation-states which are interdependent through international trade and the ownership of capital across countries. The dilemma of greater income through trade and specialization at the expense of dependency on others and the loss of national sovereignty has been with countries ever since the creation of nation-states. There are no easy ways out of the dilemma, and economists who are knowledgeable about the benefits from trade and specialization can contribute to a rational choice only by urging that the value of national sovereignty be considered carefully. How much real income would residents of a country be willing to give up in order to know that, as a result of some control measures, the decisions of domestic corporations are influenced less by noneconomic factors emanating abroad, macroeconomic stabilization and income redistribution policies are more effective, a greater research capability is maintained, traditional national culture is preserved, and foreigners threaten military security less through industrial sabotage and espionage? The debates over MNEs among scholars, politicians, and concerned citizens are, of course, the methods by which, in democracies, politicians obtain knowledge about the public's views about these matters before policy actions are undertaken. Students, as concerned citizens who are knowledgeable in economics, have to form their own judgments about the value of national sovereignty and the implied justifiable degree of interference with the operation of the MNEs which leads to a lower standard of living for all.

Externalities Due to Market Failures

The list of ways in which MNEs are alleged to produce welfare losses due to market failures is very long and encompasses nearly all of the criticisms which have been made about the failure of market economies to perform in a socially optimal manner. A few of the most important classes of criticism are as follows. First, it has been argued that MNEs exploit the national resources of countries as part of an imperalist plot to enrich capitalist countries at the expense of the poor, leaving future generations with inadequate amounts of resources and preventing economic growth. Second, MNEs are accused of having wrong social priorities in the development of industries, favoring the production of luxury goods over food and other products basic to human life. Third, it is said that MNEs have monopoly and monopsony power, exploit consumers, and the owners of factors of production. As a result, the economy is inefficient and the cost of the capital which is alleged to bring benefits through employment, growth, and so on, is too high. Often the process is seen as part of an imperialist plot against developing countries. Fourth, MNEs introduce inefficiencies into countries' foreign trade patterns because often they are part of a worldwide marketing system in which historic, political, and institutional rather than real economic factors determine exports and imports. For example, marketing arrangement may make it impossible to sell an Australian-produced good of an MNE in Southeast Asia where, instead, the Japanese subsidiary of the MNE has marketing rights. Yet, Australia rather than Japan may have the comparative advantage in supplying this market.

Allegations of this sort about the harmful effects of MNEs require careful theoretical and empirical analysis. They are often based on a misunderstanding of how the economy works, or they involve value judgments made by certain elitist or political groups in society which are not shared necessarily by the majority of the people. For example, the view that natural resources are exploited at an unduly rapid rate is held by many people who do not understand that in market economies entrepreneurs are induced to allocate resources efficiently through time by their consideration of the interest rate. After all, metal worth $100 today but expected to be worth $111 next year will be left in the ground if the interest rate is 10 percent. Price theory indicates how the interest rate tends to reflect the social rate of preference for consumption tomorrow rather than today. The interpretation that the prices of goods produced in developing countries and sold abroad are too low and involve imperalist exploitation most often are based on a misunderstanding of how market prices are determined in a free market in which MNEs, in competition with each other and with producers from other countries and industries, sell their goods. Attempts to raise prices, such as have been made in the past with coffee, cocoa and natural rubber, typically lead to the entry of new producers, the development of technical substitutes, and, eventually, excess supplies. It is quite conceivable that attempts to raise incomes of producers in this manner result in lower incomes over the longer run.

While cases of exploitation may occur, the preceding considerations imply that on average countries could not receive higher prices for their goods in the absence of MNEs. Only an explicit system of compensation on the basis of need could result in the receipt of higher prices. But such a system requires a degree of international cooperation and sharing attainable only through global agreement not foreseeable in the near future.

Views on what are essential and luxury goods differ widely. Normally the arguments that the goods that are produced and sold profitably are socially less valuable than those that are not but should be, according to the judgments of some individuals, reveal paternalistic attitudes which most economists urge should be disregarded. This recommendation is based on an understanding of the well-known model of how the invisible hand allocates resources and enables the public to obtain the goods it values most at the lowest possible cost. Governments not willing to accept the public's judgments on what goods are desired face the very uncomfortable and difficult problem of selecting goods for production by what must of necessity be undemocratic means.

As for the effects of the MNEs on the market structure of certain industries, empirical studies have shown that while MNEs in some cases have great market power, in other cases their activities have led to reduced market concentration, especially where a number of MNEs are operating in the same country and share the market with domestic and other foreign firms. Competition among MNEs from different countries tends to be stronger than competition among domestic producers alone. Similarly, empirical studies have revealed the existence of some inefficient marketing arrangements which prevent exports or imports between certain countries. However, such agreements are not frequent or quantitatively significant, because if they are inefficient they also imply a suboptimal profit situation for the MNE which it is not in the interest of the MNE to maintain.

Let us now assume that empirical studies have revealed that MNEs in fact are engaging in activities producing the sorts of market failures outlined above. Under these conditions the question still arises whether control of the MNEs is the most efficient way to eliminate these market failures. In Chapter 8 we presented an argument against the use of tariffs which is applicable directly to the case of controls on MNEs. The argument is that if there is an externality in production or consumption, policies should be aimed at its elimination directly. The use of a tariff or controls on MNEs introduces unnecessary added distortions and therefore unnecessary efficiency costs. For example, if there is considered to be wasteful consumption of luxury goods, then taxation of such goods and the subsidy of necessities can bring about the desired pattern of consumption, without incurrence of the cost of lower foreign direct investment through controls on MNEs.

Income Distribution Effects

When MNEs enter a country and establish efficient factories producing modern goods, they necessarily harm the competitive position of some domestic producers, sales of traditional goods are reduced, capital is harder to obtain, some workers and managers lose jobs, others move to the MNEs, and adjustment costs more generally are incurred. It is a very natural reaction of the traditional, native entrepreneurs and workers to complain publicly and to attempt to persuade the government that foreigners engage in "unfair" competition and create all sorts of externalities which reduce social welfare.

Governments faced with requests for the control of MNEs on such grounds must evaluate carefully the extent to which adjustment costs and the harmful effects on the incomes and relative social position of some groups in society are outweighed by the benefits accruing to the rest. As in the case of loss of national sovereignty, the problems of social change and income redistribution accompanying economic growth and development have been with societies since early history. The choices are hard, and they are not made any easier by the fact that the agents of change in this case are corporate giants from abroad. However, as in the case of externalities due to market failures discussed above, economic theory suggests that if society wishes to deal with the income redistribution and adjustment costs of MNEs, it should so so most efficiently directly through income redistribution and adjustment assistance programs, and not through the control of MNEs. Under such policies, the country as a whole can enjoy the benefits brought by the MNEs, and those who gain are required in a most equitable way to share their gains with the losers.

Methods of Control

The social calculus underlying rational dealing with MNEs is complicated further still by the availability of a wide range of methods for controlling MNEs, all of which have uncertain effects on the MNEs and on overall welfare. At one extreme of controls is the complete prohibition of foreign ownership of means of production. This approach has been used by the Soviet Union, China, and other planned economies. To obtain foreign capital and technologies, the governments of these countries have entered into special agreements with MNEs. This approach is not a viable alternative for most developing countries, unless they have totally planned economies and a bureaucracy capable of integrating the foreign influence into their domestic economic plans. Furthermore, there is the added cost that in the case of some industries it is not possible to purchase the latest technology and product designs, since they are changing continuously and the MNEs are unwilling to relinquish control over them. In

Chapter 25 Section II dealing with the determinants of direct foreign investment, we discussed industries of this sort, giving the computer, pharmaceutical, automobile, and electronic products industries as examples.

A less drastic method for the control of MNEs involves the regulation that nationals must have a controlling majority interest in the domestic branch or subsidiary. This approach has been used by Mexico, Japan, and some other countries. It is successful and leads to little cost in the form of smaller foreign investment in the case of industries with static technology and standard products. However, it does reduce the establishment of MNEs in industries with rapidly developing technologies and product design. Unfortunately these industries tend also to be the most dynamic and most capable of bringing needed technology. For reasons discussed in the preceding chapter, in these industries the technology typically is not for sale as a separate package.

A still milder method for control of MNEs has been introduced in Canada. This involves the requirement that take-overs of domestic firms by foreigners be approved by the government. Criteria determining the acceptability of take-over bids are rather general, referring to the protection of the interest of the Canadian public and other nonquantifiables in this category. The effectiveness and cost of this control method depend greatly on the manner in which it is used. In Canada it has been applied most cautiously, and it has been interpreted as a political concession to powerful and vocal groups in the economy which wanted some form of control.

Most economists oppose the use of controls on MNEs because they believe that it is more efficient to use taxes and subsidies to deal directly with the problems created by MNEs and to take advantage of the benefits brought by MNEs. However, there are two categories of policies affecting MNEs which are recommended by many economists. First, there are policies to assure that national governments have the knowledge and means for dealing with MNEs as equally well-informed bargainers. The need for such policies arises from the fact that MNEs often have better knowledge and better trained personnel than do the governments in developing and some industrial countries. For example, few governments are able to establish whether or not MNEs are avoiding tax payments by the use of transfer prices to report profits elsewhere. Similarly, it is difficult to establish whether royalties or prices received on raw-materials exports are competitively determined or fixed through the use of market power; whether agreements between governments and private individuals with MNEs are on competitive terms or whether they are rigged in favor of the MNEs drawing on more skillful negotiators; whether or not MNEs are engaging in oligopolistic market practices, and so on.

The existence of market imperfections of this sort typically cannot be handled by individual countries alone, though there have been reports of the establishment of a private firm based in Switzerland which sells information about the competitive value of goods and services required in deciding about appropriate transfer prices. In general, what appears to be required is the production of knowledge and the maintenance of a staff of technical experts in a neutral, international organization, such as the World Bank, the IMF, or GATT, which are made available to national governments for free or at cost when special investigations are required. The same international agency could also draft a code of behavior for MNEs and host countries which would make it easier to negotiate standard contracts. International cooperation in this form could do much to permit MNEs and national governments to engage in negotiations with equal knowledge and to reach equitable agreements.

Second, it is ironic that in spite of all the concern about the harmful effects of MNEs, many countries have programs to encourage MNEs to establish branches and subsidiaries through the granting of subsidies, tax concessions and other benefits. These programs may be indicative of the fact that most governments are convinced that the benefits brought by MNEs outweigh their costs, and they believe that most of the arguments discussed above have been made by vocal and articulate groups of special interests. Most important, the subsidies to MNEs are likely to be inefficient because they developed as a by-product of the competition among countries for investment by the MNEs. Initially, when only one country grants a subsidy it can draw investments away from others, but as all countries simultaneously do so, then the incentives are offsetting. The benefits accrue mainly to the MNEs, except that the subsidies may increase somewhat the overall supply of capital to all importing countries together. However, most economists agree that this effect of the subsidies is probably minor and certainly not what was expected when the program was initiated by the first few countries trying to bid investment away from others.

To eliminate the wasteful granting of subsidies to MNEs, concerted international action is required. Thus, under the leadership of a respected international agency a code of appropriate behavior by individual capital-importing countries might be drafted. International agreement would then be required to assure that all countries adhere to this code without exception. It may not be easy to reach and enforce agreement on such a code of behavior, but its adoption would represent one of the least costly ways in which developing and other capital-importing countries can reduce the costs associated with the activities of the MNEs, so many of which are highly beneficial.

Finally, we should note that in many countries MNEs have been induced to establish local manufacturing facilities because of tariffs on the goods they used to import. Here is another case where governments, through deliberate policies, have attracted MNEs, presumably considering the benefits to be greater than the cost. Now, if after some time or after a change of political parties running the government, it has been decided that the costs of the MNEs are greater than the benefits, then efficiency demands that tariffs and the implicit subsidies to MNEs should be removed. Further controls on MNEs should be contemplated only after it has become evident that the removal of the tariffs and implicit subsidies has failed to induce the MNEs to leave.

Summary and Conclusions

MNEs are potent forces in the modern world in raising the efficiency of production and distribution in all countries. Recipient countries benefit from the spillover of technology, increased competition, tax revenues, and income redistribution in favor of labor. These benefits generated by the activities of MNEs come at costs in the form of increased economic interdependence with the rest of the world. For the individual country, this interdependence can mean loss of freedom in carrying out macroeconomic stabilization policies, changing the social and economic organization of the country, maintaining specific national patterns of consumption and cultural pursuits, and having a scientific elite engaged in research. There may be aggravation of traditional negative externalities, and some segments of a country's economy may be hurt by the competition from MNEs. We have shown that the last two items of cost should be dealt with directly rather than through restrictions on MNEs. Most of the costs of interdependence can be eliminated only through regulations which, according to the modern theory of direct investment motives, reduce capital flows and therefore the benefits conveyed by the MNEs. In a world where none of these benefits or costs can be measured, the question whether individual governments would increase the welfare of their countries by restricting MNEs is one which can be expected to require much further analysis and public discussion.

II. THE BALANCE-OF-PAYMENTS EFFECTS OF DIRECT FOREIGN INVESTMENT

During the 1950s and 1960s the United States exported large quantities of capital and simultaneously suffered large balance-of-payments deficits, as we have shown in different analytical contexts above. Some observers argued that there existed a causal relationship between these capital outflows and balance-of-payments deficits, and many politicians were persuaded by their arguments. There is some question as to the importance of labor's opposition to capital exports as a determinant of the politicians' views on the problems caused by the capital outflows. Nevertheless, in order to alleviate the U.S. balance-of-payments deficits in the 1960s, a number of restrictions were imposed on U.S. capital exports, some of them "voluntary," others mandatory, and all of them since abandoned. Many economists have questioned the validity of the arguments about an identifiable causal link between foreign investment and the balance of payments, and a number of studies have been undertaken to analyze the relationship beween the two. The best known of these are by Gary Hufbauer and Michael Adler (1968) for the U.S. Treasury Department and W. B. Reddaway et al. (1967–68) for the U.K. government. We will review briefly some of the main findings of these and some other studies.

We can note first the difficulties associated generally with establishing causal relationships between changes in individual categories of transactions on the liabilities and credits side of the balance of payments, because all entries are determined simultaneously and are highly interdependent. For example, a U.S. outflow of capital leads to increased foreign exchange supplies to foreign countries. This may enable recipient countries to maintain their levels of imports of merchandise from the United States, which otherwise they would have had to lower because of domestic excess demand for foreign exchange and a lack of reserves. At the same time, excess-demand conditions in the United States may have caused a deterioration of its current account balance, which would have been even larger in the absence of the capital exports. Yet, the U.S. balance of payments during the hypothetical period under consideration might have shown an equal increase in U.S. capital outflows and overall deterioration in the balance of payments, inviting suggestions of a causal link. For this reason, it is necessary to examine in detail and with the help of economic theory the effects between capital flows and the balance of payments, rather than drawing conclusions from coincidential changes in balance-of-payments accounts.

On the most general level of analysis, it must be true that over a time horizon of sufficient length the balance-of-payments debits of a capital outflow must be balanced by a credit upon repatriation of the principal sum and of earnings during the investment period, assuming no default or expropriation of the capital. Moreover, through time, when gross investment grows at a rate smaller than the rate of return on the capital, even without amortization of the principal sum but assuming repatriation of the earnings, at some point in the future balance-of-payments income from investment must exceed the balance-of-payments debits from the outflow. In Table 26–1 we have constructed an example to illustrate this point. In Column (2) we show the balance-of-payments debits due to capital outflows growing at 5 percent per period and starting at 100. Column (3) shows the cumulative amount of foreign capital owned, and Column (4) indicates the earnings on this stock of invested capital at 10 percent per period. The difference between the gross outflows and the earnings are

TABLE 26–1
Balance of Payments Effects of Capital Flows and Investment Earnings

(1) Period	(2) Gross Investment Growing at 5%	(3) Stock of Investment	(4) Income on Investment at 10% Repatriated	(5) Net Balance-of-Payment Outflows (2) −(4)
1	100.0	100.0	10.0	90.0
2	105.0	205.0	20.5	84.5
3	110.3	315.3	31.5	78.8
4	115.8	431.1	43.1	72.7
5	121.6	552.7	55.3	66.3
6	127.6	680.3	68.0	59.6

shown in Column (5) as the net balance-of-payments debit in each period. As can be seen, this figure is falling from a peak of 90 in Period 1 to 59.6 in Period 6. It is easy to see that this decrease continues and ultimately results in the condition where the earnings on past investment exceed the gross outflows. Over a time horizon long enough, balance-of-payments imbalances associated with foreign investment tend to be solved automatically as long as the gross outflows rise at a rate slower than the rate of return on the investment which is repatriated. If the two rates are very similar, of course, the automatic diminution of the payments problems may take a very long time.

The studies of direct foreign investment and the balance of payments also found that U.S. firms investing abroad tended to purchase U.S. capital equipment worth about 21 to 27 percent of the foreign investment, which increased exports directly. Once operating, these foreign plants also tended to purchase inputs of intermediate products from U.S. affiliates. Offsetting these sources of improvement in the U.S. balance of payments were replacements of exports by U.S. firms from production by foreign affiliates. In some instances foreign affiliates actually imported into the United States goods which previously had been produced domestically. It is possible in principle to estimate the actual balance-of-payments effects of foreign investment emanating from these four sources, U.S. exports of capital goods and component parts, reduced U.S. exports, and increased imports. However, even if one obtains reliable numbers for these effects, there is the still more difficult step of deciding what would have been the U.S. and foreign investment pattern without these U.S. capital exports. Would the investment abroad have taken place anyway, financed from non–U.S. sources, and would it have led to U.S. imports and reduced exports? Or would the investment have taken place in the United States and increased exports and reduced imports? Would the investors abroad have bought U.S. capital equipment and intermediate inputs? Would income abroad have risen at a different rate and caused U.S. exports of other goods to have been lower?

These and other questions have to be answered before it is possible to arrive at a reliable conclusion about the balance-of-payments effects of direct foreign investment. From the nature of the questions posed, it is fairly obvious that economics cannot provide good answers. Consequently, the studies of the 1960s aimed at estimating the balance-of-payments effects of direct foreign investment for the United States and Britain produced interesting theoretical insights and led to the collection of some new statistics, but they were unable to provide any definitive answers to the basic questions posed. With the reform of the international monetary system taking shape in the 1970s, and the resultant greater flexibility of the dollar exchange rate, the problem of the balance-of-payments effects of direct foreign investment has diminished greatly in importance.

We should note briefly here that all of the preceding analysis of the balance-of-payments effect of direct foreign investment on the capital-exporting countries can be applied directly to the analysis of the balance-of-payments effects for capital-importing countries. After all, U.S. payments imbalances are matched exactly by imbalances with the opposite sign with the rest of the world. If we do so, we conclude that the balance-of-payments effects of direct foreign investment on recipient countries in the intermediate run is uncertain. Over the longer run, however, we conclude there will be a negative impact, due to the fact that debt-service payments tend to grow at a faster compound rate than do new capital flows. When this time comes, the capital-importing countries may well find that a more flexible exchange rate and monetary system will have reduced effectively the importance of the balance-of-payments problems for the domestic economy.

III. THE TRANSFER PROBLEM

As a result of the parity exchange rate system and the role of the dollar, the world has inherited a very large stock of U.S. monetary obligations, which represent a claim on U.S. goods and services. This overhang of dollars raises problems of how it can be repaid. To analyze this question we now turn to a body of economic literature which deals with an area known as the transfer problem. This topic is fitted into the present chapter on factor movements because it does not fit anywhere else very well and because it has been applied in the past occasionally in connection with the analysis of the balance-of-payments problems caused by foreign portfolio investment (which are even more elusive than those of direct foreign investment). The transfer problem is also useful in understanding the issues raised by the existence of the large debts of industrial nations held by petroleum-producing nations during the 1970s, as a result of the sharply higher petroleum prices after 1973, and the need to repay these debts. As an introduction to the analysis of the transfer problem it is useful to review some historic events which led to the development of the literature on the transfer mechanism in the 1930s.

In 1871 Germany defeated France in the Franco-Prussian War, and as part of the peace settlement Germany insisted on reparations payments in gold small enough so that France could make them from gold in her national treasury without any economic problems. In 1918, at the end of World War I, the Versailles Treaty imposed reparation payments obligations on Germany which vastly exceeded its gold holdings or its ability to produce the metal domestically. In order to earn gold for these reparation payments, Germany engaged in the proper exchange rate and demand-management policies to achieve a foreign trade surplus, in effect making reparations payments in the form of goods and services. However, the victorious Allies found that their economies were being swamped by cheap German imports which created unemployment and other adjustment problems. In response they raised tariffs, lowered their exchange rates, eliminated Germany's trade surplus, and insisted that the Versailles Treaty required Germany to make reparations in gold, not goods. Our understanding of the international adjustment mechanism today, on the basis of the knowledge embodied in Chapters 14–20 above, clearly points out the folly of these policies, but at the time politicians and even economists did not understand the issues fully. In the 1930s and later, as part of the Keynesian revolution in economics, a substantial body of economic analysis developed dealing with the international adjustment mechanism in a situation where one country has incurred the obligation to transfer a substantial amount of real resources to the rest of the world. This is known as the transfer problem.

The existence of large debts of one country held by another one, whether they have arisen from war reparations obligations, large private capital flows, foreign aid, or oil price increases, gives rise to two distinctly different analytical and practical problems. First, there is the need for both creditor and debtor countries to engage in the proper monetary and fiscal policies to effect the transfer of real resources in settlement of the debt. The very essence of this process is that the debtor country has to decrease domestic expenditures, and the credit country has to increase it. Difficulties in the implementation of these policies arise when there are political obstacles to the reduction in public income in the debtor country and the creditor country suffers from unemployment because of an import surplus and insufficiently compensating domestic expenditure increases. Second, there is the problem that even if the adjustment mechanism works perfectly, in the sense that it does not cause unemployment or inflation in either country, there is the question whether or not the transfer leads to a secondary burden for the debtor country, because of the need to worsen its terms of trade. Such a situation may arise if the public in the creditor country has a great preference for domestically produced and its own export goods and is willing to accept increased imports from the debtor country only if they are offered at a lower relative price than before the transfer was initiated. We will analyze these two problems separately, assuming away in the first part all complications arising from the goods composition of demand and supply. In the second part we analyze the secondary burden effects of transfer payments.

Transfer and the Adjustment Mechanism

In the framework of our analysis of the international adjustment mechanism presented above in Part Four, reparations obligations, large capital flows, and oil price increases are random disturbances to foreign exchange market equilibrium not unlike those created by bad harvests, strikes, and business cycles. The big difference between the "normal" disturbances and those giving rise to the transfer problem is that the latter are very much larger than the former and involve the vast resources of governments. However, in order to understand the solutions to the problems raised by these large disturbances, it is useful to stress their similarity with ordinary random shocks. By doing so we can apply the models of international adjustment already developed above in explaining more clearly the nature of the problem and the solutions available.

Before we do so, however, it is important to focus on the very essence of the adjustment mechanism operating in connection with the transfer problem. If a country has accumulated a large financial claim on the rest of the world, there is only one way in which this claim can be settled in real terms: For a period the rest of the world must produce more than it consumes or invests, and the country holding the financial claim must consume or invest more than it produces. When in a world of two countries there is initial payments equilibrium, and absorption in both equals production, then the economic and political difficulties associated with achieving the real transfers are an increasing function of their magnitude. If reparations payments, capital flows, or petroleum bills amount to only 1 percent of each of the two countries' total production and consumption, then the relative shifts in expenditures can be achieved without any serious problems, simply by minor exchange rate or macroeconomic policies. On the other hand, if the transfers require large changes in total consumption, on the order of 10 percent, then political and economic problems of adjustment are much more serious. Yet, once governments and the public in the two countries understand the need for the relative shifts in expenditures, economic theory is unambiguously clear about the policies needed to achieve real transfers of any size.

In order to analyze fully the transfer mechanism under a wide range of assumptions about existing institutions, such as freely floating exchange rates, managed rates, the gold standard, and flexibility of prices and of wages, we would have to review all of the models of the international adjustment mechanism presented above in Part Four, Chapters 14–20, and we cannot do this because of limitations on space. Instead, we will set out a simple model and briefly outline the transfer mechanism, drawing on the concepts developed above.

Let us assume that the world consists of two countries, A and B, with dollars and sterling, respectively, as their native currencies. Both countries initially are in external payments equilibrium, and domestic production equals expenditures. Prices are stable, there is no unemployment or growth, and the exchange rate is freely floating. Now assume that country A has obligated itself to pay $1 billion to country B for some real assetes in B, for petroleum or as reparations for a past war. Under ideal management of the problem, country A would simultaneously increase taxes on its residents by $1 billion and credit the government of country B with the money. Country B can then increase the income of its residents in different ways, the simplest of which is to use the money to purchase $1 billion of real goods in country A and distribute them in B. Under the assumption that the public in country A reduces its expenditures by the full amount of the tax, then the purchases by country B's government just fill the expenditure gap, and the equality between expenditures and production is maintained. There are no pressures on prices and employment in country A or on the exchange rate. By analogy, under the assumption that the public in country B does not reduce its normal expenditures as a result of the receipt of the $1 billion of goods from the government, expenditures and production remain in equality, and therefore there are no pressures on existing equlibrium prices, employment, or the exchange rate.

Instead of using the $1 billion to purchase goods directly in country A, the government of country B can reduce taxes by the equivalent of $1 billion in sterling at the current exchange rate and use the dollars to purchase sterling with which to maintain its normal level of expenditures. If country B residents use all of the reduced taxes to spend on goods, they generate domestic excess demand of equal value, putting upward pressure on prices and the exchange rate. Under competition the prices of goods rise only marginally, and the excess demand is satisfied by imports from country A, where the increased taxes put downward pressures on prices. The increased demand for foreign exchange (dollars) for imports into country B is just offset by the sale of the dollars by that country's government, so that the exchange rate is unchanged. Except for marginal changes in prices in both countries, the transfer of the $1 billion obligation from A to B leaves unchanged the other two key variables, employment and the exchange rate. This is as in the preceding case, when the government purchased country A goods directly.

We can retain the preceding model to analyze how the transfer can also be effected through the use of monetary policy. In this instance, country A engages in open-market operations and reduces the money supply, which reduces real expenditures as the public attempts to restore its real balances and puts downward pressures on prices and employment. At the same time, country B increases its money supply, which creates upward pressure on prices and employment. Under competition, the price pressures in B lead to an import surplus by country B which is just matched by the foreign exchange sales of the transfer payment in dollars received by that country's government, if the excess demand in B and reduction in expenditures in A are just equal to the transfer of $1 billion. In both countries, expenditures remain equal to production; the strength of pressures on prices and employment are a function of the magnitude of the money supply changes in both countries, the size of which also determines the speed at which the real transfer takes place. In the next period, when the need for the transfer has ceased, the money supplies in both countries can be restored to normal. In the example above, the tax rates can also be returned to the levels at which they were initially.

The preceding sketch of the transfer mechanism can be complicated by considering combinations of monetary and fiscal policies, the existence of managed exchange rates, time lags in adjustment, and so on. However, the key elements necessary for the successful operation of the transfer mechanism were brought out by the simple analysis just presented. First, both countries need to coordinate their policies. Second, the countries must be willing and able to decrease and increase real expenditures by the necessary amounts.

The second assumption is rarely met in the real world, because of uncertainities about the public's reaction to tax changes and monetary policy. Furthermore, countries may simply not be able to reduce expenditures enough without creating civil unrest or starvation. Countries receiving transfers may not be able to generate enough demand without incurring waste, a condition known as having limited absorptive capacity. This situation is alleged to have arisen in the case of some developing countries which could not use efficiently the foreign aid and private capital grants received during the 1950s and 1960s. The oil-producing nations, with small populations, were not able to increase their real expenditures quickly after the dramatic increases in their petroleum revenues after 1974. As a result of these problems of absorption, it is rational to set the quantity of transfer per time period at a level at which inefficiencies in the receiving country are avoided, even though the other country could have generated greater real net exports. If the mistake is made that the country reducing expenditures generates more surplus than the other country can absorb, falling prices, unemployment, and, under freely floating exchange rates, a deterioration in the terms of trade afflict the former country. On the other hand, if the transfer-receiving country expands its expenditures by more than the other country reduces its expenditures, then the terms of trade change in favor of the country owing the transfers.

Terms-of-Trade Effects Due to Demand Patterns

The preceding analysis of the international adjustments necessary to achieve the transfer of real resources in the amortization of intercountry debts is of very great real-world importance, especially for governments concerned with the maintenance of full employment, price stability, and balance-of-payments equilibrium. However, the best-known literature on the transfer mechanism deals with the welfare effects of international transfers, under the assumption that there are no problems of adjustment, employment, and price stability. The analysis is conducted in terms of the pure theory of international trade as formalized in the Heckscher-Ohlin model. The arguments were formulated originally by Paul Samuelson (1952). We will not use here a rigorous model to expound the welfare effects of transfer payments but instead try to make the argument verbally and at a more intuitive level of analysis.

Consider that Germany and France are the only two countries in the world. They have an initially balanced trade, with Germany exporting shoes and France exporting wine. We can choose the units of shoes and wine in such a way that initially they trade at a relative price of one for one. Now assume that Germany is required to transfer purchasing power worth 1,000 units of goods to France. The German government increases taxes to reduce absorption and France's government increases absorption by the required amounts. The problem now arises from the relative proportion in which the demand for shoes and wine is increased and decreased in the two countries. There are three different possibilities, assuming for convenience that German demand reduction affects equally wine and shoes by 500 units and that both countries are completely specialized in production.

First, the French public has the same tastes as Germany's, and demand increases by 500 shoes and 500 units of wine. International trade remains balanced at the initial terms of trade of 1, since no relative price effects are required to induce different consumption patterns of the world's output of goods in the two countries. Second, France has a great preference for its own export good, wine, and would increase consumption by 900, while adding only 100 to the imports of shoes if the price stayed at 1. Clearly, at this price there is an excess demand for wine and an excess supply of shoes in the world, and in order to restore equilibrium the relative price of wine for shoes has to rise, such as to discourage wine consumption and encourage shoe consumption in both countries. But since wine is France's export good, she enjoys an improvement in her terms of trade and a resultant welfare gain which is in addition to the one enjoyed because of the receipt of the transfer. By analogy, Germany suffers an additional "secondary" welfare cost. Third, the French public prefers to consume more shoes than wine at the initial price of 1. This case is the mirror image of Case 2, and it leads to an improvement in Germany's and a worsening of France's terms of trade and welfare.

The preceding analysis, under the assumption of complete specialization in production and therefore unchanged world output, can be amended to consider changes in the composition of output in response to changes in the terms of trade. Such shifts in production ameliorate the welfare effects of the terms of trade by permitting each country to increase the output of the relatively more expensive good, but they do not affect the direction of the welfare changes implied by the analysis in the simpler analytical framework.

An interesting question raised by this theoretical analysis is whether or not there is any presumption about the likely direction of the terms of trade effect. Samuelson argues that there is not and that in the case of transfer between two countries as similar as Germany and France, tastes probably are such as to leave the terms of trade unchanged. Ronald Jones (1970) has argued that there may be a presumption that the terms of trade move in favor of the country exporting the real resources, on the grounds that in most countries the marginal propensity to consume is greater for the imported than the exported good. Under these conditions, the reduction in Germany's income reduces demand for wine relatively more than for shoes, while in France the opposite effect takes place, leading to an excess demand for shoes and excess supply of wine and a consequent terms-of-trade change in favor of Germany.

Summary and Conclusions

In sum, large financial obligations of one country held by another as a result of reparations payments, portfolio investment, foreign aid, or sudden changes in the prices of important commodities such as petroleum give rise to two different problems, arising from the need to amortize the financial obligation through the transfer of real resources. The first problem relates to the coordination of expenditure-reducing and expenditure-expanding policies in debtor and creditor nations, respectively. Solutions to this problem involve difficult political and practical obstacles, since income reductions are never popular, and in a world of price rigidities and costs of moving factors of production, adjustments are never smooth. The second problem arises from the possibility that the public in the creditor and debtor countries may have different income elasticities of demand for traded goods, so that the transfer may require changes in relative prices and terms of trade. The secondary burden resulting from terms-of-trade changes for the debtor country may be neutral, positive, or negative, with some theoretical arguments suggesting a presumption for a neutral or negative secondary burden on (i.e., a benefit for) the debtor country.

IV. MIGRATION OF LABOR AND HUMAN CAPITAL

Human migration was an important form of international factor movements during the 18th and especially the 19th centuries, when waves of European workers settled in North and South America and Australia. Immigration has remained a significant source of population increase in these countries in the 20th century, and even in the 1970s the forecasts of population growth in the United States, Canada, and Australia are affected noticeably by assumptions about the rate of immigration. During the 1960s the migration of highly skilled persons from developing to developed countries, but also from some industrial countries to the United States, has become an issue of great public concern. This phenomenon is known as the brain drain. The tools of analysis developed in preceding sections of this chapter permit us to deal briefly with the motives and welfare effects of human migration, though there are some problems associated with human migration that are not found in association with capital flows and direct foreign investment. We now turn to the analysis of motives for and the welfare effects of human migration generally and of highly skilled persons in particular.

Motives

People migrate between countries in order to maximize their welfare. While the determination of welfare is a complex process for the individual which involves many elements, it is possible to generalize by distinguishing two main classes of motives: monetary and psychic. Thus, differences in money income from work in the migrants' home country and country of destination are an important determinant of migration. However, the monetary benefits from migration are not simply reflected in differences in salaries in two separate countries converted at the market exchange rate. In a rational calculus, migrants will also consider differences in taxation; costs of getting to work; the availability of public services, especially education for their children; the general cost of living, and, very importantly, the prospects for advancement in their chosen profession. The net monetary benefits through time have to be large enough to compensate for the cost of the initial move and lack of earnings between the emigration date and the finding of a new job.

Psychic costs of migration involve all of the intangible sources of pleasure and discomfort connected with social human relations and the disutility of uncertainty. At home people enjoy the pleasures of long friendships, family connections, common culture, a sense of belonging, and an orderly and reasonably certain structure of life. However, they are also subject to the discomforts of real or perceived lack of opportunity and excitement, suppression by peers, political persecution, and dissatisfaction with the traditional way of life. In the country of destination all of these elements of pleasure or discomfort have to be considered also. One of the most important deterrents to migration is the lack of reliable information about both the monetary and the psychic benefits obtainable abroad. For this reason we find a greater propensity to migrate among groups of persons who already have relatives and friends abroad able to provide reliable information about conditions and likely costs.

Welfare Effects

The welfare effects of human migration are analyzed most easily by assuming that migration is marginal, there are no externalities associated with the migrant's work in either country, and there are no government taxation and expenditures. Subsequently we relax these three assumptions, one after the other. The following analysis is applicable to the migration of unskilled labor as well as of highly skilled persons. The main difference between these two classes of migrants is that the latter may be considered as involving the flow of human capital along with labor, while the former involves the flow of labor alone.

In a world characterized by the assumptions just spelled out, there is an unambiguous gain in world welfare from the international flow of labor because the migrant increases his welfare, as is revealed by his act of voluntary migration. The people remaining behind in the country of emigration have their welfare unchanged, since the migrant who is paid his marginal product takes along both his contribution to and his claim on society's output. The assumed absence of government implies that the migrant had his schooling financed by his parents, and whatever financial obligations he has towards them on moral grounds can be met by payments from abroad as readily as from the native country. At the same time the residents in the country of settlement also have their welfare unaffected, since the migrant contributes to and claims from national output an equal amount. For the welfare calculus it is irrelevant that the migration might have changed aggregate national incomes in the countries of emigration and new settlement. It is also irrelevant that the migration of a person with above-average income, such as a highly skilled professional, changes average per capita incomes in the two countries.

The preceding analysis is logically valid, given its assumptions, but its empirical relevance for judgments about the welfare effects of migration and the brain drain depends on the realism of these assumptions. One school of economists known as the internationalists believe that by and large the assumptions are realistic, whereas other economists claim that they are inconsistent with observed facts, especially in the case of highly skilled persons. We now consider briefly the most important evidence for and against the validity of the assumptions made above.

It is difficult to define conceptually when migration ceases to involve marginal effects and becomes "nonmarginal". Is annual migration of 0.0001, 0.01, or 1 percent of a country's population or stock of skilled persons nonmarginal? Actually, observed flows in recent decades have been extremely small as a percentage of the stock of labor of most countries sending or receiving the migrants. But let us now assume that migration is nonmarginal and consider the resultant welfare effects. For this purpose we can use Figure 25–4 in Chapter 25 and assume that there are no skilled workers. Then the distance $O_A O_B$ can represent the world's labor force which, with given stocks of capital in the only two countries in the world, A and B, results in the two marginal productivity schedules in Figure 25–4 which are drawn as in the case of capital above with origins at O_A and O_B, respectively. Initially $O_A Q$ labor is in country A earning a wage of R_A, while $O_B Q$ labor in country B earns R_B. Migration of Q^*Q labor from A to B equalizes wages at R^* and increases world output by GDF, of which GDK accrues to the immigrants, who increase their total income by $HDKG$. In contrast with the case of capital flows and interest payments, the income of the "foreign" labor Q^*QKG is returned not to the residents of country A but to the migrants in country B themselves.

In country B wage rates are reduced by the immigration, and capital owners enjoy an increased consumer surplus of GKF at the expense of domestic labor. In country A wages are raised and capital owners lose a surplus of HDG. If country A is a heavily populated, developing country and country B is an industrial country, then the changes in labor income in A are in a direction which would be welcomed as a probable improvement in welfare by most people, while the gains of the migrants are also indisputably increasing their welfare. Therefore, there is a strong presumption that nonmarginal general migration of unskilled labor from developing to developed countries raises the welfare of remaining and former residents of the developing countries. This sort of migration is opposed by labor in the developed countries because it lowers its wage rates, as can be seen from Figure 25–4.

Let us now consider that the labor force of the world shown in Figure 25–4 is highly skilled, and therefore labor takes along a certain amount of human capital when it migrates. In other parts of this book we have shown that societies have an option of using savings to increase their physical or human capital stocks, and an efficient allocation requires that the marginal productivity of both forms of capital be equal. When these conditions are met initially, then the emigration of labor taking along human capital but not physical capital may make a reallocation of society's total stock of capital necessary. If the human capital per emigrant is just equal to the average human plus physical capital per worker, then the average stock of capital per worker in the country of emigration remains unchanged. As a result, after the efficient reallocation of capital in the two forms, the emigration leaves unchanged both the overall productivity of capital and the wages of skilled and unskilled workers. In terms of Figure 25-4, these conditions imply that the movement of Q^*Q skilled workers from A to B also shifts downward the marginal productivity schedule of labor, such that in the new world equilibrium it goes through point H and the skilled wage rate is unchanged at R_A. Country A does not enjoy the benefits of higher wages from emigration as in the case of unskilled workers, but in this limiting case there are also no changes in per capita incomes of those remaining behind, while the migrants themselves enjoy the same gains as in the simpler case. It is easy to see that income per capita available for distribution and the skilled wage rates in country A rise or fall, depending on whether the human capital taken along by the skilled emigrants is smaller or less than the average per capita endowment with capital. Some calculations have shown that the human capital embodied in a person with two years of college education in the United States or one year of college education in India is about equal to the total average capital stock in these two countries, respectively. From this analysis it follows that persons emigrating from India with less than one year of college education raise the income per capita of the remaining population.

The preceding argument deals with the long run, and there may be inefficiencies in the short run before the capital reallocation can be completed. However, these losses tend to be minor, since technical substitution between unskilled labor and physical and human capital is quite easy, and the resultant inefficiencies are minor. Moreover, in a growing world emigration can be anticipated, and the educational system can be made to produce a surplus of human capital so that efficiency is retained through time, in spite of the outflow of human capital. We conclude from this analysis of migration of nonmarginal quantities of unskilled labor that the changes in wages and per capita incomes in the country of emigration establish a general presumption that the welfare of those remaining behind is raised. In the case of skilled labor migration, the chances for welfare gains of the people remaining behind depends on the amount of human and real capital the emigrants take along. But even if they take along more than an average share of society's total capital, the effects on the remaining population are likely to be small, because the emigration of highly skilled persons from most countries has represented only a very small proportion of total stocks of labor and capital.

Let us now turn to the problems raised by the existence of governments. The most important aspect of government activities relevant in this context are education, the provision of public goods generally, and income redistribution. Typically migrants in recent times have had substantial parts of their education financed by governments, though we should note that about one half of the total cost of education takes the form of foregone earnings during schooling, which are borne privately. One can argue about the welfare effects of the government-financed schooling in two ways. First, education can be considered to represent an investment by society in its young, which it undertakes in order to receive future benefits such as old age security benefits from the educated through taxation. We will discuss these externalities associated with activities of skilled persons below. If these externalities are positive, then the remaining residents lose their investment in the flow of externalities when the educated people emigrate, and the public in the country of destination gains. Second, education can be considered to involve a moral obligation to their children by parents who put them into the world not as a form of investment, as the first view implies, but for their own joy and satisfaction. According to this view children are a consumption good, and they owe no repayment for their education either to their parents or to others collectively organized as taxpayers who support public education. The only obligation of educated persons is toward their own children's education. Under this view, if educated persons emigrate they do not affect the costs of the education expenditures per person remaining behind, since they take along not only their contributions to the tax revenue but also the children they would have placed into the school system. By analogy, they do not raise the welfare of the public in the country of immigration, since on average their tax payments equal the value of the services consumed by their children.

The same principle of equality between tax payment and the consumption of government services can be applied to some other important public services, such as police protection and judicial services for which consumers are not charged directly. However, in all of these public services, perhaps including education, there may be strong economies of scale. One of the most important categories of government expenditure is national defense. In this case the marginal cost of defending more or fewer migrants is effectively zero. Migration therefore lowers or raises the net tax burden for defense expenditures in the migrant's new and old countries of residence. Elements of the same welfare effects may also be present in schooling and other public goods. However, it would be misleading to consider in the welfare calculus of migration only the changes in tax revenue, without noting that citizens also consume government services whose marginal cost may not be zero.

The income redistribution function of governments is affected by migration. Unskilled labor typically pays below-average taxes and consumes above-average government services, in such forms as public parks and direct welfare payments. The opposite holds true for migrants with above-average skills and therefore incomes. As a result, in the country of emigration tax obligations on those remaining behind fall or rise when unskilled and skilled labor leaves. The converse effect is registered in the country of immigration.

Externalities generally are considered to be important only in the case of highly skilled persons who provide leadership, engage in cultural activities, make scientific discoveries, are good voters in democratic countries, and generally improve the quality of life of society. As a result, the public in countries of emigration loses and in countries of immigration gains the benefits of these externalities. However, we can note that educated persons may also have negative externalities associated with their activities. In scientific institutions and bureaucracies generally, distinguished professional persons or administrators often have great power, and they can hinder progress by limiting the creative activities of younger people. Leadership can also be demagogic and lead to revolutions and bloodshed. Scientific discoveries and contributions to the fine arts, to the extent that they are not patented or copyrighted so that the originator captures a large proportion or all of their benefits for his own use, are public goods available freely to all citizens of the world. Thus, a cancer cure or cheap, new source of energy discovered by a Pakistani scientist working at the University of California will benefit his country as much as if he had made these discoveries in Karachi. If he had not migrated to California, and therefore would not have had the laboratory equipment, research assistance, and specialist colleagues he needed for his work, the externalities of his work would never have been created for the benefits of the world as a whole, including Pakistan.

Summary and Conclusions

The preceding discussion of the effects of migration of skilled and unskilled labor on welfare in receiving and sending countries, due to the existence of government activities and externalities, merely provides a flavor of the issues and shows how complex and empirically difficult to evaluate they are. Subjective judgments inevitably determine analysts' and governments' evaluation of the welfare costs of the brain drain. Most people familiar with the analysis presented above conclude that unskilled labor migration from low- to high-income countries benefits the former substantially but has some negative effects on the latter. The brain drain, on the other hand, on balance may cause some harm to developing and result in some benefits to developed countries. Generally, however, the welfare effects are much smaller than is implied by the journalistic exploitation of individual episodes of migration of highly skilled persons and by a widely held popular view that the migrants' full personal earnings measure the welfare losses and gains of countries.

These views of the welfare effects of the brain drain may be considered as underlying the reluctance of countries to adopt severe measures to stop it. All conceivable effective administrative measures are accompanied by heavy costs in the form of even greater restrictions on the freedom of human beings to choose a place of residence and place of work than are already in existence. Furthermore, to stop the brain drain it would be necessary to curtail drastically or stop altogether tourism and programs of foreign study and apprenticeship. While these often lead to migration, they also yield great benefit to countries in which the experience gained abroad is put to use and can produce important technological spillover effects. In the view of many people, and according to the analytical considerations presented above, these costs of administrative restrictions to stem the brain drain far outweigh the benefits from doing so.

BIBLIOGRAPHICAL NOTES

Much of the literature cited at the end of the preceding chapter is relevant also for the present chapter. However, the conference volume edited by Kindleberger (1970) and the books by Dunning (1970) and Behrman (1970) deal specifically with multinational enterprises and should be consulted by anyone interested in further research in this rapidly developing field. Books with a strong nationalistic viewpoint are Levitt (1970) for Canada and Servan-Schreiber (1969) for Europe. Brash (1966) for Australia and Safarian (1966, 1969) and the Gray Report (1972) for Canada present solid evidence on the magnitude and behavior of foreign investment in these two countries.

The transfer problem has its classics in Keynes (1929) and Ohlin (1929). Its modern classic is Samuelson (1952), whose conclusion about the presumptive change in the terms of trade has been challenged by Jones (1970).

The balance-of-payments effects of foreign investment have been analyzed for the United States by Hufbauer and Adler (1968), for Britain by Reddaway et al. (1967–68), and for Canada in the Gray Report (1972). Many articles have been written on the brain drain. One of the first, which has become identified with the "internationalist" approach to the problem, is Grubel and Scott (1966). A conference volume with a number of good papers and discussion is Adams (1968). A broad and very recent review of the literature and issues is in the publication by the Foreign Affairs Division of the Congressional Research Service (1974).

CONCEPTS FOR REVIEW

Transfer problem

Secondary welfare cost of transfer
   payments

Presumptive terms of trade effects

Brain drain

Psychic costs of migration

Internationalist approach to the
   brain drain

Multinational enterprises
   and loss of national sovereignty
   and externalities
   and income effects

Codes of behavior for MNEs and
   host countries

POINTS FOR FURTHER STUDY AND DISCUSSION

1. Using *Fortune* magazine's annual lists of the largest 500 firms in the United States and the world, try to identify which of them are multinational enterprises and from what countries they originate. Classify these firms by the nature of their main output and establish the U.S. and non–U.S. shares of each industry's total output. Can you theorize about the causes of observed industry differences in U.S. dominance?

2. Study the literature arguing the case against foreign investment in Canada, Australia, France, and developing countries. Try to classify the arguments according to the principles developed in the text; that is, are they referring to externalities due to interdependencies, general externalities, or special-interest pleading?

3. Consider the arguments made about the balance-of-payments effects of foreign investment from the point of view of capital-exporting countries and analyze what they imply for the balance of payments of capital-importing countries.

4. Apply the analytical tools developed in the context of the historic transfer problem due to war reparations to the problems raised by the accumulation of large quantities of obligations of the rest of the world by Arab oil-exporting countries after 1973. How could a worldwide recession have been avoided? Are there likely to be secondary burdens due to terms-of-trade changes?

5. Interview some foreign students at your university and try to find out their attitudes toward remaining in the United States after completion of their study. Determine such factors as nationality, economic and social status of the students' families, their marital status, nationality of spouse, political stability of the native country, source of school finances, visa status, and so on. Correlate such objective characteristics with the students' likelihood of returning home after study. How important do economic criteria appear to be in migration motives?

6. List and evaluate measures which could reduce the problem of the brain drain.

27 Customs Unions and Monetary Integration

IN 1957, Belgium, Luxembourg, France, Germany, Italy, and the Netherlands signed the Rome Treaty and agreed to establish the European Economic Community (EEC). This movement toward economic and ultimately political integration of the major Western European countries has been one of the most important political and economic developments since the end of World War II, with major effects on the patterns of world trade and power. The EEC, enlarged since its inception by the addition of Britain and the associate memberships of Denmark and Ireland, has a population exceeding that of either the United States or the Soviet Union and a level of production about equal to that of the United States and greater than that of the Soviet Union. The foreign trade of the EEC with the rest of the world exceeds that of any other country. Along with this population and economic size come influence and power in world affairs which would be increased even more in the future if a political union leads to genuinely unified EEC policies on foreign and economic matters.

It is difficult to know whether the EEC might develop into a political union and a federated United States of Europe or when this might take place. There are pessimists who point to the reawakened nationalism of the 1960s, the breakdown of monetary arrangements (to be discussed below), and the lack of unity of the EEC members in dealing with the oil crisis of 1974. There are other observers who argue that the road to political union was never expected to be straight and that certain setbacks are inevitable. They point to the history of the Zollverein and Germany as an example of how long it may take to move from economic integration to political union. In 1834 the large number of small sovereign German states

582

in existence then founded a customs union known as the Zollverein, which led to a lowering of trade barriers between these sovereign states. Only in 1870, 36 years after the founding of the Zollverein, did Bismarck succeed in creating a German nation-state. The vitality of Germany after this unification, in a world previously dominated by the superpowers of the time, Britain, France and Austria-Hungary, is well known. Visionary economists and politicians see such a potential vitality for a united Western Europe as one of the main forces driving the region toward union, in spite of the strength of national and sectarian interests.

The grand vision of a United States of Europe, achieved gradually through progressively greater economic integration and the actual EEC agreements, in the past two decades has sparked a large body of literature on the nature and effects of economic and monetary integration. In this chapter we present a summary of the most important aspects of the stock of knowledge embodied in this literature. We focus on the EEC experience, though the principles to be developed are applicable to all regional associations, such as the European Free Trade Association, the Central American Common Market, the Benelux Union, and the New Zealand–Australia Free Trade Agreement, to name just a few.

Some Preliminary Definitions

The one common characteristic of the EEC and other regional associations is that member nations grant each other preferences with respect to tariffs and factor movements, which is in violation of the most-favored-nation clause of the GATT tariff agreement, though it has never been enforced. Some regional associations also coordinate among themselves the conduct of monetary, fiscal, expenditure, and exchange rate policies, excluding nonmember countries from these preferences and coordination efforts. Regional associations differ according to the extent to which they grant preferences and coordinate policies among member states. The following terminology has been developed to describe different degrees of preference granting: free trade area, customs union, common market, and economic union. In a free trade area member countries remove intra-area obstacles to free trade but retain their national barriers to trade against the rest of the world. The customs union removes obstacles to free trade among member countries, as does the free trade area, but in addition it harmonizes trade policies toward the rest of the world. In a common market, such as the EEC, countries agree to the same policies as under the customs union, but in addition they remove obstacles to the free movement of labor and capital. In an economic union, such as the EEC has announced it wishes to achieve in the future, countries surrender national sovereignty over their exchange rate, monetary, and fiscal stabilization policies and the provision of unionwide public goods to a union government, which also determines the common exchange rate toward the rest of the world.

The organization of the economic affairs of the United States may serve as a ready model of an economic union. There is a common currency, which implies a permanently fixed exchange rate among states of the union; the money supply and exchange rate are determined by the federal government; there is free trade among the states; and factors of production can move without obstacles. Public goods in principle are provided by the levels of government covering the incidence of the benefits and appropriate taxation authority. Thus, military expenditures, diplomatic, and other foreign affairs, as well as national health and retirement programs, are undertaken by the federal government, while expenditures for education, cultural affairs, conservation, welfare, police, and the judiciary are made by state and local governments. This sort of division of authority permits states of the economic union to maintain their cultural and regional identities, while collectively they present a united front toward the rest of the world.

Degrees of Coordination

There is widespread agreement on the terminology concerning degrees of regional integration, but no such agreement exists on the degree of coordination of economic policies. As we shall see below, the problem of coordination arises at the stage of moving a common market to complete economic union, which the EEC appears to be going through during the 1970s. At this point it is necessary to assign taxation and expenditure authority to appropriate government levels, which requires the surrender of some sovereignty of national governments to community agencies, such as the Common Market Agricultural Commission and the Regional Development Authority. Furthermore, fiscal policies must be harmonized so that firms are not induced to locate production facilities in countries where subsidies are granted for the establishment of factories, while profits taxes are high, and company headquarters and reported profits are kept in countries in which profits and taxes are low but no subsidies to production are paid. Analogously, it appears to be necessary to prevent the emergence of incentives for labor to work in the low-tax and low–retirement benefit countries and retire in the high-tax and high-benefit countries.

One of the most important aspects of complete economic union is that exchange rates are fixed permanently among member countries of the union. Fixity of exchange rates can be achieved increasingly through three different institutional arrangements; payments unions, financial policy coordination, and monetary integration. In a payments union countries pool their international reserve assets and provide for the financing of intraunion payments imbalances. Financial policy coordination requires in addition that countries harmonize their monetary policies and avoid the consequences of large destabilizing capital flows. Under monetary integration, countries surrender completely the right to make independent monetary policy, thus permitting the maintenance of permanently fixed exchange rates and the introduction of a common currency.

It should be noted that the theory of economic integration to be presented here could be considered to be a part of commercial policy and as such might have been presented in Part Two of this book. However, because of the interest created by the EEC integration experiment, the special treatment in this chapter was adopted. Similarly, the theory of monetary cooperation and integration might have been discussed as part of the analysis of international monetary organization. But because of the EEC monetary integration efforts it seems most appropriate to discuss this subject in the present chapter. As a final introductory point we should note that while in the EEC case there has been a historic connection between the formation of a payments union, the common market, and financial policy coordination, with monetary integration and economic union as the ultimate goal, it is logically possible for groups of countries to join in payments unions and financial policy coordination without having a common market or intentions of moving towards economic union. Similarly, there can be a common market without moves towards monetary integration. Common market member countries could have floating exchange rates; the European Payments Union was in operation during the 1950s before the Rome Treaty. As we have discussed in Chapters 18 and 19, financial policy coordination takes place in the Group of Ten, the IMF, and other regional associations, without expectation that these coordination activities will lead to preferential trading arrangements, common markets, or economic union. However, as we shall argue below as an important point, economic union and monetary integration must occur together. One is impossible without the other.

In Section I of this chapter we present the theory of customs unions, which has developed as a special branch of the pure theory of international trade presented in Part One of this book. Customs union theory captures the effects of tariff preferences and therefore is relevant for the analysis of one of the main features of the common market agreements of the EEC.

I. CUSTOMS UNION THEORY

The formation of a customs union leads to the removal of import tariffs among member countries and the establishment of common tariffs toward the rest of the world. At least when the common external tariffs of the union are no higher than the average of the individual countries before the union, it is tempting to argue that the customs union formation is a step toward trade liberalization which raises the welfare of the countries in the union and the rest of the world, for reasons familiar from our comparative statics analysis of Part One. After all, tariff restrictions between the union and the rest of the world are not increased and those between union members have moved to zero, so that by any index of tariff levels a reduction must have taken place for the world as a whole. Surprisingly, the conclusion that customs union formation necessarily increases union and world welfare is not warranted. The explanation of this conclusion is at the very heart of comparative statics of the modern customs union theory we are about to develop as one of the two main parts of this section. Presented first by Jacob Viner of the University of Chicago in a famous book in 1950, it has led James Meade of Cambridge University and Richard Lipsey and Kelvin Lancaster, then at the London School of Economics, to the generalization of the principle of the "second best," which states that in a world in which there is more than one distortion of free market equilibria the elimination of one of the distortions does not necessarily improve welfare. We return to a brief discussion of the second-best principle below, after we have established rigorously the point that customs union formation does not necessarily improve welfare of the union countries, first in partial equilibrium and then in general equilibrium, holding constant the world prices of goods traded by the small country A, all in comparative statics terms. In the second main part of this section we analyze dynamic and other effects of customs union. All arguments to be presented deal only with the welfare of country A, abstracting from effects on country B, which is assumed to be the other member of the customs union, and country C, which may be considered to represent the rest of the world. The analysis of welfare effects for the world as a whole is, in principle, the same as that for country A, but in detail it is much more complicated and we omit it here.

Comparative Static Analysis

In Figure 27–1 we reproduce the essential of Figure 7–3 (Chapter 7), measuring the quantity and price of good X in country A currency along the horizontal and vertical axes, respectively. The curves DD' and SS' represent the industry domestic demand and supply curves in country A for good X. The price at which good X can be purchased from country B is given at OB, at which, under the small-country assumption, country A faces the perfectly elastic supply curve BB'. The import price of good X from country C is OC, and the supply curve is CC'. In the presence of a uniform tariff of T per unit of imports, initial equilibrium is found with country A importing good X only from country C, since its supply price, with the tariff $C + T$, dominates country B's price $B + T$. Recall from

FIGURE 27–1

Trade Diversion and Creation: Partial Equilibrium

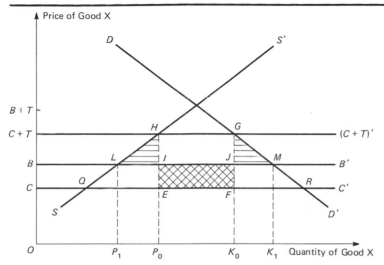

The small country A's industry demand and supply curves are given as DD' and SS'. Before the customs union imports came only from country C, whose cost of production is OC but which is burdened with an import tariff, T, so that in initial equilibrium country A imports from country C P_0K_0 units of good X.

After customs union formation with country B, imports from C stop and P_1K_1 units of X are imported tariff-free from country B at OB unit cost. Country A's welfare is increased as a result of trade creation, by an amount equal to the triangles LIH and JMG. However, country A loses, through trade diversion, a quantity represented by $EFJI$ tariff revenue formerly collected on imports from C, but in the new situation accruing as factor incomes to producers in the customs union partner, country B. The net welfare effect of customs union formation depends on the relative size of trade diversion and creation effects.

Chapter 7 that in this equilibrium position, country A produces OP_0, consumes OK_0 and imports P_0K_0 of good X. Tariff revenue is $EFGH$, and the welfare loss due to protection is equal to the sum of the two triangles of deadweight loss, $QEH + FRG$.

Now consider that countries A and B form a customs union, which causes country A's supply curve for good X to become the tariff-free BB', and this dominates the tariff-inclusive supply curve of country C. The new equilibrium is characterized by lowered production of good X in country A at OP_1, increased consumption at OK_1 and larger trade, P_1K_1. Country A's welfare is increased as a result of what is known as trade creation, which is measured by the reduction in the size of the original deadweight triangle losses by an amount equal to the sum of the two smaller shaded triangles, $LIH + JMG$ shown in Figure 27–1. However, the switch to country B imports also imposes a welfare loss which is equal to the shaded rectangle $EFJI$, which represents an amount of tariff revenue collected under the preunion conditions but which now goes as payment to country B. Country A now has to raise taxes to make up for the lost tariff revenue or cut government expenditures previously financed with the tariff revenue, by an amount equal to *EFJI*. The loss of welfare represented by this foregone tariff revenue is considered to be due to trade diversion. The net welfare effect of customs union formation depends on the relative sizes of the welfare gains due to trade creation and trade diversion. As can readily be seen from Figure 27–1, depending on the elasticities of the domestic demand and supply curves, the size of the preunion tariff, and the difference in the cost of good *X* bought from countries B and C, the relative magnitudes of the gains from trade creation and the losses from trade diversion may lead to net welfare gains or losses. There is no logical necessity that one must dominate over the other. We have thus established the important point that some policies of trade liberalization in the presence of other distortions in world trade do not necessarily lead to an increase in welfare.

In the case we have just analyzed, the customs union formation caused country A to switch its purchases of good *X* from country C to its union member B. It is possible, however, that the union does not lead to any trade diversion at all. This case can arise when, before the union, country B was the cheapest supplier of good *X* for country A. The removal of the tariffs in the union under these conditions only creates trade, and it leads to the elimination of all deadweight welfare losses. In terms of Figure 27–1, this case would be represented by reversing the C and B labels. The analysis of gains follows strictly that presented in Chapter 7 and need not be repeated here. Another case where there is no trade diversion is found when country C's good *X* price, including tariffs, is lower than country B's price without tariffs. Such a situation can readily be shown in Figure 27–1 by locating the *BB'* line above the $(C + T) - (C + T)'$ line. Under these conditions the customs union formation does not cause country A to switch its purchase of good *X* from C to B.

Empirical Studies. Numerous efforts have been made to estimate how much trade creation and trade diversion has taken place as a result of the formation of the EEC. In these studies the analysis has focused on trade flows only, rather than the estimation of welfare changes in the sense derived in connection with Figure 27–1. The essential approach of econometric estimates of trade diversion is as follows. Consider the fraction of country A's total consumption of good *X* which has been imported from country C before and after the formation of the customs union. In the simplest and earliest studies it was assumed that in the absence of the customs union this share would have remained constant. If in fact it decreased, trade was diverted. In later, more refined studies, the expected share of the total consumption of good *X* supplied by country C was estimated by taking into account country C's competitiveness in the sale of good X in country D, which was not a member of a customs union during the period under consideration. If country C's share of good X consumption in country D rose, it was assumed that it should have risen similarly in country C's consumption of good X. If country C's exports of good X to country A fell or rose by less than the expected share, trade diversion took place by an amount equal to the value of the actual trade, minus what its value would have been if the expected share had been achieved. Further refinements take into account changes in expected shares due to differences in income elasticities of demand for the particular product in countries A and D.

Trade creation, in turn, is estimated simply by considering the increased share of country A's consumption of particular goods supplied by country B. All empirical studies of the value of trade diversion and trade creation have found evidence of very little diversion relative to creation. Successive refinements of expected shares of consumption have altered the results derived from the simpler models only marginally, and we can reasonably expect that further refinements, taking into account changes in comparative advantage due to factor growth and technical change and product differentiation, will not alter these results dramatically.

General Equilibrium Approach.   We now present briefly the arguments about trade diversion and trade creation in terms of general equilibrium analysis, which reveals some aspects of the problem not apparent in the partial equilibrium approach. However, for simplicity we retain the small-country assumption and take the relative prices of X and Y in trade with country B and C as given.

Consider Figure 27–2, in which we show country A's conventional production possibility frontier with initial equilibrium production at P_0 and consumption at W_0. The line CC' is the price ratio available for trade with country C. A tariff on the import of good X results in the domestic price ratio TT', which prompts producers to be at P_0 on the production frontier. The arguments explaining this initial equilibrium condition, made in Chapter 7, need not be repeated here. The application of this model to customs union theory now requires that we introduce a second price at which country A can trade freely. In Figure 27–2 it is represented by the line B_1B_1' which is assumed to reflect the relative price prevailing in the large union partner, country B. Before union at the same tariff rate applicable to country C imports, it was not profitable for country A to import from B. But after the preferential elimination of the tariff, A is in new equilibrium with production at P_1 and consumption at W_1. Imports of good X from B have replaced those from C. The graphic representation now lends itself to making two important points.

First, the new equilibrium point of consumption, W_1, is shown to involve a level of welfare clearly superior to the original point W_0. However, it is easy to see that this gain need not achieved. For example, we could

FIGURE 27–2

Trade Diversion and Creation: General Equilibrium

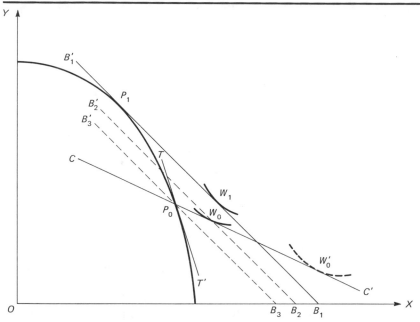

Before customs union formation with country B, country A is at P_0 and consumes at W_0, trading with the lowest cost producer country C at the price CC'. After removal of tariffs on trade with country B, production moves to P_1, trade takes place at B_1B_1' prices, and country A reaches the welfare level W_1. There has been a gain in welfare as a result of the customs union formation. However, it is equally possible that in the precustoms union situation, country A was consuming not at W_0 but at W_0'. Under these conditions, the customs union leads to a loss in welfare. Either case is possible in principle.

In the case where country A is initially at W_1, the distance B_2B_3 represents trade diversion, since it measures the loss in output of good X available for consumption if production had remained unchanged after customs union formation and country A had been forced to trade at the less favorable price ratio of country B. The distance B_3B_1 represents the value of trade creation in terms of good X. Clearly, $B_3B_2 < B_3B_1$, and trade diversion is less than trade creation, resulting in the net welfare gain. However, if the initial equilibrium is assumed to have been at W_0', then trade diversion would be greater than trade creation (the B_2B_2' line analytically equivalent for W_0' is not shown to keep the graph simple).

have assumed that in the initial equilibrium in Figure 27–2 consumption was not at W_0, but at W_0', which lies outside of the trade opportunity curve, B_1B_1', attainable after the formation of the union and the switch to trade with B. Under these conditions, the highest attainable welfare position could be below that reached before the union. We have here the interesting case where the elimination of one market distortion in the presence of another lowered rather than raised welfare.

Second, we can show, with the help of Figure 27–2, the magnitude of trade diversion and trade creation. For this purpose we consider what income, measured in terms of good X, is required at the new country B price ratio to attain the initial income bundle of X and Y which country A enjoyed before the union. The line B_2B_2' parallel to B_1B_1' and going through W_0 intersects the X axis at B_2. The quantity $0B_2$ thus represents the value of income in terms of good X at W_0, expressed in the new relative price. By analogy we now find the value of income in terms of good X attainable by country A if it had remained at its initial point of production, P_0. The intersection of the price line B_3B_3' with the X axis at B_3 gives us this value. As can be seen, the diversion of trade from country C to B causes a reduction in income of B_2B_3 of good X. This diversion must always take place if the union formation leads to a switching of suppliers, because under these conditions it must be true that the relative price at which country A can acquire its import good X is less favorable after than before the union. However, this trade diversion effect in Figure 27–2 is compensated by the gain in efficiency achieved through the movement of production from P_0 to P_1. This gain is increased in terms of good X by the distance B_3B_1. The net effect of trade diversion and creation is equal to the positive quantity B_2B_1. As we noted above, B_1 could lie between B_3 and B_2, in which case the diversion effect would be larger than the creation effect, and there would be a net loss of income from the customs union formation measured in terms of good X.

Second-Best Argument. The principle that the elimination of one distortion in the presence of others does not necessarily improve welfare (which we have just demonstrated) is known as the principle of the second best. It was given this name because the first-best solution always is to remove all obstacles to free trade and competition and to eliminate all market failures and imperfections. The removal of only one of many such impediments to efficiency is second best.

In his original discussion of the principle of the second best, Meade outlined a method whereby in theory it is possible to establish whether or not a second-best removal of impediments to efficiency increases welfare. Our analysis of the effects of customs union formation above represents a simple application of this method in a case of only two distortions. Theoretical analysis in the presence of more than two becomes vastly more complicated and involves the arithmetic weighting of positive and negative effects. Our simple analysis suffices to make the general point that in the real world it is extremely unlikely that we can ever trace through the effects on welfare of any second-best policies. From this fact we reach the very uncomfortable conclusion that, practically, economists are never able to know with certainty that any policy of removing one or more obstacles to efficiency will increase welfare.

This uncomfortable conclusion, like the argument that interpersonal comparisons of utility are impossible, implies that policy advice by economists can never be scientifically objective, however rigorous may be the theoretical models and econometric estimates underlying the policy formulation. This fact bothers many economists, but most of them have found that unless they live with their scruples, they are unable to give any advice. They also find that economic policies are made by persons with less information and understanding of the effects of these policies than trained economists have. However, the argument of the second best should serve as a constant reminder of the necessity to consider the broad, indirect effects rather than only the narrow, direct effects of all economic policies.

Terms-of-Trade Effects.   One of the obvious shortcomings of the analysis of welfare gains from customs union formation presented above is that we had to assume that country A is so small we could ignore terms-of-trade effects. In the real world, terms-of-trade effects of customs union formation may be rather important, both for the individual countries of the union in trade with each other and for the union as a whole in trade with the rest of the world. The EEC is a very large trading unit, and it is not realistic to assume that major trade policies such as the customs union formation would not have an effect on its terms of trade.

It is well known that an improvement in the terms of trade of a country raises its welfare and a worsening of the terms lowers welfare. This argument can readily be incorporated in the models presented above, but since the results are so obvious we will not do so formally. The really important question is whether customs union formation is likely to improve or worsen the union's terms of trade. Unfortunately, the conventional two-commodity model of trade-offer curves does not lend itself very well to the analysis of union formation. One of the main difficulties arises from the fact that in a three-country world with two goods, trade can take place between only two of them. This can readily be seen by considering Figure 27–3, in which we show three different possible trading combinations. In Panel I we assume that country A imports good X and exports good Y, trading in this pattern with both B and C. However, it is clear that B and C cannot trade with each other unless one of them imports and exports the same good, which of course in the simple Heckscher-Ohlin model is not possible logically. In Panels II and III we show the other combinations of pairs of countries trading with each other, all of which have the deficiency that initially there is no trade between one pair. Of course, there is no necessary reason why either one of the three panels should describe reality more closely than the other.

However, if we assume that the initial trade pattern resembles that of Panel II, that is, there is initially no trade in the two relevant goods between the union member countries A and B, then we can use the con-

FIGURE 27–3
Possible Trading Patterns in a Three-Country World

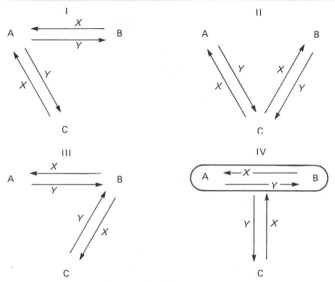

The analysis of terms of trade effects of customs union formation encounters the problem that in a model with three countries and two goods, trade cannot take place between one pair of countries without one country importing and exporting the same good. In Panel I of Figure 27–3 country A imports good X from countries B and C and exports good Y to them. No trade can logically take place between countries B and C. Analogous situations are shown in Panels II and III. Under the assumption that before the customs union formation the condition of Panel II prevails, then the customs union can induce trade between countries A and B and the new economic unit trades with country C as shown in Panel IV. Terms of trade effects of a union under these conditions are derived in Figure 27–4.

ventional offer curve analysis to speculate about the likely direction of a terms-of-trade change after the union. For this purpose, consider Figure 27–4, in which we measure goods X and Y along the horizontal and vertical axes, respectively, and show the offer curves of the three countries, A, B, and C. The offer curve, OC, of country C is constructed in the conventional manner, with X the export and Y the import good. The offer curve OO'B, on the other hand, introduces an analytical innovation by representing a sum of the offer curves of countries A and B. It is derived by drawing country A's offer curve, OA, in the conventional manner and then locating the origin of country B's offer curve at the point of intersection between OA and the terms-of-trade line OT, which is point O'. The curve O'B represents country B's offer curve drawn in the normal manner, using O' as the origin with axes going through it parallel to the ones shown in the graph. In the initial equilibrium at point E we find that country C, at the terms of trade OT, is willing to trade just the amount of X for Y which the other two countries are willing to trade at that price.

FIGURE 27–4

Customs Union Formation and Terms of Trade

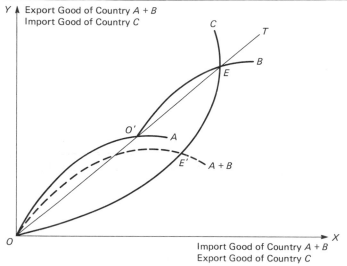

Before customs union formation country C imported good Y from both countries A and B and exported good X to both of them. Countries A and B did not trade with each other. The initial equilibrium terms of trade were OT. They were determined by the intersection of the offer curves of country C (OC) and of countries A and B (OO'B), where O' represents the origin of B's offer curve, which was drawn in the conventional way and added onto country A's offer curve. Customs union formation results in trade between countries A and B and the union offer curve O(A + B), which is derived analytically by netting out trade between A and B at different relative prices. In the new equilibrium country C suffers a deterioration of its terms of trade. However, if before customs union formation countries A and B had heavy trade restrictions, the union offer curve could also have caused an improvement in country C's terms of trade.

Now consider customs union formation between countries A and B and the development of trade between them, as is indicated in Panel IV of Figure 27–3. We will not do so, but in a graph this event would be shown by drawing offer curves of countries A and B in the manner known from Chapter 7. Nothing is known about the terms of trade between A and B, and the removal of trade barriers between the two countries is likely to expand the size of the offer curves, but this effect changes only the quantitative and not the qualitative results of our analysis. The main point is that as a result of the union the two countries are assumed to satisfy a part of their demand for good X by production within the union rather than, as initially, through import from country C. However, for any given price ratio we can net out the quantities demanded and supplied by A and B. There must be the usual equilibrium price at which intraunion demand equals supply and no trade takes place with the rest of the world. At other prices there is excess demand or supply by one or the other country.

We can plot this functional relationship between the relative price of X and Y and the quantities of the two goods offered by the community as a whole and call it the union offer curve. In Figure 27–4 such a curve is shown as $O(A + B)$. It is not possible to know whether this union offer curve is smaller or larger than either of the two individual country's curves. If before the union the two offer curves had been contracted severely by trade restrictions, it is even logically possible that the union offer curve is larger than $OO'B$. If the resultant intersection of the union offer curve with the OC offer curve leads to a flatter terms of trade, such as it would with $O(A + B)$, the union's terms of trade improve. On the other hand, we cannot rule out the possibility of an intersection of the offer curves producing a steeper terms-of-trade line and therefore a worsening of the union's terms of trade. Without much more information, we cannot know the terms-of-trade effects of customs union formation, even in the relatively simple case shown in Panel III of Figure 27–3.

Dynamic and Other Effects of Integration

Many economists believe that the gains from freer trade in the conventional Heckscher-Ohlin model of comparative statics are less important sources of welfare gains from customs union formation than are a number of other effects. These effects, which we will discuss now, do not fit readily into rigorous analytical models, and they are difficult to measure. Therefore it is impossible to establish with any reliability their magnitude, and we must appeal to indirect and fragmentary evidence. However, before we turn to analyzing the dynamic and other effects of interpretation we must clarify our approach. At first we consider only a case where countries have formed a customs union, have established free trade among themselves, and have permitted factors of production to move without restrictions, while there is no coordination or harmonization of macroeconomic and tax policies, and exchange rates among the countries of the union fluctuate freely. We then take up the case of the added welfare gains available to countries which also fix their exchange rates and genuinely unify their macroeconomic stabilization and tax policies.

Customs Union Gains. In a common market the economies of individual member countries are subjected to increasing competition, which forces workers and managers to work harder and more efficiently in order to survive. In the process, the cost of producing the output of the society falls, thus benefiting consumers. Competition from abroad brings special benefits in some national industries which through time and behind the protective wall of tariffs have become stagnant and oligopolistic. Foreign producers which typically are not members of national oligopoly "clubs" tend to increase competition through lower prices and the sale of better quality products, backed up by more efficient servicing to consumers. One of the great dangers is that the industries, after a short bout with competition, may again return to oligopolistic practices, but this time with collusion and market sharing on a common market–wide basis. This danger is real, though it is much more difficult to reach oligopolistic agreements in larger markets and among people of different nationalities than it is in a small, cohesive domestic market. Furthermore, the EEC has passed antitrust legislation and created a special staff to administer it from EEC bureaucratic headquarters in Brussels in an effort to minimize the danger of communitywide collusive agreements among producers.

It is well known that specialization in production is an increasing function of market size. For example, in large cities we tend to find specialists in branches of law and medicine; this is possible only because their specialized services are demanded by a sufficiently large number of persons in their marketing area. Such specialists charge high prices for their services, yet they are in demand because what they can do for their clients is worth the expense. Specialization of this sort effectively increases the efficiency of an economy through externalities. The specialist may be earning only a normal rate of return on his investment in training and equipment, yet the consumer gets his services at a price at least marginally lower than what he would have had to pay for this service or an inferior substitute from a nonspecialist. A customs union enlarges the market size for producers in many industries and professions, permitting the development of greater specialization and lower costs of production which are passed on to consumers through externalities. These externalities are related but not identical to the externalities arising from the conventional gains from trade due to specialization which we analyzed above in terms of the Heckscher-Ohlin model. In this model increased world welfare is due to specialization in production of a given set of products and services. In the present context we are emphasizing increases in welfare due to the development of new, specialized products and services.

For some time it had been believed that the formation of the EEC would permit industries in individual countries of the union to expand according to their comparative advantage in the conventional sense, in the process taking advantage of economies of scale in production, and that this would lead to overall lower average costs of goods for consumers. However, studies attempting to quantify potential gains from economies of scale were curiously inconclusive. As it turned out, in the major industries in which such scale economies could be expected to appear, such as automobiles, chemicals, and consumer durables, the plants in individual European countries before the union were about the same size as those in the United States. Under the apparently reasonable assumption that in the large and free U.S. market, plants would be of optimal technical size, it was concluded that union formation would probably bring few opportunities to exploit further economies of plant size. Apparently, national markets before union, together with exports, had permitted European industries to build plants of optimal technical size.

However, at this point we must bring in our analysis of intraindustry trade and product differentiation presented above in Chapter 4. As recent research by Donald Daly of York University at Toronto has shown (Daly et al., 1962), average costs of production in plants of identical size and using the same quality of labor and capital in Canada and the United States differ because Canadian plants tend to produce a wider range of differentiated goods than do their U.S. counterparts. The average U.S. costs per unit of output are lower than the Canadian costs because the smaller range of differentiated products manufactured in the United States permits the exploitation of economies of scale due to the length of runs. As we discussed in Chapter 4, these economies arise because, when a plant produces smaller varieties of a product, it can keep lower inventories of inputs and outputs, idle machine time for switching of cutting and shaping of parts is reduced, and workers and machines become more efficient in performing a specialized task. The reason why Canadian plants produce more varieties of a product than do U.S. plants is found in oligopolistic market behavior and protection. This argument has been spelled out fully in Chapter 4.

In Europe before union national markets were protected as the Canadian market, and plants tended to produce relatively large numbers of differentiated products in short runs, each to satisfy the spectrum of its national consumer tastes. The customs union formation permitted the national oligopolistic industries of each country to penetrate the markets of others. In the process national industries tended to drop certain lines of differentiated products for which foreigners were able to supply close substitutes at a lower price, while they expanded output of product lines that they could sell abroad successfully. In the process of this interpenetration of national oligopolistic markets, producers enjoyed the savings arising from longer runs in production, lowering prices or increasing the quality of the goods they sold. Unfortunately, direct evidence on this process of rationalization and welfare gains in EEC industries is not available. However, there are some empirical phenomena which are consistent with the process of increased intraindustry specialization. P. J. Verdoorn, Bela Balassa, and Herbert Grubel have shown that the growth of trade among EEC countries took the form of rapidly increasing intraindustry trade, which, Chapter 4 noted, is defined as the exchange of goods belonging to the same fairly narrowly defined "industry." Interindustry trade, defined as the net of exports minus imports, which is expected to take place according to the simple Heckscher-Ohlin model has grown only little among member countries of the EEC. The well-known relative ease of adjustment to free trade in the EEC is consistent with the view that intraindustry specialization was the major form of competitive response of national producers. Visits to retail shops in Europe easily confirm the fact that EEC producers of food, textiles, cosmetics, electronic goods, and consumer durables are marketing their special brands, styles, and qualities of substitute products in the entire community. All of this evidence may be considered to be indicative of the existence of welfare gains from increased intraindustry specialization in the EEC and the resultant lower costs due to the exploitation of economies from increased length of runs.

In a world in which technical change through process and product innovation is an important aspect of competition and welfare, the formation of a customs union has a further effect which was central to our analysis of direct foreign investment in Chapters 25 and 26. Research and development has been encouraged because the free trade access to a larger market in the customs union permits firms to spread these fixed costs over a larger quantity of output. To the extent that these are economies of scale in knowledge capital formation, or diminishing returns are less than in physical capital formation, a customs union increases the total output available from a given stock of social savings.

The promise of a large free trade market and the existence of an external tariff in Europe have been alleged to create special incentives for U.S. firms to invest in the EEC. It is difficult to prove this proposition, but if it is correct, the customs union formation has resulted in a European capital stock larger than it would have been otherwise. While interest and dividend payments are due on this foreign capital, the public in the EEC gains as a result of consumer suplus effects and the taxation of investment income, as we argued in Chapter 24.

Next, we can note that customs union formation holds out the potential of savings in the cost of administering tariffs and trade controls. In principle, when trade is entirely free, all border guards for customs purposes can be abandoned. Tourists readily notice the difference in effort and expense encountered in passing through an EEC border and the U.S., Canadian, or Australian borders. Moreover, the heavy administrative costs of trade control imposed on the private sector through bureaucratic requirements to complete and file information can be eliminated.

As a final source of welfare gains from customs union formation we can note the increased efficiency in the allocation of the factors of production brought about by the free movement of capital and labor. We have discussed the nature of these gains in the preceding chapters on factor movements and need not discuss them further here, except to note that to the extent that factor movements substitute for trade they permit the saving of transportation costs and thus an increase in total output. Complete freedom of movement of skilled and professional labor in the EEC has not yet been achieved, because of special national laws requiring lawyers, doctors, and other professionals to meet certain licensing requirements. It is doubtful that totally unrestricted international mobility of such manpower can ever be achieved. Even in the United States licensing requirements restrict the mobility of lawyers and medical doctors.

Gains from Economic Union.   In the next section of this chapter we discuss the history and problems associated with efforts to move a customs union to a complete economic union with permanently fixed exchange rates among the member countries. Without prejudging the case whether such a union is possible, desirable, or likely for the EEC in the foreseeable future, it is useful to analyze the additional economic welfare gains to be had from such a union. For this purpose we can draw on the theory of optimum currency areas presented in Chapter 22. A brief sketch of this analysis is as follows.

Recall that the permanent fixing of exchange rates between two countries that previously had freely floating exchange rates has welfare effects through changes in the level of income, the stability of income, and the loss of national economic sovereignty. The changes in income are positive because the fixity of the exchange rates lowers uncertainty and encourages the factors of production and entrepreneurs to consider the entire area as if it were one country, which leads to increased efficiency in the allocation of resources. Furthermore, in the enlarged currency area the price level is likely to be more stable than it was when the two countries each had freely floating exchange rates. This effect is due to the greater averaging of random shocks internally and the existence of a greater sector of non-traded goods whose prices are unaffected by rest-of-the-world disturbances. As a result of the greater price stability, the money of the currency area is more useful, producing externalities in its use as a medium of exchange, unit of account, and store of value. Further resources are saved because there is reduced need for foreign exchange transactions and for the elimination of risk through forward exchange commitments.

In an enlarged currency area income may become more or less stable, depending on the strength of private and public arbitrage between regions affected by different cyclical or random influences and the ability of governments to take advantage of money illusion in achieving the real wage rates that are necessary for the attainment of full employment. Finally, there are likely losses in welfare due to the fact that countries of the union, which previously had been able to choose unemployment-inflation trade-off targets and fiscal-monetary policy mixes to influence growth without constraint, are forced by the union agreements to move off their preferred targets.

It is very difficult to know whether or not, on balance, these diverse effects on welfare resulting from the formation of an economic union among EEC countries will be positive or negative. One might argue on economic grounds alone that if the EEC countries agree to establish such a union, it can be interpreted as evidence that the perceived benefits exceed the preceived costs. In other words, the EEC is an optimum currency area. But even if on balance economic union leads to economic welfare losses, the countries of the EEC may decide to proceed with it on the grounds that there are political power gains offsetting the economic costs. All of the preceding considerations touch on subjects on which there exists little agreement among economists and politicians. The analytical framework presented here, however, should be useful for understanding and giving perspective to actual developments and pronouncements of intent by politicians and bureaucrats concerning the future of the EEC.

Why not Free Trade?   We now turn to the analysis of some effects of customs union formation which have been raised as a result of the following fact: If a country wishes to enjoy the benefits from free trade, it should remove all trade barriers unilaterally, not form a customs union. The validity of this proposition can be seen most readily in the context of both Figures 27–1 and 27–2. In the partial equilibrium analysis all cost of protection could be eliminated if there were no tariffs on trade with country C and country A took advantage of the supply curve CC' in Figure 27–1. Similarly, if the price ratio CC' in Figure 27–2 were used to move to an efficient production point, the resultant trade opportunities along the CC' line would permit attainment of a higher level of welfare than is possible by free trade with country B only. To keep Figure 27–2 simple we have not shown the equilibrium position under free trade with country C, but students can do so readily by remembering the analysis of Chapter 7.

The fact that free trade raises welfare more than customs union formation has led C. A. Cooper and B. F. Massell (1965) to argue that the traditional customs union theory just presented is deficient in not providing explanations of why countries choose customs unions rather than general free trade. We can remedy this deficiency of traditional customs union theory by providing the following explanation. First, customs union such as the EEC often have been conceived as first steps towards ultimate economic union and the formation of strong regional political and military associations. To the extent that this motive is present, it leads to expectation of welfare gains which are political rather than economic in nature. The vision of a powerful United States of Europe replacing a factionalized, warring continent of small nation-states has undoubtedly been a major driving force behind the design of the Rome Treaty and later EEC agreements. Harry G. Johnson has developed an explicit analytical framework for incorporating noneconomic motives such as political and military power and industrialization for its own sake into the decision-making calculus of governments.

Second, in a world in which exchange rates are rigid through international agreements and past protectionist policies have created rents to some factors of production, unilateral trade liberalization causes balance-of-payments deficits and organized resistance from industries losing protection. These difficulties are minimized in a customs union where mutual intraunion tariff reductions, together with a common outside tariff, cause balance-of-payments effects to be small for individual countries. Also, since in most cases the industrial structures of countries in a union are very similar, only relatively minor adjustments in industry mix are required. For example, in the EEC free trade led to considerably fewer adjustment problems for the French and German textile industries than would have arisen from French and German trade liberalization with the developing countries. This explanation of the lower balance-of-payments and adjustment costs of customs unions is open to the objection that in principle it should be possible to move toward general free trade in a process of worldwide mutual tariff reductions and the elimination of opposition to adjustment through a proper program of adjustment assistance. The answer to this objection is that the difficulties of negotiating such programs on a worldwide basis are enormous, as is evident from the history of tariff negotiations under GATT discussed in Chapter 9 above. In a world where balance-of-payments and adjustment problems are important real consequences of trade liberalization, it may be welfare maximizing to form regional customs unions rather than to move toward free trade unilaterally or even multilaterally through worldwide negotiations.

II. THE PROBLEMS OF FISCAL AND MONETARY INTEGRATION

The economic analysis of problems associated with monetary and fiscal integration has been strongly stimulated by movements to unite the countries of the EEC not only in a customs union but ultimately in a complete economic union with a common currency, a central monetary authority, no "Fiscal borders," and a federalist type of taxation and expenditure pattern. These movements resulted in two official EEC reports, the Werner Report, and the Neumark Report. The former, published on October 8, 1970, set out a program for the establishment of a complete monetary union for the EEC by 1980. In this union there would be a single currency and a common central bank for the EEC as a whole, organized along the lines of the Federal Reserve System of the United States. The union would be responsible for the conduct of domestic monetary policy and of the community's foreign exchange policy, using in the process the pooled reserves of all member countries. The conduct of monetary and exchange rate policy by this EEC central bank would be responsible to a duly elected European Parliament. The 1963 *Report of the Fiscal and Financial Committee,* known as the Neumark Report, recommended that the EEC harmonize national tax programs through the adoption of a value-added tax, the abolition of fiscal frontiers for intra–EEC trade, and the equalization of value-added tax rates.

These reports were hailed by some observers as welcome steps toward the attainment of the visionary goal of a United States of Europe. This was desired by a majority of Europeans and was needed to maintain the momentum which had been created by the formation of the customs union under the Treaty of Rome but which was being lost as the customs union provisions were enacted during the 1960s. Other observers claimed that fiscal harmonization was not necessary and that the Werner Report was the work of the EEC bureaucracy in Brussels, which had lost touch with the reality of political life and reawakening nationalism in Europe. It was said the bureaucracy attempted to get into operation policies raising its own importance and power, in disregard of the economic and political problems associated with the proposed plans of unification.

In the remainder of this chapter we present a body of economic analysis needed in order to understand the arguments of those who think that the fiscal harmonization program is not necessary for the functioning of a customs union and that economic problems of monetary integration are so great that the political will to overcome them is insufficient in the foreseeable future.

Fiscal Integration

In the real world there exist two important, basic types of taxation, known technically as direct and indirect taxes. Examples of indirect taxes are sales, turnover, excise, and value-added taxes. Their common characteristic is that they are imposed on the sale or manufacture of specific goods and services, sales taxes being levied at the retail or wholesale level, while turnover and excise taxes typically are imposed on inputs at certain stages of production. The prices of these goods and services are raised by the full amount of the tax, and consumers have their incomes reduced indirectly because at a given income they can afford to buy fewer real goods and services when these indirect taxes are present. Direct taxes are imposed on the incomes of persons and corporations and reduce the disposable income of both directly. There is considerable dispute over whether or not some direct taxes are passed on to the public as a whole through higher prices of output, but it is well agreed that under perfect competition such shifting is not possible. For the sake of simplicity we will assume in the present analysis that indirect taxes are all passed on to consumers in the form of higher prices just equal to the value of the taxes, while direct taxes affect only factor incomes, leaving prices unchanged.

Indirect Taxes. Before we enter into our analysis of the effect of indirect taxes on the need for tax union, we have to discuss briefly the difference between turnover and value-added taxes. In most countries, historically, the most important indirect tax has been the turnover tax, which requires that firms pay a certain percentage of the value of their sales as taxes, adding them into the price. Taxes imposed at the retail level are still common and unpopular forms of taxation in many of the U.S. states. Such turnover or sales taxes have three important disadvantages. First, they tend to encourage the vertical integration of firms, because transfers of goods at different levels of production within the same firm are not burdened by taxes the way they are when sold between independent producers at different stages in the manufacturing process. The savings from vertical integration are increased because taxes have to be paid at every stage of production on taxes already paid at earlier stages, a phenomenon known technically as the cascading effect of turnover taxes. Second, it is easier to evade turnover taxes than any other form of taxes. In many small businesses and service industries purchases and sales without record are easy to make and very difficult to prove by tax authorities. Third, under GATT rules, countries are permitted to rebate to exporters indirect taxes paid on earlier stages of production of a good. In the case of turnover taxes it is nearly impossible to know with precision how many tax payments were made in the production of a given good, making the calculation of export rebates most difficult.

During the postwar years the French government, which was especially plagued by turnover tax evasion problems, invented and introduced a new form of indirect taxation known as the value-added tax. Under this scheme a firm pays a tax of a certain percentage only on the difference between the value of the inputs and sales, adjusted for previously paid value-added taxes on the inputs. The difference between the cost of inputs and the value of outputs is equal to the firm's value added and consists of expenditures on labor, capital, and profits. The tax rate can be set at such a level that it produces the same revenue as a turnover tax, but the value-added tax has many advantages over the turnover tax. First, the incentive for vertical integration of firms is removed, and there is no cascading of taxes. Second, since every firm's taxes are increased by its inability to document the cost of its inputs, every firm has incentives to keep perfect records of its costs. These records can be used by the authorities to ascertain that all sales at different levels of production are recorded. Under these conditions tax evasion is much more difficult and risky than under the turnover tax, where the incentives are to lose records of transactions. Finally, export rebates of value-added taxes can be calculated with precision and ease. This overwhelming case in favor of the value-added over the turnover tax system should and would have led most governments of the EEC countries to the adoption of the value-added tax, even in the absence of the customs union.

Having concluded this preliminary discussion of the difference between a turnover and value-added tax system, we now turn to the analysis of the role of indirect taxes generally in a customs and economic union. For this purpose consider a customs union between two countries, A and B, in perfect internal and external equilibrium. Now assume that country A imposes an indirect tax which has the effect of raising the GNP price index by 10 percent. Trade between the two countries of the union can be treated in two different ways, known as the destination and origin principles of taxation. Under the destination principle it is necessary to have a fiscal border between countries A and B at which exports from A receive a rebate of taxes paid and imports into A are assessed taxes at the country A rates. If country B had an indirect tax other than zero, its exports and imports would be treated analogously at the fiscal border. As a result of this treatment of trade at the border, country A's exports compete in country B, and country B's exports compete in country A, in the same manner as before the imposition of the tax. There are no pressures for changes of the exchange rates or the reallocation of resources. The great disadvantage of the destination principle of taxation is that it requires the maintenance of fiscal borders between members of the customs union, and these borders involve the expenditure of real resources by public authorities and the private sector. They also are a symbol of the failure to move the customs union toward complete economic union, in which trade and factors can move between countries without any restrictions.

The origin principle of indirect taxation requires that goods exported from country A to country B are sold in B at prices including A's taxes, while goods exported from B into A are sold at prices without taxes. This treatment of trade initially after the imposition of the tax makes country A's exports noncompetitive in B and creates incentives to import more goods from country B into A. The resultant trade deficit of country A puts downward pressure on its exchange rate which comes to an end only after it has been depreciated by 10 percent, which is equivalent to the impact of the indirect tax on country A's price level. At this new equilibrium trade patterns between A and B are the same as before the imposition of the indirect tax in country A. The advantage of the origin principle of taxation is that it can function without the need for fiscal borders. Its disadvantage is that it requires the adjustment of exchange rates whenever a country in the union changes its indirect tax rates.

The most important conclusion of the preceding analysis is that indirect taxes imposed in countries of a customs union do not affect the efficient allocation of resources if fiscal borders exist or exchange rates adjust properly under the treatment of trade according to the destination or origin principle, respectively. The analysis permits us to appreciate the program of fiscal harmonization proposed in the Neumark Report, whereby the removal of fiscal borders was to be achieved through the use of the origin principle of taxation. The equalization of value-added tax rates would permit the maintenance of fixed exchange rates among member countries of the EEC rates. The common use of the value-added tax system by all countries would facilitate the maintenance of equal rates of indirect taxation, because of the complicated nature and uncertain incidence of the conventional turnover taxes. The Neumark Report thus may be considered to be an important step for moving the EEC countries from a customs union toward a complete economic union characterized by the absence of fiscal borders and the fixity of exchange rates.

Let us now mention briefly a separate problem of fiscal harmonization important for an economic union. This problem arises from the treatment of trade with the rest of the world on the basis of the destination principle. Let us assume that intraunion trade is treated according to the origin principle so that there are no fiscal borders between countries, but country A has a 10 percent and country B a zero rate of indirect taxation, an exchange rate adjustment having taken place to assure efficiency of intracommunity trade. Now consider what happens when each country imposes at its borders with the rest of the world an indirect tax on imports and grants a rebate on exports at the rate prevailing within its borders. Under these conditions, imports into the customs union would be "deflected" to country B, where a zero indirect tax rate is imposed. Exports from the community, on the other hand would all be deflected to country A, since at its borders with the rest of the world exporters receive a 10 percent tax rebate. Obviously, such deflections of customs union trade with the rest of the world are undesirable. They can be prevented simply by the adoption of a common rate of tax adjustment, which is now in effect for the EEC.

The preceding analysis of problems for customs and economic unions caused by the existence of indirect taxes has sketched the main issues. In practice, there are several other problems, such as the existence of indirect taxes at different rates on different classes of commodities and the distribution of revenue from border tax adjustments among countries of the union, which cannot be considered here because of space limitations. Interested readers are referred to the Bibliographical Notes at the end of this chapter for references to writings in which fiscal harmonization problems are discussed further. As of 1975, fiscal borders continue to exist in the EEC because of the use of value-added taxes on different classes of commodities and the use of the destination principle. This lack of progress is due to political problems of adjustment, not a lack of understanding about the economics of fiscal harmonization in a customs union.

Direct Taxes. It is tempting to argue that if income taxes on persons or corporations are higher in country A than in country B, there will be an incentive for workers and capital to move from A to B. Therefore in a customs union in which restrictions on international factor movements are removed, the existence of differential direct tax rates leads to inefficient resource allocation, unless rates are harmonized. This argument for harmonization has only limited validity because most generally governments return to the taxed public goods and services worth an equal amount. Rational taxation and expenditure policies push the provision of public goods and services to the point where at the margin their social productivity is equal to private productivity. If there are increasing returns to public expenditures, it is possible that persons and firms located in a high-tax country receive benefits from the government exceeding the private costs of their tax payments, and the high-tax country attracts rather than pushes out labor and capital. This principle of correspondence between tax and expenditure programs of governments is apparent most readily at the local level. In U.S. school districts the amount of money spent on education and the tax rates on local residents imposed for this service differ between districts for many reasons. A person considering only taxes would be tempted to move to the low-tax district, but he would not be better off and might actually lose if the low quality of the public education system there forces him to send his children to a private school. Business firms similarly could find that, in general, the quality of judicial, police, and transportation services and the health and education level of the labor force they draw on is higher in regions or countries with high taxes than in those with low tax rates.

The general principle of neutrality of government tax and expenditure policies in the real world may often be inoperative, because of inefficiencies in government operations and the existence of social welfare programs aimed explicitly at the redistribution of income. But even a given region's strong welfare programs leading to a transfer of income from the rich to the poor do not necessarily create incentives for the poor to immigrate to and the rich to leave the region, for two reasons. First, most people in high-income brackets derive a positive utility from the efforts of their governments to attain some degree of income equality in their society and to prevent abject poverty among people at the lower ends of the income distribution. This utility may be based either on humanitarian perceptions of a desirable society or, more selfishly, on the perceived danger of drastic changes in social or economic organization threatening their own well-being, if excessive income differentials lead to violent revolution or radical legislation. Second, social welfare programs may be considered to be insurance programs to which high income earners contribute willingly as a coverage against the possibility that they or their families may some day fall victims to unfortunate circumstances which place them among the recipients of social welfare benefits.

However, we should realize that even if all regional tax authorities are efficient and there is equality between tax payments and government services, as long as individual districts have different programs of expenditure, they may induce migration of labor and capital. The reason for this migration is that people have different tastes and needs. For example, different school and taxation expenditures in U.S. school districts create incentives for people with children to move into high-tax and high– education expenditure districts, and the opposite incentives are created for persons with no children of school age. Analogous differences exist between regions of the United States and countries of the EEC with respect to expenditures on cultural affairs, higher education, public trans- portation, environmental protection, and so on. Economic union should not be aimed at eliminating through central direction such national and regional differences in taxation and expenditure patterns, because they make for cultural diversity. Welfare is raised by migration caused by people's desire to live in areas providing the mix of public expenditures they most prefer and cannot bring about in their own district through democratic processes because they are in a minority there. This is one of the most attractive features of a free and open society.

We conclude from the preceding analysis that, in general, direct taxes on individuals and capital in different countries and at various levels of governmental authority in a customs or economic union do not need to be, and for the sake of preserving national and regional identities should not be, equalized. However, extreme, separate programs of income redistri- bution may induce inefficient factor movements, and there is one class of government programs which requires some degree of harmonization. These programs relate to the subsidy of industry through tax concessions, cash payments, or other procedures which are unrelated to services pro vided and which distort the allocative efficiency of capital within the union. If these subsidy programs are big enough, they can make it impos- sible to have free trade in the goods produced by the subsidized industry. An example of such an industry is agriculture; the heavy subsidy pro- grams in effect in the EEC member countries before the customs union required the development of a Common Agricultural Policy (CAP) for the EEC.

Common Agricultural Policy.   Our analysis of the CAP starts with the given facts that for some reason the countries of Western Europe, before EEC formation, had programs for the subsidization of their agricultural sector, and this subsidy took the form of pegging the prices for agricultural products at levels above those that the free market would have resulted in. To bring out the need for harmonization of agricultural subsidy pro- grams, let us consider the following hypothetical, simplified situation. As- sume that initially France and Germany paid their farmers a price of six francs and ten marks per bushel of wheat, respectively. Now assume that the exchange rate was one franc per mark. It is clear that under these conditions free trade in wheat between the two countries is impossible. Private arbitrage would cause French wheat to be sold in Germany, and the quantities offered to the German government at the support price of 10 marks would soar. If there is to be free trade in agricultural products between Germany and France it is necessary to equalize the support price of wheat at some price such as eight francs and eight marks. In fact, the CAP, in effect since July 1968, agreed on an agricultural support price program which required Germany to lower and France to raise its internal support price. This agreement involved a major concession on the part of Germany because it implied a relative decline of German agriculture and increase of French agriculture. The fact that the CAP was adopted was hailed as evidence of good will and cooperation among EEC countries and therefore as a significant step toward economic union.

However, the seemingly easy CAP has been found to involve many problems and costs. The adoption of a high support price means high prices to consumers, which are unpopular and reduce consumption. Of necessity, since the support price is above the market clearing price and the CAP made no provisions for reductions in output, the policy must lead to excess supply of agricultural products. These have to be bought by an EEC support agency and, after some period of costly storage, typically are exported at a subsidized price. These operations of the EEC price support agency have to be financed by contributions from member governments, and Germany made another major concession by contributing to these expenditures proportionately more than the share of the expenses caused by her own agricultural sector. France again was the greatest beneficiary of this agreement. The CAP represented a major obstacle to negotiations for Britain's entry into the EEC because Britain, like the United States in recent years, had an agricultural subsidy program involving deficiency payments to farmers rather than fixed support prices for their outputs. Under the British program, farmers sold their goods at world prices, and the government provided them afterward with payments designed to raise their incomes to the desired level. In principle, this level could be the same as that derived under the price support program under the EEC scheme. The advantages of the deficiency payments program are the absence of surplus production and, politically most important, low prices of agricultural products for consumers. The increase in food prices in Britain which accompanied her joining the EEC was one of the main factors leading to the June 1975 popular referendum on British membership.

The EEC support price for agricultural products is protected by a most effective tariff system which stipulates that the height of the tariff is set at such a level that, when added to the world price for the products existing at the time, it always gives European farmers the domestic price agreed upon under the CAP. Thus, when the world price of wheat is $2 per bushel and the CAP support price is $3, then the tariff is set at $1 per bushel. If the world price were $1, ceteris paribus, the tariff would be $2. This program of protection under the CAP has made it impossible for the United States, Canada, and exporters of agricultural products from developing countries to compete with EEC producers, and because of the EEC exports of surplus products these countries' exports have suffered even further. As a result, the governments of the former food exporters to the EEC have lodged strong protests against this CAP policy. If, among the countries of the Atlantic Community, there is a longer run balancing of costs and benefits of national policies, we can expect that the EEC will sooner or later have to make concessions on other policy disputes to compensate allies for these losses from the CAP.

A final CAP problem arises from the fact that free trade in agricultural products, common support prices, and a common external tariff are incompatible with exchange rate changes among members of the EEC. For example, assume that the French franc–German mark exchange rate is one to one and that the rate to the dollar is two francs and two marks per dollar. Further assume that initially the CAP support price for wheat is eight francs and marks, while the world price is $3 per bushel. Under these conditions the common import tariff for wheat is $1, which at the given exchange rates equalizes the import plus tariff price with the support price. Now assume that Germany runs a persistent payments surplus and has to appreciate its currency by 50 percent relative to both the franc and the dollar. In the new equilibrium the mark is worth one dollar and two francs. This appreciation lowers the price of wheat in Germany to DM 4, which is equal to the sum of the world price of $3 plus the tariff of $1 converted to the new DM–$ exchange rate. On the other hand, in France the price of wheat remains at eight francs per bushel. It is clear that under these conditions the support received by German farmers has dropped dramatically in terms of industrial goods they can buy. As a result, if Germany wants to maintain the support for its farmers measured in terms of industrial goods they can buy for their output, the agricultural support price in marks has to be raised. But under these conditions the levels of support in France and Germany are unequal, different import duties have to be applied, and free trade is not possible.

These difficulties for the CAP arising from exchange rate changes among EEC members have been hailed initially as an important and welcome constraint on exchange rate changes. However, in 1969 the German mark was appreciated by 9.4 percent relative to the franc, and it was obvious that the CAP was not a sufficiently strong policy commitment to prevent an exchange rate change which had become necessary on other grounds. As a result of the 1969 exchange rate change, the CAP in effect was suspended. Germany and France instituted a complex system of border tax adjustments and subsidies to preserve otherwise free trade in agricultural products within the EEC. Since then the floating of the mark and the franc has created further difficulties for the CAP which are being handled by added changes in border tax and subsidies. The ultimate fate of the CAP is far from clear.

Monetary Integration

We introduce the subject of monetary integration by presenting first an outline of the history of European and EEC cooperation and coordination, in fact and in official proposals between the end of World War II and 1976. We then turn to a theoretical analysis of issues surrounding the costs and benefits of monetary integration which provides some useful insights about the likely future course of monetary integration in the EEC.

History of Coordination and Integration. Before World War II, the countries of Western Europe were independent nation-states which made domestic monetary and fiscal policies and changed their exchange rates according to the model of behavior we developed above in Part Four. Immediately after World War II international trade among the countries of Western Europe was guided by networks of bilateral trade and payments agreements which, in effect, bypassed the functioning of markets. Perhaps the devastation of the war made this bilateralism the only feasible method for international trade.

However, as the reconstruction of national economies proceeded, the bilateral agreements became increasingly burdensome and restrictive. With the help of U.S. Marshall Plan funds and pressures by U.S. officials after 1947, progressive steps towards multilateral trade and payments agreements were made, culminating in 1950 in the creation of the European Payments Union. Under this agreement all intra-European trade was balanced multilaterally and automatic credit was extended by surplus countries to deficit countries, up to certain limits. In an important sense this automatic credit was equivalent to a pooling of international reserves, because deficit countries did not have to use reserves useful for financing trade with the rest of the world in settlement with union partners. The European Payments Union assisted the rapid development of intra-European trade and trade with the rest of the world. These conditions led in 1958 to the restoration of the free convertibility of European currencies. It is difficult to know how much the institution of European cooperation in the form of the Payments Union contributed to recovery and trade, but many observers believe that it served as a most useful forum for international consultation and cooperation among finance ministers and central bankers. After years of nationalist policies in the 1930s and belligerence during the war such a forum was necessary to establish trust and a sense of community. As such, the Payments Union is believed to have contributed to the establishment of the EEC in 1957. The European Payments Union was replaced in 1958 by the European Monetary Agreement, which, because of the convertibility of currencies instituted simultaneously, thereafter played a much less important role than the European Payments Union it had replaced.

The next steps towards monetary integration in Europe took place within the institutional framework of the EEC, which comprised a much smaller number of countries than the European Payments Union had. The Rome Treaty envisaged only the coordination of economic policies among members necessary to the functioning of the EEC treaty objectives, not the attainment of monetary union, and it did so without providing for institutions to supervise the coordination of policies. However, in 1962 the permanent bureaucratic governing body known as the EEC Commission recommended that further steps be taken to assure that the EEC moved towards an ultimate goal of fixed exchange rates between members. Based on these recommendations, the legislative body of the EEC, the Council of Ministers, moved to set up in 1964 the Committee of Governors of Central Banks, the Budgetary Committee, and the Medium-Term Economic Policy Committee, and it broadened the mandate of the Monetary Committee. We need not review here in detail the functioning of these committees. For our purposes of analysis it is important to note their establishment as a significant step in the direction of institutionalized economic coordination of monetary and fiscal policies, which is necessary for the maintenance of fixed exchange rates and free capital flows among a group of countries such as the EEC.

After the creation of these committees in 1964 there was little need to make use of their services. The economies of the EEC member countries boomed; they ran large payments surpluses with the rest of the world, especially the United States, and accumulated large stocks of international reserves. Exchange rates were fixed but fluctuating within the plus or minus 1 percent around parity permitted under the IMF agreements. However, in 1968 the French economy was disturbed seriously by internal civil strife and student strikes. At the same time, Germany's external surpluses continued to grow and were increased dramatically by speculative capital inflows. Attempts were made to handle the crisis through the institution of exchange controls while the fixed parities were maintained, but these controls were incapable of preventing a devaluation of the franc against the dollar by 11.1 percent on August 8, 1969. On September 29, the mark was permitted to float upward and finally, in October, it was revalued upward by 9.3 percent against the dollar.

The dramatic realignment of the two major currencies of the EEC, together with the widespread use of direct controls, represented a serious setback in what had appeared to many to be a steady road toward integration and ultimate economic union. As a result, the Commission in 1969 took a new initiative and in the Barre Report urged the need for more effective procedures for consultation and policy coordination, to prevent repetition of the difficulties that had been witnessed. There also was a growing desire among EEC countries to counter the importance of the

U.S. dollar in international monetary affairs for political and prestige reasons, as we described in Chapter 23. For this purpose the Barre Report recommended that the margins of fluctuation around parities of the EEC exchange rates were to be eliminated as a step towards fusing the EEC currencies into one large unit. This program was supported by France for the further reason that it would strengthen the CAP, of which it was the main beneficiary. Finally, the Barre Report envisaged the establishment of a system whereby EEC countries in balance-of-payments disequilibria could receive automatic credit from other members.

The ideas of the Barre Report, which was issued by the bureaucratic branch of the EEC, were embraced and extended in the Werner Report, issued on October 8, 1970, in response to the political decision of the EEC heads of state meeting in The Hague on December 1 and 2, 1969, to establish an economic and monetary union in the EEC. As noted above, the Werner Report envisaged complete monetary union by 1980, by a series of stages. The main features of the first stage were to be a narrowing of the intervention margins around parity to a maximum of 0.6 percent on either side, plus a number of other programs for mutual assistance, coordination of policies, and liberalization of capital markets. In the beginning of 1971, when these policies were to be brought into effect, the world was swept by a new wave of currency speculation centering on expectations about a dollar devaluation and an appreciation of the mark and the yen. In the face of this speculation the EEC countries suspended their plan for narrowing the intervention margins and, most importantly, they could not agree on how to deal with them. Polar cases in the approach were again France and Germany, the former willing to use controls to combat speculation, the latter wanting to rely on the market through the floating of currencies. On August 15, 1971, President Richard Nixon announced the now-famous program of suspension of gold convertibility and an import surcharge.

In the negotiations following August 15 and leading to the Smithsonian Agreement on December 18, 1971, the EEC countries represented a relatively united front in pushing for a reform of the international monetary system and removing the dollar from its central role. The events of 1971 were interpreted by many Europeans as strengthening the case for European monetary integration, and it was believed that the more realistic exchange rates which emerged from the Smithsonian Agreement permitted the EEC to proceed with its plan to move toward a narrower band of fluctuations among EEC currencies. This narrowing of bands was given further impetus by the Smithsonian Agreement provision for a change in the width of the intervention margins from the previous 1 percent to a maximum of 2.25 percent on either side of par, or the "central rate," as it was newly named. This wider margin, in theory, permitted the currencies of EEC countries to diverge more widely, without declaration of changes in central, rates, because of the following technical fact.

Consider that the central rates of the French franc and German mark were defined as two each per dollar. Now assume that the franc depreciated to a maximum of 2.25 percent against the dollar, becoming worth 1.955 francs per dollar, whereas the mark appreciated to the full extent permitted, to 2.045 marks per dollar. The resultant spread between the franc and the mark is 4.5 percent, reached without any official changes of the two countries' exchange rates. Such a possibility would not aid monetary integration, and it was agreed that EEC countries would keep their exchange rates linked to each other so closely that the maximum deviation between the highest and lowest currency was 2.25 percent. In other words, at any given point in time there was to be a band of values for EEC currencies defined in terms of dollars, the maximum width of which was 2.25 percent. EEC central banks would intervene with member currencies to keep individual currencies within the band, selling the strongest and buying the weakest EEC currencies. However, the narrow, maximum 2.25 percent spread EEC band, dubbed the "snake," was permitted to find its own market-determined level against the dollar band of maximum 4.5 percent, known as the "tunnel." This technical arrangement is known as "the snake in the tunnel." Only when the snake reached the intervention margin with the dollar would EEC central banks intervene with dollars.

The snake-in-the-tunnel scheme instituted on April 24, 1972 and agreement on the institution of some further procedures for cooperation and coordination were interpreted as signs of success of the forces moving the EEC towards monetary union. Then renewed currency crises developed in 1972, and the Arab oil embargo in 1974 created new political and exchange rate strains within the EEC. At one point in the middle of 1975 the snake-in-the-tunnel agreement operated between Germany, France, the Netherlands, Belgium-Luxembourg and Denmark, while the British and Irish pounds and the Italian lira floated outside the band. In their efforts to overcome the 1974 oil embargo and assure oil supplies in the longer run, EEC countries proceeded mostly on their own, outside of the many EEC institutions which in principle would have been able to provide the forum for the development of cooperative and coordinated approaches to the problem. What was lacking was the political will to sacrifice national sovereignty in order to gain the uncertain advantages of a joint program of action.

The history of international monetary integration in the EEC is not a success story. It raises the question whether the visionary Werner Report underestimated the economic difficulties associated with complete monetary integration and overestimated the political will of EEC countries to overcome these difficulties through some economic sacrifices for the sake of the achievement of the visionary political goal of a United States of Europe. Has the experiment of narrowing exchange rate bands, which was broken by the floating of the pound and the lira, set back the case for integration by demonstrating that it cannot operate? Or has the machinery for operating the band brought together EEC technicians and politicians, taught them the benefits of cooperation and coordination, and thus aided the cause of integration in the longer run? Has the nationalistic approach to the oil crisis been a temporary setback on the road toward integration, which no one but the greatest idealists had expected to be smooth and without such setbacks? The answers to these questions will only be found in the future. We now turn to the theoretical analysis of the costs of monetary union, which will provide us with some useful insights for evaluating future trends.

The Theory of the Costs of Monetary Union

Many laymen whose fancy has been caught by the idea of creating a United States of Europe have asked the question why the EEC countries do not adopt a common currency, perhaps to be named symbolically the Europa. Readers of Part Four of this book should have no great difficulties in answering this question. A common currency for EEC countries implies the absolute and permanent fixing of exchange rates and the formation of a currency area. As we discussed in Chapter 22, the formation of a currency area gives rise to welfare gains and losses which are well understood theoretically but which are difficult to estimate empirically and to explain to politicians and the voting public. These difficulties are due to the fact that the benefits accrue in the form of externalities and in small doses to the public as a whole, while the costs are much more readily identifiable and affect special-interest groups in society. Until it is possible to establish more firmly than has been done what are the external benefits and costs of union and explain them to politicians and the public, the adoption of a common currency is equivalent to putting the cart before the horse. First there must be the will to surrender national sovereignty over monetary and fiscal policy, in order to make it possible to fix exchange rates permanently. Then the introduction of a common currency will be the crowning symbol of the achievement of a United States of Europe.

In the political and public discussions about the wisdom of a complete monetary union for the EEC, the emphasis is on the costs; there is relatively little dispute about the general gains which would accrue to Europe politically, militarily, and in economic bargaining power with the rest of the world. The sophisticated arguments about the gains from currency area formation due to the increased stability of prices and the greater usefulness of money are too difficult to be appreciated by noneconomists and enter the discussions only very marginally. Because of the importance of arguments over the costs of monetary union, we concentrate the following analysis on them, using the approach developed in our discussion of optimum currency areas developed in Chapter 22.

Dealing with Random Shocks. Let us assume that two symbolic countries of a potential monetary union, Germany and France, initially have freely floating exchange rates and pursue independent monetary and fiscal policies resulting in price stability through time. Random shocks to economic stability require the use of a monetary and fiscal policy which under the regime of freely floating rates can be applied effectively and without payments constraints. Now if these two countries link rigidly their exchange rates while floating their common currency toward the rest of the world, it is impossible to deal with random disturbances affecting each country as effectively as before the union. For example, when a boom requires tight monetary policy in France, a business downturn may require easy monetary policy in Germany. The common monetary policy must be a compromise between the needs of the two regions, imposing costs on each.

However, the costs may be smaller than the preceding analysis implies, because the union permits arbitrage between goods and factor markets to operate more effectively than before the union. Thus, scarcities of output, labor, and capital developing during the boom in France are met by supplies of goods and the flow of capital and labor from Germany. In the process, boom and recessionary pressures in the two countries are relieved. Short-term capital flows especially have an important role to play in financing intercountry payments imbalances, as James Ingram of the University of North Carolina has shown in some of his studies. In a union in which two countries' economies are firmly integrated, market forces also tend to generate relative equality in regional growth in productivity, because capital and labor are free to move to locations in which their productivity and rewards are maximized. We consider below the problems raised by the persistence of regional disparities. The union as a whole is likely to enjoy a more stable exchange rate against the rest of the world than did the two countries' independent rates averaged through time, because of the internal offsetting of random disturbances in the union. As a result of this increased stability of the union exchange rate, the fluctuations of prices are reduced and the usefulness of money as a store of value, medium of exchange, and unit of account is increased, as we argued in our analysis of the optimum currency area controversy. In sum, purely in terms of dealing with random disturbances to economic stability, monetary union is likely to result in no reduction in welfare and may even raise it.

The Phillips Curve Tradeoff. The greatest perceived cost of monetary union arises from the fact that a common monetary policy makes it impos-

sible for countries to opt for different tradeoffs between inflation and unemployment along their Phillips curves. For example, if France is willing
to accept a 3 percent inflation in order to enjoy an unemployment rate of,
say, 2 percent, whereas Germany aims for a zero rate of inflation, accepting whatever unemployment rate results, then the institution of a fixed
exchange rate between France and Germany is impossible. The loss of
France's cost competitiveness relative to Germany through time under
fixed exchange rates leads to increasing French payments deficits and
German surpluses. This would involve the lending of real resources by
Germany to France, which, one may surmise, Germany is unwilling to
undertake even if France were willing to go into debt by the amounts
involved. Therefore, sooner or later the fixed exchange rate has to be
changed and the union is less than complete. A common currency would
make such an exchange rate change impossible, but only at the cost of
either or both countries moving from their target rates of inflation and
unemployment. Critics of the concept of an EEC monetary union are
convinced that it is unrealistic to expect member countries to surrender
these policy targets and, most importantly, they feel that the welfare costs
of doing so are so much greater than any gains from union that these
countries should not surrender their targets.

A variant of the costs of the Phillips curve tradeoff involves emphasis
of the fact that labor productivity in countries of the EEC has grown at
different rates in the past and can be expected to do so in the future. With
output prices the same in all countries and rigid money wages of labor,
countries with slow productivity increases will experience increased unemployment, for the following reason. Consider that French and German
workers produce a good, X, initially requiring in each country two labor
hours, abstracting from capital costs. The wage rate per hour in the two
countries is two Europas, and the good sells competitively for four
Europas. Now consider that French workers become more productive as
a result of some innovation which they adopt readily and which permits
them to produce the good in one hour instead of two, while German
workers, perhaps because of unionization, do not adopt the innovation.
Under competition among industry X producers in France, the price of
product X falls to two Europas, and markets in the EEC and the rest of the
world previously held by German producers are taken over by the French.
German workers become unemployed until, moving along the declining
marginal productivity schedule of labor, few enough workers in the good
X industry are employed and working with a sufficiently large capital
stock so that their productivity is equal to that of the French workers.
When exchange rates are flexible, of course, under the assumed conditions
the value of the German currency would have depreciated relative to that
of the French franc, and the competitiveness of the German producers of
good X domestically and in the rest of the world would have been main-

tained. Consequently, there would have been no unemployment in Germany as a result of the differential rates of productivity growth in the two countries.

The validity of the argument about the welfare costs of giving up inflation-unemployment targets depends decisively on the existence of the Phillips curve tradeoff. Elsewhere we have noted the accumulation of theoretical and empirical evidence suggesting that this tradeoff exists only for very short periods and has no significance for long-range macroeconomic policy formation. Under these conditions, the most important source of welfare cost from monetary union is eliminated. Unification of the rate of inflation in all EEC countries brought about by the monetary union does not cause added unemployment but, through the medium of fixed exchange rates, increases price stability and encourages trade and specialization. We can see, therefore, that the outcome of this debate depends on clarification of the issue over whether or not countries have the option to trade a reduction of unemployment for inflation.

The problem over differential rates of productivity growth raises important questions about its causes. If it is due to differential rates of capital accumulation, economic union tends to alleviate its magnitude because of the free movement of capital. If it is due to deep-seated cultural attitudes of people in different countries toward work, union power, technical change, the need to mitigate market forces, and so on, then it could be argued that the cost of monetary union is that countries have to become more equal in their attitudes on these matters. It is consistent with this view that opposition to economic and monetary union of the EEC tends to come from labor organizations whose professed aim is to change the income distribution resulting from the free market and, if necessary, to replace capitalism by some form of public ownership of the means of production. Personal tastes determine how heavily one weights the costs of having to give up or transfer to an EEC–wide theater efforts to bring about these changes in free market economies, as well as the costs of giving up culturally determined attitudes towards work, and so on. Johnson, for example, has argued that monetary union would bring into public view the economic costs of militant unions in Britain and bring the majority of the British public to vote for legal restraints on their excessive power, which is harmful to the majority of nonunionized workers. Others would argue that unions in Britain are engaged in a just struggle to rectify the economic injustices and inequities brought about by the excessive power of the upper classes of landowners and industrialists. Any restraint on unions in Britain brought about by monetary union, therefore, would impose a great welfare cost on the British people. The issues appear to be rather clear. The answers to the challenge of monetary union among EEC countries will be determined by national political processes whose outcome cannot be predicted.

Regional Poverty Problems. A final form of perceived cost of monetary union is that it will cause depression and poverty in some countries in the EEC, akin to the regions of Southern Italy, the Maritime Provinces of Canada, the poor mining districts of Great Britain's Wales, and Appalachia in the United States. Every country, even the rapidly growing and prosperous Germany, has such regions of slow growth, low incomes, and high unemployment. In Germany one such region is the easternmost Bavarian Forest. In the EEC under full union, entire countries may become depressed areas.

It is difficult to know how well founded such fears are, because economists have not yet made much progress in understanding the causes of regional disparities of income within existing nation-states. There are some common elements among depressed regions. They tend to be heavily dependent on industries such as coal, fishing, forestry, or agriculture for which demand has been growing slowly and productivity increases have been small. The areas suffer from the emigration of young and educated workers and potential innovators. Typically, the regions are far from industrial and population centers, with poor transportation facilities to the rest of the world. Some theorizing about causal relationships and interdependencies among these phenomena stresses the fact that industrialization and economic growth tend to take place in central areas of countries with great population agglomeration. In these centers of development external economies of specialization in production are internalized, and the proximity of many producers and of consumers saves costs of transportation and communication. The centers attract further immigrants from outlying areas, increasing their advantage and causing further losses of efficiency away from the centers. It is quite possible that such developments may be repeated for the EEC, though the existence of centers of rapid growth and agglomeration in all countries of the union seems to diminish the risk that entire countries could become depressed regions. Germany has the Ruhr area, France has Paris, Italy has the Po Valley, and Britain has London and the Midlands, all of which have great independent strength and are capable of holding their own against a potential EEC center which appears to be developing in the area of northern France, southern Belgium, and a part of Germany and the Netherlands.

The hard-nosed but politically unpopular solution to regional disparity problems is to let the centers of growth develop and permit emigration from the depressed regions, without interference with the process through subsidies or special government assistance programs. In the longer run there is likely to develop an equilibrium in which diseconomies of agglomeration in the center slow down growth and the low density of population in the fringe areas permits people to earn a competitive income. In most countries governments have interfered with this movement toward equilibrium by subsidy and special assistance programs to depressed regions, which often, because of the federalist structure of Western democratic governments, have great political power. In the EEC provisions already have been made to assist depressed regions with the help of a European Social Fund and the Regional Fund. There is every expectation that the political power of any federated government of the EEC will enable depressed areas to attract subsidies and other support programs from the prosperous centers. The economic growth and vitality of the EEC, stimulated by a monetary union, would provide the center with the means to carry out these programs of assistance.

An Evolutionary Approach. In the Werner Report and in most discussion about an EEC monetary union, it has been assumed, either explicitly or implicitly, that agreements on permanently fixed exchange rates or a common currency would have to be reached as a discrete step involving acceptance of the full program of centralized monetary policy. Recently, proposals have been advanced, most notably those by Giovanni Magnifico, that instead it may be possible to move toward monetary union through the development of a common currency, the Europa, which would coexist with national currencies and represent an increasing fraction of the EEC money supply through time. As the public and governments became accustomed to using the Europa, its introduction as the sole currency of the EEC would be facilitated in the longer run and its administration would teach bureaucrats and politicans valuable lessons about the operation of a common EEC monetary unit.

The proposals for the gradual introduction of the Europa involve a number of technical problems and require governments to surrender some rights of national economic sovereignty. We cannot discuss the Magnifico plan here in detail; we mention only that it is based on the establishment of a European Bank which receives as assets national currencies and international reserve assets of EEC member countries. Against these assets the bank would issue Europas, which should be made acceptable in settlement of tax obligations to national governments, made to be held by commercial banks, and used in making a market for Europa-denominated short-term money market instruments and long-term debt issues, much as there now is a Eurodollar market for financial instruments. Once the Europa has become acceptable by the private sector, it is possible for the Europa Bank to use it in open-market operations in support of national currencies, according to instructions from a committee of national central banks.

The evolutionary approach to EEC monetary union seems plausible and technically feasible. It was explained first in an article published in 1971 and elaborated upon on a book published in 1973. The response to the plan by national governments and the EEC, if there is any, is not now known publicly. The future of the idea seems uncertain.

BIBLIOGRAPHICAL NOTES

A semipopular book with much useful, up-to-date institutional information is Swann (1975). An early, more rigorous text is Balassa (1961). Books of readings containing the classics, extensions, and empirical studies are Robson (1971) and Krauss (1973). The volumes edited by Shoup (1967) and Krause and Salant (1973) contain articles presented at conferences of specialists on fiscal and monetary integration, respectively.

The seminal classic on the customs union issue is Viner (1950). More rigorous and extensive treatments, with original contributions are Meade (1956) and Lipsey (1960). A limited selection of papers extending and modifying the classics consists of Gehrels (1956–57), Cooper and Massell (1965) and Arndt (1968). The theory of the second best is formulated in Lipsey and Lancaster (1956–57) and Negishi (1969). A difficult but thorough and in many ways original work is Vanek (1965).

An estimate of welfare effects before union is Johnson (1958a). Landmarks of trade diversion and creation estimates, with increasing sophistication in order, are Balassa (1967), Kreinin (1972), and Truman (1969). Sellekaerts (1973) presents a critique of such empirical studies. Verdoorn (1954), Grubel (1967b), Willmore (1972), and Adler (1970) analyze the effects of customs unions on intraindustry trade.

The best statements of the fiscal harmonization problem concerning indirect taxes are Shibata (1967) and Johnson and Krauss (1970). The theoretical classic on monetary integration is Meade (1956). Mundell (1961) and McKinnon (1963) originate the optimum currency area idea, and a rigorous restatement of it is found in Grubel (1970). Bloomfield (1973) provides a useful history of EEC monetary integration efforts. Contrasting views on the future of monetary integration are presented by Ingram (1973), Corden (1972, 1973), and Johnson (1971b). The snake-in-the-tunnel concept is discussed by Johnson (1973). Magnifico (1973) presents his proposal for a European Bank. On the agricultural problem, read Swann (1975), Ch. 6, and Josling (1973).

CONCEPTS FOR REVIEW

Common market	Trade creation
Free trade area	Theory of the second best
Tariff preferences	Common Agricultural Policy
Monetary union	Customs union
Fiscal harmonization	European Payments Union
Value-added tax	Snake-in-the-tunnel scheme
Trade diversion	

POINTS FOR FURTHER STUDY AND DISCUSSION

1. Research the history and prospects of such efforts for economic integration as the Benelux Union, the European Coal and Steel Community, Latin American Free Trade Area, Australia–New Zealand Free Trade Agreement. Analyze the methods and effects of integration and evaluate how important, relatively, economic and other motives have been in these integration efforts.

2. Evaluate the prospects that there might ever be a customs union between Iceland and Panama and that Sweden, Finalnd, and Norway will join the EEC. Use the analytical principles developed in the text in preparing your answer.

3. Discover and discuss motives underlying the opposition of some factions of the British Labour Party to U.K. membership in the EEC.

4. What public goods might ultimately be provided by the central government of a United States of Europe, and what might be its main source of tax revenue?

5. Analyze the practical and economic implications of instituting the following system in the EEC: Central banks in every country announce every morning domestic prices at which, until the next morning, they accept EEC member countries' bank notes without any brokerage charges. Commercial banks acting on behalf of the central banks are paid a fee of 3 percent of the cash collected. Would such an institution increase the acceptability of national currencies of member countries in retail shops in the EEC, lead to social savings, and pave the way for monetary integration? What are the likely costs and risks of such a system?

BIBLIOGRAPHY

BIBLIOGRAFIA

Bibliography

Adams, Walter. *The Brain Drain.* New York: Macmillan, 1968.

Adler, Michael. "Specialization in the European Coal and Steel Community." *Journal of Common Market Studies,* March 1970.

Alchian, Armen. "Costs and Outputs." In M. Abramovitz and others, *The Allocation of Economic Resources: Essays in Honor of B. F. Haley.* Stanford, Calif.: Stanford University Press, 1959.

Alexander, Sidney. "Devaluation versus Import Restriction as an Instrument for Improving Foreign Exchange Balance." *IMF Staff Papers,* 1951.

————. "The Effects of a Devaluation on a Trade Balance." *IMF Staff Paper,* 1952.

Aliber, Robert Z. (ed.). *The International Market for Foreign Exchange.* New York: Praeger, 1969.

————. *The International Money Game.* New York: Macmillan, 1973.

Allen, William (ed.). *International Trade Theory: Hume to Ohlin.* New York: Random House, 1965.

Arndt, Sven W. "On Discriminatory versus Non-Preferential Tariff Policies." *Economic Journal,* December 1968 (reprinted in Robson, 1971).

Arrow, Kenneth R. "The Economic Implications of Learning by Doing." *Review of Economic Studies,* 1962.

Balassa, Bela. *The Theory of Economic Integration.* Homewood Ill.: Richard D. Irwin, 1961.

————. "An Empirical Demonstration of Classical Comparative Cost Theory." *Review of Economics and Statistics,* August 1963.

————. "The Purchasing Power Parity Doctrine: A Reappraisal."

Journal of Political Economy, 1964 (reprinted in Cooper, 1969).

———. "Tariff Protection in Industrial Countries." *Journal of Political Economy,* December 1965 (reprinted in Caves and Johnson, 1968).

———. "Trade Creation and Trade Diversion in the European Common Market." *Economic Journal,* March 1967 (reprinted in Robson, 1971).

———. *The Structure of Protection in Developing Countries.* Baltimore: Johns Hopkins Press, 1971.

Baldwin, Robert E. (ed.). *Trade, Growth and the Balance of Payments.* Chicago: Rand McNally, 1965.

———. *Non-Tariff Distortions of International Trade.* London: Allen Unwin, 1970.

———. "Determinants of the Commodity Structure of U.S. Trade." *American Economic Review,* March 1971.

———, and Richardson, J. D. (eds.). *Selected Topics in International Trade and Finance: A Book of Readings.* Boston: Little, Brown, 1973.

Barber, C. L. "Canadian Tariff Policy." *Canadian Journal of Economics and Political Science,* November 1955.

Basevi, Georgio. "The United States Tariff Structure: Estimates of Effective Rates of Protection of United States Industries and Industrial Labor." *Review of Economics and Statistics,* May 1966.

———. "The Restrictive Effect of the U.S. Tariff." *American Economic Review,* September 1968.

Baumol, W. J., and Oates, Wallace E. *The Theory of Environmental Policy.* Englewood Cliffs, N.J.: Prentice-Hall, 1975.

Behrman, Jack N. *National Interests and the Multinational Enterprise.* Englewood Cliffs, N.J.: Prentice-Hall, 1970.

Bernstein Report. *The Balance of Payments Statistics of the United States: A Review and Appraisal.* Washington, D.C.: U.S. Government Printing Office, 1965.

Bhagwati, Jagdish. "Immiserizing Growth." *Review of Economic Studies,* June 1958 (reprinted in Caves and Johnson, 1968).

———. "Protection, Real Wages and Real Incomes." *Economic Journal,* August 1959 (reprinted in Bhagwati, 1969).

———. "The Pure Theory of International Trade: A Survey," *Economic Journal,* March 1964.

——— (ed.). *International Trade: Selected Readings* Baltimore: Penguin Books, 1969.

———, and Desai, P. *India: Planning for Industrialization.* London: Oxford University Press, 1970.

———. "The Generalized Theory of Distortions and Welfare." In Bhagwati et al. (1971a).

———, Jones, R. W., Mundell, R. A., and Vanek, J. (eds.). *Trade, Balance of Payments and Growth.* Amsterdam: North-Holland, 1971b.

Bharadwaj, R. "Factor Proportions and the Structure of India–U.S. Trade." *Indian Economic Journal,* October 1962.

Blackhurst, Richard. "International Trade and the Environment: A Review of the Literature and a

Suggested Approach." *Economic Notes,* 1975.

Blaug, Mark (ed.). *Economics of Education* (2 vols). Baltimore: Penguin Books, 1969 and 1970.

Bloomfield, Arthur I. *Capital Imports and the American Balance of Payments 1934–39.* Chicago: University of Chicago Press, 1950.

———. *Monetary Policy under the International Gold Standard, 1880–1914.* New York: Federal Reserve Bank, 1959.

———. "The Historical Setting." In Krause and Salant (1973).

Boyer de la Giroday, F. *Myths and Reality in the Development of International Affairs.* Essays in International Finance No. 105. Princeton, N.J.: Princeton University Press, 1974.

Branson, William H. *Financial Capital Flows in the U.S. Balance of Payments.* Amsterdam: North-Holland, 1968.

Brash, Donald T. *American Investment in Australian Industry.* Canberra: Australian National University Press, 1966.

Brittan, Samuel. *The Price of Economic Freedom: A Guide to Flexible Rates.* London: Macmillan, 1970.

Brown, Weir A. *The Gold Standard Re-Interpreted, 1914–34.* New York: National Bureau of Economic Research, 1934.

Buchanan, James M. *The Demand and Supply of Public Goods.* Chicago: Rand McNally, 1968.

Cairncross, Alexander K. *Factors in Economic Development.* London: Allen & Unwin, 1962 (excerpts reprinted in Meier, 1970).

Cassell, Gustav. *Money and Foreign Exchange after 1914.* New York: Macmillan, 1923.

Caves, Richard E. *Trade and Economic Structure.* Cambridge, Mass.: Harvard University Press, 1960.

———. "International Corporations: The Industrial Economics of Foreign Investment." *Economica,* 1971 (reprinted in Dunning, 1972).

———, and Johnson, H. G. (eds.). *Readings in International Economics.* Homewood, Ill.: Richard D. Irwin, 1968.

———, and Jones, Ronald W. *World Trade and Payments: An Introduction.* Boston: Little, Brown, 1973.

Chalmers, E. B. (ed.). *Forward Exchange Intervention.* London: Hutchison Educational, 1971.

Cheh, J. H. "United States Concessions in the Kennedy Round and Short Run Labor Adjustment Costs." *Journal of International Economics,* November 1974.

Clement, M. O., Pfister, F. L., and Rothwell, K. J. *Theoretical Issues in International Economics.* New York: Houghton Mifflin, 1967.

Coase, Ronald H. "The Problem of Social Cost." *Journal of Law and Economics,* October 1966.

Cohen, Benjamin J. *Balance of Payments Policy.* Baltimore: Penguin Books, 1970.

———. "International Reserves and Liquidity: A Survey." In Kenen (1975).

Cooper, C. A., and Massell, B. F. "A New Look at Customs Union Theory." *Economic Journal,* December 1965 (reprinted in

Robson, 1971, and in Krauss, 1973).

Cooper, Richard N. "The Balance of Payments in Review." *Journal of Political Economy,* August 1966.

———. *The Economics of Interdependence,* New York: McGraw-Hill, 1968.

——— (ed.). *International Finance.* Baltimore: Penguin Books, 1969.

Coppock, J. D. *International Economic Instability.* New York: McGraw-Hill, 1962.

Corden, W. M. "Economic Expansion and International Trade: A Geometric Approach." *Oxford Economic Papers,* June 1956.

———. "The Geometric Representation of Policies to Attain Internal and External Balance." *Review of Economic Studies,* 1960 (reprinted in Cooper, 1969).

———. *Recent Developments in the Pure Theory of International Trade.* Special Papers in International Economics No. 7. Princeton, N.J.: Princeton University Press, 1965.

———. "The Structure of a Tariff System and the Effective Protective Rate." *Journal of Political Economy,* June 1966.

———. "The Effects of Trade on the Rate of Growth." In Bhagwati et al. (1971a).

———. *The Theory of Protection.* London: Oxford University Press, 1971b.

———. *Monetary Integration.* Essays in International Finance No. 93. Princeton, N.J.: Princeton University Press, 1972.

———. "The Adjustment Problem." In Krause and Salant (1973).

———. *Trade Policy and Economic Welfare.* London: Oxford University Press, 1974.

———. "The Costs and Consequences of Protection: A Survey of Empirical Work." In Kenen (1975).

Curzon, Gerard. *Multilateral Commercial Diplomacy.* London: Michael Joseph, 1965.

———, and Curzon, V. *Hidden Barriers to International Trade.* London: Trade Policy Research Center, 1971.

Daly, Donald J., Keys, B. A., and Spence, E. J. *Scale and Specialization in Canadian Manufacturing.* Staff Study No. 21. Ottawa: Economic Council of Canada, 1962.

David, Paul A. "Just How Misleading are Official Exchange Rate Conversions?" *Economic Journal,* September 1972.

Despres, Emile, Kindleberger, Charles, and Salant, Walter. "The Dollar and World Liquidity: A Minority View." *The Economist,* February 5, 1966.

Dornbusch, Rudiger. "Currency Depreciation, Hoarding and Relative Prices." *Journal of Political Economy,* July–August 1973a.

———. "Devaluation, Money and Nontraded Goods." *American Economic Review,* December 1973b.

Downs, Anthony. "An Economic Theory of Political Action in a Democracy." *Journal of Political Economy,* April 1957.

Dreze, Jacques. "*Quelques Reflexions Sur l'Adaption de l'Industrie Belge au Marche Commun,*" *Comptes rendues des Travaux de la Societe Royale d'Economie Politique de Belgique*, 1960.

Dunn, Robert. "Flexible Exchange Rates and Oligopoly Pricing: A Study of Canadian Markets." *Journal of Political Economy*, January–February 1970.

Dunning, John H. *Studies in International Investment*. London: Allen & Unwin, 1970.

———, (ed.). *International Investment*. Baltimore: Penguin Books, 1972.

Einzig, Paul. *A Dynamic Theory of Forward Exchange*. London: Macmillan, 1966.

———. *The Euro-dollar System* (2nd ed.). London: Macmillan, 1973.

Ellis, Howard S., and Metzler, L. A. (eds.). *Readings in the Theory of International Trade*. Homewood, Ill.: Richard D. Irwin, 1949.

Erdman, Paul. *The Billion Dollar Killing*. New York: Hutchison, 1973.

Findlay, Ronald. *Trade and Specialization*. Baltimore: Penguin Books, 1971.

———, and Grubert, H. "Factor Intensities, Technological Progress and the Terms of Trade." *Oxford Economic Papers*, February 1959 (reprinted in Bhagwati, 1969).

Fisher, Irving. *The Theory of Interest*. New York: Macmillan, 1930.

Fleming, Marcus J. "Domestic Financial Policies under Fixed and under Floating Exchange Rates." *IMF Staff Papers*, November 1962 (reprinted in Cooper, 1969).

———. "On Exchange Rate Unification." *Economic Journal*, September 1971.

Floyd, John E. "International Capital Movements and Monetary Equilibrium." *American Economic Review*, September 1969.

Foreign Affairs Division, Congressional Research Service, Library of Congress. *Brain Drain: A Study of the Persistent Issue of International Scientific Mobility*. Washington, D.C.: U.S. Government Printing Office, 1974.

Frenkel, Jacob, and Johnson, Harry G. (eds.). *The Monetary Approach to the Balance of Payments*. London: Allen & Unwin, 1975.

Friedman, Milton. "The Case for Flexible Exchange Rates." In *Essays in Positive Economics*. Chicago: University of Chicago Press, 1953.

———. "The Role of Monetary Policy." *American Economic Review*, 1968.

———. *The Optimum Quantity of Money and Other Essays*. Chicago: University of Chicago Press, 1969.

———. "The Euro-dollar Market: Some First Principles." *Federal Reserve Bank of St. Louis Review*, July 1971.

———, and Schwartz, Anna. *A Monetary History of the United States (1867–1960)*. Princeton, N.J.: Princeton University Press, 1963.

Gehrels, Franz. "Customs Union from a Single Country Viewpoint." *Review of Economic Studies*, February, 1956.

Graaf, V. J. de. *Theoretical Welfare Economics*. Cambridge: Cambridge University Press, 1957.

Grassman, Sven. *Exchange Reserves and the Financial Structure of*

Foreign Trade. Lexington, Mass.: Lexington Books, 1973.

Gray, H. Peter. "Senile Industry Protection: A Proposal." *Southern Economic Journal,* April 1973.

Gray Report. *Foreign Direct Investment in Canada.* Ottawa: Government of Canada, 1972.

Gregory, Robert G. "U.S. Imports and Internal Pressure of Demand." *American Economic Review,* March 1971.

Grubel, Herbert G. (ed.). *International Monetary Reform: Plans and Issues.* Palo Alto, Calif.: Stanford University Press, 1963.

———. *Forward Exchange, Speculation and International Capital Flows.* Palo Alto, Calif: Stanford University Press, 1966.

———. "The Anatomy of Classical and Modern Infant Industry Arguments." *Weltwirtschaftliches Archiv,* December 1967a.

———. "Intra-Industry Specialization and the Pattern of Trade." *Canadian Journal of Economics and Political Science,* August 1967b.

———. "Internationally Diversified Portfolios: Welfare Gains and Capital Flows." *American Economic Review,* December 1968 (reprinted in Dunning, 1972).

———. "The Theory of Optimum Currency Areas." *Canadian Journal of Economics,* May 1970.

———. "The Demand for International Reserves: A Critical Review of the Literature." *Journal of Economic Literature,* December 1971a.

——— "A Non-specialist Guide to the Theory of Effective Protection." In Grubel and Johnson

(1971b) (reprinted in Baldwin and Richardson, 1973).

———. "Basic Methods for Distributing Special Drawing Rights and the Problem of International Aid." *Journal of Finance,* December 1972.

———. "The Case for Optimum Exchange Rate Stability." *Weltwirtschafiliches Archiv,* Heft 3, 1973.

———. "Taxation and the Rates of Return from Some U.S. Asset Holdings Abroad." *Journal of Political Economy,* August 1974.

———. *The International Monetary System* (3rd ed.). Baltimore: Penguin Books, 1976.

———, and Johnson, Harry G. (eds.). *Effective Tariff Protection.* Geneva: GATT and the Graduate Institute of International Studies, 1971.

———, and Lloyd, P. J. *Intra-Industry Trade: The Theory and Measurement of International Trade in Differentiated Products.* London: Macmillan, and New York: Halsted Press, 1975.

———, and Scott, A. D. "The International Flow of Human Capital." *American Economic Review,* May 1966 (reprinted in Blaug, 1969).

Gruber, William, Mehta, D. and Vernon, R. "The R + D Factor in International Trade and International Investment of United States Industries." *Journal of Political Economy,* February 1967.

Gutowski, Armin. "Flexible Exchange Rates vs. Controls." In F. Machlup, A. Gutowski, and F. A. Lutz, *International Monetary Problems.* Washington,

D.C.: American Enterprise Institute, 1972.

Haberler, Gottfried. "The Market for Foreign Exchange and the Stability of the Balance of Payments: A Theoretical Analysis." *Kyklos*, 1949 (reprinted in Cooper, 1969).

———. *The Theory of International Trade*. London: William Hodge, 1950.

———. *International Trade and Economic Development*. Cairo: National Bank of Egypt, 1959 (reprinted in Meier, 1970).

———. *A Survey of International Trade Theory* (2nd ed.). Special Papers in International Economics, No. 1. Princeton: Princeton University Press, 1961.

———, and Willett, Thomas. *U.S. Balance of Payments Policies and International Monetary Reform*. Washington, D.C.: American Enterprise Institute for Public Policy Research, 1968.

Hagen, Everett E. "An Economic Justification of Protectionism." *Quarterly Journal of Economics,* November 1958.

Harberger, A. C. "Some Evidence on the International Price Mechanism." *Journal of Political Economy*, December 1957 (reprinted in Cooper, 1969).

Heckscher, Eli F. "The Effects of Foreign Trade on the Distribution of Income." *Economisc Tidskrift,* 1919 (reprinted in Ellis and Metzler, 1949).

Heilperin, Michael. "The Case for Going Back to Gold." *Fortune,* September 1962 (reprinted in Grubel, 1963).

Helleiner, Gerald K. *International Trade and Economic Development*. Baltimore: Penguin Books, 1972.

———. "Manufactured Exports from Less Developed Countries and Multinational Firms." *Economic Journal,* March 1973.

Heller, H. Robert. "Optimal International Reserves." *Economic Journal,* June 1966.

———. *International Trade: Theory and Empirical Evidence* (2d ed.). Englewood Cliffs, N.J.: Prentice Hall, 1973.

———. *International Monetary Economics*. Englewood Cliffs, N.J.: Prentice-Hall, 1974.

Hirsch, Fred. *Money International*. Baltimore: Penguin Books, 1967.

Hirschleifer, Jack. "The Firm's Cost Function: A Successful Reconstruction?" *Journal of Business,* July 1962.

Hirschman, Albert O. *The Strategy of Economic Development*. New Haven, Conn.: Yale University Press, 1958.

Holmes, Alan, and Schott, Francis. *The New York Foreign Exchange Market*. New York: Federal Reserve Bank of New York, 1965.

Holzman, F. D. "Comparison of Different Forms of Trade Barriers." *Review of Economics and Statistics,* May 1969.

Houthakker, Hendrik. "An International Comparison of Household Expenditure Patterns." *Econometrica,* October 1957.

———. "Exchange Rate Adjustment." *Factors Affecting the United States Balance of Payments*. Washington, D.C.: U.S.

Government Printing Office, 1967.

———, and Magee, Stephen. "Income and Price Elasticities in World Trade." *Review of Economics and Statistics,* May 1969.

Hufbauer, Gary. *Synthetic Materials and the Theory of International Trade.* Cambridge, Mass: Harvard University Press, 1966.

———, and Adler, Michael. *Overseas Manufacturing Investment and the U.S. Balance of Payments.* Washington, D.C.: U.S. Treasury Department, 1968.

Hume, David. "Of Money." *Political Discourses,* 1752 (reprinted in Allen, 1965, and Cooper, 1969).

Ingram, James C. *The Case for European Monetary Integration.* Princeton Essays in International Finance No. 98. Princeton, N.J.: Princeton University Press, 1973.

Ishiyama, Y. "The Theory of Optimum Currency Areas: A Survey." *IMF Staff Papers,* July 1975.

Johnson, Harry G. "Optimum Tariffs and Retaliation." *Review of Economic Studies,* May 1954 (reprinted in Johnson, 1961).

———. "The Transfer Problem and Exchange Stability." *Journal of Political Economy,* 1956 (reprinted in Caves and Johnson, 1968, and Cooper, 1969).

———. "Factor Endowment, International Trade and Factor Prices." *Manchester School of Economic and Social Studies,* September 1957 (reprinted in Caves and Johnson, 1968).

———. "The Gains from Freer Trade with Europe: An Estimate." *Manchester School of*

Economic and Social Studies, September 1958a (reprinted in Robson, 1971).

———. "Towards a General Theory of the Balance of Payments." In *International Trade and Economic Growth.* London: Allen & Unwin, 1958b (reprinted in Cooper, 1969).

———. *International Trade and Economic Growth: Studies in Pure Theory.* Cambridge, Mass.: Harvard University Press, 1961.

———. *Money, Trade and Economic Growth.* London: Allen & Unwin, 1962.

———. "An Economic Theory of Protectionism, Tariff Bargaining, and the Formation of Customs Unions." *Journal of Political Economy,* June 1965a.

———. "Optimal Trade Intervention in the Presence of Domestic Distortions." In Baldwin (1965b).

———. "The Theory of Tariff Structure, with Special Reference to World Trade and Development." in H. G. Johnson and P. B. Kenen, *Trade and Development.* Geneva: Libraire Droz, 1965c.

———. *Economic Policies toward Less Developed Countries.* New York: Praeger, for the Brookings Institution, 1967a.

———. "International Trade Theory and Monopolistic Competition Theory." In R. E. Kuenne (ed.), *Monopolistic Theory: Studies in Impact,* New York: Wiley, 1967b.

———. "Theoretical Problems of the International Monetary System." *Pakistan Development Review,* 1967c (reprinted in Cooper, 1969).

———. *Comparative Cost and Commercial Policy Theory for a Developing World Economy.* Stockholm: Almquist & Wicksell, 1968.

———. "A New View of the Infant Industry Argument." In McDougall and Snape (1970a).

———. "The Efficiency and Welfare Implications of the International Corporation." In Kindleberger (1970b) (reprinted in Dunning, 1972).

———. *Aspects of the Theory of Tariffs.* London: Allen & Unwin, 1971a.

———. "Problems of European Monetary Union." *The Journal of World Trade Law,* July–August 1971b (reprinted in Krauss, 1973).

———. "The Monetary Approach to Balance of Payments Theory." *Monti dei Paschi Quarterly Review,* 1972 (reprinted in Frenkel and Johnson, 1975).

———. "Narrowing the Exchange Rate Bands." In Krause and Salant (1973).

———, and Krauss, M. B. "Border Taxes, Border Tax Adjustments, Comparative Advantage, and the Balance of Payments." *Canadian Journal of Economics,* November 1970 (reprinted in Krauss, 1973).

———, and Swoboda, Alexander (ed.). *Madrid Conference on Optimum Currency Areas.* Cambridge Mass.: Harvard University Press, 1973.

Jones, Ronald W. "Factor Proportions and the Heckscher-Ohlin Theorem." *Review of Economic Studies,* October 1956 (reprinted in Bhagwati, 1969).

———. "The Transfer Problem Revisited." *Economica,* May 1970.

Josling, T. "The Common Agricultural Policy of the European Economic Community." *The Journal of Agricultural Economics,* May 1969 (reprinted in Krauss, 1973).

Junz, Helen, and Rhomberg, Rudolf. "Price Competitiveness in Export Trade among Industrial Countries." *American Economic Review,* May 1973.

Keesing, Donald B. "Labor Skills and Comparative Advantage." *American Economic Review,* May 1966.

———. "The Impact of Research and Development on United States Trade." *Journal of Political Economy,* 1967.

Kemp, Murray C. *The Pure Theory of International Trade and Investment.* Englewood Cliffs, N.J.: Prentice-Hall, 1969.

Kenen, Peter B. "International Liquidity and the Balance of Payments of a Reserve-Currency Country." *Quarterly Journal of Economics,* November 1960.

———. "Nature, Capital, and Trade." *Journal of Political Economy,* October 1965.

———, (ed.). *International Trade and Finance: Frontiers for Research.* Cambridge: Cambridge University Press, 1975.

Keynes, John M. "The German Transfer Problem." *Economic Journal,* March 1929 (reprinted in Ellis and Metzler, 1949).

Kindleberger, Charles P. "Foreign Trade and Economic Growth, Lessons from Britain and France, 1850–1931," *Economic History Review,* December 1961.

————. *American Business Abroad.* New Haven, Conn.: Yale University Press, 1969.

————. *The International Corporation.* Cambridge, Mass.: M.I.T. Press, 1970.

————. *International Economics* (5th ed.). Homewood, Ill.: Richard D. Irwin, 1973.

Klopstock, F. H. "Money Creation in the Euro-Dollar Market: A Note on Professor Friedman's Views." Federal Reserve Bank of New York, *Monthly Review,* January 1970.

Kouri, Pentti, and Porter, Michael. "International Capital Flows and Portfolio Equilibrium." *Journal of Political Economy,* May–June 1974.

Krause, Lawrence B. "A Passive Balance of Payments Strategy for the United States." *Brookings Papers on Economic Activity,* no. 3, 1970.

————, and Dam, K. W. *Federal Tax Treatment of Foreign Income.* Washington, D.C.: Brookings Institution, 1964.

————, and Salant, Walter S. (eds.). *European Monetary Unification and Its Meaning for the United States.* Washington, D.C.: Brookings Institution, 1973.

Krauss, Melvyn, B. (ed.). *The Economics of Integration.* London: Allen & Unwin, 1973.

Kravis, Irving. "Wages and Foreign Trade." *Review of Economics and Statistics,* February 1956.

Kreinin, Max. *International Economics: A Policy Approach.* New York: Harcourt Brace Jovanovich, 2d ed., 1974.

————. "Effects of the EEC on Imports of Manufactures." *Economic Journal,* September 1972.

Krueger, Anne O. "Some Economic Costs of Exchange Control: The Turkish Case." *Journal of Political Economy,* October 1966.

Lancaster, Kelvin. "The Heckscher-Ohlin Trade Model: A Geometric Treatment." *Economica,* February 1957 (reprinted in Bhagwati, 1969).

Lanyi, Anthony. *The Case for Floating Exchange Rates Reconsidered.* Essays in International Finance No. 72. Princeton, N.J.: Princeton University Press, 1969.

Leamer, Edward E., and Stern, Robert. *Quantitative International Economics.* Boston: Allyn & Bacon, 1970.

Lederer, Walther. *The Balance on Foreign Transactions: Problems of Definition and Measurement.* Special Papers in International Economics No. 5. Princeton, N.J.: Princeton University Press, 1963.

Leontief, Wassily. "The Use of Indifference Curves in the Analysis of Foreign Trade." *Quarterly Journal of Economics,* May 1933 (reprinted in Bhagwati, 1969).

————. "Domestic Production and Foreign Trade: The American Position Re-examined." *Proceedings of the American Philosophical Society,* September 1953 (reprinted in Caves and Johnson, 1968, and Bhagwati, 1969).

————. "Factor Proportions and the Structure of American Trade: Further Theoretical and Empirical Analysis." *Review of Economics and Statistics,* November 1956.

Lerner, Abba P. "The Symmetry between Import and Export Taxes." *Economica,* August 1936 (reprinted in Caves and Johnson, 1968).

———. *The Economics of Control.* London: Macmillan, 1944.

———. "Factor Prices and International Trade," *Economica,* February 1952.

Levin, Jay H. *Forward Exchange and Internal-External Equilibrium. Michigan International Business Studies No. 12.* Ann Arbor: Bureau of Business Research, University of Michigan, 1970.

Levitt, Kari. *Silent Surrender: The Multinational Corporation in Canada.* Toronto: Macmillan, 1970.

Lewis, Stephen R. "Government Revenue from Foreign Trade: An International Comparison." *Manchester School of Economic and Social Studies,* January 1963.

Linder, Staffan B. *An Essay on Trade and Transformation.* New York: John Wiley and Sons, Inc., 1961.

Lipsey, Richard G. "The Theory of Customs Unions: A General Survey." *Economic Journal,* September (reprinted in Robson, 1971, and Krauss, 1973).

———, Lancaster, Kelvin. "The General Theory of Second Best." *Review of Economic Studies,* October 1956.

List, Friedrich. *National Systems of Political Economy.* New York: Longmans, Green, 1904.

Little, Ian; Scitovsky, T. and Scott, M. F. G. *Industry and Trade in Some Developing Countries.*

London: Oxford University Press, 1970.

Little, Jane S. *Euro-Dollars: The Money Market Gypsies.* New York: Harper & Row, 1975.

Lloyd, Peter J. *New Zealand Manufacturing Production and Trade with Australia.* Wellington: New Zealand Institute of Economic Research, 1971.

Macario, Santiago. "Protectionism and Industrialization in Latin America. *Economic Bulletin for Latin America,* March 1965 (reprinted in Meier, 1970).

MacBean, Alistair. *Export Instability and Economic Development.* London: Allen & Unwin, 1966.

MacDougall, G. D. A. "British and American Exports: A Study Suggested by the Theory of Comparative Costs." *Economic Journal,* December 1951 and September 1952.

———. "The Benefits and Costs of Private Investment from Abroad: A Theoretical Approach," *Economic Record,* March, 1960.

McDougall, Ian A, and Snape, Richard (eds.). *Studies in International Economics.* Amsterdam: North-Holland, 1970.

Machlup, Fritz. *International Trade and the National Income Multiplier,* Philadelphia: Blakiston, 1943. Reprints of Economic Classics. New York: August M. Kelley, 1965.

———. "The Theory of Foreign Exchanges." In *International Payments, Debts and Gold: Collected Essays by F. Machlup.* New York: Scribner, 1964.

———. *Remaking the International Monetary System.* Baltimore: Johns Hopkins Press, 1968.

————, Gutowski, Armin and Lutz, Friedrich A. (eds.). *International Monetary Problems.* Washington, D.C.: American Enterprise Institute, 1972.

McKinnon, Ronald I. "Optimum Currency Areas." *American Economic Review,* September 1963 (reprinted in Cooper, 1969).

————. *Private and Official International Money: The Case for the Dollar.* Essays in International Finance No. 74. Princeton, N.J.: Princeton University Press, 1969.

————. *Money and Capital in Economic Development.* Washington, D.C.: Brookings Institution, 1973.

Magee, Stephen P. "Currency Contracts, Pass-through and Devaluation." *Brookings Papers on Economic Activity,* no. 1, 1973.

Magnifico, Giovanni. *European Monetary Unification.* London: MacMillan Press, 1973.

Makin, John. "Identifying a Reserve Base for the Euro-Dollar System." *Journal of Finance,* June 1973.

Marshall, Alfred. *The Pure Theory of Foreign Trade,* 1879.

————. *Money, Credit and Commerce.* London: Macmillan, 1923.

Masera, Rainer S. "A Stylized Model of a Highly Open Economy under a System of Fixed Exchange Rates and its Implications for the Establishment of Currency Areas," *Economic Notes,* January–April 1974.

Massell, Benton F. "Export Concentration and Export Earnings." *American Economic Review,* March 1964.

————. "Export Instability and Economic Structure." *American Economic Review,* September 1970.

Mayer, Helmut W. *Some Theoretical Problems Relating to the Euro-Dollar Market.* Essays in International Finance No. 79. Princeton, N.J.: Princeton University Press, 1970.

Meade, James E. *Theory of International Economic Policy.* vol. 1, *The Balance of Payments.* New York: Oxford University Press, 1951.

————. *A Geometry of International Trade.* London: Allen & Unwin, 1952.

————. *Theory of International Economic Policy.* vol. 2, *Trade and Welfare.* New York: Oxford University Press, 1955.

————. *The Theory of Customs Unions.* Amsterdam: North-Holland, 1956 (excerpts reprinted in Robson, 1971).

————. "The Balance of Payments Problems of a European Free-Trade Area." *Economic Journal,* September 1957 (reprinted in Robson, 1971, and Krauss, 1973).

Meier, Gerald M. *International Trade and Development.* New York: Harper & Row, 1963.

————. *Leading Issues in Economic Development* (2d ed.). New York: Oxford University Press, 1970.

————. *Problems of Trade Policy.* London: Oxford University Press, 1973.

————. *Problems of World Monetary Order.* London: Oxford University Press, 1974.

Metzler, Lloyd. "Tariffs, The Terms of Trade, and the Distribution of

National Income." *Journal of Political Economy,* February 1949 (reprinted in Caves and Johnson, 1968).

Mill, John S. *Principles of Political Economy with Some of their Applications to Social Philosophy,* 1814.

Minhas, B. S. "The Homohypallagic Production Function, Factor Intensity Reversals and the Heckscher-Ohlin Theorem." *Journal of Political Economy,* April 1962 (reprinted in Bhagwati, 1969).

Moroney, John R. *The Structure of Production in American Manufacturing.* Chapel Hill: University of North Carolina Press, 1972.

————, and Walker, T. M. "A Regional Test of the Heckscher-Ohlin Hypothesis." *Journal of Political Economy,* December 1966.

Mundell, Robert. "International Trade and Factor Mobility." *American Economic Review,* June 1957 (reprinted in Mundell, 1968, and Caves and Johnson, 1968).

————. "A Theory of Optimum Currency Areas." *American Economic Review,* September, 1961 (reprinted in Krauss, 1973).

————. "The Appropriate Use of Monetary and Fiscal Policy for Internal and External Stability." *IMF Staff Papers,* March 1962 (reprinted in Mundell, 1968).

————. *International Economics.* New York: Macmillan, 1968.

————. *Monetary Theory: Inflation, Interest and Growth in the World Economy.* Pacific Palisades, Calif.: Goodyear, 1971.

Mussa, Michael. "A Monetary Approach to Balance of Payments Analysis." *Journal of Money Credit and Banking,* August 1974 (reprinted in Frenkel and Johnson, 1975).

Myrdal, Gunnar. *Development and Underdevelopment.* Cairo: National Bank of Egypt, 1956 (reprinted in Meier, 1970).

Naya, Seji. "Natural Resources, Factor Mix, and Factor Reversal in International Trade." *American Economic Review,* May 1957.

Negishi, T. "The Customs Union and the Theory of the Second Best." *International Economic Review,* October 1969.

Niehans, Juerg. "Monetary and Fiscal Policies in Open Economies under Fixed Exchange Rates: An Optimizing Approach." *Journal of Political Economy,* July–August 1968.

Nurkse, Ragnar. *International Currency Experience.* Princeton, N.J.: League of Nations, 1944.

Officer, Lawrence H. "The Purchasing-Power-Parity Theory of Exchange Rates: A Review Article," *IMF Staff Papers,* March 1976.

————, and Willett, T. D. (eds.). *The International Monetary System.* Englewood Cliffs, N.J.: Prentice-Hall, 1969.

Ohlin, Bertil. "The Reparation Problem: A Discussion." *Economic Journal,* June 1929 (reprinted in Ellis and Metzler, 1949).

————. *Interregional and International Trade.* Cambridge, Mass.: Harvard University Press, 1933.

Oppenheimer, Peter M. "The Case for Raising the Price of Gold."

Journal of Money, Credit and Banking, August 1969.

Pearce, Ivor F. *International Trade,* New York: Norton, 1970.

Phelps, Edmund S. "Phillips Curves, Expectations of Inflation and Optimal Unemployment Over Time." *Economica,* August 1967.

Pincus, Jonathan. "Pressure Groups and the Pattern of Tariffs." *Journal of Political Economy,* August 1975.

Posner, Michael V. "International Trade and Technical Change." *Oxford Economic Papers,* October 1961.

Power, John H. "Import Substitution as an Industrialization Strategy." *The Phillipine Economic Journal,* 1966 (reprinted in Meier, 1970).

Prachowny, Martin. "The Effectiveness of Stabilization Policy in a Small Open Economy." *Weltwirtschaftliches Archiv,* Heft 2, 1973.

Prais, S. J., and Houthakker, H. S. *The Analysis of Family Budgets.* Cambridge, Mass.: Harvard University Press, 1955.

Prebisch, Raul. *Towards a New Trade Policy for Development.* Report by the Secretary General of UNCTAD. New York: United Nations, 1964 (reprinted in Meier, 1970).

Prochnow, H. V. (ed.). *The Eurodollar.* Chicago: Rand McNally, 1970.

Reddaway, W. B., Potter, S. J., and Taylor, C. T. *The Effects of U.K. Direct Investment Overseas: Final Report.* University of Cambridge, Department of Applied Economics, Occasional Paper No. 15 (1967–68).

Ricardo, David. *Principles of Political Economy,* 1817. (reprinted New York: Penguin, 1971; Chapter 7 also in Allen, 1965).

Richardson, David J. "On Going Abroad: The Firm's Initial Foreign Investment Decision." *Quarterly Review of Economics and Business,* Winter 1971.

Robinson, Joan. "The Foreign Exchanges." In *Essays on the Theory of Employment.* Oxford: Basil Blackwell, 1947 (reprinted in Ellis and Metzler, 1949).

Robson, P. (ed.). *International Economic Integration.* Baltimore: Penguin Books, 1971.

Rueff, Jacques. "Gold Exchange Standard: a Danger to the West." *The Times,* June 27–29, 1961 (reprinted in Grubel, 1963).

Rugman, Alan. "Risk Reduction by International Diversification," *Journal of International Business Studies,* September 1976.

Rybczynski, T. M. "Factor Endowments and Relative Commodity Prices." *Economica,* November 1955.

Safarian, A. E. *Foreign Ownership of Canadian Industry.* Toronto: McGraw-Hill, 1966.

———. *The Performance of Foreign-Owned Firms in Canada.* Toronto: Canadian National Planning Association, 1969.

Samuelson, Paul. "The Gains from International Trade." *Canadian Journal of Economic and Political Science,* May 1939 (reprinted in Ellis and Metzler, 1949).

———. "International Trade and the Equilization of Factor Prices." *Economic Journal,* June 1948.

———. "International Factor Price Equalization Once Again." *Economic Journal,* June 1949 (reprinted in Caves and Johnson, 1968).

———. "The Transfer Problem and Transport Costs: The Terms of Trade When Impediments Are Absent." *Economic Journal,* June 1952.

———. "Social Indifference Curves." *Quarterly Journal of Economics,* February 1956.

Savosnick, K. M. "The Box-Diagram and the Production Possibility Curve." *Ekonomisk Tidskrift,* September 1958.

Scammell, William M. *International Trade and Payments.* Toronto: Macmillan, 1974.

Scitovsky, Tibor. "A Reconsideration of the Theory of Tariffs." *Review of Economic Studies,* No. 2, 1942 (reprinted in Ellis and Metzler, 1949).

Sellekaerts, Willy. "How Meaningful Are Empirical Studies on Trade Creation and Diversion?" *Weltwirtschaftliches Archiv,* Heft 4, 1973.

Servan-Schreiber, J. J. *The American Challenge.* New York: Avon Books, 1969.

Sharpe, William F. *Portfolio Theory and Capital Markets.* New York: McGraw-Hill, 1970.

Shibata, Hirofumi. "The Theory of Economic Unions: A Comparative Analysis of Customs Unions, Free Trade Areas, and Tax Unions." In Shoup (1967) (reprinted in Robson, 1971).

Shoup, Carl S. (ed.). *Fiscal Harmonization in Common Markets.* (Vols. 1 and 2). New York: Columbia University Press, 1967.

Singer, Hans W. "The Distribution of Gains between Investing and Borrowing Countries." *American Economic Review,* May 1950

(reprinted in Caves and Johnson, 1967).

Soedersten, Bo. *International Economics.* New York: Harper & Row, 1970.

Sohmen, Egon. *Flexible Exchange Rates: Theory and Controversy* (rev. ed.). Chicago: University of Chicago Press, 1969.

Stamp, Sir Maxwell. "The Stamp Plan—1962 Version," *Moorgate and Wall Street,* Autumn 1962 (reprinted in Grubel, 1963).

Stern, Robert. "British and American Productivity and Comparative Costs in International Trade." *Oxford Economic Papers,* October 1962.

———. "The U.S. Tariff and the Efficiency of the U.S. Economy." *American Economic Review,* May 1964.

———. *The Balance of Payments: Theory and Economic Policy.* Chicago: Aldine, 1973a.

———. "Tariffs and Other Measures of Trade Control: A Survey of Recent Developments." *Journal of Economic Literature,* March 1973b.

Stolper, Wolfgang F., and Roskamp, Karl. "Input-Output Table for East Germany, with Applications to Foreign Trade." *Bulletin of the Oxford Institute of Statistics,* November 1961.

———, and Samuelson, Paul A. "Protection and Real Wages." *Review of Economic Studies,* November 1941 (reprinted in Bhagwati, 1969).

Swan, Trevor. "Longer-run Problems of the Balance of Payments." In II. W. Arndt and W. M. Corden (eds.). *The Australian Economy: A Volume of Readings.* Melbourne: Cheshire,

1963 (reprinted in Caves and Johnson, 1969).

Swann, D. *The Economics of the Common Market* 3d ed. Baltimore: Penguin Books, 1975.

Swoboda, Alexander K. *The Eurodollar Market: An Interpretation.* Essays in International Finance No. 64 Princeton, N.J.: Princeton University Press, 1968.

————. ''Equilibrium, Quasi-equilibrium, and Macro-economic Stabilization Policy under Fixed Exchange Rates.'' *Quarterly Journal of Economics,* February 1972.

Takayama, Akira C. *International Economics.* New York: Holt, Rinehart & Winston, 1972.

Tarshis, Lorie. ''International Price Ratios and International Trade Theory.'' *American Economic Review,* March 1954.

Tatemoto, M., and Ichimura, S. ''Factor Proportions and Foreign Trade: The Case of Japan'' *Review of Economics and Statistics,* November 1959.

Taussig, Frank W. *International Trade.* New York: Macmillan, 1927.

————. *Economic Policy: Principles and Design* Amsterdam: North-Holland, 1952a.

Tinbergen, Ian. *On the Theory of Economic Policy.* Amsterdam: North-Holland, 1952b.

Tower, Edward. ''Monetary and Fiscal Policy in a World of Capital Mobility: A Respecification'', *Review of Economic Studies,* July 1972.

————. and Willett, Thomas D. ''The Theory of Optimum Currency Areas and Exchange Rate Flexibility,'' Special Papers in International Economics, No. 11, Princeton: Princeton University Press, May 1976.

Travis, William P. *The Theory of Trade and Protection.* Cambridge, Mass.: Harvard University Press, 1964.

Triffin, Robert. ''National Central Banking and the International Economy,'' *International Monetary Policies, Postwar Economic Studies,* No. 7, Board of Governors of the Federal Reserve System, 1947.

————. *Gold and the Dollar Crisis.* New Haven, Conn.: Yale University Press, 1960.

————. ''The Myth and Realities of the So-Called Gold Standard.'' In *Our International Monetary System: Yesterday, Today and Tomorrow.* New York: Random House, 1968 (reprinted in Cooper, 1969).

————, and Grubel, Herbert. ''The Adjustment Mechanism to Differential Rates of Monetary Expansion among Countries of the European Economic Community.'' *Review of Economics and Statistics,* November 1962.

Truman, Edward M. ''The European Economic Community: Trade Creation and Trade Diversion.'' *Yale Economic Essays,* Spring 1969.

Tsiang, S. C. ''The Theory of Forward Exchange and Effects of Government Intervention on the Forward Exchange Market.'' *IMF Staff Papers,* April 1959.

————. ''The Role of Money in Trade-Balance Stability: Synthesis of the Elasticity and Absorption Approaches.'' *American Economic Review,* December 1961 (reprinted in Cooper, 1969).

U.S. Commission on International Trade and Investment Policy (Williams Commission). *United States International Economic Policy in an Interdependent World*. Washington, D.C.: U.S. Government Printing Office, 1971.

Valavanis-Vail, Stefan. "Leontief's Scarce Factor Paradox." *Journal of Political Economy*, December 1954.

———. "Factor Proportion and the Structure of American Trade: Comment." *Review of Economics and Statistics*, February 1958.

Vanek, Jaroslav. "The Natural Resource Content of Foreign Trade, 1870–1955, and the Relative Abundance of Natural Resources in the United States." *Review of Economics and Statistics*, May 1959.

———. *General Equilibrium of International Discrimination: The Case of Customs Unions*. Cambridge, Mass.: Harvard University Press, 1965.

Verdoorn, P.J. "A Customs Union for Western Europe: Advantages and Feasibility." *World Politics*, July 1954.

Vernon, Raymond. "International Investment and International Trade in the Product Cycle." *Quarterly Journal of Economics*, May 1966.

Viner, Jacob. *The Customs Union Issue*. New York: Carnegie Endowment for International Peace, 1950 (excerpt reprinted in Robson, 1971).

Wahl, D. F. "Capital and Labor Requirements for Canada's Foreign Trade." *Canadian Journal of Economic and Political Science*, August 1961.

Wallich, Henry C. "Cooperation to Solve the Gold Problem," *Harvard Business Review*, May–June 1961, (reprinted in Grubel 1963).

Walter, Ingo. *International Economics*. 2d ed. New York: Ronald Press, 1975.

Whitman, Marina. *Policies for Internal and External Balance*. Special Papers in International Economics, No. 9. Princeton, N.J.: Princeton University Press, 1970.

Willett, Tom, and Tower, Edward. "The Concept of Optimum Currency Areas and the Choice between Fixed and Flexible Exchange Rates." in G. N. Halm, (ed.), *Approaches to Greater Flexibility of Exchange Rates*. Princeton, N.J.: Princeton University Press, 1970.

Williamson, John H. "Surveys in Applied Economics: International Liquidity." *Economic Journal*, September 1973.

Willmore, L. N. "Free Trade in Manufactures among Developing Countries: The Central American Experience." *Journal of Economic Development and Cultural Change*, July 1972.

Wonnacott, Ron J., and Wonnacott, Paul. *Free Trade between the United States and Canada*. Cambridge, Mass.: Harvard University Press, 1967.

Yeager, Leland B. *International Monetary Relations: Theory, History and Policy*. New York: Harper & Row. Second Edition, 1975.

INDEXES

Name Index

Subject Index

This book has been set in 10 point and 9 point Times Roman, leaded 2 points. Part numbers are 36 point Kennerly italic and chapter numbers are 60 point Bookman. Part and chapter titles are 18 point Kennerly. The size of the type pages is 27 × 45½ picas.